AN

INTRODUCTION TO THE GRAMMAR

OF THE

SANSKRIT LANGUAGE

AN

INTRODUCTION TO THE GRAMMAR

OF THE

SANSKRIT LANGUAGE,

FOR THE USE OF

EARLY STUDENTS.

BY

H. H. WILSON, M.A., F.R.S. &c. &c.

GYAN

Published by

Gyan Publishing House
5, Ansari Road
Daryaganj, New Delhi-110002
Phone: 011-47034999, 9811692060
E-mail: books@gyanbooks.com

Distribution Network
gyanbooks.com
India, USA, Canada, UK, Australia

ISBN: 978-81-212-7021-2 (PB)
First Published, 1841

2nd Impression 2024

Printed at: Gyan Press, Delhi.

AN INTRODUCTION TO THE GRAMMAR OF THE SANSKRIT LANGUAGE
Author: H. H. WILSON

AN INTRODUCTION TO THE GRAMMAR OF THE SANSKRIT LANGUAGE,

FOR THE USE OF

EARLY STUDENTS.

BY

H. H. WILSON, M.A. F.R.S. &c. &c.

BODEN PROFESSOR OF SANSKRIT IN THE UNIVERSITY OF OXFORD.

LONDON,

PUBLISHED BY J. MADDEN AND CO.,

LEADENHALL STREET.

1841.

PREFACE.

THE design of the present Grammar of the Sanskrit Language has been suggested by the experience which I have now had in teaching the language, and by the want which I have repeatedly felt of some such elementary work as that which I have here attempted to compile.

Of the Sanskrit Grammars published in Calcutta, the works of Mr. Colebrooke, Dr. Carey, and Mr. Forster are too voluminous and difficult for beginners. The Grammar of Mr. Yates is better adapted to such a class of students, but it is not readily procurable in this country. The Grammar of Professor Bopp, being composed in German and in Latin, is not universally acceptable to English students: and the only Grammar within their reach, therefore, has been that of Sir C. Wilkins. This work, however admirable in many respects, is exceptionable in some parts of its arrangement, and is inconvenient in use from its extent; it is also growing scarce. A new Grammar, therefore, on a somewhat different plan, had become necessary; and as I found no one disposed to engage in its preparation, I have thought it incumbent upon me to undertake the task.

The structure of a highly elaborated form of speech, such as is Sanskrit, abounding with grammatical inflexions, cannot be explained with that brevity of which more simply constituted languages permit: much cannot be described in a very few phrases. The present work has exceeded the limits which I originally contemplated; but I found it impossible to be more concise, without being obscure, or without omitting something that was essential. As the extent of the book, however, is in great part attributable to the multiplication of examples, rather than of rules, it will be useful for occasional reference, without being cumbrous to the memory of the student. I have endeavoured to make reference easy, by the headings of the pages and other supplementary means.

The first topic of all Sanskrit Grammars is necessarily the euphonic combination of concurrent letters, the analysis of which must be performed before the words can be separated and read. In the chapter upon the combination of letters, or Sandhi, as it is termed, I have rather added to, than diminished, the number of the rules which are to be found in the Grammar of Sir C. Wilkins: but, on the other hand, I have not imitated Professor Bopp in the copiousness with which he has explained the changes, as, however serviceable the rules which he has assembled with singular industry and correctness, they are not in all cases confined to modifications of a euphonic character: they comprise many that occur as the consequence of verbal or nominal inflexion: and although a knowledge of them will no doubt facilitate the student's subsequent acquirement of the principles of declension and conjugation, I have not found him content to be detained so long upon what appears to him to be but the threshold of the edifice, into the interior of which he is eager to enter.

The general outline of the chapter on Declension is in all essential respects the same as that followed in the

Grammars of Wilkins and Bopp; but I have thought it advisable to put more prominently forward than they have done the scheme of technical terminations, devised by native grammarians for the construction of the cases of a noun; as, notwithstanding the substitutions which they partially undergo, they are applicable in all nouns to a considerable portion of the cases, and in some nouns to all. They are easily acquired, and so are their substitutes; and familiarity with them once attained, the subject of Declension, however complicated it may appear, becomes exceedingly simple, and is mastered with facility.

It is in the chapter on Conjugation that I have departed most widely from the course pursued by my European predecessors. Professor Bopp has followed in the main the example set by Sir C. Wilkins, of exemplifying, under the head of each class or conjugation, only those tenses of the verb to which the conjugational characteristics are confined; and of illustrating the remaining tenses of verbs in general in one collective division, under the head of each several tense. I have found this arrangement peculiarly embarrassing to beginners. An entire verb is nowhere presented to them; and although the whole of the inflexions of most of those of which the conjugational tenses are exhibited are to be found in the Grammar, yet they can only be collected by a diligent and protracted search. It rarely happens that the young student is not disheartened by the labour thus imposed upon him, and a competent knowledge of the conjugation of Sanskrit verbs is in consequence comparatively seldom acquired. In the hope of removing some of the difficulties inherent in the subject, I have brought the several tenses of the verb together, and explained their formation in consecutive order. I have then detailed an entire verb in its different voices and derivative forms; and finally, under the head of each conjugation, I have given complete paradigms of a number of the most useful verbs, arranged in alphabetical succession, in the several conjugations to which they respectively belong. An example of this classification of the verbs was set by Mr. Colebrooke. In the first volume of his Grammar, the only one published, he has assembled all the verbs of the first conjugation, with paradigms more or less complete. The limits of the present work rendered it impossible to represent all the verbs of each conjugation, but I have endeavoured to make such a selection as comprehends those which are of most frequent occurrence, or anomalous construction. The forms are taken chiefly from the native Grammar, the Siddhánta Kaumudí, and from a MS. collection of verbs I had compiled in India. The first part only of Mr. Westergaard's very valuable work, 'Radices Linguæ Sanscritæ,' had reached me before my collection was completed, or it would have saved me some labour. The usefulness of the series will have been materially enhanced by the alphabetical Index to all the verbs specified, which will be found at the end of the volume, and for the preparation of which I am indebted to the promptly tendered assistance of Professor Johnson, whom I have also to thank for the careful revision of the proof sheets, with exception of those of the last hundred pages, and for the correction of many errors, ascribable to typographic inaccuracy, or to my own inadvertencies.

The chapter on Derivation does not attempt to follow the detail with which the subject is illustrated in the

Grammar of Sir C. Wilkins. The same copiousness was no longer necessary, as my Dictionary, however incomplete, offers many of the same examples, and sufficiently exhibits the principles of etymological developement. By the alphabetical arrangement, however, of the technical affixes employed in eliminating derivative from primitive words, a plan adopted from the example of Professor Bopp, reference to any particular form of derivatives will have been facilitated, and the process of their developement, perhaps, have been rendered more intelligible.

The formation of compound words is described much in the same manner, but with some slight difference of arrangement, as by Sir C. Wilkins. In the succeeding chapter on Syntax, also, I have followed much the same course, being guided, as he was, by the authority of native grammarians, although appealing to different works, and endeavouring to illustrate the rules by more diversified examples. The subject, however, is yet but imperfectly investigated. The native authorities restrict their remarks to the application of the cases of the nouns, and the tenses of the verbs; and to have supplied their deficiencies would have demanded a longer period, and ampler space, than were compatible with the plan and purposes of the present publication. My guides have been principally the Siddhánta Kaumudí and the poem of Bhaťťi, but I have drawn examples also from other printed Sanskrit books.

The Prosody of Sanskrit has been much more successfully illustrated than its Syntax; and in the Dissertation of Mr. Colebrooke, in the tenth volume of the Asiatic Researches, and in the remarks and annotations of various continental scholars and critics upon the metres prevailing in the Sanskrit works which they have edited, abundant materials exist for a comprehensive treatise upon the laws of Sanskrit metre. In the chapter upon the subject which I have added to the Grammar, nothing more has been intended than a brief explanation of the fundamental principles by which poetical metre is regulated, and an exemplification of a few of its most frequently recurring and popular varieties.

As the especial object of the present work is the introduction of the juvenile student to an elementary knowledge of the Sanskrit language, I have but rarely adverted to the affinities which connect it with other languages; and in the few allusions which I have admitted, I have purposed rather to intimate that such affinities exist, than to explain their nature, or inquire into their origin or extent. The more advanced student, who may take an interest in the investigation, will find in the writings of different continental scholars and grammarians, and especially in the Comparative Grammar of Professor Bopp, numerous and undeniable proofs of the close connexion which subsists between the sacred language of the Hindus and the languages of ancient Greece and Rome, as well as those of the Celtic, Teutonic, and Sclavonic nations.

It were superfluous in the present day to offer any observations upon the value and interest of Sanskrit literature. The study constitutes an era in the branch of intellectual inquiry just referred to, and has given an entirely new character to philology. The principles of etymological affinity have been placed upon secure grounds, and the history of languages, and through them the history of man, has received novel and important elucidation. Nor is this the only service which it has rendered to general literature. The history of philosophy and science is also largely indebted to it; and in the civil and religious codes which it has laid open to our knowledge, and in the mythological and legendary traditions, and the dramatic and heroic poems, which it offers to our curiosity, it presents a series of new, interesting, and instructive pictures of society, in which the features of a highly artificial, but original civilization are singularly blended with the characteristics of primitive manners and archaic institutions. The history of mankind can be but imperfectly appreciated without some acquaintance with the literature of the Hindus.

It is, however, to the educated youth whose manhood is to be spent in India, and who is there destined to discharge high duties, and sustain heavy responsibilities—who is to execute the offices of civilized government over millions of subject Hindus, and to make that government a blessing, not a curse, to India—a glory, not a shame, to Britain;—it is to him that the study of Sanskrit commends itself, by considerations of peculiar utility and importance.

A careful examination of the different dialects which are spoken in various parts of India is yet to be effected; but enough is known to admit of their being distinguished as belonging to two great families, that of India proper, and that of the Dakhin. Of the former, the members are, as far as we are familiar with them, recognised as Sanskrit. They have undergone great changes; have simplified their grammatical structure; have suffered in a greater or lesser degree admixture and adulteration from foreign words. They probably also comprehend a small portion of a primitive, unpolished, and scanty speech, the relics of a period prior to civilization:

but in the names of things of the most ordinary observation, in terms for the functions of life, as well as the relations of society, as much as in those words which are the offspring of civilization, and which spring from science, philosophy, law, and religion, they are almost wholly dependent upon Sanskrit; a knowledge of which consequently places the members of this family, Bengali, Hindee, Punjabi, Guzerati, Marhatha, and others, almost without effort within the power of any one to whom it may become a duty to acquire either or all of them.

In the south of India the case is somewhat different. Cultivated languages of local origin are there met with, largely supplied with words which are not of Sanskrit origin. There, however, as in the north, the introduction of Sanskrit was the precursor of civilization, and deeply impressed it with its own peculiarities. The spoken languages were cultivated in imitation and rivalry, and but partially aspired to an independent literature. The principal compositions in Tamil, Teloogoo, Canara, and Malayalam, are translations or paraphrases from Sanskrit works, and largely borrow the phraseology of their originals: and hence so large a proportion of the language of education and of society is Sanskrit, that a knowledge of it is absolutely essential to a correct understanding of the spoken dialects of the peninsula.

There is, however, a higher point of view from which the advantages to the servants of the East India Company in India of a knowledge of Sanskrit are to be contemplated, than the aid which it is calculated to afford them in their executive functions. It will not only enable them to understand the uttered words of those with whom they hold official intercourse; it will not only teach them to interpret the language of representation or complaint, or to express the decrees of justice, or the commands of power;—it will enable them to understand the people, and to be understood by them. The popular prejudices of the Hindus, their daily observances, their occupations, their amusements, their domestic and social relations, their local legends, their national traditions, their mythological fables, their metaphysical abstractions, their religious worship, all spring from, and are perpetuated by, the Sanskrit language. To know a people, these things must be known. Without such knowledge, revenue may be raised, justice may be administered, the outward shows and forms of orderly government may be maintained; but no influence with the people will be enjoyed, no claim to their confidence or attachment will be established, no affection will be either felt or inspired, and neither the disposition nor the ability to work any great or permanent improvement in the feelings, opinions, or practices of the country will be attained. It fortunately happens, it is true, that much of this indispensable information may now be acquired through the English language, in consequence of the valuable translations and dissertations of various of the Company's most distinguished servants; but knowledge from the fountain head is more precise and effective than when gleaned from subordinate, and not always pure or profound, rivulets: and in proportion as it is effective and precise, will be the respect and trust of the native population, the influence and power of their English masters.

CONTENTS.

SANSKRIT ALPHABET.

Initial.	Medial.	Equivalent and power.		Equivalent and power.
अ	–	a, *as in* America.	ञ	ṅ, *as in* singe.
आ	ा	a — casa (Italian).	ट	ṭ — true.
इ	ि	i — chi —	ठ	ṭh
ई	ी	í — cosí —	ड	ḍ — dim.
उ	ु	u — furore —	ढ	ḍh
ऊ	ू	ú — fui —	ण	n̂ — none.
ऋ	ृ	ri — ricco —	त	t — tongue.
ॠ	ॄ	rí — ríso —	थ	th
ऌ	ॢ	lri	द	d — den.
ॡ	ॣ	lrí	ध	dh
ए	े	e — che —	न	n — not.
ऐ	ै	ai — mai —	प	p — point.
ओ	ो	o — cosa —	फ	ph — up-hill.
औ	ौ	au — paura —	ब	b — bind.
अं	ं	aṅ — (ang)	भ	bh — abhor.
अः	ः	ah	म	m — man.
क		k, *as in* king.	य	y — young.
ख		kh — khan.	र	r — rain.
ग		g — gun.	ल	l — lion.
घ		gh — afghan.	व	v — voice.
ङ		ń — sing.	श	ś — session.
च		ch — church.	ष	sh — shun.
छ		chh	स	s — son.
ज		j — jet.	ह	h — house.
झ		jh	ळ	lr

Varieties: अ a, ऋ ri, ल l, ए e, झ jh, ण n̂, रु ru, रू or ऱ rú.

Numerals:	१	२	३	४	५	६	७	८	९	१०
	1	2	3	4	5	6	7	8	9	10

SANSKRIT GRAMMAR.

CHAPTER I.

LETTERS.

THE Sanskrit language is written in different parts of India in the characters which are in use for the spoken dialects; but the alphabet which is regarded as most appropriate to it, and from which the local alphabets are derived, is that which is termed Nágarí or Devanágarí, the alphabet of 'the city,' or of 'the city of the gods,' being a derivative from Nagara, 'a city,' compounded in the second form with Deva, 'deus,' 'a god.' It appears to have undergone various modifications from a period of remote antiquity down to the seventh or eighth century, when the letters assumed the form in which they now occur.

As usually enumerated, the Nágarí alphabet comprises forty-seven letters, the long vowels being considered distinct from the short; the vowels are thus fourteen: the consonants, among which the aspirated are distinguished from the corresponding unaspirated letters, are thirty-three. The consonants are classified according to the organ chiefly concerned in their articulation; and in order to effect their utterance, the short vowel 'a' is attached to their respective sounds.

Vowels.

अ a, आ á, इ i, ई í, उ u, ऊ ú, ऋ ṛi, ॠ ṛí, ऌ lṛi, ॡ lṛí, ए e, ऐ ai, ओ o, औ au.

Consonants.

Gutturals, क ka, ख kha, ग ga, घ gha, ङ ń.
Palatals, च cha, छ chha, ज ja, झ jha, ञ ṅ.
Cerebrals, ट ťa, ठ ťha, ड ďa, ढ ďha, ण ńa.
Dentals, त ta, थ tha, द da, ध dha, न na.
Labials, प pa, फ pha, ब ba, भ bha, म ma.
Semivowels, य ya, र ra, ल la, व va.
Sibilants and aspirate, श śa, ष sha, स sa, ह ha.

To these are to be added two signs, which are occasionally attached to vowels, termed Anuswára and Visarga. The first is a dot over and after a letter; the second consists of two dots after it. The first denotes a slight nasal; the second, a soft aspirate; as, अं aṅ (ang), अः ah. Another additional character is ळ, with a sound partaking of 'l' and 'r,' but it is peculiar to the Vedas. Some lists add क्ष ksha and ज्ञ jṅa, but these are compounds; the first of क k and ष sh, and the second of ज j and ञ ṅ. The first is sometimes expressed by 'x.'

In designating a letter, the word कार kára is added to it; as, अकार a-kára, the letter 'a;' ककार ka-kára, the letter 'k,' &c.

When a vowel is uttered as an initial, or before a consonant, it retains the form above given: when it is uttered after a consonant, or as a medial or final, it assumes a different form, which is written before or after, above or below, the consonant with which it is associated; with exception of अ 'a,' which, as a medial or final, is always left unwritten, being understood to be combined with the consonant, and articulated with it, as in the alphabet, unless the consonant be final, which is denoted by a mark at its foot, a Virâma or 'rest,' as

क् k; or unless it be conjoined with another consonant, as below. The forms of the vowels as medials and finals are,

ा á, ि i, ी í, ु u, ू ú, ृ ṛi, ॄ ṛí, ॢ lṛi, ॣ lṛí,
े e, ै ai, ो o, ौ au:

or in combination, अक् ak, अक aka, आका áká, इकि iki, ईकी íkí, उकु uku, ऊकू úkú, ऋकृ ṛikṛi, ॠकॄ ṛíkṛí, ऌकॢ lṛiklṛi, ॡकॣ lṛíklṛí, एके eke, ऐकै aikai, ओको oko, औकौ aukau, अकं akaṅ, अकः akah.

When two or more consonants come together, without any intermediate vowel, they are combined into one compound consonant—in which in general the component members may be recognised without much difficulty—one consonant being subjoined to the other, as in अक्क akka, अच्च achcha, where the transverse line of the lower is omitted; or one consonant following the other, as अग्ग agga, अज्ज ajja, where the perpendicular line of the first of the two is rejected. In some cases the elements of the combination are not so obvious. The letters most frequently recurring in conjunction with preceding consonants are य ya and र ra. The first is easily discernible in

क्य kya, च्य chya, त्य tya, द्य dya, प्य pya, म्य mya, &c.:

the second is usually designated by a short transverse stroke at the foot of the letter or letters; as,

क्र or क्र kra, ग्र gra, त्र or त्र tra, द्र dra, प्र pra, क्र्य krya.

When र precedes a consonant, it is placed at the top of it in the shape of a crescent; as, र्क rka in अर्क arka, 'the sun;' or र्म्म rmma in धर्म्म dharmma, 'duty.'

The difficulties from this source soon disappear with practice. Some of the most useful combinations are subjoined. It may be also here observed, that some of the single letters may be written in a different manner, of which examples are given at the foot of the Table at the head of this chapter.

Compound consonants.

क्क kka	क्त kta	क्न kna	क्म kma	क्व kwa	क्त्व ktwa
क्त्र्य ktrya	क्ष ksha	क्ष्य kshya	क्ष्व kshwa	ख्य khya	ग्र gra
ग्र्य grya	घ्न ghna	घ्म ghma	ङ्क ńka	ङ्ग ńga	ङ्घ ńgha
ङ्घ्र ńghra	च्च chcha	च्छ chchha	च्म chma	च्छ्र chchhra	ज्ज jja
ज्य jya	ज्र jra	ज्व jwa	ज्झ jjha	ञ्च ǹcha	ञ्ज ǹja
ट्ट t́t́a	ठ्य t́hya	ढ्र d́hra	ण्ट n̂t́a	ण्ठ n̂t́ha	ण्ड n̂d́a
ण्ढ n̂d́ha	ण्ण n̂a	ण्ण्य n̂n̂ya	ण्व n̂wa	त्क tka	त्त tta
त्त्य ttya	त्त्र ttra	त्न tna	त्म tma	त्म्य tmya	त्र्य trya
त्व twa	त्स tsa	त्स्न tsna	त्स्य tsya	द्ग dga	द्घ dgha
द्द dda	द्ध ddha	द्ध्य ddhya	द्न dna	द्ब dba	द्भ dbha
द्भ्य dbhya	द्म dma	द्य dya	द्र dra	द्व dwa	द्व्य dwya
ध्न dhna	ध्म dhma	ध्व dhwa	न्त nta	न्त्य ntya	न्त्र ntra
न्द nda	न्द्र ndra	न्ध ndha	न्ध्र ndhra	न्न nna	प्त pta
प्न pna	प्प ppa	प्म pma	प्ल pla	प्व pwa	प्स psa
ब्ज bja	ब्भ bbha	भ्य bhya	भ्व bhwa	म्न mna	म्प mpa
म्म mma	म्स msa	ल्प lpa	ल्म lma	व्य vya	श्च ścha
श्च्य śchya	श्न śna	श्र śra	श्व śwa	श्श śśa	ष्ट sht́a
ष्ट्य sht́ya	ष्ट्र sht́ra	ष्ट्र्य sht́rya	ष्ण shn̂a	ष्म shma	स्क ska
स्ख skha	स्त sta	स्त्र stra	स्थ stha	स्न sna	स्प spa
स्फ spha	स्म sma	स्म्य smya	स्य sya	स्र sra	स्व swa
ह्न hna	ह्म hma	ह्य hya	ह्र hra	ह्ल hla	ह्व hwa.

PRONUNCIATION.

Few observations are required regarding the pronunciation of the letters of the Sanskrit alphabet. As a general rule, the vowels are to be sounded like those of the Italian alphabet, except the first, the short 'a,' which has the obscure sound of that letter in such English verbs as 'adorn,' 'adore,' or in the word 'America[a].' The vowels ṛi and lṛi differ not in

[a] This is the only cause of embarrassment in the system here followed of expressing Sanskrit words in English characters. It is difficult to our practice to pronounce 'ban' as if it was written 'bun;' as in Sanskrit, Bandhana, 'binding,' is to be pronounced Bundhunu; but u is necessarily restricted to its proper office, as in Italian, 'fui,' 'furore.'

sound from the syllables so compounded. They take their place among vowels as subject to euphonic changes, of which as syllables they would not be susceptible. The consonants are in general pronounced as in English, and we have, it may be suspected, several of the sounds for which the Sanscrit alphabet has provided distinct signs, but of which signs are wanting with us. This seems to be the case with the nasals and the cerebrals. We write but one 'n,' but we vary its articulation, according to the consonants it precedes, as a guttural, palatal, cerebral, and dental, in such words as 'conquer,' 'singe,' 'none,' and 'content.' So we write but one 't' and one 'd,' but their sounds differ in such words as 'trumpet' and 'tongue,' 'drain' and 'den:' in the first of which they are cerebrals, in the second dentals: the term cerebral has been adopted to express the Sanskrit Múrddhanya from Múrddhan मूर्द्धन् 'the head,' as these letters are articulated by touching the palate with the tongue farther back in the mouth than is practised in other articulations. The व v when compounded with another consonant is pronounced and written 'w,' as in द्वि dwi, 'two.' Of the three sibilants, the first 's' श is less decidedly 'sh' than the second, as in our 'ss' in 'session;' it is a palatal letter: ष sha is a cerebral, as in 'shore:' and स is a dental sibilant, as in 'sun.' Anuswára is a slight nasal, rather stronger than the 'n' of the French 'bon.' It is used in writing, however, as a substitute for other nasals, and then in general retains their pronunciation; as अहं ahań for अहम् aham, 'I,' is equally pronounced Aham; and अहंकार ahańkára is pronounced अहङ्कार ahańkára, for which it is written. Before semivowels and the aspirate ह the Anuswára is most appropriately used, and, whether original or substituted, has the same nasal sound, as in अंश ańśa, 'a part,' and संशय sańśaya, 'doubt;' in the latter of which it takes the place of the final of सम् sam, 'cum.' The aspirate denoted by Visarga is rarely marked: रामः Rámah is commonly articulated as Ráma.

CLASSIFICATION.

Besides the classification of the letters of the alphabet specified above, there is another which it may be sometimes useful to refer to. In this system the letters are thus arranged:

अ इ उ ण् | ऋ ऌ क् | ए ओ ङ् | ऐ औ च् | ह य व र ट् | ल ण् | ञ म ङ ण न म् | झ भ ञ् | घ ढ ध ष् | ज ब ग ड द श् | ख फ छ ठ थ च ट त व् | क प य् | श ष स र् | ह ल्.

The object of this arrangement is to provide a convenient mode of designating any particular set of letters to the exclusion of all others, which is done by combining any prior letter with the consonant at the end of a series, so as to form a Pratyáhára or syllable, denoting all the letters that intervene: thus, अल् means the whole alphabet; अच् the vowels only; हल् the consonants only; अण् means अ इ उ, inclusive of their corresponding long vowels; अक् denotes the simple vowels; एच् the diphthongs; यण् the semivowels; and झल् all the consonants exclusive of the nasals and semivowels. Other combinations may be formed on the same principle, with a like purport.

There are some distinctions also affecting the vowels and consonants generally, which it is advisable to particularise.

1. Vowels have three times or quantities: they are, लघु Laghu, 'light' or 'short;' गुरु Guru, 'heavy' or 'long;' and प्लुत Pluta, 'prolated.' They have also three accents, and are, उदात्त Udátta, 'grave;' अनुदात्त Anudátta, 'acute;' and स्वरित Swarita, 'compounded' or 'circumflex.' The long and short vowels are separately represented, as अ a, आ á: the prolated is the long á with three lines underneath it, or a figure of three behind it, as आ or आ ३. The accents are thus severally marked; अ́, अ॒, अ॑. They are rarely used, except in MSS. of the Vedas.

In combination and in inflexion the vowels are subject to two changes, or rather substitutions, in which other vowel forms take their places. These are called गुण Guńa and वृद्धि Vriddhi, rendered by Dr. Wilkins 'conversion' and 'augmentation.'

The Guńa substitutes are अ ए ओ अर् अल्.
The Vriddhi substitutes are आ ऐ औ आर् आल्.

Thus the verb भू bhú, 'to be,' in its inflexions is subject to Guńa; that is, it becomes भो bho, 'o' being substituted for 'u.' In some of its secondary derivatives the 'u' is subject to Vriddhi: thus भूत bhúta, 'a being,' 'an element,' furnishes the adjective भौतिक bhautika, 'elementary.' This will be more intelligible as we proceed. It is only at present essential to recollect the purport of the terms Guńa and Vriddhi.

2. Consonants. It is at present more important to notice a distinction of the consonants into two classes: some of them are hard, some soft. Wilkins calls the former surds; the latter, sonants; in which he is followed by Professor Bopp. The hard or surd consonants are the two first letters of the five first classes of the alphabet and the sibilants; the soft or sonant consonants are the three last letters of each class, the semivowels, and the aspirate.

Hard or surd letters, क ख च छ ट ठ त थ प फ श ष स.
Soft or sonant, ग घ ङ ज झ ञ ड ढ ण द ध न ब भ म य र ल व ह.

CHAPTER II.

SANDHI—COMBINATION OF LETTERS.

CONTRIVANCES for avoiding the concurrence of harsh or incongruous sounds, or the unpleasing hiatus which arises from keeping sounds apart that are disposed to coalesce, are not wanting in all languages. They are in general, however, rather poetical or prosodial than grammatical; such as the elision of a final 'e' before an initial 'e' in such a concurrence as "the etherial height of heaven," which it was formerly the fashion to write, as the measure demanded, "th' etherial;" to say nothing of the synalepha and ecthlipsis of Latin verse, "Monstr' horrend' inform' ingens," &c. Other instances of a regard for euphony, however, do occur independent of prosody, and especially in Greek, in which many of the euphonic changes are analogous to those provided for in Sanskrit. In no language has the subject, however, been so systematically investigated as in Sanskrit; and the changes to which letters are subject for the sake of euphony are numerous, and carefully defined, forming that part of Sanskrit grammar which is termed सन्धि Sandhi, 'a holding together,' 'a junction;' or संहिता Saṅhitá, 'an association,' 'a conjunction;' either being derived from the verb compounded of the preposition सम् sam, 'cum,' and धा dhá, 'to have,' 'to hold.'

SECTION I.

Conjunction of vowels.

1. When a vowel terminating a word is followed by a similar vowel beginning another word, whether they both be short or both long, or one be short and one long, they combine into one long homogeneous vowel: thus

a with a makes á; as, दैत्य Daitya + अरि ari = दैत्यारि Daityári, 'a foe of the demons,' a name of Vishṅu.

á with a makes á; as, सा sá + अगच्छत् agachhat = सागच्छत् sá-gachhat, 'she went.'

i with i makes í; as, इति iti + इव iva = इतीव itíva, 'so indeed.'

í with í makes í; as, श्री S'rí + ईश ís'a = श्रीश S'rís'a, 'the lord of S'rí.'

u with u makes ú; as, भानु bhánu + उदय udaya = भानूदय bhánúdaya, 'sun-rise.'

ṛi with ṛi makes ṛí; as, नृ nṛi + ऋषि ṛishi = नॄषि nṛíshi, 'a man- (a mortal) sage.'

The concurrence of a final and initial ऌ never perhaps takes place. ऌ may however follow ऋ, and as they are considered as homogeneous, a long ॠ ṛí may be the result; as, होतृ hotṛi + ऌकार lṛikára makes होतॄकार 'the letter lṛí (a sort of incantation) of the Hotṛi,' or officiating priest. The concurrence of ऋ, however, either with another ऋ or with ऌ, is not liable to any very strict rule, and the substitute may be either a short or long ऋ; as, होतृ with either ऋकार or ऌकार may be either होतृकार or होतॄकार.

2. If a word which ends in either अ a or आ á be followed by a word beginning with a different vowel, then a Guńa element is substituted for both; that is, if अ or आ precedes इ or ई, the substitute is ए; if उ or ऊ, it is ओ; if ऋ or ॠ, it is अर्; if ऌ or ॡ, अल्; as,

उप upa + इन्द्र Indra = उपेन्द्र Upendra, a name of Kṛishńa.

यथा yathá + ईप्सितं ípsitam + यथेप्सितं yathepsitam, 'as desired.'

गङ्गा Gańgá + उदकम् udakam = गङ्गोदकम् Gańgodakam, 'Ganges water.'

मह maha + ऋषि ṛishi = महर्षि maharshi, 'a great sage.'

तव tava + ऌकार lṛikára = तवल्कार tavalkára, 'thy letter ऌ.'

3. If a word ends, as in the last case, with अ or आ, and is followed by one beginning with a diphthong, a Vṛiddhi letter is substituted for both; that is, if अ be followed by ए or ऐ, the substitute is ऐ; if by ओ or औ, it is औ; as,

कृष्ण Kṛishńa + एकत्वं ekatwam = कृष्णैकत्वं Kṛishńaikatwam, 'oneness with Kṛishńa.'

विद्या vidyá + एव eva = विद्यैव vidyaiva, 'knowledge,' 'verily.'

देव deva + ऐश्वर्यं aiśwaryam = देवैश्वर्यं devaiśwaryam, 'the divinity of a god.'

अल्प alpa + ओजस् ojas = अल्पौजस् alpaujas, 'of little radiance.'

बाला bálá + औत्सुक्यं autsukyam = बालौत्सुक्यं bálautsukyam, 'the maiden's sorrow.'

There are some exceptions to these two last rules, which it may be convenient here to insert. With regard to these and to other anomalies and exceptions, however, it may be advisable once for all to recommend to the student, in an early stage of his studies, to content himself with a passing notice of them, and not allow them to divert his attention from the general rules. Familiar with the rules, he will find no difficulty in the occasional deviations from them which occur.

a. अक्ष aksha before ऊहिणी úhiñí makes अक्षौहिणी akshauhiñí, 'a large army,' instead of अक्षोहिणी, as it should do by rule 2.

b. When ईर् ír, a radical signifying 'go,' or any of its derivatives, follows the 'a' of स्व swa, the substitute is not 'e,' but 'ai;' as स्वैरं 'self-going,' 'independence;' स्वैरिणी 'an independent female servant,' i. e. not a slave.

c. Verbal derivatives from the roots इण् iñ, 'go,' and एध् edh, 'increase,' take the Vṛiddhi substitute after the vowel अ of a preposition; as, उप + एति = उपैति 'he approaches;' उप + एधते = उपैधते 'it increases.' In general, verbs beginning with ए or ओ retain their own vowel, and cause the elision of the final अ of a preposition; as, प्र before एजते makes प्रेजते 'he trembles;' प्र before ओषति makes प्रोषति 'he sprinkles.' The ओ which is evolved from ऊह्, substituted for the व of वह् vah, 'bear,' takes Vṛiddhi after the short 'a,' as विश्ववाह् 'all-sustaining,' becomes in the acc. plur. विश्वौहः

d. Derivatives from इष् ish, 'go,' 'wish,' take the Vṛiddhi letter after the 'a' of प्र pra, as प्रैष praisha, 'a messenger;' so do those of ऊह् úh, 'reason;' as प्रौढ praudha, 'proud,' 'arrogant.' ईष् ísh, 'glean,' takes Guña after प्र, as प्रेष presha, 'a gleaner.'

e. Roots beginning with ऋ after a preposition ending in 'a,' substitute the Vṛiddhi form आर् ár, as उप + ऋच्छति makes उपार्च्छति upárchchhati, 'approaches;' by rule 2. it should have been उपर्च्छति uparchchhati. The Vṛiddhi आर् is also substituted for an initial ऋ when the word it commences is compounded with a preceding word ending in 'a,' and having the sense of the instrumental case: thus सुख sukha and ऋत ṛita may be joined together, as सुखार्त्त sukhártta, 'affected by joy;' शीत śíta and ऋत ṛita, as शीतार्त्त śítártta, 'affected by cold.' If the first member have not the sense of the instrumental case, the words combine agreeably to rule 2; as, परम parama and ऋत ṛita make परमर्त paramartta, 'last-gone:' the same if the first word retains the sign of the instrumental case, the words coalescing in virtue of their juxta-position, but not forming a compound: thus सुखेन + ऋत makes सुखेनर्त sukhenartta.

f. The word ऋण ṛíṅa doubled or preceded by प्र, वत्सतर, कम्बल, वसन, or दश, substitutes the Vṛiddhi syllable आर्, not the Guṅa अर्; as, ऋणार्ण ṛiṅárṅa, 'debt of a debt;' प्रार्ण prárṅa, 'principal debt;' वत्सतरार्ण vatsatarárṅa, 'debt of a mule;' वसनार्ण vasanárṅa, 'debt of a cloth;' दशार्ण Daśárṅa, name of a country; दशार्णा Daśárṅá, name of a river, the Dosaron of Ptolemy.

g. Verbs formed from nouns beginning with ऋ take either the Guṅa or Vṛiddhi substitute after the अ of a preposition: ऋषभीयति ṛishabhíyati, 'he resembles or acts like a ṛishabha,' i. e. a bull, with प्र pra makes either प्रर्षभीयति or प्रार्षभीयति. So with an initial ऌ, as प्रल्कारीयति or प्राल्कारीयति. When the initial is the long vowel ॠ, either no coalescence takes place, or the change is to the Guṅa syllable; as, उप and ॠकारीयति make either उपॠकारीयति or उपर्कारीयति.

h. When ऋ as the initial of a noun follows an inflected noun ending in a short vowel, it may remain unaltered, or follow rule 2: thus मह and ऋषि may make either महर्षि or महऋषि.

i. Verbs formed from nouns beginning with ए or ओ following a preposition ending in अ, either cause its elision, or substitute the Vṛiddhi letter; as, उप and एडकीयति edakíyati make either उपेडकीयति or उपैडकीयति 'he is sheepish.'

k. When the particle एव, 'verily,' 'indeed,' is used to intimate uncertainty, it causes the elision of a preceding अ; as, क्व kwa and एव eva make क्वेव kweva in such a sentence as क्वेवभोक्ष्यसे 'Where will you dine?' When certainty is affirmed, the combination follows rule 3; as, सखे त्वया सहैव भोक्ष्ये 'I shall certainly dine with you, my friend.'

l. The words ओतु otu, 'a cat,' and ओष्ठ osht́ha, 'the lip,' when compounded with a preceding word ending in अ, either follow rule 3, or cause the elision of the preceding vowel; as, स्थूल sthúla + ओतु = स्थूलौतु or स्थूलोतु 'a fat cat;' विम्ब vimba + ओष्ठ is either विम्बौष्ठ or विम्बोष्ठ 'cherry-lipped.' If the words coalesce without forming a new compound, the rule is adhered to: तव + ओष्ठ make तवौष्ठ 'the lip of thee.'

---

4. When a word ends with any simple vowel, except अ or आ, and is followed by a word that begins with a dissimilar vowel, or with a diphthong, the latter is unaltered, but the former is changed to its analogous semivowel: thus इ and ई are changed to य y, उ and ऊ to व v, ऋ ॠ to र r, and ऌ ॡ to ल l; as,

इति + आकर्ण्य = इत्याकर्ण्य ityákarńya, 'thus having heard.'
ऋजु + आयत = ऋज्वायत ṛijwáyata, 'simple-minded.'
भ्रातृ + अंश = भ्रात्रंश bhrátranśa, 'a brother's portion.'
ऌ + अनुबन्ध = लनुबन्ध lanubandha, 'the adjunct (Anubandha) . Lṛi.'

---

a. There are various rules for the correct orthography of words coalescing in this form, but they are amongst the inconveniences of Sanscrit grammar, and are little observed in practice: it is enough here to remark, that under them the first word may be also spelled इत्त्याकर्ण्य, इत्याकर्ण्य्य, or इत्त्याकर्ण्य्य, doubling the first conjunct consonant, the second, or both. In general, however, the simplest form is used, unless the first of the conjunct consonants be र, when the second should be doubled; as, गौरी 'Gaurí' (the goddess) + अत्र 'here,' is most correctly written गौर्य्यत्र Gauryyatra. So also in uncompounded words the letter र doubles the consonant conjoined with it, as कर्त्ता karttá, कर्म्म karmma, धर्म्म dharmma, although it is not uncommon to omit the duplication in writing.

b. In some instances, when the words are not compounded,

and not inflected, a final simple vowel followed by a dissimilar vowel may either conform to the rule, may remain unaltered, or, if long, may be changed to its short vowel: thus चक्री chakrí + अत्र atra, 'The discus-armed (Vishńu), here!' may make either चक्र्यत्र or चक्रि अत्र or चक्री अत्र. If a new compound be formed, the rule must be followed, and the semivowel substituted; as, हरि Hari + अर्थ artha makes हर्य्यर्थ Haryyartha, 'the object of Hari:' and so it must if an inflective termination be added to the word to form a case, as गौर्य्याः Gauryyáh, 'of the goddess Gaurí.'

---

5. When a diphthong ending a word is followed by any vowel or diphthong—even though the latter be the same—beginning a word, the following syllables are severally substituted for the antecedent diphthong:

For ए—अय् ay, as चे + अन makes चयन chayana, 'gathering.'
— ऐ—आय् áy, as नै + अक makes नायक náyaka, 'a leader.'
— ओ—अव् av, as विष्णो + ए = विष्णवे Vishńave, 'to Vishńu.'
— औ—आव् áv, as पुत्रौ + इमौ = पुत्राविमौ putrávimau, 'these two children.'

---

a. These syllables may be substituted for diphthongs before य when it is the initial of the affix यत्, forming participial nouns in certain senses.

जे from जि + यत् = जय्य jayya, 'what may be conquered.'
भो from भू + यत् = भव्य bhavya, 'what may be' or 'is to be.'
नौ + यत् = नाव्य návya, relating to 'a ship,' 'naval.'

b. गो before यत् substitutes अव् for the final, गव्य gavya, 'relating to a cow;' also before the affix यूति, as गव्यूति 'a measure;' but this is peculiar to the Vedas. In ordinary use, the words are गो यूति 'a measure of two kos.'

---

6. Concurrent heterogeneous letters in some cases do not follow any of the preceding rules, or they follow them optionally; or one of the two vowels becomes quiescent, or is ejected.

These are termed प्रगृह्य Pragṛihyá, literally 'what must be taken out,' 'excipienda.'

---

a. The finals ई ऊ and ए, when they are the terminations of nouns in the dual number, are unchanged before other vowels or diphthongs: हरी एतौ 'these two Haris;' भानू इमे 'these two suns;' अङ्गने अमू 'these two women.'

b. अमी the nom. plur. masc. of the pronoun अदस्, 'that,' does not coalesce with a following vowel: अमी ईशाः 'those lords.'

c. The उ of किमु may be unchanged, or may substitute the semivowel 'v' before a vowel, as किमु उक्तं or किम्वुक्तं 'What is said?'

d. ई or ऊ substituted, as they sometimes irregularly are, for the proper ending of the locative case, are unchanged, as सोमो गौरी अधिश्रितः 'Soma relying on Gaurí:' गौरी for गौर्याम्.

e. Prolated vowels, pluta, are incapable of combination: एहि कृष्ण३ अत्र 'Come, Kṛishńa̳ (as if in calling), here.'

f. ए and ओ being the terminations of an inflected word, cause a following अ to be ejected; its elision is however usually denoted by a peculiar character; as, अग्नेऽत्र 'O fire! here.' विष्णोऽत्र 'O Vishńu! here.'

g. The ओ of गो is subject to various modifications before अ: both may be unchanged, अ may be elided, or ओ may be changed to अव ava: thus गो and अग्रं make गो अग्रं, गोऽग्रं, or गवाग्रं. ओ is changed to अव ava before अक्ष and इन्द्र, making by rules 1. and 2. गवाक्ष 'a lattice,' and गवेन्द्र a name of Kṛishńa; also before ईश, making गवेशः; or it may be changed before this word to अव् av, by rule 5, regularly making गवीश 'lord of kine.'

h. When the short vowel अ is followed by the sacred monosyllable ओम् Om, or by the preposition आ compounded with a verb, it is rejected: thus शिवाय + ओम् becomes शिवायोंनमः 'Adoration (Om) to S'iva!' and शिव + एहि (from आ + इहि) makes शिवेहि 'O S'iva, come!'

i. Particles, when single vowels, are not changed before other vowels; as, इ इन्द्र—उ उमेश 'O Indra! O lord of Umá!' आ is an exception, if it implies diminution: आ + उष्णं makes ओष्णं oshńam, 'a little warm.' As an interjection it is unchanged: आ एवं 'Ah, indeed!' The final ओ of a particle is unchanged: अहो ईशाः 'Ho, deities.'

k. The final ओ of a vocative case takes various forms before the particle इति; as, विष्णो इति, विष्ण इति, or विष्णविति.

l. In a particular class of compound words the initial of the second word is preserved, and the last vowel of the preceding word is rejected; in one case, along with the consonant by which it is followed: thus

शक + अन्धु = शकन्धु śakandhu, 'a sort of potherb.'
कर्क + अन्धु = कर्कन्धु karkandhu, 'the jujube.'
लाङ्गल + ईशा = लाङ्गलीशा láṅgalíśá, 'the handle of a plough.'
मार्त्त + अण्ड = मार्त्तण्ड márttańḋa, 'the sun.'
मनस् + ईषा = मनीषा manísha, 'intellect.'

SECTION II.

Combination of consonants.

We must now recollect the distinction which has been pointed out (p. 7) with regard to the two classes of consonants, as hard or surd, and soft or sonant; as, in addition to such rules as affect peculiar letters, there are one or two general rules which it will be of great use to bear in mind.

7. When two consonants come together, and are affected by no special rule, there will be no change, if they are both hard or both soft; but if they are of different enunciation, and one is hard, and the other is soft, then the first of the two must be changed to a letter of the same quality as the second, which will be the hard or soft letter of the class to which it belongs; as, क to ग, or ग to क; च to ज, or ज to च; ट to ड or ड to ट; त to द or द to त; प to ब or ब to प. The further exemplification of this rule may thus be stated:—

a. If the consonants be both hard, there is no change:

thus, before the termination सु, the nouns sarvaśak, harit, ap, retain their finals, as सर्वशक्सु, हरित्सु, अप्सु. वाक् before पति is वाक्पति 'lord of speech.'

b. If both are soft, there is no change: अद् before भिस् is अद्भिः adbhih, 'by waters.'

c. A hard before a soft consonant must be changed to a soft consonant of its own class: thus भगवत् गीता 'the song of the lord,' becomes भगवद्गीता bhagavad-gíta, 't' being changed to 'd:' अप् before ज changes its final to ब, and becomes अब्ज, 'water-born,' 'a lotus.'

d. A soft consonant before a hard consonant must be changed to the hard consonant of its own class: भिद्, 'to break,' before तव्य changes द to त, भेत्तव्य 'to be broken;' so it does before सु, and गोत्रभिद् becomes गोत्रभित्सु 'in the destroyers of races.'

8. If the antecedent consonant be an aspirated letter, it is not only modified by the preceding rule, but whatever form it takes it is the unaspirated letter; an aspirate cannot precede an unaspirated letter, nor can two aspirated consonants come together. Thus in the combination दधि + अत्र dadhi-atra, where by rule 4. it makes दध्यत्र dadhyatra, and by the following remark *a.* the ध dh may be doubled, the duplication requires that the first member shall be unaspirated, and the word must be written, not दध्ध्यत्र dadhdhyatra, but दद्ध्यत्र daddhyatra: so क्रुध and ध become क्रुद्ध; लभ and ध, लब्ध; ककुभ् and भिस्, ककुब्भि; and चित्रलिख् and भ्याम्, चित्रलिग्भ्याम्, the ख, which is a hard letter, being first changed to the unaspirated क, and क being changed to ग before the soft aspirate भ.

9. A hard consonant, when final, is changed to a soft consonant; and a final aspirated consonant, to an unaspirated: thus, वाक् becomes वाग्; and चित्रलिख्, चित्रलिग्.

When however it occurs before a pause, that is, when not followed immediately by any letter, the change to a soft consonant is optional: thus the nom. sing. of वाक् is either वाक् or वाग्; of चित्रलिख्, चित्रलिक् or -लिग्.

10. Final hard consonants, followed by words beginning with vowels, are changed to soft (the vowels being soft or sonant letters); as, वाक् + ईश becomes वागीश Vágísa, 'god of speech,' a name of Vrihaspati; not 'the god of wine,' as Sir Wm. Jones conjectured, from the accidental resemblance of Vágísa and Bacchus.

When hard and aspirated consonants are followed by the terminations of the cases which open with vowels, they are no longer regarded as final, and are therefore not subject to change: सर्व्वशक् makes सर्व्वशकौ—सर्व्वशका; चित्रलिख्, चित्रलिखौ—चित्रलिखे &c.

11. A consonant of the dental class, त थ द ध न, preceding a consonant of the palatal class, च छ ज झ ञ श, or of the cerebral class, ट ठ ड ढ ण, but excepting the sibilant (ष), is changed to the corresponding letter of that class; that is, त थ are changed to च or ट; द ध to ज or ड; and न to ञ or ण.

सत् + चित् = सच्चित् 'pure reason.'
तद् + जीव = तज्जीव 'that life.'
तत् + श्रुत्वा = तच्छ्रुत्वा 'having heard that.'
शार्ङ्गिन् + जय = शार्ङ्गिञ्जय a name of Vishńu.
तत् + टीका = तट्टीका 'a comment on that.'
चक्रिन् + ढौकसे = चक्रिण्ढौकसे 'O discus-armed! thou goest.'

Before the cerebral sibilant, the dentals are unchanged, as सन् षष्ठ 'being the sixth.'

12. Dentals are also changed to cerebrals, when following cerebrals; as, the affix तृच् with the verb पिष्, 'to grind,' forms पेष्टृ peshṭṛi, 'a grinder.' They are not so changed when they are radical letters, as षट् ते 'they six.'

13. Dental consonants before the letter ल are changed to ल; as, तत् + लिखति = तल्लिखति 'he writes that;' भवान् + लिखति makes भवाल्लिखति; as σὺν and λέγω make συλλέγω. A peculiar mark is sometimes inserted to denote the change of the nasal, as भवाँल्लिखति.

14. A nasal of the same class may be substituted for any final consonant, except र or ह, before a word beginning with a nasal; as,

वाक् + नयति = वाङ् नयति váń nayati, 'speech guides.'
षट् + नवति = षण्णवति shaññavati, 'ninety-six.'
षट् + मास = षण्मास shañmása, 'six months.'
एतत् + मुरारि = एतन्मुरारि Etan-Murári, 'that Vishñu.'

a. This rule does not preclude the operation of the general rule, by which concurrent consonants must be assimilated; it only makes it optional: thus for वाङ् नयति we may also write वाग् नयति; and for एतत् मुरारि, एतद्मुरारि; the nasals being sonants.

b. The rule is absolute in one case, when the following word is a technical affix; such as मय, implying, when conjoined with nouns, 'consisting of;' and मात्र, implying 'so much,' 'merely;' as, वाक् with मय makes only वाङ्मय váńmaya, 'made of speech,' 'eloquent;' and तत् with मात्र is तन्मात्र tanmátra, 'merely that,' 'a primary element.'

15. न is changed to ण in the genitive case of षट् 'six;' also in the words नवति and नगरी after षट्; as, षण्णां shaññám, षण्णवति shaññavati, षण्णगरी shaññagarí; the ट of षट् being changed to ण by rule 14.

16. Before a sibilant, ङ and ण may insert respectively the letters क and ट; as, प्राङ् before षष्ठ makes प्राङ् क् षष्ठ or प्राङ् षष्ठ 'sixth anterior,' and सुगण् + षष्ठ = सुगण् ट् षष्ठ 'sixth numerator:' and ट or ड or न, before the dental sibilant, may insert the dental त; as, मधुलिट् सहते or मधुलिट् त्सहते 'the bee endures;' and सन् सः or सन त् सः 'he being.'

17. The nasals ङ ण न, terminating a word, when preceded by a short vowel, and followed by any vowel as the initial of a subsequent word, may be doubled; as,

प्रत्यङ् + आस्ते = प्रत्यङ्ङास्ते 'he sits facing the west.'
सुगण् + ईश = सुगण्णीश 'the lord of an excellent class.'
राजन् + इति = राजन्निति 'O king! thus.'

18. न following ऋ immediately, or र or ष either immedi-

ately or separated by an intervening guttural or labial consonant, a vowel, य, व, ह, Visarga, or Anuswára deduced from न or म, is changed to ण; as, ऋन becomes ऋण 'debt;' परि + नत = परिणत 'bowed.' If final it is unchanged, as गुरून्.

19. A final म terminating an inflected word may be changed to Anuswára before a consonant; as, for हरिम् read हरिं वन्दे 'I salute Hari;' so for तम् read तं हसति 'he laughs at him.' Before राज् the final of सम् is unalterable; as, सम्राज् 'a universal monarch.' It is unchanged before a vowel; as, अहमागतः 'I (am) come.'

20. म is optionally changed to Anuswára before ह in conjunction with म, as किम् or किं ह्मलयति; but Anuswára derived from म may become य, ल, or व, before ह combined with these semivowels severally; as, किं or किय् ह्यः, किं or किल् ह्लादयति, किं or किव् ह्वलयति. It may become न before ह combined with न, as किं or किन् ह्नुते.

21. Anuswára followed by any consonant, except the semivowels, sibilants, and ह, is changed, if in the middle of a word, to the nasal of that class to which the consonant following it belongs: अं + कित = अङ्कित 'marked;' अं + चित = अञ्चित 'worshipped.'

a. If it be the final of an inflected word, the change is optional; as, अहम् + कार = अहंकार or अहङ्कार 'egoism;' त्वं or त्वङ्करोषि 'thou doest;' त्वं or त्वन् ददासि 'thou givest.'

b. If the following consonant be a semivowel, the Anuswára may be optionally changed to the nasal form of the semivowel, which is denoted by a peculiar mark above it; as, संयम or सँय्यम 'restraint;' यंलोकं or यँल्लोकं 'to what world;' संवत्सर or सँव्वत्सर 'a year.'

22. Anuswára may be substituted for a medial न or म, when followed by a sibilant; as, धनूंषि 'bows;' यशांसि 'reputations;' कंस a proper name.

23. A final य् or व् preceded by अ or आ may be dropped before any letter except a hard consonant or a sibilant, as ते becoming तय् by rule 5. before आगताः makes त आगताः 'they

are come:' so तौ changed to ताव् before इमौ becomes ता इमौ 'those two.'

24. When श follows any consonant, except a semivowel, a nasal, or a sibilant, it is changed to छ; as, तद् + शिव S'iva = तच्छिव tach-chhiva, 'that, S'iva.'

For by rule 11. द् has been changed, before the palatal छ, to the analogous palatal ज; but the soft consonant ज, again, has been changed to the hard consonant च, before the hard consonant छ.

25. When followed by शम्भु, a final न may interpose the letter त, making सन् त् शम्भु; but by the preceding rule श is changed to छ; and by rule 11. त will then be changed to च, and न to ञ, and the compound will be सञ्च्छम्भु. By a subsequent rule, however, the terminating letter of the conjunct ञ्च् may be rejected, and the word will finally be सञ्छम्भु.

26. The augment त् may be inserted after a word ending in a short vowel, before one beginning with छ, as शिव त् छाया; but as त must be changed to च in such a position, the form is शिवच्छाया 'the shadow of S'iva.'

a. The same augment त् is optionally inserted after a long vowel, whether medial or final; as, लक्ष्मीछाया or लक्ष्मीच्छाया 'the shadow of Lakshmí;' म्लेछ or म्लेच्छ 'a barbarian.'

b. It is also inserted optionally after the particles आङ् and माङ् (leaving आ and मा) prefixed to verbal inflexions or derivatives beginning with छ (त is in like manner changed to च); as, आछादयति or आच्छादयति 'he covers;' माछिदत् or माच्छिदत् 'let him not divide.'

27. ष is changed to क before स, as द्रष् for दृश्, 'see,' makes with स्यति, द्रक्ष्यति 'will see:' (for स after a guttural becomes ष, and क and ष form the compound क्ष.)

28. Before a palatal consonant, including श, the dental स is changed to श; and before a cerebral, including ष, it is changed to ष; as, रामस् + चिनोति = रामश्चिनोति 'Ráma gathers;' रामस् + शेते = रामश्शेते 'Ráma sleeps;' रामस् + टीकते = रामष्टीकते 'Ráma goes;' रामस् + षष्ठ = रामष्षष्ठ 'Ráma, sixth.'

29. स, not being final, is changed to ष after any vowel except अ or आ, a guttural consonant, a semivowel, and ह, though the augment न, Visarga, or a sibilant intervene; thus धनुस् becomes in the plural, धनूंषि 'bows;' and शिवे and सु make शिवेषु 'in' or 'on S'ivas.'

30. When स in the verbs स्था 'to stay,' and स्तम्भ 'to stop,' and their derivatives, is preceded by the preposition उद्, it is rejected; and as the final द् becomes the hard consonant त before a hard consonant, then उद्+स्थान=उत्थान 'uprising,' and उद्+स्तम्भन=उत्तम्भन 'upholding.'

31. When ह follows any consonant, except a nasal, semivowel, or sibilant, the aspirate of the preceding letter may be substituted for it, that letter, if a hard consonant, being first changed to its corresponding soft letter; as, वाक्+हरति becomes first वाग्+हरति; and then वाग्घरति 'speech seizes.'

32. ह when final, or before any consonant except a nasal or a semivowel, is changed to ढ, as मधुलिह्, 'a bee,' becomes मधुलिढ्; such a ढ is changed to क before स, as दढ् for दह्, 'burn,' makes with स्यति, दक्ष्यति 'will burn.'

33. Any consonant may be optionally doubled after र or ह preceded by a vowel; as, अर्क or अर्क्क 'the sun;' वह्नि or वह्न्नि 'fire.'

34. Any consonant, except ह, followed by a consonant, may be doubled; as, पुत्+र may be पुत्त्र, 'a son;' मित्+र may be मित्त्र 'a friend.'

a. But when three or more consonants are joined together, by virtue of a grammatical rule, one or more of the intermediate ones, if similar, may be rejected; therefore पुत्त्र and मित्त्र are more usually written पुत्र and मित्र.

b. A semivowel following any consonant, except a semivowel, a sibilant, म, or ह, may be doubled; as, आदित्य or आदित्त्य 'the sun.'

c. But when two semivowels are preceded by a different consonant, one of them may be rejected; so आदित्त्य becomes आदित्य, as before.

35. When a conjunct consonant is final, whether terminating a syllable or a word, the second member is rejected, as खञ्ज्, 'a lame man,' becomes खन्; and हिन्स्, 'what injures,' हिन्: so after nouns ending in consonants, the sign of the nominative case स is rejected, as पतन्, 'going,' not पतन्स्.

If the preceding letter be र the final is retained, as ऊर्ज् 'strong;' but not if the second member be a sibilant, as चिकीर्ष्, 'who wishes to do,' becomes चिकीर्.

There are other rules affecting the mode of combining consonants, and the changes to which the combinations are subject; but their validity is matter of dispute: accordingly, as different rules are followed, the derivatives of the compound of सम् 'cum,' and कृ 'to make,' may be written in a variety of manners: संस्कर्ता, for instance, may be written in a hundred and eight ways. These are, however, matters merely of ortho-epical conceit, and in practice the simplest spelling, consistent with the essential elements of a word, is to be preferred.

36. When a word ending with र is followed by one beginning with र, one is rejected, and the preceding vowel, if short, is made long; as, पुनर् + रमते = पुनारमते 'he again sports;' निर् + रक्त = नीरक्त 'unimpassioned.'

SECTION III.

Changes of Visarga.

As preliminary to the rules for those changes to which the soft aspirate termed Visarga is subject, it may be useful to premise, that they contemplate the reciprocal equivalency of (:) Visarga, स, and र; these signs being, according to circumstances, mutually interchangeable. There are, as is well known, indications of similar reciprocity in the classical languages. The Greek ἕξ, ἑπτα, ἅλς, become in Latin, sex, septem, sal. In the older Latin writers a final 's' was commonly elided, at least for prosodial purposes; and Pott suggests that its place may have been supplied by something like

Visarga. Lucilius, according to Quintilian, wrote "Serenu' fuit et dignu' loco;" and Cicero observes, "Plures antiquorum sic locutos." The substitution of 'r' for 's' was also common in Latin, and arbor, labor, clamor, were originally written arbos, labos, clamos. The 's' was also sometimes preserved in the nominative, but changed in other inflexions, as flos, floris, and the like.

The meaning of Visarga विसर्ग is literally 'abandoning,' 'ejecting;' and that of its synonyme विसर्जनीय Visarjjaníya is 'that which may' or 'is to be ejected, or abandoned.' It has been a question, therefore, whether the symbol to which it is applied (:) be a simple mark of elision, a kind of apostrophe, or whether it designates a sound. It would be out of place to discuss the question at present. It is usually considered to denote a very soft and almost imperceptible breathing, and it is sufficient for our purpose so to regard it.

37. A final स् is changed to Visarga: रामस् Rámas becomes रामः Rámah; and रामैस् Rámais, रामैः Ramaih.

38. Before a hard consonant Visarga again becomes स: विष्णु + त्राता = विष्णुस्त्राता 'Vishńu the preserver.'

a. It is not so changed before a hard letter followed by a sibilant, as कः त्सरुः, 'Which (is) the sword-hilt?'

b. Before a sibilant the change is optional, as रामः शेते or रामश्शेते. (The dental sibilant is changed to the sibilant of the class of the consonant by which it is followed: see rule 28.)

c. Before the hard consonants of the guttural and labial classes, Visarga may be unchanged: कः करोति 'who does;' सः पचति 'he cooks.'

d. Before these letters a different sign ᳵ called Arddha-visarga, 'a half Visarga,' is sometimes used, as कᳵ करोति, कᳵ पचति. The sign before a guttural is described as जीह्वामूलीय 'proceeding from the root of the tongue;' and before a labial, उपध्मानीय 'to be gently blown or aspirated.' Modifications of aspiration are no doubt intended, which might have been of consequence when the language was spoken, but are now of no importance.

e. The permanence of Visarga before क is liable to exception, and it is changed to स before, 1. the pronoun क, as कस्कः 'quisquis;' 2. the affix क, as यशस्क 'famous;' and the particles कल्प and काम्य, as यशस्कल्प 'of little fame;' यशस्काम्य 'desirous of fame.' It is also changed before पाश, as यशस्पाश 'of slight renown.'

f. But it is not changed before कल्प, if that follows an indeclinable word; as, प्रातः कल्प 'nigh to morning;' nor before काम्य, if it be derived from a radical final; thus गिर् makes गीः 'speech,' whence गीः काम्य 'desirous of speech.'

g. It is changed before verbs and verbal derivatives commencing with क when compounded with नमः, पुरः, आवीः, and दुः; as, नमस्कार 'salutation;' पुरस्करोति 'he places before;' आविष्कृत 'manifested;' दुष्कृति 'evil-doing.'

h. The numerals द्विः त्रिः and चतुः change Visarga to स before क, as द्विष्करोति, त्रिष्करोति, चतुष्करोति, 'he makes two, three, four.' But if repetition is implied, the change is optional, as द्विःकरोति or द्विष्करोति 'he does (any thing) twice.'

i. तिरः optionally changes its final, as तिरः कार or तिरस्कार 'abuse.'

j. निर् becoming निः also optionally changes Visarga to स before क, as निः कासित or निष्कासित 'expelled.'

k. Visarga is changed to स after सर्पिः compounded with the particles कल्प and पाश, as सर्पिष्कल्प, सर्पिष्पाश, 'a little butter.'

l. It is changed after अधः and शिरः compounded with पद, as अधस्पद 'foot below;' शिरस्पद 'foot on the top.' If the words are uncompounded, the change does not take place, as अधः पद, शिरः पद.

39. The letter र (in technical grammar called रु ru, to distinguish it from the mere alphabetical sign) is substituted for Visarga after any vowel except अ or आ, and before a vowel or a soft consonant; as, गुणैः उपेत becomes गुणैरुपेत 'endowed with qualities;' अग्निः दहति = अग्निर्दहति 'fire burns;' नौर्याति 'the boat goes;' शम्भुर्हरति 'S'ambhu takes.'

40. If the Visarga be preceded by अ, and the initial of the word following be अ, or a soft consonant, उ is substituted in place of र, and उ with the penultimate अ forms the final diphthong ओ; as, कः अत्र makes कोऽत्र 'Who here?' कः गतः makes को गतः 'Who (is) gone?'

a. An initial अ following ओ so formed is rejected, but its place is marked by the sign ऽ. See rule 6. *f.*

b. मनस् changed by rule 37. to मनः becomes by this rule मनो in such compounds as मनोज, मनोभव, 'mind-born;' मनोरम 'mind-delighting.'

41. After the short vowel अ, and before any vowel except अ, Visarga may be changed to य्, which by rule 23. may be rejected; as, देवः and आस्ते become देवयास्ते or देव आस्ते 'a god sits;' देवः and इन्द्र become देवयिन्द्रः or देव इन्द्रः 'the god Indra;' नलः उवाच 'Nalah spoke,' makes नलयुवाच or more commonly नल उवाच.

42. After the long vowel आ, and before any vowel or soft consonant, य् is substituted for Visarga; it is optionally rejected before the vowels, absolutely before the consonants; as, देवाः अत्र make देवायत्र or देवा अत्र 'the gods (are) here;' देवाः and नम्याः make देवा नम्याः 'the gods are to be reverenced;' देव्याः अभिहितं, said of Deví, makes देव्यायभिहितं or देव्या अभिहितं; श्रियाः माला, 'the garland of Srí,' makes श्रिया माला.

a. After the interjections भोस्, भगोस्, अघोस्, the Visarga, to which the final is changed, is said to be again changed to य्, which is ejected before a vowel or soft consonant; as, भो इन्द्र 'O Indra!' भगो देव 'O god!'

43. Visarga substituted for a radical final र may become र again before a vowel or a soft consonant; as, प्रातः for प्रातर् + अत्र becomes प्रातरत्र 'the dawn (is) here.'

a. Such a Visarga may also optionally become र again before a hard consonant; as, गीः for गिर् before पति may make गीर्पति 'lord of speech,' or, by rule 38, गीष्पति, Visarga being changed to ष.

b. Visarga substituted for the final of अहर् for अहन् 'a day,' becomes र again before any consonant except र and भ; as, अहर्पति 'lord of day;' अहर्गण 'a number of days.' Before र and भ, उ is substituted for it; as, अहोरात्र 'day and night;' अहोभिः 'by days.'

44. Visarga is substituted for a final न, except in the word प्रशान्, before a hard consonant of the palatal, cerebral, and dental classes, if followed by a vowel, a semivowel, or a nasal. Anuswára is prefixed to the sibilant to which by rule 38. Visarga is changed; as, शार्ङ्गिन् + छिन्धि becomes शार्ङ्गिंश्छिन्धि 'O bow-armed, cut!' राजन् + तर = राजंस्तर 'O king, cross!' but प्रशान् चिनोतु 'let the quiet man collect.'

a. Before प the substitution is optional, and the Visarga does not become a sibilant, as by rule 38. *c*, but may or may not substitute the Arddha-visarga: नॄन् पाहि 'cherish men,' is therefore written, नॄन्पाहि, नॄंः पाहि, or नॄं ⨯ पाहि, also with a mark denoting the Visarga to be nasal, as नॄँः पाहि, or नॄँ ⨯ पाहि.

b. सम् in combination with कृ and its derivatives, the word कान् repeated, and पुम् derived from पुंस् prefixed to a word beginning with a hard consonant, insert the augment स्, in which case Visarga is said to be substituted for their proper finals, preceded by Anuswára, and changed before स् to स्: सम् before कार therefore becomes संस् स्कार; कान् before कान्, कांस् स्कान्; and पुम् before कोकिल, पुंस् स्कोकिल. By clause *a.* of rule 34, however, one of the sibilants is rejected, leaving संस्कार 'initiation;' कांस्कान् 'whom! whom!' and पुंस्कोकिल 'a male koïl (Indian cuckoo)'.

45. The Visarga which is the sign of the masculine nominative of the pronouns तद् and एतद्, or सः 'he,' एषः 'that person,' is commonly dropped before a consonant; as, स चरति 'he goes;' स ददाति, 'he gives;' एष विष्णुः 'that Vishńu;' but not if the negative अ is prefixed, as असः शिवः 'not that S'iva.'

a. In verse, for the convenience of the metre, स not only rejects the Visarga, but allows the final अ to be conjoined with a following vowel, by the rules of vowel-Sandhi; as, सेन्द्रो राजा जयति, 'that Indra the king conquers,' for स इन्द्रः; so सैष

दाशरथी रामः, 'that very Ráma, the son of Daśaratha,' for स एषः.

CHAPTER III.

DECLENSION.

SECTION I.

General rules.

46. Most nouns in the Sanskrit language are declinable in one or more of three genders. They admit, with very few exceptions, of three numbers, singular, dual, and plural; and of seven cases in each number; 1. the nominative, 2. accusative, 3. instrumental, 4. dative, 5. ablative, 6. genitive, 7. locative: of these it may be remarked, that the third or instrumental has the sense of 'by' or 'with;' the ablative, 'from;' and the locative, 'in' or 'on:' the rest have the usual powers.

47. Inflexion, whether of declension or conjugation, is contrived by the Sanskrit grammarians on the same principle. It consists of two parts; 1. the Anga, 'body,' or inflective base, that is, the word itself; and, 2. of certain particles, which, being attached to the base, complete the inflected word. The inflectional terminations of conjugation will be hereafter specified. We are concerned at present with those of declension only.

48. The inflectional terminations of nouns are twenty-one; some of them are repetitions: they are attached to the inflective base in each of the seven cases of the three numbers, and are as follows:

nom.	सि	औ	जस्
acc.	अम्	औ	शस्
instr.	टा	भ्यां	भिस्
dat.	ङे	भ्यां	भ्यस्
abl.	ङसि	भ्यां	भ्यस्
gen.	ङस्	ओस्	आम्
loc.	ङि	ओस्	सुप्

E 2

The vocative has no separate termination, being considered as a modification only of the nominative.

49. Now of these inflectional terminations it is to be remarked, that some of the letters serve only to form syllables, and facilitate enunciation: they are rejected, therefore, when those letters which are essential are applied to the base. These auxiliary letters are the इ् of सि; the ज of जस्; the श of शस्; the ट of टा; the ङ of the terminations ङे, ङसि (in which also इ् is subordinate), ङस्, and ङि: and the प of सुप्. It is also to be recollected, that by rule 37. a final स् is changed to Visarga. The actual terminations therefore will be,

nom.	:	औ	अः
acc.	अं	औ	अः
instr.	आ	भ्यां	भिः
dat.	ए	भ्यां	भ्यः
abl.	अः	भ्यां	भ्यः
gen.	अः	ओः	आम्
loc.	इ्	ओः	सु

50. In applying these terminations to the final letter of the inflective base, a recollection must be preserved of the modifications which that final letter must undergo, whether it be a vowel or a consonant, before the initial letters of the terminations; as in the following example:

नौ 'navis,' 'a ship.'

nom.	नौः	नावौ	नावः
acc.	नावं	नावौ	नावः
instr.	नावा	नौभ्यां	नौभिः
dat.	नावे	नौभ्यां	नौभ्यः
abl.	नावः	नौभ्यां	नौभ्यः
gen.	नावः	नावोः	नावां
loc.	नावि	नावोः	नौषु

It will be observed, that before the consonants, the word नौ is unchanged; before the vowels, औ becomes आव् by rule 5. The स of सु is changed after औ to ष by rule 29.

It is worth while to pause for a moment upon this scheme of inflectional terminations, and to understand it fully, as it furnishes a useful clue to all the varieties of nominal inflexion which follow. If it were rigidly applied, nothing would be so simple as Sanskrit declension; and even as it is, we are authorized to affirm that there is but one general declension in Sanskrit grammar. There are however various modifications, both of the bases and of the terminations, in the individual nouns, which render it convenient to divide them into classes; and no arrangement admits of more ready reference than that which classes them according to their final letters; first, as they are vowels or consonants; and secondly, according to the letter or class of letters in each of those two divisions.

SECTION II.

Nouns ending in vowels.

Class I. Nouns ending in अ and आ.

51. Nouns ending in अ form by far the most numerous class of nouns, and commonly admit of three genders, forming the feminine by adding आ; as, masc. शिव S'iva, the god; fem. शिवा the goddess S'ivá.

52. In forming the inflexions of all nouns, such changes as may occur are of two descriptions; 1. those affecting the base, 2. those affecting the termination.

53. Nouns ending in अ substitute आ for the final before य substituted for ए in the dat. sing.; before the dual termination भ्यां; and before the augment न, in the genitive case plural, and in the nominative and accusative plural neuter. They substitute ए for their final अ before ओस् in the dual, and भ्यस् and सु in the plural. They insert न before the signs of the genitive case plural, and the nominative and accusative plural neuter. The feminine noun changes आ to ए before the आ of the instrumental case singular, the ओस् of the dual, and in the vocative case; and inserts या before the four last cases of the singular, and न् before आम् in the gen. plural.

54. Nouns in अ substitute other terminations for those of the scheme, in some of the cases: thus,

Singular.			Plural.		
acc.	म्	for अम्	acc.	न्	for स्
instr.	इन	— टा	instr.	ऐस्	— भिस्
dat.	य	— ङे			
abl.	आत्	— ङसि			
gen.	स्य	— ङस्			

a. The feminine noun substitutes ई for औ in the nom. and acc. dual, and आम् for ङि in the locative case sing.

b. The neuter substitutes in the three numbers of the nom. and accus. severally म् ई इ, the latter with न prefixed, as नि, in place of the terminations of the masculine: in all the other cases it adopts the terminations of the masculine.

55. We are now prepared to understand the construction of the following forms of शिव, bearing in mind the alterations dependent upon the laws of combination, in joining the inflectional terminations to the inflective base.

Masc. शिव S'iva the deity.

nom.	शिवः	शिवौ	शिवाः	S'iva, &c.
acc.	शिवं	शिवौ	शिवान्	S'iva, &c.
instr.	शिवेन	शिवाभ्यां	शिवैः	By or with S'iva, &c.
dat.	शिवाय	शिवाभ्यां	शिवेभ्यः	To S'iva, &c.
abl.	शिवात्	शिवाभ्यां	शिवेभ्यः	From S'iva, &c.
gen.	शिवस्य	शिवयोः	शिवानां	Of S'iva, &c.
loc.	शिवे	शिवयोः	शिवेषु	In or on S'iva, &c.
voc.	शिव	शिवौ	शिवाः	O S'iva! &c.

Fem. शिवा the goddess S'ivá.

nom.	शिवा	शिवे	शिवाः
acc.	शिवां	शिवे	शिवाः
instr.	शिवया	शिवाभ्यां	शिवाभिः

dat.	शिवायै	शिवाभ्यां	शिवाभ्यः
abl.	शिवायाः	शिवाभ्यां	शिवाभ्यः
gen.	शिवायाः	शिवयोः	शिवानां
loc.	शिवायां	शिवयोः	शिवासु
voc.	शिवे	शिवे	शिवाः

Neuter शिव 'auspicious.'

Nom. and accus. शिवं शिवे शिवानि.

The rest as the masculine.

a. Other nouns declinable on the above models are,

Masculine.	Feminine.	Neuter.
अश्वः a horse	अङ्गना a woman	अण्डं an egg
आकाशः the sky	आशा hope	आसनं a seat
उष्ट्रः a camel	इच्छा wish	इन्द्रियं an organ of sense
काकः a crow	कन्या a girl	कुलं a family
गुणः a quality	ग्रीवा the neck	गृहं a house
चन्द्रः the moon	चन्द्रिका moonlight	छत्रं an umbrella
ज्वरः fever	जरा decay	जलं water
तर्कः reasoning	तारा a star	तीरं a shore
देवः a god	दोला a swing	दुःखं pain
धर्म्मः virtue	धारा an edge	धनं wealth
नखः a nail	नासा the nose	नृत्यं dancing
पर्व्वतः a mountain	पूजा worship	पत्रं a leaf
मत्स्यः a fish	भार्य्या a wife	मूलं a root
यज्ञः sacrifice	माला a garland	यौवनं youth
रसः flavour	रक्षा preserving	रक्तं blood
लोहः iron	लज्जा modesty	लवणं salt
वकः a crane	वीणा a lute	वनं a wood
शृगालः a jackall	शोभा beauty	शास्त्रं a scripture
समुद्रः the ocean	सभा an assembly	सूत्रं a rule
हस्तः the hand	हिंसा injury	हिमं frost

b. Many adjectives and participles declinable in the three genders belong to this class.

c. The feminine nouns अम्बा, अल्ला, अक्का, signifying chiefly in poetic language 'mother,' make their vocatives अम्ब, अल्ल, अक्क. If the penultimate be not a conjunct consonant, other synonymes follow the usual form, as हे अम्बिके, अम्बाले, अम्बाडे, 'O mother!'

56. Besides those nouns which are formed from masculine nouns in अ, by adding, as it is said, the feminine ending टाप्, that is, आ, there are nouns derived immediately from verbs ending in आ, as पा, मा, ध्मा, and the like, in which the final आ is an essential, not an accidental letter. Such nouns admit of a variety of gender. The declension of the masculine and feminine noun is the same. In the neuter the final is made short, and the word is declined like शिवं.

57. Nouns in आ, then, in which the final is a radical letter, combine with the terminations of the nominative case, and with those of the singular and dual accusative, agreeably to the laws of Sandhi. In the accusative plural and the following cases the final आ is cut off before the vowel terminations, and they are affixed at once to the word, as if it ended in a consonant: before the consonantal terminations there is no change; as,

Masc. and fem. विश्वपा 'all-preserving.'

nom.	विश्वपाः	विश्वपौ	विश्वपाः
acc.	विश्वपां	—	विश्वपः
instr.	विश्वपा	विश्वपाभ्यां	विश्वपाभिः
dat.	विश्वपे	—	विश्वपाभ्यः
abl.	विश्वपः	—	—
gen.	—	विश्वपोः	विश्वपां
loc.	विश्वपि	—	विश्वपासु
voc.	विश्वपा &c.		

So सोमपा 'who drinks the soma juice;' शङ्खध्मा 'a shell-blower.'

58. The word हाहा, the name of an inferior divinity, a Gandharba, is considered as a primitive, and is inflected therefore throughout without any elision of the final, which combines with the vowel terminations agreeably to the rules of Sandhi, and is consequently in every way regularly declined.

nom.	हाहाः	हाहौ	हाहाः
acc.	हाहां	—	हाहाः or हाहान्
instr.	हाहा	हाहाभ्यां	हाहाभिः
dat.	हाहै	—	हाहाभ्यः
abl.	हाहाः	—	—
gen.	—	हाहौः	हाहां
loc.	हाहे	—	हाहासु
voc.	हाहा &c.		

Class II. Nouns ending in इ and उ.

59. Nouns ending in these two vowels may be conveniently classed together, as they are analogously inflected; recollecting only that the semivowels to which they are changeable before other vowels are respectively य् and व्.

60. In the masculine gender the changes of the base are, the substitution of the long vowel for the final in the dual nom. and accus., and in the accus. and gen. plural; the Guńa letter ए or ओ is substituted for the final before जस्, ङे, ङसि, and ङस्, and in the vocative; and the final is dropped before the termination of the locative case: न् is inserted before the terminations of the instrumental case singular and the gen. plural.

61. In the same gender the dual termination औ is rejected; म् is substituted for अम्, and न् for the अस् of शस्; the vowel of अस् in the ablative and genitive is dropped; and औ is substituted for ङि; as follows:

	अग्नि 'fire.'			वायु 'wind.'		
nom.	अग्निः	अग्नी	अग्नयः	वायुः	वायू	वायवः
acc.	अग्निं	—	अग्नीन्	वायुं	—	वायून्
instr.	अग्निना	अग्निभ्यां	अग्निभिः	वायुना	वायुभ्यां	वायुभिः
dat.	अग्नये	—	अग्निभ्यः	वायवे	—	वायुभ्यः
abl.	अग्नेः	—	—	वायोः	—	—
gen.	—	अग्न्योः	अग्नीनां	—	वाय्वोः	वायूनां
loc.	अग्नौ	—	अग्निषु	वायौ	—	वायुषु
voc.	अग्ने &c.			वायो &c.		

F

62. There are some anomalies in nouns in इ. Thus सखि, 'a friend,' substitutes आ for the final in the first five inflexions, and inserts य before their vowel terminations. In the other cases of the singular, and in the gen. and loc. dual, it is more regular than अग्नि, the final इ becoming य before a vowel. In the abl. and gen. singular उस् is substituted for ङसि and ङस्.

सखि 'a friend.'

nom.	सखा	सखायौ	सखायः
acc.	सखायं	—	सखीन्
instr.	सख्या	सखिभ्यां	सखिभिः
dat.	सख्ये	—	सखिभ्यः
abl.	सख्युः	—	—
gen.	—	सख्योः	सखीनां
loc.	सख्यौ	—	सखिषु
voc.	सखे &c.		

a. In composition this word may be inflected regularly in all the cases, or in all except the two first; सुसखिः or सुसखा 'a good friend;' सुसख्ये or सुसखये 'to a good friend,' &c.

b. पति, 'a master,' is declined like सखि in the five last cases singular; as, पत्या, पत्ये, पत्युः, पत्यौ. In the rest like अग्नि.

पति in composition is declined like अग्नि; as, भूपति 'a king,' (lord of the earth,) भूपतिः भूपती भूपतयः भूपतये, &c.

63. Feminine nouns in इ and उ differ from the masculine in the accus. plural, and in the third and following cases singular. They do not substitute न् for the Visarga of शस्, nor insert न् before टा. In the dative and following cases they have two forms, one like the masculine: in the other they insert आ before the affixes of the dative, ablative, and genitive cases; and, like feminine nouns in आ, substitute आम् for the sign of the locative ङि; as,

	Fem. मति 'Mind.'			धेनु 'a milch cow.'		
nom.	मतिः	मती	मतयः	धेनुः	धेनू	धेनवः
acc.	मतिं	—	मतीः	धेनुं	—	धेनूः
instr.	मत्या	मतिभ्यां	मतिभिः	धेन्वा	धेनुभ्यां	धेनुभिः

dat.	मतये or मत्यै	मतिभ्यां	मतिभ्यः	धेनवे or धेन्वै	धेनुभ्यां	धेनुभ्यः
abl.	मतेः or मत्याः	—	—	धेनोः or धेन्वाः	—	—
gen.	———	मत्योः	मतीनां	———	धेन्वोः	धेनूनां
loc.	मतौ or मत्यां	—	मतिषु	धेनौ or धेन्वां	—	धेनुषु
voc.	मते &c.			धेनो &c.		

64. Neuter nouns in इ and उ reject the terminations of the nom. and accus. singular, substitute ई and इ for the dual and plural terminations, and insert न् before them and all other terminations beginning with a vowel. They lengthen the final before न् in the plural.

	वारि 'water.'			मधु 'honey.'		
nom. acc.	वारि	वारिणी	वारीणि	मधु	मधुनी	मधूनि
instr.	वारिणा	वारिभ्यां	वारिभिः	मधुना	मधुभ्यां	मधुभिः
dat.	वारिणे	—	वारिभ्यः	मधुने	—	मधुभ्यः
abl.	वारिणः	—	—	मधुनः	—	—
gen.	—	वारिणोः	वारीणां	मधुनः	मधुनोः	मधूनां
loc.	वारिणि	—	वारिषु	मधुनि	—	मधुषु
voc.	वारि or वारे &c.			मधु &c.		

65. There are a few neuter nouns in इ which before the vowel terminations of all the cases except the two first, and optionally before ङि, drop the final vowel; as,

	अस्थि 'a bone.'		
nom. acc.	अस्थि	अस्थिनी	अस्थीनि
instr.	अस्थ्ना	अस्थिभ्यां	अस्थिभिः
dat.	अस्थ्ने	—	अस्थिभ्यः
abl.	अस्थ्नः	—	—
gen.	—	अस्थ्नोः	अस्थ्नां
loc.	अस्थ्नि or अस्थनि	—	अस्थिषु
voc.	अस्थि &c.		

a. अक्षि 'an eye,' दधि 'ghee,' and सक्थि 'a thigh,' are similarly declined: the fact being, in all probability, that as nouns in इ they are defective, and their deficiencies are supplied before the vowel terminations by analogous but obsolete nouns ending in न्, as अस्थन्, अक्षन्, दधन्, सक्थन्.

b. Other nouns in इ and उ, declinable on the above models, are,

Masc. in इ.	Fem. in इ.	Masc. in उ.
असिः a sword	कृषिः agriculture	आयुः life
ऋषिः a sage	क्षान्तिः patience	इक्षुः sugar cane
कविः a poet	गतिः going	ऋतुः a season
गिरिः a mountain	जातिः caste, sort	गुरुः a teacher
मणिः a jewel	दीप्तिः light	बन्धुः a relation
रविः the sun	धृतिः firmness	भानुः the sun
राशिः a heap	प्रकृतिः nature	मृत्युः death
विधिः an ordinance	बुद्धिः understanding	विष्णुः Vishńu
सारथिः a charioteer	वृष्टिः rain	वेणुः a bambu
हरिः a name of Vishńu	स्मृतिः remembrance	शत्रुः an enemy

c. There are not many feminine substantive nouns in उ, and but few neuter either in इ or उ. Adjectives of course, or substantives used attributively, may, with few exceptions, be declined in three genders.

d. When a noun in इ or उ, whether substantive or attributive, is used in the neuter gender in the same sense in which it is employed in the masculine, it is optionally declinable in all cases of which the terminations begin with vowels, except the two first, either after the masculine or neuter form; as अनादि 'eternal:' neuter nom. and acc. अनादि, अनादिनी, अनादीनि; instr. अनादिना; dat. अनादये or अनादिने; abl. and gen. अनादेः or अनादिनः; loc. अनादौ or अनादिनि; gen. and loc. dual, अनाद्योः or अनादिनोः. If the sense differs, the neuter form only is admissible: पीलु masc. 'a kind of tree;' neut. 'the fruit of the Pílu tree:' dat. पीलुने, abl. and gen. पीलुनः, loc. पीलुनि, &c.

e. Other neuter nouns in इ and उ are derived from nouns terminating in the long vowels ई and ऊ.

CLASS III. Nouns ending in ई and ऊ.

66. The chief peculiarity affecting the inflective base, or the word itself, in nouns terminating in ई and ऊ, regards the substitution in some cases of the syllables इय् and उव् for the finals ई and ऊ before those inflective terminations which begin with vowels. When these syllables are substituted, the nouns are inflected before the vowel terminations as if they ended with the semivowels य् and व्. When those syllables are not substituted, the final vowels combine with the vowels of the terminations, agreeably to the laws of Sandhi, with very few exceptions.

67. After the syllables इय् and उव् the inflective terminations undergo no changes; after the finals ई and ऊ they undergo a few, chiefly after feminine nouns, analogous to those already observable in feminine nouns of the preceding classes, and depending on the same conditions.

68. इय् and उव् are severally substituted for the final ई and ऊ of masculine nouns, when they are monosyllabic verbal derivatives, or when the finals are preceded by a conjunct consonant; as, धी (for ध्यै) 'to think,' लू 'to cut,' श्री 'to serve.'

Masc. धी 'who understands.'				Masc. लू 'who cuts.'		
nom.	धीः	धियौ	धियः	लूः	लुवौ	लुवः
acc.	धियं	—	धियः	लुवं	—	—
instr.	धिया	धीभ्यां	धीभिः	लुवा	लूभ्यां	लूभिः
dat.	धिये	—	धीभ्यः	लुवे	—	लूभ्यः
abl.	धियः	—	—	लुवः	—	—
gen.	—	धियोः	धियां	—	लुवोः	लुवां
loc.	धियि	—	धीषु	लुवि	—	लूषु
voc.	धीः &c.			लूः &c.		

a. Nouns of this description are not considered as ceasing to be monosyllabic by having particles prefixed to them, which merely qualify their application; therefore सुधीः 'a man of good understanding,' परमधीः 'a man of excellent understanding,' and the like, substitute इय् for the final; सुधीः, सुधियौ, सुधियः. So

स्वयम्भूः 'self-existent,' from स्वयं 'self,' and भू 'being,' a name of Brahmá, makes स्वयम्भूः, स्वयम्भुवौ, स्वयम्भुवः.

b. They are considered as polysyllabic if derived from a compound verb, as प्रधी 'a man of superior understanding,' which is a derivative, not from the simple verb धी, but the compound verb प्रधी, and therefore is declined प्रधीः, प्रध्यौ, प्रध्यः, &c., the final becoming य् before a vowel, by rule 4: and they are also considered as polysyllabic if the first member of the compound is a subordinate term, or one not in opposition, as वर्षाभूः 'born in the rains,' 'a frog.' There are also certain compounds of भू which are by special rule excepted from substituting उव्; as, पुनर्भू 'born again,' दृन्भू 'a snake,' काराभू 'born in a prison,' करभू 'produced from the hand:' these are all declined, as वर्षाभूः, वर्षाभ्वौ, वर्षाभ्वः, वर्षाभ्वं, &c.

69. Masculine nouns ending in ई or ऊ, when consisting of more than one syllable in consequence of being compounded with another noun as a subordinate term, or being derived from a modification of the verb, merely follow the rules of combination; that is, ई becomes य्, and ऊ, व्, before a vowel affix.

	सेनानी 'a general' (from सेना 'an army,' and नी 'who leads.')			खलपू 'a sweeper' (खल 'a place,' & पू 'who cleans').		
nom.	सेनानीः	सेनान्यौ	सेनान्यः	खलपूः	खलप्वौ	खलप्वः
acc.	सेनान्यं	—	—	खलप्वं	—	—
instr.	सेनान्या	सेनानीभ्यां	सेनानीभिः	खलप्वा	खलपूभ्यां	खलपूभिः
dat.	सेनान्ये	—	—	खलप्वे	—	खलपूभ्यः
abl.	सेनान्यः	—	—	खलप्वः	—	—
gen.	—	सेनान्योः	सेनान्यां	—	खलप्वोः	खलप्वां
loc.	सेनान्यां	—	सेनानीषु	खलप्वि	—	खलपूषु
voc.	सेनानीः &c.			खलपूः &c.		

a. नी, 'to lead,' and its compounds substitute आम् for ङि in the locative.

b. पपी 'who drinks (moisture),' i. e. the sun, derived from पा 'to drink;' यायी 'a road,' from या 'to go;' वातप्रमी 'an antelope,' from वात 'the wind' and प्रमी 'who outstrips;' and हूहू a demigod so named; differ from सेनानी in three cases:

acc. sing.	पपीं	acc. plur.	पपीन्	loc. sing.	पपी
—	ययीं	—	ययीन्	—	ययी
—	वातप्रमीं	—	वातप्रमीन्	—	वातप्रमी
—	हूहूं	—	हूहून्	—	हूह्वि

They may, however, be also regularly declined in these cases, as पप्यं, पप्यः, पप्यि, &c.

c. लू in composition, as यवलू 'who cuts barley,' makes either यवल्वां or यवलूनां in the gen. plur., and यवल्वां in the loc. singular.

70. Feminine nouns in ई and ऊ, like masculine nouns, are declined in two ways: if they are monosyllables, or contain a conjunct consonant, they substitute इय् and उव् for their finals; if polysyllabic, they change the finals, agreeably to the laws of Sandhi, to य् and व् before the affixes commencing with vowels.

71. Feminine nouns of the first description optionally prefix आ to the affixes marked by a mute ङ, like feminine nouns in the short इ and उ.

72. They optionally prefix न् to आम् in the gen. plural, and substitute आम् for ङि in the loc. singular; as, श्री 'prosperity,' and भू 'the earth.'

nom.	श्रीः	श्रियौ	श्रियः	भूः	भुवौ	भुवः
acc.	श्रियं	—	—	भुवं	—	—
instr.	श्रिया	श्रीभ्यां	श्रीभिः	भुवा	भूभ्यां	भूभिः
dat.	श्रिये or श्रियै	—	श्रीभ्यः	भुवे or भुवै	—	भूभ्यः
abl.	श्रियः or श्रियाः	—	—	भुवः or भुवाः	—	—
gen.	———	श्रियोः	श्रियां or श्रीणां	———	भुवोः	भुवां or भूणां
loc.	श्रियि or श्रियां	—	श्रीषु	भुवि or भुवां	—	भूषु
voc.	श्रीः &c.			भूः &c.		

73. Feminine nouns of the second description, having more than one syllable, and being derivative nouns from masculine nouns by the substitution of the terminations ई and ऊ for the masculine final, insert आ before the terminations having a mute ङ्, make the vowel short in the voc. singular, and prefix न् to the termination of the gen. plural.

The स् of the nominative is rejected after such nouns in ई, but not after ऊ. After both, म् is substituted for अम्, स् for the अस् of शस्, and आम् for ङि; as,

	नदी 'a river.'			वधू 'a wife.'		
nom.	नदी	नद्यौ	नद्यः	वधूः	वध्वौ	वध्वः
acc.	नदीं	—	नदीः	वधूं	—	वधूः
instr.	नद्या	नदीभ्यां	नदीभिः	वध्वा	वधूभ्यां	वधूभिः
dat.	नद्यै	—	नदीभ्यः	वध्वै	—	वधूभ्यः
abl.	नद्याः	—	—	वध्वाः	—	—
gen.	—	नद्योः	नदीनां	—	वध्वोः	वधूनां
loc.	नद्यां	—	नदीषु	वध्वां	—	वधूषु
voc.	नदि &c.			वधु &c.		

a. The rejection of स् after a feminine noun ending in ई depends upon that ई being the feminine termination, or sign of the feminine gender. If it is part of the word itself, the sibilant becomes Visarga, as usual; as, लक्ष्मीः 'the goddess Lakshmí,' तन्त्रीः 'a lute,' तरीः 'a boat.'

b. स्त्री, 'a woman,' is inflected in the nom. and voc. like नदी, and optionally so in the accus. singular and plural: in the other cases like श्री. But the insertion of न् before the gen. plural, and of आ before the terminations with a mute ङ्, and the substitution of आम् for ङि are absolute, not optional as in श्री.

nom.	स्त्री	स्त्रियौ	स्त्रियः
acc.	स्त्रियं or स्त्रीं	—	स्त्रियः or स्त्रीः
instr.	स्त्रिया	स्त्रीभ्यां	स्त्रीभिः
dat.	स्त्रियै	—	स्त्रीभ्यः
abl.	स्त्रियाः	—	—
gen.	—	स्त्रियोः	स्त्रीणां *
loc.	स्त्रियां	—	स्त्रीषु
voc.	स्त्रि &c.		

* Wilkins has स्त्रीणां or स्त्रियां, but the Kaumudí expressly excepts स्त्री from the alternative.

c. Feminine nouns in ई and ऊ, when compounded so as to form attributes, are to be declined like nouns masculine, when used in the sense of a masculine noun, as सुश्री, 'a prosperous man,' takes, in the dative, ablative, genitive, and locative cases, only one form, viz. सुश्रिये, सुश्रियः, and सुश्रियि. If the compound is only a qualification of the substantive, the feminine form may be followed, as सुश्री, 'good fortune,' makes सुश्रिये or सुश्रियै, &c. If the noun is a word invariably feminine, it retains its feminine terminations, although used as an attribute of a male, as बहुश्रेयसी, 'a man of many good qualities,' makes बहुश्रेयस्यै, बहुश्रेयस्याः, बहुश्रेयस्यां.

d. Feminine nouns formed from verbal roots, and compounded with subordinate terms, however, when used in a sense analogous to that of the masculine, take exactly the same form, as ग्रामणी 'a female head of a village,' खलपू 'a female sweeper,' make, accus. sin. and plur. ग्रामण्यं, ग्रामण्यः, खलप्वं, खलप्वः; dat. ग्रामण्ये, खलप्वे; abl. and gen. ग्रामण्यः, खलप्वः; gen. plur. ग्रामण्यां, खलप्वां; loc. ग्रामण्यां (see rule 69. *a.*), खलप्वि; voc. ग्रामणीः, खलपूः.

e. So पुनर्भू 'twice-being,' if it be applied to man or woman indifferently, is declined in the same manner; mf. पुनर्भ्वं, पुनर्भ्वः, पुनर्भ्वि; but if it mean 'a woman twice married,' it is declined like वधू; पुनर्भ्वै, पुनर्भ्वाः, &c.

f. The object of these rules, and of others affecting nouns ending in ई and ऊ, is to intimate that a word which may be applied to an object either male or female is declined in a form common to both; that is, with the masculine terminations: when it is limited to a distinct female object, it is declinable only with the feminine terminations, as in the instance of पुनर्भू. So also वर्षाभू for instance, being 'a male' or 'female frog,' is declined alike, वर्षाभ्वे, -भ्वः, -भ्वि, -भूः; but the same word being the name of a plant, in which sense there is no male, is declined only, वर्षाभ्वै, वर्षाभ्वाः, वर्षाभ्वां, वर्षाभु.

74. Nouns in ई and ऊ which are susceptible of the neuter gender, substitute the short vowels इ and उ for their finals.

If the word is an attributive, and the sense of the neuter is analogous to that of the other genders, the word is declined in all the cases of which the affixes begin with vowels, except the two first, optionally, as if it were a noun ending in ई long; that is, the final becomes य् or व् before the vowel: otherwise न is inserted, as after वारि. Thus ग्रामणी 'who leads or is chief over a village;' ग्रामणीः ब्राह्मणः 'a head man, Bráhman;' ग्रामणी ब्राह्मणी 'a Bráhman woman head of a village;' ग्रामणि कुलं 'a family, chief over a village.' The inflexion of the latter is,

nom. acc.	ग्रामणि	ग्रामणिनी	ग्रामणीनि
instr.	ग्रामण्या or ग्रामणिना	ग्रामणिभ्यां	ग्रामणिभिः
dat.	ग्रामण्ये or ग्रामणिने	—	ग्रामणिभ्यः
abl.	ग्रामण्यः or ग्रामणिनः	—	—
gen.	——	ग्रामण्योः or ग्रामणिनोः	ग्रामणीनां
loc.	ग्रामण्यां	——	ग्रामणिषु

a. Nouns ending in ई and ऊ as derived from simple verbal roots are not numerous, the roots not being in any number; but they admit of being multiplied as compounded with other words. Feminine nouns formed by the affixes ई and ऊ, and especially the former, are more frequent.

प्रणीः m. a leader, a guide.	प्रतिभूः m. a surety.
कुमारी f. a damsel.	चमूः f. an army.
पृथिवी f. the earth.	भ्रूः f. the eyebrow.
भगिनी f. a sister.	श्वश्रूः f. a mother-in-law.
विपणी f. a shop.	सुभ्रूः f. a woman with good eyebrows.

Class IV. Nouns in ऋ and ॠ, ऌ and ॡ.

75. Masculine nouns in ऋ substitute अन् for the final, and, according to the analogy of nouns in अन्, form the nominative in आ; as, पितृ 'a father,' nom. पिता.

76. In one class of nouns in ऋ, अर्, in another आर्, is substituted for the final before the vowel terminations of the nominative dual and plural, and of the accusative sing. and dual. Before the accus. and gen. plur. the vowel is made

long. न् is inserted before आम्. Before the vowel terminations of the instr. and dat. singular, and gen. and loc. dual, ऋ is changed to the semivowel र्: it is changed to अर् in the locative and vocative cases.

77. The only changes in the affixes are, the rejection of स् in the nominative; the substitution of न् for शस् in the accus. plural, and of उस् for अस् in the abl. and gen. singular; स् is rejected; and the उ of उस् is prefixed to the semivowel र्, which as a final is changed to Visarga.

	पितृ 'a father.'			कर्तृ 'a doer.		
nom.	पिता	पितरौ	पितरः	कर्ता	कर्तारौ	कर्तारः
acc.	पितरं	—	पितॄन्	कर्तारं	—	कर्तॄन्
instr.	पित्रा	पितृभ्यां	पितृभिः	कर्त्रा	कर्तृभ्यां	कर्तृभिः
dat.	पित्रे	—	पितृभ्यः	कर्त्रे	—	कर्तृभ्यः
abl.	पितुः	—	—	कर्तुः	—	—
gen.	—	पित्रोः	पितॄणां	—	कर्त्रोः	कर्तॄणां
loc.	पितरि	—	पितृषु	कर्तरि	—	कर्तृषु
voc.	पितः &c.			कर्तः &c.		

a. Most masculine nouns implying affinity are declined like पितृ; as, भ्रातृ 'a brother,' जामातृ 'a son-in-law,' देवृ 'a husband's brother:' but नप्तृ, 'a grandson,' makes नप्ता, नप्तारौ, नप्तारः, नप्तारं, नप्तारौ, in the first five inflexions.

b. Feminine nouns of affinity are declined also like पितृ, except in the accus. plural; as मातृ, 'a mother,' makes माता, मातरौ, मातरः, मातरं, मातरौ, मातॄः; so दुहितृ 'a daughter:' but स्वसृ, 'a sister,' is declined like नप्ता; स्वसा, स्वसारौ, &c.; acc. plural, स्वसॄः.

c. नृ, 'a man,' is declined like पितृ, except in the gen. plural, where the vowel is optionally short, as नृणां or नॄणां.

d. Nouns formed from roots by the addition of the particles तृच् or तृन् (in which the finals are used merely to distinguish them from each other) are nouns of agency, and are declined like कर्तृ. They are also declinable in three genders.

e. The feminine is formed with the affix ई, before which

the semivowel र् is substituted for ऋ: thus कर्तृ becomes कर्त्री in the feminine, and कर्त्री is declined like नदी.

f. The neuter is formed analogously to neuter nouns in इ and उ; and as there are no substantive neuter nouns in ऋ, the neuter of attributives being mostly usable in the same sense as the masculine, then by a similar analogy the neuter nouns in ऋ admit also of two forms before the vowel terminations of all the cases except the two first; either inserting न before them, or taking the same form as the masculine: thus, nom. and accus. कर्तृ, कर्तृणी, कर्तॄणि; sing. instr. कर्तृणा or कर्त्रा; dat. कर्तृणे or कर्त्रे; abl. and gen. कर्तृणः or कर्तुः; loc. कर्तृणि or कर्तरि; gen. and loc. dual, कर्तृणोः or कर्त्रोः. Before the other terminations the forms are the same as in the masculine.

g. क्रोष्टृ, 'a jackal,' has lost some of its cases, and they are in part supplied by the inflexions of क्रोष्टु, which are those of nouns in उ. Some of the cases belong to both nouns.

nom.	क्रोष्टा	क्रोष्टारौ	क्रोष्टारः
acc.	क्रोष्टारं	—	क्रोष्टून्
instr.	क्रोष्ट्रा or क्रोष्टुना	क्रोष्टुभ्यां	क्रोष्टुभिः
dat.	क्रोष्ट्रे or क्रोष्टवे	—	क्रोष्टुभ्यः
abl.	क्रोष्टुः or क्रोष्टोः	—	—
gen.	———	क्रोष्ट्रोः or क्रोष्ट्वोः	क्रोष्टूनां
loc.	क्रोष्टरि or क्रोष्टौ	———	क्रोष्टुषु
voc.	क्रोष्टः or क्रोष्टो &c.		

h. To the preceding examples of nouns in ऋ may be added क्षत्तृ, 'a man of the military caste;' जेतृ m. 'a conqueror,' or mfn. 'victorious;' दातृ m. 'a donor,' or mfn. 'liberal;' धातृ m. 'a creator;' mfn. 'cherishing;' योद्धृ 'a warrior,' mfn. 'warlike;' and होतृ m. 'a priest.'

78. There are a few roots ending in ॠ, from which verbal nouns may be formed; as, from कॄ, 'scatter,' comes कॄ 'who or what scatters.' These are usually inflected by substituting इर् for the radical; agreeably to which, कॄ becomes किर्, and is then declined like nouns ending in र्; as किर्, nom. कीः, किरौ, किरः,

&c. If this change does not take place, the noun is regularly declined, substituting the semivowel र् before the vowel terminations; as कॄ 'who injures;' nom. कॄः, क्रौ, क्रः, &c. These forms are of rare occurrence.

79. The same may be said, with still greater truth, of nouns ending in ऌ and ॡ; but grammarians admit the possibility of their occurrence: thus गमॢ, the root गम् 'to go,' with the affix ऌ, may be declined analogously to nouns ending in ऋ; as गमा, गम्लौ, गम्लः. In the ablative and genitive उ is substituted for the अ of अस्, and prefixed to the final semivowel; स् is rejected, as being the last member of a conjunct consonant: the form is therefore गमुल्. This is of little practical value.

Class V. Nouns in ए.

80. There are no simple nouns ending in ए, but compounds are exhibited to illustrate the declension of nouns so terminating; as से, which is compounded of स, 'with,' and इ, 'love;' 'one who loves.' The declension is regular, except in the abl. and gen. singular, where the initial of अस् is rejected; as, sing. nom. सेः, acc. सयं, instr. सया, dat. सये, abl. and gen. सेः, loc. सयि; dual nom. and acc. सयौ, instr. dat. and abl. सेभ्यां, gen. and loc. सयोः; plural nom. and acc. सयः, instr. सेभिः, dat. and abl. सेभ्यः, gen. सयां, loc. सेषु.

Class VI. Nouns in ऐ.

81. Nouns ending in ऐ are declined regularly, the terminations are unchanged; the inflective base substitutes आ for its final before the consonantal terminations, and is changed to आय्, agreeably to the laws of Sandhi, before the vowels; as रै mf., 'wealth,' makes

nom.	राः	रायौ	रायः
acc.	रायं	—	रायः
instr.	राया	राभ्यां	राभिः
dat.	राये	—	राभ्यः

abl.	रायः	राभ्यां	राभ्यः
gen.	—	रायोः	रायां
loc.	रायि	—	रासु

82. The neuter of nouns in ऐ is formed by changing the final before the vowel terminations to इ, and inflecting it like neuters in इ. Before the consonants, आ is substituted for the final; as प्रै 'wealthy;' n. प्रि; sing. nom. and acc. प्रि, instr. प्रिणा, dat. प्रिणे, abl. and gen. प्रिणः, loc. प्रिणि; dual nom. and acc. प्रिणी, instr. dat. and abl. प्राभ्यां, gen. and loc. प्रिणोः; plural nom. and acc. प्रीणि, instr. प्राभिः, dat. and abl. प्राभ्यः, gen. प्रिणां, loc. प्रासु.

a. Some grammarians affirm, that when it is used attributively, a neuter noun ending in ऐ, like those ending in इ or उ &c. (see rule 74), may take also the masculine form before the vowel terminations टा &c., as प्रिणा or प्रायाः; but this is denied by the best authorities.

Class VII. Nouns in ओ.

83. Nouns in ओ, both masculine and feminine, substitute the Vṛiddhi letter औ for the final before the three terminations of the nominative case and that of the accusative dual. They substitute आ for the final before the terminations of the accusative singular and plural. Before the other vowel terminations ओ becomes अव् by rule of Sandhi 5, except before ङसि and ङस्, which reject their initial अ, and consequently the final is unchanged.

गो 'a cow.'

nom.	गौः	गावौ	गावः
acc.	गां	—	गाः
instr.	गवा	गोभ्यां	गोभिः
dat.	गवे	—	गोभ्यः
abl.	गोः	—	—
gen.	गोः	गवोः	गवां
loc.	गवि	—	गोषु

84. In the neuter the final is changed to उ, as उपगु तृणं 'pasture near the cow;' which is declined like neuters in उ.

a. Here also authorities differ as to the alternative of inflecting the neuter optionally as the masculine in the instrumental and other cases singular, उपगुना or उपगवा &c.: the former is to be preferred.

Class VIII. Nouns in औ.

85. Nouns in औ, masculine and feminine, are strictly regular, as in the example already given of नौ 'navis,' 'a boat.' In the neuter the final becomes उ; as अतिनु जलं 'the water, beyond the boat;' अतिनु, अतिनुनी, अतिनूनि, &c.

a. The nouns that end in diphthongs are not numerous. To the preceding may be added द्यौ mf. 'heaven,' and ग्लौ m. 'the moon.'

SECTION II.

Nouns ending in consonants.

86. Nouns ending in consonants may also be conveniently arranged according to the classification of the letters by analogy of articulation; distinguishing those ending with the nasals, semivowels, sibilants, and with ह, as constituting separate classes.

87. Nouns ending in consonants modify their finals before the inflectional terminations, agreeably to the rules of Sandhi: thus a hard consonant is optionally changed to a soft when it is final, that is, in the nominative singular: absolutely, before the terminations of the dual and plural beginning with भ. A soft consonant must be changed to a hard consonant before सु.

88. Whatever other special modifications the inflective base may undergo, they are, with a few exceptions, confined to the first five inflections; that is, to the nominative in the three numbers, and the accusative in the singular and the dual. Whatever form the word assume before the termination of the accusative plural, is preserved before all subsequent terminations beginning with vowels.

89. The inflectional terminations are attached unchanged to the final consonant of the base: the only seeming irregularity is the rejection of स् as the termination of the nominative singular; but this is the result of the rule, that of a final conjunct consonant the last member shall be rejected. (See rule 35.)

90. As the inflectional terminations are unchanged, there is of course but one form for both masculine and feminine nouns. In the neuter gender the terminations of the two first cases dual and plural are changed to ई and इ, and न् is prefixed to the latter.

Class I. Nouns ending in the gutturals क, ख, ग, घ.

91. There is no peculiarity in the declension of these nouns; their inflexion is conformable to the rules of Sandhi. The final of the nominative may be either of the unaspirated letters, क् or ग्: thus सर्व्वशक्, 'omnipotent,' makes सर्व्वशक् or सर्व्वशग्; and चित्रलिख्, 'a painter,' makes also चित्रलिक् or चित्रलिग्. Before the vowels the termination of the base is unchanged, as सर्व्वशकौ; चित्रलिखौ. Before भ the final must be the unaspirated soft consonant, सर्व्वशग्भ्यां, चित्रलिग्भ्यां. Before the स of सु the unaspirated hard consonant must be placed, सर्व्वशक् सु, चित्रलिक् सु, or the sibilant being changeable after a guttural to ष, the form may be सर्व्वशक् षु, or in the compound letter, सर्व्वशक्षु.

In the neuter, the nominative and accusative forms are,

सर्व्वशक् or ग्	सर्व्वशकी	सर्व्वशङ्कि
चित्रलिक् or ग्	चित्रलिखी	चित्रलिङ्खि

Class II. Nouns ending in the palatals च, छ, ज, झ.

92. Nouns ending in a palatal commonly substitute क् for the final before the inflectional terminations beginning with consonants; which again is subject to the usual euphonic changes.

	वाच् 'speech.'			भुज् 'who eats.'		
nom.	वाक् or वाग्	वाचौ	वाचः	भुक् or भुग्	भुजौ	भुजः
acc.	वाचं	—	—	भुजं	—	—
instr.	वाचा	वाग्भ्यां	वाग्भिः	भुजा	भुग्भ्यां	भुग्भिः
dat.	वाचे	—	वाग्भ्यः	भुजे	—	भुग्भ्यः
abl.	वाचः	—	—	भुजः	—	—
gen.	—	वाचोः	वाचां	—	भुजोः	भुजां
loc.	वाचि	—	वाक्सु or वाक्षु	भुजि	—	भुक्षु
voc.	वाक् &c.			भुक्, &c.		

n. वाक् or वाग् वाची वाञ्चि
भुक् or भुग् भुजी भुञ्जि

93. There are several anomalies in this class, as regarding, not the inflectional terminations, but the inflective base.

a. Derivatives from the roots व्रश्च् 'cut,' भ्रस्ज् 'fry,' सृज् 'create,' मृज् 'rub,' यज् 'worship,' राज् 'shine,' भ्राज् 'shine,' व्रज् 'go,' substitute ष् for their final in the nom. sing., and before the terminations beginning with भ and स; that is, they are declined like nouns ending in ष्, which in those cases substitute ट् before a hard, and ड् before a soft consonant.

b. भ्रस्ज् is further changed to भृज्, 'who fries,' before the terminations beginning with consonants; and to भृज्ज् before those beginning with vowels.

nom.	भृट् or भृड्	भृज्जौ	भृज्जः
acc.	भृज्जं	—	—
instr.	भृज्जा	भृड्भ्यां	भृड्भिः
dat.	भृज्जे	—	भृड्भ्यः
abl.	भृज्जः	—	—
gen.	—	भृज्जोः	भृज्जां
loc.	भृज्जि	—	भृट्सु

c. So व्रश्च्, 'who cuts,' makes, वृट् or वृड्, वृश्चौ, वृश्चः, वृड्भ्यां, वृट्सु. विश्वसृज्, 'creator of the universe,' makes, nom. sing. विश्वसृट् or -सृड्, nom. dual विश्वसृजौ, nom. acc. plur. विश्वसृजः, instr. dual विश्वसृड्भ्यां, loc. plur. विश्वसृट्सु; but स्रज्,

a garland,' derived from the same root, makes, nom. स्रक् or स्रग्, स्रजौ, स्रजः; instr. dual स्रग्भ्यां, loc. plur. स्रक्षु; and असृज्, 'blood,' is differently inflected, as will be noticed below. परिमृज्, 'who cleanses,' makes, nom. sing. परिमृट् or -मृड्, nom. dual -मृजौ, instr. dual -मृड्भ्यां, &c. देवेज्, 'a worshipper of the gods,' makes, देवेट् or देवेड्, nom. dual देवेजौ, instr. dual देवेड्भ्यां, &c.; but ऋत्विज्, 'a ministering priest,' which is also derived from यज्, 'to worship,' is regular; nom. sing. ऋत्विक् or ऋत्विग्, nom. dual ऋत्विजौ, instr. dual ऋत्विग्भ्यां, &c. राज्, 'a ruler,' makes, nom. sing. राट् or राड्, nom. dual राजौ, instr. dual राड्भ्यां; but विश्वराज्, 'a universal ruler,' has this peculiarity, that when the final of राज् is changed, the short final vowel of विश्व is made long; as, nom. sing. विश्वाराट् or -राड्, nom. dual विश्वराजौ, acc. sing. विश्वराजं, instr. dual विश्वाराड्भ्यां, &c. विभ्राज्, 'who shines much,' makes, nom. sing. विभ्राट् or -भ्राड्, nom. dual विभ्राजौ, instr. dual विभ्राड्भ्यां; but this is a derivative from the root, which is marked in the lists of radicals, as टु-भ्राजृ. There is another root, भ्राजृ 'to shine,' without the prefix टु, and its derivatives are regular; as, nom. sing. विभ्राक् or विभ्राग्, nom. dual विभ्राजौ, instr. dual विभ्राग्भ्यां, &c. प्रव्राज्, 'a mendicant,' 'an errant,' makes, nom. sing. परिव्राट् or ड्, nom. dual परिव्राजौ, instr. dual परिव्राड्भ्यां, &c.

94. Derivatives from roots ending in च् or ज्, formed by adding the affix technically termed क्विन्, insert a nasal before the final in the first five inflexions; as, युज्, 'who joins,' from युज्, 'join,' makes, nom. युङ्, युञ्जौ, युञ्जः; acc. युञ्जं, युञ्जौ; in the rest it is regular, acc. plur. युजः, instr. sing. युजा, instr. dual युग्भ्यां, loc. plur. युक्षु. It is regular throughout in composition; as, अश्वयुज्, a constellation so named, makes, nom. अश्वयुक् or -ग्, अश्वयुजौ, अश्वयुजः. युज् also, if derived from युजिर्, is regular; as, युज् 'one who meditates;' nom. युक् or युग्, &c.

a. क्रुञ्च्, 'a curlew,' retains the nasal throughout; as, nom. क्रुङ्, क्रुञ्चौ, क्रुञ्चः; instr. क्रुञ्चा, क्रुङ्भ्यां, क्रुङ्भिः; loc. plur. क्रुङ्षु or क्रुङ्क्षु.

95. Derivations of अञ्च् in the sense of 'going,' compounded

with prepositions and with certain other words, are very irregular. They are,

प्राच् eastern.	विष्वद्र्यच् moving all round.
प्रत्यच् western.	सम्यच् moving equally.
उदच् northern.	सध्र्यच् moving with.
अवाच् southern.	तिर्य्यच् moving crookedly.

Which are thus inflected:

	प्राच् 'eastern.'			प्रत्यच् western.		
nom.	प्राङ्	प्राञ्चौ	प्राञ्चः	प्रत्यङ्	प्रत्यञ्चौ	प्रत्यञ्चः
acc.	प्राञ्चं	—	प्राचः	प्रत्यञ्चं	—	प्रतीचः
instr.	प्राचा	प्राग्भ्यां	प्राग्भिः	प्रतीचा	प्रत्यग्भ्यां	प्रत्यग्भिः
dat.	प्राचे	—	प्राग्भ्यः	प्रतीचे	—	प्रत्यग्भ्यः
abl.	प्राचः	—	—	प्रतीचः	—	—
gen.	—	प्राचोः	प्राचां	—	प्रतीचोः	प्रतीचां
loc.	प्राचि	—	प्राक्षु	प्रतीचि	—	प्रत्यक्षु

a. They form the feminines by dropping the nasal, and adding the termination ई, as प्राची, प्रतीची, and are declined like नदी. The neuters are regular; as, nom. and acc. प्राक्, प्राची, प्राञ्चि; प्रत्यक्, प्रतीची, प्रत्यञ्चि; the rest like the masculine. अवाच् is declined like प्राच्. उदच् substitutes ई for the antepenultimate before the accus. plur. and following terminations; as, उदङ्, उदञ्चौ; उदञ्चं, उदीचः, उदीचा, &c. Those derivatives also in which the semivowel य occurs, change it to ई, analogously to the similar change in प्रत्यच्. तिर्य्यच् changes its nasal to a sibilant before the vowel terminations beginning with the accus. plur.

nom.	तिर्य्यङ्	तिर्य्यञ्चौ	तिर्य्यञ्चः
acc.	तिर्य्यञ्चं	—	तिरश्चः
instr.	तिरश्चा	तिर्य्यग्भ्यां	तिर्य्यग्भिः
dat.	तिरश्चे	—	तिर्य्यग्भ्यः
abl.	तिरश्चः	—	—
gen.	—	तिरश्चोः	तिरश्चां
loc.	तिरश्चि	—	तिर्य्यक्षु

b. When the derivatives are from a similar root, but which has a different meaning, namely, अञ्च् 'to worship,' they follow the rules of Sandhi only; that is, च is rejected when final, and before a consonant, when also the palatal nasal becomes the guttural; as, प्राञ्च् 'who worships:' sing. nom. प्राङ्, acc. प्राञ्चं, instr. प्राञ्चा, dat. प्राञ्चे, abl. and gen. प्राञ्चः, loc. प्राञ्चि; dual nom. and acc. प्राञ्चौ, instr. dat. and abl. प्राङ्भ्यां, gen. and loc. प्राञ्चोः; plur. nom. and acc. प्राञ्चः, instr. प्राङ्भिः, dat. and abl. प्राङ्भ्यः, gen. प्राञ्चां, loc. प्राङ्क्षु. Fem. sing. nom. प्राञ्ची, प्राञ्च्यौ, प्राञ्च्यः; neut. nom. and acc. प्राङ्, प्राञ्ची, प्राञ्चि.

96. There are not many nouns ending in छ, but they follow the model of व्रश्च &c. before the consonants, and optionally change छ to श before the vowels: thus सर्व्वप्राच्छ्, 'who asks all,' makes,

nom.	सर्व्वप्राट् or -ड्	सर्व्वप्राच्छौ or -प्राशौ	सर्व्वप्राच्छः or -प्राशः
acc.	सर्व्वप्राच्छं or -प्राशं	———	———
instr.	सर्व्वप्राच्छा or -प्राशा	सर्व्वप्राड्भ्यां	सर्व्वप्राड्भिः
dat.	सर्व्वप्राच्छे or -प्राशे	—	सर्व्वप्राड्भ्यः
abl.	सर्व्वप्राच्छः or -प्राशः	—	—
gen.	———	सर्व्वप्राच्छोः or -प्राशोः	सर्व्वप्राच्छां or -प्राशां
loc.	सर्व्वप्राच्छि or -प्राशि	———	सर्व्वप्राट्सु

97. यज, 'to sacrifice,' when compounded with the preposition अव, lengthens its penultimate vowel before the vowel inflectional terminations, and is declined like a noun ending in स् before the consonants, as if it was an imperfect noun supplied in part by the obsolete noun अवयस्. Thus अवयज्, 'an inferior worshipper,' makes,

nom.	अवयाः	अवयाजौ	अवयाजः
acc.	अवयाजं	—	—
instr.	अवयाजा	अवयोभ्यां	अवयोभिः
dat.	अवयाजे	—	अवयोभ्यः
abl.	अवयाजः	—	—
gen.	अवयाजः	अवयाजोः	अवयाजां
loc.	अवयाजि	—	अवयःसु
voc.	अवयः, &c.		

98. खञ्ज्, 'a lame man,' drops, agreeably to the rules of combination, the last member of its conjunct, when final, or when followed by a consonant: hence, sing. nom. खन्, instr. dual खन्भ्यां; plur. खन्भिः, loc. plur. खन्सु. Before the vowels there is no change; खञ्जौ, खञ्जः, खञ्जा, &c.

99. ऊर्ज्ज्, 'strong,' may reject one ज before a pause or a consonant, but is in other respects regular: sing. nom. ऊर्क् or ऊर्ग्, acc. ऊर्ज्जं, instr. ऊर्ज्जा; dual instr. ऊर्ग्भ्यां; plur. instr. ऊर्ग्भिः, loc. ऊर्क्षु, &c. The neuter plural may be ऊंर्ज्जि or ऊर्न्जि; but in composition with बहु, 'much,' the nasal, if inserted, must precede the final consonant; as, plur. nom. and acc. बहूर्न्जि or बहूर्ञ्जि 'very strong.'

100. असृज्, 'blood,' a neuter noun, optionally borrows its inflexions in the accus. plur. and following cases from an obsolete noun, असन्, which is inflected like other nouns in न्.

nom.	असृक्	असृजी	असृञ्जि
acc.	—	—	— or असानि
instr.	असृजा or अस्ना	असृग्भ्यां or असभ्यां	असृग्भिः or असभिः
dat.	असृजे or अस्ने	———	असृग्भ्यः or असभ्यः
abl.	असृजः or अस्नः	———	———
gen.	———	असृजोः or अस्नोः	असृजां or अस्नां
loc.	असृजि or असनि	———	असृक्षु or असःसु

CLASS III. Nouns ending in cerebrals, or ट, ठ, ड, ढ.

101. Nouns terminating in these letters do not, as far as is yet known, occur; but ट and ड are used as the substitutes of nouns ending in ष. The first, as a hard consonant, is changed optionally when final, and absolutely before the inflexions beginning with भ, to ड.

CLASS IV. Nouns terminating in the dentals, त, थ, द, ध.

102. Nouns terminating in consonants of the dental class are for the most part regular, being subject to no other

changes than those which the laws of Sandhi require. The final in the nominative is either the unaspirated hard or soft letter त or द; before भ it is the soft द; and before सु the hard consonant त; as in the following paradigmas of हरित् 'green,' अग्निमथ् 'one who kindles fire,' ककुद् 'a bull's hump,' समिध् 'fuel.'

	हरित् mfn.	अग्निमथ् mfn.	ककुद् f.	समिध् f.
s. nom.	हरित् or -द्	अग्निमत् or -द्	ककुत् or -द्	समित् or -द्
— acc.	हरितं	अग्निमथं	ककुदं	समिधं
— inst.	हरिता	अग्निमथा	ककुदा	समिधा &c.
d. inst. &c.	हरिद्भ्यां	अग्निमद्भ्यां	ककुद्भ्यां	समिद्भ्यां &c.
pl. inst.	हरिद्भिः	अग्निमद्भिः	ककुद्भिः	समिद्भिः
— loc.	हरित्सु	अग्निमत्सु	ककुत्सु	समित्सु

The neuter form of the two first is in the nom. and acc.; हरित् or -द्, हरिती, हरिन्ति; अग्निमत् or -द्, अग्निमथी, अग्निमन्थि; but बेभिद्, 'who cuts much,' and similar derivatives, do not insert the nasal in the plural; as, बेभित् or -द्, बेभिदी, बेभिदि.

a. दत्, 'a tooth,' and पृत्, 'an army,' are considered as optionally substituted for दन्त and पृतना; as, sing. nom. दत् or दद् or दन्तः, acc. दतं or दन्तं, instr. दता or दन्तेन; dual instr. &c. दद्भ्यां or दन्ताभ्यां, &c.

b. So पद्, 'a foot,' is the optional substitute for पाद in all cases, and absolutely for पाद् in composition, but only in the accus. plur. and subsequent cases beginning with vowels; as, sing. nom. पत् or पद् or पादः, acc. पदं or पादं, instr. पदा or पादेन; dual instr. &c. पद्भ्यां पादाभ्यां, &c.: but व्याघ्रपाद्, 'tiger-foot,' a plant so named, makes, nom. व्याघ्रपात् or पाद्, व्याघ्रपादौ, व्याघ्रपादः; acc. व्याघ्रपादं, व्याघ्रपादौ, व्याघ्रपदः; instr. व्याघ्रपदा, व्याघ्रपाद्भ्यां, व्याघ्रपाद्भिः, &c. In like manner, हृद्, 'the heart,' is a substitute for हृदय; nom. हृत् or हृद्, हृदी, हृन्दि, &c.

103. यकृत्, 'the spleen,' and शकृत्, 'ordure,' neuter nouns, are declined analogously to असृज्; that is, they optionally substitute in the accusative plural and subsequent cases the inflexions of obsolete nouns ending in न्, as यकन् and शकन्.

nom.	यकृत्	यकृती	यकृन्ति
acc.	—	—	— or यकानि
instr.	यकृता or यक्ना	यकृद्भ्यां or यकृभ्यां	यकृद्भिः or यकभिः
dat.	यकृते or यक्ने	———	यकृद्भ्यः or यकृभ्यः
abl.	यकृतः or यक्नः	———	———
gen.	———	यकृतोः or यक्नोः	यकृतां or यक्नां
loc.	यकृति or पक्नि	———	यकृत्सु or यकसु

So शकृन्ति or शकानि, शकृता or शक्ना, &c.

a. बुध् 'who knows,' changes its initial to भ whenever it changes its final to the unaspirated letter, that is, in the nominative singular, and before the inflectional terminations beginning with a consonant.

nom.	भुत् or भुद्	बुधौ	बुधः
instr.	बुधा	भुद्भ्यां	भुद्भिः &c.
loc. plur.	भुत्सु &c.		

104. Besides nouns of a general character ending in dentals, there are certain declinable participles ending in अत् and वत्, and certain possessive nouns ending in वत् and मत्, which undergo some modification of the inflective base before the terminations of the nominative, and before the accusative singular and dual. In all the other cases they are regularly declined like other nouns ending in त्; that is, the vowel affixes are attached to the final; त is unaltered before सु, and becomes द before भ.

105. These participial and possessive nouns prefix an न to their final त् before the terminations of the five first inflexions: thus पचत् 'cooking,' becomes पचन्त्. Those ending in वत् or मत् also make the penultimate vowel long in the nominative, and accordingly कृतवत् becomes कृतवान्त् 'doing:' but by the rule that the second member of a final conjunct consonant is to be rejected, the final त् is thrown out, and the words remain in the nominative singular पचन्, कृतवान्. Before the vowels the compound is unchanged, as पचन्तौ, कृतवन्तौ, &c.: thus,

	भवत् 'being.'			गतवत् 'going.'		
nom.	भवन्	भवन्तौ	भवन्तः	गतवान्	गतवन्तौ	गतवन्तः
acc.	भवन्तं	—	भवतः	गतवन्तं	—	गतवतः
instr.	भवता	भवद्भ्यां	भवद्भिः &c.	गतवता	गतवद्भ्यां	गतवद्भिः &c.

So धनवत् 'having wealth;' masc.

nom.	धनवान्	धनवन्तौ	धनवन्तः
acc.	धनवन्तं	—	धनवतः
instr.	धनवता &c.		

and श्रीमत् 'having prosperity;' masc.

nom.	श्रीमान्	श्रीमन्तौ	श्रीमन्तः
acc.	श्रीमन्तं	—	श्रीमतः &c.

a. To form the feminine gender of these nouns, ई is added to the termination, and the noun is declined like नदी; as, गतवती, धनवती, श्रीमती. The neuter is regular; as, गतवत्, गतवती, गतवन्ति.

b. Participles of the present tense formed with अत् sometimes retain the nasal augment in the feminine noun throughout, and in the nominative and accusative dual of the neuter; as, भवत् makes भवन्ती, भवन्त्यौ, भवन्त्यः, &c. in the feminine; and in the neuter, भवत्, भवन्ती, भवन्ति.

c. This insertion of the nasal is imperative in the participles of all verbs of the first, fourth, and tenth conjugations. It is optionally inserted after verbs of other conjugations, which either in their simple form or in their conjugational bases end with अ or आ. It is not inserted after any others.

	Verb.	Part. pres. masc.	Fem.
1st conj.	भू to be	भवत्	भवन्ती
2d —	अद् to eat	अदत्	अदती
	भा to shine	भात्	भाती or भान्ती
3d —	हु to sacrifice; repeated, जुहु	जुह्वत्	जुह्वती
4th —	दिव to play	दीव्यत्	दीव्यन्ती
5th —	सु to bear; with increment सुनु	सुन्वत्	सुन्वती

6th conj.	तुद to torment	तुदत्	तुदती or तुदन्ती
7th —	रुध् to obstruct	रुन्धत्	रुन्धती
8th —	तन to stretch; with increment तनु	तन्वत्	तन्वती
9th —	क्री to buy; with increment क्रीणा	क्रीणत्	क्रीणती or क्रीणन्ती
10th —	चुर to steal	चोरयत्	चोरयन्ती

So in the nominative and accusative dual of the neuter, भवन्ती; अदती, भाती or भान्ती, &c.

d. The participles of the present tense of verbs, which take a reduplicate form, even though the crude verb originally terminates in अ or आ, do not insert an न before their final त्, but are declined like nouns in general ending in that consonant; as दा 'to give:' part. pres. ददत्; masc. nom. ददत् or ददद्, ददतौ, ददतः; acc. ददतं, ददतौ, ददतः; instr. ददता, दद्भ्यां, &c.: fem. sing. nom. ददती; neut. nom. acc. dual ददती; plur. ददन्ति or ददति.

e. There are certain other verbs which are analogously inflected in their present participles; as, जक्ष 'to eat;' जक्षत्, जक्षतौ, जक्षतः, &c.: शास 'govern;' शासत्, शासतौ, शासतः, &c.

f. भवत्, when a term of address, as 'Sir,' 'Your worship,' is declined amongst the pronouns.

g. पृषत् 'a deer,' जगत् 'the world,' and बृहत् 'great,' are declined like participles in the three numbers of the nominative and in the accusative singular and dual; in the rest they are regular.

nom.	पृषन्	पृषन्तौ	पृषन्तः
	जगन्	जगन्तौ	जगन्तः
	बृहन्	बृहन्तौ	बृहन्तः
acc.	पृषन्तं	पृषन्तौ	पृषतः
	जगन्तं	जगन्तौ	जगतः
	बृहन्तं	बृहन्तौ	बृहतः
instr.	पृषता	पृषद्भ्यां	पृषद्भिः &c.

106. महत्, 'great,' makes its penultimate long before the first five inflexions of the masculine, and that of the two first cases plural of the neuter; as,

nom. महान्	महान्तौ	महान्तः
acc. महान्तं	—	महतः
instr. महता	महद्भ्यां &c.	

Fem. महती; neut. nom. and acc. महत्, महती, महान्ति.

a. Nouns of every description ending in dentals are numerous; of which the following are a few.

Substantives.	Attributives.
उपनिषद् f. a sacred treatise	कृत् who or what cuts
कुमुद् n. a lotus	चित् who or what gathers
क्रव्याद् mf. a cannibal	पत् who or what falls
दृशद् f. a stone	वृत् who or what is or abides
प्रतिपद् f. 1st day of lunar fortnight	कथ् who speaks
मरुत् m. wind	मथ् who or what churns
विद्युत् f. lightning	तुद् what torments
शरद् f. autumn	नुद् who sends or drives
सम्पत् f. wealth	भिद् who or what breaks
संविद् f. agreement	विद् who or what knows

Possessives.	Participles.
आयुष्मत् long-lived	कुर्वत् doing
कुमुद्वत् abounding in lotuses	गच्छत् going
धीमत् sensible	चरत् going
परवत् dependant	जयत् conquering
पुत्रवत् having children	जानत् knowing
मूर्त्तिमत् having form	तरत् crossing
भगवत् majestic, divine	दमत् taming
यशस्वत् famous	धरत् holding
लक्ष्मीवत् prosperous	नदत् sounding
सरस्वत् having elegance	स्रवत् flowing

Class V. Nouns ending in labials, प, फ, ब, भ.

107. These, which are few in number, are for the most part regular. The nominative ends in प् or ब्. The final remains before the vowel terminations, and is ब before भ, and प before सु; as गुप् 'who preserves:' nom. गुप् or गुब्, गुपौ, गुपः; acc. गुपं, गुपौ, गुपः; instr. गुपा, गुब्भ्यां, गुब्भिः; loc. plur. गुप्सु. So ककुभ् 'a quarter of the horizon:' nom. ककुप् or ककुब्, ककुभौ, ककुभः; acc. ककुभं, ककुभौ, ककुभः; instr. ककुभा, ककुब्भ्यां; loc. plur. ककुप्सु.

108. There is one irregular noun in this class, अप् 'water,' declinable only in the plural number: plur. nom. आपः, acc. अपः, instr. अद्भिः, dat. and abl. अद्भ्यः, gen. अपां, loc. अप्सु.

In composition it may be declined like any other noun in प्; as, स्वप्, from सु 'good,' and अप् 'water,' 'having good water,' makes, nom. sing. स्वप् or स्वब्, nom. dual स्वपौ, nom. plur. स्वपः, instr. dual स्वब्भ्यां, loc. plur. स्वप्सु, &c.

Class VI. Nouns ending in nasals, ङ, ञ, ण, न, म.

109. Of words terminating in nasals of the two first classes no instances are known, and but few are met with ending in ण्. They are quite regular, but may optionally insert ट् before सु; as सुगण् 'of a good class:' nom. सुगण्, सुगणौ, सुगणः; instr. &c. dual सुगण्भ्यां; loc. plur. सुगण्सु or सुगण्ट्सु.

110. Nouns ending in न् are numerous, and present many peculiarities. They may be divided into two orders; one ending in अन्, the other in इन्.

Nouns ending in अन्.

111. When regularly inflected, nouns in अन् drop the final in the nominative singular, and before the terminations beginning with consonants; and in the masculine and feminine genders they make the penultimate letter long before all the terminations of the nominative, and those of the accusative singular and dual: the vocative singular is unchanged. Thus आत्मन्, 'soul,' is declined as follows:

nom.	आत्मा	आत्मानौ	आत्मानः
acc.	आत्मानं	—	आत्मनः
instr.	आत्मना	आत्मभ्यां	आत्मभिः
dat.	आत्मने &c.		loc. आत्मसु
voc.	आत्मन्		

In the neuter form the vowel is made long only, agreeably to general rule, in the plural; where however a nasal is not inserted before a nasal: ब्रह्मन् 'Brahma,' 'the Supreme;' nom. acc. ब्रह्म, ब्रह्मणी, ब्रह्माणि.

112. In these two examples, आत्मन् and ब्रह्मन्, the final अन् is preceded by a conjunct consonant, of which the final letter is म. If the last of such conjunct be व, the noun is similarly inflected; as यज्वन् 'a sacrificer:' nom. यज्वा, यज्वानौ, यज्वानः; acc. यज्वानं, यज्वानौ, यज्वनः, &c.: but if no such conjunct precede, then in the accusative plural and following cases, of which the terminations begin with vowels, the penultimate अ is rejected, and the antepenultimate and final coalesce; as राजन् 'a king:' nom. राजा, राजानौ, राजानः; acc. राजानं, राजानौ, राज्ञः; instr. राज्ञा, राजभ्यां, राजभिः; voc. राजन्, &c. In the locative sing. the rejection is optional; as राज्ञि or राजनि.

a. The same takes place before the feminine affix ई; as राज्ञी 'a queen:' and optionally before the neuter dual; as व्योमन् 'the sky:' nom. acc. व्योम, व्योम्नी or व्योमनी, व्योमानि.

b. When a noun ending in अन् is derived from a root ending in र् or व्, preceded by इ, उ, or ऋ, the vowel is made long before the conjunct consonant of the accusative plural, &c.; as परिदिवन् 'who sports:' nom. परिदिवा, परिदिवानौ, परिदिवानः; acc. परिदिवानं, परिदिवानौ, परिदीव्नः; instr. परिदीव्ना, परिदिवभ्यां, परिदिवभिः, &c.

c. मघवन्, a name of Indra, may substitute त् for its final, and be declined like a noun in वत्; as, nom. मघवान्, मघवन्तौ, मघवन्तः; acc. मघवन्तं, मघवन्तौ, मघवतः, &c.: but it is also declinable as a noun in न् when it changes its semivowel व to उ before the vowel terminations of the accusative plural and following cases, and ओ is substituted for उ and the अ of मघ; in the other cases it is declined like आत्मन्; as,

nom.	मघवा	मघवानौ	मघवानः
acc.	मघवानं	मघवानौ	मघोनः
instr.	मघोना	मघवभ्यां	मघवभिः
dat.	मघोने		loc. मघवसु
voc.	मघवन्		

d. श्वन्, 'a dog,' and युवन्, 'a youth,' are declined so far analogously to मघवन्, that they change व to उ before the accusative plural and the following cases, of which the terminations begin with vowels. In श्वन् the उ is of course merely subjoined to the श; in युवन् it is preceded by the उ of यु, and consequently the two short vowels combine into one long one; they then follow the analogy of राजन्, as by rule 112, and reject the penultimate अ; in consequence of which, उ or ऊ immediately precedes the final न्. श्वन्, κυων, 'canis,' 'a dog:' nom. श्वा, श्वानौ, श्वानः; acc. श्वानं, श्वानौ, शुनः; instr. शुना, श्वभ्यां, श्वभिः; dat. शुने, श्वभ्यां, &c. युवन्, 'juvenis,' 'a youth:' nom. युवा, युवानौ, युवानः; acc. युवानं, युवानौ, यूनः; instr. यूना, युवभ्यां, युवभिः; dat. यूने, युवभ्यां, &c.

e. अर्य्यमन्, 'the sun,' is irregular in not making the penultimate long before the terminations of the nominative dual and plural, and accusative singular and dual; in the rest it follows राजन्; its न् is changed to ण् by virtue of the र् in अर्य्य.

nom.	अर्य्यमा	अर्य्यमणौ	अर्य्यमणः
acc.	अर्य्यमणं	—	अर्य्यम्णः
instr.	अर्य्यम्णा	अर्य्यमभ्यां	अर्य्यमभिः
loc.	अर्य्यम्णि or अर्य्यमणि	—	अर्य्यमसु
voc.	अर्य्यमन्		

f. Compounds with हन्, 'to kill,' follow the analogy of अर्य्यमन्, i. e. they do not make the vowel long in the nom.

dual, &c. They also change ह to घ before the vowel terminations of the accusative plural, and following cases, in which also the penultimate vowel is rejected, and accordingly the antepenultimate and final consonants combine.

ब्रह्महन्, 'the murderer of a Brahman.'

nom.	ब्रह्महा	ब्रह्महणौ	ब्रह्महणः
acc.	ब्रह्महणं	—	ब्रह्मघ्नः
instr.	ब्रह्मघ्ना	ब्रह्महभ्यां	ब्रह्महभिः
dat.	ब्रह्मघ्ने &c.		

g. पूषन्, 'the sun,' is inflected after the model of अर्यमन्; but in the accusative plural, and analogous cases, an imperfect noun, पूष्, is optionally substituted.

nom.	पूषा	पूषणौ	पूषणः
acc.	पूषणं	—	पूष्णः or पूषः
instr.	पूष्णा or पूषा	पूषभ्यां	पूषभिः
dat.	पूष्णे or पूषे &c.		

h. अर्वन्, 'a horse,' belongs to nouns in अन् in one case only, the nom. sing.: in all the rest it is declined like a noun in त्, or अर्वत्; as,

nom.	अर्वा	अर्वन्तौ	अर्वन्तः
acc.	अर्वन्तं	—	अर्वतः
instr.	अर्वता	अर्वद्भ्यां	अर्वद्भिः
dat.	अर्वते &c.		

If compounded with a negative, and used attributively, it is declined regularly as a noun ending in अन् preceded by a conjunct consonant, of which the last member is व; as अनर्वन् 'one who has not a horse:' nom. अनर्वा, अनर्वाणौ, अनर्वाणः; acc. अनर्वाणं, अनर्वाणौ, अनर्वणः; instr. अनर्वणा, अनर्वभ्यां, &c.

113. अहन् neut., 'a day,' is very irregular, substituting र् for the final in the nominative singular and locative plural, and उ convertible to ओ with the short vowel of अह before भ. In the other cases it conforms to व्योमन्; as,

nom. acc.	अहः	अह्नी or अहनी	अहानि
instr.	अह्ना	अहोभ्यां	अहोभिः
dat.	अह्ने	—	अहोभ्यः
abl.	अह्नः	—	—
gen.	—	अह्नोः	अह्नां
loc.	अह्नि or अहनि	—	अहःसु or अहस्सु

a. Compounded with numerals, with वि, or with साय, अह्न is substituted before all the terminations, and is declined like a noun ending in अ; as सायाह्न 'the afternoon:' सायाह्नः, सायाह्नौ, सायाह्नाः, &c.: but in the locative case singular these compounds take different forms; as सायाह्ने, सायाह्नि or सायाहनि.

b. Compounded with other words, अहन् is declined in the masculine and feminine like other nouns in अन्, except before the terminations of the dual and plural that begin with भ, where it substitutes उ for न्; as दीर्घाहन् 'a long day:' nom. दीर्घाहा, दीर्घाहानौ, दीर्घाहानः; acc. दीर्घाहानं, दीर्घाहानौ, दीर्घाह्नः; instr. दीर्घाह्ना, दीर्घाहोभ्यां, दीर्घाहोभिः; dat. दीर्घाह्ने, &c.; loc. sing. दीर्घाह्नि or दीर्घाहनि, plur. दीर्घाहःसु or दीर्घाहस्सु, voc. दीर्घाहः, &c.

Nouns in इन्.

114. Many possessive nouns are formed with the affixes इन्, विन्, and मिन्; as, धनिन् 'having wealth,' 'opulent;' दण्डिन् 'having a staff,' 'an ascetic;' तपस्विन् 'having devotion,' 'a devotee;' वाग्मिन् 'having speech,' 'eloquent:' all of which are declined on one model. They reject the न् before the consonants; retain it before the vowels; and make the penultimate of the base long in the nom. singular; in all the other cases the inflectional terminations are added, without any change, to the final of the base: as धनिन् mfn. 'rich.'

masc.	nom.	धनी	धनिनौ	धनिनः
	acc.	धनिनं	—	धनिनः
	instr.	धनिना	धनिभ्यां	धनिभिः
	dat.	धनिने &c.		loc. धनिषु
	voc.	धनिन्		

The feminine affixes ई, as धनिनी, and is declined like नदी. The neuter is regular; nom. acc. धनि, धनिनी, धनीनि.

115. There are three irregular nouns of this class; पथिन् 'a road,' मथिन् 'a churning stick,' and ऋभुक्षिन् 'a name of Indra.' These substitute आ for the final syllable before the affix of the nominative singular, and for इ before the other affixes of the nominative, and those of the accusative singular and dual: before the vowel terminations of the accusative plural and other cases they reject the final syllable altogether: before the consonants they reject the न्.

The two first also prefix a nasal to the consonant थ, before the first five inflexions; viz. those of the nominative, and the singular and dual accusative; as पथिन् 'a path,' 'a road.'

nom.	पन्थाः	पन्थानौ	पन्थानः
acc.	पन्थानं	—	पथः
instr.	पथा	पथिभ्यां	पथिभिः
dat.	पथे &c.	loc.	पथिषु
voc.	पथिन्		

So मथिन् makes मन्थाः, मन्थानौ, मथा, मथिभ्यां, &c.

Compounded with other words, these are declined in the masculine in the same manner as the uncompounded word: in the feminine, the final syllable is rejected, and the affix ई is added to the antepenultimate consonant: in the neuter, न् is rejected in the singular and dual, and prefixed to थ before the plural: as सुपथिन्, 'having a good road,' makes, masc. सुपन्थाः, &c.; fem. सुपथी, सुपथ्यौ, &c.; neut. nom. and acc. सुपथि, सुपथी, सुपन्थानि.

ऋभुक्षिन् makes, nom. ऋभुक्षाः, ऋभुक्षाणौ, ऋभुक्षाणः; acc. ऋभुक्षाणं, ऋभुक्षाणौ, ऋभुक्षः; instr. ऋभुक्षा, ऋभुक्षिभ्यां, &c.

116. Nouns ending in म् are few: before the consonantal terminations it is changed to न्; as प्रशाम् 'mild,' 'quiet,' makes, nom. प्रशान्, प्रशामौ, प्रशामः; instr. प्रशामा, प्रशान्भ्यां, प्रशान्भिः; loc. plur. प्रशांसु or प्रशान्त्सु.

CLASS VII. Nouns ending in semivowels, य, र, ल, व.

117. Nouns ending in य् and ल् are of rare occurrence: if they occur, they are regular.

118. Nouns derived from verbal roots ending in र् or व् make a preceding vowel long before the inflectional terminations which begin with consonants. र् is changed to Visarga in the nominative singular; but not before the locative plural, if it be a radical letter. स followed by a vowel, as in सु, is not doubled after र्. Thus गिर् fem. 'speech:' nom. गीः, गिरौ, गिरः; acc. गिरं, गिरौ, गिरः; instr. गिरा, गीर्भ्यां, गीर्भिः; loc. plur. गीर्षु.

Nouns ending in semivowels do not insert a nasal before the neuter plural. वार् n., 'water,' makes, nom. and acc. वाः, वारी, वारि; instr. वारा, वार्भ्यां, वार्भिः, &c.

a. दिव्, 'sky,' changes व to औ in the nominative, and to उ before the consonantal terminations. The इ of दि becomes य् by the rules of Sandhi. दिव् f. 'sky:' nom. द्यौः, दिवौ, दिवः; acc. दिवं, दिवौ, दिवः; instr. दिवा, द्युभ्यां, द्युभिः; loc. plur. द्युषु.

b. Used attributively, as in सुदिव्, 'having a clear sky (a day),' the neuter form is, nom. and acc. सुद्यु, सुदिवी, सुदिवि; the rest like the masculine.

CLASS VIII. Nouns ending in sibilants, श, ष, स.

श.

119. Nouns formed from verbal roots ending in श्, with the affix technically termed क्विन्, substitute for the final the guttural letter क् before all the terminations beginning with consonants; as दिश् f. 'space.'

nom.	दिक् or दिग्	दिशौ	दिशः
acc.	दिशं	—	दिशः
instr.	दिशा	दिग्भ्यां	दिग्भिः &c.
loc.	दिशि	दिशोः	दिक्षु

When formed with any other affix, it is said that ष् is substituted for the final; and for ष् the cerebral ट् is substituted in the same cases.

विश् (विष्) 'who enters.'

nom.	विट् or विड्	विशौ	विशः
acc.	विशं	—	—
instr.	विशा	विड्भ्यां	विड्भिः &c.
loc.	विशि	विशोः	विट्सु

neuter nom. and acc. विट् or विड्, विशी, विंशि

a. नश्, 'who or what destroys,' takes either form.

nom.	नक्-नग् or नट्-नड्	नशौ	नशः
acc.	नशं	—	—
instr.	नशा	नग्भ्यां or नड्भ्यां	नग्भिः or नड्भिः
loc.	नशि	———	नक्षु or नट्सु

b. दृश् 'who sees,' with its compounds ईदृश्, तादृश्, सदृश्, 'such-like,' 'similar,' take the guttural substitute: so do the derivatives of स्पृश् 'to touch;' तादृक् or तादृग्, तादृशौ, तादृशा, तादृग्भ्यां, &c.: so घृतस्पृश् 'who touches Ghee;' घृतस्पृक् or ग्, घृतस्पृशौ, घृतस्पृशा, घृतस्पृग्भ्यां, &c.

c. निश् may be substituted for निशा 'night,' and is then declined like विश्; according to some, a palatal may be substituted for the cerebral before the consonants, except in the nominative singular; as निड्भ्यां or निज्भ्यां, निट्सु or निच्सु.

ष.

120. Nouns ending in ष् are inflected in one of three ways; 1. by substituting ट् for the final before the consonantal inflexions; 2. by substituting क् in the similar cases; and 3. by substituting before the same inflexions 'ru' or र्.

The substitution of ट् is considered the regular form of inflecting verbal derivative forms in ष्; as त्विष् f., 'light,' from त्विष् 'to shine.'

nom.	त्विट् or त्विड्	त्विषौ	त्विषः
acc.	त्विषं	—	—
instr.	त्विषा	त्विड्भ्यां	त्विड्भिः
dat.	त्विषे &c.	loc.	त्विट्सु or त्विट्त्सु

121. As in the case of nouns ending in श्, those in ष् formed from verbs by the affix क्विन् take the guttural substitute; as दधृष् 'arrogant,' from धृष् 'to be proud.'

nom.	दधृक् or -धृग्	दधृषौ	दधृषः
acc.	दधृषं	—	—
instr.	दधृषा	दधृग्भ्यां &c.	

122. In the case of सजुष् 'a friend,' and some other words, particularly those in which the final is properly स्, but has become ष् in consequence of being preceded by some other vowel than अ or आ (see rule 29), र् is substituted for the final before the consonantal inflexions, and the nouns are declined like nouns ending in र्.

सजुष् 'a friend.'

nom.	सजूः	सजुषौ	सजुषः
acc.	सजुषं	—	—
instr.	सजुषा	सजूर्भ्यां	सजूर्भिः
dat.	सजुषे &c.	loc. सजूःषु or सजूष्षु	

a. आशिष् for आशिस् f. 'a benediction,' is similarly inflected.

nom.	आशीः	आशिषौ	आशिषः
acc.	आशिषं	—	—
instr.	आशिषा	आशीर्भ्यां	आशीर्भिः
dat.	आशिषे &c.	loc. आशीःषु or आशीष्षु	

b. दोष् for दोस्, 'the arm,' besides being declined in this manner, admits before the vowel terminations of the accusative plural and following cases the optional use of दोषन्, declined like nouns in अन्.

nom.	दोः	दोषौ	दोषः
acc.	दोषं	—	— or दोष्णः
instr.	दोषा or दोष्णा	दोर्भ्यां	दोर्भिः
dat.	दोषे or दोष्णे	—	दोर्भ्यः
abl.	दोषः or दोष्णः	—	—
gen.	दोषः or दोष्णः	दोषोः or दोष्णोः	दोषां or दोष्णां
loc.	दोषि or दोष्णि	———	दोःषु or दोष्षु

It is also neuter: nom. and acc. दोः, दोषी, दोंषि.

c. Neuter nouns with a penultimate इ or उ short, make the vowel long only before the nasal augment of the nominative and accusative plural; as, धनुष् 'a bow,' चक्षुष् 'the eye,' रोचिष् 'light,' हविष् 'Ghee,' severally for धनुस्, चक्षुस्, &c.; as, nom. and acc. रोचिः, रोचिषी, रोचींषि; instr. रोचिषा, रोचिर्भ्यां, रोचिर्भिः, &c.: so, nom. and acc. चक्षुः, चक्षुषी, चक्षूंषि; instr. चक्षुषा, चक्षुर्भ्यां, चक्षुर्भिः.

d. Nouns derived from the desiderative form of the verb are declined after this manner; as पिपठिष्, 'one who wishes to read,' makes, mf. पिपठीः, पिपठिषौ, पिपठीर्भ्यां, &c.; neuter nom. and acc. पिपठिः, पिपठिषी, पिपठिषि. It does not insert the nasal in the neuter plural. चिकीर्ष्, 'one who wishes to do,' rejects the sibilant before a consonantal inflection (see rule 35); as, चिकीः, चिकीर्षौ, चिकीर्षः, चिकीर्भ्यां, &c.

123. Nouns formed from verbs ending in the compound letter क्ष् reject before the consonantal inflexions either the first member of the compound or क्, and are then declined like nouns in ष्; or they reject the second member ष्, and are declined as if ending in क्.

The same words, accordingly as they are said to be formed with different affixes, may take both modifications; as तक्ष् mf. 'who or what pares' or 'makes thin:' nom. sing. तट् or तड्, तक् or तग्; instr. dual, &c. तड्भ्यां or तग्भ्यां; loc. plur. तट्सु or तक्षु; so गोरक्ष्, 'a cow-keeper,' makes, nom. sing. गोरट् or गोरड्, गोरक् or -रग्; instr. dual, &c. गोरड्भ्यां or गोरग्भ्यां; loc. plur. गोरट्सु or गोरक्षु. Before the vowels the final is of course unchanged; as तक्षौ, गोरक्षौ.

a. Nouns in क्ष् formed from desideratives reject the sibilant only; as पिपक्ष्, 'who desires to cook,' makes, पिपक् or -ग्, पिपक्षौ, पिपग्भ्यां, पिपक्षु, &c. विवक्ष् 'who wishes to speak,' दिधक्ष् 'what desires to burn,' are similarly inflected.

स.

124. Nouns masculine and feminine ending in स्, when preceded by अ, make the penultimate long in the nominative singular, and substitute उ for the sibilant before the inflexions beginning with भ, which with a preceding अ makes ओ.

वेधस् 'Brahmá.'

nom.	वेधाः	वेधसौ	वेधसः
acc.	वेधसं	—	—
instr.	वेधसा	वेधोभ्यां	वेधोभिः
dat.	वेधसे	—	वेधोभ्यः
abl.	वेधसः	—	—
gen.	—	वेधसोः	वेधसां
loc.	वेधसि	—	वेधःसु or वेधस्सु
voc.	वेधः		

a. The vowel is not made long in the nominative, if the noun retain the form of the radical whence it is derived; as, वस् 'to clothe;' सुवस् 'who dresses well;' nom. sing. सुवः. So पिण्डग्रस् 'who takes a funeral cake,' from पिण्ड and ग्रस् 'to take;' nom. sing. पिण्डग्रः.

b. Three masculine nouns in अस् are irregular, अनेहस् 'time,' उशनस् 'the regent of the planet Venus,' and पुरुदंशस् a name of Indra. They are declined in the nominative singular as if ending in अन्; अनेहा, उशना, पुरुदंशा. In the vocative the first and last are regular, अनेहः, पुरुदंशः; the second has three forms, उशनः, उशन, or उशनन्.

125. Neuter nouns in अस् do not make the penultimate long in the nominative and accusative singular, but make it long in the plural; as पयस् 'water:' nom. and acc. पयः, पयसी, पयांसि; पयसा, पयोभ्यां, पयोभिः, &c.; पयःसु or पयस्सु.

126. Nouns ending in स् in conjunction with a consonant drop the final (by rule 35) before the consonantal inflexions; so हिन्स् mf., 'who or what injures,' becomes, nom. हिन्, हिन्सौ, हिन्सः; acc. हिन्सं, हिन्सौ, हिन्सः; instr. हिन्सा, हिन्भ्यां, हिन्भिः, &c.

a. Derivatives from संस् and ध्वंस्, 'to fall,' with the affix क्विन्, substitute द् for the final (which becomes ट् and ड्) before the consonants, and reject the nasal throughout. ध्वंस् 'who falls:' nom. ध्वट् or ध्वड्, ध्वसौ, ध्वसः; acc. ध्वसं, ध्वसौ, ध्वसः; instr. ध्वसा, ध्वड्भ्यां, ध्वड्भिः, &c.

127. पुंस्, 'a man,' drops the final sibilant before the consonantal inflexions; and it is otherwise peculiar in the nominative, and in the singular and dual of the accusative; as,

nom.	पुमान्	पुमांसौ	पुमांसः
acc.	पुमांसं	—	पुंसः
instr.	पुंसा	पुंभ्यां	पुंभिः
dat.	पुंसे	—	पुंभ्यः
abl.	पुंसः	—	—
gen.	पुंसः	पुंसोः	पुंसां
loc.	पुंसि	—	पुंसु or पुंषु
voc.	पुमन् &c.		

It may be declined in three genders as an epithet; as सुपुंस् 'of a good man:' mf. सुपुमान् &c.; neut. nom. and acc. सुपुम्, सुपुंसी, सुपुमांसि.

128. There are some participial nouns formed with वस्, which before the inflexions of the nominative, and of the accusative singular and dual, prefix a nasal to the sibilant, and make the preceding vowel long. In the nominative singular the स् is rejected, as the final of a conjunct consonant: before the accusative plural, and following vowel inflexions, व is changed to उ, as also before a feminine formed with ई, and the dual neuter: the sibilant, when final (as in the neuter singular), and before the consonantal inflexions, is changed to द्.

विद्वस् 'who is knowing, wise.'

masc.	nom.	विद्वान्	विद्वांसौ	विद्वांसः
	acc.	विद्वांसं	—	विदुषः
	instr.	विदुषा	विद्वद्भ्यां	विद्वद्भिः
	dat.	विदुषे &c.	loc.	विद्वत्सु
	voc.	विद्वन्		
	fem.	विदुषी	विदुष्यौ	विदुष्यः
	neut.	विद्वत्	विदुषी	विद्वांसि

a. If the termination वस् be preceded by इ, that vowel is rejected when the व is changed to उ; as सेदिवस् 'who is sitting:' nom. सेदिवान्, सेदिवांसौ, सेदिवांसः; acc. सेदिवांसं, सेदिवांसौ, सेदुषः; instr. सेदुषा, सेदिवद्भ्यां, &c.: fem. nom. sing. सेदुषी: neut. nom. and acc. सेदिवत्, सेदुषी, सेदिवांसि.

129. Superlatives formed with the termination ईयस् are declined in the three numbers of the nominative, and in the singular and dual accusative, analogously to participles in वस्; in the other cases they follow the analogy of nouns in अस्; as गरीयस् 'most heavy.'

masc.	nom.	गरीयान्	गरीयांसौ	गरीयांसः
	acc.	गरीयांसं	—	गरीयसः
	instr.	गरीयसा	गरीयोभ्यां	गरीयोभिः
	dat.	गरीयसे &c.		loc. गरीयःसु or गरीयस्सु
	voc.	गरीयन्		
	fem.	गरीयसी	गरीयस्यौ	गरीयस्यः
	neut.	गरीयः	गरीयसी	गरीयांसि

Class IX. Nouns ending in ह्.

130. Nouns ending in ह् substitute ढ् for it, agreeably to rule 32: ढ् undergoes the changes to which the rules of Sandhi subject it. मधुलिह् 'a bee,' from मधु 'honey,' and लिह् 'who or what sips,' is thus declined:

nom.	मधुलिट् or -लिड्	मधुलिहौ	मधुलिहः
acc.	मधुलिहं	—	—
instr.	मधुलिहा	मधुलिड्भ्यां	मधुलिड्भिः
dat.	मधुलिहे	—	मधुलिड्भ्यः
abl.	मधुलिहः	—	—
gen.	—	मधुलिहोः	मधुलिहां
loc.	मधुलिहि	—	मधुलिट्सु or -लिट्त्सु
voc.	मधुलिट्		

The feminine is the same as the masculine. लिह् in the neuter makes, nom. and acc. लिट् or -ड्, लिही, लिंहि.

a. तुरासाह्, a name of Indra, is inflected like मधुलिह्, but has the peculiarity of changing स to ष when the final is changed; as तुराषाट् or -ड्, तुरासाहौ, तुराषाड्भ्यां, &c.

131. Words formed with the affix क्विन् substitute घ् for a final ह्, which becomes क् or ग्, agreeably to the rules of Sandhi, before the consonantal inflexions; as उष्णिह्, 'a metre of the Vedas.'

nom.	उष्णिक् or ग्	उष्णिहौ	उष्णिहः
acc.	उष्णिहं	—	—
instr.	उष्णिहा	उष्णिग्भ्यां	उष्णिग्भिः
dat.	उष्णिहे &c.		loc. उष्णिक्षु

a. Other verbal nouns formed with the same affix substitute either a guttural or a cerebral for the final; as मुह् mf. 'one who is perplexed.'

nom.	मुट्-मुड् or मुक्-मुग्	मुहौ	मुहः
acc.	मुहं	—	—
instr.	मुहा	मुड्भ्यां or मुग्भ्यां	मुड्भिः or मुग्भिः
dat.	मुहे &c.		loc. मुट्सु or मुक्षु

So स्नुह् 'one who vomits;' स्निह् 'one who is kind;' द्रुह् 'one who hates.'

b. But, monosyllabic verbal derivatives, ending in an aspirated soft consonant, change their initial, if it be any unaspirated soft consonant, except ज, to its corresponding aspirate, whenever the final is changed: therefore द्रुघ् for द्रुह् becomes, nom. sing. ध्रुक् or ध्रुग्, ध्रुट् or ध्रुड्; instr. dat. and abl. dual ध्रुग्भ्यां or ध्रुड्भ्यां; instr. plur. ध्रुग्भिः; dat. and abl. plur. ध्रुग्भ्यः or ध्रुड्भ्यः; loc. plur. ध्रुक्षु or ध्रुट्सु; in the other cases, द्रुहौ, द्रुहः, द्रुहा, &c. So दह् 'what burns:' धक् or धग्, धट् or धड्; धग्भ्यां or धड्भ्यां &c. दुह्, who or what milks,' takes the guttural substitute only; as,

nom.	धुक् or धुग्	दुहौ	दुहः
acc.	दुहं	—	—
instr.	दुहा	धुग्भ्यां	धुग्भिः
dat.	दुहे &c.		loc. धुक्षु

c. वाह्, 'what bears or carries,' substitutes ऊ for the first two letters in several compound nouns before the accusative plural and subsequent vowel inflexions: this ऊ (by rule 3. clause *c.*) makes, with a preceding अ, औ not ओ; as विश्ववाह् mf. 'all-sustaining.'

nom.	विश्ववाट् or -वाड्	विश्ववाहौ	विश्ववाहः
acc.	विश्ववाहं	—	विश्वौहः
instr.	विश्वौहा	विश्ववाड्भ्यां	विश्ववाड्भिः
dat.	विश्वौहे &c.		loc. विश्ववाट्सु

fem. nom. sing. विश्वौही

If the preceding vowel be not अ or आ, the ऊ to which वा is changed combines with it, according to rule: thus भूवाह् 'earth-sustaining;' nom. भूवाट्, भूवाहौ, भूवाहः; acc. plur. भूहः; instr. sing. भूहा, &c.

d. श्वेतवाह्, 'Indra,' (he who is borne on a white horse,) presents several anomalies. In the nominative and vocative singular, and before the consonantal inflexions, it is declined as if ending in वस्; as श्वेतवस्. In the accusative plural and following cases with vowel inflexions it retains its final, but optionally substitutes ऊ for वा; as,

nom.	श्वेतवाः	श्वेतवाहौ	श्वेतवाहः
acc.	श्वेतवाहं	—	श्वेतौहः or श्वेतवाहः
instr.	श्वेतौहा or श्वेतवाहा	श्वेतवोभ्यां	श्वेतवोभिः
dat.	श्वेतौहे or श्वेतवाहे	—	श्वेतवोभ्यः
abl.	श्वेतौहः or श्वेतवाहः	—	—
gen.	———	श्वेतौहोः or श्वेतवाहोः	श्वेतौहां or श्वेतवाहां
loc.	श्वेतौहि or श्वेतवाहि	———	श्वेतवःसु or श्वेतवस्सु

e. उपानह् f. 'a slipper,' substitutes ध् for the final before the consonantal inflexions; making उपानत् or उपानद्, उपानद्भ्यां, उपानद्भिः, उपानद्भ्यः, उपानत्सु; before the vowels, उपानहौ, &c.

f. अनडुह्, 'an ox,' is very anomalous. In the nominative and vocative singular न् is substituted for the final; and in all the numbers of the nominative, and in the accusative singular and dual, आ is prefixed to the final; before which, उ regularly becomes व्. Before the consonantal inflexions ह् is changed to द्.

nom.	अनड्वान्	अनड्वाहौ	अनड्वाहः
acc.	अनड्वाहं	—	अनडुहः
instr.	अनडुहा	अनडुद्भ्यां	अनडुद्भिः
dat.	अनडुहे &c.		loc. अनडुत्सु
voc.	अनड्वन्		

Compounded so as to form an epithet, this word may become feminine and neuter; as स्वनडुह्, 'having good cattle,' makes, fem. nom. स्वनडुही, neut. nom. and acc. स्वनडुत्, स्वनडुही, स्वनड्वांहि.

SECTION III.

Adjectives.

132. Adjective or attributive nouns are inflected in the same manner as substantive nouns: admitting of the three genders, and varying as to their inflectional terminations according to their proper finals, agreeably to the rules already given for the inflexions of nouns.

133. Adjectives admit of the variations of degree common in other languages, as comparatives and superlatives. When regular, they are formed by adding to the crude noun the terminations तर and तम (technically called तरप् and तमप्): in the former of which we have the Greek τερος, and in the latter an approximation to τατος and the 'timus' of the Latin. Thus,

पुण्य holy	पुण्यतर more holy	पुण्यतम most holy.
पटु eloquent	पटुतर more eloquent	पटुतम most eloquent.

a. Before these affixes a final न् is rejected, and the final स् of the participial affix वस् is changed to त्; as,

युवन् young	युवतर younger	युवतम youngest.
विद्वस् wise	विद्वत्तर wiser	विद्वत्तम wisest.

b. The same affixes, with a like import, are added to some particles; as अति, 'more than,' may make अतितर and अतितम 'still more' or 'most:' and although different etymologies are assigned to उत्तर and उत्तम, which, besides other meanings, denote degrees of excellence, or 'better,' 'best,' they are most probably formed from उद् 'up,' with the terminations of the comparative and superlative degrees.

c. The terminations are sometimes added to substantive nouns; as, नृप 'a king;' नृपतर 'more a king;' नृपतम 'most a king.'

d. When added to feminine nouns in ई or ऊ, the finals may be made short; as, श्रितर or श्रीतर 'more fortunate;' श्रितम or श्रीतम 'most fortunate.'

e. The same terms, with the syllable आम् added, give a comparative and superlative force to the personal inflexions of verbs; as, जल्पति 'he talks;' जल्पतितराम् 'he talks more than he ought;' जल्पतितमाम् 'he talks without stint or measure.'

134. Attributives formed with तर and तम are declined in three genders like other nouns in अ, and like them offer a marked resemblance to Latin attributives in 'us;' as पुण्यतरः, पुण्यतरा, पुण्यतरं, &c.

135. Attributives of comparison are also formed with the affixes ईयस् and इष्ठ, which are analogous to the *ιων* and *ιστος* of the Greek; the former properly denoting the comparative, the latter the superlative; although the distinction is not always carefully observed. Those which are formed with इष्ठ are declined like nouns in अ; those with ईयस् in the manner explained under nouns ending in स् (see rule 129). They take the three genders; as, बल 'strong;' बलीयस् 'stronger,' nom. बलीयान्, बलीयसी, बलीयः; बलिष्ठ 'strongest,' बलिष्ठः, बलिष्ठा, बलिष्ठं, &c.

a. These affixes have the effect of causing, as in the example given, a final vowel to be dropped. बल rejects its own अ,

and consequently the vowels ई and इ are attached at once to the consonant; so पटु, 'eloquent,' makes पटीयस् and पटिष्ठ. If the word be a monosyllable, however, the final अ is not rejected, and the usual change by Sandhi takes place; as प्र for प्रिय, 'dear,' with ईयस् and इष्ठ makes प्रेयस्, प्रेष्ठ; and श्र for प्रशस्य, 'excellent,' श्रेयस्, श्रेष्ठ. They also cause the elision of the possessive affixes मत्, इन्, विन्, and of तृ when an affix forming nouns of agency; so मतिमत्, 'having sense,' 'sensible,' becomes मतीयस् 'more sensible,' मतिष्ठ 'most sensible;' मेधाविन्, 'possessed of intelligence,' makes मेधीयस् 'more intelligent,' मेधिष्ठ 'most intelligent;' धनिन्, 'having wealth,' 'rich,' धनीयस् 'richer,' धनिष्ठ 'most rich;' कर्तृ from कृ 'to do,' 'an agent,' 'active,' करीयस् 'more' or 'very active,' करिष्ठ 'most active.'

b. The affixes ईयस् and इष्ठ are attached, however, most commonly to modifications of the original noun, or to what are considered as substitutes for it; although possibly in some cases they are the proper originals become obsolete. The following is a list of the principal instances.

Primitive.	Substitute.	Comparative.	Superlative.
अन्तिक near	नेद	नेदीयस्	नेदिष्ठ
अल्प little, young	कण कन	कणीयस् कनीयस्	कणिष्ठ कनिष्ठ
उरु large	वर	वरीयस्	वरिष्ठ
कृश thin	क्रश	क्रशीयस्	क्रशिष्ठ
क्षिप्र quick	क्षेप	क्षेपीयस्	क्षेपिष्ठ
क्षुद्र small or mean	क्षोद	क्षोदीयस्	क्षोदिष्ठ
गुरु heavy	गर	गरीयस्	गरिष्ठ
तृप्र content	त्रप	त्रपीयस्	त्रपिष्ठ
दीर्घ long	द्राघ	द्राघीयस्	द्राघिष्ठ
दूर distant	दव	दवीयस्	दविष्ठ
दृढ firm	द्रढ	द्रढीयस्	द्रढिष्ठ
परिवृह large	परिव्रह	परिव्रहीयस्	परिव्रहिष्ठ
पृथु large	प्रथ	प्रथीयस्	प्रथिष्ठ
प्रशस्य excellent	श्र ज्या	श्रेयस् ज्येयस्	श्रेष्ठ ज्येष्ठ

प्रिय dear	प्र	प्रेयस्	प्रेष्ठ
बहु much	बंह	बंहीयस्	बंहिष्ठ
भृश much	भ्रश	भ्रशीयस्	भ्रशिष्ठ
मृदु soft	म्रद	म्रदीयस्	म्रदिष्ठ
युवन् young	यव	यवीयस्	यविष्ठ
	कण	कणीयस्	कणिष्ठ
	कन	कनीयस्	कनिष्ठ
बाढ heavy	साध	साधीयस्	साधिष्ठ
वृद्ध old	वर्ष	वर्षीयस्	वर्षिष्ठ
	ज्या	ज्येयस्	ज्येष्ठ
वृन्दारक excellent	वृन्द	वृन्दीयस्	वृन्दिष्ठ
स्थिर firm, stable	स्थ	स्थेयस्	स्थेष्ठ
स्थूल gross, bulky	स्थव	स्थवीयस्	स्थविष्ठ
स्फिर much	स्फ	स्फेयस्	स्फेष्ठ
ह्रस्व short	ह्रस	ह्रसीयस्	ह्रसिष्ठ

c. बहु, 'much,' substitutes भूय, and is anomalous in the first form, as भूयस्, भूयिष्ठ.

d. Occasionally the regular terminations are superadded to these superlatives to imply excess in a still greater degree; as, श्रेष्ठतर 'more excellent;' श्रेष्ठतम 'most excellent,' 'most best.'

SECTION IV.

Pronouns and Pronominal Nouns.

136. Pronouns and certain other nouns are classed together, as agreeing in some peculiarities of inflexion, by which they are distinguished from all other nouns. The list commences with the distributive pronoun सर्व 'all;' whence they are called सर्वादि or Sarva and others.

137. Besides the meaning 'all,' सर्व is a name of S'iva, and in that sense it is declined like any other noun in अ; but when it is a pronominal noun it differs from its regular inflexion in the following respects:

nom. plur. ए	is substituted for	आः, as सर्व्वे	for सर्व्वाः
dat sing. स्मै	———	ङे — सर्व्वस्मै	— सर्व्वाय
abl. sing. स्मात्	———	ङसि — सर्व्वस्मात्	— सर्व्वात्
loc. sing. स्मिन्	———	ङि — सर्व्वस्मिन्	— सर्व्वे
gen. plur. स्	———	न — सर्व्वेषाम्	— सर्व्वाणां

138. After the feminine form सर्व्वा, स्य is prefixed to the terminations of the dative, ablative, genitive, and locative singular; and the final of the inflective base is made short. In the genitive plural स is prefixed to आम्.

सर्व्व 'all.'

	Masculine.			Feminine.		
nom.	सर्व्वः	सर्व्वौ	सर्व्वे	सर्व्वा	सर्व्वे	सर्व्वाः
acc.	सर्व्वं	—	सर्व्वान्	सर्व्वां	—	—
instr.	सर्व्वेण	सर्व्वाभ्यां	सर्व्वैः	सर्व्वया	सर्व्वाभ्यां	सर्व्वाभिः
dat.	सर्व्वस्मै	—	सर्व्वेभ्यः	सर्व्वस्यै	—	सर्व्वाभ्यः
abl.	सर्व्वस्मात्	—	—	सर्व्वस्याः	—	—
gen.	सर्व्वस्य	सर्व्वयोः	सर्व्वेषां	—	सर्व्वयोः	सर्व्वासां
loc.	सर्व्वस्मिन्	—	सर्व्वेषु	सर्व्वस्यां	—	सर्व्वासु

Neuter nom. and acc. सर्व्वं सर्व्वे सर्व्वाणि &c.

139. All the words of this class follow this model, as far as regards the inflectional terminations, with exception of the two first personal pronouns, which are altogether anomalous. The class consists of the following pronouns and pronominal nouns.

1. Personal pronouns.

अस्मद् I.

युष्मद् thou.

तद्, त्यद् } that, or he, she, it.

2. Demonstrative pronouns.

अदस् this or that.

एतद् this.

इदम् this.

3. Relative.

यद् who, which, or what.

4. Interrogative.

किम् who? or what?

5. Honorific.

भवत् your honour, your excellency.

6. Pronominal nouns.

1. Distributives.

सर्व्व, विश्व } all.
एक one.
एकतर one of two.
एकतम one of many.
अन्य other.
अन्यतर either.
इतर other.
कतर which of two.
कतम which of many.
यतर whether of two.
यतम whether of many.
द्वय two, twofold.
उभ, उभय } both.

द्वितय, द्वितीय } second.
त्रितय, तृतीय } third.
प्रथम first.
चरम last.
अर्द्ध half.
अल्प few.
कतिपय how many.
सम all.
सिम whole.
नेम half.
त्व all.
स्व own.

2. Locatives.

पूर्व्व prior, east.
पर after.
अवर posterior, west.
अपर inferior, other.

अधर inferior, west.
दक्षिण south, right.
उत्तर subsequent, north.
अन्तर outer.

140. The pronouns of the first and second persons are very anomalous, but their irregularities are of exceeding interest, as they present striking analogies to those of the pronouns of the same persons in the classical and teutonic languages.

अस्मद् 'I.'

nom.	अहम्	आवां	वयं
acc.	मां or मा	आवां or नौ	अस्मान् or नः
instr.	मया	आवाभ्यां	अस्माभिः
dat.	मह्यम् or मे	आवाभ्यां or नौ	अस्मभ्यम् or नः
abl.	मत्	आवाभ्यां	अस्मत्
gen.	मम or मे	आवयोः or नौ	अस्माकम् or नः
loc.	मयि	आवयोः	अस्मासु

युष्मद् 'thou.'

nom.	त्वं	युवां	यूयं
acc.	त्वां or त्वा	युवां or वाम्	युष्मान् or वः
instr.	त्वया	युवाभ्यां	युष्माभिः
dat.	तुभ्यम् or ते	युवाभ्यां or वाम्	युष्मभ्यम् or वः
abl.	त्वत्	युवाभ्यां	युष्मत्
gen.	तव or ते	युवयोः or वाम्	युष्माकम् or वः
loc.	त्वयि	युवयोः	युष्मासु

141. The other pronouns are declinable in three genders, and follow more nearly the model of the class, सर्व्व, in their inflexions.

Those which end in द्, as तद् &c., reject their final consonant before all the inflexions, except in the nominative singular of the neuter; and they thus become words terminating in अ.

Before the nominative masculine and feminine, तद्, त्यद्, and एतद् change their त to स; becoming therefore स, सा, स्य, स्या, एष, एषा; as,

तद् 'that,' or 'he, she, it.'

	Masculine.			Feminine.		
nom.	सः	तौ	ते	सा	ते	ताः
acc.	तं	तौ	तान्	तां	ते	ताः
instr.	तेन	ताभ्यां	तैः	तया	ताभ्यां	ताभिः
dat.	तस्मै	—	तेभ्यः	तस्यै	—	ताभ्यः
abl.	तस्मात्	—	—	तस्याः	—	—
gen.	तस्य	तयोः	तेषां	—	तयोः	तासां
loc.	तस्मिन्	—	तेषु	तस्यां	—	तासु

Neuter तद् or तत् ते तानि.

So त्यद्, 'that,' makes, | and एतद्, 'this:'

masc.	स्यः	त्यौ	त्ये	एषः	एतौ	एते
fem.	स्या	त्ये	त्याः	एषा	एते	एताः
neut.	त्यद्	त्ये	त्यानि	एतद्	एते	एतानि

The other inflexions are also like those of तद्; but in the accusative singular, dual, and plural, in the instrumental singular, and the genitive dual, in the three genders, एन is sometimes used for एत; as,

masc.	acc.	एतं or एनं	एतौ or एनौ	एतान् or एनान्
	instr. s.	एतेन or एनेन		
	gen. d.	एतयोः or एनयोः		
fem.	acc.	एतां or एनां	एते or एने	एताः or एनाः
	instr. s.	एतया or एनया		
	gen. d.	एतयोः or एनयोः		
neut.	acc.	एनं	एने	एनानि

a. The second form is employed in the subsequent member of a sentence in which the first has already been used; as, एतेन व्याकरणमधीतमेनं हितोपदेशं पाठय, 'The grammar has been studied by him; now set him to read the Hitopadeśa.'

142. The other two demonstrative pronouns, अदस् 'this' or 'that,' and इदम् 'this,' undergo various modifications, chiefly of the inflective bases.

अदस् 'this' or 'that.'

	Masculine.			Feminine.		
nom.	असौ	अमू	अमी	असौ	अमू	अमूः
acc.	अमुं	—	अमून्	अमुं	—	—
instr.	अमुना	अमूभ्यां	अमीभिः	अमुया	अमूभ्यां	अमूभिः
dat.	अमुष्मै	—	अमीभ्यः	अमुष्यै	—	अमूभ्यः
abl.	अमुष्मात्	—	—	अमुष्याः	—	—
gen.	अमुष्य	अमुयोः	अमीषां	—	अमुयोः	अमूषां
loc.	अमुष्मिन्	—	अमीषु	अमुष्यां	—	अमूषु

Neuter nom. and acc. अदः अमू अमूनि.

इदम् 'this,' or 'that.'

	Masculine.			Feminine.		
nom.	अयं	इमौ	इमे	इयं	इमे	इमाः
acc.	इमं	—	इमान्	इमां	—	—
instr.	अनेन	आभ्यां	एभिः	अनया	आभ्यां	आभिः
dat.	अस्मै	—	एभ्यः	अस्यै	—	आभ्यः
abl.	अस्मात्	—	—	अस्याः	—	—
gen.	अस्य	अनयोः	एषां	—	अनयोः	आसां
loc.	अस्मिन्	—	एषु	अस्यां	—	आसु

Neuter nom. and acc. इदम् इमे इमानि.

This pronoun also substitutes एन for the base in the same cases as एतद्. See above, rule 141.

143. The relative pronoun यद्, 'who' or 'which,' is declined like तद्; as, masc. nom. यः, यौ, ये; fem. nom. या, ये, याः; neut. nom. and acc. यद्, ये, यानि, &c.

144. किम्, 'who' or 'what,' is also declined analogously to तद्, substituting अ for its final and preceding vowel, except in the nom. neuter, and thus becoming a noun in अ; as,

क for किम् 'who,' 'which.'

	Masculine.			Feminine.		
nom.	कः	कौ	के	का	के	काः
acc.	कं	कौ	कान्	कां	के	काः
instr.	केन	काभ्यां	कैः	कया	काभ्यां	काभिः
dat.	कस्मै	—	केभ्यः	कस्यै	—	काभ्यः
abl.	कस्मात्	—	—	कस्याः	—	—
gen.	कस्य	कयोः	केषां	—	कयोः	कासां
loc.	कस्मिन्	—	केषु	कस्यां	—	कासु

Neuter nom. and acc. किम् के कानि.

a. किम् to various of its inflexions may affix चित् or चन, giving to it a more general and indefinite signification; as, कश्चित् 'some one,' 'any one,' 'a certain one;' कस्मैचित् 'to some one;' केचित् 'some ones,' 'any ones;' किञ्चित् 'something,' 'any thing.' The neuter also occurs in the obsolete form of चित्; as कश्चित् 'any thing.' चन is also added to inflexions of किम् in a like sense; as, कश्चन 'some one;' किञ्चन 'any thing, something.'

b. The preceding pronouns may be compounded with दृश्, दृश, or दृक्ष, derivatives from दृश् 'to see,' to signify 'similarity:' when तद्, एतद्, यद्, &c. become ता &c. ई is substituted for अदस् and इदम्, and की for किम्; as,

> तादृश्, तादृश, or तादृक्ष, such like.
> एतादृश्, एतादृश, or एतादृक्ष, this like.
> यादृश्, यादृश, or यादृक्ष, how or what like.
> ईदृश्, ईदृश, or ईदृक्ष, that or this like.
> कीदृश्, कीदृश, or कीदृक्ष, how like.

These are declinable in three genders, forming the feminine in ई; mn. तादृक्, f. तादृशी; or as nouns ending in अ, as तादृशः, तादृशी, तादृशं, &c.

b. To तद्, एतद्, यद्, may be added वत्, implying 'quantity,' when they are similarly changed; as, तावत् 'so much;' एतावत् 'so much;' यावत् 'how much;' which are declinable like nouns in वत्; as, तावान्, तावती, तावत्, &c.: they are also used in the neuter form as adverbs, as, यावत् 'how much,' तावत् 'so much;' and correlatively, as यावत् तावत् 'as much as.'

c. इदम् and किम् in a similar sense have यत् joined to the vowel of the base; as, इयत् 'so much;' कियत् 'how much:' nom. इयान्, इयती, इयत्, &c.

d. To क substituted for किम् may be also added ति, to form कति 'quot,' 'how much,' 'how many.' It is the same for all genders, and is declinable in the plural only; as, nom. and acc. कति, instr. कतिभिः, dat. and abl. कतिभ्यः, gen. कतीनाम्, loc. कतिषु. Similar derivatives may be formed from तद् and यद्, as तति and यति, but they are of very rare occurrence.

145. भवत्, an honorific term for युष्मद्, and which, like 'Your honour,' 'Vossignoria,' &c., although used for the second, is a pronoun of the third person: it is declined like other nouns in अत्; as,

M 2

nom. भवान्	भवन्तौ	भवन्तः
acc. भवन्तं	—	भवतः
instr. भवता	भवद्भ्यां	भवद्भिः
dat. भवते &c.		loc. भवत्सु
fem. भवती	भवत्यौ	भवत्यः
neut. भवत्	भवती	भवन्ति

146. With respect to some of the following pronominal nouns, a few observations will be necessary.

a. एक, 'one,' 'some one,' is also the numeral 'one,' and will be again noticed. In this place it admits of three numbers; as, एकः 'one;' एकौ 'two ones;' एके 'some;' as एके वदन्ति 'some ones,' or 'some, say.'

b. अन्य and the six following words in the list of pronominal nouns, which are analogous to comparatives and superlatives, differ from them in being inflected like सर्व. They are also peculiar in forming the neuter in त्; as, अन्यत्, अन्यतरत्, अन्यतमत्. The two terms preceding अन्य, एकतर and एकतम, make their neuters like other nouns in अ, as एकतरं, एकतमं.

c. उभ, 'both,' is declinable in the dual only; as, उभौ, उभाभ्यां, उभयोः.

d. उभय, 'both,' has no singular: nom. dual उभयौ, pl. उभये.

e. द्वितय and त्रितय have two forms in the nom. plural, द्वितये or द्वितयाः &c.; so have द्वितीय, तृतीय; and the two last have also two forms in both the masculine and feminine before the inflexions of the dat., abl., gen., and loc. sing.; as, द्वितीयाय or द्वितीयस्मै, द्वितीयायै, द्वितीयस्यै, &c.

f. प्रथम 'first,' चरम 'last,' अल्प 'few,' कतिपय 'how many,' have two forms in the nom. plur., प्रथमाः or प्रथमे, चरमाः or चरमे, &c.

g. सम, when meaning 'equal,' 'same,' is not a pronoun: it is declined like nouns in अ; nom. plur. समाः, dat. sing. समाय.

h. नेम has two forms in the nom. plur., नेमे, नेमाः.

i. स्व, when implying 'property,' is a noun; as a pronoun it has two forms in the abl. and loc. sing., स्वात् or स्वस्मात्, स्वे or स्वस्मिन्.

j. पूर्व and the remaining terms have two forms in the abl. and loc. sing., and nom. plural, पूर्वात् or पूर्वस्मात्, पूर्वे or पूर्वस्मिन्, पूर्वे or पूर्वाः; so परात् or परस्मात्, &c. They are pronouns only as signifying relation in time or space; 'before,' 'after,' 'east,' 'west,' and the like. In any other sense they are nouns; as दक्षिण 'clever:' nom. plur. दक्षिणाः, dat. sing. दक्षिणाय.

k. अन्तर is a pronoun in the sense only of 'outer;' as, अन्तराः or अन्तरे गृहाः 'outer houses;' अन्तरस्याः शाटकायाः 'of the outer petticoat:' but if a city be intended, it does not take the pronominal form; as अन्तरायां (not अन्तरस्यां) पुरि 'in the outer town,' the suburb or Pettah.

SECTION V.

Numerals.

147. The first ten numerals are, एक one, द्वि two, त्रि three, चतुर् four, पञ्चन् five, षष् six, सप्तन् seven, अष्टन् eight, नवन् nine, दशन् ten.

148. The nine first are compounded with दशन्, 'ten,' to form the next nine, undergoing in some instances slight changes of termination; as,

एकादशन् eleven.	षोडशन् sixteen.
द्वादशन् twelve.	सप्तदशन् seventeen.
त्रयोदशन् thirteen.	अष्टादशन् eighteen.
चतुर्दशन् fourteen.	नवदशन् nineteen or
पञ्चदशन् fifteen.	ऊनविंशति one less than twenty.

149. With विंशति, 'twenty,' the simple numerals are combined on much the same plan; as,

एकविंशति twenty-one.	षड्विंशति twenty-six.
द्वाविंशति twenty-two.	सप्तविंशति twenty-seven.
त्रयोविंशति twenty-three.	अष्टाविंशति twenty-eight.
चतुर्विंशति twenty-four.	नवविंशति twenty-nine or
पञ्चविंशति twenty-five.	ऊनत्रिंशत् one less than thirty.

150. The rest of the series and its decimal subdivisions are composed analogously to विंशति and its subdivisions.

त्रिंशत् thirty. | सप्तति seventy.
चत्वारिंशत् forty. | अशीति eighty.
पञ्चाशत् fifty. | नवति ninety.
षष्टि sixty.

Higher numbers have distinct denominations.

शतं a hundred.
सहस्रं a thousand.
अयुतः or अयुतं ten thousand.
लक्षं or लक्षा a lac, a hundred thousand.
नियुतः or -तं } one million.
प्रयुतः or -तं }
कोटिः a krore, ten millions.
अर्बुदः or -दं a hundred millions.
महार्बुदः or -दं a thousand millions.
पद्मं ten thousand millions.
महापद्मं a hundred thousand millions.
खर्वः a billion.

a. Numerals, when declinable, are inflected upon the same principles as other nouns, but in some cases they undergo peculiar modifications of the base, which it is necessary to notice.

b. एक, 'one,' is declined as a numeral in the singular number only, in the three genders, एकः, एका, एकं. It retains the pronominal form of inflexion; as, एकस्मै 'to one;' एकस्मात् 'from one,' &c.

c. द्वि is declined in the dual only, substituting अ for its final; as, nom. and acc. masc. द्वौ, fem. and neut. द्वे, instr. &c. द्वाभ्यां, gen. and loc. द्वयोः.

d. त्रि and the rest are declined in the plural only. त्रि substitutes तिसृ in the feminine gender.

	Masc.	Fem.
nom.	त्रयः	तिस्रः
acc.	त्रीन्	तिस्रः
instr.	त्रिभिः	तिसृभिः

dat. abl.	त्रिभ्यः	तिसृभ्यः
gen.	त्रयाणां	तिसृणां
loc.	त्रिषु	तिसृषु

Neuter nom. and acc. त्रीणि. The rest as the masculine.

e. चतुर्, 'four,' inserts आ before the final in the nom. masc. and nom. and acc. neuter, and substitutes तसृ for the last syllable before the inflexions of the feminine.

nom.	चत्वारः	f. चतस्रः	n. चत्वारि
acc.	चतुरः	चतस्रः	चत्वारि &c.
instr.	चतुर्भिः	चतसृभिः	
dat. abl.	चतुर्भ्यः	चतसृभ्यः	
gen.	चतुर्णाम्	चतसृणां	
loc.	चतुर्षु	चतसृषु	

f. The remaining numbers to twenty, declinable in the plural only, are the same in all genders. A final न् is rejected before all the affixes, and the terminations of the nominative and accusative are dropped: अष्टन् substitutes औ for its final vowel in the two first cases, and optionally elongates it in the rest: thus पञ्चन्, 'five,' makes, nom. and acc. पञ्च, instr. पञ्चभिः, dat. and abl. पञ्चभ्यः, gen. पञ्चानाम्, loc. पञ्चसु. After which model are inflected सप्तन्, नवन्, दशन्, एकादशन्, &c.

षष् 'six,' makes, nom. and acc. षट्, instr. षड्भिः, dat. and abl. षड्भ्यः, gen. षण्णां, loc. षट्सु.

अष्टन् 'eight;' nom. and acc. अष्टौ, instr. अष्टभिः or अष्टाभिः, dat. and abl. अष्टभ्यः or अष्टाभ्यः, gen. अष्टानां, loc. अष्टसु or अष्टासु.

g. विंशति 'twenty,' त्रिंशत् 'thirty,' &c. are declined like other nouns with similar terminations; but they are confined to the feminine gender, and to the singular number, unless multiples of them be signified, when they take the other numbers; as, sing. विंशति 'twenty,' dual विंशती 'two twenties,' plur. विंशतयः 'many twenties:' otherwise the number does not vary with the substantive with which it may be connected; as

विंशत्या, त्रिंशता, चत्वारिंशता शरैः, 'with twenty, thirty, forty arrows, &c. Instances however do occur where they take the plural number, to agree with a plural substantive; as पञ्चाशद्भिर्हयैः 'with fifty horses.'

h. शतं 'a hundred,' and सहस्रं 'a thousand,' are both neuter nouns, and are usually limited to the singular, except when repetition of them is intended; as, शते 'two hundreds,' सहस्रे 'two thousands,' शतानि 'many hundreds,' सहस्राणि 'many thousands.' In construction they are commonly employed with nouns in the genitive plural, as शतं दासीनां 'a hundred (of) female slaves;' although they are also used attributively with plural nouns, as सहस्रं पितरः 'a thousand ancestors.' The other numerals are inflected, like nouns in general, according to their gender and termination.

151. Numerals in composition with nouns to form attributives are inflected, like other nouns, according to their finals; as, प्रियत्रिः मनुष्यः 'a man having three friends;' प्रियत्रिः स्त्री 'a woman having three lovers;' प्रियत्रि कुलं 'a family having three agreeable persons:' but प्रियतिसृ, 'a man who has three mistresses,' makes प्रियतिस्रा, प्रियतिस्रौ, प्रियतिस्रः, प्रियतिसृभ्यां, &c. The same term may be used in the neuter; as प्रियतिसृ कुलं 'a family with three beloved females;' nom. and acc. प्रियत्रि, प्रियतिसृणी, प्रियतिसृणि, &c. चतुर् in such a compound becomes चत्वार् in the nominative and in the accusative singular and dual; as, nom. प्रियचत्वाः, प्रियचत्वारौ, प्रियचत्वारः; acc. प्रियचत्वारं, प्रियचत्वारौ, प्रियचतुरः; instr. प्रियचतुरा, &c.

a. Similar compounds of षष् are inflected like nouns in ष्, and those of the numerals ending with न् like nouns in अन्; but अष्टन् may in composition be inflected like a noun in अन् (p. 59), or like a primitive noun masculine in आ (p. 33), or in the plural number like the simple numeral; as, nom. प्रियाष्टा, प्रियाष्टानौ, प्रियाष्टानः, or प्रियाष्टाः, प्रियाष्टौ, प्रियाष्टाः or प्रियाष्टौ; acc. प्रियाष्टानं, प्रियाष्टानौ, प्रियाष्टनः, or प्रियाष्टां, प्रियाष्टौ, प्रियाष्टाः, प्रियाष्टान् or प्रियाष्टौ; instr. प्रियाष्टना, प्रियाष्टभ्यां, प्रियष्टभिः, or प्रियाष्टा, प्रियाष्टाभ्यां, प्रियाष्टाभिः, &c.

b. ऊन, implying ‘less,’ is used alone, as above exhibited, to signify one less than the numeral to which it is prefixed; as, ऊनविंशतिः ‘twenty minus one,’ i. e. nineteen; ऊनत्रिंशत् ‘thirty minus one,’ i. e. twenty-nine. It may also be used with a definite number; as, एकोनविंशतिः ‘twenty minus one;’ पञ्चोनत्रिंशत् ‘thirty minus five,’ i. e. twenty-five; दशोनशतं ‘a hundred minus ten,’ i. e. ninety. The term अधिक, ‘more,’ but which is declinable, is also compounded with numerals to denote addition, as पञ्चाधिकं शतं ‘a hundred plus five,’ or ‘one hundred and five.’

Ordinals.

152. The ordinal equivalent of ‘one’ or ‘first’ is most commonly प्रथम, declinable in three genders, प्रथमः, -मा, -मं, and according to the rules of pronominal inflexion (p. 77). Other synonymes are, आदिः, आद्यः, आदिमः; the first is restricted to the masculine gender, the others are declinable in three genders.

153. In forming ordinals from the other cardinal numbers, certain terminations are either added to or are substituted for their proper finals, and the word is declinable in the three genders. In the case of चतुर्, ‘four,’ other words are optionally substituted.

द्वितीयः	-या	-यं	second.	षष्ठः	-ष्ठी	-ष्ठं	sixth.
तृतीयः	-या	-यं	third.	सप्तमः	-मी	-मं	seventh.
चतुर्थः	-र्थी	-र्थं	fourth.	अष्टमः	-मी	-मं	eighth.
तुरीयः	-या	-यं	fourth.	नवमः	-मी	-मं	ninth.
तुर्यः	-या	-यं	fourth.	दशमः	-मी	-मं	tenth.
पञ्चमः	-मी	-मं	fifth.				

154. The termination अ, derived from the technical affix डट्, being added to एकादशन् and the rest as far as twenty, is substituted for the final syllable, leaving एकादशः, -शी, -शं, ‘eleventh;’ द्वादशः, -शी, -शं, ‘twelfth,’ &c.

155. The same affix, causing the elision either of the final syllable or final vowel, is also added to the numerals from twenty upwards. In another form they add तम to their finals; as,

विंशतितमः or विंशः twentieth.
त्रिंशत्तमः or त्रिंशः thirtieth.
चत्वारिंशत्तमः or चत्वारिंशः fortieth.
पञ्चाशत्तमः or पञ्चाशः fiftieth.
षष्टितमः or षष्टः sixtieth.
सप्ततितमः or सप्ततः seventieth.
अशीतितमः or अशीतः eightieth.
नवतितमः or नवतः ninetieth.
शततमः or शतः hundredth.

a. In these as in the cardinal numbers the decimal subdivisions are expressed by prefixing the numeral, as एकविंशतितमः or एकविंशः 'one and twentieth.'

b. There are other modifications of the numerals, declinable or indeclinable, in different shades of meaning; as, द्वयम् 'a two,' 'a duad;' त्रयम्, त्रयी, 'a triad;' also द्वितयम् and त्रितयम् in similar senses. द्विः 'twice;' त्रिः 'thrice;' एककृत्व or एकधा 'once;' द्विधा 'twice,' &c.: but these belong more especially to the subject of derivation.

CHAPTER IV.

INDECLINABLES.

156. THE indeclinable words of the Sanskrit language comprehend nouns used as nouns, and nouns or particles used as particles, that is, in some other sense than that which is expressed by a noun or a verb.

157. I. Nouns which retain their character of the names of things or notions, but which are employed in one unalterable inflexion, whatever may be their relation to the other members of the sentence in which they stand, may be either simple monoptote nouns, or compounds of the indeclinable class: the latter will be noticed when treating of the different classes of compounds: the former are not numerous; the principal are the following:

अस्तम् setting, decline, of the sun or of fortune.
अस्ति what is, existence.
आदि remainder, et cetera.
कम् water, head, happiness.
क्षमा patience, pardon.

अनस् food.
नमस् reverence, salutation.
नास्ति non-existence.
बदि the fortnight of the moon's wane.
भुवर् sky, atmosphere.
भू earth.
मिथुर् a pair.
संवत् a year.
सुदि the fortnight of the moon's increase.
स्वर् heaven.
स्वस्ति salutation, greeting.

a. Besides अस्ति, as specified in the above list, there are a few other verbal inflexions which may be used in the sense of nouns; as भवति and विद्यते 'what is,' 'existence;' स्यात् 'what may be,' 'scepticism:' or of pronouns; as, अस्मि 'I,' properly 'I am;' असि 'thou,' properly 'thou art.' They are also used absolutely, or as particles; as, अस्तु, भवतु 'so be it,' implying assent; एहि 'come,' 'begin;' पश्य and पश्यत 'see!' 'lo!' 'behold!' and a few others of rarer occurrence.

158. 2. The other division of Indeclinables, termed निपाताः, comprises a variety of terms, the origin and character of which are sometimes of difficult determination, but which, from the functions they fulfil, may be considered as adverbs, prepositions, conjunctions, interjections, expletives; and particles properly so termed; that is, syllables which are affixed or prefixed to words to modify their meaning, although in themselves they are apparently insignificant.

Adverbs.

159. Adverbs are numerous, and are variously formed, but they are in most instances, and very possibly in all, attributive nouns adverbially employed in some one or other unvarying inflexion. The prevailing form is that of the neuter accusative; offering in this respect an analogy to such Latin adverbs as 'facile,' 'difficile,' 'dulce,' 'ceterum,' 'multum,' and the like: but other inflexions, either regularly or irregularly constructed, are also in use as adverbs. Thus सत्यम्, 'truth,' means also 'truly;' सुखम्, 'happiness,' occurs as सुखम् 'happily;' कृतः, -ता, -तं, 'done,' furnishes कृतम् 'done with,' 'enough:'

from स्थानं, 'place,' comes स्थाने 'in place,' 'suitably,' 'fitly;' and from बलं, 'strength,' 'force,' बलात् 'by force,' 'forcibly,' 'violently.' It may be a question if every Sanskrit noun which is capable of being used attributively may not be employed as an adverb, to denote the variations of mode, circumstance, kind, degree, or those modifications which adverbs are intended to express. The following list furnishes some of those in most familiar use. The manner in which such are formed as differ from the inflexions of the nouns hitherto described, belongs to the head of derivation.

अकस्मात् suddenly, unexpectedly, without a wherefore.

अग्रतस् before, preceding.

अग्रे before, in front of.

अचिरम्, अचिरात्, अचिरेण } without delay.

अजस्रम् continuously, continually.

अज्ञानतस् ignorantly.

अञ्जसा quickly.

अतस् hence, hereafter, moreover.

अतीव very much.

अत्र here.

अथ so, thus.

अथकिम् how-else, yes.

अद्धा rightly, truly, clearly.

अद्य to day.

अद्यत्वे now, at present.

अध, अधस् } down, downwards.

अधस्तात् below.

अपरम् moreover, further.

अपरेद्युस् the day after.

अधुना now.

अनिशम् always, eternally.

अन्तरम्, अन्तरा, अन्तरे, अन्तरेण } without, except; within, among.

अन्यच्च moreover.

अन्यत् other, otherwise.

अन्यत्र elsewhere.

अन्यथा otherwise.

अभितस् quickly, entirely, around, near.

अभीक्ष्णम् repeatedly, quickly.

अम् quickly, a little.

अमुत्र there, in the next world.

अरम् quickly.

अर्वाक् behind in time or place.

अलम् enough; it is also a prefix.

अवस् without, outside.

असकृत् repeatedly, more than once.

असम्प्रति improperly, unfitly.

असाम्प्रतम् improperly, unseasonably.

अह्नाय by day.

आनुषक् / आनुषट् successively, seriatim.

आरात् near, afar.

आर्य्यहलम् forcibly, violently.

आविस् present, in sight.

इतस् hence, from hence.

इतस्ततस् here and there.

इति so, thus, ita.

इतरम् again, another.

इतरेद्युस् either day.

इतिह traditionally.

इत्थम् thus.

इदानीम् now.

इद्धा clearly, truly.

इव like, as, so.

इह here, in this place, in this world.

ईषत् a little.

उच्चैस् high, loud.

उत्तरम् subsequently.

उत्तरेद्युस् a subsequent day.

उपांशु secretly, privately, in a whisper.

उभयतस् on both sides.

उभयद्युस् / उभयेद्युस् both days.

उषा dawn.

ऋतम् rightly, truly.

ऋधक् rightly, truly.

एकत्र at one place, together.

एकदा at one time.

एकधा once.

एकपदे at the same moment.

एतर्हि at this time.

एव also, verily, so.

एवम् thus, so, as.

ओम् yes, so be it: it is also an inceptive mystical term prefixed to prayers and charms.

कश्चन / कश्चित् What if, how, if ever.

कथम् how.

कथञ्चन / कथञ्चित् some how.

कथन्नाम how then, how indeed.

कदा when.

कदाचित् some when, some time: न कदाचित् never.

कर्हि when, at what time.

कर्हिचित् some when, at some time.

किङ्खिल what truly, what indeed.

किञ्च further, moreover.

किञ्चन / किञ्चित् a little, something; as with a negative न किञ्चन nothing.

किन्तु but, also.

किन्नु but what, but how.

किम् what.

किमुत् what, what how.

किमुत or what, or also.

किमुह what, how.

किंवा or, either, but how.

किंस्वित् or perhaps.

किल indeed, possibly.

किमु what then, how.

कुतस् whence, how.

कुत्र where.

कुत्रचित् somewhere.

कुचित् abundantly.

कुषत् excellently.

कूपत् excellently, well.

कृतम् enough.

क्व where.

क्वचित् somewhere; न क्वचित् nowhere.

खलु certainly.

चिरम् a long time. Other cases of this noun are used in the same sense, as चिराय, चिरेण, चिरात्, चिरस्य, चिरे.

चिररात्राय for a long time.

जातु sometimes, some-when.

जोषम् silently, happily.

ज्योक् quickly, frequently.

झगिति / झटिति quickly.

तत् (तद्) therefore, then.

ततस् thence, from or after that.

तत्र there.

तदा then, at that time.

तदानीम् then.

तथा thus, so.

तथाहि thus, thus even.

तथैव in like manner.

तस्मात् therefore, from that.

तर्हि then, at that time.

तावत् so far, so much.

तिरस् / तिर्यक् crookedly; also dishonestly.

तुम् thouing.

तूष्णीकाम् silently.

तूष्णीम् silently.

तेन by that, therefore.

दिवा by day.

दिष्ट्या fortunately, luckily.

दुःसमम् vilely, badly.

दुष्ठु badly.

दूरम् far off, distant.

दोषा in the evening.

द्राक् / द्राङ् speedily.

नकिम् / नकिर् no-what, nothing, except.

नक्तम् by night.

न / नञ् no, not.

नवरम् only.

नह / नहि no, not.

नाना many, various.

नाम evidently, verily.

निकषा near.

निकामम् willingly, readily, very.

नुषा perhaps.

नूनम् certainly, truly.

नो no, not.

न्वै perhaps.

परम् after, afterwards.

परश्वस् day after to-morrow.

परितस् all round.

परेद्यवि the morrow, the day after.

पर्याप्तम् sufficiently, abundantly.

पशु well, good, right.

पश्चात् after, afterwards, behind, east.

पुनर् again; पुनः पुनर् again and again, repeatedly.

पुरतस्, पुरस्, पुरस्तात् before either in place or time, in front, formerly.

पुरा in the east, in front, formerly.

पूर्वतस् formerly, in front.

पूर्वेद्युस् day before, yesterday, forenoon.

पृथक् separately, distinctly, apart.

प्रगे in the morning.

प्रतान् widely.

प्रताम्, प्रशाम् wearily, with fatigue.

प्रतिदिनम् daily, day by day.

प्रत्युत on the contrary, otherwise.

प्रभाते early, in the morning.

प्रवाहिका, प्रवाहुकम् at the same time.

प्रसह्य violently, forcibly.

प्राक् before in place or time, in front, formerly, in presence of, east, hereafter.

प्रातर् early, in the morning.

प्राध्वम् in a contrary way, continuously.

प्रायस् mostly, for the most part.

प्राह्णे in the forenoon.

प्रेत्य after death, in the next world.

बलवत्, बलात् violently, by violence or force.

बहिस् out, without, outside.

भाजक् speedily, quickly.

भूयस् again, repeatedly; much, abundantly.

भृशम् much, very much.

मंक्षु speedily, quickly.

मनाक् a little, slowly, dully.

मा or माङ्, मास्म no, not; prohibitive 'do not.'

माकिम्, माकिर् no, not, except.

माचिरम् without delay.

मिथस्, मिथो together, mutually, in conjunction.

मिथ्या falsely.

मुधा vainly, idly, unprofitably.

मुहुर् repeatedly.

मृषा falsely.

यत् (यद्) what; यत्, तत्, that-which.

यतस् whence, wherefore.

यत्र where.

यथा as; यथा, तथा, so-as.

यथाकथाच any how; seldom.

यथाक्रमम् in order or succession.

यथातथा properly, rightly.

यदा when.

यावत् as far as, as much as; यावत्, तावत्, as much as, so much.

युक् bad, ill.

युक्तम् fitly, properly.

युगपत् (-पद्) at once.

युत् bad, ill.

येन wherefore, why, because.

रात्रौ by night.

वाद् like, as.

वाव only.

विभाषा in two ways, optionally, alternately.

विष्वक् universally.

विषु many.

विहायसा aloft, in the air.

वृथा vainly, idly.

वै verily, indeed.

शनैस् slowly.

शाश्वत् eternally, continually.

शुकम् quickly.

सकृत् once.

संक्षु speedily.

सत् well, good, right.

सततम् always.

सदा always.

सद्यस् at the same time.

सनत्
सना
सनात् } always, continually, eternally.

सनुतर् in concealment, privily.

सपदि at once.

समन्ततस् wholly, altogether, all about, all round, on every side.

समम् together, equally.

समया near to.

समीपम्
समीपे } near to, in the presence of.

समीचीनम् entirely, rightly.

समुपजोषम् happily.

सम्प्रति now, at this time.

सम्मुखम् before, in the presence or face of.

सम्यक् entirely, completely; rightly, properly.

सर्व्वतस् wholly, every way, every where.

सर्व्वत्र every where.

सर्व्वदा always.

सहसा hastily, precipitately.

साक्षात् visibly, manifestly; before or in sight.

साचि awry, indirectly.

सामि half, equally.

साम्प्रतम् now, opportunely, fitly.

सायम् evening.

सुकम् very, exceedingly.

सुचिरम् for a long time.

सुधा uselessly, idly.

सुष्ठु good, excellent, very.

स्वयम् of one's-self.

हि verily, for, because.

हिरुक् without, except.

हेतोः
हेतौ } because, by reason or on account of.

ह्यस् yesterday.

The same difficulty that exists in other languages applies to various terms in the preceding list, and they may be sometimes thought to be rather conjunctions or prepositions than adverbs. Several, no doubt, fulfil either office, and in any case the embarrassment is that rather of denomination than of application, as the connexion of the sentence will readily point out the sense in which they are to be employed.

Prepositions.

160. The most important of these are used chiefly in combination with simple verbs, and form with them compound or derivative verbs, which, either in their own inflexions, or those of the nouns derived from them, constitute the bulk of the language. The verbs thus compounded sometimes retain the meaning of the original, or more frequently they have the sense of their component elements; but in many instances they express significations which depart widely from those which they might be expected from their composition to convey. In all these respects they offer striking analogies to the compound verbs of the Greek, Latin, and German languages. A preposition combined with a verb is termed an Upasarga (उपसर्गः). The name Gati (गतिः) is also given to it, as well as to other verbal prefixes. The Upasargas are twenty-one in number.

a. The principal or primary notion conveyed by these prepositions is in general sufficiently obvious, and may be rendered by equivalents in English or in the classical languages. Usage, convention, and metaphor, however, extend the primary notion through a variety of modifications, which can become familiar only by practice. The explanation of them all is the province of a dictionary, and in this place all that can be attempted is the explanation of, 1. the principal purport of each preposition; 2. the equivalents by which it is usually translated; and 3. its exemplification by nouns of frequent occurrence, derived from verbs compounded of a simple verb and a preposition; as in the following arrangement.

अति 1. Going beyond a real or imaginary limit: 2. 'over,' 'beyond,' 'trans,' 'ex:' 3. अतिक्रमः (1) 'going over or beyond;' (2) 'transgression;' अतिशयः 'excess.'

अधि 1. Being above in place or degree: 2. 'over,' 'above,' 'upon,' 'super:' 3. अधिगमः (1) 'going over or on;'

(2) 'going over or through,' as a book; अधिकारः 'office,' 'superintendence;' अध्यात्मा 'presiding spirit.'

अनु 1. After in order or manner: 2. 'after,' 'like:' 3. अनुचरः 'a follower;' अनुक्रमः 'an index,' 'a series;' अनुकृतिः 'imitation.'

अन्तर् 1. Coming within a space or interval: 2. 'inner,' 'within,' 'inter,' 'unter:' 3. अन्तर्द्धानं 'disappearance;' अन्तर्यामी 'the pervading or inner soul.'

अप 1. Taking away in substance or kind: 2. 'from,' 'away,' 'off,' ἀπὸ, 'de,' 'dis,' 'ex:' 3. अपहारः 'carrying off;' अपवादः 'detraction,' 'censure.'

अपि 1. Affirming of a certainty: 2. 'verily,' 'indeed' (but this is more frequently used alone, as an adverb or conjunction): 3. अपिधानं 'a covering:' it is also पिधानं, the initial being rejected.

अभि 1. Being present, opposite, or near to; also, being above in place or degree: 2. 'to,' 'unto,' 'ad;' 'before,' 'opposite,' 'ob;' 'up,' 'super:' 3. अभिमुखं 'in front or in presence of;' अभिगमः 'approach;' अभिसारः 'a high land;' अभिजनः 'a person of high rank.'

अव 1. Being below in place or degree; also, being separated: 2. 'down,' 'off,' 'from,' 'de,' 'dis,' 'ex:' 3. अवतारः 'coming down as from heaven to earth;' अवकर्त्तनं 'cutting off,' 'excision;' अवगतः 'gone away,' 'departed;' अवगीतः 'despised.'

आ or आङ् 1. Bounding or limiting; also reversing: 2. 'to,' 'unto,' 'as far as,' 'ad,' 're:' 3. आकारः 'form;' आकाशः 'sky;' गमनं 'going;' आगमनं 'coming;' दानं 'gift' or 'giving;' आदानं 'taking.' It is also used conjunctively with nouns in the ablative case: as, आग्रामात् 'as far as to the village;' आसमुद्रात् 'as far as to the ocean.'

उत् or उद् 1. Being high in place or excellent in kind: 2. 'up,' 'above,' 'superior,' 'super,' 'valde:' उड्डीनं 'flying up;' उत्कृष्टः 'excellent;' उद्यमः 'great effort.'

उप 1. Being near or next to; whence also, being less than:

2. 'near,' 'less,' ὑπὸ, 'sub,' 'infra:' 3. उपगमः 'approach;' उपवेदः 'a minor Veda or scripture.'

दुर् 1. Condition of badness, pain, difficulty, and the like: 2. 'in,' 'un,' δυς, 'dis:' 3. दुराचारः 'wicked;' दुःखं 'unhappiness,' 'pain;' दुस्सहः 'unbearable;' दुर्धर्षः 'difficult of access.'

नि 1. Being within, below, or under; also, being contrary or reverse: 2. 'in,' 'on,' ἐν, 'in;' 'down,' 'sub;' 'un' or 'in,' 're:' 3. निकेतः 'a dwelling;' निचयः 'a heap;' निपतनं 'coming down;' निकृतिः 'iniquity.'

निर् 1. Being out or exempt from; whence also affirmation, as excluding doubt: 2. 'out,' 'without,' 'ex,' 'ab,' 'ne:' 3. निर्गमः 'going forth,' 'exit;' निश्चयः 'certainty;' निर्दोषः 'faultless.'

परा 1. Being opposite or opposed to; whence also reverse: 2. 'over,' 'back,' παρὰ, 'ob,' 're,' 'de:' 3. पराञ्च् 'turned back;' पराजयः 'defeat.'

परि 1. Being all round or about; whence also fulness, completeness: 2. 'about,' 'around,' περὶ, 'per,' 'circum:' 3. परिधिः 'circumference;' परिणामः 'maturity;' परिष्कारः 'perfection of fabric.'

प्र 1. Being before in time, place, or quality: 2. 'fore,' 'before,' 'above,' πρὸ, 'pro,' 'præ:' 3. प्रभवः 'first birth;' प्रयाणं 'going forth,' 'proceeding;' प्रभावः 'preeminence.'

प्रति 1. Reverted, or reflected, or repeated action or condition: 2. 'again,' 'back,' 're:' 3. प्रतिकारः 'retaliation,' 'requital;' प्रतिभाषा 'reply;' प्रतिबिम्बं 'a reflected image;' प्रतिदिनं 'day by day.'

वि 1. Being several or separate; whence also privation: 2. 'apart,' 'away,' 'without,' 'dis,' 'de,' 'se:' 3. विकारः 'separate or new form,' 'change of form;' वियोगः 'disjunction,' 'separation;' विशेषः 'distinction;' विकर्णः 'without ears.'

सम् 1. Being conjoined with; whence also completeness: 2. 'with,' 'together with,' σὺν, 'con:' 3. सङ्गमः 'association;' संयोगः 'union;' संस्कारः 'perfect fabric or performance.'

सु 1. The opposite of दुर्, or condition of happiness, ease, and the like: 2. 'good,' 'well,' εὖ, 'bene:' सुखं 'happiness;' सुरूपः 'handsome.'

b. Some of these prepositions are used separately or without verbs, especially अति, अधि, अनु, अन्तर्, अप, अभि, आ, उप, परि, and प्रति; and there are others which are not subject to be compounded with verbs; as, अन्तरेण 'except,' अमा 'with,' ऋते 'except,' विना 'without' or 'except,' and सजुस्, सह, सहितम्, साकम्, or सार्द्धम्, 'with,' 'together with.' Some of the words given as adverbs may be considered as prepositions; as समीपं, समीपे, 'near to.'

c. Besides prepositions in the sense in which they are usually understood, a number of words which are actually or were originally nouns, of which some are included in the above list of adverbs, are prefixed in one unvarying or uninflected form, analogously to particles, to the verbs अस 'to be,' भू 'to be' or 'become,' and कृ 'to do.' To these, in native grammars, the term Gati, 'motion' or 'transition,' is extended; and a few of them may be conveniently specified here, as illustrative of the manner in which they are used with nouns derived from the verbs above specified.

अन्वाजे assisting the weak;	अन्वाजेकरणं giving such assistance.
अलम् ornament;	अलङ्कारः decoration.
आविस् manifestation;	आवीर्भूतः appeared.
उररी उरी ऊररी ऊरी } assent;	{ उरीकरणं &c. promising, making assent.
कवाली केवाली केवासी } striking;	केवालीभूतः &c. wounded, slain.
ताली diffusion;	तालीभूतः diffused.
नमस् reverence;	नमस्कारः reverential salutation.
पशु an animal, a victim;	पशुभूतः hurt, slain.

पाणौ in the hand;	पाणीकरणं marriage.
प्रादुस् manifestation;	प्रादुरस्ति appearance.
प्राध्वम् continuity;	प्राध्वकृतं tied in regular order.
श्रद्धा faith;	श्रद्धाकरणं believing, trusting.
सत् good;	सत्कारः treating kindly or hospitably.
साक्षात् manifestly;	साक्षाद्भवः being manifest.

Most nouns may also be combined in this manner with verbs by the substitution of the technical affix च्वि, leaving the vowel ई for their finals; as, कृष्ण 'black;' कृष्णीकरणं 'blackening,' 'making black,' &c.: but this subject belongs to derivation.

Conjunctions.

161. The principal conjunctions are the following:

अथ, अथो inceptive, used to begin a sentence or a subject; 'now,' 'then,' 'thus.'
अपि and, also.
आह, आहो but, how.
आहोस्वित् inceptive, and implying doubt.
इति conclusive, used to finish a sentence or a subject; 'so it is,' 'finis.'
उत also, or.
उताह, उताहो whether; implying doubt or interrogation.
एव also.
किञ्च but.
किन्तु but.
किमु but how; implying doubt.
किमु how, but.
किमुत or how, or also.
किमुह or how, or what.
किंवा but, or, moreover.
किंस्वित् or, perhaps.
च and, or, but.
चेत् if.
चैव and also.
तु but.
त्वै but how; implying doubt.
नतु but not.
ननु but, if, is not, nonne.
नवा or not, if not.
नु if, how; implying doubt.
नुकम् either, or.
नुवा perhaps, or if.
नेत् if.
नोचेत् if not.
न्वै if, perhaps.
यदि if.
वा or, either.
वेट् if.
हि for, because.

Interjections.

162. These are numerous: they are mostly sounds devoid of signification, other than the unpremeditated utterance of natural emotions: some are significant words, and of them some are capable in other senses of inflexion, although others appear to have become obsolete both in inflexion and meaning.

Of the simple exclamations the principal are the vowels, as अ आ, इ ई, उ ऊ, ऋ ॠ, ए, ओ, which may express surprise or sorrow, like 'ah!' 'eh!' and अयि, अह, अहह, अहो, अहोवत, ह, हा, हाहा, are exclamations of a similar kind. Others are, कित् implying 'contempt;' धिक् importing the same, also 'grief,' 'alas!' 'ah me!' बत implying 'grief;' हस 'anger' or 'sorrow;' हाहा or हाहो 'grief;' हिम् 'alarm;' हुम् 'displeasure,' &c.

a. Vocative particles, used in speaking or calling to, are frequently employed; some of which are respectful, others disrespectful. Of the former class are, अयो, अह, अहो, अहोवत, ए, ऐ, ओ, औ, पाट, प्याट्, भगोस् भोस्, हंहो, हे, है, हो. Of the latter are, अरे, अवे, रे, रै. अङ्ग may be used in either.

b. Some ejaculatory syllables are mystical, like the monosyllable ओम्, which is typical of the three great deities of the Hindu mythology, Brahmá, Vishńu, and S'iva, and of the three Vedas, and should never be uttered in the hearing of ears profane. Others are used with charms and mystical prayers peculiar to certain sects; as हं, हुम्, ह्रीं, फट्. Others, again, of which some are significant words, are uttered in the act of pouring oiled butter on the sacrificial fire, as a libation to the manes or the gods; as वाट, वेट्, वषट्, वौषट्, श्रौषट्, स्वधा, and स्वाहा.

Expletives.

163. Syllables used mostly to complete the metre of a line are considered to be devoid of signification; they are, किल, खलु, च, तु, नु, वै, स्म, ह, हि; being identical, therefore, for the most part with the conjunctions.

Particles.

164. These are syllables added to words, either as prefixes or affixes, to qualify their purport. The specification of them properly belongs to derivation, but a few may be advantageously noticed here.

अ may be prefixed to nouns of any kind, to give them a contrary or negative sense; as, धर्म्मः 'virtue,' अधर्म्मः 'vice;' सत् 'being,' असत् 'non-existent.' Before a vowel it is changed to अन्; as, अन्तः 'finite,' अनन्तः 'infinite,' 'eternal.'

अद् is a prefix implying 'surprise;' अद्भुतं 'wonderful!'

का prefixed to nouns gives them a depreciatory sense; as, पुरुषः 'a man,' कापुरुषः 'a contemptible man,' 'a wretch.' It also signifies 'diminution;' as, का + उष्ण = कोष्णं 'a little warm.'

कु is also a depreciatory prefix; कुकृत्यं 'wickedness.'

चन } These are added to pronouns and adverbs to give them
चित् } a more extended sense; as, कश्चन, कश्चित् 'any one,' 'some one;' कथञ्चन, कथञ्चित् 'any how;' कहिंचित् 'any where,' &c.

वत् implies 'resemblance,' as ब्राह्मणवत् 'like a Brahman.'

स्म is usually an expletive, but when affixed to a verb in a present tense it gives it a past signification; as, भवति 'it is,' भवतिस्म 'it was.' It is also used with the prohibitive मा or माङ्; as, मास्म 'no,' 'not,' 'do not.'

स्वित् is added to particles to imply 'doubt and interrogation;' as, किंस्वित् 'How is it?' 'Is it so?' अहोस्वित् 'Whether?' 'Is it so?' and the like.

स्वी prefixed to कृ and its derivatives implies 'consent;' स्वीकारः 'assent,' 'promise.'

CHAPTER V.

CONJUGATION.

SECTION I.

Roots and indicatory letters.

165. The धातु or 'radical' of the Sanskrit language, although in strictness it fulfils no specific grammatical function, and is equally the theme of a noun as of a verb, may be most conveniently considered as identical with the latter, or as the crude verb; in which condition it undergoes the usual modification of conjugation, and the varieties of voice, mood, and tense.

166. As arranged in the Dhátu-páťhas (धातुपाठाः) or 'glossaries of roots,' the root is usually interpreted by an active or abstract noun in the locative case; as, अंश-विभागे 'in' division; गम-गतौ 'in' going; भू-सतायां 'in' being; ज्ञा-ज्ञाने 'in' knowledge; and the like; intimating one general and comprehensive idea to which the different modifications expressed by its derivatives may be referred.

167. All the roots, with a few doubtful exceptions, as आन्दोल 'swinging,' अवधीर 'ascertaining,' कुमाल 'playing,' गवेष 'seeking,' are monosyllables: many of them are uniliteral, as इ 'going,' ऋ 'injuring:' the greater number, however, terminate in consonants, as तर्क् 'discussion,' गज् 'sounding,' भास् 'shining.' In all cases, however, the root has some vowel, most usually the short अ, attached to the final consonant, not as a radical letter, but for the sake of pronunciation or accentuation, and the mark of quiescence is therefore not subjoined: the roots specified, although ending as radicals in consonants, are written, तर्क, गज, भास. The whole number is about nineteen hundred.

168. In the original lists the roots have attached to them certain supernumerary letters or Anubandhas (अनुबन्धाः), which have one of two objects; 1. Some of them denote the class or conjugation in which the verb is inflected; 2. Others intimate those peculiarities to which each single verb is subject in its inflexions. It will be useful to specify the principal of either class for the sake of occasional reference.

1. *General Anubandhas.*

Sign.	Verb.	Conjugation.
ल	अद ल	second.
लि	हु लि	third.
य	दिव य	fourth.
न	सु न	fifth.
श	तुद श	sixth.
म	रुध म	seventh.
द	तन द	eighth.
ग	क्री ग	ninth.
क	चुर क	tenth
ङृक	द्युत ङृक	a subdivision of the first conjugation, द्युत and other verbs.
ऐ	यज ऐ	another subdivision.

2. *Special Anubandhas.*

अ is added to all roots not terminating in any other radical or indicatory vowel; as एध (एध् + अ). This vowel should be accented, and the accents mark the voice in which the verb is conjugated. The grave shews that the verb takes the voice which is termed the Átmane-pada, 'the reflective;' the acute accent indicates the Parasmai-pada or 'transitive;' and the circumflex denotes that the verb takes both voices. The accents, however, are no longer marked in manuscripts.

आ denotes the optional insertion of इ before the affix of one of the past participles, and its absolute insertion before another; as, श्विदा (श्विद् + आ) 'to perspire;' indef. past part. स्वेदितः or स्विन्नः; perfect past part. सिष्विद्वस्.

इ indicates the insertion of a nasal after a radical vowel in all the tenses; as, निदि for निद् 'to abuse;' निन्दति, निनिन्द, निन्दिता, &c.

इर् indicates two modes of inflecting the indefinite past; as, स्फुटिर् (स्फुट् + इर्), 'to swell,' makes either अस्फोटीत् or अस्फुटत्.

ई prohibits the insertion of इ in the past participle; as, उन्दी (उन्द् + ई) 'to wet;' past part. उन्नः.

उ marks the optional insertion of इ in the indeclinable past participle; as, दमु 'to tame' (दम् + उ), दमित्वा or दान्त्वा.

ऊ indicates the optional insertion of इ in certain of the tenses; as, षिधू (षिध् + ऊ), 'to accomplish;' definite future, सेद्धा or सेधिता; indefinite future, सेत्स्यति or सेधिष्यति; indef. past असैत्सीत् or असेधीत्.

ऋ prohibits the substitution of a short vowel for a radical long one in the indefinite past of the causal verb; as, शीकृ (शीक् + ऋ) 'to sprinkle,' अशिशीकत्.

ॠ denotes that this is optional; as, भाजॄ (भाज् + ॠ), 'to shine,' makes either अबिभाजत् or अबिभजत्.

ऌ restricts the indefinite past of the simple verb to one form; as, घसॢ (घस् + ऌ) 'to eat;' indef. past अघसत्.

ए prohibits the substitution of a Vriddhi letter in the indefinite past; as, कटे (कट् + ए) 'to encompass;' indef. past अकटीत् not अकाटीत्.

ओ indicates the change of the usual termination of the past participle, त to न; as, भञ्जो (भञ्ज + ओ) 'to break;' past part. भग्नः.

औ prohibits the insertion of इ in those tenses in which it might else be inserted; as रभौ (रभ + औ) 'to begin;' def. fut. रब्धा; indef. fut. रप्स्यति; indef. past अरब्ध.

ङ indicates the reflective voice; as, ष्मिङ् (ष्मि + ङ्) 'to smile,' स्मयते.

ञ indicates both voices; as, श्रिञ् (श्रि + ञ्) 'to serve,' श्रयति or श्रयते.

ञि indicates the optional employment of the past participle in the sense of the present; as, ञिष्विदा 'to perspire;' स्विन्नः 'perspiring,' 'perspired.' This is an instance of what is not uncommon, the annexation of more than one Anubandha to a verb. The present occurs in the lists, as ञिष्विदा.

टु indicates that the verb may take the affix अथु to form abstract or active nouns; as, टुवेपृ 'to tremble;' वेपथुः 'a trembling,' 'a tremor.'

डु indicates the formation of participial nouns with the affix क्त्रिम; as, डुपच 'to cook' or 'ripen;' पक्त्रिम 'cooked,' 'ripened.'

ष indicates the formation of feminine derivatives with टाप्, as in the case of the last quoted verb पच, which occurs डुपचष्, and therefore forms the derivative, पचा 'cooking,' 'maturing.'

With regard to the roots themselves it may be added, that those which in the lists are marked as beginning with the cerebral nasal or sibilant, ण or ष, change usually those letters in inflexion to the corresponding dentals; so णम, 'to bow,' makes नमति 'he bows;' षह, 'to bear,' सहते 'he bears.' There are a few exceptions.

SECTION II.

Classes or Conjugations of Verbs.

169. The conjugational inflexion of Sanskrit verbs is effected by a scheme similar to that which has been described under the head of the Declension of nouns. The verb in its inflected form is composed of two elements; 1. the Anga or 'base,' the modified verb to which the inflexions are subjoined; and 2. certain letters or syllables which constitute the inflectional terminations, and are subjoined to the base. These terminations, which will be presently specified, are subject to but few changes in themselves; but there is some variety in the manner of attaching them to the base. The crude verb, on the contrary, is liable to a greater number of modifications, most of which are special; that is, they are restricted to the individual instance; and, as not being reducible to general rules, they constitute the chief difficulty of Sanskrit grammar.

170. Certain changes, affecting a greater or lesser number of verbs alike, have the effect of distributing them into *ten* classes or conjugations. These changes regard the manner in which the base is fitted to receive the affixes, either immediately, or mediately through the intervention of a vowel or a syllable, accompanied in some instances by the substitution of a Guńa vowel for the vowel either of the base or of the adjunct, when it is capable of such substitution.

a. Each conjugation is designated by a word compounded of the first verb of the conjugation with the term आदि, equivalent to 'et cetera,' added to it. They are severally, 1. भ्वादि or भू 'to be,' and other verbs; 2. अदादि or अद् 'to eat,' and others; 3. जुह्वादि or हु 'to sacrifice,' &c.; 4. दिवादि or दिव 'to sport,' &c.; 5. स्वादि or सु 'to bear,' &c.; 6. तुदादि or तुद 'to tease,' &c.; 7. रुधादि or रुध 'to obstruct,' &c.; 8. तनादि or तन 'to stretch,' &c.; 9. क्र्यादि or क्री 'to buy,' &c.; 10. चुरादि or चुर 'to steal,' &c. The following are the characteristic peculiarities.

1. The first conjugation, भ्वादि, interposes अ between the final of the verb and the inflectional termination, and requires the Guńa change of the simple vowel. Thus before ति, the affix of the third person singular of the present tense, the verb भू 'to be' substituting Guńa becomes भो, and अ being inserted, ओ with अ becomes अव; the entire form therefore is (भव-ति) भवति. Before the letters व, म, of a termination this अ is made long; as, भवामि 'I am.'

2. In the second conjugation, अदादि, the affixes are attached immediately to the base, with only such change as the rules of Sandhi require: अद्, 'to eat,' with ति makes (अत्-ति) अत्ति.

3. The third conjugation, called जुह्वादि, requires the reduplication of the base, and the substitution of the Guńa vowel before certain terminations: no vowel is interposed. हु, 'to sacrifice,' becomes जुहु; and with ति, (जुहो-ति) जुहोति.

4. The fourth conjugation, दिवादि, interposes य, and in some cases elongates a radical vowel: दिव, 'to sport,' thus makes (दीव्य-ति) दीव्यति.

5. The fifth conjugation, स्वादि, is characterised by the addition of नु to the base; the उ of which substitutes the Guńa letter ओ before certain affixes; as सु, 'to bear young,' becomes सुनु, and in inflexion (सुनो-ति) सुनोति.

6. The sixth conjugation, तुदादि, like the first, interposes अ; but it differs from the first in not substituting a Guńa letter for the vowel of the base: तुद, 'to torment,' makes (तुद-ति) तुदति.

7. The seventh conjugation, रुधादि, subjoins न् to the last vowel of the base: रुध, 'to obstruct,' becomes therefore रुन्ध्. The vowel अ is however inserted between the members of the conjunct consonant before certain affixes; and in combination with ति the verb makes (रुणद्-धि) रुणद्धि.

8. The eighth conjugation, तनादि, adds उ to the final of the base; for which, before certain affixes, the Guńa element ओ is substituted: thus तनु for तन्, 'to stretch,' makes (तनो-ति) तनोति.

9. The verbs of the ninth conjugation, क्र्यादि, take ना after the final; as क्री 'to buy,' (क्रीणा-ति) क्रीणाति.

10. The tenth conjugation, चुरादि, inserts अय before the affixes, and substitutes the Guńa letter for a radical vowel: चुर, 'to steal,' becomes (चोरय-ति) चोरयति.

b. Of these conjugational distinctions it may be remarked, that their especial object is obviously, in every conjugation except the second and third, to interpose a vowel between the base and the terminations. In four of them the vowel is either mediately or immediately अ, and consequently an analogous mode of adapting the terminations to the base prevails in all of them; that is, in the first, fourth, sixth, and tenth. The vowel of the fifth and eighth classes is उ; of the ninth आ. The second and third dispense with any vowel. Professor Bopp has accordingly distributed the verbs into two principal conjugations; the first composed of the first, fourth, sixth, and tenth; and the second of the remaining conjugations. The first he considers as agreeing most nearly with Greek verbs in *ω*; the second with those in *μι*.

c. It is also to be borne in mind with regard to these conjugational characteristics, that they are limited to four tenses, the present, the first præterite, the imperative, and the potential, in all the conjugations except the tenth, in which the distinctive sign is preserved in some other tenses. In the other nine conjugations the tenses beyond the four above named have not the conjugational characteristic distinctions. Accordingly Dr. Wilkins has given the four tenses specified above alone under each conjugation, and has classed the other tenses promiscuously together. Professor Bopp has followed a similar distinction in regard to the same, under the denomination of "Tempora specialia" and "Tempora generalia." The inconvenience however of searching for different tenses of the same verb in different places, seems to be more than equivalent to any advantage resulting from the more distinct exhibition of conjugational peculiarities in the four special or conjugational tenses; and although the peculiarities of these will be noted in the following pages, yet the whole of the tenses of each verb, when particularised, will be kept together.

SECTION III.

Moods and Tenses.

171. The moods are not distinguished from the tenses by native grammarians, who arrange the inflexions of the verb under nine subdivisions. One of these, however, being again subdivided, we have ten divisions, tenses and moods, of which the verb consists. There is another, an imperative, peculiar to the Vedas; which, not occurring in other books, need not be farther noticed in this place. Adopting the principle of classification common in European grammatical systems, we shall arrange the Sanskrit verb in the following manner:

Indicative mood.

1. Present Tense.
2. First præterite or imperfect tense.
3. Second præterite or perfect tense.
4. Third præterite, indefinite præterite, or aorist.
5. Absolute future.
6. Indefinite future.
7. Imperative mood.

8. Potential mood.
9. Benedictive mood.
10. Conditional mood.

On which distinctions a few observations may be necessary.

172. The present tense requires no remark; it is defined as denoting present action—action begun, and not completed: स करोति 'he does' or 'is doing;' सा गच्छति 'she goes' or 'is going.'

173. The first præterite corresponds in the adoption of the temporal augment, and apparently in application, with the imperfect of the Greek verb. It is defined as denoting action recently past—action only not of to-day. But it seems especially used to signify action past, but not perfected; or "it represents a past action continuing during another past action, and accompanying it;" as, ऋषयो मनुमभिगम्येदं वचनमब्रुवन् 'The Rishis having gone to Manu, spake this speech.' What they said then follows; so that the act of speaking was not then perfected. Again; न तानगणयन् सर्वानास्कन्दंश्च रिपून् द्विषः 'The hostile Rakshasas regarded not all those (omens), but attacked their enemies.' In both cases we have the action accompanying another action, and only begun, not done and past.

174. The second præterite is the absolute past; it relates to an action entirely out of sight, or concluded, and also agrees in purport, as well as construction by reduplication, with the Greek præterite; as, जम्बुमाली जहौ प्राणान् ग्राव्णा मारुतिना हतः 'Jambumálí abandoned life, slain by the son of the wind with a stone.'

175. The third præterite is the past of any period, but usually remote; as, आसीद्राजा 'There was a king;' अभूनृपो विबुधसखः 'There was a prince, a friend of the gods;' that is, they were, at some time or other, in fact long ago; but this is undetermined. The application of this tense is both that of the Greek aorists and "plusquam-perfectum;" and in its forms it varies so as to correspond more or less with them, sometimes

taking only the augment, and sometimes taking the reduplication and the augment also. It has hence been termed by Professor Bopp the "Præteritum augmentatum multiforme," and may be suspected of being an aggregate of more than one tense under a common denomination.

176. The first future is the definite future, denoting action which will be after a fixed period, not remote, although not immediate; as, अयोध्यां श्वः प्रयातासि 'Thou shalt depart tomorrow to Ayodhyá.'

177. The second future defines no limit to the commencement of the action: it will be at some future period, or it will be contingent on some future event; as, रविस्तप्स्यति निःशङ्कं वास्यत्यनियतं मरुत् 'The sun will shine without fear; the wind will blow unrestrained;' that is, when the power of the enemy Rávańa shall be overturned.

178. The imperative mood is defined as implying not simply command, but the various significations of the potential. In general, however, it denotes, in the second and third persons, injunction, advice, or command; as, हिंस्रा भवतु ते बुद्धिरेतासु कुरु निष्ठुरं 'Let thy purpose be cruel, shew sternness, to these (thy guards).' In the first person the senses are those of intention or volition, and the verb is commonly put interrogatively, as asking for acquiescence or command; as, किं करवाणि ते 'What may I do for thee?' करवामैतत्प्रियं देवि वयं तव 'Let us do that which is agreeable to thee, O queen.'

179. The senses of the potential, which may be also expressed by the imperative, are said to be, 1. प्रेरणं 'commanding;' as, त्वं ग्रामं गच्छेः 'Thou mayest go (i. e. Go thou) to the village:' 2. निमन्त्रणं 'directing;' as, इह दौहित्रो भुञ्जीत 'Let the daughter's son eat in this place:' 3. आमन्त्रणं 'inviting;' as, भवानिह आसीत 'Let your honour sit here:' 4. अधीष्टं 'expression of wish;' as, गुरुः पुत्रमध्यापयेत् 'Let the Guru teach the boy:' 5. सम्प्रश्नः 'interrogation' or 'inquiring;' as, वेदमधीयीय उत तर्कमधीयीय 'Shall I peruse the Veda? or shall I study logic?' and 6. प्रार्थना 'asking;' as, भो भोजनं लभेय 'O may I obtain (i. e.

give me) food. It is also very commonly used as the subjunctive mood with the conjunction 'if;' as, म्रियेय न स्यास्त्वं यदि मे गतिः 'If thou be not my protector, then I may (or shall) die.'

180. The benedictive or optative mood is considered as a modification of the potential; as, धेया धीरत्वमच्युतं स्थेयाः कार्य्येषु बन्धूनां 'Mayest thou preserve unshaken firmness, and be steady in the affairs of thy friends.'

181. The last tense is the conditional, which is susceptible, like the moods, of all times, and is commonly used with the conjunctions यदि and चेत्; as, नाभविष्यदियं शुद्धा यद्यपास्यमहं न तां 'She (Sita) would not have been purified, if I had not protected her;' यावज्जीवमशोचिष्यो नाहास्यश्चेदिदं तमः 'You will grieve as long as you live, if you do not relinquish this error.'

SECTION IV.

Voices.

182. The preceding moods and tenses are common to the usual distinctions of active and passive voices; but the Sanskrit verb, like the Greek, has two active voices, as well as one passive: they are called severally Parasmai-pada and Átmane-pada, which terms are retained by Professor Bopp, and rendered by Dr. Wilkins 'common' and 'proper' forms.

183. The Parasmai-pada is that inflected word or verb (pada) the action of which is addressed to another than the agent (from Parasmai, dative of Para, 'another'). Átmane-pada is a word or verb the action of which is addressed or reverts to the agent himself (from Átmane, dative of Átman, 'self'). These might be rendered therefore 'transitive' and 'reflective' verbs, but that it is in a peculiar sense that the action is said to affect either a different agent or the agent himself: it is the result rather than the action, and this is therefore compatible with an intransitive verb. Thus, 'Devadatta cooks:' in the one case he cooks for his master, the verb is then put in the Parasmai-pada, देवदत्तः पचति; but in another case he

cooks for himself, the Átmane-pada is then employed, and the phrase is देवदत्तः पचते. In ordinary usage, however, the distinction of import is little observed, and some verbs are conjugated in one voice, some in the other, and some in both, without much attention being paid to their signification or relations.

184. The passive voice takes the terminations of the Átmane-pada, and prefixes य ya or in some cases य् to them before those of the four conjugational tenses. Before य the radical vowel takes neither Guńa nor Vṛiddhi. In the other tenses the form is the same as in the active, with a few special changes to be hereafter noticed.

SECTION V.

Numbers and Persons.

185. The Sanskrit verb in its different tenses has three numbers, singular, dual, and plural; and three persons in each number. They are arranged in native grammars in an inverse order to that which we follow, the third person being placed first, and the first person last; but it may be more convenient to follow the European order. The terminations by which the persons are distinguished are shewn in the following scheme.

Indicative mood.

Present tense.

	Parasmai-pada.			Átmane-pada.		
Pers.	Sing.	Dual.	Plural.	Sing.	Dual.	Plural.
1.	मिप्	वस्	मस्	ए	वहे	महे
2.	सिप्	थस्	थ	से	आथे	ध्वे
3.	तिप्	तस्	अन्ति	ते	आते	अन्ते

First præterite or imperfect.

1.	अमिप्	व	म	इ	वहि	महि
2.	सिप्	तं	त	थास्	आथां	ध्वं
3.	दिप्	तां	अन्	तन्	आतां	अन्त

Second præterite or perfect.

1.	णप्	व	म	ए	वहे	महे
2.	थप्	अथुस्	अ	से	आथे	ध्वे
3.	णप्	अतुस्	उस्	ए	आते	इरे

Third præterite or indefinite past.

1.	सम्	स्व	स्म	सि	स्वहि	स्महि
2.	सीस्	स्तं	स्त	स्थास्	साथां	ध्वं
3.	सीत्	स्तां	सुस्	स्त	सातां	सत

First or definite future.

1.	तास्मि	तास्वस्	तास्मस्	ताहे	तास्वहे	तास्महे
2.	तासि	तास्थस्	तास्थ	तासे	तासाथे	ताध्वे
3.	ता	तारौ	तारस्	ता	तारौ	तारस्

Second or indefinite future.

1.	स्यामिप्	स्यावस्	स्यामस्	स्ये	स्यावहे	स्यामहे
2.	स्यसिप्	स्यथस्	स्यथ	स्यसे	स्याथे	स्यध्वे
3.	स्यतिप्	स्यतस्	स्यन्ति	स्यते	स्याते	स्यन्ते

Imperative mood.

1.	आनिप्	आवप्	आमप्	ऐप्	आवहैप्	आमहैप्
2.	हि	तं	त	स्व	आथां	ध्वं
3.	तुप्	तां	अन्तु	तां	आतां	अन्तां

Potential or subjunctive mood.

1.	यां	याव	याम	ईय	ईवहि	ईमहि
2.	यास्	यातं	यात	ईथास्	ईयाथां	ईध्वं
3.	यात्	यातां	युस्	ईत	ईयातां	ईरन्

Benedictive or optative mood.

1.	यासं	यास्व	यास्म	सीय	सीवहि	सीमहि
2.	यास्	यास्तं	यास्त	सीष्ठास्	सीयास्थां	सीध्वं
3.	यात्	यास्तां	यासुस्	सीष्ट	सीयास्तां	सीरन्

Conditional mood.

1.	स्यम्	स्याव	स्याम	स्ये	स्यावहि	स्यामहि
2.	स्यस्	स्यतं	स्यत	स्यथास्	स्याथां	स्यध्वं
3.	स्यत्	स्यतां	स्यन्	स्यत	स्यातां	स्यन्त

a. In the passive voice इ is substituted for त, the termination of the third person singular of the Átmane-pada.

b. Of these inflectional terminations it is to be remarked, that, like those employed for the construction of the cases of nouns, they comprehend some letters which are not retained in the inflexion, being introduced merely for the sake of enunciation, or of indicating some change in the base.

c. प in तिप्, सिप्, मिप्, and every where else, is rejected; but it is an indicatory letter, denoting that, where there is no rule to the contrary, the vowel of the base is to be changed to its Guńa substitute: thus विद् v. 2d conj. 'to know,' before the terminations of the singular in the present tense, makes वेद्मि, वेत्सि, वेत्ति. Before those inflexions which have not an indicatory प् the vowel is unchanged; as, वित्थ, विदन्ति, &c.

d. In the first præterite the इ of दिप्, सिप्, अमिप्, is inserted merely for articulation: the real terminations are therefore द्, स्, म्. In the Átmane-pada in this tense the न् of तन् is superfluous.

e. In the second præterite ण is indicatory, and denotes that in some cases the Vṛiddhi, and in others the Guńa element is to be substituted for a radical. A final स् is every where commuted to Visarga, agreeably to the rules of Sandhi (see rule 37). Other modifications of a less general nature we shall now proceed to notice under each tense separately, together with such modifications of the base as are not exclusively of a special or conjugational character.

General principles of Conjugation.

186. Present tense. The inflective terminations are subject to few changes. The initial अ of the third person plural is rejected after an inflective base ending in अ; that is, after those of the first, fourth, sixth, and tenth conjugations; so that चर, 'to go,' makes चरन्ति not चरान्ति 'they go;' एध, 'to increase,' एधन्ते not एधान्ते 'they grow.' In other cases it is preserved; as, अद् 'to eat,' अदन्ति; युनु 'to mix,' युन्वन्ति. After verbs which are either polysyllabic, or become so by reduplication, the nasal is rejected; as, दरिद्रा, 'to be poor,' makes दरिद्रति 'they are poor;' जुहु for हु 'to sacrifice,' जुह्वति 'they sacrifice.' Verbs of which, although monosyllabic, the inflective base ends in a consonant, or in any vowel except अ, also reject the nasal in the A'tmane-pada; as, शास 2d conj. 'to rule;' शासते 'they rule;' कृ 'to do;' कुर्वते 'they do.' The same applies to the analogous terminations of the first præterite and imperative, अन्त and अन्तां. For the initial आ of the second and third persons dual, and for इ of the first person singular, in the A'tmane-pada of the first, fourth, sixth, and tenth conjugations, इ is substituted, which with the conjugational affix अ becomes ए; as, चरे, चरेथे, चरेते. The initial त or थ of a termination in this or any other tense, when following an inflective base ending with an aspirate, is changed to ध, before which the aspirate becomes the unaspirated letter (r. 8); as, रुध, 'to oppose,' makes रुणद्धि.

The changes of the base in this tense will be specified under each conjugation.

187. First præterite. The अ of अमिप्, अन्, and अन्त is rejected after अ; and after some verbs उस् is substituted for अन्. The आ of आतां and आथां substitute इ, as in the present tense.

Besides the special changes to which the base is subject in this tense, there is one modification which is universal, the prefixing of the temporal augment अ to a verb beginning with a consonant; thus चर makes अचरत् 'he went;' and आ to one beginning with a vowel. In prefixing the temporal augment to a verb beginning with a consonant, no change takes place. For आ and the radical vowel the Vṛiddhi equivalent of the latter is substituted; as, अट 'to go,' आटत् 'he went;' ईह 'to wish,' ऐहत 'he wished.' If the verb be a compound with a preposition, the augment is inserted between the preposition and the simple verb: thus from भाष, 'to speak,' comes प्रतिभाष 'to speak again,' 'to reply;' first præterite, प्रत्यभाषत 'he replied.'

188. Second præterite. In general the terminations undergo no other changes than those which arise from the rejection of the indicatory or servile letters. After roots in आ, औ is substituted for the vowel अ left by णप्; as, दा 'to give;' first and third pers. sing. ददौ.

The changes of the base are more numerous, and the most important may be conveniently noticed here. One of these, which may be regarded as universal, although subject to a few exceptions, is the reduplication of the root; in effecting which, certain substitutions for the radical letters sometimes take place.

a. If the verb commences with the vowel अ, the repeated vowel is आ, which combines with the radical अ; as, अद् 'to eat,' आद 'he ate.' But if the verb contain a double consonant, न is inserted after the reduplication, and before the radical vowel; as, अर्च 'to worship,' आनर्च he 'worshipped.' It is also inserted before अश 'to spread;' as, आनशे 'he spread:' but not before अश 'to eat;' as, आश 'he ate.'

b. If the verb begins with इ or उ, convertible to the Vṛiddhi or Guṅa element, the substitutes in the reduplication are इय् and उव्; as, इ 'to go,' इयाय 'he has gone,' इयेथ 'thou hast gone;' उख 'to wither,' उवोख 'it has withered:' when the initial is not so changed, the reduplication of the initial produces a long vowel; as, ईयतुः, ऊखतुः.

c. An initial ऋ substitutes आ; as, ऋ 'to go,' आर 'he went:' followed by a consonant it inserts न; as, ऋज, 'to be firm,' makes आनृजे 'it was firm.'

d. A verb beginning with a single consonant, not a guttural nor an aspirate, is simply reiterated; as, रद् 'to sound,' रराद; पच 'to cook,' पपाच.

e. A guttural consonant is changed to the corresponding palatal, or क ख to च, and ग घ to ज; as, कृ 'to make,' चकार; खन 'to dig,' चखान; ग्रह 'to take,' जग्राह; घस 'to eat,' जघास. ज is also substituted for ह; as, हृ 'to take,' जहार. In some cases the reduplication of an initial semivowel is the corresponding vowel; as, यज 'to sacrifice, इयाज; and वच 'to speak,' उवाच.

f. The unaspirated is substituted for an aspirated consonant; as, भ्रम 'to whirl,' बभ्राम.

g. When the initial is a double consonant, the first only is reduplicated; as, श्रि 'to serve,' शिश्राय; क्षिप 'to throw,' चिक्षेप. If the compound be a sibilant and a hard consonant, the latter is reduplicated; as, ष्टु 'to praise,' तुष्टाव; स्था 'to stay' or 'stand,' तस्थौ. If the consonant is soft, the sibilant is repeated; as, स्मृ 'to remember,' सस्मार. If a sibilant and hard consonant followed by य occur, the medial is repeated; as, श्चुत 'to ooze,' चुश्च्योत.

h. अ is the reduplicate of a medial or final अ, आ, ऋ, ॠ, and for a final ए, ऐ, ओ; as, कृ 'to make,' चकार; भा 'to shine, बभौ; गै 'to sing,' जगौ; also for the ऊ of भू 'to be,' बभूव.

i. Any other short vowel, medial or final, is repeated; as, मुद 'to be pleased,' मुमुदे. A long vowel is made short; as, श्रीक 'to sprinkle,' शिश्रीके. For a medial diphthong the analogous short vowel is repeated; as, पेल 'to go,' पिपेल; लोक 'to see,' लुलोके.

k. Verbs which begin and end with a simple consonant, having a medial अ, and of which the first consonant is unaltered in the repetition, do not double the verb before the terminations of this tense beginning with a vowel, whether it be the vowel of the termination or the augment इ, to be presently noticed. Such verbs change the radical अ to ए; thus पच makes, dual and plural in the third person, पेचतुः, पेचुः; and in the first, पेचिव, पेचिम.

l. Of those changes which affect the primitive or unreduplicated syllable of the inflective base, some are special, and will be hereafter noticed: the most general are the following, and concern chiefly the vowels.

m. The terminations of the first and third persons singular having an indicatory ण are said to require the substitution of the Vṛiddhi letter; but this affects only final vowels and a medial अ; as, णी 'to guide,' third pers. sing. निनाय; द्रु 'to run,' दुद्राव (इ and उ becoming severally ऐ and औ, changeable before a vowel to आय् and आव्; see rule 5); गम 'to go,' जगाम. The termination of the first person singular is optionally अ, and it has therefore two forms, जगम or जगाम.

n. An initial short vowel, and a medial, except अ, takes the Guńa substitute before णप्; as, इष, 'to wish,' makes इयेष; बुध 'to know,' बुबोध. A vowel long either by nature or position, when initial, requires a different form of inflexion, as will be presently explained: when medial, it is unaltered; as, जीव 'to live,' जिजीव; शिक्ष 'to learn,' शिशिक्ष.

o. The second person, थप्, requires the Guńa change of any final vowel, and of a short medial vowel; as, जि 'to conquer,' जिगेथ; द्विष 'to hate,' दिद्वेष्ठ. The same if इ is inserted; as, जिगयिथ, दिद्वेषिथ.

p. Before the other terminations of this tense in the Parasmai-pada, and all those of the Átmane-pada, the radical vowel, if initial or medial, is unaltered; as, उष 'to burn,' ऊषतुः (उ becoming ऊ by virtue of the reduplication only, as above, clause *b*); द्विष 'to hate,' दिद्विषतुः, दिद्विषे. A final vowel is unaltered before the consonants; as, कृ 'to do,' चकृव, चकृम; and is changed before the vowels only according to the rules of Sandhi, चक्रतुः, चक्रे. A final आ is rejected before a vowel; as, दा 'to give,' ददतुः, ददे; and roots ending in diphthongs change them, with few exceptions, to आ, and are similarly inflected. इ and ई final undergo the changes of Sandhi, as, चि 'to gather,' चिच्यतुः, except when the root consists of a single vowel, or when इ is preceded by a conjunct consonant, in which cases इय् is substituted; as, इ 'to go,' ईयतुः; श्रि 'to serve,' शिश्रियतुः. A final उ or ऊ substitutes उव्, as, द्रु 'to run,' दुद्रुवतुः, except भू, which substitutes ऊव्, बभूवतुः. A final ॠ substitutes the Guńa अर्, and so does ऋ when preceded by a double consonant; as, स्मृ 'to remember,' सस्मरतुः, सस्मरुः. There are some anomalies in regard to the changes of the radical vowels; but these will be pointed out as they occur.

q. Initial semivowels are sometimes changed to their corresponding vowels, and the verb is inflected as if commencing with them; as, वच 'to speak,' उवाच, ऊचतुः, ऊचुः.

r. Some verbs, having अ between two consonants, of which the latter is a nasal, reject the medial before all the terminations except those of the singular in the Parasmai-pada; as, जन 'to be born,' जजान, जज्ञतुः, जज्ञे; गम 'to go,' जग्मतुः, &c.

s. Before थप् and the other affixes of the second præterite beginning with consonants, as व, म, वहे, महे, से, ध्वे, all roots, except कृ, सृ, भृ, वृ, द्रु, स्रु, श्रु, स्तु, insert इ; as, पच makes पेचिथ, पेचिव, पेचिम, पेचिषे, पेचिढ्वे, पेचिवहे, पेचिमहे. Before थप् it is sometimes optional; as, पेचिथ or पपक्थ; the ध in ध्वे is changed to ढ.

189. Besides the formation of the second præterite upon the principle of reduplication, there is another form of it, which may be regarded as a compound præterite tense, the radical verb being combined with the inflexions of the auxiliary verbs अस 'to be,' भू 'to be,' and कृ 'to make.' The syllable आम् is interposed between the radical verb and the auxiliary inflexion: thus एध, 'to increase,' becomes in this tense,

एधामास	एधामासिव	एधामासिम
एधामासिथ	एधामासथुः	एधामास
एधामास	एधामासतुः	एधामासुः
एधांबभूव	एधांबभूविव	एधांबभूविम
एधांबभूविथ	एधांबभूवथुः	एधांबभूव
एधांबभूव	एधांबभूवतुः	एधांबभूवुः
एधाञ्चक्रे	एधाञ्चकृवहे	एधाञ्चकृमहे
एधाञ्चकृषे	एधाञ्चक्राथे	एधाञ्चकृढ्वे
एधाञ्चक्रे	एधाञ्चक्राते	एधाञ्चक्रिरे

a. Verbs of which the initial is any vowel except अ or आ, and which is long either by nature or position, before two consonants (except ऋच्छ 'to go,' and ऊर्णु 'to cover'), also the roots अय 'to go,' आस 'to sit,' and दय 'to hurt'—verbs of more than one syllable—all verbs of the tenth conjugation—

and all derivative verbs, as causals, frequentatives, desideratives, and nominals—take the compound form of the second præterite.

b. In inflexion, भू and अस always follow the Parasmai-pada; कृ takes either Pada, according to the voice of the primary verb.

c. काश and कास 'to shine,' दरिद्रा 'to be poor,' विद 'to know,' जागृ 'to be awake,' and उष 'to burn,' may be conjugated either in the reduplicate or compound præterite.

190. Third præterite or indefinite past. The inflexions of this tense are so various, that it has been termed by Professor Bopp the "præteritum multiforme;" and Dr. Wilkins has specified eleven modes in which they are formed. In these latter, however, he comprises not merely changes of termination, but modifications of the base, and those affecting the terminations by the insertion of certain augments.

a. The alterations of the terminations are not many, but the terminations themselves are referrible to two classes. They are, 1. the terminations of the tense, as specified in the scheme, p. 115; or they are, 2. those of the first præterite, as found in the same place, p. 114.

b. The changes of the first class are confined to the elision of the स् combined with त or थ after a short vowel, or any consonant except a nasal, a semivowel, and ह. स्तां, स्तं, स्त of the Parasmai-pada, and स्त, स्थां of the Átmane-pada, become तां, तं, त, and त, थां. The only change of the second class is the optional substitution of उस् for अन्, the termination of the third person plural.

c. The principal modifications, however, arise from prefixing certain augments to these terminations. To the terminations of the first class इ is prefixed, either singly or with स, as सि; to those of the second class, in like manner, अ is prefixed, either singly or with the sibilant, as स.

d. When इ is prefixed alone to the terminations of the first class, the स of the second and third persons singular of the

Parasmai-pada is rejected. In the other persons the dental sibilant is changed, of course, to the cerebral after इ (rule 29). We have then,

Parasmai-pada.			Átmane-pada.		
इषं	इष्व	इष्म	इषि	इष्वहि	इष्महि
ईः	इष्टं	इष्ट	इष्ठाः	इषाथां	इढ्वं or इड्ढ्वं
ईत्	इष्टां	इषुः	इष्ट	इषातां	इषत

In the Parasmai-pada only, स् may be prefixed to these terminations, making सिषम्, सिष्व, सिष्म; सीः, सिष्टं, सिष्ट; सीत्, सिष्टां, सिषु.

e. The inflexions of the third præterite becoming those of the first, the tense preserves an analogy throughout, and instead of inserting the augment इ, which cannot belong to the first præterite, inserts अ, which does belong to it in several conjugations. The terminations of the base then become,

Parasmai-pada.			Átmane-pada.		
अं	आव	आम	ए	आवहि	आमहि
अः	अतं	अत	अथाः	एथां	अध्वं
अत्	अतां	अन् or उः	अत	एतां	अन्त or अत

Here, agreeably to rules already specified, अ has become आ before व and म; the initial of अम्, अन्, अन्त is rejected after a vowel; अ is dropped before उस्; and the आ of आतां and आथां, having been changed to इ, form ए with the augment अ; so does the इ of the first person singular.

f. Sometimes, but rarely, and only after a verb ending in a vowel, the augment अ is rejected, when the terminations of the first præterite are attached directly to the base. It is more usual, however, to prefix स् to them in both voices; making therefore,

Parasmai-pada.			Átmane-pada.		
सम्	साव	साम	सि	स्वहि	स्महि
सः	सतं	सत	सथा	साथां	सध्वं
सत्	सतां	सुः	सत	सातां	सन्त

g. Modifications of the base. These are for the greater part of a special description, and will best be adverted to under each particular case. A few of the most general ones may be here inserted.

h. The indefinite præterite prefixes the temporal augment, whether it retains its own terminations, or adopts those of the first præterite; as, या 'to go, अयासीत्; भू 'to be,' अभूत्. In a few verbs, which take the terminations of the first præterite, the root is also doubled; as, श्रि 'to serve,' अशिश्रियत्.

i. Before the terminations of the first class, or those which are its own, verbs having simple final vowels commonly substitute for them the Vṛiddhi element in the Parasmai-pada, and the Guńa in the Átmane-pada; as, णी 'to take,' अनैषीत्, अनेष्ट; धु 'to shake,' अधावीत्, अधोष्ट; कृ 'to make,' अकार्षीत्. A short vowel is however sometimes unchanged before स, when, agreeably to clause *b*, the sibilant is dropped; as, third pers. sing. Átmane-pada, अकृत. Verbs ending in diphthongs commonly change this to आ; as, धो, 'to destroy,' makes अधासीत् or अधात्.

Of roots ending in consonants, those which take the augment इ, either with or without the sibilant, and have a medial अ, optionally substitute the Vṛiddhi आ in the Parasmai-pada; but not if they end in म, य, ह, or a double consonant, or are distinguished by an Anubandha ए; nor do the roots क्षण् and श्वस् admit of the alternative; as, पठ, 'to read,' makes अपाठीत् or अपठीत्; but भ्रम 'to wander,' अभ्रमीत्; यम 'to restrain,' अयंसीत्. If they end with र् or ल्, the vowel is invariably long; as, चर or चल 'to go,' अचारीत्, अचालीत्. So it is in वद् 'to speak,' and व्रज 'to go,' अवादीत्, अव्राजीत्. In the Átmane-pada the change does not take place; as, त्वर 'to hasten,' अत्वरिष्ट.

j. Any other medial short vowel substitutes the Guńa element in both voices, except in certain verbs. If the final is a double consonant no change takes place, nor is a long vowel changed; as, विद् 'to know,' अवेदीत्; पुष्प 'to flower,' अपुष्पीत्; दीप 'to shine,' अदीपिष्ट.

k. Of those which do not take the augment इ, and which are marked in lists of roots by the Anubandha औ, the medial vowel substitutes the Vṛiddhi element in the Parasmai-pada, before the proper inflexions of the tense; as, यज 'to worship,' अयाक्षीत्; but not in the Átmane-pada; as, मुच 'to liberate,' अमुक्त; स of स्त being rejected (clause *b*), and च becoming क before त, as in declension (rule 92).

l. Before the terminations of the first præterite—and before which, it should be remembered, the augment इ cannot be inserted—verbs ending in vowels undergo the Guńa change when the affix begins with अ; when the augment अ is not inserted, they are unchanged; as, सृ 'to go,' makes असरत्; दा 'to give,' अदात्; and final diphthongs are changed to आ; so that धे, 'to drink,' makes अधात्. The verbs that insert the sibilant before the terminations of the first præterite in the sense of the third, are those which end in श, ष, or ह, having any other penultimate than अ or आ. There are a few exceptions. The final sibilant or aspirate is changed to क before स, and that again is changed to ष (rules 27, 28), making the compound क्ष; as, दिश 'to shew,' अदिक्षत्; कृश 'to be thin,' अकृक्षत्. Before a double consonant a vowel is unchanged. Verbs of the fourth conjugation of the class पुषादि are inflected with the terminations of the first præterite in the Parasmai-pada with the augment अ, when the radical vowel is unaltered; as, पुष 'to nourish,' अपुषत्. So are verbs of the class द्युतादि of the first conjugation, अद्युतत्; and verbs distinguished by an Anubandha ऌ; as, शक्ॢ 'to be able,' अशकत्. In the Átmane-pada some of these verbs may take इ, and undergo the usual changes; as, द्युत, 'to shine,' makes अद्योतिष्ट.

m. Verbs which have an Anubandha इर् are conjugated in the indefinite præterite with both classes of terminations; as, (छिदिर्) छिद, 'to cut,' makes either अच्छैत्सीत् or अच्छिदत्.

n. Verbs having an Anubandha औ do not insert इ before the terminations of the third præterite; as, (रुधौ) रुध 'to obstruct,' अरौत्सीत्, अरौत्तां, अरौत्सुः; or Átmane-pada, अरुद्ध, अरुत्सातां, अरुत्सत.

o. Verbs with an Anubandha ऊ optionally insert इ; as,

(षिधू) षिध 'to be perfect,' असैत्सीत्, असैद्धां, असैत्सुः; or असेधीत्, असेधिष्टां, असेधिषुः.

p. All the verbs of the eighth conjugation, except कृ 'to do,' besides taking इ, and being inflected on the principle of clause *d*, may dispense with the इ in the Átmane-pada, before the terminations of the second and third persons singular; before which also they drop their own finals; as, तन 'to stretch,' अतत, अतथाः (the स of स्त and स्थास् being rejected by clause *b*).

q. All verbs of the tenth conjugation, and causal verbs, are inflected with the terminations of the first præterite with the augment अ. The root is doubled before them, according to rules to be given when treating of the causal præterite; thus, चुर, 'to steal,' makes अचूचुरत्.

Of the augment इ.

191. The insertion of this augment is not restricted to the cases in which it has already been pointed out in the second and third præterite, but is extended to the terminations beginning with consonants in the other tenses which are not comprised within those that take the conjugational distinctions, except the benedictive of the Parasmai-pada. The objects of the insertion and exception may be easily understood. In the former case it is intended to supply the place of the conjugational vowel; in the latter, the initial of the termination is the semivowel य, which may be united with a preceding consonant, and does not need the interposition of a vowel.

a. Although, however enjoined in most cases, there are many exceptions to its insertion. In the two futures, the conditional, and the benedictive Átmane-pada, as in the third præterite, इ is not inserted after verbs distinguished by an indicatory औ; रभ-औ 'to begin,' रब्धा 'he will begin:' and it is optionally inserted in verbs having an indicatory ऊ; as, षिधू, 'to accomplish,' makes in the first future सेद्धा or सेधिता. In the tenses now named, however, a more general prohibition to the insertion of इ, and which is not applicable to the præterites, is when the vowel of a verb has the grave accent. These verbs are specified as follows.

b. Monosyllables ending in any vowels except ऊ and ॠ, and except क्षु, क्ष्णु, डी, णु, यु (2d conj.), रु, वृ, शी, श्रि, श्वि, स्नु. Verbs ending in ऋ also insert इ before the terminations of the indefinite future.

c. The following verbs ending in consonants do not insert this prefix.

अद् to eat.
आप् to obtain.
कृष् to attract. (1. 6.)
क्रुध् to be angry.
क्रुश् to cry aloud.
क्षिप् to throw.
क्षुद् to pound.
क्षुध् to be hungry.
खिद् to be distressed.
गम् to go.
घस् to eat.
छिद् to cut.
छुप् to touch.
णम् to bow.
णह् to tie.
णिज् to cleanse.
णुद् to send.
तप् to inflame. (1. 4. 10.)
तिप् to drop.
तुद् to torment.
तुष् to be satisfied.
तृप् to be satisfied. (4.)
त्यज् to abandon.
त्विष् to shine.
दंश् to bite.
दह् to burn.
दिश् to shew.
दिह् to smear.
दुष् to do wrong.
दुह् to milk. (2.)
दृप् to be proud.
दृश् to see.
द्विष् to hate.
पच् to cook.
पद् to go.
पिष् to grind.
पुष् to cherish. (4.)
प्रच्छ् to ask.
बध् to bind.
बन्ध् to bind.
भज् to serve.
भञ्ज् to break.
भिद् to break.
भुज् to enjoy.
भ्रस्ज् to fry.
मन् to think.
मस्ज् to merge.
मिह् to urine.
मुच् to be free.
मृश् to perceive.
यज् to sacrifice.
यभ् to copulate.

यम to stop.
युज to join.
युध to fight.
रञ्ज to colour.
रभ to begin.
रम to sport.
राध to accomplish.
रिच to purge.
रिश to hurt.
रुज to be sick.
रुध to obstruct.
रुश to hurt.
रुह to ascend.
लभ to acquire.
लिप to smear.
लिश to lessen.
लिह to lick.
लुप to disturb.
वच to speak.
वप to sow.
वस to dwell. (1.)
वह to bear.
विच to differ.
विज to differ.
विद् to know. (4. 6. 7.)
विश to enter.
विष to pervade. (1. 3. 9.)
व्यध to pierce.
शक to be able. (5.)
शद् to wither.
शप to vow.
शिष to hurt, to distinguish. (1. 7.)
शुध to be pure. (4.)
शुष to dry.
श्लिष to embrace. (4.)
षञ्ज to embrace.
षद् to wither.
षिच to sprinkle.
षिध to accomplish.
ष्वञ्ज to embrace.
ष्वप to sleep.
साध to accomplish.
सृज to abandon.
सृप to creep.
स्कन्द् to go.
स्पृश to touch.

The figures mark the conjugations in which the verbs are inflected without इ; in any others they may insert it. The same verb sometimes belongs to more than one conjugation, either with the same or with a different sense.

192. First future. The terminations undergo no change whatever, except when the verb ends with an aspirate, when त is changed to ध, as in the present tense. The changes of the base are few and simple. The final vowels इ, ई, उ, ऊ, ऋ, ॠ, substitute the Guña elements, ए, ओ, अर्, whether the augment इ be inserted or not. If inserted, the first two are changed by the rules of Sandhi to अय्, अव्; as,

जि 'to conquer,' जेता 'he will conquer;' शी 'to sleep,' शयिता 'he will sleep;' रु 'to cry,' रविता. A final ए and ऐ are changed to आ, and this vowel, as well as ओ, undergoes no change; as, दा 'to give,' दाता 'he will give;' पै 'to drink,' पाता; शो 'to sharpen,' शोता. The medial vowels इ, उ, ऋ, if followed by a single consonant, also substitute the Guńa letters; but ऋ is sometimes changed to र्; long vowels are unchanged; as, सिच 'to sprinkle,' सेक्ता; शुच 'to be sad,' शोचिता; दृश 'to see,' द्रष्टा; जीव 'to live,' जीविता. The final consonants when not separated by the augment इ from the dental त, which is the initial of all the terminations of this tense, combine with it, according to the rules of Sandhi: thus पच makes पक्ता; गम, गन्ता. After an aspirate, त is changed to ध; as, लभ 'to gain,' लब्धा. ध after ढ derived from a final ह (rule 32) is changed to ढ, and the first ढ is rejected; as, रुह 'to grow,' रोढा.

193. Indefinite future. The terminations of this tense differ from those of the present only in having स्य prefixed to them, on the same principles as verbs of the first conjugation; making therefore स्यन्ति, स्यन्ते, not स्यान्ति, &c.; स्येथे, स्येते, not स्याथे, स्याते. After इ the sibilant is changed to ष; and after a final vowel or consonant it undergoes such changes as the rules of Sandhi enjoin.

a. The changes of the base are not numerous. A final or medial short vowel, the latter not being long by position, substitutes the Guńa element, which before इ is changed to the form which the laws of combination require. Final consonants are also modified according to the same rules. A final palatal is changed before स to the hard guttural क, and स after क becoming ष, the compound क्ष is formed; as, पच 'to cook,' पक्ष्यति; णिजि 'to wash,' निंक्ष्यति. After a final cerebral sibilant the same change takes place; as, दृष for दृश, 'to see,' makes द्रक्ष्यति. ह also is changed to क; and as in the declension of nouns in ह, when the final is so changed the initial is changed to its aspirate (rule 131, *b*), so दह, 'to burn,' makes धक्ष्यति; दुह 'to milk,' धोक्ष्यति.

194. Imperative. The changes of the terminations are

few, and where the terminations are analogous to those of the present, as अन्तु, अन्तां, आथां, आतां, they undergo similar modifications, when such are necessary, as in the first, fourth, sixth, and tenth conjugations. In the same conjugations, हि, the sign of the second person singular, is rejected, leaving only the conjugational sign अ; as, भू+हि becomes भव 'be thou.' In the other conjugations, after any consonant except a semivowel or a nasal or ह, धि is substituted for हि; as, वच 'to speak,' वग्धि; also after हु 'to sacrifice,' as जुहुधि. तात is substituted for the terminations of the second and third persons singular in a benedictive sense; as, भवतात् 'may thou' or 'may he be.'

a. The changes of the base are conjugational, and analogous to those of the present.

195. Potential. इ is substituted for the या of all the terminations of this mood, and is prefixed to यां, which becomes यं, and also to युस्, in the Parasmai-pada of the first class of conjugations, and with their conjugational sign अ becomes by the rules of Sandhi (rule 2) ए; as, भवेत्, दीव्येत्, तुदेत्, चोरयेत्. In the second series या is unchanged; as, अद्यात्, &c. In the first class of conjugations the initial ई of the terminations of the Átmane-pada becomes with the conjugational अ, ए; as, रभेत, रभेयातां. In the second class it is unchanged; as, आस 'to sit,' आसीत, आसीयातां, आसीरन्, &c.

a. The changes of the base are conjugational.

196. Benedictive mood. The terminations are not liable to change: इ may be inserted before those of the Átmane-pada, when स becomes ष.

a. The following are the principal changes to which the inflective base is subject in the Parasmai-pada, and when इ is not inserted in the Átmane-pada.

b. Of verbs ending in vowels, most of those which terminate in आ, either as a primitive or as derived from ए or ऐ, substitute ए in the Parasmai-pada; they are unchanged in the Átmane-pada; as, दा 'to give,' देयात्, दासीष्ट. Some change it optionally before य; as, गै 'to sing,' गायात् or गेयात्. Those in which आ is preceded by a conjunct consonant, except स्था 'to stay,' do not change the आ; as, ध्मा 'to blow,' ध्मायात्.

Those ending in इ or ई substitute ई in the Parasmai-pada, and the Guńa letter ए in the Átmane-pada; as, नी 'to take,' नीयात्, नेषीष्ट. Those ending in उ and ऊ substitute ऊ and ओ; as, श्रु 'to hear,' श्रूयात्; स्तु 'to praise,' स्तूयात्, स्तोषीष्ट. ऋ short substitutes रि, and ॠ long ईर्, in the Parasmai-pada; as, कृ 'to make,' क्रियात्; तॄ 'to cross,' तीर्यात्. Verbs ending in ऋ, and beginning with a compound consonant, substitute the Guńa अर् for their final; as, स्तॄ 'to spread,' स्तर्यात्. In the Átmane-pada the vowel is unchanged; as, कृ 'to make,' कृषीष्ट. A final ओ is unchanged; as, शो 'to wither,' शोयात्.

c. Verbs ending in consonants change their finals according to the rules of Sandhi, or others of an analogous application, only before the sibilants of the Átmane-pada; nor do their preceding vowels undergo any alteration; as, छिद 'to cut,' छिद्यात्, छित्सीष्ट; पच 'to cook,' पच्यात्, पक्षीष्ट. If the final be a compound, of which a nasal is the first member, it is rejected in the Parasmai-pada, as दंश 'to bite,' दश्यात्; not in the Átmane-pada, as स्वञ्ज 'to embrace,' स्वंक्षीष्ट; nor does this apply to roots inserting a nasal in consequence of an Anubhandha इ; as, नदि 'to rejoice,' नन्द्यात्.

d. Some verbs containing semivowels change them to their corresponding vowels in the Parasmai-pada; as, प्रच्छ 'to ask,' पृच्छ्यात्; वच 'to speak,' उच्यात्; वप 'to sew,' उप्यात्; यज 'to worship,' इज्यात्; वह 'to bear,' उह्यात्; वस 'to dwell,' उष्यात्; वश 'to subdue,' उश्यात्. There are a few verbs containing the semivowel व, and ending in ए, which admit of a similar modification, and reject the diphthong; as, वे 'to weave,' ऊयात्; व्ये 'to conceal,' वीयात्; and ह्वे 'to call,' हूयात्.

e. When इ is prefixed to the terminations of this tense in the Atmane-pada, the changes of the base are analogous to those of the other tenses before the same augment.

197. Conditional mood. The terminations generally follow the analogy of those of the indefinite future (see p. 115).

a. The base prefixes the temporal augment, but in all other respects is analogous to the inflective base of the indefinite future; as, ind. fut. भविष्यति 'will be,' cond. अभविष्यत्; अत्स्यति 'will eat,' cond. आत्स्यत्.

SECTION VI.

Formation of the Verb.

198. From this general view of the formation of the tenses, we may now proceed to trace an entire verb through all its inflexions in the two active voices and in the passive voice. In following the example of Mr. Colebrooke, and offering भू, 'to be,' as an example, we select a verb of general usefulness, and frequent recurrence. भू is a verb of the first conjugation: it is properly confined to the Parasmai-pada, and in its character of a substantive verb cannot well admit of any other. With prepositions, however, it takes a transitive sense, and may then be both active and passive; as, अनुभवते 'he perceives;' अनुभूयते 'it is perceived.' We may, however, lay aside the preposition for the present, that the purpose for which the verb is exhibited, that of supplying a model of extensive application, may not be embarrassed by unnecessary complexity.

199. भू as a verb of the first conjugation changes its vowel to ओ before the sign of the conjugation अ. It changes it to ओ also before the augment इ, which it admits: and before अ and इ, ओ becomes अव्. The inflective base with the augments is therefore भव and भवि. In the second præterite व् is added to the radical vowel, and the verb being repeated, the base is बभूव्. In the third præterite in the Parasmai-pada the verb takes the terminations of the first: in the Átmane-pada it retains its own terminations with the augment इ.

भू 'to be.'

Indicative mood.

Present tense, 'I am,' &c.

Parasmai-pada.			Átmane-pada.		
भवामि	भवावः	भवामः	भवे	भवावहे	भवामहे
भवसि	भवथः	भवथ	भवसे	भवेथे	भवध्वे
भवति	भवतः	भवन्ति	भवते	भवेते	भवन्ते

First præterite or imperfect, 'I was,' &c.

अभवम्	अभवाव	अभवाम	अभवे	अभवावहि	अभवामहि
अभवः	अभवतं	अभवत	अभवथाः	अभवेथां	अभवध्वं
अभवत्	अभवतां	अभवन्	अभवत	अभवेतां	अभवन्त

Second præterite or perfect, 'I was or have been,' &c.

बभूव	बभूविव	बभूविम	बभूवे	बभूविवहे	बभूविमहे
बभूविथ	बभूवथुः	बभूव	बभूविषे	बभूवाथे	बभूविध्वे (ढ्वे)
बभूव	बभूवतुः	बभूवुः	बभूवे	बभूवाते	बभूविरे

Third præt., indefinite, or aorist past, 'I was or had been,' &c.

अभूवम्	अभूव	अभूम	अभविषि	अभविष्वहि	अभविष्महि
अभूः	अभूतं	अभूत	अभविष्ठाः	अभविषाथां	अभविध्वं (ढ्वं)
अभूत्	अभूतां	अभूवन्	अभविष्ट	अभविषातां	अभविषत

First or definite future, 'I will be,' &c.

भवितास्मि	भवितास्वः	भवितास्मः	भविताहे	भवितास्वहे	भवितास्महे
भवितासि	भवितास्थः	भवितास्थ	भवितासे	भवितासाथे	भविताध्वे
भविता	भवितारौ	भवितारः	भविता	भवितारौ	भवितारः

Second or indefinite future, 'I will or shall be,' &c.

भविष्यामि	भविष्यावः	भविष्यामः	भविष्ये	भविष्यावहे	भविष्यामहे
भविष्यसि	भविष्यथः	भविष्यथ	भविष्यसे	भविष्येथे	भविष्यध्वे
भविष्यति	भविष्यतः	भविष्यन्ति	भविष्यते	भविष्येते	भविष्यन्ते

Imperative mood, 'May I be,' &c.

भवानि	भवाव	भवाम	भवै	भवावहै	भवामहै
भव	भवतं	भवत	भवस्व	भवेथां	भवध्वं
भवतु	भवतां	भवन्तु	भवतां	भवेतां	भवन्तां

Potential or subjunctive mood, 'I may be,' &c.

भवेयं	भवेव	भवेम	भवेय	भवेवहि	भवेमहि
भवेः	भवेतं	भवेत	भवेथाः	भवेयाथां	भवेध्वं
भवेत्	भवेतां	भवेयुः	भवेत	भवेयातां	भवेरन्

Benedictive or optative mood, 'I wish I may be,' &c.

भूयासम्	भूयास्व	भूयास्म	भविषीय	भविषीवहि	भविषीमहि
भूयाः	भूयास्तं	भूयास्त	भविषीष्ठाः	भविषीयास्थां	भविषीध्वं (ढ्वं)
भूयात्	भूयास्तां	भूयासुः	भविषीष्ट	भविषीयास्तां	भविषीरन्

Conditional mood, 'I shall be, if,' &c.

अभविष्यम्	अभविष्याव	अभविष्याम	अभविष्ये	अभविष्यावहि	अभविष्यामहि
अभविष्यः	अभविष्यतं	अभविष्यत	अभविष्यथाः	अभविष्येथां	अभविष्यध्वं
अभविष्यत्	अभविष्यतां	अभविष्यन्	अभविष्यत	अभविष्येतां	अभविष्यन्त

Passive voice.

200. In this voice य् is prefixed to the terminations of the conjugational tenses in the Átmane-pada; and before य् the radical vowel is unchangeable. In the non-conjugational tenses the radical vowel optionally substitutes the Guńa or Vṛiddhi diphthong, and thus भू becomes भो or भौ; making consequently before a vowel भव् or भाव्. It takes the latter only before the termination इ of the third præterite. In every other respect there is no difference between the tenses of the passive voice and those of the active in the Átmane-pada of the first conjugation.

Present tense.	भूये	भूयावहे	भूयामहे
	भूयसे	भूयेथे	भूयध्वे
	भूयते	भूयेते	भूयन्ते
First præter.	अभूये	अभूयावहि	अभूयामहि &c.
Second præter.	बभूवे	बभूविवहे	बभूविमहे &c.
Third præter.			
1st pers.	अभविषि	अभविष्वहि	अभविष्महि
	अभाविषि	अभाविष्वहि	अभाविष्महि
2d pers.	अभविष्ठाः	अभविषाथां	अभविढ्वं
	अभाविष्ठाः	अभाविषाथां	अभाविढ्वं
3d pers.	अभावि	अभविषातां	अभविषत
		अभाविषातां	अभाविषत:
First future.	भविताहे	भवितास्वहे	भवितास्महे &c.
	भाविताहे	भावितास्वहे	भावितास्महे
Second future.	भविष्ये	भविष्यावहे	भविष्यामहे &c.
	भाविष्ये	भाविष्यावहे	भाविष्यामहे
Imperative.	भूयै	भूयावहै	भूयामहै &c.
Potential.	भूयेय	भूयेवहि	भूयेमहि &c.
Benedictive.	भविषीय	भविषीवहि	भविषीमहि &c.
	भाविषीय	भाविषीवहि	भाविषीमहि

Conditional.	अभविष्ये	अभविष्यावहि	अभविष्यामहि	&c.
	अभाविष्ये	अभाविष्यावहि	अभाविष्यामहि	

SECTION VII.

Derivative Verbs.

201. Before proceeding to any detail of individual verbs, it is desirable that some notion should be entertained of those secondary or derivative forms of which the simple verb admits. Some of these might perhaps be more correctly designated as moods; for causality, desire, frequency, or intensity, are but different modes or conditions of the same action; and the modifications by which they are expressed are no more to be regarded as distinct verbs because they take all the tenses of the simple verb, than are the moods of the Greek verb, of which the same circumstance may be predicated. As however the derivative forms have been hitherto given separately, and as their annexation to the simple verb as moods would present to the learner a rather formidable array of verbal inflexion, the distinct explanation of them may be here also observed.

Causals.

202. All verbs admit of a modification implying causality, as causing to be, to do, &c. In the language of the original grammarians, णिच् is added to the verb; that is, the vowel इ, which is convertible to ए, and becomes अय् before a vowel; the ण in the affix indicates the substitution of the Vṛiddhi element for the radical vowel; भू therefore becomes भौ, which with इ makes भावि, or before a vowel भावय्.

a. The causal verb may be conjugated with the terminations of either voice; with those of the Parasmai-pada when it is strictly transitive; with the Átmane-pada when it is reflective, or when the consequence of the action reverts to the causer or instigator. अ is inserted before the terminations in the conjugational tenses, and इ in the non-conjugational;

except in the third præterite, which takes the terminations of the first præterite. The second præterite is formed with the auxiliary verbs कृ, भू, अस्.

b. Verbs ending in आ, whether primitive or derived from the change of a final diphthong to आ, insert प, ल, or य, before the causal augment; as, पा 'to drink,' पाययति 'he causes to drink;' पा 'to preserve,' पालयति 'he causes to preserve;' ज्ञा 'to know,' ज्ञापयति 'he causes to know,' 'he teaches.' In some instances the radical vowel is optionally made short; as, शा 'to sharpen' or 'kill,' शापयति or शपयति 'he causes to kill;' स्ना 'to bathe,' स्नापयति or स्नपयति 'he causes to bathe.'

c. Roots ending in इ or ई when substituting the Vṛiddhi element ऐ change the latter of course before the vowel of the causal form to आय्; as, चि 'to collect,' चाययति 'he causes to collect:' but य is sometimes replaced by प, and the vowel in both cases made optionally short; so that चि makes also चापयति, चययति, or चपयति. Roots in ई long sometimes either change the radical to the Guṇa element, or preserve it unchanged, interposing a consonant before the causal augment; as, ह्री 'to be ashamed,' ह्रेपयति; प्री 'to be pleased,' प्रीणयति or प्रीययति, Roots ending in उ, ऊ, ऋ, and ॠ, mostly change their finals to the Vṛiddhi substitutes.

d. Roots ending in consonants usually change a medial अ to आ; and इ, उ and ऋ to ए, ओ and अर्. Long vowels are unchanged. There are exceptions, as in the class of roots called घटादि or घट 'to endeavour,' with other verbs of the first conjugation, which do not make the vowel long, as घट, घटयति. Of roots ending in म, some do and some do not make the vowel long; as, गम 'to go,' गमयति; कम 'to wish,' कामयति. हन्, 'to kill,' substitutes घात; as, घातयति 'he causes to kill.' रुह्, 'to ascend,' optionally substitutes प for the final; as, रोहयति or रोपयति 'he causes to ascend or grow,' 'he plants.'

e. These general rules for the modification of the base are applicable to all the tenses except the benedictive in the Parasmai-pada, and the third præterite. In the former the causal augment is rejected, although the vowel of the base undergoes the change to which it is liable in this form, as भू becomes भावयाम्. In the third præterite, which takes the terminations of the first, and the conjugational augment अ before them, the root undergoes reduplication, with some peculiar modifications of the radical vowel. With very few exceptions the causal augment is rejected; as, याच्, 'to ask,' makes अययाचत् not अययाचयत्. In general the radical vowel, if long, is made short; as, प्री 'to please,' अपीप्रियत् 'he caused to please; धू 'to shake,' अदूधुनत् 'he caused to shake.' There are some exceptions, as in the instance of याच्; so also शास्, 'to govern,' makes अशशासत्. Some verbs take both forms; as, भाष् 'to speak,' अबिभाषत् or अबीभषत् 'he caused to speak.'

f. In doubling the root before the third præterite of the causal, the general rules are mostly to be observed (see p. 118); but there are also some peculiarities.

g. If the verb consists of a vowel followed by a consonant, the first member of the reduplication is the entire root, with the vowel modified as usual: to this, इ is added, with the radical consonant; as, अट् 'to go,' आटिटत् 'he sent,' or 'caused to go;' इल् 'to worship,' ऐलिलत् 'he caused to worship.'

h. If the verb begin with a consonant, the reduplicated consonant will conform to preceding rules (p. 118). The reduplicate vowel will be अ, इ, or उ.

i. अ is repeated for a radical अ prosodially long; as, लभ्, 'to obtain,' makes अललम्भत् 'he caused to obtain;' and for अ when it is preceded by a double consonant; as, मृद् 'to trample,' अममर्दत् 'he caused to trample:' for आ medial, which is preserved in the inflexion; as, शास् 'to govern,' अशशासत्; and for ऋ and ॠ in some verbs; as, वृत् 'to be,' अववर्तत् 'he caused to be;' दॄ 'to tear,' अददरत् 'he caused to tear.'

j. इ, becoming ई before a single consonant followed in its inflected form by a short vowel, and remaining unchanged before a double consonant, or before a single consonant if followed in its inflected form by a long vowel, is repeated—

1, for अ or आ when not followed by a double consonant; as, पच् 'to cook,' अपीपचत्; क्ष्मा 'to shake,' अचिक्ष्मपत्; स्था 'to stand,' अतिष्ठिपत् 'he caused to stand:' 2, for इ, ई, ए, ऐ; as, जि 'to conquer,' अजीजपत्; वेष्ट 'to surround,' अविवेष्टत्: 3, for उ or ऊ preceded by ज, a labial, or a semivowel; as, जु 'to make haste,' अजीजवत् 'he caused to make haste;' भू 'to be,' अबीभवत् 'he caused to be;' लू 'to cut,' अलीलवत्: 4, optionally for उ or ऊ preceded by the same consonants in composition with others; as, श्रु 'to hear,' अशिश्रवत् or अशुश्रवत्: 5, for ऋ, when that does not substitute अर्; as, वृत 'to be,' अवीवृतत्, otherwise अववर्तत्; or in some cases where it does take Guṇa; as, कृ 'to make,' अचीकरत् 'he caused to make.'

k. उ, liable to be changed to ऊ by the same circumstances which require the alteration of इ to ई, is repeated for उ, ऊ, ओ, औ; as, रुह 'to grow,' अरूरुहत् 'he caused to grow,' 'he raised;' ढौक 'to seek,' अडुढौकत् 'he caused to seek;' स्वप 'to sleep,' असूषुपत् 'he caused to sleep.'

l. Some of the forms of this tense are apparently anomalous, although they arise out of previous rules: thus इ 'to go,' with अधि prefixed, 'to read,' makes अध्यापिपत् or अध्यजीगपत् 'he taught' or 'caused to read;' घ्रा 'to smell,' अजिघ्रिपत् or अजिघ्रपत् 'he caused to smell;' हन 'to kill,' अजीघतत्; and पा 'to drink,' अपीप्यत् 'he caused to drink.'

m. It is not necessary, either in the case of causal derivatives or those about to be described, to multiply examples under their several rules. In the succeeding pages paradigmas will be given of many of the most useful verbs, and these will include examples of their derivative verbal inflexions.

Desideratives.

203. When the agent wishes, intends, or expects to do the action, or be in the condition, which the verb imports, स, technically called सन्, is added to the root. The अ is rejected before the terminations of the non-conjugational tenses. The root undergoes reduplication, and is conjugated in the same voice in which the primitive is conjugated.

a. Before सन् the augment इ is very commonly prefixed. Its exclusion occurs for the most part after those roots which do not take the same augment before the non-conjugational tenses (see p. 127). This does not prevent the use of the augment before the personal terminations in those tenses in which it is enjoined in all derivative verbs. After इ the स of सन् is changed to ष.

b. The reduplication of the radical syllable follows the rules affecting consonants (r. 188. cl. *d* to *g*). There are some peculiarities in regard to the vowels; इ being usually substituted for a radical medial or final अ, आ, इ, ई, ऋ, ॠ, ए, ऐ; and उ for उ, ऊ, ओ, औ. When the root begins with a vowel, the reduplication is the radical syllable itself, followed by the final consonant with इ prefixed; as, अश् 'to eat,' अशिशिष् 'to wish to eat.' Very commonly, however, there is no reduplication, but the initial letter or the whole syllable is changed; as, आप् 'to obtain,' ईप्स् 'to wish to obtain;' ऋध 'to increase,' ईर्त्स् 'to wish to increase,' &c. The same occurs with verbs beginning with consonants; as, दा 'to give,' दित्स्, दित्सति 'he wishes to give;' मि 'to scatter,' and मी 'to kill,' मित्स्, मित्सति 'he wishes to scatter' or 'kill;' शक 'to be able,' शिक्ष्, as शिक्षति 'he wishes to be able,' 'he learns;' लभ 'to obtain,' लिप्स्, as लिप्सति 'he desires to obtain;' पद 'to go,' पित्सते 'he wishes to go;' पत 'to fall,' पित्सति 'he expects to fall,' &c.

c. Besides the changes to which the radical vowels are subject in the syllable of reduplication, they are occasionally subject to the same or similar changes in the radical syllable also. When इ is not prefixed to सन्, a radical short इ and उ become long; as, जि, 'to conquer,' makes जिगीषति; यु 'to join,' युयूषति. The long vowels remain for the most part unaltered; as, ज्ञा 'to know,' जिज्ञासति 'he wishes to know;' भू 'to be,' बुभूषति 'he wishes to be.' ऋ and ॠ are commonly changed to ईर्; as, कृ 'to make,' चिकीर्षति 'he wishes to make:' but when preceded by a labial, the substitute is उर्; as, मृ, 'to die,' makes मुमूर्षति 'he wishes to die.'

d. When इ is prefixed to सन्, a final आ may be dropped; as, दरिद्रा 'to be poor,' दरिद्रिषति; otherwise दरिद्रासति. Other final vowels may substitute the Guṇa or Vṛiddhi elements, changed before इ agreeably to the rules of Sandhi. Thus श्रि, 'to serve,' makes शिश्रयिषति; otherwise शिश्रीषति. इ, 'to go,' substitutes गम, which takes इ and makes जिगमिषति; but not if अधि be prefixed, as अधिजिगांसते. पू, 'to purify,' substitutes इ for its radical, which becomes the Guṇa ए, and by Sandhi अय् before the augment पिपयिषति. ऊर्णु, 'to cover,' takes different forms, ऊर्णुनुविषति, ऊर्णुनविषति, or ऊर्णुनूषति. Those verbs in ऋ or ॠ which prefix इ to स, change the radical letter to र; as, ऋ 'to go,' अरिरिषति 'he wishes to go.' तॄ 'to cross,' with इ, is तितरिषति; without it तितीर्षति.

e. Most roots ending with consonants prefix इ to सन्. When they do not, the finals combine with the sibilant, agreeably to the laws of Sandhi; as, पच 'to cook,' पिपक्ष् 'to wish to cook.' पिपक्षति; पठ, which takes इ, makes पिपठिषति 'he wishes to read.' तन 'to spread,' and सन 'to serve,' take both forms; as, तितांसति or तितनिषति, सिसांसति or सिसनिषति.

f. Verbs having a medial इ, ई, उ, ऊ, when इ is prefixed to स, optionally substitute the Guṇa letter; as, रुच 'to please,' रुरुचिषति or रुरोचिषति. There are a few exceptions; as, रुद 'to weep,' रुरुदिषति. When the final is व it is changed to ऊ, when इ is not inserted; so दिव, 'to play,' makes दिदूषति, दिदिविषति, or दिदेविषति 'he wishes to play.' A medial ऋ or ॠ is usually changed to अर् when इ is inserted, but remains unchanged when it is not; as, नृत, 'to dance,' makes either निनर्तिषति or निनृत्सति.

g. Some verbs take the form of the desiderative, although they have the meaning only of the simple verb; as, गुप 'to blame,' जुगुप्सते 'he blames;' कित 'to cure,' चिकित्सति 'he cures;' मान 'to investigate,' मीमांसते; and a few others.

Frequentatives.

204. When repetition or intensity of the action or condition is signified, य्, technically called यङ्, is added to the verb. The nasal ङ् intimates that it is to be conjugated in the Átmane-pada only. The root is doubled. Again, it is said that the affix is rejected; when य् is not inserted, although the verb retains the reduplication. In that case the frequentative form may, according to some authorities, be conjugated in either voice, although others restrict it to the Parasmai-pada.

a. Verbs implying motion take the frequentative form in the sense of tortuous motion, and some others in an ill sense of the verb.

b. When conjugated with य्, the verb follows the model of verbs of the first conjugation; that is, it inserts अ before the terminations of the four conjugational tenses. When य् has been rejected, it follows that of verbs of the second conjugation, or is inflected without the intermediate vowel अ.

Frequentatives inserting य्.

205. In the reduplication initial consonants are repeated, agreeably to general rules (p. 118). A verb beginning with a vowel repeats the whole, and makes the vowel of the primitive syllable, if short, long; as, अट 'to wander,' अटाट्यते 'he wanders much.' A monosyllabic vowel is changed to its Guńa representative in both syllables; as, ऋ 'to go,' अरार्यते 'he goes often.'

a. A medial अ or आ is represented in the reduplicate syllable by आ; as, पच 'to cook,' पापच्यते; याच 'to ask,' यायाच्यते. If a root with a medial अ ends in a nasal, the nasal is repeated; as, गम 'to go,' जङ्गम्यते 'he goes frequently,' or 'crookedly.' Some follow different forms; as, जन, 'to be born,' makes either जञ्जन्यते or जाजायते; and हन 'to kill,' जंहन्यते, जङ्घन्यते, or जेघ्नीयते. Some verbs insert a nasal in the reduplicate syllable; as, जल्प 'to speak,' जञ्जल्प्यते 'he talks much.' Some with a nasal in the primitive, retain it only in the reduplication; as, दंश 'to bite,' दन्दश्यते 'he bites much:' and verbs ending in य, ल, व, insert a nasal optionally; as, चल 'to go,' चंचल्यते or चाचल्यते 'he goes crookedly' or 'repeatedly;' फल, 'to bear fruit,' has only one form, पंफुल्यते. The verb चर, 'to go,' also inserts a nasal, चञ्चूर्य्यते. Some verbs, having a medial अ, require नी to be placed after the reduplicated consonant, and if they have nasals, drop them; as, पद 'to go,' पनीपद्यते; or ध्वंस 'to fall,' दनीध्वस्यते.

b. The simple vowels इ, ई, उ, ऊ, ऋ, ॠ, final or medial, and whether radical or derived from the changes to which a radical vowel or diphthong is subject in this form, substitute the Guńa letter in the reduplication; as, विद 'to know,' वेविद्यते; भू 'to be,' बोभूयते. दा 'to give,' becoming दी, makes देदीयते; and गै 'to sing,' first changed to गा, makes गी, and then जेगीयते. The vowel ई is put after the Guńa substitute of ऋ; as, नृत 'to dance,' नरीनृत्यते.

c. The radical syllable is also subject to various modifications, affecting chiefly the vowels. A final आ, whether primitive or substituted for a final diphthong, is changed to ई; as, दा 'to give,' देदीयते. इ and उ, when final, are made long; and if long, are unchanged; as, चि 'to gather,' चेचीयते; कु 'to coo,' चोकूयते or कोकूयते. ऋ preceded by a single consonant is changed to री; as, कृ, 'to make,' becomes चेक्रीयते 'he makes' or 'does incessantly.' If the initial is a double consonant, the vowel is changed to अर्; as, स्मृ, 'to remember,' makes सास्मर्य्यते. When medials, the radical vowels are for the most part unchanged.

d. Some verbs containing semivowels combined with consonants change them, and the vowels following them, to their analogous vowels: thus व्ये, 'to cover,' becomes वी; as, वेवीयते 'he hides repeatedly:' श्वि, 'to increase,' becomes शु, and makes शोशूयते 'he increases constantly:' स्वप्, 'to sleep,' becomes सुप्; as, सोषुप्यते 'he sleeps frequently' or 'soundly:' स्यम, 'to make a noise,' becomes सिम्; as, सेसिम्यते 'he makes a great noise:' गॄ, 'to swallow,' becomes गिर्, and again changes र to ल; as, जेगिल्यते 'he swallows voraciously.' In others, the changes are arbitrary; as, चर, 'to go,' changes its च to ज: and फल, 'to bear fruit,' changes it to ञ; as, पम्फुल्यते, पंफुल्यते.

Frequentatives rejecting य्.

206. The rules regarding reduplication are generally the same for this as for the preceding form of the frequentative verb.

a. The vowel of the reduplicate syllable is the Guńa equivalent of that of the base; or ए for इ, ई; ओ for उ, ऊ; अर् for ऋ, ॠ. The vowel इ or ई may be optionally subjoined to अर्; thus कृ, 'to make,' in its reduplication becomes चरीकृ, चरिकृ, or चर्कृ; ऋ, 'to go,' becomes अर्ऋ or अरियृ. The final ॠ of गॄ 'to swallow,' and तॄ 'to cross,' becomes आ; as, जागॄ, तातॄ. The changes of medial vowels, and the rules affecting the insertion or ejection of a nasal in the reduplicate syllable, are the same as those of the preceding class of frequentatives.

b. As being inflected in the second conjugation, no vowel is interposed between the terminations and the base: दा, 'to give,' therefore makes दादाति, and पच 'to cook,' पापक्ति, in the third pers. sing. present tense. Optionally, however, ई may be prefixed to terminations containing a mute प्, and beginning with a consonant. Before the same terminations a final, and if short, a medial vowel undergoes the usual Guńa substitution; and when ई is inserted, the final combines with it, according to the rules of Sandhi; as, शी 'to sleep,' शेशेति or शेशयीति; and भू 'to be,' बोभोति or बोभवीति.

c. Verbs ending in आ change the final to ई before the terminations of the conjugational tenses beginning with consonants not having a mute प्; as, हा 'to abandon,' जाहीवः, जाहीमः; but दा 'to give,' and धा 'to have,' before the same, drop their final vowel, as दाद्वः, दाद्मः. Before terminations containing प् the change is optional, as जाहाति or जाहेति; ई being changed to its Guńa equivalent. Before vowels the final is dropped, as, third pers. plur. जाहति, दादति; the nasal being rejected after a reduplicate (r. 186). Before य the final is optionally changed to ए, as जाहायात् or जाहेयात्, ध्मा and घ्रा, change the final to ई, and are inflected like verbs ending with ई.

d. The changes of इ, ई, उ, ऊ, ऋ, ॠ, when final, are analogous to those to which they are subject in conjugational inflexion. Before those terminations which reject प् they substitute the Guńa letters ए, ओ, अर्, which undergo the usual changes before vowels. Before a termination beginning with a vowel, and not containing a mute प्, they are changed according to the rules of Sandhi, or in some cases इ ई make इय्, and उ ऊ become उव्, before such a vowel. Before similar terminations beginning with consonants they are unchanged. In like manner medial short vowels are changed to Guńa vowels before the terminations rejecting प्.

e. There are some special modifications, which will be noticed in the paradigmas. We may now give the continuation of भू in its derivative modifications.

Causal form of भू 'to be:' भावि 'to cause to be.'

Present tense, 'I cause to be,' &c.

Parasmai-pada.			Átmane-pada.		
भावयामि	भावयावः	भावयामः	भावये	भावयावहे	भावयामहे
भावयसि	भावयथः	भावयथ	भावयसे	भावयेथे	भावयध्वे
भावयति	भावयतः	भावयन्ति	भावयते	भावयेते	भावयन्ते

First præterite, 'I caused to be,' &c.

अभावयम्	अभावयाव	अभावयाम	अभावये	अभावयावहि	अभावयामहि
अभावयः	अभावयतं	अभावयत	अभावयथाः	अभावयेथां	अभावयध्वं
अभावयत्	अभावयतां	अभावयन्	अभावयत	अभावयेतां	अभावयन्त

Second præterite, 'I have caused to be,' &c.

भावयाञ्चकार	भावयाञ्चकृव	भावयाञ्चकृम	भावयाञ्चक्रे	भावयाञ्चकृवहे	भावयाञ्चकृमहे
भावयाञ्चकर्थ	भावयाञ्चक्रथुः	भावयाञ्चक्र	भावयाञ्चकृषे	भावयाञ्चक्राथे	भावयाञ्चकृढ्वे
भावयाञ्चकार	भावयाञ्चक्रतुः	भावयाञ्चक्रुः	भावयाञ्चक्रे	भावयाञ्चक्राते	भावयाञ्चक्रिरे

Third præterite, 'I had caused to be,' &c.

अबीभवम्	अबीभवाव	अबीभवाम	अबीभवे	अबीभवावहि	अबीभवामहि
अबीभवः	अबीभवतं	अबीभवत	अबीभवथाः	अबीभवेथां	अबीभवध्वं
अबीभवत्	अबीभवतां	अबीभवन्	अबीभवत	अबीभवेतां	अबीभवन्त

First future, 'I will cause to be,' &c.

भावयितास्मि	भावयितास्वः	भावयितास्मः	भावयिताहे	भावयितास्वहे	भावयितास्महे
भावयितासि	भावयितास्थः	भावयितास्थ	भावयितासे	भावयितासाथे	भावयिताध्वे
भावयिता	भावयितारौ	भावयितारः	भावयिता	भावयितारौ	भावयितारः

Second future, 'I shall or will cause to be,' &c.

भावयिष्यामि	भावयिष्यावः	भावयिष्यामः	भावयिष्ये	भावयिष्यावहे	भावयिष्यामहे
भावयिष्यसि	भावयिष्यथः	भावयिष्यथ	भावयिष्यसे	भावयिष्येथे	भावयिष्यध्वे
भावयिष्यति	भावयिष्यतः	भावयिष्यन्ति	भावयिष्यते	भावयिष्येते	भावयिष्यन्ते

Imperative, 'May I cause to be,' &c.

भावयानि	भावयाव	भावयाम	भावयै	भावयावहै	भावयामहै
भावय	भावयतं	भावयत	भावयस्व	भावयेथां	भावयध्वं
भावयतु	भावयतां	भावयन्तु	भावयतां	भावयेतां	भावयन्तां

Potential, 'May I cause to be,' &c.

भावयेयं	भावयेव	भावयेम	भावयेय	भावयेवहि	भावयेमहि
भावयेः	भावयेतं	भावयेत	भावयेथाः	भावयेयाथां	भावयेध्वं
भावयेत्	भावयेतां	भावयेयुः	भावयेत	भावयेयातां	भावयेरन्

Benedictive or optative, 'I pray I may cause to be,' &c.

भाव्यासम्	भाव्यास्व	भाव्यास्म	भावयिषीय	भावयिषीवहि	भावयिषीमहि
भाव्याः	भाव्यास्तं	भाव्यास्त	भावयिषीष्ठाः	भावयिषीयास्थां	भावयिषीढ्वं
भाव्यात्	भाव्यास्तां	भाव्यासुः	भावयिषीष्ट	भावयिषीयास्तां	भावयिषीरन्

Conditional, 'I shall cause to be, if,' &c.

अभावयिष्यम्	अभावयिष्याव	अभावयिष्याम	अभावयिष्ये	अभावयिष्यावहि	अभावयिष्यामहि
अभावयिष्यः	अभावयिष्यतं	अभावयिष्यत	अभावयिष्यथाः	अभावयिष्येथां	अभावयिष्यध्वं
अभावयिष्यत्	अभावयिष्यतां	अभावयिष्यन्	अभावयिष्यत	अभावयिष्येतां	अभावयिष्यन्त

Desiderative form of भू 'to be:' बुभूष् 'to wish to be.'

Present tense, 'I wish to be,' &c.

Parasmai-pada.			Átmane-pada.		
बुभूषामि	बुभूषावः	बुभूषामः	बुभूषे	बुभूषावहे	बुभूषामहे
बुभूषसि	बुभूषथः	बुभूषथ	बुभूषसे	बुभूषेथे	बुभूषध्वे
बुभूषति	बुभूषतः	बुभूषन्ति	बुभूषते	बुभूषेते	बुभूषन्ते

First præterite, 'I wished to be,' &c.

अबुभूषम्	अबुभूषाव	अबुभूषाम	अबुभूषे	अबुभूषावहि	अबुभूषामहि
अबुभूषः	अबुभूषतं	अबुभूषत	अबुभूषथाः	अबुभूषेथां	अबुभूषध्वं
अबुभूषत्	अबुभूषतां	अबुभूषन्	अबुभूषत	अबुभूषेतां	अबुभूषन्त

Second præterite, 'I have wished to be,' &c.

बुभूषाञ्चकार or -चकर	बुभूषाञ्चकृव	बुभूषाञ्चकृम	बुभूषाञ्चक्रे	बुभूषाञ्चकृवहे	बुभूषाञ्चकृमहे
बुभूषाञ्चकर्थ	बुभूषाञ्चक्रथुः	बुभूषाञ्चक्र	बुभूषाञ्चकृषे	बुभूषाञ्चक्राथे	बुभूषाञ्चकृढ्वे
बुभूषाञ्चकार	बुभूषाञ्चक्रतुः	बुभूषाञ्चक्रुः	बुभूषाञ्चक्रे	बुभूषाञ्चक्राते	बुभूषाञ्चक्रिरे

Third præterite, 'I had wished to be,' &c.

अबुभूषिषम्	अबुभूषिष्वः	अबुभूषिष्मः	अबुभूषिषि	अबुभूषिष्वहि	अबुभूषिष्महि
अबुभूषीः	अबुभूषिष्टं	अबुभूषिष्ट	अबुभूषिष्ठाः	अबुभूषिषाथां	अबुभूषिढ्वं
अबुभूषीत्	अबुभूषिष्टां	अबुभूषिषुः	अबुभूषिष्ट	अबुभूषिषातां	अबुभूषिषत

First future, 'I will wish to be,' &c.

बुभूषितास्मि	बुभूषितास्वः	बुभूषितास्मः	बुभूषिताहे	बुभूषितास्वहे	बुभूषितास्महे
बुभूषितासि	बुभूषितास्थः	बुभूषितास्थ	बुभूषितासे	बुभूषितासाथे	बुभूषिताध्वे
बुभूषिता	बुभूषितारौ	बुभूषितारः	बुभूषिता	बुभूषितारौ	बुभूषितारः

Second future, 'I will or shall wish to be,' &c.

बुभूषिष्यामि	बुभूषिष्यावः	बुभूषिष्यामः	बुभूषिष्ये	बुभूषिष्यावहे	बुभूषिष्यामहे
बुभूषिष्यसि	बुभूषिष्यथः	बुभूषिष्यथ	बुभूषिष्यसे	बुभूषिष्येथे	बुभूषिष्यध्वे
बुभूषिष्यति	बुभूषिष्यतः	बुभूषिष्यन्ति	बुभूषिष्यते	बुभूषिष्येते	बुभूषिष्यन्ते

Imperative, 'May I wish to be,' &c.

बुभूषाणि	बुभूषाव	बुभूषाम	बुभूषै	बुभूषावहै	बुभूषामहै
बुभूष	बुभूषतं	बुभूषत	बुभूषस्व	बुभूषेथां	बुभूषध्वं
बुभूषतु	बुभूषतां	बुभूषन्तु	बुभूषतां	बुभूषेतां	बुभूषन्तां

Potential, 'I may wish to be,' &c.

बुभूषेयं	बुभूषेव	बुभूषेम	बुभूषेय	बुभूषेवहि	बुभूषेमहि
बुभूषेः	बुभूषेतं	बुभूषेत	बुभूषेथाः	बुभूषेयाथां	बुभूषेध्वं
बुभूषेत्	बुभूषेतां	बुभूषेयुः	बुभूषेत	बुभूषेयातां	बुभूषेरन्

Benedictive, 'I pray I may wish to be,' &c.

बुभूष्यासम्	बुभूष्यास्व	बुभूष्यास्म	बुभूषिषीय	बुभूषिषीवहि	बुभूषिषीमहि
बुभूष्याः	बुभूष्यास्तं	बुभूष्यास्त	बुभूषिषीष्ठाः	बुभूषिषीयास्थां	बुभूषिषीध्वं
बुभूष्यात्	बुभूष्यास्तां	बुभूष्यासुः	बुभूषिषीष्ट	बुभूषिषीयास्तां	बुभूषिषीरन्

Conditional 'I shall wish to be, if,' &c.

अबुभूषिष्यम्	अबुभूषिष्याव	अबुभूषिष्याम	अबुभूषिष्ये	अबुभूषिष्यावहि	अबुभूषिष्यामहि
अबुभूषिष्यः	अबुभूषिष्यतं	अबुभूषिष्यत	अबुभूषिष्यथाः	अबुभूषिष्येथां	अबुभूषिष्यध्वं
अबुभूषिष्यत्	अबुभूषिष्यतां	अबुभूषिष्यन्	अबुभूषिष्यत	अबुभूषिष्येतां	अबुभूषिष्यन्त

Frequentative form of भू 'to be,' with the affix यङ्; बोभूय् 'to be repeatedly;' conjugated in the Átmane-pada only.

Present tense, 'I am repeatedly,' &c.

बोभूये	बोभूयावहे	बोभूयामहे
बोभूयसे	बोभूयेथे	बोभूयध्वे
बोभूयते	बोभूयेते	बोभूयन्ते

First præterite, 'I was frequently,' &c.

अबोभूये	अबोभूयावहि	अबोभूयामहि
अबोभूयथाः	अबोभूयेथां	अबोभूयध्वं
अबोभूयत	अबोभूयेतां	अबोभूयन्त

Second præterite, 'I have been frequently,' &c.

बोभूयाञ्चक्रे	बोभूयाञ्चकृवहे	बोभूयाञ्चकृमहे
बोभूयाञ्चकृषे	बोभूयाञ्चक्राथे	बोभूयाञ्चकृढ्वे
बोभूयाञ्चक्रे	बोभूयाञ्चक्राते	बोभूयाञ्चक्रिरे

Third præterite, 'I had been frequently,' &c.

अबोभूयिषि	अबोभूयिष्वहि	अबोभूयिष्महि
अबोभूयिष्ठाः	अबोभूयिषाथां	अबोभूयिध्वं (ढ्वं)
अबोभूयिष्ट	अबोभूयिषातां	अबोभूयिषत

First future, 'I will be frequently,' &c.

बोभूयिताहे	बोभूयितास्वहे	बोभूयितास्महे
बोभूयितासे	बोभूयितासाथे	बोभूयिताध्वे
बोभूयिता	बोभूयितारौ	बोभूयितारः

Second future, 'I will or shall be frequently,' &c.

बोभूयिष्ये	बोभूयिष्यावहे	बोभूयिष्यामहे
बोभूयिष्यसे	बोभूयिष्येथे	बोभूयिष्यध्वे
बोभूयिष्यते	बोभूयिष्येते	बोभूयिष्यन्ते

Imperative, 'May I be frequently,' &c.

बोभूयै	बोभूयावहै	बोभूयामहै
बोभूयस्व	बोभूयेथां	बोभूयध्वं
बोभूयतां	बोभूयेतां	बोभूयन्तां

Potential, 'I may be frequently,' &c.

बोभूयेय	बोभूयेवहि	बोभूयेमहि
बोभूयेथाः	बोभूयेयाथां	बोभूयेध्वं
बोभूयेत	बोभूयेयातां	बोभूयेरन्

Benedictive, 'I wish I may be frequently,' &c.

बोभूयिषीय	बोभूयिषीवहि	बोभूयिषीमहि
बोभूयिषीष्ठाः	बोभूयिषीयास्थां	बोभूयिषीध्वं (ढ्वं)
बोभूयिषीष्ट	बोभूयिषीयास्तां	बोभूयिषीरन्

Conditional, 'I will be frequently, if,' &c.

अबोभूयिष्ये	अबोभूयिष्यावहि	अबोभूयिष्यावहि
अबोभूयिष्यथाः	अबोभूयिष्येथां	अबोभूयिष्यध्वं (ढ्वं)
अबोभूयिष्यत	अबोभूयिष्येतां	अबोभूयिष्यन्त

Frequentative form of भू 'to be,' after rejecting the affix यङ् in the Parasmai-pada.

Present tense, 'I am frequently,' &c.

बोभवीमि or बोभोमि	बोभूवः	बोभूमः
बोभवीषि or बोभोषि	बोभूथः	बोभूथ
बोभवीति or बोभोति	बोभूतः	बोभुवति

First præterite, 'I was frequently,' &c.

अबोभवम्	अभोभूव	अबोभूम
अबोभवीः or अबोभोः	अबोभूतं	अबोभूत
अबोभवीत् or अबोभोत्	अबोभूतां	अबोभवुः

Second præterite, 'I have been frequently,' &c.

बोभवाञ्चकार	बोभवाञ्चकृव	बोभवाञ्चकृम &c.

or

बोभाव or बोभूव	बोभुविव or बोभूविव	बोभुविम or बोभूविम
बोभूविथ	बोभुवथुः or बोभूवथुः	बोभुव or बोभूव
बोभाव or बोभूव	बोभुवतुः or बोभूवतुः	बोभुवुः or बोभूवुः

Third præterite, 'I had been frequently,' &c.

अबोभूवम्	अबोभूव	अबोभूम
अबोभवीः or अबोभोः	अबोभूतं	अबोभूत
अबोभवीत् or अबोभोत् / अबोभूवीत् or अबोभूत्	अबोभूतां	अबोभूवुः or अबोभवुः
	or	
अबोभाविषम्	अबोभाविष्व	अबोभाविष्म
अबोभाविषीः	अबोभाविष्टं	अबोभाविष्ट
अबोभावीत्	अबोभाविष्टां	अबोभाविषुः

First future, 'I will be frequently,' &c.

बोभवितास्मि	बोभवितास्वः	बोभवितास्मः
बोभवितासि	बोभवितास्थः	बोभवितास्थ
बोभविता	बोभवितारौ	बोभवितारः

Second future, 'I will or shall be frequently,' &c.

बोभविष्यामि	बोभविष्यावः	बोभविष्यामः
बोभविष्यसि	बोभविष्यथः	बोभविष्यथ
बोभविष्यति	बोभविष्यतः	बोभविष्यन्ति

Imperative, 'May I be frequently,' &c.

बोभवानि	बोभवाव	बोभवाम
बोभूहि	बोभूतं	बोभूत
बोभवीतु or बोभोतु	बोभूतां	बोभुवतु

Potential, 'I may be frequently,' &c.

बोभूयां	बोभूयाव	बोभूयाम
बोभूयाः	बोभूयातं	बोभूयात
बोभूयात्	बोभूयातां	बोभूयुः

Benedictive, 'I wish I may be frequently,' &c.

बोभूयासं	बोभूयास्व	बोभूयास्म
बोभूयाः	बोभूयास्तं	बोभूयास्त
बोभूयात्	बोभूयास्तां	बोभूयासुः

Conditional, 'I shall be frequently, if,' &c.

अबोभविष्यम्	अबोभविष्याव	अबोभविष्याम
अबोभविष्यः	अबोभविष्यतं	अबोभविष्यत
अबोभविष्यत्	अबोभविष्यतां	अबोभविष्यन्

The conjugation of the frequentative form of the verb, after rejecting यङ्, in the Átmane-pada, is not admitted by all grammarians, and it is unnecessary therefore to exhibit it at length. The following exemplification of it in the third person singular of each tense will be sufficient.

Pres. बोभूते, 1st præt. अबोभूत, 2d præt. बोभवाञ्चक्रे, 3d præt. अबोभविष्ट, 1st fut. बोभविता, 2d fut. बोभविष्यते, imp. बोभूतां, pot. बोभवीत, bened. बोभविषीष्ट, cond. अबोभविष्यत.

These derivative forms or moods may be used also in the passive as well as in the active voice; as, भाव्यते 'it is caused to be;' बुभूष्यते 'he is desired to be;' बोभूय्यते 'he is to be frequently.' They may also take other derivative forms; as, the causal of the passive, भावयते 'he is caused to be;' the desiderative of the causal, भावयिषति 'he wishes to cause to be:' or more than one desiderative may be combined; as, बोभूययिषयति 'he causes the wish to occasion frequent existence.' These complex forms, and even the simple derivative forms, seldom occur, except the causal. The desiderative form is most frequently met with in the derivative nouns; as, जिज्ञासा 'the wish to know;' मुमूर्षु 'one who desires to die.' The frequentative is rarely used.

Impersonals.

There is another specified form of a verb, which can scarcely be considered as distinct—that of the impersonal—as it is nothing else than the third person singular of each tense of the passive form, either of the simple or derivative verb, being used with a noun in the instrumental case; as, भूयते 'it is;' मया भूयते 'it is by me,' i. e. I am; बभूवे 'it was;' भविता 'it will be;' बुभूष्यते 'it is desired to be;' बोभूयते 'it is frequently,' &c.

Nominals.

Nouns are also not unfrequently employed as verbs. Instances of this are not wanting in other languages, but not perhaps to a like extent. At the same time it is to be remarked, that the verbal form of the noun occurs only in specific inflexions, and that its conjugation in every person and tense is only theoretically allowable. The most common inflexion is that which is usually given in example of the formation of such verbs, the third person singular of the present tense, and it is that of the first conjugation. There is no peculiarity in the mode of inflexion: the modification is confined to the base, and is chiefly the insertion of काम्य, or of य called technically क्यच् or क्यङ्, between the noun and the verbal terminations.

काम्य is inserted before the terminations to imply desire; as, पुत्रकाम्यति 'he wishes for a son;' स्वःकाम्यति 'he desires heaven.'

य is more extensively employed, and in most cases with some modification of the vowel of the noun. The principal changes are the substitution of आ for अ; ई for अ and इ; ऊ for उ; and री for ऋ. A final न or स is usually rejected. The senses expressed by these forms may mostly be resolved into desire and imitative action: thus from पुत्र, 'a son,' comes पुत्रीयति, 1. 'he wishes for a son;' 2. 'he treats as a son:' राजीयति, 1. 'he wishes for a king;' 2. 'he acts like a king:' धनीयति 'he desires wealth;' धनायति 'he longs to acquire wealth:' विष्णु 'Vishńu;' विष्णूयति द्विजम् 'he treats the Brahman as if he was Vishńu:' प्रासाद 'a palace;' प्रासादीयति कुट्यां भिक्षुः 'the beggar acts or lives in his hut as if he were in a palace;' श्येन 'a kite;' श्येनायते काकः 'the crow acts like a kite:' अप्सरस् 'a nymph;' अप्सरायते 'she acts like a nymph.' A final स् is sometimes retained; as, यशस्, 'fame,' makes either यशायते or यशस्यते कापुरुषः 'the vile man acts as if he were famous.'

In some cases स is prefixed to य, implying desire; as, क्षीर 'milk;' क्षीरस्यति बालः 'the child longs for milk:' अश्व 'a horse;' अश्वस्यति वडवा 'the mare longs for the horse.'

Sometimes the augment is dropped; as, 'he acts like Krishńa' may be either कृष्णायते or कृष्णति; 'he acts like a father' may be पित्रीयति or पितरति; गल्भ 'arrogant,' गल्भते or गल्भायते 'he acts arrogantly.'

The class of words called भृशादि takes य in the Átmane-pada to imply becoming or acquiring that which the word denotes; they lengthen a final vowel before य; and optionally adopt the Parasmai-pada, rejecting the augment; as, भृश 'much,' 'many;' भृशायते, भृशति, 'becomes much:' पण्डित 'learned;' पण्डितायते, पण्डितति, 'becomes learned,' &c. The class termed लोहितादि in a similar sense may take य in either Pada, or reject it in the Parasmai-pada; as, लोहितायते, लोहितायति, or लोहितति 'becomes red,' 'reddens.'

शब्द and other words are conjugated with य, in the Átmane-pada only, to signify making; as, शब्दायते 'he makes a noise.' सुख and others are so conjugated to signify feeling or experiencing;' as, सुखायते 'he enjoys happiness;' कष्टायते 'he suffers pain.' The last also denotes, doing what will incur pain; as, कष्टायते दुर्जनः 'the wicked man commits what will bring him pain,' i. e. sin. धूम 'smoke,' उष्मन् 'heat,' फेन 'froth,' वाष्प steam,' are used exactly as in English: धूमायते 'it smokes;' उष्मायते 'it grows warm,' 'it heats;' फेनायते 'it froths' or 'foams;' वाष्पायते 'it steams.'

नमस् 'reverence,' तपस् 'penance,' वरिवस् 'service,' do not reject स before य; as, नमस्यति देवान् 'he salutes the gods;' तपस्यति तपः 'he performs penance;' वरिवस्यति गुरुं 'he serves his Guru.'

A class of words called कण्ड्वादि is conjugated with य in the sense of doing or suffering what the noun implies; as, कण्डु 'scratching,' कण्डूयति or कण्डूयते 'he scratches;' मन्तु 'sin,' मन्तूयति or मन्तूयते 'he sins;' उषस् 'dawn,' उषस्यति 'it dawns;' मही 'worship,' महीयते 'he is worshipped,' &c.

There is no apparent limit to this conversion of a noun into a verb, but the pleasure of the writer, or the practice of his predecessors. Little or no difficulty can arise from it, however, as the context will sufficiently explain the meaning of such a term, whenever it occurs in a sentence.

The general construction of the Sanskrit verb having been thus premised, we now proceed to offer paradigmas of individual verbs which are of most frequent occurrence, with such occasional remarks as they may seem to require; arranging them under the conjugation to which they severally belong, in alphabetical order. The person given is the third person of each tense in the primitive, and of the present tense in the derivative forms; with an occasional notice of other persons in the former, and other tenses in the latter. When there is no sufficient authority for the derivatives they will be omitted.

SECTION VIII.

1. *First Conjugation.*

212. The modifications of the inflectional terminations in this conjugation have been pointed out (rules 186, 187, 194, 195). Those of the inflective base arise out of the characteristic insertion of अ before the terminations beginning with consonants, and its elongation before व and म. As it is derived from the syllable शप्, which contains a mute प्, a medial or final radical vowel is changed to its Guṅa substitute, and the latter is combined with अ agreeably to the rules of Sandhi; that is, इ and ई become ए, which before a vowel is changed to अय्; उ and ऊ becomes ओ, which is also changed to अव् before अ; ऋ and ॠ are changed to अर्. Thus, as has been seen, भू, 'to be,' makes भवामि, अभवं, &c. As further exemplifications of the peculiarities of this conjugation, the following conjugational tenses of जि 'to conquer,' and एध 'to increase,' are subjoined.

जि 'to conquer.' एध 'to increase.'

Present.

I conquer, &c.			I increase, &c.		
जयामि	जयावः	जयामः	एधे	एधावहे	एधामहे
जयसि	जयथः	जयथ	एधसे	एधेथे	एधध्वे
जयति	जयतः	जयन्ति	एधते	एधेते	एधन्ते

First præterite.

I conquered, &c.			I increased, &c.		
अजयम्	अजयाव	अजयाम	ऐधे	ऐधावहि	ऐधामहि
अजयः	अजयतं	अजयत	ऐधथाः	ऐधेथां	ऐधध्वं
अजयत्	अजयतां	अजयन्	ऐधत	ऐधेतां	ऐधन्त

Imperative.

May I conquer, &c.			May I increase, &c.		
जयानि	जयाव	जयाम	एधै	एधावहै	एधामहै
जय	जयतं	जयत	एधस्व	एधेथां	एधध्वं
जयतु	जयतां	जयन्तु	एधतां	एधेतां	एधन्तां

Potential.

I may conquer, &c.			I may increase, &c.		
जयेयम्	जयेव	जयेम	एधेय	एधेवहि	एधेमहि
जयेः	जयेतं	जयेत	एधेथाः	एधेयाथां	एधेध्वं
जयेत्	जयेतां	जयेयुः	एधेत	एधेयातां	एधेरन्

a. Of the remaining tenses of जि it may be observed, that, as a monosyllable ending in a short vowel, it does not take the augment इ (rule 191, *b*). In the reduplication of the second præterite and of the desiderative it substitutes गि for जि in the radical syllable, thus:

2d præt. जिगाय (जिग्यतुः, जिग्युः, जिगेथ or जिगयिथ, जिग्यिव, &c.); 3d præt. अजैषीत् (अजैष्टां &c.); 1st fut. जेता; 2d fut. जेष्यति; bened. जीयात्; cond. अजेष्यत्. Pass. pres. जीयते; 3d præt. अजायि; 1st fut. जयिता or जायिता. Caus. pres. जापयति; 3d præt. अजीजपत्. Desid. जिगीषति. Freq. जेजीयते, and जेजेति or जेजयीति. Other verbs ending in इ will be analogously conjugated.

b. एध्, as beginning with a diphthong prosodially long, is conjugated in the second præterite with the auxiliary verbs. It takes the augment इ.

2d præt. एधाञ्चक्रे, एधाम्बभूव, एधामास; 3d præt. ऐधिष्ट; 1st fut. एधिता; 2d fut. एधिष्यते; bened. एधिषीष्ट; cond. ऐधिष्यत. Pass. एध्यते. Caus. एधयति or -ते. Desid. एदिधिषते.

The most useful verbs of this conjugation are the following.

अक (अकि) 'to mark.'

The इ which is added to the verb in the list of roots is indicatory, and denotes the insertion of a nasal before the final consonant in all the inflexions (p. 105).

Pres. अङ्कते; 1st præt. आङ्कत; 2d præt. आनङ्के; 3d præt. आङ्किष्ट; 1st fut. अङ्किता; 2d fut. अङ्किष्यते; imp. अङ्कतां; pot. अङ्केत; bened. अङ्किषीष्ट; cond. आङ्किष्यत. Pass. अंक्यते. Caus. अङ्कयति or -ते. Desid. अञ्चिकिषते.

अक्ष (अक्षू) 'to pervade.'

The indicatory ऊ shews the insertion of इ before the non-conjugational tenses to be optional (p. 106). The क of क्ष is rejected before a त and थ, with which the sibilant combines, and they become cerebrals after ष.

Pres. अक्षति; 1st præt. आक्षत्; 2d præt. आनक्ष (आनक्षिथ or आनष्ठ); 3d præt. आक्षीत्, आक्षिष्टां, आक्षिषुः, or आक्षीत्, आष्टां, आक्षुः; 1st fut. अक्षिता or अष्टा; 2d fut. अक्षिष्यति or अक्ष्यति; imp. अक्षतु; pot. अक्षेत्; bened. अक्ष्यात्; cond. आक्षिष्यत् or आक्ष्यत्. Pass. अक्ष्यते. Caus. अक्षयति; 3d præt. आचिक्षत्. Desid. अचिक्षिषति.

This is also a verb of the fifth conjugation, q. v.

अज 'to go.'

This verb is defective in the non-conjugational tenses, and its place is supplied by वी before the terminations beginning with a vowel or with य, and optionally before the rest; when वी does not, and अज does, take the augment इ.

Pres. अजति; 1st præt. आजत्; 2d præt. विवाय (विव्यतुः, विव्युः, विवयिथ, विवेथ or आजिथ, विव्यिव or आजिव, विव्यिम or आजिम); 3d præt. अवैषीत् or आजीत्; 1st fut. वेता or अजिता; 2d fut. वेष्यति or अजिष्यति; imp. अजतु; pot. अजेत्; bened. वीयात्; cond. अवेष्यत् or आजिष्यत्. Pass. वीयते. Caus. वाययति. Desid. अजिजिषति or विवीषति. Freq. वेवीयते.

अट 'to go.'

This and the next are examples of a verb regular throughout.

Pres. अटति; 1st præt. आटत्; 2d præt. आट; 3d præt. आटीत्;

1st fut. अटिता; 2d fut. अटिष्यति; imp. अटतु; pot. अटेत्; bened. अट्यात्; cond. आटिष्यत्. Pass. अट्यते. Caus. आटयति or -ते. Desid. अटिटिषति. Freq. (but meaning 'to go crookedly') अटाट्यते, आट्टि or आटीति.

अर्ह 'to be fit' or 'worthy.'

Pres. अर्हति; 1st præt. आर्हत्; 2d præt. आनर्ह; 3d præt. आर्हीत्; 1st fut. अर्हिता; 2d fut. अर्हिष्यति; imp. अर्हतु; pot. अर्हेत्; cond. आर्हिष्यत्. Pass. अर्ह्यते. Caus. अर्हयति or -ते. Desid. अर्जिहिषति. Freq. अर्हर्ह्यते.

इ 'to go.'

In the conjugational tenses इ is changed to the Guṇa element ए, which becomes अय् before the vowel अ. It does not take इ except in the 2d præt., and becomes ईय् before a vowel termination, and ए before a consonant. Its derivative forms are those of the same root conjugated as a verb of the second conjugation, in which it is most usually inflected.

Pres. अयति; 1st præt. आयत्; 2d præt. इयाय (ईयतुः, ईयुः, इययिथ or इयेथ, ईयिव, ईयिम); 3d præt. ऐषीत्; 1st fut. एता; 2d fut. एष्यति; imp. अयतु; pot. अयेत्; bened. ईयात्; cond. ऐष्यत्.

ईक्ष 'to see.'

Pres. ईक्षते; 1st præt. ऐक्षत; 2d præt. ईक्षांचकार; 3d præt. ऐक्षिष्ट; 1st fut. ईक्षिता; 2d fut. ईक्षिष्यते; imp. ईक्षतां; pot. ईक्षेत; bened. ईक्षिषीष्ट; cond. ऐक्षिष्यत. Pass. ईक्ष्यते. Caus. ईक्षयति. Desid. ईचिक्षिषते.

ईर्ष्य 'to envy.'

Pres. ईर्ष्यति; 1st præt. ऐर्ष्यत्; 2d præt. ईर्ष्यांचक्रे; 3d præt. ऐर्ष्यीत्; 1st fut. ईर्ष्यिता; 2d fut. ईर्ष्यिष्यति; imp. ईर्ष्यतु; pot. ईर्ष्येत्; bened. ईर्ष्यात्; cond. ऐर्ष्यिष्यत्. Pass. ईर्ष्यते. Caus. ईर्ष्ययति; 3d præt. ऐर्ष्यियत् or ऐर्ष्यिष्यत्. Desid. ईर्ष्यियिषति or ईर्ष्यिषिषति.

उ 'to sound.'

Pres. अवते (अवसे, अवे); 1st præt. आवत; 2d præt. ऊवे (ऊविषे);

3d præt. औष्ट; 1st fut. ओता; 2d fut. ओष्यते; imp. अवतां; pot. अवेत; bened. ओषीष्ट; cond. औष्यत. Pass. ऊयते. Caus. आवयते. Desid. ऊषिषते. Freq. अवूयते.

So other verbs ending in उ; as, कु 'to sound;' द्रु 'to go;' प्लु 'to jump,' &c.

उख 'to go.'

Pres. ओखति; 1st præt. औखत्; 2d præt. उवोख (ऊखतुः, उवोखिथ); 3d præt. औखीत्; 1st fut. ओखिता; 2d fut. ओखिष्यति; imp. ओखतु; pot. ओखेत्; bened. उख्यात्; cond. औखिष्यत्. Pass. उख्यते. Caus. ओखयति. Desid. ओचिखिषति.

ऊह 'to reason.'

Pres. ऊहते; 1st præt. औहत; 2d præt. ऊहाञ्चक्रे; 3d præt. औहिष्ट; 1st fut. ऊहिता; 2d fut. ऊहिष्यते; imp. ऊहतां; pot. ऊहेत; bened. ऊहिषीष्ट; cond. औहिष्यत. Pass. ऊह्यते. Caus. ऊहयते. Desid. ऊजिहिषते.

With a preposition it takes both Padas; as, समूहति or समूहते 'he assembles.'

ऋ 'to go,' 'to gain.'

This substitutes ऋच्छ् before the conjugational tenses. Its other changes are to the Guṅa or Vṛiddhi substitutes required by rules previously stated.

Pres. ऋच्छति; 1st præt. आर्च्छत्; 2d præt. आर (आरिथ, आरिव, आरिम); 3d præt. आर्षीत् (आर्ष्ट); 1st fut. अर्ता; 2d fut. अरिष्यति; imp. ऋच्छतु; pot. ऋच्छेत्; bened. अर्यात्; cond. आरिष्यत्. Pass. अर्यते. Caus. अर्पयति. Desid. अरिरिषति. Freq. अरार्यते, and अरर्त्ति, अरियर्त्ति, अररीति or अरियरीति.

With सम् it takes the Átmane-pada, if used intransitively; as, समृच्छते 'it collects.'

ऋज 'to be straight' or 'honest,' 'to gain,' 'to go,' 'to live.'

Pres. अर्जते; 1st præt. आर्जत; 2d præt. आनृजे; 3d præt. आर्जिष्ट; 1st fut. अर्जिता; 2d fut. अर्जिष्यते; imp. अर्जतां; pot. अर्जेत; bened. अर्जिषीष्ट; cond. आर्जिष्यत. Pass. ऋज्यते. Caus. अर्जयति; 3d præt. आर्जिजत्. Desid. अर्जिजिषते. Freq. अर्जार्ज्यते.

ओखृ 'to be dry' or 'arid.'

Pres. ओखति; 1st præt. औखत्; 2d præt. ओखाञ्चकार; 3d præt. औखीत्; 1st fut. ओखिता; 2d fut. ओखिष्यति; imp. ओखतु; pot. ओखेत्; bened. ओख्यात्; cond. औखिष्यत्. Pass. ओख्यते. Caus. ओखयति; 3d præt. औचिखत्. Desid. ओचिखिषति.

कमु 'to desire.'

This verb by special rule becomes कामय् in the conjugational tenses, and optionally so in the non-conjugational.

Pres. कामयते; 1st præt. अकामयत; 2d præt. चकमे or कामयाञ्चक्रे; 3d præt. अचीकमत or अचकमत; 1st fut. कामयिता or कमिता; 2d fut. कामयिष्यते or कमिष्यते; imp. कामयतां; pot. कामयेत; bened. कामयिषीष्ट or कमिषीष्ट; cond. अकामयिष्यत or अकमिष्यत. Pass. काम्यते; 3d præt. अकामि. Caus. कामयति. Desid. चिकामयिषते.

कित 'to cure.'

In this sense the verb is conjugated in the desiderative form only.

Pres. चिकित्सति; 1st præt. अचिकित्सत्; 2d præt. चिकित्साञ्चकार; 3d præt. अचिकित्सीत्; 1st fut. चिकित्सिता; 2d fut. चिकित्सिष्यति; imp. चिकित्सतु; pot. चिकित्सेत्; bened. चिकित्स्यात्; cond. अचि-कित्सिष्यत्.

कृपू 'to be able.'

The Anubandha ऊ renders the insertion of इ optional (p. 106); the radical vowel is changed throughout to ऌ, which becomes अल्, the Guṇa substitute of ऌ, where that substitution is required. As belonging to the class द्युतादि, it may be conjugated in the third præterite in the Parasmai-pada also. This verb may likewise be conjugated in both voices in the two future and the conditional tenses.

Pres. कल्पते; 1st præt. अकल्पत; 2d præt. चक्लृपे (चक्लृपिषे or चक्लृप्से); 3d præt. अक्लृपत् and अकल्पिष्ट or अक्लृप्त; 1st fut. कल्प्ता or कल्पिता (कल्प्तासे or कल्पितासे, and कल्प्तासि or कल्पितासि); 2nd fut. कल्प्स्यते or कल्पिष्यते, and कल्प्स्यति or कल्पिष्यति; imp. कल्पतां; pot. कल्पेत; bened. कल्पिषीष्ट or क्लृप्सीष्ट; cond. अकल्प्स्यत

or अकल्पिष्यत, and अकल्प्स्यत् or अकल्पिष्यत्. Pass. कॢप्यते. Caus. कल्पयति. Desid. चिकल्पिषते or चिकॢप्सते.

क्रम ‘to go,’ ‘to walk.’

This verb, under different circumstances, may be conjugated in either voice. In the Parasmai-pada it makes the radical vowel long in the conjugational tenses, and prefixes इ to the terminations of the rest. Not so in the A'tmane-pada. In the conjugational tenses it is also optionally conjugated in the fourth or the first class. The vowel is short in the causal, as the verb ends in म.

Pres. क्रामति or क्राम्यति, क्रमते or क्रम्यते; 1st præt. अक्रामत् or अक्राम्यत्, अक्रमत or अक्रम्यत; 2d præt. चक्राम, चक्रमे; 3d præt. अक्रमीत्, अक्रंस्त; 1st fut. क्रमिता, क्रन्ता; 2d fut. क्रमिष्यति, क्रंस्यते; imp. क्रामतु or क्राम्यतु, क्रमतां or क्रम्यतां; pot. क्रामेत् or क्राम्येत्, क्रमेत or क्रम्येत; bened. क्रम्यात्, क्रंसीष्ट; cond. अक्रमिष्यत्, अक्रंस्यत. Pass. क्रम्यते. Caus. क्रमयति; 3d præt. अचिक्रमत्. Desid. चिक्रमिषति. Freq. चंक्रम्यते, चंक्रमीति or चंक्रन्ति.

क्रुश ‘to cry.’

This does not take इ except in the second præterite. The third præterite is formed with the terminations of the first. A final palatal sibilant, not followed by a vowel or य, is changed to ष; and ष before स becomes क, which with the following sibilant forms क्ष; see rule 27.

Pres. क्रोशति; 1st præt. अक्रोशत्, 2d præt. चुक्रोश (चुक्रोशिथ, चुक्रुशतुः, चुक्रुशिव); 3d præt. अक्रुक्षत्; 1st fut. क्रोष्टा; 2d fut. क्रोक्ष्यति; imp. क्रोशतु; pot. क्रोशेत्; bened. क्रुश्यात्; cond. अक्रोक्ष्यत्. Pass. क्रुश्यते. Caus. क्रोशयति; 3d præt. अचुक्रुशत्. Desid. चुक्रुक्षति. Freq. चोक्रुश्यते, चोक्रोशीति, चोक्रोष्टि.

क्षमू ‘to bear’ or ‘be patient.’

The final म becomes न in conjunction with the व or म of a termination, and is changed to ण by virtue of the preceding ष. It becomes Anuswára before any other consonant: see rules 14, 18–22, &c.

Pres. क्षमते; 1st præt. अक्षमत; 2d præt. चक्षमे (चक्षमिषे or चक्षंसे, चक्षमिध्वे or चक्षंध्वे, चक्षमिवहे or चक्षण्वहे, चक्षमिमहे or चक्षण्महे); 3d præt. अक्षमिष्ट or अक्षंस्त; 1st fut. क्षमिता or क्षंता; 2d fut. क्षमिष्यते, क्षंस्यते; imp. क्षमतां; pot. क्षमेत; bened. क्षमिषीष्ट or क्षंसीष्ट; cond. अक्षमिष्यत or अक्षंस्यत. Pass. क्षम्यते. Caus. क्षमयति; 3d præt. अचिक्षमत. Desid. चिक्षमिषते or चिक्षंसते. Freq. चंक्षम्यते, and चंक्षमीति or चंक्षंति.

क्षि 'to waste.'

It takes इ only in the second præterite: इय् is substituted for the radical vowel before a vowel termination not requiring Guña or Vṛiddhi.

Pres. क्षयति; 1st præt. अक्षयत्; 2d præt. चिक्षाय (चिक्षियतुः, चिक्षयिथ, or चिक्षेथ, चिक्षियिव); 3d præt. अक्षैषीत्; 1st fut. क्षेता; 2d fut. क्षेष्यति; imp. क्षयतु; pot. क्षयेत्; bened. क्षीयात्; cond. अक्षेष्यत्. Pass. क्षीयते. Caus. क्षाययति or -ते. Desid. चिक्षीषति. Freq. चेक्षीयते, चेक्षयीति or चेक्षेति.

क्षै 'to waste' or 'decay.'

Verbs ending in ऐ adapt their final to the अ of the conjugational tenses, agreeably to the laws of Sandhi; that is, they change it to आय्. Before the terminations of the non-conjugational tenses they change the final to आ. Verbs ending in आ change the final to औ in the first and third persons singular of the second præterite of the Parasmai-pada, and reject it before the terminations of the same tense in either Pada beginning with a vowel, and before the augment इ. In the benedictive they change आ to ए; optionally if beginning with a conjunct consonant.

Pres. क्षायति; 1st præt. अक्षायत्; 2d præt. चक्षौ (चक्षतुः, चक्षाथ, or चक्षिथ, चक्ष, चक्षिव, चक्षिम); 3d præt. अक्षासीत्; 1st fut. क्षाता; 2d fut. क्षास्यति; imp. क्षायतु; pot. क्षायेत्; bened. क्षायात् or क्षेयात्; cond. अक्षास्यत्. Pass. क्षीयते. Caus. क्षपयति. Desid. चिक्षासति. Freq. चेक्षीयते.

So कै 'to sound,' गै 'to sing,' ग्लै 'to be weary,' दै 'to cleanse,' ध्यै 'to meditate,' रै 'to sound,' श्यै 'to melt,' षै 'to decay,' and others; as कायति, चकौ, काता; गायति, जगौ, गाता; ध्यायति, दध्यौ, ध्याता. ध्यै has but one form in the benedictive, ध्यायात्.

खन ' to dig.'

This takes both Padas. The penultimate is rejected before the terminations of the second præterite, not having a mute प, except that of the second person plural, and becomes optionally long, with rejection of न् before य.

Pres. खनति or -ते; 1st præt. अखनत्, अखनत; 2d præt. चखान (चख्नतुः, चख्नुः), चख्ने; 3d præt. अखानीत्, अखनिष्ट; 1st fut. खनिता; 2d fut. खनिष्यति or -ते; imp. खनतु, खनतां; pot. खनेत्, खनेत; bened. खन्यात् or खायात्, खनिषीष्ट; cond. अखनिष्यत्, अखनिष्यत. Pass. खन्यते or खायते. Caus. खानयति; 3d præt. अचीखनत्. Desid. चिखनिषति or -ते. Freq. चंखन्यते or चाखायते, and चंखनीति or चंखन्ति.

गमॢ ' to go.'

This verb substitutes गच्छ in the conjugational tenses. It takes इ only in the second præterite and second future. In the former the penultimate is rejected, as in the last example. The indicatory ऌ denotes the inflexion of the third præterite with the terminations of the first.

Pres. गच्छति; 1st præt. अगच्छत्; 2d præt. जगाम (जग्मतुः, जगन्थ or जगमिथ, जग्मिव); 3d præt. अगमत्; 1st fut. गन्ता; 2d fut. गमिष्यति; imp. गच्छतु; pot. गच्छेत्; bened. गम्यात्; cond. अगमिष्यत्. Pass. गम्यते. Caus. गमयति; 3d præt. अजीगमत्. Desid. जिगमिषति. Freq. जङ्गम्यते, जङ्गमीति or जङ्गन्ति.

With certain prepositions this verb may be conjugated in the Átmane-pada, as सङ्गच्छते. In this Pada the nasal of the verb is optionally rejected before the terminations of the third præterite and benedictive tenses, as संगम, 'to go together,' making समगत or समगंस्त, संगसीष्ट or संगंसीष्ट. It is inflected also in the Átmane-pada of the causal, when compounded with आ to signify delay; आगमयस्व तावत् 'wait a little:' with आ in the Parasmai-pada it means 'to come;' अत्रागच्छ 'come hither.'

गाहू 'to agitate.'

The changes of the final before a consonant are those of Sandhi (rule 32), and in some cases require the aspiration of the initial, as in declension (rule 131, *b*): ह being changed to the aspirate ढ, a following त or थ is changed (rule 186) also to ध; that again becomes also ढ, and the first ढ is rejected. The sibilant of स्त स्थास् is rejected between two consonants not being nasals or semivowels, and the त and थ are permuted to ढ as before: इ is optionally inserted.

Pres. गाहते; 1st præt. अगाहत; 2d præt. जगाहे (जघाक्षे or जगाहिषे, जघाढ्वे or जगाहिध्वे -ढ्वे); 3d præt. अगाढ (अघाक्षातां, अगाढाः, अघाढ्वं, अघाक्षि) or अगाहिष्ट (अगाहिषातां &c.); 1st fut. गाढा or गाहिता; 2d fut. घाक्ष्यते or गाहिष्यते; imp. गाहतां; pot. गाहेत; bened. घाक्षीष्ट or गाहिषीष्ट; cond. अघाक्ष्यत or अगाहिष्यत. Pass. गाह्यते. Caus. गाहयते. Desid. जगाहिषते. Freq. जागाह्यते.

गुपू 'to protect.'

This verb with a few others, as विच्छ 'to go,' and पण and पन 'to praise,' inserts आय् before the terminations of the conjugational tenses, and optionally before those of the rest. It takes इ optionally.

Pres. गोपायति; 1st præt. अगोपायत्; 2d præt. गोपायाञ्चकार or जुगोप (जुगुपतुः, जुगोपिथ, or जुगोप्थ); 3d præt. अगोपायीत्, अगोपीत्, or अगौप्सीत्; 1st fut. गोपायिता, गोपिता, गोप्ता; 2d fut. गोपायिष्यति, गोपिष्यति, गोप्स्यति; imp. गोपायतु; pot. गोपायेत्; bened. गोपाय्यात्; गुप्यात्; cond. अगोपायिष्यत्, अगोपिष्यत्, अगोप्स्यत्. Pass. गुप्यते. Caus. गोपाययति or गोपयति; 3d præt. अजुगोपायत् or अजूगुपत्. Desid. जुगोपायिषति, जुगुप्सति, जुगोपिषति. Freq. जोगुप्यते.

गुप 'to blame.'

This takes the desiderative form (see कित्), but is in other respects regular.

Pres. जुगुप्सते; 1st præt. अजुगुप्सत; 2d præt. जुगुप्साञ्चक्रे; 3d præt. अजुगुप्सिष्ट; 1st fut. जुगुप्सिता; 2d fut. जुगुप्सिष्यते; imp.

जुगुप्सतां; pot. जुगुप्सेत; bened. जुगुप्सिषीष्ट; cond. अजुगुप्सिष्यत. Pass. जुगुप्स्यते. Desid. जुगुप्सिषते.

गृहू 'to take.'

When इ is not inserted, the changes of the final are those specified under गाहृ. This is also a verb of the ninth conjugation.

Pres. गर्हते; 1st præt. अगर्हत; 2d præt. जगृहे (जगृहिषे or जघृक्षे); 3d præt. अगार्हिष्ट or अघृक्षत; 1st fut. गर्हिता or गर्ढा; 2d fut. गर्हिष्यते or घृक्ष्यते; imp. गर्हतां; pot. गर्हेत; bened. गर्हिषीष्ट or घृक्षीष्ट; cond. अगर्हिष्यत or अघर्क्ष्यत. Pass. गृह्यते. Caus. गर्हयति. Desid. जिगर्हिषते or जिघृक्षते. Freq. जरीगृह्यते, जरीगर्हीति or जरीगर्ढि.

घस्लृ 'to eat.'

In the second præterite, before the vowel terminations, this verb rejects its radical vowel, and घ in composition with स necessarily becomes क, which with the sibilant makes क्ष. Before a termination beginning with स, the final is changed to त. The verb is imperfect, and wants the third præterite and benedictive in the active voice, and all the tenses except the two futures and conditional in the passive.

Pres. घसति; 1st præt. अघसत्; 2d præt. जघास (जक्षतुः, जक्षुः); 1st fut. घस्ता; 2d fut. घत्स्यति; imp. घसतु; pot. घसेत्; bened. घस्यात्; cond. अघत्स्यत्. Pass. 1st fut. घस्ता; 2d fut. घत्स्यते; cond. अघत्स्यत.

घ्रा 'to smell.'

This in the conjugational tenses has for its base जिघ्र. In the other tenses it is unchanged. It is one of the verbs which optionally attach to the final the affixes of the first præterite in the third.

Pres. जिघ्रति; 1st præt. अजिघ्रत्; 2d præt. जघ्रौ; 3d præt. अघ्रात् or अघ्रासीत् (अघ्रातां, अघ्रास्तां, अघ्रुः, or अघ्रासुः, &c.); 1st fut. घ्राता; 2d fut. घ्रास्यति; imp. जिघ्रतु; pot. जिघ्रेत्; bened. घ्रायात् or घ्रेयात्; cond. अघ्रास्यत्. Pass. घ्रायते. Caus. घ्रापयति; 3d præt. अजिघ्रपत् or अजिघ्रिपत्. Desid. जिघ्रासति. Freq. जेघ्रीयते, and जेघ्रेति or जेघ्रयीति.

चम् 'to eat.'

As a verb having a short अ between two consonants, of which the former is repeated without change in the reduplication, it substitutes ए for the radical vowel, and is not doubled before the terminations of the second præterite, which begin with a vowel except that of the second plural.

Pres. चमति; 1st præt. अचमत्; 2d præt. चचाम (चेमतुः, चेमुः, चचमिथ, &c.); 3d præt. अचमीत्; 1st fut. चमिता; 2d fut. चमिष्यति; imp. चमतु; pot. चमेत्; bened. चम्यात्; cond. अचमिष्यत्. Pass. चम्यते. Caus. चामयति. Desid. चिचमिषति. Freq. चंचम्यते.

With आ prefixed, in the sense of sipping water, it lengthens the radical vowel, आचामति.

चर् 'to go.'

As ending in र्, the radical vowel is made long in the third præterite: rule 190, *i*. See p. 124.

Pres. चरति; 1st præt. अचरत्; 2d præt. चचार (चेरतुः); 3d præt. अचारीत्; 1st fut. चरिता; 2d fut. चरिष्यति; imp. चरतु; pot. चरेत्; bened. चर्यात्; cond. अचरिष्यत्. Pass. चर्यते. Caus. चारयति Desid. चिचरिषति. Freq. चंचूर्यते, चंचूरीति or चंचूर्त्ति.

It is conjugated in the Átmane-pada, preceded by उत् with a transitive import; धर्ममुच्चरते 'he goes beyond or transgresses duty:' and by सम् with a noun in the instrumental case; रथेन संचरते 'he travels with a chariot.'

च्युतिर् 'to drop' or 'sprinkle.'

The indicatory इर् denotes the optional inflexion of the third præterite with the affixes of the first preceded by अ.

Pres. च्योतति; 1st præt. अच्योतत्; 2d præt. चुच्योत (चुच्योतिथ, चुच्युततुः, चुच्युतिव); 3d præt. अच्युतत् or अच्योतीत्; 1st fut. च्योतिता; 2d fut. च्योतिष्यति; imp. च्योततु; pot. च्योतेत्; bened. च्युत्यात्; cond. अच्योतिष्यत्. Pass. च्युत्यते. Caus. च्योतयति or -ते; 3d præt. अचुच्युतत् or अचुच्यतत्. Desid. चुच्युतिषति or चुच्योतिषति. Freq. चोच्युत्यते or चोच्युतीति, चोच्योत्ति.

So श्च्युतिर् in the same senses. The reduplication is as in the second præterite, चुश्च्योत.

जभ 'to yawn.'

This verb prefixes न् to the final, whenever that is followed by a vowel. In the frequentative the nasal is confined to the reduplication. न before any consonant except a semivowel or a nasal becomes Anuswára, which before भ is changed to म.

Pres. जम्भते; 1st præt. अजम्भत; 2d præt. जजम्भे; 3d præt. अजम्भिष्ट; 1st fut. जम्भिता; 2d fut. जम्भिष्यते; imp. जम्भतां; pot. जम्भेत; bened. जम्भिषीष्ट; cond. अजम्भिष्यत. Pass. जभ्यते. Caus. जम्भयति. Desid. जिजम्भिषते. Freq. जंजभ्यते, जंजभीति, जंजब्धि.

जीव 'to live.'

Pres. जीवति; 1st præt. अजीवत्; 2d præt. जिजीव; 3d præt. अजीवीत्; 1st fut. जीविता; 2d fut. जीविष्यति; imp. जीवतु; pot. जीवेत्; bened. जीव्यात्; cond. अजीविष्यत्. Pass. जीव्यते. Caus. जीवयति; 3d præt. अजिजीवत् or अजीजिवत्. Desid. जिजीविषति. Freq. जेजीव्यते.

So ष्ठीव 'to spit,' and मीव or पीव 'to be fat,' &c.

जृभि 'to yawn.'

This verb inserts a nasal by virtue of the indicatory इ. In the frequentative, री is substituted for the vowel.

Pres. जृम्भते; 2d præt. जजृम्भे; 1st fut. जृम्भिता. Caus. जृम्भयति. Desid. जजृम्भिषते. Freq. जरीजृंभ्यते, जरीजृम्भीति.

ज्वर 'to have fever.'

Pres. ज्वरति; 1st præt. अज्वरत्; 2d præt. जज्वार; 3d præt. अज्वारीत्; 1st fut. ज्वरिता; 2d fut. ज्वरिष्यति; imp. ज्वरतु; pot. ज्वरेत्; bened. ज्वर्यात्; cond. अज्वरिष्यत्. Pass. ज्वर्यते. Caus. ज्वरयति; 3d præt. अजिज्वरत्. Desid. जिज्वरिषति. Freq. जाज्वर्यते, जाज्वरीति or जाजूर्ति.

त्वर, 'to hasten,' takes the Átmane-pada: it is else similarly conjugated.

ढौकृ 'to go.'

Pres. ढौकते; 1st præt. अढौकत; 2d præt. डुढौके; 3d præt. अढौकिष्ट; 1st fut. ढौकिता; 2d fut. ढौकिष्यते; imp. ढौकतां; pot.

ढौकेत; bened. ढौकिषीष्ट; cond. अढौकिष्यत. Pass. ढौक्यते. Caus. ढौकयति. Desid. डुढौकिषते. Freq. डुढौक्यते.

णम 'to bow.'

This verb takes इ only in the second and third præterites, and prefixes स to the latter; in which, यम 'to refrain,' and रम 'to sport,' agree with it.

Pres. नमति; 1st præt. अनमत्; 2d præt. ननाम (नेमतुः, नेमिथ or ननन्थ, नेमिव); 3d præt. अनंसीत् (अनंसिष्टां, अनंसिषुः); 1st fut. नन्ता; 2d fut. नंस्यति; imp. नमतु; pot. नमेत्; bened. नम्यात्; cond. अनंस्यत्. Pass. नम्यते. Caus. नमयति or नामयति. Desid. निनंसति. Freq. नंनम्यते, नंनमीति or नंनन्ति.

णी (णीञ्) 'to lead.'

The ञ intimates its being conjugated in both voices.

Pres. नयति or -ते; 1st præt. अनयत्, अनयत; 2d præt. निनाय (निनयिथ or निनेथ, निन्यतुः), निन्ये (निन्यिषे); 3d præt. अनैषीत् (अनैष्टां), अनेष्ट (अनेषातां); 1st fut. नेता; 2d fut. नेष्यति or -ते; imp. नयतु, नयतां; pot. नयेत्, नयेत; bened. नीयात्, नेषीष्ट; cond. अनेष्यत् or -ष्यत. Pass. नीयते. Caus. नाययति or -ते. Desid. निनीषति or -ते. Freq. नेनीयते, नेनयीति or नेनेति.

णी is used in the Átmane-pada in the sense of preceding or worshipping, as नयते 'he leads' or 'precedes,' 'he worships;' also after different prepositions, as उत्, उन्नयते 'he leads up' or 'raises;' उप, उपनयते 'he gives' or 'pays' or 'averts:' but if it is transitively used, it is regular, विनयति; also if it concerns part of the body, as गण्डं विनयति 'he averts or turns away the cheek.'

णिदि 'to blame.'

Pres. निन्दति; 1st præt. अनिन्दत्; 2d præt. निनिन्द; 3d præt. अनिन्दीत् (अनिन्दिष्टां); 1st fut. निन्दिता; 2d fut. निन्दिष्यति; imp. निन्दतु; pot. निन्देत्; bened. निन्द्यात्; cond. अनिन्दिष्यत्. Pass. निन्द्यते. Caus. निन्दयति. Desid. निनिन्दिषति. Freq. नेनिन्द्यते.

So may other verbs ending in द्, with an indicatory इ, as

कदि, क्रदि, 'to call;' क्लिदि 'to be moist;' नदि 'to be happy,' &c.

तिज 'to endure.'

The verb in this sense is conjugated in the desiderative form: in the sense of 'sharpen' it is a regular verb of the tenth conjugation.

Pres. तितिक्षते; 1st præt. अतितिक्षत; 2d præt. तितिक्षाञ्चक्रे; 3d præt. अतितिक्षिष्ट; 1st fut. तितिक्षिता; 2d fut. तितिक्षिष्यते; imp. तितिक्षतां; pot. तितिक्षेत; bened. तितिक्षिषीष्ट; cond. अतितिक्षिष्यत.

तॄ 'to cross over.'

The verb substitutes the Guña syllable अर् in the conjugational tenses, and changes अ to ए in the second præterite, except in the first and third persons singular. The augment इ may be made long every where except in the third præterite of the Parasmai-pada; and it may be omitted in that tense, as well as in the benedictive of the Átmane-pada. When इ is not inserted, ॠ is changed to ईर्. In some senses the verb is conjugated in both voices.

Pres. तरति or -ते; 1st præt. अतरत्, अतरत; 2d præt. ततार (तेरतुः, तेरिथ, तेर, ततार or ततर), तेरे; 3d præt. अतारीत् (अतारिष्टां)—Átmane-pada अतीर्ष्ट, अतरिष्ट or अतरीष्ट; 1st fut. तरिता or तरीता; 2d fut. तरिष्यति -ते or तरीष्यति -ते; imp. तरतु, तरतां; pot. तरेत्, तरेत; bened. तीर्य्यात्, तरिषीष्ट or तरीषीष्ट or तीर्षीष्ट; cond. अतरिष्यत् -ष्यत or अतरीष्यत् -ष्यत. Pass. तीर्य्यते. Caus. तारयति. Desid. तितरिषति, तितरीषति or तितीर्षति. Freq. तेतीर्य्यते, तातरीति or तातर्त्ति.

त्यज 'to abandon.'

The root does not take इ; and before a hard consonant the soft final palatal is changed, agreeably to rule 7, *d*, to क.

Pres. त्यजति; 1st præt. अत्यजत्; 2d præt. तत्याज (तत्यजतुः, तत्यजिथ or तत्यक्थ); 3d præt. अत्याक्षीत् (अत्याक्तां, अत्याक्षुः); 1st fut. त्यक्ता; 2d fut. त्यक्ष्यति; imp. त्यजतु; pot. त्यजेत्; bened. त्यज्यात्; cond. अत्यक्ष्यत्. Pass. त्यज्यते. Caus. त्याजयति. Desid. तित्यक्षति. Freq. तात्यज्यते, तात्यजीति or तात्यक्ति.

दद 'to give.'

This is an exception to rule 188, *k*, not substituting ए for the vowel in the second præterite.

Pres. ददते; 1st præt. अददत; 2d præt. दददे (दददाते, दददिरे); 3d præt. अददिष्ट; 1st fut. ददिता; 2d fut. ददिष्यते; imp. ददतां; pot. ददेत; bened. ददिषीष्ट; cond. अददिष्यत. Pass. दद्यते. Caus. दादयति or -ते. Desid. दिददिषते. Freq. दादद्यते, and दाददीति or दादत्ति.

दध 'to have' or 'hold.'

Pres. दधते; 1st præt. अदधत; 2d præt. देधे (देधाते, देधिरे); 3d præt. अदधिष्ट; 1st fut. दधिता; 2d fut. दधिष्यते; imp. दधतां; pot. दधेत; bened. दधिषीष्ट; cond. अदधिष्यत. Pass. दध्यते. Caus. दाधयति or -ते. Desid. दिदधिषते. Freq. दादध्यते, दादधीति or दादद्धि.

दंश 'to bite.'

This verb drops its nasal in the conjugational tenses; also before any termination beginning with य, and in the radical syllable of the frequentative. The final श before a consonant becomes ष, and ष before a sibilant becomes क (rule 27).

Pres. दशति; 1st præt. अदशत्; 2d præt. ददंश (ददंशिथ or ददंष्ठ); 3d præt. अदांक्षीत् (अदांष्टां); 1st fut. दंष्टा; 2d fut. दंक्ष्यति; imp. दशतु; pot. दशेत्; bened. दश्यात्; cond. अदंक्ष्यत्. Pass. दश्यते. Caus. दंशयति. Desid. दिदंक्षति. Freq. दंदश्यते or दंदशीति or दंदष्टि.

दह 'to burn.'

The changes of the final before a sibilant, and the concurrent change of the initial, are like those of गाह; p. 62. Before a dental the substitute of ह is घ; त or थ after an aspirate become ध; and घ as the initial of a compound is changed to ग.

Pres. दहति; 1st præt. अदहत्; 2d præt. ददाह (देहतुः, देहिथ or ददग्ध); 3d præt. अधाक्षीत् (अदाग्धां); 1st fut. दग्धा; 2d fut. धक्ष्यति; imp. दहतु; pot. दहेत्; bened. दह्यात्; cond. अधक्ष्यत्. Pass. दह्यते. Caus. दाहयति or ते. Desid. दिधक्षति. Freq. दादह्यते, दादहीति or दादग्धि.

दा (दाण्) 'to give.'

दा is also a verb of the second and third conjugation, and in order to distinguish it from them, an indicatory ण् is added to it in the first. This verb substitutes यच्छ् in the conjugational tenses. In the third præterite it takes the terminations of the first, and substitutes ए for आ in the benedictive; in which some other verbs ending in आ, either as a primitive or as substituted for a diphthong, concur: see धे and घ्रा.

Pres. यच्छति; 1st præt. अयच्छत्; 2d præt. ददौ (ददिथ or दाथ, ददतुः); 3d præt. अदात्; 1st fut. दाता; 2d fut. दास्यति; imp. यच्छतु; pot. यच्छेत्; bened. देयात्; cond. अदास्यत्. Pass. दीयते. Caus. दापयति. Desid. दित्सति. Freq. देदीयते, दादाति or दादेति.

With आ or उप prefixed in the sense of receiving, and with सम् or सम् and प्र in its own of giving, it takes the Átmanepada; as, आयच्छते 'he takes;' संयच्छते or संप्रयच्छते 'he gives.'

द्रु 'to run.'

Pres. द्रवति; 1st præt. अद्रवत्; 2d præt. दुद्राव (दुद्रुवतुः, दुद्रविथ or दुद्रोथ); 3d præt. अद्रावीत्, अद्रौषीत्; 1st fut. द्रोता; 2d fut. द्रोष्यति; imp. द्रवतु; pot. द्रवेत्; bened. द्रूयात्; cond. अद्रोष्यत्. Pass. द्रूयते. Caus. द्रावयति. Desid. दुद्रूषति. Freq. दोद्रूयते, दोद्रवीति or दोद्रोति.

दृश (दृशिर्) 'to see.'

This is another verb of the first conjugation inflected by a substitution, as it takes पश्य् before the conjugational tenses. Before the terminations of the other tenses beginning with any consonant except य, ऋ is changed to र. The changes of the sibilant are as usual. इर् indicates two forms of the third præterite (p. 106).

Pres. पश्यति; 1st præt. अपश्यत्; 2d præt. ददर्श (ददृशतुः, ददर्शिथ or दद्रष्ठ); 3d præt. अदर्शत् or अद्राक्षीत्; 1st fut. द्रष्टा; 2d fut. द्रक्ष्यति; imp. पश्यतु; pot. पश्येत्; bened. दृश्यात्; cond. अद्रक्ष्यत्. Pass. दृश्यते. Caus. दर्शयति; 3d præt. अदीदृशत् or अददर्शत्. Desid. दिदृक्षते. Freq. दरीदृश्यते or दरीदृशीति or दर्दर्ष्टि.

With सम् prefixed in an intransitive sense it takes the Átmane-pada; सम्पश्यते 'he contemplates.'

दे (देङ्) 'to protect.'

The ङ denotes its being restricted to the Átmane-pada. In the conjugational tenses it is regularly inflected, ए becoming अय् before अ. In the second præterite it substitutes दिगि for the reduplicate; and in the third, इ for the final; after which the स of स्त and स्यास् is rejected. In the rest it is conjugated like verbs in आ.

Pres. दयते; 1st præt. अदयत; 2d præt. दिग्ये (दिग्याते, दिग्यिषे); 3d præt. अदित (अदिषातां, अदिषत, अदिथाः, अदिषि); 1st fut. दाता; 2d fut. दास्यते; imp. दयतां; pot. दयेत; bened. दासीष्ट; cond. अदास्यत. Pass. दीयते. Caus. दापयति. Desid. दित्सते. Freq. देदीयते, दादेति.

द्युत 'to shine.'

This gives name to a class of verbs, द्युतादि, of which the third præterite takes two forms; one being that of the first præterite of the Parasmai-pada, without change of the radical vowel; the other being regular. There are in all twenty-two verbs of this class.

क्लृप to be able.	लुट, लुठ to resist.
क्षुभ to agitate.	वृत to be.
घुट to exchange.	वृध to grow.
णभ to hurt.	शुभ to be beautiful.
तुभ to hurt.	शृध to break wind.
द्युत to shine.	श्वित to be white.
ध्वंस, भ्रंस to fall down.	ष्विद to sweat.
मिद to be unctuous.	स्यन्द to drop.
रुच to shine.	स्रंभ to trust in.
रुट to resist.	स्रंस to fall down.

Several of these will be found in their places.

Pres. द्योतते; 1st præt. अद्योतत; 2d præt. दिद्युते; 3d præt. अद्युतत् or अद्योतिष्ट; 1st fut. द्योतिता; 2d fut. द्योतिष्यते; imp. द्योततां; pot. द्योतेत; bened. द्योतिषीष्ट; cond. अद्योतिष्यत. Pass. द्युत्यते. Caus. द्योतयति. Desid. दिद्युतिषते or दिद्योतिषते. Freq. देद्युत्यते, देद्युतीति or देद्योत्ति.

द्रु 'to run.'

This is one of the few exceptions to the insertion of इ in the second præterite: rule 188, *s*.

Pres. द्रवति; 1st præt. अद्रवत्; 2d præt. दुद्राव (दुद्रुवतुः, दुद्रोथ); 3d præt. अदुद्रुवत्; 1st fut. द्रोता; 2d fut. द्रोष्यति; imp. द्रवतु; pot. द्रवेत्; bened. द्रूयात्; cond. अद्रोष्यत्. Pass. द्रूयते. Caus. द्रावयति; 3d præt. अदुद्रवत् or अदिद्रवत्. Desid. दुद्रूषति. Freq. दोद्रूयते, दोद्रवीति or दोद्रोति.

So ध्रु 'to be firm.'

धे 'to drink.'

Before the conjugational tenses धे becomes धय्; before the rest it is inflected like a verb in आ; but it has three forms in the third præterite: see दा 'to give,' दे 'to protect,' &c.

Pres. धयति; 1st præt. अधयत्; 2d præt. दधौ (दधतुः, दधिथ); 3d præt. अदधत् (अदधतां, अदधन्), or अधात् (अधातां, अधुः), or अधासीत् (अधासिष्टां, अधासिषुः); 1st fut. धाता; 2d fut. धास्यति; imp. धयतु; pot. धयेत्; bened. धेयात्; cond. अधास्यत्. Pass. धीयते. Caus. धापयति or -ते; 3d præt. अदीधपत् or -पत. Desid. धित्सति. Freq. देधीयते, दाधेति or दाधाति.

धोर्ऋ 'to be quick,' 'to gallop.'

The ऋ in every case becomes र.

Pres. धोरति; 1st præt. अधोरत्; 2d præt. दुधोर; 3d præt. अधोरीत्; 1st fut. धोरिता; 2d fut. धोरिष्यति; imp. धोरतु; pot. धोरेत्; bened. धोर्य्यात्; cond. अधोरिष्यत्. Pass. धोर्य्यते. Caus. धोरयति; 3d præt. अदुधोरत्. Desid. दुधोरिषति. Freq. दुधोर्य्यते, दुधोरीति or दधोर्त्ति.

ध्मा 'to blow,' as fire or an instrument.

This verb substitutes धम् before the conjugational augment.

Pres. ध्मति; 1st præt. अधमत्; 2d præt. दध्मौ; 3d præt. अध्मासीत्; 1st fut. ध्माता; 2d fut. ध्मास्यति; imp. धमतु; pot. धमेत्; bened. ध्मेयात् or ध्मायात्; cond. अध्मास्यत्. Pass. ध्मायते. Caus. ध्मापयति. Desid. दिध्मासते. Freq. देध्मीयते, दाध्मेति or दाध्माति.

पच ‘to cook.’

A final palatal, as च् or ज्, becomes क्, when not followed by any other letter, and before a termination beginning with any consonant except a semivowel or a nasal, and combines with it according to the rules of Sandhi. The vowel is changed to ए in the persons of the second præterite not having an indicatory प्. In the third præterite the स preceding स्तां &c. is rejected, and the radical vowel is made long in the Parasmai-pada only. The verb takes both Padas.

Pres. पचति -ते; 1st præt. अपचत्, अपचत; 2d præt. पपाच, पेचे; 3d præt. अपाक्षीत् (अपाक्तां, अपाक्षुः), अपक्त (अपक्षातां, अपक्षत); 1st fut. पक्ता; 2d fut. पक्ष्यति -ते; imp. पचतु -तां; pot. पचेत् -त; bened. पच्यात्, पक्षीष्ट; cond. अपक्ष्यत् -त. Pass. पच्यते. Caus. पाचयति -ते; 3d præt. अपीपचत्. Desid. पिपक्षति -ते. Freq. पापच्यते, पापचीति or पापक्ति.

पत (पतॢ) ‘to go.’

The indicatory ॡ denotes the inflexion of the third præterite with the terminations of the first, and before them प् is prefixed to the radical final. In the desiderative the vowel may be changed to इ; and in the frequentative, नी is added to the reduplicate syllable.

Pres. पतति; 1st præt. अपतत्; 2d præt. पपात; 3d præt. अपप्तत्; 1st fut. पतिता; 2d fut. पतिष्यति; imp. पततु; pot. पतेत्; bened. पत्यात्; cond. अपतिष्यत्. Pass. पत्यते. Caus. पातयति. Desid. पिपतिषति or पित्सति. Freq. पनीपत्यते, पनीपतीति or पनीपत्ति.

पा ‘to drink.’

This verb substitutes पिब् before the conjugational अ; in the other tenses it agrees with other verbs in आ.

Pres. पिबति; 1st præt. अपिबत्; 2d præt. पपौ; 3d præt.

अपात्; 1st fut. पाता; 2d fut. पास्यति; imp. पिबतु; pot. पिबेत्; bened. पेयात्; cond. अपास्यत. Pass. पीयते. Caus. पाययति -ते. Desid. पिपासति. Freq. पेपीयते, पापेति or पापाति.

पा, 'to preserve,' is a verb of the second conjugation, q. v.

(ओ) प्यायी 'to grow.'

In the third person singular of the third præterite this verb optionally substitutes इ for त.

Pres. प्यायते; 1st præt. अप्यायत; 2d præt. पिप्ये (पिप्यिषे); 3d præt. अप्यायि or अप्यायिष्ट; 1st fut. प्यायिता; 2d fut. प्यायिष्यते; imp. प्यायतां; pot. प्यायेत; bened. प्यायिषीष्ट; cond. अप्यायिष्यत. Pass. प्याय्यते. Caus. प्याययते.

फण 'to approach.'

As this verb changes its फ to प in the reduplication of the second præterite, it should not substitute ए for अ (r. 188, *k*); it does so optionally by special rule.

Pres. फणति; 1st præt. अफणत्; 2d præt. पफाण (पफणतुः or फेणतुः, पफणिथ or फेणिथ, &c.); 3d præt. अफणीत् or अफाणीत्; 1st fut. फणिता; 2d fut. फणिष्यति; imp. फणतु; pot. फणेत्; bened. फण्यात्; cond. अफणिष्यत्. Pass. फण्यते. Caus. फणयति. Desid. पिफणिषति. Freq. पंफण्यते, पंफणीति or पंफण्टि.

फल 'to bear fruit.'

This differs from the preceding only in the change of अ to ए in the second præterite being absolute, and the vowel being long only, in the third præterite, as the verb ends in ल. In the frequentative the radical vowel is changed to उ.

Pres. फलति; 1st præt. अफलत्; 2d præt. पफाल (फेलतुः); 3d præt. अफालीत्; 1st fut. फलिता; 2d fut. फलिष्यति; imp. फलतु; pot. फलेत्; bened. फल्यात्; cond. अफलिष्यत्. Pass. फल्यते. Caus. फालयति. Desid. पिफलिषति. Freq. पंफुल्यते, पंफुलीति or पंफुल्ति.

बध 'to despise;' 'to bind.'

This takes the frequentative form.

Pres. बीभत्सते; 1st præt. अबीभत्सत; 2d præt. बीभत्साञ्चक्रे; 3d præt. अबीभत्सिष्ट; 1st fut. बीभत्सिता; 2d fut. बीभत्सिष्यते; imp. बीभत्सतां; pot. बीभत्सेत; bened. बीभत्सिषीष्ट; cond. अबीभत्सिष्यत. Pass. बीभत्स्यते. Caus. बीभत्सयते.

बुध, or with इर्, बुधिर् 'to know.'

There is some difference as to whether these are distinct roots or not. With इर् there are two forms in the third præterite (see p. 106); without it, only one. The causal of बुध also is restricted to the Parasmai-pada. There is another verb बुध, 'to know,' of the fourth conjugation, which also substitutes इ for the third person singular of the third præterite in the Átmane-pada. They are both inflected like other verbs with a medial उ, except in the desiderative, which does not insert इ, and changes the radical consonant to भ.

Pres. बोधति -ते; 1st præt. अबोधत् - त; 2d præt. बुबोध, बुबुधे; 3d præt. (of बुध) अबोधीत्, (of बुधिर्) अबोधीत् or अबुधत्, अबोधिष्ट; 1st fut. बोधिता; 2d fut. बोधिष्यति -ते; imp. बोधतु, बोधतां; pot. बोधेत् -त; bened. बुध्यात्, बोधिषीष्ट; cond. अबोधिष्यत् -त. Pass. बुध्यते. Caus. बोधयति or (बुधिर्) बोधयति -ते. Desid. बुभुत्सति. Freq. बोबुध्यते, बोबुधीति, बोबोद्धि.

भृञ् 'to nourish.'

It takes both Padas. Before a य, ऋ becomes रि or री. In the third præterite, Átmane-pada, the स of स्त is rejected after a short vowel. In the desiderative, उ is optionally substituted for the radical vowel, being preceded by a labial.

Pres. भरति -ते; 1st præt. अभरत् -त; 2d præt. बभार (बभ्रतुः, बभर्थ, बभृव), बभ्रे; 3d præt. अभार्षीत्, अभृत (अभृषातां); 1st fut. भर्ता; 2d fut. भरिष्यति -ते; imp. भरतु -तां; pot. भरेत् -त; bened. भ्रियात्, भृषीष्ट; cond. अभरिष्यत् -त. Pass. भ्रियते. Caus. भारयति; 3d præt. अबीभरत्. Desid. बिभरिषति -ते or बुभूर्षति -ते. Freq. बेभ्रीयते, बर्भर्ति, बरिभर्ति or बरीभर्ति.

धृञ् 'to hold,' and हृञ् 'to take,' are similarly inflected.

भ्रम 'to wander' or 'whirl.'

This verb optionally takes the form of the fourth conjugation.

Pres. भ्रमति, भ्राम्यति; 1st præt. अभ्रमत्, अभ्राम्यत्; 2d præt. बभ्राम (भ्रेमतुः); 3d præt. अभ्रमीत्; 1st fut. भ्रमिता; 2d fut. भ्रमिष्यति; imp. भ्रमतु, भ्राम्यतु; pot. भ्रमेत्, भ्राम्येत्; bened. भ्रम्यात्; cond. अभ्रमिष्यत्. Pass. भ्रम्यते. Caus. भ्रमयति; 3d præt. अबिभ्रमत्. Desid. बिभ्रमिषति. Freq. बंभ्रम्यते, बंभ्रमीति or बंभ्रन्ति.

मन्थ 'to churn.'

The nasal is rejected before a य.

Pres. मन्थति; 1st præt. अमन्थत्; 2d præt. ममन्थ (ममन्थिथ); 3d præt. अमन्थीत्; 1st fut. मन्थिता; 2d fut. मन्थिष्यति; imp. मन्थतु; pot. मन्थेत्; bened. मथ्यात्; cond. अमन्थिष्यत्. Pass. मथ्यते. Caus. मन्थयति -ते. Desid. मिमन्थिषति. Freq. मामथ्यते, मामन्थीति or मामंत्ति.

मव्य 'to bind.'

There is nothing peculiar in the simple inflexion of this verb. Before a य the final is optionally rejected; and in the frequentative form, which rejects य, its conjunct final may be rejected altogether before a termination beginning with a consonant not a nasal, and having an indicatory प्; whilst before any other consonant य is rejected, and व changed to ऊ, which then substitutes the Vṛiddhi element औ.

Pres. मव्यति; 3d præt. अमव्यीत्; 1st fut. मव्यिता; bened. मव्यात् or मव्य्यात्. Pass. मव्यते or मव्य्यते. Desid. मामव्यिषति.

Frequentative, present tense.

मामव्यीमि or मामौमि	मामौवः	मामौमः
मामव्यीषि or मामसि	मामौथः	मामौथ
मामव्यीति or मामति	मामौतः	मामव्यति

These modifications are rather curious than useful, as the verb is of unfrequent occurrence.

मान 'to investigate.'

This verb takes the form of the desiderative, मीमांस्.

Pres. मीमांसते; 1st præt. अमीमांसत; 2d præt. मीमांसाञ्चक्रे; 3d præt. अमीमांसिष्ट; 1st fut. मीमांसिता; 2d fut. मीमांसिष्यते; imp. मीमांसतां; pot. मीमांसेत; bened. मीमांसिषीष्ट; cond. अमीमांसिष्यत. Pass. मीमांस्यते. Caus. मीमांसयते.

मे (मेङ्) 'to barter.'

The final diphthong becomes अय् before vowels, and आ before consonants: it is changed to इत् in the desiderative.

Pres. मयते; 1st præt. अमयत; 2d præt. ममे; 3d præt. अमास्त; 1st fut. माता; 2d fut. मास्यते; imp. मयतां; pot. मयेत; bened. मासीष्ट; cond. अमास्यत. Pass. मीयते. Caus. मापयते. Desid. मित्सते. Freq. मेमीयते, मेमयीति, मामेति or मामाति.

म्ना 'to remember.'

This substitutes मन् in the conjugational tenses.

Pres. मनति; 1st præt. अमनत्; 2d præt. मम्नौ; 3d præt. अम्नासीत्; 1st fut. म्नाता; 2d fut. म्नास्यति; imp. मनतु; pot. मनेत्; bened. म्नायात् or म्नेयात्; cond. अम्नास्यत्. Pass. म्नायते. Caus. म्नापयति; 3d præt. अमिम्नपत्. Desid. मिम्नासति. Freq. मामम्नायते, माम्नाति or माम्नेति.

यज 'to worship.'

इ is substituted for the semivowel before the terminations of the second præterite, except in the singular of the Parasmaipada, where it is the letter of reduplication. It is substituted for य before य. यज is one of those verbs which change ज to ष before त and थ, and to क before a sibilant, analogously to their derivatives when nouns (see Declension, rules 92, 93).

Pres. यजति -ते; 1st præt. अयजत् -त; 2d præt. इयाज (ईजतुः, इयजिथ or इयष्ठ, ईजिव), ईजे; 3d præt. अयाक्षीत्, अयष्ट (अयक्षातां); 1st fut. यष्टा; 2d fut. यक्ष्यति -ते; imp. यजतु -तां; pot. यजेत् -त; bened. इज्यात्, यक्षीष्ट; cond. अयक्ष्यत् -त. Pass. इज्यते; 1st præt. ऐज्यत. Caus. याजयति -ते; 3d præt. अयीयजत्. Desid. यियक्षति -ते. Freq. यायज्यते, यायष्टि.

यत 'to make effort.'

This is in every respect regular.

Pres. यतते ; 1st præt. अयतत ; 2d præt. येते ; 3d præt. अयतिष्ट ; 1st fut. यतिता ; 2d fut. यतिष्यते ; imp. यतताम् ; pot. यतेत ; bened. यतिषीष्ट ; cond. अयतिष्यत. Pass. यत्यते. Caus. यातयति -ते ; 3d præt. अयीयतत्. Desid. यियतिषते. Freq. यायत्यते, यायतीति or यायत्ति.

यम ' to restrain.'

This substitutes च्छ for its final before the terminations of the conjugational tenses. Although it does not take इ in the futures, it does in the second and third præterites.

Pres. यच्छति ; 1st præt. अयच्छत् ; 2d præt. ययाम (येमिथ or ययंथ) ; 3d præt. अयंसीत् (अयंसिष्टां) ; 1st fut. यन्ता ; 2d fut. यंस्यति ; imp. यच्छतु ; pot. यच्छेत् ; bened. यम्यात् ; cond. अयंस्यत्. Pass. यम्यते. Caus. यामयति or यमयति. Desid. यियंसति. Freq. यंयम्यते, यंयमीति or यंयन्ति.

यम is conjugated in the Átmane-pada when preceded by आ in an intransitive sense ; as, आयच्छते तरुः ' the tree spreads :' by उप in the sense of marrying ; रामः सीतामुपायंस्त ' Ráma married Sítá :' also by आ or उद् or सम्, signifying to heap together for one's own use ; व्रीहीन् संयच्छते ' he heaps up the rice.'

रञ्ज ' to colour.'

This drops its nasal whenever अ is inserted before the terminations and before य. Before consonants ज becomes क.

Pres. रजति -ते ; 1st præt. अरजत् -त ; 2d præt. रराज (ररंक्थ or ररंजिथ, ररंजतुः), ररंजे ; 3d præt. अरांक्षीत् (अरांक्तां), अरंक्त (अरंक्षातां) ; 1st fut. रंक्ता ; 2d fut. रंक्ष्यति -ते ; imp. रजतु -तां ; pot. रजेत् -त ; bened. रज्यात्, रंक्षीष्ट ; cond. अरंक्ष्यत् -त. Pass. रज्यते. Caus. रंजयति or रजयति. Desid. रिरंजिषति -ते. Freq. रारज्यते, रारजीति.

रभ ' to commence.'

This verb is invariably conjugated with the preposition आ. The final is changed before a consonant, agreeably to the laws of Sandhi. Before a vowel, except in the conjugational tenses and second præterite, न् is inserted, which becomes Anuswára, and then again म् before भ, as in the causal. In the desiderative, इ is substituted for the vowel, and the root is not repeated.

Pres. आरभते; 1st præt. आरभत; 2d præt. आरेभे (आरेभाते, आरेभिरे); 3d præt. आरब्ध (आरप्साताम्); 1st fut. आरब्धा; 2d fut. आरप्स्यते; imp. आरभताम्; pot. आरभेत; bened. आरप्सीष्ट; cond. आरप्स्यत. Pass. आरभ्यते. Caus. आरम्भयति; 3d præt. आररम्भत्. Desid. आरिप्सते. Freq. आरारभ्यते, आरारम्भीति, आरारब्धि.

With exception of prefixing आ, लभ 'to gain' is similarly inflected. Pres. लभते; 2d præt. लेभे; 3d præt. अलब्ध; 2d fut. लप्स्यते. Caus. लम्भयति. Desid. लिप्सते, &c.

रम 'to sport.'

It is conjugated analogously to other verbs ending with म.

Pres. रमते; 1st præt. अरमत; 2d præt. रेमे; 3d præt. अरंस्त; 1st fut. रन्ता; 2d fut. रंस्यते; imp. रमताम्; pot. रमेत; bened. रंसीष्ट; cond. अरंस्यत. Pass. रम्यते. Caus. रमयति; 3d præt. अरीरमत्. Desid. रिरंसते. Freq. रंरम्यते, रंरमीति or रंरन्ति.

विरम, 'to rest,' makes विरमति; but when it means 'to lead a married life,' विरमति or विरमते.

रुह 'to grow' or 'ascend.'

For the changes to which a final ह is subject, see गाह (p. 162). In the causal the verb optionally substitutes प for य.

Pres. रोहति; 1st præt. अरोहत्; 2d præt. रुरोह (रुरुहतुः, रुरोहिथ); 3d præt. अरुक्षत् (अरुक्षताम्); 1st fut. रोढा; 2d fut. रोक्ष्यति; imp. रोहतु; pot. रोहेत्; bened. रुह्यात्; cond. अरोक्ष्यत्. Pass. रुह्यते. Caus. रोहयति or रोपयति; 3d præt. अरूरुहत् or अरूरुपत्. Desid. रुरुक्षति. Freq. रोरुह्यते, रोरुहीति or रोरोढि.

लोच (लोचृ) 'to see.'

Pres. लोचते; 1st præt. अलोचत; 2d præt. लुलोचे; 3d præt. अलोचिष्ट; 1st fut. लोचिता; 2d fut. लोचिष्यते; imp. लोचताम्; pot. लोचेत; bened. लोचिषीष्ट; cond. अलोचिष्यत. Pass. लोच्यते. Caus. लोचयति. Desid. लुलोचिषते. Freq. लोलोच्यते, लोलोचीति or लोलोक्ति.

लोकृ, 'to see,' is similarly inflected.

वद 'to speak.'

This and the following substitute उ for the semivowel in the second præterite and before य.

Pres. वदति; 1st præt. अवदत्; 2d præt. उवाद (ऊदतुः, उवदिथ, ऊद, उवद or उवाद, ऊदिम); 3d præt. अवादीत्; 1st fut. वदिता; 2nd fut. वदिष्यति; imp. वदतु; pot. वदेत्; bened. उद्यात्; cond. अवदिष्यत्. Pass. उद्यते. Caus. वादयति; 3d præt. अवीवदत्. Desid. विवदिषति. Freq. वावद्यते, वावदीति or वावत्ति.

It is sometimes inflected in the A'tmane-pada, especially after certain prepositions, and in particular applications; as, अनुवद 'to repeat,' अनुवदते; अपवद 'to reproach (oneself),' अपवदते; विवद 'to dispute,' विवदते; सम्प्रवद 'to repeat together,' सम्प्रवदते.

वप 'to weave.'

Pres. वपति -ते; 1st præt. अवपत् -त; 2d præt. उवाप (उवप्थ or उवपिथ, ऊपतुः), ऊपे; 3d præt. अवाप्सीत्, अवप्त; 1st fut. वप्ता; 2d fut. वप्स्यति -ते; imp. वपतु -तां; pot. वपेत् -त; bened. उप्यात्, वप्सीष्ट; cond. अवप्स्यत् -त. Pass. उप्यते. Caus. वापयति -ते. Desid. विवप्सति -ते. Freq. वावप्यते, वावपीति or वावप्ति.

वस 'to dwell.'

त is substituted for the final before a sibilant immediately following it, and not conjoined with त.

Pres. वसति; 1st præt. अवसत्; 2d præt. उवास (उवसिथ or उवस्थ, ऊषतुः); 3d præt. अवात्सीत् (अवात्तां, अवात्सुः); 1st fut. वस्ता; 2d fut. वत्स्यति; imp. वसतु; pot. वसेत्; bened. उष्यात्; cond. अवत्स्यत्. Pass. उष्यते. Caus. वासयति -ते. Desid. विवत्सति. Freq. वावस्यते, वावसीति, वावस्ति.

वह 'to bear.'

The changes of ह before a following consonant are those already noticed (see गाह &c.); but whenever ह is changed to ढ, this verb substitutes ओ for its vowel.

Pres. वहति -ते; 1st præt. अवहत् -त; 2d præt. उवाह (ऊहतुः, उवहिथ or उवोढ), ऊहे; 3d præt. अवाक्षीत् (अवोढां, अवाक्षुः) अवोढ; imp. वहतु -तां; pot. वहेत् -त; bened. उह्यात्, वक्षीष्ट; cond.

अवक्ष्यत् -त. Pass. उह्यते; 1st præt. औह्यत; 3d præt. अवाहि. Caus. वाहयति -ते. Desid. विवक्षति -ते. Freq. वावह्यते, वावोढि.

Preceded by प्र or परि the verb is conjugated in the Parasmai-pada only; as, प्रवहति, परिवहति.

वृक 'to accept.'

Pres. वर्कते; 1st præt. अवर्कत; 2d præt. ववृके; 3d præt. अवर्किष्ट; 1st fut. वर्किता; 2d fut. वर्किष्यते; imp. वर्कतां; pot. वर्केत; bened. वर्किषीष्ट; cond. अवर्किष्यत. Pass. वृक्यते. Caus. वर्कयति; 3d præt. अववर्कत् or अवीवृकत्. Desid. विवर्किषते. Freq. वरीवृक्यते, वरिवर्क्ति, वरीवर्क्ति or वर्वर्क्ति, वर्वृकीति, वरिवृकीति or वरीवृकीति (see rule 206, *a*).

वृत 'to be.'

This is peculiar in optionally inflecting the second future and conditional in the Parasmai-pada, and rejecting the augment इ before their terminations and those of the desiderative. As one of the class द्युतादि, it has two forms in the third præterite: see p. 169.

Pres. वर्तते; 1st præt. अवर्तत; 2d præt. ववृते (ववृताते, ववृतिषे); 3d præt. अवृतत् or अवर्तिष्ट; 1st fut. वर्तिता; 2d fut. वर्तिष्यते or वर्त्स्यति; imp. वर्ततां; pot. वर्तेत; bened. वर्तिषीष्ट; cond. अवर्तिष्यत or अवृत्स्यत्. Pass. वृत्यते. Caus. वर्तयति. Desid. विवर्तिषते or विवृत्सति. Freq. वरीवृत्यते, वरिवृतीति or वरिवर्त्ति, or वरीवृतीति, &c. as in the last.

वे (वेञ्) 'to weave.'

The final becomes आ before the consonants of the non-conjugational tenses. In the second præterite there are two forms; in one the reduplicated root is उवे before the terminations rejecting प्, and ऊय् or ऊव् before the rest; in the other the substitute is ववे, and ए being changed to आ, as in धे &c., the tense is inflected accordingly: see दा.

Pres. वयति -ते; 1st præt. अवयत् -त; 2d præt. उवाय (ऊवतुः, ऊवुः, उवयिथ, उवाय or उवय, ऊविव, ऊविम) or ववौ (ववतुः, ववुः), ऊये (ऊयाते, ऊयिरे); 3d præt. अवासीत् (अवासिष्टां), अवास्त; 1st fut. वाता; 2d fut. वास्यति -ते; imp. वयतु -तां; pot. वयेत् -त; bened.

जयात्, वासीष्ट; cond. अवास्यत् -त. Pass. जयते. Caus. वाययति -ते. Desid. विवासति -ते. Freq. वावायते, वावाति or वावेति.

व्ये 'to cover.'

The initial is not changed. The verb as usual is inflected as if ending in आ in the non-conjugational tenses, except in the singular of the second præterite of the Parasmai-pada: in the reduplication य becomes इ. Before a य, व्ये is changed to वी.

Pres. व्ययति -ते; 1st præt. अव्ययत् -त; 2d præt. विव्याय (विव्यतुः, विव्युः), विव्ये; 3d præt. अव्यासीत्, अव्यास्त; 1st fut. व्याता; 2d fut. व्यास्यति -ते; imp. व्ययतु -तां; pot. व्ययेत् -त; bened. वीयात्, व्यासीष्ट; cond. अव्यास्यत् -त. Pass. वीयते. Caus. व्याययति. Desid. विव्यासति -ते. Freq. वेवीयते, वेवयीति, वेवेत्ति.

शद (शद्ऌ) 'to wither' or 'decay;' 'to go.'

This substitutes शीय् before the terminations of the conjugational tenses, which are those of the Átmane-pada. Those of the other tenses are the terminations of the Parasmai-pada.

Pres. शीयते; 1st præt. अशीयत; 2d præt. शशाद (शेदतुः); 3d præt. अशदत्; 1st fut. शत्ता; 2d fut. शत्स्यति; imp. शीयतां; pot. शीयेत; bened. शद्यात्; cond. अशत्स्यत्. Pass. शीयते. Caus. शातयति. Desid. शिशत्सति. Freq. शाशद्यते, शाशदीति or शाशत्ति.

When the verb means 'to go,' the causal retains the final, शादयति 'he causes to go,' or 'drives.'

शंसि 'to desire;' 'to bless.'

This is never used without आ prefixed.

Pres. आशंसते; 1st præt. आशंसत; 2d præt. आशशंसे; 3d præt. आशंसिष्ट; 1st fut. आशंसिता; 2d fut. शंसिष्यते; imp. आशंसतां; pot. आशंसेत; bened. आशंसिषीष्ट; cond. आशंसिष्यत. Pass. आशंस्यते. Caus. आशंसयति. Desid. आशिशंसिषते. Freq. आशाशंस्यते, आशाशंसीति or आशाशंस्ति.

The root शंस, 'to praise,' differs from this in being inflected in the Parasmai-pada, and as its nasal is not derived from an indicatory इ, in dropping it before य; as, pres. शंसति; bened. शस्यात्; pass. शस्यते, &c.

शीकृ 'to sprinkle.'

Pres. शीकते; 1st præt. अशीकत; 2d præt. शिशीके; 3d præt. अशीकिष्ट; 1st fut. शीकिता; 2d fut. शीकिष्यते; imp. शीकतां; pot. शीकेत; bened. शीकिषीष्ट; cond. अशीकिष्यत. Pass. शीक्यते. Caus. शीकयति -ते; 3d præt. अशीशिकत् -त. Desid. शिशीकिषते. Freq. शेशीक्यते, शेशीकीति or शेशीक्ति.

शुच 'to sorrow.'

Before the sign of the desiderative, a radical medial इ or उ, when the final is neither य, व, nor ह, is optionally changed to the Guña vowel when the augment इ is inserted.

Pres. शोचति; 1st præt. अशोचत्; 2d præt. शुशोच (शुशुचतुः); 3d præt. अशोचीत्; 1st fut. शोचिता; 2d fut. शोचिष्यति; imp. शोचतु; pot. शोचेत्; bened. शुच्यात्; cond. अशोचिष्यत्. Pass. शुच्यते. Caus. शोचयति -ते. Desid. शुशुचिषति or शुशोचिषति. Freq. शोशुच्यते, शोशुचीति or शोशोक्ति.

So शुभ 'to shine;' except that, as belonging to द्युतादि (p. 169), it makes in the third præterite अशुभत् or अशोभीत्.

श्रि (श्रिञ्) 'to serve.'

This verb, as indicated by the Anubandha ञ, takes both forms. Before a vowel termination not requiring the Guña or Vṛiddhi change of the final, इय् is substituted for it. In the third præterite of the Parasmai-pada it takes the terminations of the first, with reduplication: and in the frequentative form it optionally rejects the augment इ, which augment it takes as an exception to the general rule, 191, *b*.

Pres. श्रयति -ते; 1st præt. अश्रयत् -त; 2d præt. शिश्राय (शिश्रियतुः, शिश्रयिथ, शिश्रियिव), शिश्रिये; 3d præt. अशिश्रियत् -त; 1st fut. श्रयिता; 2d fut. श्रयिष्यति -ते; imp. श्रयतु, श्रयतां; pot. श्रयेत् -त; bened. श्रीयात्, श्रयिषीष्ट; cond. अश्रयिष्यत् -त. Pass. श्रीयते. Caus. श्राययति -ते; 3d præt. अशिश्रयत् -त. Desid. शिश्रयिषति -ते or शिश्रीषति -ते. Freq. शेश्रीयते, शेश्रयीति or शेश्रेति.

श्रु 'to hear.'

This changes the vowel to शृ, and adds नु, the proper termination of the fifth conjugation, in the conjugational tenses. उ before a vowel becomes व by the rules of Sandhi; or before व and म it may be ejected. In the second præterite, even थप् does not insert इ (rule 188, *s*). In the third præterite of the causal, इ is optionally substituted in the reduplication.

Pres. शृणोति (शृणुतः, शृण्वन्ति, शृणुवः or शृण्वः, शृणुमः or शृण्मः); 1st præt. अशृणोत् (अशृणुतां, अशृण्वन्); 2d præt. शुश्राव (शुश्रुवतुः, शुश्रोथ); 3d præt. अश्रौषीत् (अश्रौष्टां, अश्रौषुः); 1st fut. श्रोता; 2d fut. श्रोष्यति; imp. शृणोतु (शृणुतां, शृण्वन्तु); pot. शृणुयात्; bened. श्रूयात्; cond. अश्रोष्यत्. Caus. श्रावयति; 3d præt. अशुश्रवत् or अशिश्रवत्. Desid. शुश्रूषते. Freq. शोश्रूयते, शोश्रवीति, शोश्रोति.

The verb is conjugated in the Átmane-pada preceded by सम् with an intransitive sense, संशृणुते 'he hears:' otherwise, as, वाक्यं संशृणोति 'he hears the speech.' Preceded by प्रति or आङ् it retains the Parasmai-pada in the desiderative form, आशुश्रूषति or प्रतिशुश्रूषति 'he serves or attends upon.'

श्वि (ओश्वि) 'to increase.'

This verb optionally substitutes उ for वि in the second præterite; absolutely before the य of the benedictive and the passive; and optionally before the य of the frequentative. In the third præterite it has three forms; being conjugated with its own terminations and the augment इ, or with those of the first præterite with or without reduplication: in the latter case it rejects its own final.

Pres. श्वयति; 1st præt. अश्वयत्; 2d præt. शिश्वाय (शिश्वियतुः शिश्वयिथ) or शुशाव (शुशुवतुः, शुशविथ, शुशव or शुशाव); 3d præt. अश्वयीत् (अश्वयिष्टां), अशिश्वियत् (अशिश्वियतां) or अश्वत् (अश्वतां); 1st fut. श्वयिता; 2d fut. श्वयिष्यति; imp. श्वयतु; pot. श्वयेत्; bened. शूयात्; cond. अश्वयिष्यत्. Pass. शूयते. Caus. श्वाययति; 3d præt. अशिश्वत् or अशूशवत्. Desid. शिश्वयिषति. Freq. शेश्वीयते or शोशूयते, शेश्वयीति or शेश्वेति.

षञ्ज 'to embrace.'

This root rejects its nasal before the terminations of the conjugational tenses.

Pres. सजति; 1st præt. असजत्; 2d præt. ससञ्ज (ससञ्जिथ or ससंक्थ); 3d præt. असांक्षीत् (असांक्तां); 1st fut. संक्ता; 2d fut. संक्ष्यति; imp. सजतु; pot. सजेत्; bened. सज्यात्; cond. असंक्ष्यत्. Pass. सज्यते. Caus. संजयति. Desid. सिसंक्षति. Freq. सनीसज्यते, सासञ्जीति or सासंक्ति.

षद (षद्लृ) 'to decay,' 'to be sad,' 'to go.'

This substitutes सीद् before the terminations of the conjugational tenses.

Pres. सीदति; 1st præt. असीदत्; 2d præt. ससाद (सेदतुः, ससत्थ or सेदिथ); 3d præt. असदत् (असदतां); 1st fut. सत्ता; 2d fut. सत्स्यति; imp. सीदतु; pot. सीदेत्; bened. सद्यात्; cond. असत्स्यत्. Pass. सद्यते. Caus. सादयति; 3d præt. असीषदत्. Desid. सिषत्सति. Freq. सासद्यते, सासदीति or सासत्ति.

With नि prefixed, the initial becomes ष, as निषीदति 'he sits;' and this is repeated in the reduplication of the desiderative, as निषिषत्सति, and third præterite causal, as न्यषीषदत्; the sibilant following in fact इ and ई; otherwise it is not changed, as, 2d præt. निषसाद; nor is it changed after the इ of प्रति, as प्रतिसीदति 'he opposes.'

षस्ज 'to go.'

This verb changes स to ज throughout.

Pres. सज्जति -ते; 1st præt. असज्जत् -त; 2d præt. ससज्ज, ससज्जे; 3d præt. असज्जीत्, असज्जिष्ट; 1st fut. सज्जिता; 2d fut. सज्जिष्यति -ते; imp. सज्जतु -तां; pot. सज्जेत् -त; bened. सज्ज्यात्, सज्जिषीष्ट; cond. असज्जिष्यत् -त. Pass. सज्ज्यते. Caus. सज्जयति -ते. Desid. सिसज्जिषति -ते. Freq. सासज्ज्यते, सासज्जीति, सासक्ति.

षह 'to bear,' 'to suffer.'

This verb takes the augment इ, but optionally rejects it before the terminations of the first future: for the change that ensues, see गाह, वह, &c. In the desiderative the initial sibilant is not changed after a vowel in the reduplicate syllable, because such change does not take place when the स, which is the sign of the desiderative itself, is changed to ष in consequence of the augment इ preceding it.

Pres. सहते; 1st præt. असहत; 2d præt. सेहे; 3d præt. असहिष्ट; 1st fut. सहिता or सोढा; 2d fut. सहिष्यते; imp. सहतां; pot. सहेत; bened. सहिषीष्ट; cond. असहिष्यत. Pass. सह्यते. Caus. सहयति; 3d præt. असीषहत्. Desid. सिसहिषते. Freq. सासह्यते, सासहीति or सासोढि.

The initial is changed to ष after the इ of नि, परि, and वि, as निषहते; if the temporal augment intervene, the change is optional, as न्यसहत or न्यषहत; it does not take place when ह has been changed to ढ, as निषहिता or निसोढा.

षिध (षिधू) 'to accomplish.'

Pres. सेधति; 1st præt. असेधत्; 2d præt. सिषेध (सिषिधतुः, सिषेधिथ or सिषेद्ध); 3d præt. असेधीत् (असेधिष्टां) or असैत्सीत् (असैद्धां, असैत्सुः); 1st fut. सेधिता or सेद्धा; 2d fut. सेधिष्यति or सेत्स्यति; imp. सेधतु; pot. सेधेत्; bened. सिध्यात्; cond. असेधिष्यत् or असेत्स्यत्. Pass. सिध्यते. Caus. सेधयति; 3d præt. असीषिधत्. Desid. सिषिधिषति or सिषित्सति. Freq. सेषिध्यते, सेषिधीति or सेषेद्धि.

There is also a verb षिध, 'to go,' which is without the Anubandha ऊ, and which therefore inserts the augment इ invariably; as, सिषेधिथ, सेधिता, असेधीत्, &c. The initial स of either verb is not changed after the इ of a preposition, except नि, when meaning prohibition; as, निषेधति 'he forbids.'

षु 'to bear children.'

This takes इ optionally in the third præterite.

Pres. सवति; 1st præt. असवत्; 2d præt. सुषाव (सुषुवतुः, सुषविथ or सुषोथ); 3d præt. असौषीत् or असावीत्; 1st fut. सोता; 2d fut. सोष्यति; imp. सवतु; pot. सवेत्; bened. सूयात्; cond. असोष्यत्. Pass. सूयते. Caus. सावयति. Desid. सुसूषति. Freq. सोसूयते, सोषवीति or सोषोति.

The same root is also inflected in the second and fifth classes.

षूद 'to hurt' or 'kill.'

Pres. सूदते; 1st præt. असूदत; 2d præt. सुषूदे; 3d præt. असूदिष्ट; 1st fut. सूदिता; 2d fut. सूदिष्यते; imp. सूदतां; pot. सूदेत; bened. सूदिषीष्ट; cond. असूदिष्यत. Pass. सूद्यते. Caus. सूदयति -ते; 3d præt. असुषूदत् -त. Desid. सुसूदिषते. Freq. सोषूद्यते, सोषूदीति, सोषूत्ति.

षेव (षेवृ) 'to serve.'

The reduplication of ए is इ (rule 188, *i*).

Pres. सेवते; 1st præt. असेवत; 2d præt. सिषेवे; 3d præt. असेविष्ट; 1st fut. सेविता; 2d fut. सेविष्यते; imp. सेवतां; pot. सेवेत; bened. सेविषीष्ट; cond. असेविष्यत. Pass. सेव्यते. Caus. सेवयति; 3d præt. असिषेवत्. Desid. सिसेविषते. Freq. सेषेव्यते, सेषेवीति, सेषेत्ति.

So similar, but less frequent roots, गेवृ, पेवृ, मेवृ, &c. meaning also 'to serve' or 'gratify by service.'

ष्टभि 'to stop' or 'hinder.'

The sibilant being changed, the following letter also becomes a dental.

Pres. स्तम्भते; 1st præt. अस्तम्भत; 2d præt. तस्तम्भे; 3d præt. अस्तम्भिष्ट; 1st fut. स्तम्भिता; 2d fut. स्तम्भिष्यते; imp. स्तम्भतां; pot. स्तम्भेत; bened. स्तम्भिषीष्ट; cond. अस्तम्भिष्यत. Pass. स्तम्भ्यते. Desid. तिस्तम्भिषते. Freq. तास्तम्भ्यते, तास्तम्भीति or तास्तंभ्मि.

ष्ठा 'to stand' or 'stay.'

This verb substitutes तिष्ठ् before the terminations of the conjugational tenses. Although properly conjugated in the Parasmai-pada, yet in various senses, or after certain prepositions, it may take the Átmane-pada also. Before य the आ becomes ए or ई. In the third præterite the verb takes the terminations of the first; and in the Átmane-pada changes its vowel to इ. In the causal form it inserts प.

Pres. तिष्ठति -ते; 1st præt. अतिष्ठत् -त; 2d præt. तस्थौ, तस्थे; 3d præt. अस्थात्, अस्थित (अस्थिषातां); 1st fut. स्थाता; 2d fut. स्थास्यति -ते; imp. तिष्ठतु -तां; pot. तिष्ठेत् -त; bened. स्थेयात्, स्थासीष्ट; cond.

अस्थास्यत् -त. Pass. स्थीयते. Caus. स्थापयति -ते; 3d præt. अतिष्ठिपत् -त. Desid. तिष्ठासति. Freq. तेष्ठीयते, तास्थेति or तास्थाति.

ष्ठा is used in the Átmane-pada to signify 'to appeal to' or 'rely on;' also with the prepositions सम्, अव, प्र, and वि; also with आ, meaning 'to affirm;' with उद्, except it mean 'to stand up' or 'rise;' and with उप, if the sense be intransitive, or it mean 'to praise' or 'worship,' or 'to have a regard for,' &c.

ष्ठिव 'to spit.'

The vowel becomes long in the conjugational tenses: the initial sibilant is unchanged. In the reduplication त is substituted for the cerebral optionally in the second præterite. The desiderative optionally commutes the final semivowel to ऊ.

Pres. ष्ठीवति; 1st præt. अष्ठीवत्; 2d præt. तिष्ठेव or टिष्ठेव (तिष्ठिवतुः or टिष्ठिवतुः); 3d præt. अष्ठेवीत्; 1st fut. ष्ठेविता; 2d fut. ष्ठेविष्यति; imp. ष्ठीवतु; pot. ष्ठीवेत्; bened. ष्ठीव्यात्; cond. अष्ठेविष्यत्. Pass. ष्ठीव्यते. Caus. ष्ठेवयति. Desid. तिष्ठीविषति or तुष्ठ्यूषति. Freq. तेष्ठीव्यते, तेष्ठीवीति.

ष्मि (ष्मिङ) 'to smile.'

Pres. स्मयते; 1st præt. अस्मयत; 2d præt. सिष्मिये; 3d præt. अस्मेष्ट; 1st fut. स्मेता; 2d fut. स्मेष्यते; imp. स्मयतां; pot. स्मयेत; bened. स्मेषीष्ट; cond. अस्मेष्यत. Pass. स्मीयते. Caus. स्माययति -ते. Desid. सिस्मयिषते. Freq. सेष्मीयते, सेष्मयीति, सेष्मेति.

With वि prefixed, and in the causal form, it makes विस्मापयति 'he or it astonishes;' that is, the object itself astonishes: when the object differs, the Parasmai-pada is used, either in the regular form, or with प substituted for य; as, सा रूपेण तं विस्माययति or विस्मापयति 'she astonishes him by her form.'

ष्विद (ञिष्विदा) 'to melt,' 'to perspire.'

The verb belongs to the class द्युतादि; see p. 170.

Pres. स्वेदते; 1st præt. अस्वेदत; 2d præt. सिष्विदे; 3d præt. अस्वेदिष्ट or अस्विदत्; 1st fut. स्वेदिता; 2d fut. स्वेदिष्यते; imp. स्वेदतां; pot. स्वेदेत; bened. स्वेदिषीष्ट; cond. अस्वेदिष्यत. Pass. स्विद्यते. Caus. स्वेदयति -ते. Desid. सिस्वेदिषते. Freq. सेष्विद्यते, सेष्विदीति or सेष्वेत्ति.

सृ 'to go.'

When it means 'to go quickly' or 'to run,' धौ is optionally substituted for the root before the conjugational tenses (i. e. a different, but imperfect root, धौ or धाव् is also admissible in these tenses). For other particulars, see the analogous roots ह्व, भृ.

Pres. सरति, धावति; 1st præt. असरत्, अधावत्; 2d præt. ससार (सस्रुः); 3d præt. असार्षीत् or असरत्; 1st fut. सर्ता; 2d fut. सरिष्यति; imp. सरतु, धावतु; pot. सरेत्, धावेत्; bened. स्रियात्; cond. असरिष्यत्. Pass. स्रियते. Caus. सारयति -ते. Desid. सिसीर्षति. Freq. सेस्रीयते, सरीसरीति, सरीसर्त्ति or सर्सर्त्ति.

सृप (सृपॢ) 'to go,' 'to creep' or 'glide.'

The medial may be changed to र in the two futures and conditional. It is also optional to double the final after a conjunct र; as, सर्प्पति &c.

Pres. सर्पति; 1st præt. असर्पत्; 2d præt. ससर्प; 3d præt. असृपत् (असृपतां); 1st fut. स्रप्ता or सर्प्ता; 2d fut. स्रप्स्यति or सर्प्स्यति; imp. सर्पतु; pot. सर्पेत्; bened. सृप्यात्; cond. अस्रप्स्यत्. Pass. सृप्यते. Caus. सर्पयति -ते. Desid. सिसृप्सति. Freq. सरीसृप्यते, सरीसृपीति or सरीसर्प्ति.

स्कन्द (स्कन्दिर) 'to go' or 'approach.'

The nasal is rejected before य, and in one form of the third præterite: in the frequentative, नी is added to the reduplicated syllable.

Pres. स्कन्दति; 1st præt. अस्कन्दत्; 2d præt. चस्कन्द (चस्कन्दिथ or चस्कंत्थ); 3d præt. अस्कदत् (अस्कदतां), अस्कांसीत् (अस्कांत्तां, अस्कांत्सुः); 1st fut. स्कंत्ता; 2d fut. स्कंत्स्यति; imp. स्कन्दतु; pot. स्कन्देत्; bened. स्कद्यात्; cond. अस्कंत्स्यत्. Pass. स्कद्यते. Caus. स्कन्दयति -ते. Desid. चिस्कंत्सति. Freq. चनीस्कद्यते, चनीस्कन्दीति or चनीस्कंत्ति.

स्पर्द्ध 'to envy' or 'emulate.'

Pres. स्पर्द्धते; 1st præt. अस्पर्द्धत; 2d præt. पस्पर्द्धे; 3d præt. अस्पर्द्धिष्ट; 1st fut. स्पर्द्धिता; 2d fut. स्पर्द्धिष्यते; imp. स्पर्द्धतां; pot. स्पर्द्धेत; bened. स्पर्द्धिषीष्ट; cond. अस्पर्द्धिष्यत. Pass. स्पर्द्ध्यते.

Caus. स्पर्द्धयति -ते. Desid. पिस्पर्द्धिषते. Freq. पास्पर्द्ध्यते, पास्पर्द्धीति or पास्पर्द्धि.

स्फाय (स्फायी) 'to increase.'

In the causal the final is changed to व.

Pres. स्फायते; 1st præt. अस्फायत; 2d præt. पस्फाये; 3d præt. अस्फायिष्ट; 1st fut. स्फायिता; 2d fut. स्फायिष्यते; imp. स्फायतां; pot. स्फायेत; bened. स्फायिषीष्ट; cond. अस्फायिष्यत. Pass. स्फाय्यते. Caus. स्फावयति; 3d præt. अपिस्फवत्. Desid. पिस्फायिषते. Freq. पास्फाय्यते, पास्फायीति, पास्फाति.

स्मृ 'to remember.'

Pres. स्मरति -ते; 1st præt. अस्मरत् -त; 2d præt. सस्मार, सस्मरे; 3d præt. अस्मार्षीत्, अस्मृत; 1st fut. स्मर्त्ता; 2d fut. स्मरिष्यति -ते; imp. स्मरतु -तां; pot. स्मरेत् -त; bened. स्मर्य्यात्, स्मृषीष्ट; cond. अस्मरिष्यत् -त. Pass. स्मर्य्यते. Caus. स्मारयति -ते. Desid. सुस्मूर्षते. Freq. सास्मर्य्यते, सास्मरीति, सास्मर्त्ति.

स्यन्द (स्यन्दू) 'to ooze' or 'drop.'

This belongs to the class द्युतादि (p. 170). For the effect of ऊ, see p. 106. The second future and conditional are optionally conjugated in the Parasmai-pada, and so is the desiderative: see वृत and क्लृप.

Pres. स्यन्दते; 1st præt. अस्यन्दत; 2d præt. सस्यन्दे (सस्यन्दिषे or सस्यंत्से, सस्यन्दिवहे or सस्यंद्वहे); 3d præt. अस्यदत (अस्यदतां), अस्यन्दिष्ट or अस्यंत्त (अस्यन्दिषातां or अस्यंत्सातां); 1st fut. स्यन्दिता or स्यंत्ता; 2d fut. स्यन्दिष्यति -ते, स्यंत्स्यति -ते; imp. स्यन्दतां; pot. स्यन्देत; bened. स्यन्दिषीष्ट or स्यंत्सीष्ट; cond. अस्यन्दिष्यत् -त, अस्यंत्स्यत् -त. Pass. स्यद्यते. Desid. सिस्यन्दिषते and सिस्यंत्सति -ते. Freq. सास्यद्यते, सास्यन्दीति or सास्यंत्ति.

स्रंस (स्रंसु) 'to fall down.'

This verb also belongs to the class द्युतादि.

Pres. स्रंसते; 1st præt. अस्रंसत; 2d præt. सस्रंसे; 3d præt. अस्रसत् or अस्रंसिष्ट; 1st fut. स्रंसिता; 2d fut. स्रंसिष्यते; imp. स्रंसतां; pot. स्रंसेत; bened. स्रंसिषीष्ट; cond. अस्रंसिष्यत. Pass. स्रस्यते. Caus.

स्रंसयति -ते. Desid. सिस्रंसिषते. Freq. सनीस्रंस्यते, सनीस्रंसीति or सनीस्रंस्ति.

ध्वंसु and भ्रंसु, 'to fall down,' are similarly inflected.

स्रु 'to drop.'

This is one of the exceptions to the insertion of इ in the second person singular of the second præterite (p. 121). The root takes both the augment and reduplication in the third præterite.

Pres. स्रवति; 1st præt. अस्रवत्; 2d præt. सुस्राव (सुस्रोथ, सुस्रुव); 3d præt. असुस्रुवत्; 1st fut. स्रोता; 2d fut. स्रोष्यति; imp. स्रवतु; pot. स्रवेत्; bened. स्रूयात्; cond. अस्रोष्यत्. Pass. स्रूयते. Caus. स्रावयति; 3d præt. असुस्रवत् or असिस्रवत्. Desid. सुस्रूषति. Freq. सोस्रूयते, सोस्रवीति, सोस्रोति.

हृ (हृञ्) 'to take.'

Pres. हरति -ते; 1st præt. अहरत् -त; 2d præt. जहार (जह्रतुः, जहर्थ), जह्रे; 3d præt. अहार्षीत्, अहृत; 1st fut. हर्ता; 2d fut. हरिष्यति -ते; imp. हरतु -तां; pot. हरेत् -त; bened. ह्रियात्, हृषीष्ट; cond. अहरिष्यत् -त. Pass. ह्रियते. Caus. हारयति -ते. Desid. जिहीर्षति -ते. Freq. जेह्रियते, जर्हरीति, जरी- or जरिहरीति, or जरी- or जरिहर्त्ति.

ह्लाद 'to be or make glad.'

Pres. ह्लादते; 1st præt. अह्लादत; 2d præt. जह्लादे; 3d præt. अह्लादिष्ट; 1st fut. ह्लादिता; 2d fut. ह्लादिष्यते; imp. ह्लादतां; pot. ह्लादेत; bened. ह्लादिषीष्ट; cond. अह्लादिष्यत. Pass. ह्लाद्यते. Caus. ह्लादयति -ते. Desid. जिह्लादिषते. Freq. जाह्लाद्यते, जाह्लादीति or जाह्लात्ति.

स्वाद 'to taste,' and ह्राद 'to sound,' are similarly inflected.

ह्वे (ह्वेञ्) 'to call.'

When the root is doubled, or before य, the semivowel and following diphthong are changed to उ. The third præterite takes the terminations of the first in the Parasmai-pada, and optionally in the Átmane-pada. In the passive, the third præterite, second future, and conditional, optionally insert इ.

Pres. ह्वयति -ते; 1st præt. अह्वयत् -त; 2d præt. जुहाव (जुहुवतुः,

जुहविथ or जुहोथ), जुहुवे; 3d præt. अह्वत् (अह्वतां), अह्वत (अह्वेतां) or अह्वास्त (अह्वासातां); 1st fut. ह्वाता; 2d fut. ह्वास्यति -ते; imp. ह्वयतु -तां; pot. ह्वयेत् -त; bened. हूयात्, ह्वासीष्ट; cond. अह्वास्यत् -त. Pass. हूयते; 3d præt. अह्वायि, अह्वायिष्ट, अह्वत or अह्वास्त; 2d fut. ह्वास्यते or ह्वायिष्यते; cond. अह्वास्यत or अह्वायिष्यत. Caus. ह्वाययति; 3d præt. अजूहवत्. Desid. जुहूषति -ते. Freq. जोहूयते, जोहवीति, जोहोति.

Second Conjugation.

213. The characteristic peculiarity of this conjugation is the attachment of the inflectional terminations of the conjugational tenses immediately to the termination of the base, without the interposition of any vowel (rule 170, *a.* 2).

a. There is but one general change of the terminations; हि in the second persons of the imperative is changed to धि after any consonant except a nasal, semivowel, or ह. It is said, indeed, that the terminations of the first and second persons of the first præterite, त् and स् left by तिप् and सिप् (p. 114), are rejected after an inflective base ending in a consonant; but this arises from a general rule not restricted to conjugational inflexion. A conjunct consonant, when final, loses the second member of the compound (rule 35): therefore हन 'to kill,' 1st præt., making in the first instance अहन्त्, अहन्स्, must become अहन्, rejecting the finals त् and स्. The same in other verbs ending in consonants, of whatever conjugation.

b. The changes of the vowels of the base are analogous to those of the first conjugation, before the terminations having an indicatory प्. A final इ or ई is in general changed to ए; उ and ऊ to ओ; and ऋ ॠ to अर्. An initial or medial short vowel is similarly changed before the same. A long vowel is unaltered. Other changes are special, or follow the general rules of Sandhi.

c. Final consonants are combined with the terminations agreeably to the laws of Sandhi, or to special rules, or to rules affecting all similar combinations in whatever conjugation.

Some of these have been noticed under individual verbs of the first conjugation; but it may be useful to collect them in this place, as they particularly apply to the conjugational tenses of verbs of the second and third conjugations.

1. Final consonants are unaltered before a nasal, a semivowel, or ह, except by special rule.

2. A final palatal before other consonants, or when not followed by any letter, is changed to क, which before a soft consonant becomes ग (rule 7, *c*), and makes with a sibilant, क्ष (rule 27).

3. A final द or ध may be changed optionally to र in the second person singular of the first præterite; and र final becomes Visarga.

4. A final श or छ is changed to ष before any consonant except a nasal, &c., as above.

5. A final ष is unchanged before त or थ, but they become the cerebrals ट and ठ in conjunction with it (rule 12). ष before स is converted into क्ष (rule 27). Before धि and ध्व, ष is changed to ट; and after ट, ध becomes ढ (rule 12); when ड takes the place of the hard consonant ट (rule 7, *c*).

6. A final स is changed to द before any soft consonant except a nasal, &c., as above; and to त before a sibilant, except in the present tense and imperative mood. Before सि and से it is sometimes retained, sometimes rejected: it is usually rejected before स्त; it is also sometimes rejected before धि, else it is changed to द.

7. A final क्ष rejects क, and leaves ष final before any consonant except a nasal, semivowel, or ह.

8. A final ह before any consonant except a nasal, &c. is changed to घ, if the verb begin with द followed by any vowel except ऋ; if it begin with ह, or with any other consonant, ह final becomes ढ; except in णह, when it becomes ध: some verbs, as मुह, take both. After an aspirate, त and थ become ध (rule 186), when other modifications occur, which, although previously noticed, may be repeated. Thus ष and ढ become क

before a sibilant, and क forms with it क्ष (rule 29, 32): घ becomes ग, and ढ, ड, before any soft consonant (rule 7, *b*): ष after ट becomes ठ (rule 12); and when ट is repeated in a conjunct, one ट is rejected. The initial of a root ending in an aspirate, being ग, ड, द, or ब, is changed to its corresponding aspirate, घ, ढ, ध, or भ, when its final is followed by स or ध्व, or by no other letter.

d. This conjugation includes a class of five verbs, called रुदादि or रुद 'to weep,' स्वप 'to sleep,' श्वस 'to breathe,' अन 'to breathe,' जक्ष 'to eat,' which form a partial exception to the non-interposition of a vowel between the base and inflectional termination, as they insert इ before any consonant except य, and अ or ई if the termination consists of a single consonant, as in the second and third persons singular of the first præterite.

e. Another class, termed जक्षादि, is also included in this conjugation, the verbs of which are termed अभ्यस्त or 'reduplicated;' they are, जक्ष 'to eat,' जागृ 'to wake,' दरिद्रा 'to be poor,' चकास 'to shine,' शास 'to govern,' दीधी 'to shine,' and वेवी 'to obtain.' These cause the nasal of the terminations of the third person plural of the present and imperative to be rejected, as also of the same person of the first præterite, Átmane-pada; and उस् to be substituted for अन् in the same person of the Parasmai-pada.

The verb which is given as a model of this conjugation, अद 'to eat,' is inflected in its simple form in the Parasmai-pada only; but in composition with some prepositions, as with वि and अति, it may be conjugated in the Átmane-pada, as व्यत्यत्ते 'he eats much reciprocally.' It may therefore be exhibited in both forms, omitting the prefixes of the compound verb for the present, for the sake of comparison. The final of अद् becomes त् before a hard or surd consonant (rule 7, *d*): अ is inserted by special rule before the terminations of the second and third persons singular of the first præterite, Parasmai-pada. The nasal of the third person plural in the present, first præterite, and imperative of the Átmane-pada is rejected.

अद् 'to eat.'

Present tense, 'I eat,' &c.

Parasmai-pada.			Átmane-pada.		
अद्मि	अद्वः	अद्मः	अदे	अद्वहे	अद्महे
अत्सि	अत्थः	अत्थ	अत्से	अदाथे	अद्ध्वे
अत्ति	अत्तः	अदन्ति	अत्ते	अदाते	अदते

First præterite, 'I ate' or 'have eaten,' &c.

आदम्	आद्व	आद्म	आदि	आद्वहि	आद्महि
आदः	आत्तं	आत्त	आत्थाः	आदाथां	आद्ध्वं
आदत्	आत्तां	आदन्	आत्त	आदातां	आदत

Imperative, 'May I eat,' &c.

अदानि	अदाव	अदाम	अदै	अदावहै	अदामहै
अद्धि	अत्तं	अत्त	अत्स्व	अदाथां	अद्ध्वं
अत्तु	अत्तां	अदन्तु	अत्तां	अदातां	अदतां

Potential, 'I may eat,' &c.

अद्याम्	अद्याव	अद्याम	अदीय	अदीवहि	अदीमहि
अद्याः	अद्यातं	अद्यात	अदीथाः	अदीयाथां	अदीध्वं
अद्यात्	अद्यातां	अद्युः	अदीत	अदीयातां	अदीरन्

Of the remaining tenses it is only to be remarked, that the second præterite is optionally borrowed from घस (see p. 163); and the third præterite and desiderative mode are formed with the same verb. अद् does not insert इ (p. 127), except in the second præterite.

2d præt. जघास or आद (आदतुः, आदुः), जक्षे or आदे; 3d præt. अघसत् -त; 1st fut. अत्ता; 2d fut. अत्स्यति -ते; bened. अद्यात्, अत्सीष्ट; cond. आत्स्यत् -त. Pass. अद्यते. Caus. आदयति -ते; 3d præt. आदिदत् -त. Desid. जिघत्सति.

For the remaining verbs of this conjugation, selected as most useful or remarkable, the paradigmas, as in the first conjugation, with occasional observations, will be sufficient.

अन 'to breathe.'

This is one of the class रुदादि; see rule 213, *d*.

Pres. अनिति (अनितः, अनन्ति); 1st præt. आनत् or आनीत् (आनितां, आनन्); 2d præt. आन (आनतुः, आनुः); 3d præt. आनीत् (आनिष्टां, आनिषुः); 1st fut. अनिता; 2d fut. अनिष्यति; imp. अनितु; pot. अन्यात् (अन्यातां); bened. अन्यात् (अन्यास्तां); cond. आनिष्यत्. Pass. अन्यते. Caus. आनयति. Desid. अनिनिषति.

The न of this verb becomes ण after a preposition giving cause for it, even in both syllables of a reduplication; as, प्राणिति 'he breathes' or 'lives,' प्राणिणिषति 'he desires to live.'

अस 'to be.'

This auxiliary verb admits of the four conjugational tenses only, except in composition, when it has a fifth tense, the second præterite (p. 121). The other tenses are supplied by भू 'to be' (p. 132). Before those terminations which do not require a change in the radical vowel of a verb, the initial of अस is rejected: the final is rejected before a termination beginning with स. In the first præterite, the second and third persons singular are borrowed from a defective third præterite, prefixing ई to the terminations. The second person singular of the imperative substitutes ए for the root, and हि is changed to धि. Like some other verbs, अस takes the A'tmane-pada, compounded with prepositions, in a reciprocal sense; as, व्यतस (व्यतस्ते) 'to be mutually.' In this Pada ह is substituted for the root in the first person singular, present tense: स is changed to द before ध. As this verb is useful, the inflexions may be exhibited in detail, omitting the prepositions of the A'tmane-pada.

Present tense, 'I am,' &c.

Parasmai-pada.			A'tmane-pada.		
अस्मि	स्वः	स्मः	हे	स्वहे	स्महे
असि	स्थः	स्थ	से	साथे	द्धे
अस्ति	स्तः	सन्ति	स्ते	साते	सते

First præterite, 'I was,' &c.

आसम्	आस्व	आस्म	आसि	आस्वहि	आस्महि
आसीः	आस्तं	आस्त	आस्थाः	आसाथां	आध्वं
आसीत्	आस्तां	आसन्	आस्त	आसातां	आसत

Imperative, 'May I be,' &c.

असानि	असाव	असाम	असै	असावहै	असामहै
एधि	स्तं	स्त	स्व	साथां	ध्वं
अस्तु	स्तां	सन्तु	स्तां	सातां	सतां

Potential, 'I may be,' &c.

स्यां	स्याव	स्याम	सीय	सीवहि	सीमहि
स्याः	स्यातं	स्यात	सीथाः	सीयाथां	सीध्वं
स्यात्	स्यातां	स्युः	सीत	सीयातां	सीरन्

The second and third persons singular of the benedictive are considered to be स्तात्.

आस 'to sit.'

The final is optionally doubled before a consonantal termination, except ध्व, before which it is rejected.

Pres. आस्ते or आस्स्ते (आसे or आस्से, आसाथे, आध्वे); 1st præt. आस्त; 2d præt. आसाञ्चक्रे; 3d præt. आसिष्ट; 1st fut. आसिता; 2d fut. आसिष्यते; imp. आस्तां (आस्स्व, आसानि); pot. आसीत; bened. आसिषीष्ट; cond. आसिष्यत. Pass. आस्यते. Caus. आसयति. Desid. आसिसिषते.

इ (इक्) 'to remember.'

This is always combined with the preposition अधि, and with no other: the final indicatory क् distinguishes it from इ (इण्), as below. In the second and third præterites and in the derivative forms it substitutes the inflexions of गम.

Pres. अध्येति (अधीतः, अधियन्ति); 1st præt. अध्यैत्; 2d præt. अधिजगाम; 3d præt. अध्यगात्; 1st fut. अध्येता; 2d fut. अध्येष्यति; imp. अध्येतु; pot. अधीयात्; bened. अधीयात्; cond. अध्यैष्यत्. Pass. अधीयते. Caus. अधिगमयति. Desid. अधिजिगमिषति.

इ (इङ्) 'to go;' अधी 'to study.'

The indicatory ङ् restricts this to the Átmane-pada; and it is invariably combined with the preposition अधि; as, अधी 'to go over,' as a book, 'to read,' 'to study.' It borrows the forms of गा, 'to go,' in the second præterite and frequentative, and optionally in the third præterite and conditional, of the active voice, and the causal mode. Before a vowel termination, इय् is substituted for the radical vowel.

Pres. अधीते (अधीयाते, अधीयते); 1st præt. अध्यैत (अध्यैयातां, अध्यैयत); 2d præt. अधिजगे (अधिजगाते, अधिजगिरे); 3d præt. अध्यैष्ट or अध्यगीष्ट; 1st fut. अध्येता; 2d fut. अध्येष्यते; imp. अधीतां; pot. अधीयीत; bened. अध्येषीष्ट; cond. अध्यगीष्यत, अध्यैष्यत. Pass. अधीयते. Caus. अध्यापयति; 3d præt. अध्यापिपत् or अध्यजीगपत्. Desid. अधिजिगांसते.

इ (इण्) 'to go.'

The indicatory ण् distinguishes this from the two preceding verbs, as well as from इ of the first conjugation (see p. 156). Before the vowel terminations of the present and imperative, य् is substituted for the root; before other terminations, इय्. The third præterite is borrowed from गा in both the active and passive voices; and the causal and desiderative are derived from गम.

Pres. एति (इतः, यन्ति, एषि, इथः, इथ, एमि, इवः, इमः); 1st præt. ऐत् (ऐतां, आयन्, ऐः, ऐतं, आयम्); 2d præt. इयाय (ईयतुः, ईयुः); 3d præt. अगात्; 1st fut. एता; 2d fut. एष्यति; imp. एतु (इतां, यन्तु, इहि, यानि, याव, याम); pot. इयात्; bened. ईयात् (with a prep. short, निरियात्, निरियास्तां); cond. ऐष्यत्. Pass. ईयते; 3d præt. अगायि. Caus. गमयति. Desid. जिगमिषति.

ईड 'to praise.'

After the cerebral of the base, the त and थ of a termination are changed to ट and ठ; and as they are hard, the radical final is then changed to the hard consonant of its class, ट. This and ईश, as below, insert इ before से and ध्वे in the present, and स्व and ध्वं in the imperative.

Pres. ईड्डे (ईडाते, ईडते, ईडिषे, ईडाथे, ईडिड्ढ्वे, ईडे, ईड्वहे, ईड्महे); 1st præt. ऐड्ड; 2d præt. ईडाञ्चक्रे; 3d præt. ऐडिढ; 1st fut. ईडिता; 2d fut. ईडिष्यते; imp. ईड्डां, pot. ईडीत; bened. ईडिषीढ; cond. ऐडिष्यत. Pass. ईड्यते. Caus. ईडयति. Desid. ईडिडिषते.

ईर् 'to go,' 'to shake.'

Pres. ईर्ते; 1st præt. ऐर्त; 2d præt. ईराञ्चक्रे; 3d præt. ऐरिढ; 1st fut. ईरिता; 2d fut. ईरिष्यते; imp. ईर्तां; pot. ईरीत; bened. ईर्षीढ; cond. ऐरिष्यत. Pass. ईर्यते. Caus. ईरयति. Desid. ईरिरिषते.

ईश 'to rule.'

For the changes of the final श, see rule 214. इ is inserted in the present and imperative tenses before स and ध्व; see ईड.

Pres. ईष्टे (ईशिषे, ईशिध्वे); 1st præt. ऐष्ट; 2d præt. ईशाञ्चक्रे; 3d præt. ऐशिढ; 1st fut. ईशिता; 2d fut. ईशिष्यते; imp. ईष्टां; pot. ईशीत; bened. ईशिषीढ; cond. ऐशिष्यत. Pass. ईश्यते. Caus. ईशयति. Desid. ईशिशिषते.

ऊर्णु (ऊर्णुञ्) 'to cover.'

This verb takes both Padas. Before terminations rejecting प्, and having more than one letter, the Vṛiddhi change of the vowel is optional: before a vowel, उव् is substituted for the final; but optionally before the augment इ, prefixed to which the final may also take the Guṅa change or ओ, which becomes अव्. In the reduplication the second syllable only is repeated, and the proper radical consonant न resumes its dental character when detached from र. The desiderative takes various forms (rule 203, *d*).

Pres. ऊर्णोति, ऊर्णौति (ऊर्णुतः, ऊर्णुवन्ति), ऊर्णुते; 1st præt. और्णोत् (और्णोः, और्णुतां, और्णुवम्), और्णुत; 2d præt. ऊर्णुनाव, ऊर्णुनुवे; 3d præt. और्णवीत्, और्णुवीत् or और्णावीत् (और्णविष्टां &c.), और्णविष्ट, और्णुविष्ट; 1st fut. ऊर्णविता, ऊर्णुविता; 2d fut. ऊर्णविष्यति -ते, ऊर्णुविष्यति -ते; imp. ऊर्णोतु or ऊर्णौतु, ऊर्णुतां; pot. ऊर्णुयात्, ऊर्णुवीत; bened. ऊर्णूयात्, ऊर्णविषीष्ट or ऊर्णुविषीष्ट; cond. और्णविष्यत् -त or और्णुविष्यत् -त. Pass. ऊर्णूयते. Caus. ऊर्णावयति; 3d præt. और्णुनुवत्. Desid. ऊर्णुनूषति -ते, ऊर्णुनविषति -ते, ऊर्णुनुविषति -ते. Freq. ऊर्णोनूयते, ऊर्णोनवीति or ऊर्णोनोति.

चक्ष् (चक्षिङ्) ' to speak' or ' say.'

For the changes of क्ष, see rule 213, *c*, 7. The verb has but the conjugational tenses, and optionally the second præterite. In all other forms ख्या or क्शा is substituted for the root. The substitutes may be inflected in both Padas.

Pres. चष्टे (चक्षाते, चक्षते, चक्षे, चड्ढ्वे, चक्ष्वहे, चक्ष्महे); 1st præt. अचष्ट (अचक्षातां, अचक्षत); 2d præt. चचक्षे, चख्ये or चख्यौ, चक्शे, चक्शौ; 3d præt. अख्यत्, अख्यत, अक्शास्त, अक्शासीत्; 1st fut. ख्याता, क्शाता; 2d fut. ख्यास्यति -ते, क्शास्यति -ते; imp. चष्टां (चक्ष्व, चड्ढ्वं); pot. चक्षीत; bened. ख्यासीष्ट, ख्येयात्, ख्यायात्, क्शासीष्ट, क्शेयात्, क्शायात्; cond. अख्यास्यत् -त, अक्शास्यत् -त. Pass. ख्यायते, क्शायते. Caus. ख्यापयति, क्शापयति; 3d præt. अचिख्यपत्, अचिक्शपत्. Desid. चिख्यासति ते, चिक्शासति -ते. Freq. चाख्यायते, चाक्शायते.

चकास् ' to shine.'

This is one of the class जक्षादि, or reduplicated verbs. स may be rejected before the terminations of the second and third persons singular, first præterite, or changed to द् when they are dropped: it is also rejected or changed to द् before धि (rule 213, *c*, 6).

Pres. चकास्ति (चकास्तः, चकासति); 1st præt. अचकात्, अचकाद् (अचकाः or अचकाद्); 2d præt. चकासाञ्चकार; 3d præt. अचकासीत् (अचकासिष्टां); 1st fut. चकासिता; 2d fut. चकासिष्यति; imp. चकास्तु (चकाधि or चकाद्धि); pot. चकास्यात्; bened. चकास्यात् (चकास्यास्तां); cond. अचकासिष्यत्. Pass. चकास्यते. Caus. चकासयति; 3d præt. अचीचकासत् or अचचकासत्. Desid. चिचकासिषति.

जक्ष् ' to eat.'

This is the type of the Abhyasta or reiterated roots in its inflexions, although not itself a reduplicate. It also belongs to the class रुदादि (rule 213, *d*).

Pres. जक्षिति (जक्षितः, जक्षति); 1st præt. अजक्षीत् or अजक्षत् (अजक्षुः); 2d præt. जजक्ष; 3d præt. अजक्षीत् (अजक्षिष्टां); 1st fut. जक्षिता; 2d fut. जक्षिष्यति; imp. जक्षितु; pot. जक्ष्यात्; bened. जक्ष्यात्; cond. अजक्षिष्यत्. Pass. जक्ष्यते. Caus. जक्षयति. Desid. जिजक्षिषति. Freq. जाजक्ष्यते, जाजक्षीति or जाजष्टि.

जागृ 'to wake.'

The final becomes अर् before a consonantal termination rejecting प्; and in the first præterite, when the inflectional termination is rejected (rule 213, *c*, 3); the र् of अर् becomes Visarga. Before other consonants the vowel is unchanged. Before the vowels ऋ is changed to र्, except in the second præterite, and before इ, when it becomes अर्. The second præterite has two forms.

Pres. जागर्त्ति (जागृतः, जाग्रति); 1st præt. अजागः (अजागृतां, अजागरुः, अजागः, अजागृतं, &c.); 2d præt. जागराञ्चकार or जजागार (जजागरतुः); 3d præt. अजागरीत् (अजागरिष्टां); 1st fut. जागरिता; 2d fut. जागरिष्यति; imp. जागर्त्तु (जागृतां, जाग्रतु); pot. जागृयात्; bened. जागर्य्यात्. Pass. जागर्य्यते. Caus. जागरयति. Desid. जिजागरिषति.

णिज (णिजि) 'to cleanse.'

For the changes of the palatal final before consonants, see rule 213, *c*, 2.

Pres. निंक्ते (निंजाते, निंजते), निंक्षे (निंजाथे, निंग्ध्वे); 1st præt. अनिंक्त; 2d præt. निनिञ्जे (निनिञ्जिषे); 3d præt. अनिञ्जिष्ट; 1st fut. निञ्जिता; 2d fut. निञ्जिष्यते; imp. निंक्तां (निंक्ष्व, निंग्ध्वं); pot. निंजीत; bened. निंजिषीष्ट; cond. अनिञ्जिष्यत. Pass. निंज्यते. Caus. निञ्जयति -ते. Desid. निनिञ्जिषते. Freq. नेनिञ्जते, नेनिञ्जीति, नेनिंक्ति.

So पिजि 'to paint,' and शिजि 'to tinkle.'

दरिद्रा 'to be poor.'

In the conjugational tenses आ is changed to इ before a termination beginning with a consonant, and not having a mute प्. It is rejected in all tenses before a vowel termination of the same kind, or one not having प्; also before the augment इ, and before य in the benedictive. As a reduplicate root, it rejects the nasals of the third person plural, present tense, &c., and substitutes उस् for अन् in the first præterite (rule 213, *e*). In the second and third præterites it has two forms.

Pres. दरिद्राति (दरिद्रितः, दरिद्रति); 1st præt. अदरिद्रात् (अदरिद्रितां,

अदरिद्रुः); 2d præt. दरिद्राञ्चकार or ददरिद्रौ (ददरिद्रतुः, ददरिद्रुः); 3d præt. अदरिद्रीत् (अदरिद्रिष्टां, अदरिद्रिषुः) or अदरिद्रासीत् (अदरिद्रासिष्टां); 1st fut. दरिद्रिता; 2d fut. दरिद्रिष्यति; imp. दरिद्रातु (दरिद्रितां, दरिद्रतु, दरिद्राहि, दरिद्राव, दरिद्राम); pot. दरिद्रियात्; bened. दरिद्र्यात्; cond. अदरिद्रिष्यत्. Pass. दरिद्र्यते. Desid. दिदरिद्रिषति or दिदरिद्रासति.

दा (दाप्) 'to cut.'

This retains its final unchanged in all the tenses except the second præterite.

Pres. दाति; 1st præt. अदात् (अदान् or अदुः); 2d præt. ददौ (ददतुः, ददुः); 3d præt. अदासीत् (अदास्तां, अदासुः); 1st fut. दाता; 2d fut. दास्यति; imp. दातु (दाहि); pot. दायात्; bened. दायात्; cond. अदास्यत्. Pass. दायते. Caus. दापयति. Desid. दिदासति. Freq. दादायते, दादाति or दादेति.

In this manner a number of other verbs in आ, belonging to this conjugation, may be inflected; as,

द्रा to go badly, to fly.	या to go.
पा to preserve.	रा } to give, to take.
प्सा to eat.	ला }
प्रा to fill.	वा to blow.
भा to shine.	श्रा to cook or mature.
मा to measure.	ष्णा to bathe.

ख्या is conjugated only in the non-conjugational tenses: see चक्ष्. पा takes ल in the causal, पालयति. ष्णा makes the vowel of the causal optionally short, स्नापयति or स्नपयति.

दीधी (दीधीङ्) 'to shine.'

This is one of the class of reduplicated roots, and is usually considered peculiar to the Vedas.

Pres. दीधीते; 1st præt. अदीधीत; 2d præt. दीध्याञ्चक्रे; 3d præt. अदीधिष्ट; 1st fut. दीधिता; 2d fut. दीधिष्यते; imp. दीधीतां; pot. दीधीत; bened. दीधिषीष्ट; cond. अदीधिष्यत. Pass. दिधीयते.

दुह् 'to milk.'

For the changes of the final and initial, see rule 213, *c*, 8.

Pres. दोग्धि (दुग्धः, दुहन्ति, धोक्षि, दुग्धः, दुग्ध, दोह्मि दुह्वः, दुह्मः), दुग्धे (दुहाते, दुहते, धुक्षे, धुग्ध्वे); 1st præt. अधोक् (अदुग्ध); 2d præt. दुदोह, दुदुहे; 3d præt. अधुक्षत् (अधुक्षतां, अधुक्षन्), अधुक्षत (अधुक्षातां, अधुक्षन्त, अधुक्षथाः, अधुक्षध्वं, अधुक्षि, अधुक्षावहि) or अदुग्ध (अदुग्धाः, अधुग्ध्वं); 1st fut. दोग्धा; 2d fut. धोक्ष्यति -ते; imp. दोग्धु, दुग्धां; pot. दुह्यात्, दुहीत; bened. दुह्यात्, धुक्षीष्ट; cond. अधोक्ष्यत् -त. Pass. दुह्यते. Caus. दोहयति; 3d præt. अदूदुहत्. Desid. दुधुक्षति -ते. Freq. दोदुह्यते, दोदुहीति or दोदोग्धि.

दिह्, 'to anoint,' is analogously conjugated.

द्विष 'to hate.'

The verb is regularly inflected. उस् is optionally substituted for अन्. The changes of the final are either those of Sandhi, or of the declension of nouns in ष् (see also rule 213, c, 5).

Pres. द्वेष्टि, द्विष्टे; 1st præt. अद्वेट् (अद्विष्टां, अद्विषन् or अद्विषुः, अद्वेट्, अद्विष्टं, &c.), अद्विष्ट (अद्विषातां); 2d præt. दिद्वेष, दिद्विषे; 3d præt. अद्विक्षत् -त; 1st fut. द्वेष्टा; 2d fut. द्वेक्ष्यति -ते; imp. द्वेष्टु (द्विड्ढि, द्वेषाणि), द्विष्टां (द्विक्ष्व, द्विड्ढ्वं); pot. द्विष्यात्, द्विषीत; bened. द्विष्यात्, द्विक्षीष्ट; cond. अद्वेक्ष्यत् -त. Pass. द्विष्यते. Caus. द्वेषयति. Desid. दिद्विक्षति -ते. Freq. देद्विष्यते, देद्विषीति or देद्वेष्टि.

ब्रू 'to speak.'

This is an imperfect verb, admitting of the conjugational tenses only. It inserts ई before the consonantal terminations rejecting प्; and before it the Guṅa substitute ओ becomes अव्. उव् is substituted for the final before other vowel terminations. In the present tense the inflexions of आह in the three numbers of the third person, and singular and dual of the second, in the same sense, 'he speaks,' &c., but with the terminations of the second præterite, are considered to be optionally substitutes for those of ब्रू. For the non-conjugational tenses, see वच.

Pres. ब्रवीति (ब्रूतः, ब्रुवन्ति, ब्रवीषि, ब्रूथः, ब्रूथ, ब्रवीमि, ब्रूवः, ब्रूमः) or आह (आहतुः, आहुः, आत्थ, आहथुः), ब्रूते; 1st præt. अब्रवीत्, अब्रूत; imp. ब्रवीतु (ब्रूतां, ब्रुवन्तु, ब्रूहि, ब्रवाणि), ब्रूतां; pot. ब्रूयात्, ब्रुवीत.

मृज (मृजू) 'to clean,' 'to sweep.'

The vowel takes the Vṛiddhi change before the terminations of the conjugational tenses beginning with consonants having a mute प्, and optionally before those beginning with vowels not having such letter. It is so changed throughout in the non-conjugational tenses. The final ज is changed to ष before a termination beginning with any consonant except a nasal, a semivowel, or ह्. The changes to which such final ष is subject before other consonants, or to which it subjects them, are those of Sandhi: see also rule 213, *c*, 5.

Pres. मार्ष्टि (मृष्टः, मार्जन्ति or मृजन्ति, मार्क्षि, मार्ज्मि, मृज्वः, मृज्मः); 1st præt. अमार्ट् or अमार्ड् (अमृष्टां, अमृजन् or अमार्जन्, अमार्ट्, अमार्जम्, अमृज्म); 2d præt. ममार्ज (ममार्जिथ or ममार्ष्ठ); 3d præt. अमार्जीत् (अमार्जिष्टां, अमार्जिषुः) or अमार्क्षीत् (अमार्ष्टां, अमार्क्षुः); 1st fut. मार्जिता or मार्ष्टा; 2d fut. मार्जिष्यति or मार्क्ष्यति; imp. मार्ष्टु (मृष्टां, मृजन्तु or मार्जन्तु, मृड्ढि, मार्जानि); pot. मृज्यात्; bened. मृज्यात्; cond. अमार्जिष्यत् or अमार्क्ष्यत्. Pass. मृज्यते. Caus. मार्जयति; 3d præt. अममार्जत्. Desid. मिमार्जिषति or मिमृक्षति. Freq. मरीमृज्यते, मरीमार्जीति or मरिमार्ष्टि.

यु 'to join.'

This verb takes the Vṛiddhi substitute before a consonantal termination having an indicatory प्; and उव् before one beginning with a vowel. It inserts the augment इ् (rule 191, *b*), before which उ is changed to ओ, and that becomes अव्.

Pres. यौति (युतः, युवन्ति, यौषि, यौमि, युवः, युमः); 1st præt. अयौत् (अयुतां, अयौः, अयुवन्); 2d præt. युयाव (युयुवतुः, युयविथ); 3d præt. अयावीत्; 1st fut. यविता; 2d fut. यविष्यति; imp. यौतु (युहि, युवानि); pot. युयात्; bened. यूयात्; cond. अयविष्यत्. Pass. यूयते. Caus. यावयति. Desid. युयूषति or युयविषति. Freq. योयूयते, योयवीति or योयोति.

So क्षु 'to sneeze,' क्ष्णु 'to whet' or 'sharpen,' णु 'to praise,' ष्णु 'to distil' or 'drop;' which all take इ्. Other verbs in उ are conjugated in the same manner, except that they do not take इ्; as, कु 'to coo' or 'sound;' 1st fut. कोता, 2d fut. कोष्यति, 3d præt. अकौषीत्: द्यु 'to assail;' द्योता, द्योष्यति, अद्यौषीत्: षु 'to bring forth,' 'to be rich;' सोता, सोष्यति, असोषीत्. See also सू and सु.

रु 'to sound.'

This verb optionally prefixes ई to any termination beginning with a consonant in the conjugational tenses. It also takes इ.

Pres. रौति or रवीति (रुतः or रुवीतः, रौषि or रवीषि); 1st præt. अरौत् or अरवीत्; 2d præt. रुराव (रुरुवतुः); 3d præt. अरावीत्; 1st fut. रविता; 2d fut. रविष्यति; imp. रौतु or रवीतु; pot. रुयात् or रुवीयात्; bened. रूयात्; cond. अरविष्यत्. Pass. रूयते. Caus. रावयति. Desid. रुरूषति. Freq. रोरूयते, रोरवीति, रोरोति.

रुद् (रुदिर्) 'to weep.'

This is the leading root of the class रुदादि (rule 213, *d*).

Pres. रोदिति (रुदितः, रुदन्ति); 1st præt. अरोदत् or अरोदीत् (अरुदितां, अरोदः or अरोदीः); 2d præt. रुरोद (रुरोदिथ); 3d præt. अरुदत् (अरुदः) or अरोदीत् (अरोदिष्टां); 1st fut. रोदिता; 2d fut. रोदिष्यति; imp. रोदितु (रुदिहि); pot. रुद्यात्; bened. रुद्यात्; cond. अरोदिष्यत्. Pass. रुद्यते. Caus. रोदयति; 3d præt. अरूरुदत्. Desid. रुरुदिषति. Freq. रोरुद्यते, रोरुदीति or रोरोत्ति.

लिह् 'to lick.'

See rule 213, *c*, 8. Where the final is changed to ढ, and one ढ has been rejected, the vowel, if not changed to the Guṇa letter, is made long.

Pres. लेढि (लीढः, लिहन्ति, लेक्षि, लीढः, लेह्मि, लिह्वः, लिह्मः), लीढे (लिक्षे, लीढ्वे); 1st præt. अलेट् (अलीढां, अलेट्, अलिहं), अलीढ (अलिहातां, अलिहत); 2d præt. लिलेह, लिलिहे; 3d præt. अलिक्षत्, अलिक्षत or अलीढ; 1st fut. लेढा; 2d fut. लेक्ष्यति -ते; imp. लेढु (लीढि), लीढां (लिक्ष्व); pot. लिह्यात्, लिहीत; bened. लिह्यात्, लिक्षीष्ट; cond. अलेक्ष्यत् -त. Pass. लिह्यते. Caus. लेहयति. Desid. लिलिक्षति -ते. Freq. लेलिह्यते, लेलिहीति or लेलेढि.

वच् 'to speak.'

The final becomes क before some terminations (rule 213, *c*, 2). In the tenses in which this verb is substituted for ब्रू, it may take the A'tmane-pada. The third person plural of the present and imperative is wanting. In the third præterite, उ, convertible to ओ, is substituted for the radical vowel. The tense is formed with the affixes of the first præterite, with अ prefixed (rule 190, *a*).

Pres. वक्ति (वक्तः, वक्षि, वच्मि, वच्वः, वच्मः); 1st præt. अवक्, अवग् (अवक्तां, अवचन्, अवक्, अवचम्); 2d præt. उवाच (ऊचतुः, ऊचुः), ऊचे; 3d præt. अवोचत् (अवोचतां), अवोचत (अवोचेतां); 1st fut. वक्ता; 2d fut. वक्ष्यति -ते; imp. वक्तु (वग्धि); pot. वच्यात्; bened. उच्यात्, वक्षीष्ट; cond. अवक्ष्यत् -त. Pass. उच्यते. Caus. वाचयति. Desid. विवक्षति -ते. Freq. वावच्यते, वावक्ति.

वश ' to subdue.'

The final is changed to ष् (rule 213, *c*, 4), and व to उ, where the terminations have no mute प्, or where इ् is not inserted.

Pres. वष्टि (उष्टः, उशन्ति, वक्षि, वश्मि); 1st præt. अवट् (औष्टां, औशन्, अवट्, औष्टं, अवशम्); 2d præt. उवाश (ऊशतुः); 3d præt. अवाशीत् or अवशीत्; 1st fut. वशिता; 2d fut. वशिष्यति; imp. वष्टु (उड्ढि, वशानि); pot. उश्यात्; bened. उश्यात्; cond. अवशिष्यत्. Pass. उश्यते. Caus. वाशयति. Desid. विवशिषति. Freq. वावश्यते.

विद् ' to know.'

This verb is anomalous in some respects. In the present tense it admits the terminations of the second præterite, without the reduplication, as well as those of the present. It optionally forms the second præterite with the auxiliary verbs (rule 189, *c*), and the imperative with कृ.

Pres. वेत्ति or वेद (वित्तः or विदतुः, विदन्ति or विदुः, वेत्सि or वेत्थ, वित्थः or विदथुः, वित्थ or विद, वेद्मि or वेद, विद्वः or विद्व, विद्मः or विद्म; 1st præt. अवेत् (अवित्तां, अविदुः, अवेत् or अवेः); 2d præt. विवेद (विविदथुः), विदाञ्चकार, विदामास, विदाम्बभूव; 3d præt. अवेदीत्; 1st fut. वेदिता; 2d fut. वेदिष्यति; imp. वेत्तु or विदाङ्करोतु; pot. विद्यात्; bened. विद्यात् (विद्यास्तां); cond. अवेदिष्यत्. Pass. विद्यते. Caus. वेदयति. Desid. विविदिषति. Freq. वेविद्यते, वेविदीति, वेवेत्ति.

With सम् prefixed, it takes the Átmane-pada, as संविते; in the third person plural of the present, first præterite, and imperative, र may be added to the final, as संविदते or संविद्रते, &c.

वी 'to go,' &c.

According to some authorities, इय is not substituted for the radical before a vowel; the change is that of Sandhi only.

Pres. वेति (वीतः, वियन्ति); 1st præt. अवेत् (अवियन् or अव्यन्); 2d præt. विवाय (विवियतुः or विव्यतुः); 3d præt. अवैषीत्; 1st fut. वेता; 2d fut. वेष्यति; imp. वेतु; pot. and bened. वीयात्; cond. अवेष्यत्. Pass. वीयते. Caus. वाययति. Desid. विवीषति. Freq. वेवीयते, वेवयीति or वेवेति.

The verb has many meanings; as, 'to throw,' 'to eat,' 'to conceive,' &c. In the latter, the causal, 'to impregnate,' is वाययति or वापयति.

वेवी, a synonymous verb, is similarly inflected; but in the Átmane-pada: Pres. वेवीते (वेव्याते, वेव्यते), &c.

शास (शासु) 'to bless,' 'to teach.'

The vowel is changed to इ before terminations beginning with consonants which have not a mute प in the Parasmai-pada. For the change of the final, see rule 213, *c*, 6.

Pres. शास्ति (शिष्टः, शासति), शास्ते (शासते); 1st præt. अशात् (अशिष्टां, अशासुः, अशाः or अशात्), अशात; 2d præt. शशास, शशासे; 3d præt. अशिषत्, अशासिष्ट; 1st fut. शासिता; 2d fut. शासिष्यति -ते; imp. शास्तु (शाधि), शास्तां; pot. शिष्यात्, शासीत; bened. शिष्यात्, शासिषीष्ट; cond. अशासिष्यत् -त. Pass. शिष्यते. Caus. शासयति. Desid. शिशासिषति. Freq. शेशिष्यते, शाशासीति or शाशास्ति.

In the sense of 'blessing,' आ is usually prefixed, आशास्ते or आशिष्टे; for, according to some, the vowel is altered in the Átmane-pada also.

शी (शीङ्) 'to sleep.'

This verb changes the final to the Guńa element ए in all the tenses except the second præterite. ए before a vowel becomes अय्, except in the plurals of the present, first præterite, and imperative, where र is inserted before the terminations from which the nasal has been rejected. The verb inserts इ (rule 191, *l*).

Pres. शेते (शयाते, शेरते, शेषे, शेध्वे, शेये, शेवहे, शेमहे); 1st præt. अशेत (अशेरत); 2d præt. शिश्ये (शिश्याते, शिश्यिरे); 3d præt. अशयिष्ट; 1st fut. शयिता; 2d fut. शयिष्यते; imp. शेतां (शयातां, शेरतां); pot. शयीत; bened. शयिषीष्ट. Pass. शय्यते. Caus. शाययति. Desid. शिशयिषते. Freq. शाशय्यते, शेशयीति, शेशेति.

श्वस 'to breathe.'

This belongs to the class रुदादि (rule 213, *d*: see also rule 213, *c*, 6).

Pres. श्वसिति; 1st præt. अश्वसीत् or अश्वसत्; 2d præt. शश्वास; 3d præt. अश्वसीत्; 1st fut. श्वसिता; 2d fut. श्वसिष्यति; imp. श्वसितु; pot. and bened. श्वस्यात्; cond. अश्वसिष्यत्. Pass. श्वस्यते.

षू (षूङ्) 'to bring forth,' as a child.

The verb optionally admits इ.

Pres. सूते (सुवाते, सुषते, सूषे); 1st præt. असूत; 2d præt. सुषुवे; 3d præt. असविष्ट or असोष्ट; 1st fut. सोता, सविता; 2d fut. सोष्यते, सविष्यते; imp. सूतां (सूष्व, सवै, सवावहै); pot. सुवीत; bened. सोषीष्ट, सविषीष्ट; cond. असोष्यत, असविष्यत. Pass. सूयते; 3d præt. असावि. Caus. सावयति; 3d præt. असीषवत्. Desid. सुसूषते. Freq. सोषूयते, सोषवीति or सोषोति.

ष्टु (ष्टुञ्) 'to praise.'

This optionally admits ई before the consonants of the conjugational tenses, except य.

Pres. स्तौति or स्तवीति, स्तुते or स्तुवीते; 1st præt. अस्तौत् or अस्तवीत्, अस्तुत or अस्तुवीत; 2d præt. तुष्टाव (तुष्टुवतुः), तुष्टुवे; 3d præt. अस्तावीत्, अस्तोष्ट; 1st fut. स्तोता; 2d fut. स्तोष्यति -ते; imp. स्तौतु or स्तवीतु, स्तुतां, स्तुवीतां; pot. स्तुयात्, स्तुवीत; bened. स्तूयात्, स्तोषीष्ट; cond. अस्तोष्यत् -त. Pass. स्तूयते. Caus. स्तावयति. Desid. तुष्टुषति -ते. Freq. तोष्टूयते, तोष्टोति.

ष्वप 'to sleep.'

A verb of the class रुदादि (rule 213, *d*). The vowel is substituted for the semivowel in the second præterite, in the reduplicate syllable, and before the vowel terminations in the radical syllable also. Before the य of the benedictive and passive and frequentative the same change occurs, and in the third præterite of the causal.

Pres. स्वपिति; 1st præt. अस्वपत् or अस्वपीत्; 2d præt. सुष्वाप (सुषुपतुः, सुषुपुः); 3d præt. अस्वाप्सीत् (अस्वाप्तां, अस्वाप्सुः); 1st fut. स्वप्ता; 2d fut. स्वप्स्यति; imp. स्वपितु; pot. स्वप्यात्; bened. सुप्यात्; cond. अस्वप्स्यत्. Pass. सुप्यते. Caus. स्वापयति; 3d præt. असूषुपत्. Desid. सुषुप्सति. Freq. सोषुप्यते, सास्वपीति or सास्वप्ति.

हन ‘to kill.’

The final is rejected before the terminations of the conjugational tenses beginning with any consonant except a nasal or a semivowel, and not having an indicatory प्. In the same tenses and second præterite घन् is substituted for the root, which becomes घ्न before a vowel termination, not having a mute प. ज is substituted in the second person singular of the imperative. In the benedictive and third præterite वध् is substituted; घन् is substituted in some tenses of the passive, in the desiderative and frequentative modes; and घात् is substituted in the causal. हन् takes इ in the second future and conditional in the active voice: घन् admits the augment in both futures, conditional, and third præterite of the passive. वध् also takes the augment इ.

Pres. हन्ति (हतः, घ्नन्ति, हंसि, हन्मि); 1st præt. अहन् (अहतां, अघ्नन्, अहन्, अहनम्); 2d præt. जघान (जघ्नतुः, जघ्नुः, जघनिथ or जघन्थ); 3d præt. अवधीत् (अवधिष्टां); 1st fut. हन्ता; 2d fut. हनिष्यति; imp. हन्तु (हताम्, घ्नन्तु, जहि, हनानि); pot. हन्यात्; bened. वध्यात्; cond. अहनिष्यत्. Pass. pres. हन्यते; 3d præt. अवधि or अघानि (अवधिषातां or अहंसातां or अघानिषातां); 1st fut. हन्ता or घानिता; 2d fut. हनिष्यते or घानिष्यते; bened. वधिषीष्ट or घानिषीष्ट. Caus. घातयति; 3d præt. अजीघतत्. Desid. जिघांसति. Freq. जघन्यते or जेघ्नीयते, जंघनीति or जंघन्ति or जंहनीति, जंहन्ति or जंहति.

Third Conjugation.

214. The characteristic peculiarity of this conjugation is the reduplication of the radical syllable before the terminations of the conjugational tenses.

a. The reduplication takes place according to general rules, and whatever other change of the base occurs is special, except the substitution of a Guńa for a radical vowel before those terminations which reject प्, and the modifications of the final which the rules of Sandhi require. A final vowel is changed to the Guńa letter before उस् in the first præterite.

b. The terminations are also unaltered, except those of the third person plural, present and imperative, which reject न; and the third person plural of the first præterite, which substitutes उस् for अन्. The compound form of the second præterite is optionally used in four verbs, भी, ह्री, भृ, and हु.

c. The model of the class is हु 'to sacrifice;' the only peculiarities in the inflexion of which are the optional change of the vowel to the semivowel before the terminations of the first person dual and plural of the present tense, and the substitution of धि for हि in the imperative. It is thus inflected in the conjugational tenses:

Present, 'I sacrifice,' &c.

जुहोमि	जुहुवः or जुह्वः	जुहुमः or जुह्मः
जुहोषि	जुहुथः	जुहुथ
जुहोति	जुहुतः	जुह्वति

First præterite, 'I sacrificed,' &c.

अजुहवं	अजुहुव	अजुहुम
अजुहोः	अजुहुतं	अजुहुत
अजुहोत्	अजुहुतां	अजुहवुः

Imperative, 'May I sacrifice,' &c.

जुहवानि	जुहवाव	जुहवाम
जुहुधि	जुहुतं	जुहुत
जुहोतु	जुहुतां	जुह्वतु

Potential, 'I may sacrifice,' &c.

जुहुयाम्	जुहुयाव	जुहुयाम
जुहुयाः	जुहुयातं	जुहुयात
जुहुयात्	जुहुयातां	जुहुयुः

In the non-conjugational tenses the reduplication does not take place, except where required by general rules.

2d præt. जुहाव or जुहवाञ्चकार; 1st fut. होता; 2d fut. होष्यति; bened. हूयात्; cond. अहोष्यत्. Pass. हूयते. Caus. हावयति. Desid. जुहूषति. Freq. जोहूयते, जोहवीति, जोहोति.

ऋ 'to go.'

इयृ is substituted for the root in the reduplication. The verb rarely occurs in this form, except in the Vedas. In the first and second persons of the first præterite, the final of the conjunct having been rejected, the र् of the Guṇa substitute for ऋ or अर् becomes Visarga.

Pres. इयर्ति (इयृतः, इयृति); 1st præt. ऐयः; imp. इयर्तु; pot. इयृयात्.

For the other forms, see ऋ, p. 157.

जन 'to produce.'

Before terminations beginning with consonants, not containing an indicatory प्, the vowel of this verb is made long; and before such a termination beginning with a vowel, the medial radical अ is rejected: see जन, fourth conjugation.

Pres. जजन्ति (जजातः, जज्ञति); 1st præt. अजजन् (अजजातां, अजज्ञुः); 2d præt. जजान (जज्ञतुः, जज्ञुः); 3d præt. अजानीत् or अजनीत्; 1st fut. जनिता; 2d fut. जनिष्यति; imp. जजन्तु (जजातां, जज्ञतु); pot. जजन्यात्; bened. जन्यात्; cond. अजनिष्यत्. Pass. जन्यते. Caus. जानयति. Desid.. जिजनिषति. Freq. जंजन्यते or जाजायते, जंजनीति or जंजन्ति or जाजनीति, जाजन्ति.

णिज (णिजिर्) 'to cleanse.'

This takes both Padas, and in the reduplication changes इ to ए; see णिजि, second conjugation, p. 200.

Pres. नेनेक्ति (नेनिक्तः, नेनिजति), नेनिक्ते; 1st præt. अनेनेक्, अनेनिक्त; 2d præt. निनेज (निनिजतुः), निनिजे; 3d præt. अनैक्षीत् or अनिजत्, अनिक्त; 1st fut. नेक्ता; 2d fut. नेक्ष्यति -ते; imp. नेनेक्तु, नेनिक्तां; pot. नेनिज्यात्, नेनिजीत; bened. निज्यात्, निक्षीष्ट; cond. अनेक्ष्यत् -त. Pass. निज्यते. Caus. नेजयति. Desid. निनिक्षति. Freq. नेनिज्यते, नेनिजीति or नेनेक्ति.

दा (दाञ्) 'to give.

This drops आ before all the terminations of the conjugational tenses not containing an indicatory प्, making consequently दद्. In the second person singular of the imperative it substitutes दे for the reduplicated verb. It takes both Padas. It is unnecessary to give more than the conjugational tenses, as the rest are the same as those of दा, first conjugation, p. 169.

Pres. ददाति (दत्तः, ददति), दत्ते; 1st præt. अददात् (अदत्तां, अददुः), अदत्त; imp. ददातु (दत्तां, ददतु, देहि), दत्तां, (दत्स्व, ददै); pot. दद्यात्, ददीत.

धा (धाञ्) 'to have' or 'hold.'

This is inflected like the preceding, but the initial is unchanged before a termination beginning with any consonant except a nasal, a semivowel, or ह, which does not contain an indicatory प्. The other tenses are analogous to those of दा, first conjugation.

Pres. दधाति (धत्तः, दध्वः, दध्मः), धत्ते (दधाते); 1st præt. अदधात्, अधत्त; 2d præt. दधौ, दधे; 3d præt. अधात्, अधित or अधिषत; 1st fut. धाता; 2d fut. धास्यति -ते; imp. दधातु (धेहि), धत्तां (धत्स्व); pot. दध्यात्, दधीत; bened. धेयात्, धासीष्ट; cond. अधास्यत् -त. Pass. धीयते. Caus. धापयति. Desid. धित्सति -ते. Freq. देधीयते, दाधेति or दाधाति.

भस 'to shine.'

Before a termination beginning with a vowel, not containing a mute प्, this verb, like जन, rejects the medial vowel: भ being then conjoined with स, necessarily becomes प् (rule 7, *d*: see also, for the changes of स, rule 213, *c*, 6).

Pres. बभस्ति (बभस्तः, बप्सति); 1st præt. अबभः (अबभस्तां, अबप्सुः,

अबभः); 2d præt. बभास; 3d præt. अभासीत्; 1st fut. भसिता; 2d fut. भसिष्यति; imp. बभस्तु (बभस्तां, बप्सतु, बभद्धि, बभसानि); pot. बभस्यात्; bened. भस्यात्; cond. अभसिष्यत्. Pass. भस्यते. Caus. भासयति. Desid. बिभासिषति. Freq. बाभस्यते, बाभसीति, बाभस्ति.

भी 'to fear.'

This may make the vowel before a termination beginning with a consonant, and not containing an indicatory प्, short. It optionally takes the compound form of the second præterite (rule 214, *b*).

Pres. बिभेति (बिभीतः or बिभितः, बिभ्यति); 1st præt. अबिभेत् (अबिभीतां or अबिभितां, अबिभयुः); 2d præt. बिभाय (बिभ्युः) or बिभयाञ्चकार; 3d præt. अभैषीत् (अभैष्टां, अभैषुः); 1st fut. भेता; 2d fut. भेष्यति; imp. बिभेतु (बिभीतां or बिभितां); pot. बिभीयात्, बिभियात्; bened. भीयात्; cond. अभेष्यत्. Pass. भीयते. Caus. भाययति, भाययते, भापयते or भीषयते. Desid. बिभीषति. Freq. बेभीयते, बेभयीति or बेभेति.

भृ (भृञ्) 'to nourish' or 'support.'

Pres. बिभर्ति (बिभृतः, बिभ्रति); 1st præt. अबिभः (अबिभृतां, अबिभरुः); imp. बिभर्तु; pot. बिभृयात्.

The other tenses are the same as those of भृ of the first conjugation, p. 174.

मा (माङ्) 'to measure.'

This verb, हा 'to go,' and हा 'to abandon,' drop their final vowel before a termination beginning with a vowel, and not containing an indicatory प्: before such a termination beginning with a consonant, they change it to ई. The vowel of reduplication is इ.

Pres. मिमीते (मिमाते, मिमते); 1st præt. अमिमीत (अमिमातां, अमिमत); 2d præt. ममे; 3d præt. अमास्त; 1st fut. माता; 2d fut. मास्यते; imp. मिमीतां; pot. मिमीत; bened. मासीष्ट; cond. अमास्यत. Pass. मीयते. Caus. मापयति -ते; 3d præt. अमीमपत् -त. Desid. मित्सति -ते. Freq. मेमीयते, मामाति or मामेति.

विज (विजिर्) 'to discriminate.'

The verb, like णिज, changes इ to ए in the reduplicate syllable. For the effect of the Anubandha, see p. 106; and for the changes of the final, rule 213, c, 2.

Pres. वेवेक्ति (वेविक्तः, वेविजति, वेवेक्षि, वेवेज्मि, वेविज्वः, वेविज्मः); 1st præt. अवेवेक् (अवेविक्तां, अवेविजुः, अवेवेक्); 2d præt. विवेज; 3d præt. अवेक्षीत् (अवेक्तां, अवेक्षुः), अविजत्; 1st fut. वेक्ता; 2d fut. वेक्ष्यति; imp. वेवेक्तु (वेविग्धि, वेविजानि); pot. वेविज्यात्; bened. विज्यात्; cond. अवेक्ष्यत्. Pass. विज्यते. Caus. वेजयति. Desid. विविक्षति. Freq. वेविज्यते, वेवेक्ति.

विष 'to surround.'

Pres. वेवेष्टि, वेविष्टे; 1st præt. अवेवेट्, अवेविष्ट; 2d præt. विवेष, विविषे; 3d præt. अवेक्षीत्, अवेष्ट; 1st fut. वेष्टा; 2d fut. वेक्ष्यति -ते; imp. वेवेष्टु, वेविष्टां; pot. वेविष्यात्, वेविषीत; bened. विष्यात्, विक्षीष्ट; cond. अवेक्ष्यत् -त. Pass. विष्यते. Caus. वेषयति. Desid. विविक्षति. Freq. वेविष्यते, वेवेष्टि.

सृ 'to go.'

Pres. सिसर्ति; 1st præt. असिसः; 2d præt. ससार; 3d præt. असार्षीत् or असरत्; 1st fut. सर्ता; 2d fut. सरिष्यति; imp. सिसर्तु; pot. सिसृयात्; bened. स्रियात्; cond. असरिष्यत्. Pass. स्रियते. Caus. सारयति. Desid. सिसीर्षति. Freq. सेस्रीयते, सर्सर्ति.

हा (हाङ्) 'to go.'

See मा above.

Pres. जिहीते; 1st præt. अजिहीत; 2d præt. जहे; 3d præt. अहास्त; 1st fut. हाता; 2d fut. हास्यते; imp. जिहीतां; pot. जिहीत; bened. हासीष्ट; cond. अहास्यत. Pass. हायते. Caus. हापयति. Desid. जिहासते. Freq. जाहायते, जाहाति or जाहेति.

हा (हाक्) 'to abandon.'

The Anubandha क् is to distinguish this root from the preceding. The reduplicate is regular in other respects. The inflexion is analogous to that of मा. In the second person singular of the imperative, जहिहि or जहीहि is optionally substituted for the root: आ is dropped before the य of the potential.

Pres. जहाति (जहीतः, जहति); 1st præt. अजहात्; 2d præt. जहौ; 3d præt. अहासीत्; 1st fut. हाता; 2d fut. हास्यति; imp. जहातु (जहिहि, जहीहि or जहाहि); pot. जह्यात्; bened. हेयात्; cond. अहास्यत्. Pass. हीयते. Caus. हापयति; 3d præt. अजीहपत्. Desid. जिहासति. Freq. जेहीयते, जाहेति or जाहाति.

ह्री 'to be ashamed.'

Pres. जिह्रेति (जिह्रीतः, जिह्रियति); 1st præt. अजिह्रेत्; 2d præt. जिह्राय or ह्रीयाञ्चकार; 3d præt. अह्रैषीत्; 1st fut. ह्रेता; 2d fut. ह्रेष्यति; imp. जिह्रेतु; pot. जिह्रीयात्; bened. ह्रीयात्; cond. अह्रेष्यत्. Pass. ह्रीयते. Caus. ह्रेपयति. Desid. जिह्रीषति. Freq. जेह्रीयते, जेह्रयीति or जेह्रेति.

Fourth Conjugation.

215. The syllable य, technically termed श्यन्, is interposed between the inflective base and inflectional terminations of the conjugational tenses.

a. The terminations of the conjugational tenses are the same in this as in the first conjugation (rules 170, 186, &c).

b. Before य, as has already been seen in the preceding conjugation, a radical vowel is not capable of a Guńa substitute, and a consonant is unchanged.

c. The terminations of the first præterite are substituted for those of the third in the Parasmai-pada, and sometimes in the Átmane-pada, after verbs belonging to the class पुषादि or पुष, &c.; comprehending nearly a third of the whole conjugation.

d. A final ॠ is changed to ईर्, and a final ओ is rejected, before य. ओ is changed to आ before other terminations.

e. The class of roots called शमादि or शम, &c.—all of which, except मद 'to be glad' or 'intoxicated,' end with म—make a medial अ long; and roots which end with र् or व् usually prolong a medial इ, उ, ऋ, ऌ.

f. Any other changes are special. The verbs of this class are somewhat numerous: most of them are to be found in other conjugations, sometimes in the same, sometimes in different acceptations, when the non-conjugational tenses often adopt different modes of inflexion.

g. The model of the class is दिव (दिवु) 'to play,' 'to shine,' &c., which by the clause *e*, above, becomes दीव in the conjugational tenses.

Present tense, 'I play,' &c.

दीव्यामि	दीव्यावः	दीव्यामः
दीव्यसि	दीव्यथः	दीव्यथ
दीव्यति	दीव्यतः	दीव्यन्ति

First præterite, 'I played,' &c.

अदीव्यम्	अदीव्याव	अदीव्याम
अदीव्यः	अदीव्यतं	अदीव्यत
अदीव्यत्	अदीव्यतां	अदीव्यन्

Imperative, 'May I play,' &c.

दीव्यानि	दीव्याव	दीव्याम
दीव्य	दीव्यतं	दीव्यत
दीव्यतु	दीव्यतां	दीव्यन्तु

Potential, 'I may play,' &c.

दीव्येयं	दीव्येव	दीव्येम
दीव्येः	दीव्येतं	दीव्येत
दीव्येत्	दीव्येतां	दीव्येयुः

There are no peculiarities in the non-conjugational tenses. In the desiderative there are three forms (rule 203, *f*): in the frequentative, rejecting य, the final is changed to उ.

2d præt. दिदेव; 3d præt. अदेवीत् (अदेविष्टां, अदेविषुः); 1st fut. देविता; 2d fut. देविष्यति; bened. दीव्यात्; cond. अदेविष्यत्. Pass. दीव्यते. Caus. देवयति. Desid. दिदिविषति, दिदेविषति or दिद्यूषति or दुद्यूषति. Freq. देदीव्यते, देदिवीति or देद्योति.

अस (असु) 'to throw.'

This is a verb of the class पुषादि (rule 213, *c*), and subjoins थ् to the final in the third præterite.

Pres. अस्यति; 1st præt. आस्यत्; 2d præt. आस; 3d præt. आस्थत् (आस्थतां, आस्थन्); 1st fut. असिता; 2d fut. असिष्यति; imp. अस्यतु; pot. अस्येत्; bened. अस्यात्; cond. आसिष्यत्. Pass. अस्यते. Caus. आसयति. Desid. असिसिषति.

ई 'to go.'

Pres. ईयते; 1st præt. ऐयत; 2d præt. अयाञ्चक्रे; 3d præt. ऐष्ट; 1st fut. एता; 2d fut. एष्यते; imp. ईयतां; pot. ईयेत; bened. एषीष्ट; cond. ऐष्यत. Pass. ईयते.

For the derivative forms, see इ, second conjugation.

ऋधु 'to increase.'

Pres. ऋध्यति; 1st præt. आर्ध्यत्; 2d præt. आनर्ध; 3d præt. आर्धत्; 1st fut. अर्धिता; 2d fut. अर्धिष्यति; imp. ऋध्यतु; pot. ऋध्येत्; bened. ऋध्यात्; cond. आर्धिष्यत्. Pass. ऋध्यते. Caus. अर्धयति. Desid. अर्दिधिषति or ईर्त्सति.

क्षिप 'to throw' or 'send.'

Pres. क्षिप्यति; 1st præt. अक्षिप्यत्; 2d præt. चिक्षेप; 3d præt. अक्षैप्सीत्; 1st fut. क्षेप्ता; 2d fut. क्षेप्स्यति; imp. क्षिप्यतु; pot. क्षिप्येत्; bened. क्षिप्यात्; cond. अक्षेप्स्यत्. Pass. क्षिप्यते. Caus. क्षेपयति. Desid. चिक्षिप्सति. Freq. चेक्षिप्यते, चेक्षेप्मि.

जन (जनी) 'to be born.'

This verb is changed to जा before the conjugational tenses.

Pres. जायते; 1st præt. अजायत; 2d præt. जज्ञे; 3d præt. अजनिष्ट; 1st fut. जनिता; 2d fut. जनिष्यते; imp. जायतां; pot. जायेत; bened. जनिषीष्ट; cond. अजनिष्यत.

For the rest, see जन, third conjugation.

जॄ (जूष) 'to grow old.'

See rule 215, *d.* It optionally substitutes ए for the reduplication of the second præterite; takes the terminations of the first præterite for those of the third; and elongates the augment इ in the futures and conditional.

Pres. जीर्यति; 1st præt. अजीर्यत्; 2d præt. जजार (जजरतुः, जेरतुः, जजरुः, जेरुः); 3d præt. अजारीत्, अजरत्; 1st fut. जरिता,

जरीता; 2d fut. जरिष्यति, जरीष्यति; imp. जीर्य्यतु; pot. जीर्य्येत्; bened. जीर्य्यात्; cond. अजरिष्यत्, अजरीष्यत्. Pass. जीर्य्यते. Caus. जरयति, जारयति. Desid. जिजरिषति, जिजरीषति, जिजीर्षति. Freq. जेजीर्य्यते, जाजर्ति.

डी (डीङ्) 'to fly.'

It takes the augment इ (rule 191, *b*).

Pres. डीयते; 1st præt. अडीयत; 2d præt. डिड्ये; 3d præt. अडयिष्ट; 1st fut. डयिता; 2d fut. डयिष्यते; imp. डीयतां; pot. डीयेत; bened. डयिषीष्ट; cond. अडयिष्यत. Pass. डीयते. Caus. डाययति. Desid. डिडयिषते. Freq. डेडीयते, डेडयीति, डेडेति.

It is also a verb of the first conjugation; डयते, अडयत, डयतां, डयेत.

णश (णशू) 'to perish.'

It belongs to the class पुषादि, and may in the third præterite change अ to ए. It inserts a nasal before any consonant except a nasal or semivowel, and optionally inserts इ.

Pres. नश्यति; 1st præt. अनश्यत्; 2d præt. ननाश (नेशतुः, नेशुः, नेशिथ, नेष्ठ); 3d præt. अनशत्, अनेशत्; 1st fut. नंष्टा, नशिता; 2d fut. नंक्ष्यति, नशिष्यति; imp. नश्यतु; pot. नश्येत्; bened. नश्यात्; cond. अनंक्ष्यत् or अनशिष्यत्. Pass. नश्यते. Caus. नाशयति. Desid. निनंक्षति, निनशिषति. Freq. नानश्यते, नानशीति, नानष्टि.

णह 'to bind.'

The final is changed to ध, which undergoes no other change than conversion to द before a soft, and त before a hard consonant, by the rules of Sandhi. It takes both Padas.

Pres. नह्यति -ते; 1st præt. अनह्यत् -त; 2d præt. ननाह (ननद्ध or नेहिथ, नेहतुः), नेहे; 3d præt. अनात्सीत् (अनाद्धां), अनद्ध (अनत्सातां); 1st fut. नद्धा; 2d fut. नत्स्यति -ते; imp. नह्यतु -तां; pot. नह्येत्, नह्येत; bened. नह्यात्, नत्सीष्ट; cond. अनत्स्यत् -त. Pass. नह्यते. Caus. नाहयति. Desid. निनत्सति -ते. Freq. नानह्यते, नानहीति, नानद्धि.

तप 'to heat,' 'to perform penance.'

Pres. तप्यते; 1st præt. अतप्यत; 2d præt. तेपे; 3d præt. अतप्त; 1st fut. तप्ता; 2d fut. तप्स्यते; imp. तप्यतां; pot. तप्येत; bened.

तप्सीष्ट; cond. अतप्स्यत. Pass. तप्यते. Caus. तापयति. Desid. तितप्सते. Freq. तातप्यते, तातप्ति.

तृप 'to satisfy,' 'to be satisfied.'

As belonging to the class पुषादि, it should take the form of the third præterite which that class requires; and as a verb of the fourth conjugation, it should not insert इ. In both respects, however, it offers optional deviations. It may be conjugated also in the fifth, sixth, and tenth conjugations, to which the different forms should perhaps be restricted: they are always, however, given together in this conjugation.

Pres. तृप्यति; 1st præt. अतृप्यत्; 2d præt. ततर्प (ततृपतुः, ततर्पिथ, ततर्प्थ, तत्रप्थ); 3d præt. अतृपत्, अतर्पीत्, अतार्प्सीत्, अत्राप्सीत्; 1st fut. तर्प्ता, त्रप्ता, तर्पिता; 2d fut. तर्प्स्यति, त्रप्स्यति, तर्पिष्यति; imp. तृप्यतु; pot. तृप्येत्; bened. तृप्यात्; cond. अतर्प्स्यत्, अत्रप्स्यत्, अतर्पिष्यत्. Pass. तृप्यते. Caus. तर्पयति. Desid. तितर्प्सति, तित्रप्सति, तितर्पिषति. Freq. तरीतृप्यते, तरीतृपीति, तरीतर्प्ति.

दृप, 'to be proud,' is similarly conjugated.

दी 'to decay.'

This root changes its final to आ in the non-conjugational tenses, except in the second præterite.

Pres. दीयते; 1st præt. अदीयत; 2d præt. दिदीये; 3d præt. अदास्त; 1st fut. दाता; 2d fut. दास्यते; imp. दीयतां; pot. दीयेत; bened. दासीष्ट; cond. अदास्यत. Caus. दाययति. Desid. दिदीषते or दिदासते. Freq. देदीयते, देदयीति or देदेति.

So मीङ् 'to injure,' and लीङ् 'to embrace;' but the latter takes two forms in the non-conjugational tenses; as, अलेष्ट, अलास्त; लेता, लाता; लेष्यते, लास्यते; लेषीष्ट, लासीष्ट; and अलेष्यत or अलास्यत.

दीप 'to shine.'

This verb optionally inflects the third person of the third præterite like the same in the passive voice: see ध्याय, p. 173.

Pres. दीप्यते; 1st præt. अदीप्यत; 2d præt. दिदीपे; 3d præt. अदीपिष्ट or अदीपि; 1st fut. दीपिता; 2d fut. दीपिष्यते; imp. दीप्यतां;

pot. दीप्येत; bened. दीपिषीष्ट; cond. अदीपिष्यत. Caus. दीपयति. Desid. दिदीपिषते. Freq. देदीप्यते, देदीपीति or देदीप्ति.

दुह 'to oppress,' 'to injure.'

This optionally substitutes घ or ढ for the final (rule 213, *c*, 8).

Pres. द्रुह्यति; 1st præt. अद्रुह्यत्; 2d præt. दुद्रोह; 3d præt. अद्रुहत्; 1st fut. द्रोग्धा, द्रोढा, द्रोहिता; 2d fut. द्रोहिष्यति, ध्रोक्ष्यति; imp. द्रुह्यतु; pot. द्रुह्येत्; bened. द्रुह्यात्; cond. अद्रोहिष्यत्, अध्रोक्ष्यत्. Pass. द्रुह्यते. Caus. द्रोहयति. Desid. दुद्रोहिषति, दुध्रुक्षति. Freq. दोद्रुह्यते, दोद्रुहीति, दोद्रोग्धि or दोद्रोढि.

So स्निह 'to be kind,' and ष्णुह 'to vomit.'

नृत 'to dance.'

This verb optionally takes the augment इ before स in the non-conjugational tenses.

Pres. नृत्यति; 1st præt. अनृत्यत्; 2d præt. ननर्त; 3d præt. अनर्तीत्; 1st fut. नर्तिता; 2d fut. नर्तिष्यति or नर्त्स्यति; imp. नृत्यतु; pot. नृत्येत्; bened. नृत्यात्; cond. अनर्तिष्यत् or अनर्त्स्यत्. Pass. नृत्यते. Caus. नर्तयति. Desid. निनर्तिषति or निनृत्सति. Freq. नरीनृत्यते, नरीनृतीति, नरीनर्ति.

पद 'to go.'

This forms the third singular of the third præterite in इ. It does not take the augment इ.

Pres. पद्यते; 1st præt. अपद्यत; 2d præt. पेदे; 3d præt. अपादि (अपत्सातां, अपत्सत); 1st fut. पत्ता; 2d fut. पत्स्यते; imp. पद्यतां; pot. पद्येत; bened. पत्सीष्ट; cond. अपत्स्यत. Pass. पद्यते. Caus. पादयति. Desid. पित्सते. Freq. पापद्यते, पापदीति or पापत्ति.

पुष 'to nourish.'

This is the first verb of a class which in this conjugation requires the terminations of the first præterite to be substituted for those of the third, when the radical vowel is unchanged (rule 190, *l*. p. 125).

Pres. पुष्यति; 1st præt. अपुष्यत्; 2d præt. पुपोष (पुपुषतुः);

3d præt. अपुषत् (अपुषतां, अपुषन्); 1st fut. पोष्टा; 2d fut. पोक्ष्यति; imp. पुष्यतु; pot. पुष्येत्; bened. पुष्यात्; cond. अपोक्ष्यत्. Pass. पुष्यते. Caus. पोषयति. Desid. पुपूषति. Freq. पोपुष्यते, पोपुषीति, पोपोष्टि.

The class पुषादि consists of the following verbs.

अस to throw.
उच to assemble.
ऋधु to increase.
कुप to be angry.
कुस to embrace.
कृश to become thin.
क्रुध to be angry.
क्लिद to become moist.
क्षिद to let loose.
क्षुध to be hungry.
क्षुभ to be agitated.
गुप to disturb.
गृध to be greedy.
जस to let loose.
डिप to throw.
णभ to hurt.
णश to perish.
तस to toss.
तुभ to hurt.
तुष to be pleased.
तृप to satisfy or be satisfied.
तृष to thirst.
दस to toss.
दुष to become bad.
द्रुह to oppress or wrong.
प्लुष to burn.
भृंश, भ्रंश to fall.
मस to weigh.
मुस to break.
मुह to be perplexed or foolish.
यस to take pains.
युप to disturb.
रध to hurt.
रुप to disturb.
रुष to be angry.
लुट to roll on the ground.
लुप to be lost.
लुभ to covet.
वस to fix.
विस to convey.
वुस to cast off.
शुध to be clean or pure.
शुष to become dry.
श्लिष to embrace.
षिध to become perfect.
ष्णिह to be kind or bland.
ष्विद to sweat.
हृष to rejoice.

Many of these verbs, however, take other forms also in the third præterite, as belonging originally perhaps to different conjugations; but they are now so blended, that they are usually placed together under this conjugation, however inconsistent with their classification under the head पुषादि; see तृप.

प्री 'to please or be pleased.'

It is a verb also of the first and ninth conjugations.

Pres. प्रीयते; 1st præt. अप्रीयत; 2d præt. पिप्रीये; 3d præt. अप्रेष्ट; 1st fut. प्रेता; 2d fut. प्रेष्यते; imp. प्रीयतां; pot. प्रीयेत; bened. प्रेषीष्ट; cond. अप्रेष्यत. Pass. प्रीयते. Caus. प्राययति or प्रीणयति. Desid. पिप्रीषति -ते. Freq. पेप्रीयते, पेप्रयीति, पेप्रेति.

So धी 'to uphold,' पी 'to drink,' री 'to injure,' व्री 'to choose,' &c.

बुध 'to understand.'

This forms the third person singular of the third præterite optionally in इ (see दीप). When the final is changed by the rules of Sandhi before a sibilant, ब becomes भ.

Pres. बुध्यते; 1st præt. अबुध्यत; 2d præt. बुबुधे; 3d præt. अबोधि or अबुद्ध (अभुत्सातां, अभुत्सत); 1st fut. बोद्धा; 2d fut. भोत्स्यते; imp. बुध्यतां; pot. बुध्येत; bened. भुत्सीष्ट; cond. अभोत्स्यत.

For the other forms, see बुध, first conjugation, p. 174.

भ्रंश (भ्रंशु) 'to fall.'

This drops its nasal before य, and in the third præterite.

Pres. भ्रश्यति; 1st præt. अभ्रश्यत्; 2d præt. बभ्रंश; 3d præt. अभ्रशत्; 1st fut. भ्रंशिता; 2d fut. भ्रंशिष्यति; imp. भ्रश्यतु; pot. भ्रश्येत्; bened. भ्रश्यात्; cond. अभ्रंशिष्यत्. Pass. भ्रश्यते.

For the other forms, see स्रंसु, first conjugation, p. 189.

मद 'to be mad,' 'to be delighted,' 'to be intoxicated.'

As belonging to the class श्यमादि, the vowel is made long in the conjugational tenses (rule 215, *e*).

Pres. माद्यति; 1st præt. अमाद्यत्; 2d præt. ममाद; 3d præt. अमादीत्; 1st fut. मदिता; 2d fut. मदिष्यति; imp. माद्यतु; pot. माद्येत्; bened. मद्यात्; cond. अमदिष्यत्. Pass. मद्यते. Caus. मादयति. Desid. मिमदिषति. Freq. मामद्यते, मामदीति, मामत्ति.

मन 'to know' or 'to respect.'

Pres. मन्यते; 1st præt. अमन्यत; 2d præt. मेने; 3d præt. अमंस्त; 1st fut. मन्ता; 2d fut. मंस्यते; imp. मन्यतां; pot. मन्येत; bened.

मंसीष्ट ; cond. अमंस्यत. Pass. मन्यते. Caus. मानयति. Desid. मिमंसते. Freq. मामन्यते, मामन्ति.

मिद (ञिमिदा) 'to be unctuous.'

This verb takes the Guńa substitute of the vowel in all the persons of the conjugational tenses.

Pres. मेद्यति ; 1st præt. अमेद्यत् ; 2d præt. मिमेद ; 3d præt. अमिदत् ; 1st fut. मेदिता ; 2d fut. मेदिष्यति ; imp. मेद्यतु ; pot. मेद्येत् ; bened. मिद्यात् ; cond. अमेदिष्यत्. Pass. मिद्यते. Caus. मेदयति. Desid. मिमेदिषति or मिमिदिषति. Freq. मेमिद्यते, मेमेत्ति.

मुह 'to be silly,' 'to be bewildered.'

It is conjugated like द्रुह, &c.

Pres. मुह्यति ; 1st præt. अमुह्यत् ; 2d præt. मुमोह (मुमोग्ध, मुमोढ or मुमोहिथ, मुमुहिव or मुमुह्व) ; 3d præt. अमुहत् ; 1st fut. मोग्धा, मोढा or मोहिता ; 2d fut. मोक्ष्यति or मोहिष्यति ; imp. मुह्यतु ; pot. मुह्येत् ; bened. मुह्यात् ; cond. अमोक्ष्यत् or अमोहिष्यत्. Pass. मुह्यते. Caus. मोहयति. Desid. मुमुहिषति or मुमोहिषति, मुमुक्षति or मुमोक्षति. Freq. मोमुह्यते, मोमुहीति, मोमोग्धि or मोमोढि.

युध 'to fight.'

Pres. युध्यते ; 1st præt. अयुध्यत ; 2d præt. युयुधे ; 3d præt. अयुद्ध (अयुत्सातां) ; 1st fut. योद्धा ; 2d fut. योत्स्यते ; imp. युध्यतां ; pot. युध्येत ; bened. योत्सीष्ट ; cond. अयोत्स्यत. Pass. युध्यते. Caus. योधयति. Desid. युयुत्सते. Freq. योयुध्यते, योयोद्धि.

युज, 'to engage in devotion,' is similarly conjugated: Pres. युज्यते ; 3d præt. अयुक्त ; 1st fut. योक्ता, &c.

रञ्ज 'to colour.'

Pres. रज्यते ; 1st præt. अरज्यत ; imp. रज्यतां ; pot. रज्येत.

The rest as in रञ्ज, Átmane-pada, of the first conjugation, p. 177.

रध 'to hurt.'

This verb inserts न in the second præterite, but optionally before the augment इ: it takes इ optionally in the futures and conditional. In the third præterite it belongs to the class पुषादि.

Pres. रध्यति; 1st præt. अरध्यत्; 2d præt. ररन्ध (ररन्धतुः, ररन्धिथ or ररन्ध, ररन्धिव, रेध्म); 3d præt. अरधत् (अरधतां); 1st fut. रधिता or रद्धा; 2d fut. रधिष्यति or रत्स्यति; imp. रध्यतु; pot. रध्येत्; bened. रध्यात्; cond. अरधिष्यत्, अरत्स्यत्. Pass. रध्यते. Caus. रन्धयति. Desid. रिरधिषति. Freq. ररध्यते, &c.

राध (राधौ) tr. 'to propitiate;' intr. 'to be finished' or 'accomplished.'

Pres. राध्यति; 1st præt. अराध्यत्; 2d præt. रराध; 3d præt. अरात्सीत्; 1st fut. राद्धा; 2d fut. रात्स्यति; imp. राध्यतु; pot. राध्येत्; bened. राध्यात्; cond. अरात्स्यत्. Pass. राध्यते. Caus. राधयति. Desid. रित्सति or रिरात्सति. Freq. राराध्यते, &c.

षाध and साध in the same senses are similarly conjugated.

लुभ 'to covet.'

It takes इ optionally in the first future, absolutely in the second.

Pres. लुभ्यति; 1st præt. अलुभ्यत्; 2d præt. लुलोभ; 3d præt. अलुभत्; 1st fut. लोब्धा, लोभिता; 2d fut. लोभिष्यति; imp. लुभ्यतु; pot. लुभ्येत्; bened. लुभ्यात्; cond. अलोभिष्यत्. Pass. लुभ्यते. Caus. लोभयति. Desid. लुलुप्सति. Freq. लोलुभ्यते, लोलोब्धि.

विद 'to be,' 'to exist.'

Pres. विद्यते; 1st præt. अविद्यत; 2d præt. विविदे; 3d præt. अवेत्त; 1st fut. वेत्ता; 2d fut. वेत्स्यते; imp. विद्यतां; pot. विद्येत; bened. वेत्सीष्ट; cond. अवेत्स्यत. Pass. विद्यते.

For the rest, see विद 'to know,' second conjugation.

व्यध (व्यधौ) 'to pierce' or 'injure.'

This changes the semivowel and following अ to इ in the conjugational tenses, and also in the benedictive, and before the terminations of the second præterite beginning with vowels.

Pres. विध्यति; 1st præt. अविध्यत्; 2d præt. विव्याध (विविधतुः); 3d præt. अव्यात्सीत्; 1st fut. व्यद्धा; 2d fut. व्यत्स्यति; imp. विध्यतु;

pot. विध्येत्; bened. विध्यात्; cond. अव्यत्स्यत्. Pass. विध्यते. Caus. व्याधयति. Desid. विव्यत्सति. Freq. वेविध्यते, वाव्यधीति, वाव्यद्धि.

शक ‘to be able.’

This is also a root of the fifth conjugation, q. v. According to some, it may take इ.

Pres. शक्यति -ते; 1st præt. अशक्यत् -त; 2d præt. शशाक, शेके; 3d præt. अशकत्, अशकीत्, अशक्त, अशकिष्ट; 1st fut. शक्ता, शकिता; 2d fut. शक्ष्यति -ते, शकिष्यति -ते; imp. शक्यतु, शक्यतां; pot. शक्येत् -त; bened. शक्यात्, शक्षीष्ट, शकिषीष्ट; cond. अशक्ष्यत् -त, अशकिष्यत् -त. Pass. शक्यते. Caus. शाकयति. Desid. शिक्षति -ते. Freq. शाशक्यते, शाशकीति, शाशक्ति.

शम (शमु) ‘to be tranquil.’

This is the first of a class of which the vowel is made long in the conjugational tenses.

Pres. शाम्यति; 1st præt. अशाम्यत्; 2d præt. शशाम (शेमतुः); 3d præt. अशमत् or अशमीत्; 1st fut. शमिता, शन्ता; 2d fut. शमिष्यति, शंस्यति; imp. शाम्यतु; pot. शाम्येत्; bened. शम्यात्; cond. अशमिष्यत्, अशंस्यत्. Pass. शम्यते. Caus. शामयति. Desid. शिशमिषति, शिशंसति. Freq. शाशम्यते, शाशन्ति.

The other roots of this class are,

क्लम to be sad.	भ्रम to wander or whirl.
क्षम to be patient.	श्रम to be weary.
तम to be distressed.	मद to be mad.
दम to tame.	

श्लिष ‘to embrace,’ ‘to adhere to.’

In the first sense this verb inserts स before the terminations of the first præterite in the third: in any other it does so optionally. It may also take the Átmane-pada in the third præterite, and इ in the third person singular. In the sense of embracing, आ is usually prefixed.

Pres. श्लिष्यति; 1st præt. अश्लिष्यत्; 2d præt. शिश्लेष; 3d præt. अश्लिक्षत् अश्लिषत् or अश्लिषि (अश्लिक्षातां, अश्लिक्षत, अश्लिष्ठाः, अश्लिड्ढ्वं); 1st fut. श्लेष्टा; 2d fut. श्लेक्ष्यति; imp. श्लिष्यतु; pot. श्लिष्येत्; bened.

क्षिप्यात्; cond. अक्षेप्स्यत्. Pass. क्षिप्यते. Caus. क्षेपयति. Desid. चिक्षिप्सते. Freq. चेक्षिप्यते, चेक्षेप्ति.

षह 'to bear.'

Pres. सह्यति; 1st præt. असह्यत्; 2d præt. ससाह; 3d præt. असहीत्; 1st fut. सहिता or सोढा; 2d fut. सहिष्यति; imp. सह्यतु; pot. सह्येत्; bened. सह्यात्; cond. असहिष्यत्.

For the rest, see षह, first conjugation.

षिव (षिवु) 'to sew.'

This makes the vowel long in the conjugational tenses, and before य.

Pres. सीव्यति; 1st præt. असीव्यत्; 2d præt. सिषेव; 3d præt. असेवीत्; 1st fut. सेविता; 2d fut. सेविष्यति; imp. सीव्यतु; pot. सीव्येत्; bened. सीव्यात्; cond. असेविष्यत्. Pass. सीव्यते. Caus. सेवयति. Desid. सिसिविषति. Freq. सेषीव्यते, सेषीमि.

ष्ठिवु, 'to eject saliva,' is similarly conjugated.

षू 'to bear,' as children.

Pres. सूयते; 1st præt. असूयत; 2d præt. सुषुवे (सुषुविषे); 3d præt. असोष्ट, असविष्ट; 1st fut. सोता, सविता; 2d fut. सोष्यते, सविष्यते; imp. सूयतां; pot. सूयेत; bened. सोषीष्ट; cond. असोष्यत, असविष्यत. Pass. सूयते; 1st fut. साविता; 3d præt. असावि.

For the other forms, see षु first conjugation, and षू second conjugation.

षो 'to destroy.'

Verbs ending in ओ lose it before the य of this conjugation (rule 215, *d*): in other tenses आ is substituted for the final.

Pres. स्यति; 1st præt. अस्यत्; 2d præt. ससौ (ससतुः); 3d præt. असात् or असासीत्; 1st fut. साता; 2d fut. सास्यति; imp. स्यतु; pot. स्येत्; bened. सेयात्; cond. असास्यत्. Pass. सीयते. Caus. साययति. Desid. सिषासति. Freq. सेषीयते, सासाति or सासेति.

In like manner are conjugated छो 'to cut,' दो 'to cut,' and शो 'to pare.' दो has but one form, अदात्, in the third præterite.

सृज 'to abandon.'

For the changes of the final, see यज, first conj., p. 176.

Pres. सृज्यते; 1st præt. असृज्यत; 2d præt. ससृजे (ससृजिषे); 3d præt. असृष्ट (असृक्षातां); 1st fut. स्रष्टा; 2d fut. स्रक्ष्यते; imp. सृज्यतां; pot. सृज्येत; bened. सृक्षीष्ट; cond. अस्रक्ष्यत. Caus. सर्जयति -ते. Desid. सिसृक्षते. Freq. सरीसृज्यते, सरीसृजीति, सरिसर्ष्टि.

Fifth Conjugation.

216. In the conjugational tenses the verbs of this class affix the syllable नु to the base.

a. Before those terminations which reject प् the vowel is changed to the Guńa letter ओ, which combines with a following vowel, agreeably to the rules of Sandhi. Before the vowel of any other termination उ becomes व when the root ends with a vowel; but उव् if it ends with a consonant, with which न combines. Before the consonant of a termination not containing प्, the उ of नु is unchanged, but it may be dropped before व or म, if it be not preceded by a conjunct consonant.

b. The termination of the second person singular of the imperative हि is dropped after नु attached to a final vowel in the root: if attached to a final radical consonant, हि is retained.

c. The type of the class is षुञ् 'to extract,' as a juice or spirit: of which the conjugational tenses in both forms are the following:

Present tense, 'I extract (the Soma) juice,' &c.

Parasmai-pada			Átmane-pada		
सुनोमि	सुनुवः सुन्वः	सुनुमः सुन्मः	सुन्वे	सुनुवहे सुन्वहे	सुनुमहे सुन्महे
सुनोषि	सुनुथः	सुनुथ	सुनुषे	सुन्वाथे	सुनुध्वे
सुनोति	सुनुतः	सुन्वन्ति	सुनुते	सुन्वाते	सुन्वते

First præterite, 'I have extracted juice,' &c.

असुनवम्	{ असुनुव, असुन्व }	असुनुम, असुन्म	असुन्वि	{ असुनुवहि, असुन्वहि }	असुनुमहि, असुन्महि
असुनोः	असुनुतं	असुनुत	असुनुथाः	असुन्वाथां	असुनुध्वं
असुनोत्	असुनुतां	असुन्वन्	असुनुत	असुन्वातां	असुन्वत

Imperative, 'May I extract juice,' &c.

सुनवानि	सुनवाव	सुनवाम	सुनवै	सुनवावहै	सुनवामहै
सुनु	सुनुतं	सुनुत	सुनुष्व	सुन्वाथां	सुनुध्वं
सुनोतु	सुनुतां	सुन्वन्तु	सुनुतां	सुन्वातां	सुन्वतां

Potential, 'I may extract juice,' &c.

सुनुयां	सुनुयाव	सुनुयाम	सुन्वीय	सुन्वीवहि	सुन्वीमहि
सुनुयाः	सुनुयातं	सुनुयात	सुन्वीथाः	सुन्वीयाथां	सुन्वीध्वं
सुनुयात्	सुनुयातां	सुनुयुः	सुन्वीत	सुन्वीयातां	सुन्वीरन्

The other tenses are not dissimilar from those of षु of the second conjugation. It takes इ in the third præterite of the Parasmai-pada, and, according to some, optionally in the Ắtmane-pada also.

2d præt. सुषाव, सुषुवे; 3d præt. असावीत्, असोष्ट, असविष्ट; 1st fut. सोता; 2d fut. सोष्यति -ते; bened. सूयात्, सोषीष्ट; cond. असोष्यत् -त. Pass. सूयते. Caus. सावयति; 3d præt. असूषवत्. Desid. सुसूषति -ते. Freq. सोषूय`, सोषवीति, सोषोति.

There are not many verbs in this conjugation. The following are amongst those of most frequent occurrence. A few which have been met with in previous conjugations, are repeated here for the sake of the difference which their inflexions present.

अशू 'to pervade.'

For the effect of the Anubandha ऊ, see p. 106.

Pres. अश्नुते (अश्नुवाते, अश्नुवते); 1st præt. आश्नुत; 2d præt. आनशे (आनशाते, आनशिरे); 3d præt. आष्ट (आक्षातां), आशिष्ट (आशिषातां); 1st fut. अष्टा, अशिता; 2d fut. अक्ष्यते, अशिष्यते; imp. अश्नुतां; pot. अश्नुवीत; bened. अशिषीष्ट, अक्षीष्ट; cond. आक्ष्यत, आशिष्यत. Pass. अश्यते. Caus. आशयति. Desid. अशिशिषते.

आप (आपॢ) 'to obtain.'

For the effect of ऌ, see p. 106.

Pres. आप्नोति (आप्नुतः, आप्नुवन्ति); 1st præt. आप्नोत्; 2d præt. आप (आपतुः, आपुः); 3d præt. आपत्; 1st fut. आप्ता; 2d fut. आप्स्यति; imp. आप्नोतु (आप्नुहि); pot. आप्नुयात्; bened. आप्यात्;

cond. आप्स्यत्. Pass. आप्यते. Caus. (with प्र prefixed) प्रापयति. Desid. ईप्सति.

ऋध (ऋधु) 'to increase.'

Pres. (ऋध्नोति (ऋध्नुतः, ऋध्नुवन्ति); 1st præt. आर्ध्नोत्; imp. ऋध्नोतु; pot. ऋध्नुयात्.

For the rest, see ऋध, second conjugation.

कृ (कृञ्) 'to injure.'

Pres. कृणोति, कृणुते; 1st præt. अकृणोत्, अकृणुत; imp. कृणोतु, कृणुतां; pot. कृणुयात्, कृण्वीत.

The rest like कृ 'to do:' see eighth conjugation.

कृवि 'to injure.'

This verb and धिवि, 'to go,' drop the semivowel before नु; and the influence of इ is suspended in the conjugational tenses.

Pres. कृणोति; 1st præt. अकृणोत्; 2d præt. चकृण्व; 3d præt. अकृण्वीत्; 1st fut. कृण्विता; 2d fut. कृण्विष्यति; imp. कृणोतु; pot. कृणुयात्; bened. कृण्व्यात्; cond. अकृण्विष्यत्. Pass. कृण्व्यते. Caus. कृण्वयति.

चि (चिञ्) 'to collect.'

The palatal becomes optionally the guttural in the reduplicate base, in the second præterite, and desiderative.

Pres. चिनोति, चिनुते; 1st præt. अचिनोत्, अचिनुत; 2d præt. चिचाय or चिकाय, चिच्ये or चिक्ये; 3d præt. अचैषीत्, अचेष्ट; 1st fut. चेता; 2d fut. चेष्यति -ते; imp. चिनोतु, चिनुतां; pot. चिनुयात्, चिन्वीत; bened. चीयात्, चेषीष्ट; cond. अचेष्यत् -त. Pass. चीयते. Caus. चाययति. Desid. चिचीषति or चिकीषति. Freq. चेचीयते, चेचयीति, चेचेति.

दम्भु 'to deceive.'

The nasal is rejected before नु, and before य. In the second præterite it is optionally conjugated as if it ended in a single consonant (rule 188, *k*).

Pres. दभ्नोति (दभ्नुतः); 1st præt. अदभ्नोत्; 2d præt. ददम्भ (ददम्भतुः, देभतुः; ददम्भिथ, देभिथ; ददम्भिव, देभिव); 3d præt. अदम्भीत्; 1st fut. दम्भिता; 2d fut. दम्भिष्यति; imp. दभ्नोतु; pot. दभ्नुयात्; bened.

दभ्यात्; cond. अदम्भिष्यत्. Pass. दभ्यते. Caus. दम्भयति. Desid. दिदम्भिषति, धिप्सति or धीप्सति. Freq. दन्दभ्यते.

धु (धुञ्) 'to shake' or 'tumble.'

Pres. धुनोति, धुनुते; 1st præt. अधुनोत्, अधुनुत; 2d præt. दुधाव, दुधुवे; 3d præt. अधौषीत्, अधोष्ट; 1st fut. धोता; 2d fut. धोष्यति -ते; imp. धुनोतु, धुनुतां; pot. धुनुयात्, धुन्वीत; bened. धूयात्, धोषीष्ट; cond. अधोष्यत् -त. Pass. धूयते. Caus. धूनयति or धावयति. Desid. दुधूषति. Freq. दोधूयते, दोधवीति, दोधोति.

धू (धूञ्) 'to shake' or 'tumble.'

It inserts इ before the usual terminations optionally, except व and म of the second præterite, where it is absolute.

Pres. धूनोति, धूनुते; 1st præt. अधूनोत्, अधूनुत; 2d præt. दुधाव (दुधविथ, दुधोथ, दुधुविव), दुधुवे; 3d præt. अधावीत्, अधविष्ट or अधोष्ट; 1st fut. धविता, धोता; 2d fut. धविष्यति -ते, धोष्यति -ते; imp. धूनोतु, धूनुतां; pot. धूनुयात्, धून्वीत; bened. धूयात्, धविषीष्ट, धोषीष्ट; cond. अधविष्यत् -त, अधोष्यत् -त.

The other forms are the same as in the preceding.

पृ 'to delight.'

Pres. पृणोति; 1st præt. अपृणोत्; 2d præt. पपार; 3d præt. अपार्षीत्; 1st fut. पर्ता; 2d fut. परिष्यति; imp. पृणोतु; pot. पृणुयात्; bened. प्रियात्; cond. अपरिष्यत्. Pass. प्रियते. Caus. पारयति. Desid. पुपूर्षति. Freq. पेप्रीयते, पेपरीति, पेपर्ति.

मि (मिञ्) 'to throw.'

This substitutes आ for its final in all the non-conjugational tenses except the second præterite Átmane-pada, and before य.

Pres. मिनोति, मिनुते; 1st præt. अमिनोत्, अमिनुत; 2d præt. ममौ, मिम्ये; 3d præt. अमासीत्, अमास्त; 1st fut. माता; 2d fut. मास्यति -ते; imp. मिनोतु, मिनुतां; pot. मिनुयात्, मिन्वीत; bened. मीयात्, मासिष्ट; cond. अमास्यत् -त. Pass. मीयते. Caus. मापयति. Desid. मित्सति -ते. Freq. मेमीयते, मेमयीति, मेमेति.

राध 'to accomplish,' 'to injure.'

In the second sense it substitutes ए for the radical vowel before the vowel terminations and the augment इ of the second præterite.

Pres. राध्नोति; 1st præt. अराध्नोत्; 2d præt. रराध (रराधतुः, रराधिथ, रराधिव or रेधतुः, रेधिथ, रेधिव); imp. राध्नोतु; pot. राध्नुयात्.

For the rest, see राध, fourth conjugation.

वृ (वृञ्) 'to choose.'

This optionally prolongs the augment इ, except before थ in the second præterite: before the other consonantal terminations of the same it does not take इ. It optionally inserts इ in the benedictive, and may change its vowel to ऊ in that tense, the benedictive, and third præterite, A'tmane-pada. In the latter it has different forms.

Pres. वृणोति, वृणुते; 1st præt. अवृणोत्, अवृणुत; 2d præt. ववार (ववरिथ, वव्रतुः, वव्रुः or ववरुः, ववृव), ववरे or वव्रे (ववृवहे); 3d præt. अवारीत्, अवरिष्ट, अवरीष्ट, अवृत, अवूर्ष्ट; 1st fut. वरिता, वरीता; 2d fut. वरिष्यति -ते, वरीष्यति -ते; imp. वृणोतु, वृणुतां; pot. वृणुयात्, वृण्वीत; bened. व्रियात् or वूर्यात्, वरिषीष्ट, वृषीष्ट, वूर्षीष्ट; cond. अवरिष्यत् -त, अवरीष्यत् -त. Pass. व्रियते. Caus. वारयति -ते. Desid. विवरिषति -ते, विवरीषति -ते, वुवूर्षति -ते. Freq. वेव्रीयते, वोवूर्यते, वर्वरीति, वर्वर्ति.

शक (शक्लृ) 'to be able.'

Pres. शक्नोति; 1st præt. अशक्नोत्; imp. शक्नोतु; pot. शक्नुयात्.

For the rest, see शक, fourth conjugation.

स्तृ (स्तृञ्) 'to cover.'

This inserts इ optionally, except in the second future and conditional where its insertion is absolute, and may prolong it when inserted.

Pres. स्तृणोति, स्तृणुते; 1st præt. अस्तृणोत्, अस्तृणुत; 2d præt. तस्तार, तस्तरे; 3d præt. अस्तारीत् or अस्तार्षीत्, अस्तरिष्ट, अस्तरीष्ट, अस्तीर्ष्ट or अस्तृत; 1st fut. स्तर्ता, स्तरिता, स्तरीता; 2d fut. स्तरिष्यति -ते, स्तरीष्यति -ते; imp. स्तृणोतु, स्तृणुतां; pot. स्तृणुयात्, स्तृण्वीत; bened.

स्तर्यात्, स्तृषीष्ट, स्तरिषीष्ट; cond. अस्तरिष्यत् -त, अस्तरीष्यत् -त. Pass. स्तर्यते. Caus. स्तारयति. Desid. तिस्तरिषति -ते, तिस्तरीषति -ते. Freq. तास्तर्यते, तास्तरीति, तास्तर्ति.

Sixth Conjugation.

217. This class is characterised by the insertion, before the terminations of the conjugational tenses, of श, that is, of the short vowel अ, with the effect of precluding the operation of an indicatory प; and the vowel of the root therefore is unchanged either to the Guṅa or Vṛiddhi element.

a. The terminations of the conjugational tenses undergo the same modifications as in the first conjugation.

b. Verbs ending with vowels change इ ई to इय्, उ ऊ to उव्, ऋ to रिय्, and ॠ to इर्, before the अ of the conjugation.

c. A class of verbs called from the first of them मुचादि insert a nasal before the finals in the conjugational tenses.

d. The class of verbs termed कुटादि extend the prohibition of the Guṅa or Vṛiddhi change to the non-conjugational tenses, except the first and third persons singular of the second præterite.

e. The type of the conjugation is तुद, 'to inflict pain.' It takes both Padas.

Present, 'I inflict pain,' &c.

तुदामि	तुदावः	तुदामः	तुदे	तुदावहे	तुदामहे
तुदसि	तुदथः	तुदथ	तुदसे	तुदेथे	तुदध्वे
तुदति	तुदतः	तुदन्ति	तुदते	तुदेते	तुदन्ते

First præterite, 'I have inflicted pain,' &c.

अतुदम्	अतुदाव	अतुदाम	अतुदे	अतुदावहि	अतुदामहि
अतुदः	अतुदतं	अतुदत	अतुदथाः	अतुदेथां	अतुदध्वं
अतुदत्	अतुदतां	अतुदन्	अतुदत	अतुदेतां	अतुदन्त

Imperative, 'May I inflict pain,' &c.

तुदानि	तुदाव	तुदाम	तुदै	तुदावहै	तुदामहै
तुद	तुदतं	तुदत	तुदस्व	तुदेथां	तुदध्वं
तुदतु	तुदतां	तुदन्तु	तुदतां	तुदेतां	तुदन्तां

Potential, 'I may inflict pain,' &c.

तुदेयं	तुदेव	तुदेम	तुदेय	तुदेवहि	तुदेमहि
तुदेः	तुदेतं	तुदेत	तुदेथाः	तुदेयाथां	तुदेध्वं
तुदेत्	तुदेतां	तुदेयुः	तुदेत	तुदेयातां	तुदेरन्

The other tenses are,

2d præt. तुतोद, तुतुदे; 3d præt. अतौत्सीत्, अतुत्त (अतुत्सातां, अतुत्सत); 1st fut. तोत्ता; 2d fut. तोत्स्यति -ते; bened. तुद्यात्, तोत्सीष्ट; cond. अतोत्स्यत् -त. Pass. तुद्यते. Caus. तोदयति. Desid. तुतुत्सति -ते. Freq. तोतुद्यते, तोतोत्ति.

इष 'to wish.'

This makes इच्छ, 'to wish,' in the conjugational tenses. It may insert इ in the first future.

Pres. इच्छति; 1st præt. ऐच्छत्; 2d præt. इयेष; 3d præt. ऐषीत्; 1st fut. एषिता or एष्टा; 2d fut. एष्यति; imp. इच्छतु; pot. इच्छेत्; bened. इष्यात्; cond. ऐष्यत्. Pass. इष्यते. Caus. एषयति.

कु (कुङ्) 'to sound,' 'to coo.'

According to some, the vowel is unchanged in the non-conjugational tenses.

Pres. कुवते; 1st præt. अकुवत; 2d præt. चुकुवे; 3d præt. अकुत; 1st fut. कुविता, कुता; 2d fut. कुविष्यते, कुष्यते; imp. कुवतां; pot. कुवेत; bened. कुविषीष्ट, कुषीष्ट; cond. अकुविष्यत, अकुष्यत. Pass. कूयते. Caus. कावयति. Desid. चुकूषते. Freq. चोकूयते or कोकूयते.

कुट 'to be crooked.'

This is the first of a class of verbs which retain the vowel unchanged, except before णप्.

Pres. कुटति; 1st præt. अकुटत्; 2d præt. चुकोट (चुकुटिथ); 3d præt. अकुटीत्; 1st fut. कुटिता; 2d fut. कुटिष्यति; imp. कुटतु; pot. कुटेत्; bened. कुट्यात्; cond. अकुटिष्यत्. Pass. कुट्यते. Caus. कुटयति. Desid. चुकुटिषति. Freq. चोकूट्यते, चोकोट्टि.

The class consists of a number of verbs having, with few exceptions, a medial उ: the most useful of them are,

कुच to contract.
कुड to be childish.
कृड to be thick.
गुज to sound.
गुड to preserve.
गुर to make effort.
चुट, छुट, छुर to cut.
जुट to bind.
डिप to throw.
तुट to make a riot.
तुड to inflict pain.
त्रुट to cut.
पुड to abandon.
स्फुट to bud, to expand.
स्फुर to throb.

कृष 'to draw furrows,' 'to plough.'

This takes different forms in the third præterite.

Pres. कृषति -ते; 1st præt. अकृषत् -त; 2d præt. चकर्ष, चकृषे; 3d præt. अक्राक्षीत्, अकार्क्षीत् or अकृक्षत्, and अकृष्ट or अकृक्षत; 1st fut. कर्ष्टा or क्रष्टा; 2d fut. कर्क्ष्यति -ते or क्रक्ष्यति -ते; imp. कृषतु, कृषतां; pot. कृषेत् -त; bened. कृष्यात्, कर्क्षीष्ट or क्रक्षीष्ट; cond. अकर्क्ष्यत् -त, अक्रक्ष्यत् -त. Pass. कृष्यते. Caus. कर्षयति. Desid. चिकृक्षति. Freq. चरीकृष्यते, चरीकर्ष्टि.

कॄ 'to throw.'

Pres. किरति; 1st præt. अकिरत्; 2d præt. चकार (चकरतुः, चकरुः); 3d præt. अकारीत्; 1st fut. करिता or करीता; 2d fut. करिष्यति or करीष्यति; imp. किरतु; pot. किरेत्; bened. कीर्यात्; cond. अकरिष्यत्, अकरीष्यत्. Pass. कीर्यते. Caus. कारयति. Desid. चिकरिषति. Freq. चेकीर्यते, चाकर्ति.

गॄ 'to swallow.'

This verb optionally substitutes ल for the र which is derived from the radical final, except before य.

Pres. गिरति, गिलति; 1st præt. अगिरत्, अगिलत्; 2d præt. जगार, जगाल; 3d præt. अगारीत्, अगालीत्; 1st fut. गरिता, गरीता, गलिता, गलीता; 2d fut. गरिष्यति, गरीष्यति, गलिष्यति, गलीष्यति; imp. गिरतु, गिलतु; pot. गिरेत्, गिलेत्; bened. गीर्यात्; cond. अगरिष्यत्, अगरीष्यत्, अगलिष्यत्, अगलीष्यत्. Pass. गीर्यते. Caus. गारयति, गालयति. Desid. जिगरिषति, जिगलिषति. Freq. जेगिल्यते, जागर्त्ति.

चृत (चृती) 'to hurt.'

Pres. चृतति; 1st præt. अचृतत्; 2d præt. चचर्त; 3d præt. अचर्तीत्; 1st fut. चर्तिता; 2d fut. चर्तिष्यति or चर्त्स्यति; imp. चृततु; pot. चृतेत्; bened. चृत्यात्; cond. अचर्तिष्यत्, अचर्त्स्यत्. Pass. चृत्यते. Caus. चर्तयति. Desid. चिचर्तिषति or चिचृत्सति. Freq. चिचृत्यते, चिचर्त्ति.

णु 'to praise.'

This root takes इ (rule 191, *b;* see also यु &c. in the second conjugation).

Pres. नुवति; 1st præt. अनुवत्; 2d præt. नुनाव; 3d præt. अनावीत्, अनुवीत्; 1st fut. नविता, नुविता; 2d fut. नविष्यति, नुविष्यति; imp. नुवतु; pot. नुवेत्; bened. नूयात्; cond. अनविष्यत्, अनुविष्यत्. Pass. नूयते. Caus. नावयति. Desid. नुनूषति. Freq. नोनूयते, नोनोति.

णू, 'to praise,' is similarly conjugated; so is कू 'to sound.'

तृप 'to satisfy.'

Pres. तृपति; 1st præt. अतृपत्; 3d præt. अतर्पीत्; imp. तृपतु; pot. तृपेत्.

For the rest, see तृप, fourth conjugation.

ध्रुव 'to be firm.'

Pres. ध्रुवति; 1st præt. अध्रुवत्; 2d præt. दुध्रोव; 3d præt. अध्रुवीत्; 1st fut. ध्रुविता; 2d fut. ध्रुविष्यति; imp. ध्रुवतु; pot. ध्रुवेत्; bened. ध्रुव्यात्; cond. अध्रुविष्यत्. Pass. ध्रुव्यते. Caus. ध्रुवयति. Desid. दुध्रुविषति. Freq. दोध्रूयते, दोध्रुवीति.

पृ (पृङ्) 'to extend.'

Pres. प्रियते; 1st præt. अप्रियत; 2d præt. पप्रे; 3d præt. अपृत (अपृषातां); 1st fut. पर्त्ता; 2d fut. परिष्यते; imp. प्रियतां; pot. प्रियेत; bened. पृषीष्ट; cond. अपरिष्यत. Pass. प्रियते. Caus. पारयति. Desid. पुपूर्षति. Freq. पेप्रीयते. पापर्त्ति.

The verb is commonly used with वि and आङ् prefixed; व्याप्रियते 'he conducts business.'

प्रच्छ 'to ask.'

This verb changes र to ऋ in the conjugational tenses. The final छ becomes ष before a consonant (rule 213).

Pres. पृच्छति; 1st præt. अपृच्छत्; 2d præt. पप्रच्छ; 3d præt. अप्राक्षीत्; 1st fut. प्रष्टा; 2d fut. प्रक्ष्यति; imp. पृच्छतु; pot. पृच्छेत्; bened. पृच्छ्यात्; cond. अप्रक्ष्यत्. Pass. पृच्छ्यते. Caus. प्रच्छयति -ते. Desid. पिप्रच्छिषति. Freq. परीपृच्छ्यते, पाप्रष्टि.

भ्रस्ज 'to fry.'

This verb also substitutes the vowel ऋ for the semivowel in the conjugational tenses, and optionally in the non-conjugational tenses, when it becomes the Guṇa अर्. It also converts the penultimate consonant to ज throughout: see मस्ज, first conjugation. A final ज becomes ष before a consonant. It takes both Padas.

Pres. भृज्जति -ते; 1st præt. अभृज्जत् -त; 2d præt. बभर्ज, बभ्रज्ज, बभर्जे, बभ्रज्जे; 3d præt. अभार्क्षीत्, अभ्राक्षीत्, अभार्ष्ट, अभ्राष्ट; 1st fut. भर्ष्टा, भ्रष्टा; 2d fut. भर्क्ष्यति -ते, भ्रक्ष्यति -ते; imp. भृज्जतु, भृज्जतां; pot. भृज्जेत् -त; bened. भृज्ज्यात्, भर्क्षीष्ट, भ्रक्षीष्ट; cond. अभर्क्ष्यत् -त, अभ्रक्ष्यत् -त. Pass. भृज्ज्यते. Caus. भर्जयति. Desid. बिभर्क्षति -ते, बिभ्रक्षति -ते. Freq. बरीभृज्ज्यते, बाभ्रष्टि.

लस्ज, 'to be ashamed,' becomes in like manner लज्ज (लज्जति, लज्जते).

मस्ज 'to be immersed in water,' 'to sink,' 'to drown.'

This also converts the sibilant to ज. In the non-conjugational tenses it inserts a nasal before the conjunct final, and one ज is rejected (rule 34, *a*).

Pres. मज्जति; 1st præt. अमज्जत्; 2d præt. ममज्ज (ममंक्थ, ममज्जिथ); 3d præt. अमांक्षीत् (अमांक्तां); 1st fut. मंक्ता; 2d fut. मंक्ष्यति; imp. मज्जतु; pot. मज्जेत्; bened. मज्ज्यात्; cond. अमंक्ष्यत्. Pass. मज्ज्यते. Caus. मज्जयति. Desid. मिमंक्षति. Freq. मामंक्ष्यते. मामंक्ति.

मुच (मुच्लृ) 'to liberate' or 'loose.'

The class of which this verb is the first, inserts a nasal in the conjugational tenses (rule 217, *c*).

Pres. मुञ्चति- ते; 1st præt. अमुञ्चत् -त; 2d præt. मुमोच, मुमुचे; 3d præt अमुचत्, अमुक्त; 1st fut. मोक्ता; 2d fut. मोक्ष्यति -ते; imp.

मुञ्चतु, मुञ्चतां; pot. मुञ्चेत्, मुञ्चेत; bened. मुच्यात्, मोक्षीष्ट; cond. अमोक्ष्यत् -त. Pass. मुच्यते. Caus. मोचयति. Desid. मुमुक्षति -ते. Freq. मोमुच्यते, मोमोक्ति.

The other verbs of this class are,

कृत (कृन्तति) to cut. लुप (लुम्पति -ते) to cut.
खिद (खिन्दति) to hurt. विद (विन्दति -ते) to find.
पिश (पिंशति) to be organised. षिच (सिञ्चति -ते) to sprinkle.
लिप (लिम्पति -ते) to smear.

Of these, the three last have an Anubandha ऌ, and therefore make one form only in the third præterite, Parasmai-pada: लिप and षिच have two forms in the Átmane-pada, अलिपत or अलिप्त, असिचत or असिक्त; कृत and खिद take इ, कर्तिता, खेदिता, &c.

मृ (मृङ्) 'to die.'

This verb follows the Parasmai-pada in the second præterite, futures, and conditional. In the desiderative, उ is substituted for ऋ.

Pres. म्रियते; 1st præt. अम्रियत; 2d præt. ममार (मम्रतुः, ममर्थ, मम्रिव); 3d præt. अमृत; 1st fut. मर्ता; 2d fut. मरिष्यति; imp. म्रियतां; pot. म्रियेत; bened. मृषीष्ट; cond. अमरिष्यत्. Pass. म्रियते. Caus. मारयति. Desid. मुमूर्षति. Freq. मेम्रीयते, मामर्ति.

व्यच 'to deceive.'

This substitutes इ for the semivowel in the conjugational tenses, and in the second præterite; and before य.

Pres. विचति; 1st præt. अविचत्; 2d præt. विव्याच (विविचतुः); 3d præt. अव्यचीत् or अव्याचीत्; 1st fut. व्यचिता; 2d fut. व्यचिष्यति; imp. विचतु; pot. विचेत्; bened. विच्यात्; cond. अव्यचिष्यत्. Pass. विच्यते. Caus. व्याचयति. Desid. विव्यचिषति. Freq. वेविच्यते, वाव्यचीति, वाव्यक्ति.

व्रश्च (ओव्रश्चू) 'to cut.'

This substitutes the vowel for the semivowel in the conjugational tenses, and before य. In the non-conjugational tenses it optionally inserts इ; and when it does not, the final च is rejected.

Pres. वृश्चति; 1st præt. अवृश्चत्; 2d præt. वव्रश्च (वव्रश्चिथ, वव्रष्ठ);

3d præt. अव्रश्चीत्, अव्राक्षीत्; 1st fut. व्रश्चिता, व्रष्टा; 2d fut. व्रश्चिष्यति, व्रक्ष्यति; imp. वृश्चतु; pot. वृश्चेत्; bened. वृश्च्यात्; cond. अव्रश्चिष्यत्, अव्रक्ष्यत्. Pass. वृश्च्यते. Caus. व्रश्चयति. Desid. विव्रश्चिषति or विव्रक्षति. Freq. वरीवृश्च्यते, वरीवृश्चीति, वरीव्रष्टि.

सृज 'to let go,' 'to abandon,' 'to create.'

Pres. सृजति; 1st præt. असृजत्; 2d præt. ससर्ज; 3d præt. अस्राक्षीत्; 1st fut. स्रष्टा; 2d fut. स्रक्ष्यति; imp. सृजतु; pot. सृजेत्; bened. सृज्यात्; cond. अस्रक्ष्यत्. Pass. सृज्यते.

For the rest, see सृज, fourth conjugation.

स्पृश 'to touch.'

This optionally substitutes the Guña syllable or the semi-vowel only in the third præterite, futures, and conditional.

Pres. स्पृशति; 1st præt. अस्पृशत्; 2d præt. पस्पर्श (पस्पृशतुः); 3d præt. अस्पार्क्षीत्, अस्प्राक्षीत् or अस्पृक्षत्; 1st fut. स्पर्ष्टा, स्प्रष्टा; 2d fut. स्पर्क्ष्यति, स्प्रक्ष्यति; imp. स्पृशतु; pot. स्पृशेत्; bened. स्पृश्यात्; cond. अस्पर्क्ष्यत् or अस्प्रक्ष्यत्. Pass. स्पृश्यते. Caus. स्पर्शयति. Desid. पिस्पर्क्षति or पिस्प्रक्षति. Freq. परीस्पृश्यते, परीस्पर्ष्टि.

Seventh Conjugation.

218. The characteristic peculiarity of this conjugation is the insertion before the radical final of न, before the terminations which contain an indicatory प, and न् before the rest.

a. All the verbs of this class, which are not many, end in consonants; and the union of them with the initial consonants of the terminations takes place according to the rules of Sandhi. धि is substituted for हि in the imperative. The single consonants of the first præterite are rejected after a consonant (rule 213).

b. A verb containing a penultimate nasal compounded with its final, rejects it in favour of the conjugational sign before the conjugational tenses.

c. The type of the conjugation is रुध 'to hinder' or 'obstruct:' it takes both Padas.

d. After an aspirated consonant the त and थ of an inflexional termination become ध (rule 186): न preceded by र is changed to ण (rule 18).

Present, 'I obstruct,' &c.

रुणध्मि	रुंध्वः	रुंध्मः	‖	रुंन्धे	रुंध्वहे	रुंध्महे
रुणत्सि	रुंद्धः	रुंद्ध	‖	रुंत्से	रुन्धाथे	रुंद्ध्वे
रुणद्धि	रुंद्धः	रुन्धन्ति	‖	रुंद्धे	रुन्धाते	रुन्धते

First præterite, 'I obstructed,' &c.

अरुणधं	अरुंध्व	अरुंध्म	‖	अरुन्धि	अरुंध्वहि	अरुंध्महि
अरुणत् -द् अरुणः	अरुंद्धं	अरुंद्ध	‖	अरुंद्धाः	अरुन्धाथां	अरुंद्ध्वं
अरुणत् -द्	अरुंद्धां	अरुन्धन्	‖	अरुंद्ध	अरुन्धातां	अरुन्धत

Imperative, 'May I obstruct,' &c.

रुणधानि	रुणधाव	रुणधाम	‖	रुणधै	रुणधावहै	रुणधामहै
रुंद्धि	रुंद्धं	रुंद्ध	‖	रुंत्स्व	रुन्धाथां	रुंद्ध्वं
रुणद्धु	रुंद्धां	रुंधन्तु	‖	रुंद्धां	रुन्धातां	रुन्धतां

Potential, 'I may obstruct,' &c.

रुन्ध्यां	रुन्ध्याव	रुन्ध्याम	‖	रुन्धीय	रुन्धीवहि	रुन्धीमहि
रुन्ध्याः	रुन्ध्यातं	रुन्ध्यात	‖	रुन्धीथाः	रुन्धीयाथां	रुन्धीध्वं
रुन्ध्यात्	रुन्ध्यातां	रुन्ध्युः	‖	रुन्धीत	रुन्धीयातां	रुन्धीरन्

The rest are,

2d præt. रुरोध, रुरुधे; 3d præt. अरुधत् or अरौत्सीत्, अरुद्ध (अरुत्सातां, अरुत्सत); 1st fut. रोद्धा; 2d fut. रोत्स्यति -ते; bened. रुध्यात्, रुत्सीष्ट; cond. अरोत्स्यत् -त. Pass. रुध्यते. Caus. रोधयति. Desid. रुरुत्सति -ते. Freq. रोरुध्यते, रोरोद्धि.

अञ्ज (अञ्जू) 'to become manifest.'

Notwithstanding the Anubandha ऊ, the augment इ is inserted in the third præterite. This and the two following reject the nasal penultimate (rule 218, *b*).

Pres. अनक्ति (अंक्तः, अञ्जन्ति); 1st præt. आनक्; 2d præt. आनञ्ज; 3d præt. आञ्जीत्; 1st fut. अंक्ता, अञ्जिता; 2d fut. अंक्ष्यति, अञ्जिष्यति; imp. अनक्तु (अङ्ग्धि, अनजानि); pot. अंज्यात्; bened. अज्यात्; cond. आंक्ष्यत्, आञ्जिष्यत्. Pass. अज्यते. Caus. अञ्जयति. Desid. अञ्जिजिषति.

इन्ध (इन्धी) 'to shine.'

Pres. इंद्धे (इंत्से); 1st præt. ऐंद्ध; 2d præt. इन्धाञ्चक्रे; 3d præt. ऐन्धिष्ट; 1st fut. इन्धिता; 2d fut. इन्धिष्यते; imp. इंद्धां; pot. इन्धीत; bened. इन्धिषीष्ट; cond. ऐन्धिष्यत. Pass. इध्यते. Caus. इन्धयति. Desid. इन्दिधिषते.

उन्द (उन्दी) 'to wet.'

Pres. उनत्ति (उन्तः, उन्दन्ति); 1st præt. औनत्; 2d præt. उन्दाञ्चकार; 3d præt. औन्दीत्; 1st fut. उन्दिता; 2d fut. उन्दिष्यति; imp. उनत्तु; pot. उंद्यात्; bened. उद्यात्; cond. औन्दिष्यत्. Pass. उद्यते. Caus. उन्दयति. Desid. उन्दिदिषति.

छृद (छृदिर्) 'to play,' 'to shine.'

The augment इ is optionally inserted before स in any of the non-conjugational tenses.

Pres. छृणत्ति, छृन्ते; 1st præt. अछृणत्, अछृन्त; 2d præt. चच्छर्द, चच्छृदे (चच्छृदिषे or चच्छृत्से); 3d præt. अछृदत्, अच्छर्दीत्, अछृदत, अच्छर्दिष्ट; 1st fut. छर्दिता; 2d fut. छर्दिष्यति -ते or छर्त्स्यति -ते; imp. छृणत्तु, छृन्तां; pot. छृन्द्यात्, छृन्दीत; bened. छृद्यात्, छर्दिषीष्ट, छृत्सीष्ट; cond. अच्छर्दिष्यत् -त, अच्छृत्स्यत् -त. Pass. छृद्यते. Caus. छर्दयति. Desid. चिच्छर्दिषति -ते, चिच्छृत्सति -ते. Freq. चरीछृद्यते, चर्छर्दीति, चर्छर्त्ति.

तृह 'to injure.'

This verb inserts इ before the conjugational sign before the terminations beginning with consonants which reject प्. For the changes of ह, see rule 213, *c*, 8.

Pres. तृणेढि (तृणेक्षि, तृणेह्मि, तृण्ढः, तृंहन्ति, तृंह्मः); 1st præt. अतृणेट् (अतृण्ढां); 2d præt. ततर्ह; 3d præt. अतर्हीत्; 1st fut. तर्हिता; 2d fut. तर्हिष्यति; imp. तृणेढु (तृण्ढां, तृंहन्तु); pot. तृंह्यात्; bened. तृह्यात्; cond. अतर्हिष्यत्. Pass. तृह्यते. Caus. तर्हयति. Desid. तितर्हिषति. Freq. तरीतृह्यते, तर्तर्ढि.

भिद भिदिर्) 'to break,' 'to divide.'

Pres. भिनत्ति, भिंत्ते; 1st præt. अभिनत्, अभिंत्त; 2d præt. बिभेद, बिभिदे; 3d præt. अभिदत् or अभैत्सीत्, अभित्त; 1st fut. भेत्ता; 2d fut. भेत्स्यति -ते; imp. भिनत्तु, भिंत्तां; pot. भिंद्यात्, भिन्दीत;

bened. भिद्यात्, भित्सीष्ट; cond. अभेत्स्यत् -त. Pass. भिद्यते. Caus. भेदयति. Desid. बिभित्सति -ते. Freq. बेभिद्यते, बेभेत्ति.

There are several other verbs in this conjugation similarly inflected; as,

क्षुद (क्षुदिर्) 'to send:' क्षुणत्ति, क्षुंत्ते, क्षोत्ता, अक्षुदत् or अक्षौत्सीत्, अक्षुत्त.

छिद (छिदिर्) 'to cut:' छिनत्ति, छिंत्ते, छेत्ता, अच्छिदत् or अच्छैत्सीत्, अच्छित्त.

युज (युजिर्) 'to join,' 'to unite:' युनक्ति, युंक्ते, योक्ता, अयुजत् or अयौक्षीत्, अयुक्त.

रिच (रिचिर्) 'to purge:' रिणक्ति, रिंक्ते, रेक्ता, अरिचत् or अरैक्षीत्, अरिक्त.

विच (विचिर्) 'to separate:' विनक्ति, विंक्ते, वेक्ता, अविचत् or अवैक्षीत्, अविक्त.

भञ्ज 'to break.'

See rule 218, *b*.

Pres. भनक्ति; 1st præt. अभनक्; 2d præt. बभञ्ज; 3d præt. अभांक्षीत्; 1st fut. भंक्ता; 2d fut. भंक्ष्यति; imp. भनक्तु; pot. भंज्यात्; bened. भज्यात्; cond. अभंक्ष्यत्. Pass. भज्यते. Caus. भञ्जयति. Desid. बिभंक्षति. Freq. बंभज्यते, बंभंक्ति.

भुज 'to eat,' 'to enjoy,' 'to cherish.'

Pres. भुनक्ति, भुंक्ते; 1st præt. अभुनक्, अभुंक्त; 2d præt. बुभोज, बुभुजे; 3d præt. अभौक्षीत्, अभुक्त; 1st fut. भोक्ता; 2d fut. भोक्ष्यति -ते; imp. भुनक्तु, भुंक्तां; pot. भुंज्यात्, भुञ्जीत; bened. भुज्यात्, भुक्षीष्ट; cond. अभोक्ष्यत् -त. Pass. भुज्यते. Caus. भोजयति. Desid. बुभुक्षति -ते. Freq. बोभुज्यते, बोभोक्ति.

विज (ओविजी) 'to fear,' 'to tremble.'

This verb does not change its radical vowel when इ is inserted.

Pres. विनक्ति; 1st præt. अविनक्; 2d præt. विवेज (विविजिथ); 3d præt. अविजीत्; 1st fut. विजिता; 2d fut. विजिष्यति; imp. विनक्तु; pot. विंज्यात्; bened. विज्यात्; cond. अविजिष्यत्. Pass. विज्यते. Caus. वेजयति. Desid. विविजिषति. Freq. वेविज्यते, वेवेक्ति.

शिष (शिषृ) 'to distinguish.'

Pres. शिनष्टि; 1st præt. अशिनट्; 2d præt. शिशेष (शिशेषिथ); 3d præt. अशिषत्; 1st fut. शेष्टा; 2d fut. शेक्ष्यति; imp. शिनष्टु (शिण्ढि or शिड्ढि, शिनषाणि); pot. शिंष्यात्; bened. शिष्यात्; cond. अशेक्ष्यत्. Pass. शिष्यते. Caus. शेषयति. Desid. शिशिक्षति. Freq. शेशिष्यते, शेशेष्टि.

पिष (पिषृ), 'to grind,' is similarly conjugated.

हिस (हिसि) 'to injure' or 'kill.'

The nasal which the verb derives from the Anubandha is replaced by the conjugational sign in the conjugational tenses.

Pres. हिनस्ति; 1st præt. अहिनत् (अहिंस्ताम्, अहिनः or अहिनत्, अहिनसम्); 2d præt. जिहिंस; 3d præt. अहिंसीत्; 1st fut. हिंसिता; 2d fut. हिंसिष्यति; imp. हिनस्तु; pot. हिंस्यात्; bened. हिंस्यात्; cond. अहिंसिष्यत्. Pass. हिंस्यते. Caus. हिंसयति. Desid. जिहिंसिषति. Freq. जेहिंस्यते, जेहिंस्ति.

Eighth Conjugation.

219. In this conjugation उ is subjoined to the root, which before a termination containing an indicatory प् becomes ओ.

a. Before a termination beginning with व or म the augment उ may be rejected (see rule 216, *a*).

b. हि in the imperative is rejected.

c. In the third præterite of the Átmane-pada the sibilant of स्त, स्थास्, may be rejected, when a radical final consonant is dropped.

d. There are but few verbs in this conjugation, and with one exception, that of कृ, they all end in nasals; being therefore exactly analogous to verbs of the fifth conjugation, which insert नु.

e. Such verbs as have a penultimate short vowel, other than अ, change it optionally to its Guńa equivalent in the conjugational tenses.

The type of the conjugation is तन 'to stretch,' which takes both Padas.

Present, 'I stretch,' &c.

तनोमि	तनुवः तन्वः	तनुमः तन्मः	तन्वे	तनुवहे तन्वहे	तनुमहे तन्महे
तनोषि	तनुथः	तनुथ	तनुषे	तन्वाथे	तनुध्वे
तनोति	तनुतः	तन्वन्ति	तनुते	तन्वाते	तन्वते

First præterite, 'I stretched,' &c.

अतनवम्	अतनुव / अतन्व	अतनुम / अतन्म	अतन्वि	अतनुवहि / अतन्वहि	अतनुमहि / अतन्महि
अतनोः	अतनुतं	अतनुत	अतनुथाः	अतन्वाथां	अतनुध्वं
अतनोत्	अतनुतां	अतन्वन्	अतनुत	अतन्वातां	अतन्वत

Imperative, 'May I stretch,' &c.

तनवानि	तनवाव	तनवाम	तनवै	तनवावहै	तनवामहै
तनु	तनुतं	तनुत	तनुष्व	तन्वाथां	तनुध्वं
तनोतु	तनुतां	तन्वन्तु	तनुतां	तन्वातां	तन्वतां

Potential, 'I may stretch,' &c.

तनुयां	तनुयाव	तनुयाम	तन्वीय	तन्वीवहि	तन्वीमहि
तनुयाः	तनुयातं	तनुयात	तन्वीथाः	तन्वीयाथां	तन्वीध्वं
तनुयात्	तनुयातां	तनुयुः	तन्वीत	तन्वीयातां	तन्वीरन्

The other tenses are,

2d præt. ततान, तेने; 3d præt. अतनीत् or अतानीत्, अतत or अतनिष्ट; 1st fut. तनिता; 2d fut. तनिष्यति -ते; bened. तन्यात्, तनिषीष्ट; cond. अतनिष्यत् -त. Pass. तन्यते or तायते. Caus. तानयति. Desid. तितनिषति -ते, तितांसति -ते, तितंसति -ते Freq. तन्तन्यते, तन्तनीति, तन्तन्मि.

The remaining verbs of this class, which, except कृ, end in a nasal, are the following: they all may take both Padas.

ऋण 'to go:' अर्णोति, अर्णुते or ऋणोति, ऋणुते, अर्णिता, आर्णीत्, आर्त्त or आर्णिष्ट.

क्षण 'to kill or hurt:' it does not elongate the vowel in the third præterite: क्षणोति, क्षणुते, क्षणिता, अक्षणीत्, अक्षत or अक्षणिष्ट.

क्षिण 'to kill or hurt:' क्षिणोति or क्षेणोति, क्षिणुते or क्षेणुते, क्षेणिता, अक्षेणीत्, अक्षित or अक्षेणिष्ट.

घृण 'to shine:' घर्णोति, घर्णुते or घृणोति, घृणुते, घृणिता, घर्णिता, अघर्णीत्, अघर्त or अघर्णिष्ट.

तृण 'to eat grass:' तृणोति or तर्णोति, तृणुते or तर्णुते, तर्णिता, अतर्णीत्, अतर्त or अतर्णिष्ट.

मन 'to understand:' मनुते, मनिता, अमत or अमनिष्ट.

वन 'to ask:' वनोति, वनुते, वनिता, अवनीत् or अवानीत्, अवत or अवनिष्ट.

षण, 'to give,' optionally rejects the final, and makes the vowel long before य; it does the same before the त and थास् of the third præterite: सनोति, सनुते, सनिता, सन्यात् or सायात्, असनीत् or असानीत्, असात or असनिष्ट (असाथाः or असनिष्ठाः).

कृ 'to do.'

In the conjugational tenses the radical vowel substitutes, as usual, the Guṅa letter before the conjugational sign in the inflexions which have an indicatory प्; but before the rest it substitutes उर्. It rejects the conjugational sign before व, म, and य. It takes both Padas.

Pres. करोति (कुरुतः, कुर्वन्ति, कुर्वः कुर्मः), कुरुते (कुर्वाते, कुर्वते); 1st præt. अकरोत् (अकुरुतां, अकरवम्), अकुरुत (अकुर्वातां, अकुर्वत); 2d præt. चकार (चक्रतुः, चकर्थ, चकृव, चकार or चकर, चकृम), चक्रे (चकृषे); 3d præt. अकार्षीत् (अकार्ष्टां, अकार्षुः), अकृत (अकृषातां, अकृषत, अकृथाः, अकृषाथां, अकृढ्वं, अकृषि); 1st fut. कर्त्ता; 2d fut. करिष्यति -ते; imp. करोतु (कुरु, करवाणि, करवाव), कुरुतां (कुर्वातां, कुर्वतां); pot. कुर्यात्, कुर्वीत; bened. क्रियात्, कृषीष्ट; cond. अकरिष्यत् -त. Pass. क्रियते; 3d præt. अकारि. Caus. कारयति -ते; 3d præt. अचीकरत् -त. Desid. चिकीर्षति -ते. Freq. चेक्रीयते, चर्करीति, चरिकरीति or चरीकरीति, चर्कर्ति, चरिकर्ति or चरीकर्ति.

Ninth Conjugation.

220. The verbs of this class subjoin ना to the root before terminations beginning with consonants which reject प्; नी before the other terminations beginning with a consonant; and न् before those which begin with a vowel.

a. The terminations undergo no change.

b. Verbs ending in consonants substitute आन for the conjugational sign and the termination हि, in the imperative.

c. A class of verbs called प्वादि from पू 'to purify,' ending in vowels, make them short in the conjugational tenses. Some others make the vowel short only before the terminations of the second præterite not requiring Guṇa.

The model of the class is क्री 'to buy,' which takes both Padas. The न of the conjugational augment becomes ण (rule 18).

Present, 'I buy,' &c.

क्रीणामि	क्रीणीवः	क्रीणीमः	क्रीणे	क्रीणीवहे	क्रीणीमहे
क्रीणासि	क्रीणीथः	क्रीणीथ	क्रीणीषे	क्रीणाथे	क्रीणीध्वे
क्रीणाति	क्रीणीतः	क्रीणन्ति	क्रीणीते	क्रीणाते	क्रीणते

First præterite, 'I bought,' &c.

अक्रीणां	अक्रीणीव	अक्रीणीम	अक्रीणि	अक्रीणीवहि	अक्रीणीमहि
अक्रीणाः	अक्रीणीतं	अक्रीणीत	अक्रीणीथाः	अक्रीणाथां	अक्रीणीध्वं
अक्रीणात्	अक्रीणीतां	अक्रीणन्	अक्रीणीत	अक्रीणातां	अक्रीणत

Imperative, 'May I buy,' &c.

क्रीणानि	क्रीणाव	क्रीणाम	क्रीणै	क्रीणावहै	क्रीणामहै
क्रीणीहि	क्रीणीतं	क्रीणीत	क्रीणीष्व	क्रीणाथां	क्रीणीध्वं
क्रीणातु	क्रीणीतां	क्रीणन्तु	क्रीणीतां	क्रीणातां	क्रीणतां

Potential, 'I may buy,' &c.

क्रीणीयां	क्रीणीयाव	क्रीणीयाम	क्रीणीय	क्रीणीवहि	क्रीणीमहि
क्रीणीयाः	क्रीणीयातं	क्रीणीयात	क्रीणीथाः	क्रीणीयाथां	क्रीणीध्वं
क्रीणीयात्	क्रीणीयातां	क्रीणीयुः	क्रीणीत	क्रीणीयातां	क्रीणीरन्

The other tenses are,

2d præt. चिक्राय (चिक्रियतुः, चिक्रयिथ or चिक्रेथ), चिक्रिये; 3d præt. अक्रैषीत्, अक्रेष्ट; 1st fut. क्रेता; 2d fut. क्रेष्यति -ते; bened. क्रीयात्, क्रेषीष्ट; cond. अक्रेष्यत् -त. Pass. क्रीयते. Caus. क्रापयति. Desid. चिक्रीषति -ते. Freq. चेक्रीयते, चेक्रयीति, चेक्रेति.

So प्रीञ् 'to desire,' and मीञ् 'to injure' or 'kill:' the latter in the non-conjugational tenses substitutes आ for the final: see मि, fifth conjugation.

अश 'to eat.'

Pres. अश्नाति; 1st præt. आश्नात्; 2d præt. आश; 3d præt.

आशीत्; 1st fut. अशिता; 2d fut. अशिष्यति; imp. अश्नातु; pot. अश्नीयात्; bened. अश्यात्; cond. आशिष्यत्.

For the rest, see अश, fifth conjugation.

ऋ 'to go.'

As belonging to the class प्वादि, the vowel is short in the conjugational tenses.

Pres. ऋणाति; 1st præt. आर्णात्; 2d præt. अराञ्चकार; 3d præt. आरीत्; 1st fut. अरिता, अरीता; 2d fut. अरिष्यति, अरीष्यति; imp. ऋणातु; pot. ऋणीयात्; bened. ईर्यात्; cond. आरिष्यत्.

See ऋ of the first conjugation.

क्लिश (क्लिशू) 'to be distressed.'

Pres. क्लिश्नाति; 1st præt. अक्लिश्नात्; 2d præt. चिक्लेश; 3d præt. अक्लेशीत् or अक्लिक्षत्; 1st fut. क्लेशिता, क्लेष्टा; 2d fut. क्लेशिष्यति, क्लेक्ष्यति; imp. क्लिश्नातु; pot. क्लिश्नीयात्; bened. क्लिश्यात्; cond. अक्लेशिष्यत्, अक्लेक्ष्यत्. Pass. क्लिश्यते. Caus. क्लेशयति. Desid. चिक्लेशिषति, चिक्लिशिषति, चिक्लिक्षति. Freq. चेक्लिश्यते, चेक्लेष्टि.

क्षुभ 'to be agitated.'

Pres. क्षुभ्नाति; 1st præt. अक्षुभ्नात्; 2d præt. चुक्षोभ; 3d præt. अक्षोभीत्; 1st fut. क्षोभिता; 2d fut. क्षोभिष्यति; imp. क्षुभ्नातु (क्षुभाण); pot. क्षुभ्नीयात्; bened. क्षुभ्यात्; cond. अक्षोभिष्यत्. Pass. क्षुभ्यते. Caus. क्षोभयति. Desid. चुक्षुभिषति. Freq. चोक्षुभ्यते, चोक्षोब्धि.

ग्रन्थ 'to arrange in order.'

This rejects the radical nasal in favour of the conjugational sign; also before य, and optionally before the terminations of the second præterite, when before those which do not require the change of a radical vowel, ए may be substituted for अ.

Pres. ग्रथ्नाति; 1st præt. अग्रथ्नात्; 2d præt. जग्रन्थ, जग्राथ (जग्रन्थतुः, ग्रेथतुः); 3d præt. अग्रन्थीत्; 1st fut. ग्रन्थिता; 2d fut. ग्रन्थिष्यति; imp. ग्रथ्नातु; pot. ग्रथ्नीयात्; bened. ग्रथ्यात्; cond. अग्रन्थिष्यत्. Pass. ग्रथ्यते. Caus. ग्रन्थयति. Desid. जिग्रन्थिषति. Freq. जाग्रथ्यते, जंग्रन्थीति, जंग्रंद्धि.

Other verbs are similarly inflected; as, कुन्थ 'to suffer pain:'

कुथ्नाति, कुन्थिता, चुकुन्थ or चुकोथ, कुथ्यात्.—मन्थ 'to churn:' मथ्नाति, मन्थिता, ममन्थ or ममाथ (ममन्थतुः, मेथतुः), मथ्यात्.—ग्रन्थ 'to loosen:' ग्रथ्नाति, ग्रन्थिता, जग्रन्थ or जग्राथ (जग्रन्थतुः, ग्रेथतुः), ग्रथ्यात्, &c.

ग्रह 'to take.'

This substitutes ऋ for the semivowel in the conjugational tenses. It makes the augment इ long in every tense except the second præterite.

Pres. गृह्णाति, गृह्णीते; 1st præt. अगृह्णात्, अगृह्णीत; 2d præt. जग्राह (जगृहतुः, जग्रहिथ, जगृहिव); 3d præt. अग्रहीत्, अग्रहीष्ट; 1st fut. ग्रहीता; 2d fut. ग्रहीष्यति -ते; imp. गृह्णातु (गृहाण), गृह्णीतां; pot. गृह्णीयात्, गृह्णीत; bened. गृह्यात्, ग्रहीषीष्ट; cond. अग्रहीष्यत् -त. Pass. गृह्यते. Caus. ग्राहयति -ते. Desid. जिघृक्षति -ते. Freq. जरीगृह्यते, जाग्रहीति, जाग्रढि.

ज्ञा 'to know.'

This becomes जा before the conjugational terminations.

Pres. जानाति, जानीते; 1st præt. अजानात्, अजानीत; 2d præt. जज्ञौ, जज्ञे; 3d præt. अज्ञासीत्, अज्ञास्त; 1st fut. ज्ञाता; 2d fut. ज्ञास्यति -ते; imp. जानातु, जानीतां; pot. जानीयात्, जानीत; bened. ज्ञेयात्, ज्ञायात्, ज्ञासीष्ट; cond. अज्ञास्यत् -त. Pass. ज्ञायते. Caus. ज्ञापयति. Desid. जिज्ञासति -ते. Freq. जाज्ञायते, जाज्ञेति or जाज्ञाति.

ज्या 'to become old.'

The semivowel is changed to इ in the conjugational tenses, and to ई before य.

Pres. जिनाति; 1st præt. अजिनात्; 2d præt. जिज्यौ; 3d præt. अज्यासीत्; 1st fut. ज्याता; 2d fut. ज्यास्यति; imp. जिनातु; pot. जिनीयात्; bened. जीयात्; cond. अज्यास्यत्. Pass. जायते, जीयते. Caus. ज्यापयति. Freq. जेजीयते, ज्याज्याति.

धु (धुञ्), धू (धूञ्), 'to tremble.'

As the verb with the long final vowel shortens this in the conjugational tenses, there is no difference in the inflexions: in the other tenses the difference is that of the insertion or omission of इ, except in the third præterite Parasmai-pada, where it is inserted in both verbs.

Pres. धुनाति, धुनीते; 1st præt. अधुनात्, अधुनीत; 2d præt. दुधाव, दुधुवे; 3d præt. अधावीत्, अधविष्ट or अधोष्ट; 1st fut. धोता, धविता; 2d fut. धोष्यति -ते, धविष्यति -ते; imp. धुनातु, धुनीतां; pot. धुनीयात्, धुनीत; bened. धूयात्, धोषीष्ट, धविषीष्ट; cond. अधोष्यत् -त, अधविष्यत् -त.

For the rest, see धु and धू, fifth conjugation.

पुष 'to nourish.'

In this conjugation it takes इ.

Pres. पुष्णाति; 1st præt. अपुष्णात्; 2d præt. पुपोष; 3d præt. अपोषीत्; 1st fut. पोषिता; 2d fut. पोषिष्यति; imp. पुष्णातु; pot. पुष्णीयात्; bened. पुष्यात्; cond. अपोषिष्यत्.

The rest as पुष, fourth conjugation.

पू 'to purify.'

This is the first verb of a class ending in long vowels, of which the final is made short before the conjugational sign.

Pres. पुनाति, पुनीते; 1st præt. अपुनात्, अपुनीत; 2d præt. पुपाव, पुपुवे; 3d præt. अपावीत्, अपविष्ट; 1st fut. पविता; 2d fut. पविष्यति -ते; imp. पुनातु, पुनीतां; pot. पुनीयात्, पुनीत; bened. पूयात्, पविषीष्ट; cond. अपविष्यत् -त. Pass. पूयते. Caus. पावयति. Desid. पुपूषति -ते or पिपविषति -ते. Freq. पोपूयते, पोपोति.

The following verbs belong to the class ल्वादि:

लू 'to go;' as above.
कॄ 'to injure:' कृणाति, कृणीते, करिता, करीता, अकारीत्, अकरिष्ट, कीर्य्यात्.
गॄ 'to sound:' गृणाति, गरिता, गरीता, अगारीत्, गीर्य्यात्.
जॄ 'to decay:' जृणाति, जरिता, जरीता, अजारीत्, जीर्य्यात्.
दॄ 'to tear:' दृणाति, दरिता, दरीता, अदारीत्, दीर्य्यात्.
धू 'to shake;' as above.
पॄ 'to fill:' पृणाति, परिता, परीता, अपारीत्, पूर्य्यात्.
भॄ 'to threaten:' भृणाति, भरिता, भरीता, अभारीत्, भीर्य्यात्.
भ्री 'to support:' भ्रिणाति, भ्रेता, अभ्रैषीत्.
मॄ 'to injure:' मृणाति, मरिता, मरीता, अमारीत्, मीर्य्यात्.
री 'to roar:' रिणाति, रेता, अरैषीत्.
ली 'to cling to:' लिनाति, लेता, अलैषीत्.

लू 'to cut:' लुनाति, लुनीते, लविता, अलावीत्, अलविष्ट.
वृ 'to choose:' see वृ below.
व्री 'to choose:' व्रिणाति, व्रेता, अव्रैषीत्.
व्ली 'to support:' व्लिनाति, व्लेता, अव्लैषीत्.
शृ 'to injure:' see below.
स्तृ 'to spread:' see below.

प्री (प्रीञ्) 'to please,' 'to desire.'

This and several other verbs of the class ending in long vowels do not make them short, as not belonging to the class प्वादि.

Pres. प्रीणाति, प्रीणीते; 1st præt. अप्रीणात्, अप्रीणीत; 2d præt. पिप्राय, पिप्रिये; 3d præt. अप्रैषीत्, अप्रेष्ट; 1st fut. प्रेता; 2d fut. प्रेष्यति -ते; imp. प्रीणातु, प्रीणीतां; pot. प्रीणीयात्, प्रीणीत; bened. प्रीयात्, प्रेषीष्ट; cond. अप्रेष्यत् -त. Pass. प्रीयते. Caus. प्रीणयति. Desid. पिप्रीषति -ते. Freq. पेप्रीयते, पेप्रयीति, पेप्रेति.

So क्नू 'to sound,' क्नूणाति, क्नूणीते, &c.; and श्री 'to cook,' श्रीणाति, श्रीणीते. भ्री 'to cook,' and व्री 'to choose,' are optionally long or short; भ्रीणाति, भ्रिणाति; व्रीणाति, व्रिणाति.

बन्ध 'to bind.'

This drops its nasal in the conjugational tenses, and before य.

Pres. बध्नाति; 1st præt. अबध्नात्; 2d præt. बबन्ध (बबन्धिथ or बबन्द्ध); 3d præt. अभांत्सीत् (अबंद्धां, अभांत्सुः); 1st fut. बंद्धा; 2d fut. भंत्स्यति; imp. बध्नातु; pot. बध्नीयात्; bened. बध्यात्; cond. अभंत्स्यत्. Pass. बध्यते. Caus. बन्धयति. Desid. बिभंत्सति. Freq. बाबध्यते, बाबन्धीति, बाबंद्धि.

मी 'to kill' or 'injure.'

This verb, like मि in the fifth conjugation, is inflected as if it ended in मा in the non-conjugational tenses, except before the terminations of the second præterite beginning with vowels, and before य.

Pres. मीनाति, मीनीते; 1st præt. अमीनात्, अमीनीत; 2d præt. ममौ or ममाय (मिम्यतुः, ममिथ or ममाथ); 3d præt. अमासीत्, अमास्त;

1st fut. माता; 2d fut. मास्यति -ते; imp. मीनातु, मीनीतां; pot. मीनीयात्, मीनीत; bened. मीयात्; cond. अमास्यत् -त.

For the rest, see मि, fifth conjugation.

यु 'to join.'

Pres. युनाति, युनीते; 1st præt. अयुनात्, अयुनीत; imp. युनातु, युनीतां; pot. युनीयात्, युनीत.

For the rest, see यु, second conjugation.

वृ (वृञ्) 'to choose.'

Pres. वृणाति, वृणीते; 1st præt. अवृणात्, अवृणीत; imp. वृणातु, वृणीतां; pot. वृणीयात्, वृणीत.

For the rest, see वृ of the fifth conjugation. वृ (वृङ्) and वॄ (वॄञ्), verbs having the same meaning, are similarly conjugated: the first is of course restricted to the Átmane-pada.

शॄ 'to hurt.'

It is one of the class प्वादि.

Pres. शृणाति; 1st præt. अशृणात्; 2d præt. शशार (शशरतुः or शश्रतुः); 3d præt. अशारीत्; 1st fut. शरिता, शरीता; 2d fut. शरिष्यति, शरीष्यति; imp. शृणातु; pot. शृणीयात्; bened. शीर्यात्; cond. अशरिष्यत्, अशरीष्यत्. Pass. शीर्यते. Caus. शारयति. Desid. शिशरिषति, शिशरीषति, शिशीर्षति. Freq. शेशीर्यते, शाशर्ति.

षि (षिञ्) 'to bind.'

Pres. सिनाति, सिनीते; 1st præt. असिनात्, असिनीत; 2d præt. सिषाय, सिष्ये; 3d præt. असैषीत्, असेष्ट; 1st fut. सेता; 2d fut. सेष्यति -ते; imp. सिनातु, सिनीतां; pot. सिनीयात्, सिनीत; bened. सीयात्, सेषीष्ट; cond. असेष्यत् -त. Pass. सीयते. Caus. साययति. Desid. सिसीषति -ते. Freq. सेषीयते, सेषयीति, सेषेति.

स्कु (स्कुञ्) 'to leap,' 'to cover.'

Pres. स्कुनाति, स्कुनीते; 1st præt. अस्कुनात्, अस्कुनीत; 2d præt. चुस्काव, चुस्कुवे; 3d præt. अस्कौषीत्, अस्कोष्ट; 1st fut. स्कोता; 2d fut. स्कोष्यति -ते; imp. स्कुनातु, स्कुनीतां; pot. स्कुनीयात्, स्कुनीत; bened.

स्कूयात्, स्कोषीष्ट; cond. अस्कोष्यत् -त. Pass. स्कूयते. Caus. स्कावयति. Desid. चुस्कूषति -ते. Freq. चोस्कूयते, चोस्कोति.

It is also a verb of the fifth conjugation.

स्तम्भ (स्तम्भु) 'to stop.'

This rejects its nasal before the conjugational sign, and before य.

Pres. स्तभ्नाति; 1st præt. अस्तभ्नात्; 2d præt. तस्तम्भ; 3d præt. अस्तभत् or अस्तम्भीत्; 1st fut. स्तम्भिता; 2d fut. स्तम्भिष्यति; imp. स्तभ्नातु; pot. स्तभ्नीयात्; bened. स्तभ्यात्; cond. अस्तम्भिष्यत्. Pass. स्तभ्यते. Caus. स्तम्भयति. Desid. तिस्तम्भिषति. Freq. तास्तभ्यते, तास्तम्भीति, तास्तंभि.

It is also a verb of the fifth conjugation, स्तभ्नोति, &c. In the same manner are inflected स्तुम्भु, स्कम्भु, and स्कुम्भु, having the same meaning.

स्तॄ (स्तॄञ्) 'to cover.'

Pres. स्तृणाति, स्तृणीते; 1st præt. अस्तृणात्, अस्तृणीत; 2d præt. तस्तार, तस्तरे; 3d præt. अस्तारीत्, अस्तरिष्ट, अस्तरीष्ट or अस्तीर्ष्ट; 1st fut. स्तरिता, स्तरीता; 2d fut. स्तरिष्यति -ते, स्तरीष्यति -ते; imp. स्तृणातु, स्तृणीतां; pot. स्तृणीयात्, स्तृणीत; bened. स्तीर्यात्, स्तरिषीष्ट or स्तीर्षीष्ट; cond. अस्तरिष्यत् -त. Pass. स्तीर्यते. Caus. स्तारयति. Desid. तिस्तरिषति -ते, तिस्तरीषति -ते, तिस्तीर्षति -ते. Freq. तेस्तीर्यते, तास्तर्ति.

Tenth Conjugation.

221. Verbs of this conjugation take for their conjugational sign इ, technically termed णिच्; and they extend the insertion to all the tenses except the benedictive, Parasmai-pada. इ is converted to ए, and ए becomes अय्, before a vowel. The indicatory ण of the sign requires the substitution of आ for a radical medial अ, and of the Guṅa equivalent for any other short medial vowel.

a. Before the terminations of the conjugational tenses all verbs of this class insert शप्, that is, अ; whilst as they all take the augment इ in the two futures and conditional, there is in all these tenses a vowel, before which the conjugational sign इ becomes ए, and then अय्.

b. In these modifications of the base, verbs of the tenth class are analogous to the causal mode of verbs; and this analogy extends to other particulars, such as the insertion of certain augments, as प, य, न, &c., before the conjugational sign.

c. The analogy to the causal mode is still more evident in the identity of the construction of the third præterite. It is formed with the terminations of the first præterite, preceded by अ (rule 190, *e.* p. 123), and with a reduplication of the root, agreeably to the rules already given for the causal (rule 202, *e* to *l.* p. 136, &c.).

d. Although not peculiar to the causal, an analogy is also presented to it in common with derivative forms in the second præterite, which in this class is formed with the auxiliary verbs (rule 189. p. 121).

e. Verbs having a medial अ do not make it long when they are said to belong to the class मित्, that is, have an indicatory म; and अ or any other radical short vowel is unchanged in the class कथादि, the verbs of which are said to have an indicatory final अ.

f. Verbs of this conjugation, with the conjugational sign attached, are considered to be polysyllabic, and therefore do not take the frequentative mode; nor can they be considered as having a causal mode, since it is the same with their own, and it is only necessary to substitute a causal for an active signification to the same inflexions.

g. All verbs signifying 'to speak' or 'to kill' may be conjugated in the tenth, as well as in the class to which they belong, as may a variety of other verbs; and most of the verbs which belong to this conjugation may be inflected also in the first. The number of verbs is therefore somewhat indefinite; but from the uniformity which prevails amongst them, not only in the employment of the conjugational sign, but in the formation of the second and third præterites, and the insertion of the augment इ in the other tenses, they may be regarded as offering fewer difficulties than the verbs of any other conjugation.

The verb which is given as the type of the conjugation is चुर् 'to steal,' which admits of both Padas.

Present, 'I steal,' &c.

चोरयामि	चोरयावः	चोरयामः	चोरये	चोरयावहे	चोरयामहे
चोरयसि	चोरयथः	चोरयथ	चोरयसे	चोरयेथे	चोरयध्वे
चोरयति	चोरयतः	चोरयन्ति	चोरयते	चोरयेते	चोरयन्ते

First præterite, 'I stole,' &c.

अचोरयम्	अचोरयाव	अचोरयाम	अचोरये	अचोरयावहि	अचोरयामहि
अचोरयः	अचोरयतं	अचोरयत	अचोरयथाः	अचोरयेथां	अचोरयध्वं
अचोरयत्	अचोरयतां	अचोरयन्	अचोरयत	अचोरयेतां	अचोरयन्त

Second præterite (in both Padas), 'I have stolen,' &c.

चोरयामास	चोरयामासिव	चोरयामासिम
चोरयामासिथ	चोरयामासथुः	चोरयामास
चोरयामास	चोरयामासतुः	चोरयामासुः

or चोरयाम्बभूव, चोरयाञ्चकार or चोरयाञ्चक्रे, &c.

Third præterite, 'I had stolen,' &c.

अचूचुरम्	अचूचुराव	अचूचुराम	अचूचुरे	अचूचुरावहि	अचूचुरामहि
अचूचुरः	अचूचुरतं	अचूचुरत	अचूचुरथाः	अचूचुरेथां	अचूचुरध्वं
अचूचुरत्	अचूचुरतां	अचूचुरन्	अचूचुरत	अचूचुरेतां	अचूचुरन्त

First future, 'I shall steal,' &c.

चोरयितास्मि	चोरयितास्वः	चोरयितास्मः	चोरयिताहे	चोरयितास्वहे	चोरयितास्महे
चोरयितासि	चोरयितास्थः	चोरयितास्थ	चोरयितासे	चोरयितासाथे	चोरयिताध्वे
चोरयिता	चोरयितारौ	चोरयितारः	चोरयिता	चोरयितारौ	चोरयितारः

Second future, 'I will or shall steal,' &c.

चोरयिष्यामि	चोरयिष्यावः	चोरयिष्यामः	चोरयिष्ये	चोरयिष्यावहे	चोरयिष्यामहे
चोरयिष्यसि	चोरयिष्यथः	चोरयिष्यथ	चोरयिष्यसे	चोरयिष्येथे	चोरयिष्यध्वे
चोरयिष्यति	चोरयिष्यतः	चोरयिष्यन्ति	चोरयिष्यते	चोरयिष्येते	चोरयिष्यन्ते

Imperative, 'Let me steal,' &c.

चोरयाणि	चोरयाव	चोरयाम	चोरयै	चोरयावहै	चोरयामहै
चोरय	चोरयतं	चोरयत	चोरयस्व	चोरयेथां	चोरयध्वं
चोरयतु	चोरयतां	चोरयन्तु	चोरयतां	चोरयेतां	चोरयन्तां

Potential, 'I may steal,' &c.

चोरयेयम्	चोरयेव	चोरयेम	चोरयेय	चोरयेवहि	चोरयेमहि
चोरयेः	चोरयेतं	चोरयेत	चोरयेथाः	चोरयेयाथां	चोरयेध्वं
चोरयेत्	चोरयेतां	चोरयेयुः	चोरयेत	चोरयेयातां	चोरयेरन्

Benedictive, 'I pray I may steal,' &c.

चोर्य्यासम्	चोर्य्यास्व	चोर्य्यास्म	चोरयिषीय	चोरयिषीवहि	चोरयिषीमहि
चोर्य्याः	चोर्य्यास्तं	चोर्य्यास्त	चोरयिषीष्ठाः	चोरयिषीयास्थां	चोरयिषीध्वं
चोर्य्यात्	चोर्य्यास्तां	चोर्य्यासुः	चोरयिषीष्ट	चोरयिषीयास्तां	चोरयिषीरन्

Conditional, 'I will steal, if,' &c.

अचोरयिष्यम्	अचोरयिष्याव	अचोरयिष्याम	अचोरयिष्ये	अचोरयिष्यावहि	अचोरयिष्यामहि
अचोरयिष्यः	अचोरयिष्यतं	अचोरयिष्यत	अचोरयिष्यथाः	अचोरयिष्येथां	अचोरयिष्यध्वं
अचोरयिष्यत्	अचोरयिष्यतां	अचोरयिष्यन्	अचोरयिष्यत	अचोरयिष्येतां	अचोरयिष्यन्त

The remaining forms are,

Pass. चुर्य्यते; 3d præt. अचोरि. Caus. चोरयति. Desid. चुचोरयिषति.

अट्ट 'to disrespect.'

This substitutes इ for the radical vowel in the reduplication of the third præterite.

Pres. अट्टयति; 1st præt. आट्टयत्; 2d præt. अट्टयामास; 3d præt. आट्टितत्; 1st fut. अट्टयिता; 2d fut. अट्टयिष्यति; imp. अट्टयतु; pot. अट्टयेत्; bened. अट्ट्यात्; cond. आट्टयिष्यत्. Pass. अट्ट्यते. Desid. अट्टिट्टयिषति.

अर्ह 'to hurt,' 'to pain.'

Pres. अर्हयति; 1st præt. आर्हयत्; 2d præt. अर्हयाञ्चकार; 3d præt. आर्हिदत्; 1st fut. अर्हयिता; 2d fut. अर्हयिष्यति; imp. अर्हयतु; pot. अर्हयेत्; bened. अर्ह्यात्; cond. आर्हयिष्यत्. Pass. अर्ह्यते. Desid. अर्हिदयिषति.

इल 'to send.'

Pres. इलयति; 1st præt. ऐलयत्; 2d præt. इलयामास; 3d præt. ऐलिलत्; 1st fut. इलयिता; 2d fut. इलयिष्यति; imp. इलयतु; pot. इलयेत्; bened. इल्यात्; cond. ऐलयिष्यत्. Pass. इल्यते. Desid. इलिलयिषति.

कण 'to wink,' 'to close.'

This and most other verbs make the medial अ long throughout (rule 221). They have the vowel optionally short in the third præterite; when the reduplicated vowel is इ, changeable to ई (rule 202, *j.* p. 137).

Pres. काणयति; 1st præt. अकाणयत्; 2d præt. काणयामास; 3d præt. अचकाणत् or अचीकणत्; 1st fut. काणयिता; 2d fut. काणयिष्यति; imp. काणयतु; pot. काणयेत्; bened. काण्यात्; cond. अकाणयिष्यत्. Pass. काण्यते. Desid. चिकाणयिषति.

कथ 'to speak.'

This is the first of a class rejecting a final अ, and the radical vowel therefore is unchanged: it is optionally changed to इ in the reduplication of the third præterite.

Pres. कथयति; 1st præt. अकथयत्; 2d præt. कथयामास; 3d præt. अचकथत् or अचीकथत्; 1st fut. कथयिता; 2d fut. कथयिष्यति; imp. कथयतु; pot. कथयेत्; bened. कथ्यात्; cond. अकथयिष्यत्. Pass. कथ्यते. Desid. चिकथयिषति.

Other verbs of this class are,

कल 'to count:' कलयति, अचकलत्.

कुट 'to contract:' कुटयति, अचुकुटत्.

कुह 'to astonish:' कुहयति, अचुकुहत्.

गण 'to count:' गणयति. But this optionally inserts इ in the third præterite: अजगणत् or अजीगणत्.

गद 'to speak:' गदयति, अजगदत्.

गुण 'to advise:' गुणयति, अजुगुणत्.

गृह 'to take:' गृहयते, अजगृहत.

ध्वन 'to sound:' ध्वनयति, अदध्वनत्.

पट 'to tie:' पटयति, अपपटत्.

पद 'to go:' पदयति, अपपदत्.

पश 'to tie:' पशयति, अपपशत्.
पुट 'to contract:' पुटयति, अपुपुटत्.
मृग 'to seek:' मृगयते, अममृगत.
रच 'to make:' रचयति, अररचत्.
रह 'to leave:' रहयति, अररहत्. It also makes अरीरहत्.
वट 'to surround:' वटयति, अववटत्.
वर 'to choose:' वरयति, अववरत्.
शठ 'to speak ill:' शठयति, अशशठत्.
श्रथ 'to be weak:' श्रथयति, अशश्रथत्.
स्तन 'to sound:' स्तनयति, अतस्तनत्.
स्पृह 'to envy:' स्पृहयति, अपस्पृहत्.
स्वर 'to sound:' स्वरयति, असस्वरत्.

कुमार 'to play,' as a child.

Pres. कुमारयति; 1st præt. अकुमारयत्; 2d præt. कुमारयामास; 3d præt. अचुकुमारत्; 1st fut. कुमारयिता; 2d fut. कुमारयिष्यति; imp. कुमारयतु; pot. कुमारयेत्; bened. कुमार्य्यात्; cond. अकुमारयिष्यत्.

कृप 'to be feeble.'

Pres. कृपयति; 1st præt. अकृपयत्; 2d præt. कृपयाञ्चभूव; 3d præt. अचीकृपत्; 1st fut. कृपयिता; 2d fut. कृपयिष्यति; imp. कृपयतु; pot. कृपयेत्; bened. कृप्यात्; cond. अकृपयिष्यत्. Pass. कृप्यते. Desid. चिकृपयिषति.

कृप 'to be able.'

This substitutes कल्प in its inflexions: see the same root in the first conjugation, p. 158.

Pres. कल्पयति; 1st præt. अकल्पयत्; 2d præt. कल्पयामास; 3d præt. अचिकल्पत्; 1st fut. कल्पयिता; 2d fut. कल्पयिष्यति; imp. कल्पयतु; pot. कल्पयेत्; bened. कल्प्यात्; cond. अकल्पयिष्यत्.

कृत 'to sound' or 'utter,' 'to celebrate.'

This substitutes ईर् for the radical penultimate in all the tenses except the third præterite, where it is optional.

Pres. कीर्त्तयति; 1st præt. अकीर्त्तयत्; 2d præt. कीर्त्तयामास; 3d præt. अचीकृतत् or अचिकीर्त्तत्; 1st fut. कीर्त्तयिता; 2d fut

कीर्त्तयिष्यति; imp. कीर्त्तयतु; pot. कीर्त्तयेत्; bened. कीर्त्यात्; cond. अकीर्त्तयिष्यत्. Pass. कीर्त्यते. Desid. चिकीर्त्तयिषति.

घुष 'to proclaim.'

Pres. घोषयति; 1st præt. अघोषयत्; 2d præt. घोषयाञ्चकार; 3d præt. अजूघुषत्; 1st fut. घोषयिता; 2d fut. घोषयिष्यति; imp. घोषयतु; pot. घोषयेत्; bened. घोष्यात्; cond. अघोषयिष्यत्. Pass. घुष्यते. Desid. जुघोषयिषति.

चि (चिञ्) 'to collect.'

This verb optionally substitutes आ for its vowel, when it also substitutes प for य. As belonging to the class मित्, it makes the vowel short, so that आ becomes अ.

Pres. चपयति -ते, चययति -ते; 1st præt. अचपयत् -त, अचययत् -त; 2d præt. चपयाञ्चकार, चपयाञ्चक्रे; 3d præt. अचीचपत् -त, अचीचयत् -त; 1st fut. चपयिता, चययिता; 2d fut. चपयिष्यति -ते, चययिष्यति -ते; imp. चपयतु -तां, चययतु -तां; pot. चपयेत् -त, चययेत् -त; bened. चप्यात् or चय्यात्, चपयिषीष्ट, चययिषीष्ट; cond. अचपयिष्यत् -त, अचययिष्यत् -त.

See चि, fifth conjugation.

चित (चिति) 'to think.'

Pres. चिन्तयति; 1st præt. अचिन्तयत्; 2d præt. चिन्तयामास; 3d præt. अचिचिन्तत्; 1st fut. चिन्तयिता; 2d fut. चिन्तयिष्यति; imp. चिन्तयतु; pot. चिन्तयेत्; bened. चिन्त्यात्; cond. अचिन्तयिष्यत्. Pass. चिन्त्यते. Desid. चिचिन्तयिषति.

ज्ञप 'to know,' 'to make known.'

This verb is one of those said to have an indicatory म.

Pres. ज्ञपयति; 1st præt. अज्ञपयत्; 2d præt. ज्ञपयाञ्चकार; 3d præt. अजज्ञपत् or अजीज्ञपत्; 1st fut. ज्ञपयिता; 2d fut. ज्ञपयिष्यति; imp. ज्ञपयतु; pot. ज्ञपयेत्; bened. ज्ञप्यात्; cond. अज्ञपयिष्यत्. Pass. ज्ञप्यते. Desid. जिज्ञपयिषति.

The other verbs of the class मित् in this conjugation are,

चप 'to pound:' चपयति, अचचपत्, अचीचपत्.

चह 'to pound:' चहयति, अचचहत् or अचीचहत्.

चि; as above.

यम 'to feed:' यमयति, अययमत्, अयीयमत्.
बल 'to live:' बलयति, अबबलत्, अबीबलत्.

पीड 'to give pain.'

This makes the radical vowel optionally short in the third præterite, when the vowel of the reduplication is made long.

Pres. पीडयति; 1st præt. अपीडयत्; 2d præt. पीडयाञ्चकार; 3d præt. अपीपिडत् or अपिपीडत्.

The same applies to the following verbs:

जीव 'to live:' जीवयति, अजिजीवत् or अजीजिवत्.
दीप 'to shine:' दीपयति, अदिदीपत् or अदीदिपत्.
भाष 'to speak:' भाषयति, अबिभाषत् or अबीभषत्.
भास 'to shine:' भासयति, अबिभासत् or अबीभसत्.
भास 'to shine:' भासयति, अबिभ्रासत् or अबीभ्रसत्.
मील 'to close:' मीलयति, अमिमीलत् or अमीमिलत्.

पृथ 'to throw.'

A penultimate ऋ may remain unchanged in the third præterite.

Pres. पार्थयति; 1st præt. अपार्थयत्; 2d præt. पार्थयामास; 3d præt. अपीपृथत् or अपपर्थत्; 1st fut. पार्थयिता; &c.

पॄ 'to fill.'

Pres. पारयति; 1st præt. अपारयत्; 2d præt. पारयामास; 3d præt. अपीपरत्; 1st fut. पारयिता; 2d fut. पारयिष्यति; imp. पारयतु; pot. पारयेत्; bened. पार्यात्; cond. अपारयिष्यत्.

So पॄ, third conjugation. पार, 'to cross over,' is given in similar forms, except in the third præterite, which is अपपारत्.

प्रथ 'to declare.'

This and some other verbs do not substitute इ for the radical vowel in the reduplicate syllable of the third præterite.

Pres. प्राथयति; 1st præt. अप्राथयत्; 2d præt. प्राथयाञ्चकार; 3d præt. अपप्रथत्; 1st fut. प्राथयिता; imp. प्राथयतु; &c.

The other verbs that come under this example are,

दॄ 'to tear:' दारयति, अददरत्.

त्वर 'to hasten:' त्वारयति, अतत्वरत्.

म्रद 'to trample:' म्रादयति, अमम्रदत्.

स्पश 'to touch:' स्पाशयति, अपस्पशत्.

स्मृ 'to remember:' स्मारयति, असस्मरत्.

स्तॄ 'to spread:' स्तारयति, अतस्तरत्.

चेष्ट 'to make effort,' and वेष्ट 'to surround,' have two forms: अचचेष्टत् or अचिचेष्टत्, अववेष्टत् or अविवेष्टत्.

प्री 'to please.'

This verb optionally prefixes न to the sign of the conjugation.

Pres. प्रीणयति -ते, प्राययति -ते; 1st præt. अप्रीणयत् -त, अप्राययत् -त; 2d præt. प्रीणयामास, प्राययामास; 3d præt. अपीप्रिणत् -त, अपीप्रयत् -त; 1st fut. प्रीणयिता, प्राययिता; 2d fut. प्रीणयिष्यति -ते, प्राययिष्यति -ते; imp. प्रीणयतु -तां, प्राययतु -तां; pot. प्रीणयेत् -त, प्राययेत् -त; bened. प्रायात्, प्रीणयिषीष्ट, प्राययिषीष्ट; cond. अप्रीणयिष्यत् -त, अप्राययिष्यत् -त.

For the rest, see प्री of the ninth conjugation. So also धू, 'to shake,' makes धूनयति or धावयति, &c.

मन्त्र (मत्रि) 'to advise.'

Pres. मन्त्रयति -ते; 1st præt. अमन्त्रयत् -त; 2d præt. मन्त्रयामास; 3d præt. अमिमन्त्रत् -त; 1st fut. मन्त्रयिता; 2d fut. मन्त्रयिष्यति -ते; imp. मन्त्रयतु -तां; pot. मन्त्रयेत् -त; bened. मंत्र्यात्, मन्त्रयिषीष्ट; cond. अमन्त्रयिष्यत् -त. Pass. मंत्र्यते. Desid. मिमन्त्रयिषति -ते.

So कुद्रि 'to speak falsely,' तत्रि 'to support,' as a family, and यत्रि 'to contract.'

ली 'to melt.'

This optionally takes the augment प before the conjugational sign.

Pres. लापयति or लाययति; 1st præt. अलापयत्, अलाययत्; 2d præt. लापयामास, लाययामास; 3d præt. अलीलपत्, अलीलयत्; 1st fut. लापयिता, लाययिता; 2d fut. लापयिष्यति, लाययिष्यति; imp. लापयतु, लाययतु; pot. लापयेत्, लाययेत्; bened. लायात्; cond. अलापयिष्यत्, अलाययिष्यत्.

ली is also a verb of the ninth conjugation.

शृध 'to laugh at.'

Pres. शर्द्धयति; 1st præt. अशर्द्धयत्; 2d præt. शर्द्धयामास; 3d præt. अशशर्द्धत् or अशीशृधत्; 1st fut. शर्द्धयिता; 2d fut. शर्द्धयिष्यति; imp. शर्द्धयतु; pot. शर्द्धयेत्; bened. शर्द्ध्यात्; cond. अशर्द्धयिष्यत्. Pass. शृध्यते. Desid. शिशर्द्धयिषति.

साम 'to tranquillize.'

Pres. सामयति; 1st præt. असामयत्; 2d præt. सामयाञ्चकार; 3d præt. அससामत् or असीषमत्; 1st fut. सामयिता; 2d fut. सामयिष्यति; imp. सामयतु; pot. सामयेत्; bened. साम्यात्; cond. असामयिष्यत्. Pass. साम्यते. Desid. सिसामयिषति.

On the conjugation of Verbs in different voices, &c.

222. The forms of the roots which have been given in the preceding pages are those which are usually assigned to them by native grammarians. The student must not be surprised, however, if he finds occasional departures from the models here specified, or a verb inflected in a different conjugation, or in a different Pada, from that in which he will have found it here represented. As to variations of meaning, they will be frequent; for in the examples cited, the principal signification only of each verb has been purposely stated, in order not to occasion doubt or perplexity in an early period of study. The other senses will become familiar by practice. Of the variations of inflexion, the greater number are ascribed by grammarians to poetical license, or even to error (प्रमाद); but it may be doubted if they do not, sometimes at least, arise from circumstances which have been yet imperfectly investigated in the history of the grammar of the Sanskrit language. The variations of import are no doubt often imputable to the liberties taken by Sanskrit writers, relying upon the purport in which they employ any particular verb being rendered intelligible by the context of the passage in which it occurs. Some part of the uncertainty, however, proceeds from an incomplete analysis, and the want of examples to illustrate the abstract term which is used to express the meaning of the root. Authors consequently disagree as to the interpretation. However, these difficulties need not embarrass the student: he must be contented to take the verb as he finds it, and must not look upon its regular grammatical type as absolutely unalterable.

223. There is one class of modifications, and that the most frequent, which is recognised by grammarians. A simple verb may be inflected in one Pada, and when compounded with a preposition may be inflected in the other, either in its primitive, or in a modified sense. A few of these compound verbs have been already noticed, but it may be useful to extend the number of instances, arranging them in alphabetical order.

असु 'to throw,' preceded by any preposition, may take either Pada; as, with निर् 'to throw off:' बन्धं निरस्यति or निरस्यते 'he casts off the bond.'

ऊह 'to reason,' preceded by any preposition, may take either Pada; as, with अप 'to throw off' or 'repel,' अपोहेत पापं 'let him remove sin;' तदपोहति 'he removes that:' also with सम्, as समूहति -ते.

कृ, which in its simple state admits of either Pada, is restricted to one or other according to the prepositions with which it is compounded, and the meanings thence derived: अनुकरोति 'he imitates;' अधिकुरुते 'he overcomes;' उत्कुरुते 'he informs against;' उदाकुरुते 'he reviles;' उपकुरुते हरिं 'he worships Hari;' उपस्कुरुते 'he changes' (as a property); उपस्करोति 'he polishes;' पराकरोति 'he does well;' प्रकुरुते 'he offers violence to,' as a female; सीताम् प्रकुरुते रावणः 'Rávaṅa carries off Sítá:' also 'to recite;' as, गाथाः प्रकुरुते 'he recites hymns.' कृ is used with वि to imply change or production of some kind or other; and when the verb is used intransitively, or the production is confined to sounds, the Átmane-pada only is employed; otherwise, the Parasmai-pada; as, छात्रा विकुर्वते 'the scholars change,' i. e. they learn;' स्वरान् विकुरुते गायकः 'the singer varies his notes;' but चित्तं विकरोति कामः 'passion transforms the heart.'

कॄ 'to scatter,' when the act of an animal or bird, takes the Átmane-pada after अप, and inserts a sibilant: अपस्किरते कुक्कुटः 'the cock throws up (the earth, either for pleasure, or to make a hole to lie down in);' but कुसुमान्यपकिरति स्त्री 'the woman scatters flowers.'

क्रम, 'to go,' without a preposition takes the Átmane-pada, signifying 'being engaged in' or 'assiduous,' or 'becoming manifest' or 'developed in;' as, ऋचि क्रमते बुद्धिः 'the understanding is engaged in (the study of) the Rig-veda;' अध्ययनाय क्रमते 'he is assiduous for study;' क्रमन्तेऽस्मिन् शास्त्राणि 'the S'ástras are manifested (or fully understood) in him.' So with उप and परा in the same meanings: उपक्रमते, पराक्रमते; but not with सम्, as संक्रामति. So with आ prefixed, meaning 'to ascend,' as a heavenly body, not as any thing else: आक्रमते सूर्यः 'the sun ascends;' but आक्रामति धूमः 'the smoke rises.' Also with वि, meaning 'motion of the feet:' साधु विक्रमते वाजी 'the horse trots well;' but विक्रामति सन्धिः 'the joint splits.' So with उप or प्र, implying 'power' or 'valour:' उपक्रमते, प्रक्रमते 'he is mighty' or 'valiant;' but उपक्रामति 'he comes' or 'approaches;' प्रक्रामति 'he goes' or 'departs.'

क्री, 'to buy,' is restricted to the Átmane-pada, when preceded by अव, परि, or वि. The two first have the same meaning as the simple verb, 'to buy;' the latter means 'to sell:' अवक्रीणीते, परिक्रीणीते, 'he buys;' विक्रीणीते 'he sells.'

क्रीड, 'to play,' takes the Átmane-pada after आ, अनु, परि, and सम्; as, आक्रीडते 'he plays much;' अनुक्रीडते 'he plays like;' परिक्रीडते 'he plays again;' संक्रीडते 'he plays well' or 'completely:' but not if अनु influences the government of the case; as, माणवकमनुक्रीडति 'he plays with the boy;' nor if, with सम्, it denotes 'making a noise;' as, संक्रीडति चक्रं 'the wheel creaks.'

क्षिप 'to throw,' preceded by अति, अभि, or प्रति, is confined to the Parasmai-pada: अतिक्षिपति 'he throws much' or 'beyond;' अभिक्षिपति 'he throws on;' प्रतिक्षिपति 'he throws or sends back.'

क्ष्णु with सम् takes the Átmane-pada: संक्ष्णुते शस्त्रं 'he sharpens the weapon;' उत्कण्ठाम् संक्ष्णुते 'it aggravates (his) grief.'

गम 'to go,' has a variety of prefixes, and consequent modifications of form and sense. With आ prefixed, and used in the causal form to signify 'to have patience,' it takes the Átmane-pada: आगमयस्व तावत् 'wait or delay a little.' With सम् it takes the Átmane-pada in an intransitive sense: वाक्यं संगच्छते 'the sentence is plain' (or is coherent); सखिभिः संगच्छते 'he goes with his friends:' but ग्रामं संगच्छति 'he goes to the village.'

गॄ 'to swallow,' preceded by सम्, takes the meaning of 'promising' or 'uttering,' and is conjugated in the Átmane-pada: शतं संगिरते 'he promises a hundred (rupees);' स्वामिनो गुणान् संगिरते 'he proclaims the qualities of the prince:' otherwise संगिरति ग्रासं 'he swallows a mouthful.' It takes the Átmane-pada after अव; अवगिरते शोणितं पिशाचः 'the goblin swallows blood.'

चर 'to go,' with उद् in the sense of 'going astray' or 'departing from,' takes the Átmane-pada; as, धर्म्ममुच्चरते 'he deviates from virtue:' not if it is intransitive; वाष्पमुच्चरति 'the tear overflows: but it is so used with सम्, or with सम्, उद्, and आ, connected with a noun in the instrumental case; रथेन सञ्चरते (or समुदाचरते) राजा 'the king rides with (in) a chariot.'

जि, 'to conquer,' is limited to the Átmane-pada after परा and वि; as, पराजयते, विजयते, 'he conquers.'

ज्ञा 'to know,' without a preposition, if used in certain senses intransitively, is conjugated in the Átmane-pada; सर्पिषो जानीते 'he engages (in sacrifice by means of) Ghee:' also after अप, in the sense of 'denying;' शतमपजानीते 'he denies the (debt of a) hundred rupees:' after प्रति, in the sense of 'acknowledging;' शतं प्रतिजानीते 'he acknowledges the hundred:' and after सम्, in that of 'demanding' or 'expecting;'

शतं सञ्जानीते. It is used in the Átmane-pada without a preposition, and transitively when the result of the action reverts to the agent; as, गां जानीते 'he obtains a cow:' not else; as, मातरं जानाति 'he knows (the dwelling of) his mother:' nor if the verb be preceded in such a sense by a preposition; as, स्वर्गलोकं न प्रजानाति मूढः 'the fool does not recognise (or obtain) heaven.'

णी, 'to guide,' in certain senses takes the Átmane-pada: as, 'to excel in;' शास्त्रे नयते 'he excels in the Śástra:'—'to determine;' तत्त्वं नयते 'he ascertains the principle.' Also after उद्, meaning 'to lift up;' दण्डमुन्नयते 'he lifts up a staff.' After उप, implying 'to invest with the sacred cord;' बालमुपनयते 'he invests the boy with the string:'—'to hire;' कर्म्मकरानुपनयते 'he hires servants.' After वि, signifying 'to pay;' करं विनयते 'he pays the tax:'—'to grant' or 'endow;' शतं विनयते 'he grants a hundred' (for some religious purpose):—'to restrain,' when the object is in the person; क्रोधं विनयते 'he restrains wrath:' but not if the object be in another; गुरोः क्रोधं विनयति छात्रः 'the pupil assuages the wrath of the teacher:' nor if the object be corporeal; गण्डं विनयति 'he turns away his cheek.'

णु, 'to praise,' is conjugated in the Átmane-pada after आ; आनुते 'he praises.'

तप, used intransitively after उत् and वि, takes the Átmane-pada; उत्तपते, वितपते सूर्य्यः 'the sun shines:' also if it mean 'to warm or heat a part of one's own body;' उत्तपते, वितपते पाणिं 'he warms his hand:' not if a part of another; चैत्रो मैत्रस्य पाणिमुत्तपति 'Chaitra warms or burns the hand of Maitra:' nor when it means 'to burn or melt substances;' as, सुवर्णमुत्तपति स्वर्णकारः 'the goldsmith melts the gold.' When it means 'to practise devotion,' it is used in the fourth conjugation in the Átmane-pada; तप्यते तपस्तापसः 'the ascetic practises penance.' According to some, it is confined to the Átmane-pada after अनु, in the sense of 'penitence;' as, अनुतपते 'he repents.'

दा (दाम) 'to give,' when preceded by आ, in any other sense than that of 'setting open,' as the mouth, &c., takes the Átmane-pada; as, धनमादत्ते 'he receives wealth;' विद्यामादत्ते 'he acquires knowledge:' but मुखं व्याददाति 'he opens his mouth,' 'he yawns:' not, it is said, if it be another's mouth; as, व्याददते पिपीलिकाः पतङ्गस्य मुखं 'the ants open the mouth of the grasshopper.' The Parasmai-pada is also used after आ in other senses; as, विपादिकां व्याददाति वैद्यः 'the physician lays open the boil;' नदी कूलं व्याददाति 'the river lays open (undermines) the bank.'

दा (दाण), 'to give,' is used in the Átmane-pada after सम्, either singly or with another preposition, with a noun in the third case, having the sense of the fourth: दास्या संयच्छते or सम्प्रयच्छते 'he gives to the female slave.' If the sense of the third case is preserved, the Parasmai-pada is retained: दास्या धनं सम्प्रयच्छति विप्राय 'he gives wealth by the slave girl to the Brahman.'

दृश 'to see,' with सम्, and used intransitively, takes the Átmane-pada; सम्पश्यते 'he considers well:' so does नाथ 'to ask,' as a boon; as, सर्पिषो नाथते 'he asks for Ghee:' and प्रच्छ 'to ask,' with आ; as, आपृच्छते 'he takes leave of:' and with सम्, used intransitively; as, सम्पृच्छते 'he inquires.'

भुज, 'to eat,' takes the Átmane-pada; ओदनं भुंक्ते 'he eats boiled rice:' also 'to possess;' बुभुजे पृथिवीपालः पृथिवीम् 'the king possessed the earth:' also 'to suffer;' वृद्धो दुःखशतानि भुंक्ते 'the old man suffers hundreds of pains:' not if it mean 'to protect;' as, महीम्भुनक्ति राजा 'the king protects the earth.'

मृष 'to bear,' with परि prefixed, is conjugated in the Parasmai-pada: परिमृष्यति 'he endures' or 'forgives.'

यम, 'to restrain,' varies the Pada according to different meanings and prefixes. With आ used intransitively it takes the Átmane-pada; आयच्छते तरुः 'the tree spreads:' but आयच्छति कूपाद्रज्जुं 'he draws the rope from the well:' unless part of one's own body be intended; as, आयच्छते पाणिं 'he stretches out his hand.' Also with उप, meaning 'to take as a wife;' उपयच्छते कन्यां 'he takes the maiden to wife.' In this form the third præterite optionally rejects the nasal; रामः सीतामुपायत or उपायंस्त 'Ráma wedded Sítá.' If it implies taking the wife of another, it is परस्य भार्य्यामुपयच्छति: if it signifies acceptance in general, it is restricted to the Átmane-pada; दानमुपयच्छते 'he accepts the donation.' It also takes the same voice after आ, उद्, and सम्, not signifying any thing relating to books; as, वस्त्रमायच्छते 'he puts on the clothes;' भारमुद्यच्छते 'he takes up the load;' व्रीहीन् संयच्छते 'he stacks the corn:' but उद्यच्छति वेदान् 'he studies diligently the Veda.'

युज takes the Átmane-pada after उद्, and prepositions ending with vowels; as, उद्युंक्ते 'he makes effort;' अनुयुंक्ते 'he sets after' or 'according to;' नियुंक्ते 'he appoints;' प्रयुंक्ते 'he arranges:' unless it refer to sacrificial vessels; यज्ञपात्राणि प्रयुनक्ति 'he sets in order the vessels of sacrifice.'

रम 'to sport,' preceded by आ, परि, or वि, is restricted to the Parasmai-pada; आरमति 'he rests;' परिरमति 'he goes about;' विरमति 'he takes rest.' Preceded by उप, in the sense of 'dwelling with as a wife,' it takes either voice; as, उपरमति or उपरमते भार्य्यां 'he takes a wife.'

वद, 'to speak,' is conjugated in the Átmane-pada, when signifying 'to excel in' or 'to be acquainted with;' as, शास्त्रे वदते 'he is learned in the S'ástra:'—'to labour;' क्षेत्रे वदते 'he labours in the field.' Also after अनु, used intransitively, and in the sense of 'articulate speech;' as, अनुवदते कठः कलापस्य 'Kat́ha speaks after or like Kalápa:' otherwise, उक्तमनुवदति 'he repeats the speech;' and अनुवदति वीणा 'the lute sounds.' Also after उप, used transitively to mean 'pacifying;' as, भृत्यानुपवदते 'he pacifies the servants:'—'advising;' as, शिष्यमुपवदते 'he advises the scholar:'—or 'communicating with privately;' परदारानुपवदते 'he intrigues with another's wife.' Also after वि, and प्र optionally, implying difference of opinion expressed articulately, 'dispute;' as, विप्रवदन्ते or विप्रवदन्ति वैद्याः 'the doctors dispute.' Also after सम् and प्र, to signify articulate speech uttered simultaneously; as, सम्प्रवदन्ते ब्राह्मणाः 'the Brahmans speak or chaunt together:' but सम्प्रवदन्ति खगाः 'the birds sing together.' Also after अप, when the result of the action reverts to the agent; अपवदते धनकामोऽन्यायं 'the man desirous of wealth reviles improperly:' otherwise, अपवदति 'he speaks against' or 'prohibits.'

वह 'to bear,' preceded by प्र, takes the Parasmai-pada, used intransitively; नदी प्रवहति 'the river flows.'

विद्, 'to know,' takes the Átmane-pada after सम्, and optionally affixes र् to the final in the third person plural; संविदते or संविद्रते 'they know well.'

विश्, 'to enter,' takes the Átmane-pada after नि; निविशते 'he enters in.'

शप 'to swear,' when the effect of the oath reverts to the speaker, is conjugated in the Átmane-pada; कृष्णाय शपते गोपी 'the nymph swears by Kṛishńa.'

श्रु 'to hear,' after सम्, used intransitively, makes संशृणुते 'he hears well:' otherwise, शब्दं संशृणोति 'he hears the sound.'

स्था, 'to stay' or 'stand,' takes a variety of prepositions, and is conjugated in the Átmane-pada after, अव, प्र, वि, सम्, used intransitively; अवतिष्ठते 'he waits patiently;' प्रतिष्ठते 'he stands or sets forth;' वितिष्ठते 'he stands apart' or 'still;' सन्तिष्ठते 'he stops or stays with' or 'proceeds.' Also after आ, used transitively; as, शब्दं नित्यमातिष्ठते 'he assents to the eternal word.' It occurs with आ also in the Parasmai-pada; विधिमातिष्ठति 'he observes the rite.' Also after उद्, not implying to stand up or rise, or to exact or demand; as, मुक्तावुत्तिष्ठते 'he aspires to salvation:' but पीठादुत्तिष्ठति 'he rises from the stool;' ग्रामाच्छतमुत्तिष्ठति 'he levies a hundred (rupees) from the village.' After उप, in the sense of performing religious rites, of worshipping, of doing homage to, of uniting with, of shewing affection to, or of tending towards, as a road, स्था takes the Átmane-pada; as, आग्नेय्याग्नीध्रमुपतिष्ठते 'the Brahman preserves the sacred fire;' आदित्यमुपतिष्ठते 'he worships the sun;' नृपमुपतिष्ठते 'he attends on, or does homage to, the king;' गङ्गा यमुनामुपतिष्ठते 'the Ganges unites with the Jumna;' साधुमुपतिष्ठते 'he befriends the pious;' पन्था ग्राममुपतिष्ठते 'the road leads to the village.' It is also used intransitively in the Átmane-pada after उप; as, भोजनकाले उपतिष्ठते 'he waits or stands by at the time of eating:' and transitively in either Pada, when expectation, or service not religious, is implied; भिक्षुकः प्रभुमुपतिष्ठति or उपतिष्ठते 'the mendicant waits upon the master' (for alms); भर्तारमुपतिष्ठति or उपतिष्ठते नारी 'a woman waits upon, or ministers to, her husband.' ष्ठा is also used in the Átmane-pada, without a preposition, to signify 'to manifest dependence upon;' as, गोपी कृष्णाय तिष्ठते 'the nymph places her trust in Krishńa:' or 'to adhere to,' as a leader; कर्णादिषु तिष्ठते 'he adheres to, or follows, Karńa and the rest.'

स्वृ, 'to sound, takes the Átmane-pada after आ; आस्वरते 'he sounds.'

हन, 'to strike' or 'kill,' takes the Átmane-pada after आ, if used intransitively; or when the object is part of one's self, transitively; as, आहते 'he strikes;' or आहते शिरः 'he strikes his head:' but परस्य शिर आहन्ति 'he strikes the head of another.'

हृ 'to take,' preceded by अनु, implying 'to take after,' or 'act like,' takes the Átmane-pada;' पैतृकमश्वा अनुहरन्ते 'horses take the nature of the father:' but not if actual presence is implied; as, पितुरनुहरति 'he takes after his father.'

ह्वे, 'to call,' used intransitively, takes the Átmane-pada after उप, नि, वि, and सम्; as, उपह्वयते, निह्वयते, विह्वयते, संह्वयते 'he calls out,' 'exclaims,' &c.: also after आ, used transitively in the sense of 'defiance;' शत्रुमाह्वयते 'he defies or challenges the enemy:' but पुत्रमाह्वयति 'he calls his son.'

Causal verbs ordinarily take the Parasmai-pada, and seldom appear in any other; but, as observed already, they may assume the Átmane-pada when the effect of the action reverts to the individual; as, स्थानं मार्जयति 'he causes the place to be cleaned;' आत्मानं मार्जयते 'he causes himself to be cleansed' or 'purified.' There are certain causal verbs, however, which are limited to one or other Pada, according to their meanings. गृध 'to be greedy,' in the sense of 'deceiving,' takes the Átmane-pada; बालं गर्धयते 'he deceives the child:' otherwise, श्वानं गर्धयति 'he excites the dog to be greedy.' So वञ्च, 'to deceive,' makes कन्यां वञ्चयते 'he deceives the girl:' but अहिं वञ्चयति 'he drives away the snake.' So कृ, combined with a word signifying 'falsely' or 'erroneously,' takes the Átmane-pada; as, मिथ्या कारयते घोषणां 'he causes a false alarm or proclamation to be made:' but सुष्ठु कारयति पदं 'he causes the word to be accurately repeated.'

According to some authoritics, thc following verbs do not admit the Parasmai-pada in the causal mode. पा 'to drink,' दम 'to tame,' यम 'to restrain,' and यस 'to make effort,' preceded by आ; मुह 'to be perplexed,' preceded by परि; रुच 'to shine,' नृत 'to dance,' वद 'to speak,' वस 'to dwell;' as, पाययते, दमयते, आयामयते, आयासयते, परिमोहयते, रोचयते, नर्तयते, वादयते, वासयते. So also धे 'to give suck;' धापयते. This limitation is however qualified as above; and when the object of the action is different from the agent, these verbs take the Parasmai-pada; as, वत्सान् पाययति पयः 'he causes the calves to drink the milk,' &c.

It is unnecessary to prosecute this subject farther, as it would be impossible in this place to collect all the variations that occur in books, and they will be readily recognised when they are met with.

CHAPTER VI.

DERIVATION.

SECTION I.

Verbal Derivatives.

224. The derivatives of the Sanskrit language are arranged under two principal classes; the first comprises those nouns

which are formed from the verb; the second, those which are formed from other nouns. To the first is assigned the name Kṛidanta, or nouns formed with terminations attached to verbal roots: to the second, the denomination Taddhita, or nouns which import relation to other nouns. We may be permitted to distinguish them as verbal and nominal derivatives, and proceed to treat of the former.

225. One principal class of verbal derivatives consists of what we are accustomed to consider as parts of the verb itself, or the infinitive and the participles.

Infinitive.

226. The infinitive of the Sanskrit verb is regarded by native grammarians as an indeclinable noun, formed from the root by affixing to it the syllables तुमुन्, leaving तुम्.

a. Whatever modifications the root undergoes in the first future before the affix ता (rule 192), it equally undergoes in the infinitive before तुम्, inserting or not inserting इ, and combining with the augment, or with the first letter of the termination, conformably to the plan pursued in the first future tense; as a few examples will suffice to prove.

Verb.	First future.	Infinitive.
इ to go	एता	एतुम्
ऋ to go	अर्त्ता	अर्त्तुम्
एध to grow	एधिता	एधितुम्
कृ to do	कर्त्ता	कर्त्तुम्
गम to go	गन्ता	गन्तुम्
चुर to steal	चोरयिता	चोरयितुम्
गै to sing	गाता	गातुम्
जन to bear	जनिता	जनितुम्
जि to conquer	जेता	जेतुम्
दह to burn	दग्धा	दग्धुम्
दा to give	दाता	दातुम्
दो to cut	दाता	दातुम्
दृश to see	द्रष्टा	द्रष्टुम्

पच् to cook	पक्ता	पक्तुम्
भू to be	भविता	भवितुम्
रम् to sport	रन्ता	रन्तुम्
सह् to bear	{ सोढा	सोढुम्
	{ सहिता	सहितुम्
स्था to stay	स्थाता	स्थातुम्
सृप् to creep	{ सर्प्ता	सर्प्तुम्
	{ स्रप्ता	स्रप्तुम्
हिंस् to hurt	हिंसिता	हिंसितुम्
हृ to take	हर्ता	हर्तुम्

b. The Sanskrit infinitive presents a general analogy to the Latin supine in 'um,' and in many instances the words are the same; as, स्थातुम् 'statum;' दातुम् 'datum;' पातुम् 'potum;' योक्तुम् 'junctum;' स्वापयितुम् 'sopitum.' In others, we have the same principles of formation displayed; as पच् makes पक्तुम्, so 'facio' makes 'factum;' as अञ्ज् makes अंक्तुम्, so 'unguo' makes 'unctum;' as स्तम्भ may make स्तब्धुम्, so 'rumpo' makes 'ruptum.' The augment इ also is observable in such supines, as 'monitum,' 'domitum,' &c.; and in some cases we have it optionally inserted or omitted, as in 'altum' or 'alitum,' and the like.

Participles.

227. The participles are of two kinds, declinable and indeclinable: to the latter the denomination of Gerunds has been given by Professor Bopp.

228. The declinable participles are of the present, past, and future times, diversified according to the Pada, or the voice, to which they are considered to belong.

a. The indeclinable participles, or Gerunds, are indeterminately past.

Present Participles.

229. The present participle may be active or passive; and the active is distinguished as belonging to the Parasmai or Átmane-pada.

230. The present participle, Parasmai-pada, is formed by adding the syllable अत्, technically called शतृ, to the root: the initial श indicates that the base undergoes, before the participial affix अत्, modifications which it derives from its conjugational peculiarities, especially before the termination of the third person plural of the present tense: thus भू makes भवत् 'being;' जि, जयत् 'conquering;' पच्, पचत् 'cooking;' गम्, गच्छत् 'going;' पा, पिबत् 'drinking;' स्था, तिष्ठत् 'staying;' अद्, अदत् 'eating;' हन्, घ्नत् 'killing;' हु, जुह्वत् 'sacrificing;' दिव्, दीव्यत् 'playing;' सु, सुन्वत् 'producing;' तुद्, तुदत् 'tormenting;' रुध्, रुन्धत् 'obstructing;' कृ, कुर्वत् 'doing;' क्री, क्रीणत् 'buying;' चुर्, चोरयत् 'stealing;' and the like.

a. The present participle ending in अत् is declinable in the three genders, according to rules already given: see p. 55, rule 104, &c.

b. In the case of विद्, 'to know,' वस् is optionally affixed in place of अत्, making विद्वस् 'knowing,' 'wise' (see p. 70); as well as विदत्.

231. The present participle of the Átmane-pada is formed by adding शानच्, that is, आन, to the inflective base of the verb, as modified for conjugation in the present tense. When, as in the first, fourth, sixth, and tenth conjugations, the inflective base ends with अ, then म is prefixed to the termination; as, एध, एधमान 'increasing;' पच, पचमान 'cooking:' in the other conjugations the termination is added at once to the verb; as, शी, शयान 'sleeping;' धा, दधान 'having;' कृ, कुर्वाण 'making;' &c. These participles are declined in the three genders like nouns in अ; पचमानः, पचमाना, पचमानं. See p. 30.

a. There are some participial nouns formed with terminations of an analogous character, and having the same letters; as, भुज, भुञ्जानः 'enjoying;' भृ, बिभ्राणः 'wearing;' हन, निघ्नानः 'slaying,' &c., formed with चानश्: also पू, पवमानः 'purifying,' 'a purifier,' 'the air;' and यज 'to sacrifice,' यजमानः 'sacrificing,' 'a sacrificer,' &c., formed with शानन्.

b. आस, 'to sit,' makes आसीनः, -ना, -नं, 'sitting,' 'seated.'

232. The present participle of the passive voice is formed with मान attached to the inflective base of the present tense; as, कृ 'to do,' क्रियते; क्रियमाणः -णा -णं 'being to be made:' दा 'to give,' दीयते; दीयमानः -ना -नं 'being to be given:' णश; नश्यते, नश्यमानः -ना -नं 'being to be destroyed:' गम 'to go;' गम्यमान 'being to be traversed;' गम्यमानं न तेनासीदगतं क्रामता पुरा 'That which was to be gone over before (by the sun), was not untraversed by him (Hanuman):' बाणौघैः कीर्य्यमाणो भीमः 'Bhíma being overwhelmed with arrows.'

Past Participles.

233. There are two participles which follow the analogy of the second or reduplicate præterite, one for the Parasmai, the other for the Átmane-pada; which latter serves also for the passive voice.

Participles of the second præterite.

234. The participle past of the second præterite, Parasmai-pada, is formed by adding वस्, technically termed क्वसु, to the inflective base, as it occurs before the terminations of the dual and plural numbers of the reduplicate præterite (see p. 118, rule 188).

a. The augment इ is prefixed to वस् when the inflective base consists of a single vowel followed by a consonant; also after certain other verbs. When the verb is reduplicated, so that the inflective base contains more than one vowel, इ is ordinarily not inserted; as in the following examples.

b. Participles in वस् are declined in the three genders; as in p. 70, rule 128.

इ to go; ईयिवस् did go; ईयिवान्, ईयुषी, ईयिवत्.

ऋ to go; आरिवस् did go; आरिवान्, आरुषी, आरिवत्.

कृ to make; चकृवस् did make; चकृवान्, चक्रुषी, चकृवत्.

गम to go; जग्मिवस् or जगन्वस् did go; जग्मिवान्, जगन्वान्, जग्म्युषी, जग्मुषी, जग्मिवत्, जगन्वत्.

घस to eat; जक्षिवस् did eat; जक्षिवान्, जक्ष्युषी, जक्षिवत्.

जागृ to be awake; जजागर्वस्, जजागृवस् did wake; जजागर्वान्, जजागृवान्, जजागरुषी, जजागृषी, जजागर्वत्, जजागृवत्.

दाश to give; दाश्वस् did give; दाश्वान्, दाशुषी, दाश्वत्.
दृश to see; ददृशिवस् or ददृश्वस् did see; ददृशिवान्, ददृश्वान्, ददृश्युषी, ददृशुषी, ददृशिवत्, ददृश्वत्.
पच to cook; पेचिवस् did cook; पेचिवान्, पेचुषी, पेचिवत्.
मिह to urine; मीढ्वस् did urine; मीढ्वान्, मीढुषी, मीढ्वत्.
रुद to weep; रुरुद्वस् did weep; रुरुद्वान्, रुरुदुषी, रुरुद्वत्.
विद to know; विविद्वस् or विविदिवस् did know; विविद्वान्, विविदुषी, विविद्वत् or विविदिवान्, विविद्युषी, विविदित्.
विश to enter; विविश्वस् or विविशिवस् did enter, &c.; as in विद.
षह to bear; साह्वस् did bear; साह्वान्, साहुषी, साह्वत्.
हन to kill; जघ्निवस् or जघन्वस् did kill; जघ्निवान्, जघन्वान्, &c.

236. The past participle of the reduplicate præterite in the Átmane-pada is formed by adding आन to the inflective base, as it occurs before the termination of the third person singular: thus पच, 'to cook,' makes पेचान; कृ, 'to do,' चक्राण; वच, 'to speak,' 2d præt. ऊचे, part. ऊचान; श्रु, 'to hear,' 2d præt. शुश्रुवे, part. शुश्रुवाण; &c. These participles are declined in the three genders like nouns in अ.

Indefinite past Participle.

237. The indefinite past participles are two; one having an active, the other a passive signification. Neither can be said to appertain to any particular tense, as they do not, like the preceding, follow any analogy of construction.

238. The indefinite past participle active is formed by adding क्तवतु to the root or crude verb, leaving तवत्; the effect of the क in this or any technical termination being to preclude the Guńa or Vṛiddhi change of the radical vowel, and to occasion the rejection of a radical nasal penultimate: कृ, 'to do,' therefore makes कृतवत्, 'was making' or 'made;' दृश 'to see,' दृष्टवत् 'was seeing' or 'saw;' दंश 'to bite,' दष्टवत् 'was biting.' It is commonly used with an auxiliary verb; as, अहं कृतवानस्मि 'I was doing' or 'I did.' The declension of the participles so formed has already been described (p. 55, r. 104).

239. The indefinite past participle passive is formed by adding to the root or crude verb the affix क्त, that is, त; the object of the क being, as just mentioned, to bar the substitution of the Guṅa or Vṛiddhi equivalent of the radical vowel, and eject a penultimate nasal: thus जि, 'to conquer,' makes जित, 'conquered;' श्रु 'to hear,' श्रुत 'heard;' भू 'to be,' भूत 'been;' हृ 'to take,' हृत 'taken;' चित 'to think,' चित्त 'thought;' दंश 'to bite,' दष्ट 'bitten;' and the like.

a. When following a verb ending in an aspirated consonant or ह, the termination त is changed to ध, and combined with the final, analogously to the combinations of the same verb before the त and थ of the tenses (rule 213, *c*, 8); as, दह 'to burn,' दग्ध 'burnt;' सह 'to bear,' सोढ 'borne.'

b. In verbs ending in consonants the augment इ is occasionally prefixed to the termination त, when a medial इ or उ may be optionally changed to the Guṅa equivalent; as, रुद 'to weep,' रुदित or रोदित 'wept;' विद 'to know,' विदित or वेदित 'known.' ग्रह, 'to take,' makes the इ long, and optionally substitutes the vowel for the semivowel; as, ग्रहीत or गृहीत 'taken.' वस 'to dwell,' and वच and वद 'to speak,' substitute the vowel for the initial; as, उषित 'dwelt,' उक्त and उदित 'said.'

c. Verbs ending with म commonly reject the nasal; so गम, 'to go,' makes गत, 'gone;' यम 'to refrain,' यत; रम 'to be engaged in,' रत: but कम, 'to desire,' makes कान्त, &c.

d. The termination of this participle is sometimes changed to न; as, श्रा, 'to cook,' makes श्राण, 'cooked;' धू 'to shake,' धून 'shaken:' also after verbs ending in द or र, not inserting इ; as, भिद 'to break,' भिन्न 'broken;' पूर 'to fill,' पूर्ण 'filled.' Verbs taking this form are denoted in the lists of roots by an indicatory ओ (see p. 106).

e. Although not changeable to a Guṅa or Vṛiddhi letter, a radical final vowel sometimes substitutes a different vowel. Thus, of verbs ending in आ, ष्ठा 'to stay' makes स्थित; मा 'to mete,' मित 'meted;' पा 'to drink,' पीत 'drank;' हा 'to abandon,' हीन 'abandoned:' or a final आ may be dropped; as, दा, 'to give,' makes दत्त: and in this root the initial may be rejected, when a preposition ending in a vowel precedes; as, प्रत्त or प्रदत्त 'given away.' If the vowel of the preposition be इ or उ, it must be made long, when the initial of दा is rejected; as, परीत्त or परिदत्त 'completely given;' सूत्त or सुदत्त 'well given.' दरिद्रा, 'to be poor,' makes दरिद्रित 'poor,' 'impoverished.'

f. Verbs ending in ॠ substitute ईर् for the final, and न for त; as, कॄ 'to scatter,' कीर्ण 'scattered;' जॄ 'to be old,' जीर्ण 'old.' पॄ 'to fill,' and मॄ 'to kill,' substitute ऊर्; as, पूर्ण 'filled,' मूर्ण 'killed.'

g. Verbs ending in ए are anomalous in their participles past: दे, 'to cherish,' makes दत्त; धे 'to suck,' धीत; मे 'to barter,' मीत; वे 'to weave,' उत; व्ये 'to cover,' वीत; ह्वे 'to invoke,' हूत.

h. Verbs ending in ऐ usually change it to आ; as, ध्यै, 'to meditate,' makes ध्यात, 'meditated;' म्लै 'to be dirty,' म्लान; but गै, 'to sing,' makes गीत, 'sung;' षै 'to waste,' सीत. श्यै, 'to shrink,' makes, when it signifies 'being cold,' शीत; when it means 'congealed,' शीन; when it denotes 'shrunk,' श्यान. क्षै, 'to decay,' makes क्षाम; and स्त्यै 'to surround,' स्तीम or स्तीत.

i. Verbs ending in ओ optionally substitute इ; as, छो 'to cut,' छात or छित; दो 'to cut,' दात or दित; शो 'to pare,' शात or शित.

j. Whether ending in त or न, the past indefinite participle is declined like nouns in अ; कृतः, कृता, कृतं; विदितः, विदिता, विदितं; भिन्नः, भिन्ना, भिन्नं; &c.

k. The participles formed with क्त from verbs signifying motion, श्लिष 'to embrace,' शी 'to sleep,' स्था 'to stay,' आस 'to sit,' वस 'to dwell,' जन 'to be born,' रुह 'to mount,' जॄ 'to grow old,' may be used in an active sense; as, गङ्गां गतः 'he went to the Ganges;' अश्वमारूढः 'he mounted the horse;' पुत्रमाश्लिष्टः 'he embraced his son.' They are also sometimes used absolutely, in place of the past tense; as, स स्थितः 'he stood;' स गतः 'he went.'

l. The past participle in the neuter gender is often used as an abstract noun; as, भाषितं 'speech,' 'that which is spoken;'

शयितं 'sleep,' 'repose;' जल्पितं 'prattle;' हसितं 'laughter;' हितं 'good.'

The following alphabetical list contains many of the verbs ending in vowels which form the participle past with न, or are in other ways anomalous, and most of those ending in consonants which do not insert the augment इ.

अक्ष to pervade, अष्ट.
अञ्च to move, अक्त; but 'to worship,' अञ्चित.
अञ्ज to anoint, अक्त.
अद to eat, अत्त or अन्न, and sometimes जग्ध. अन्नं food; what is eaten.
अश to spread, अष्ट; but 'to eat,' अशित.
आप to obtain, आप्त.
इन्ध to kindle, इद्ध.
उन्द to be wet, उत्त or उन्न.
उर्व्व to injure, उर्ण.
ऊर्णु to cover, ऊर्णुत.
ऊय to weave, ऊत.
ऋ to go, ऋत gone; also, true: but when meaning a debt, ऋण due, owed.
ऋष to go, ऋष्ट.
कन to shine, कन्न.
कम to desire, कान्त or कमित.
कुष to extract, कुष्ट.
कृत to cut, कृत्त.
कृश to grow thin, कृश.
कृष to draw lines, to plough, कृष्ट.
कॄ to scatter, कीर्ण.
क्नूय to stink, क्नूत.
क्रम to go, क्रान्त.
क्रुध to be angry, क्रुद्ध.
क्रुश to cry, क्रुष्ट.
क्लम to be weary, क्लान्त.
क्लिश to be distressed, क्लिष्ट or क्लिशित.
खन to dig, खात.
क्षम to be patient, क्षान्त.
क्षि to waste, क्षित or क्षीण.
क्ष्विद to be moist, क्ष्विण्ण.
क्षिप to throw, क्षिप्त.
क्षीव to be drunk, क्षीब.
क्षुभ to agitate, क्षुब्ध.
क्ष्माय to shake, क्ष्मीत.
खिद to be distressed, खिन्न.
गम to go, गत.
गाह to be thick, गाढ.
गु to void excrement, गून.
गुप to preserve, गुप्त.
गुर to take pains, गुर्ण.
गुह to hide, गूढ.
गॄ to swallow, गीर्ण.
ग्लै to be sad, ग्लान.
घुष to proclaim, घुष्ट or घुषित.
घ्रा to smell, घ्रात or घ्राण.
चित to be sensible, चित्त.
चुर, चूर } to burn { चुर्ण, चूर्ण.
छद to cover, छन्न or छादित.
छिद to cut, छिन्न.
छुप to touch, छुप्त.

जन to be born, जात.
जप to pray silently, जप्त or जपित.
जर्व्व to kill, जर्ण.
जुष to be pleased, जुष्ट.
जूर to decay, जूर्ण.
जृभ to yawn, जृब्ध.
जॄ to grow old, जीर्ण.
ज्ञप to know, ज्ञप्त or ज्ञपित.
ज्या to decay, जीन.
ज्यो to instruct, जीत.
ज्री to grow old, ज्रीण.
डी to fly, डीन or डीत.
णम to bow, नत.
णश to perish, नष्ट.
णह to tie, नद्ध.
णिज to clean, निक्त.
णुद to send, नुन्न or नुत्त.
तक्ष to parc, तष्ट.
तन to stretch, तत.
तप to be hot, तप्त.
तुद to torment, तुन्न.
तुर्व्व to kill, तूर्ण.
तुष to be satisfied, तुष्ट.
तृप to be satisfied, तृप्त.
तॄ to cross over, तीर्ण.
त्यज to abandon, त्यक्त.
त्रप to be ashamed, त्रप्त.
त्रस to be afraid, त्रस्त.
त्रै to preserve, त्रात or त्राण.
त्वक्ष to pare, त्वष्ट.
त्वर to hasten, तूर्ण or त्वरित.
त्विष to shine, त्विष्ट.
दंश to bite, दष्ट.
दम to tame, दान्त or दमित.
दह to burn, दग्ध.

दिव to play, द्यून; to game, द्यूत.
दिश to show, दिष्ट.
दिह to smear, दिग्ध.
दी to waste, दीत or दीन.
दीप to shine, दीप्त.
दु to suffer pain, दुत or दुन.
दुर्व्व to kill, दूर्ण.
दुष to be made bad, दुष्ट.
दुह to milk, दुग्ध.
दृभ to fear, to arrange, दृब्ध.
दृश to see, दृष्ट.
दृह to be firm, दृढ.
दॄ to tear, दीर्ण.
द्यै to despise, द्यान.
द्राह to awake, द्राढ.
द्रै to sleep, द्राण.
द्विष to hate, द्विष्ट.
धा to have, हित.
धुर to injure, धूर्ण.
धुर्व्व to injure, धूर्ण.
धू to shake, धून.
धूर to injure, धूर्ण.
धृष to be proud, धृष्ट.
ध्रै to satisfy, ध्राण.
पच to cook, पक्व.
पद to go, पन्न.
पिष to grind, पिष्ट.
पुष to cherish, पुष्ट.
पूय to stink, पूत.
पूर to fill, पूर्ण or पूरित.
पृच to mix, पृक्त.
पॄ to fill, पूर्ण.
प्याय to grow fat, पीन or पीत.
प्रच्छ to ask, पृष्ट.
प्रा to fill, पूर्त.

फुल्ल to blow, as a flower, फुल्ल with प्र prefixed, प्रफुल्लित.

बन्ध to bind, बद्ध.

बुध to know, बुद्ध.

भज to worship, भक्त.

भञ्ज to break, भग्न.

भिद् to break or divide, भिन्न.

भुज to eat, भुक्त; to be crooked, भुग्न.

भ्रम to wander, भ्रान्त.

भ्रस्ज to fry, भृष्ट.

भ्री to serve, भ्रीण.

मद् to be mad, मत्त.

मन to mind, मत.

मस्ज to be immersed, मग्न.

मिद् to be unctuous, मिन्न.

मिह् to urine, मीढ.

मुच to liberate, मुक्त.

मुर्व्व to fasten, मूर्ण.

मुह् to be foolish, मूढ or मुग्ध.

मूर्च्छ to faint, मूर्त्त or मूर्च्छित.

मृज to clean, मृष्ट.

मृश to consult, मृष्ट.

मृ to kill, मूर्ण.

म्लेच्छ to speak barbarously, म्लिष्ट.

म्लै to be dull or dirty, म्लान.

यज to worship, इष्ट.

यत to strive, यत्त.

यम to restrain, यत.

युज to join, युक्त.

युध to fight, युद्ध.

रञ्ज to colour, रक्त.

रभ to be engaged in, रब्ध; so with आ prefixed, to begin, आरब्ध.

रम to sport, to be intent on, रत.

रिच to be separate, रिक्त.

रिश to injure, रिष्ट.

री to kill, रीण.

रुज to break, रुग्न.

रुध to obstruct, रुद्ध.

रुश to injure, रुष्ट.

रुष to be angry, रुष्ट or रुषित.

रुह् to ascend, रूढ.

रेभ to sound, रिब्ध.

लग to be in contact, लग्न.

लभ to gain, लब्ध.

लस्ज to be ashamed, लग्न or लज्जित.

लिप to smear, लिप्त.

लिश to be small, लिष्ट.

लिह् to lick, लीढ.

ली to embrace, लीन.

लुप to lop, लुप्त.

लुभ to covet, लुब्ध.

लुह् to covet, लूढ.

लू to cut, लून.

वच to speak, उक्त.

वप to weave, to sow seed, उप्त.

वम to vomit, वान्त or वमित.

वह् to bear, ऊढ.

वा to blow, वात or वान; निर्व्वाण blown out, extinguished.

वाह् to shine, वाढ.

विच to divide, विक्त.

विज to divide, विक्त; to be agitated, विग्न.

विद् to gain, to find, वित्त or विन्न.

विश to enter, विष्ट.

विष to surround, विष्ट.

वृज to leave, वृक्त.
वृत to be, वृत्त.
वृह to be great, वृढ.
व्रश्च to break, वृक्ण.
व्री to choose, व्रीण.
व्ली to go, व्लीन.
शक to be able, शक्त.
शद to fall, शन्न.
शप to curse, शप्त.
शम to be quiet, शान्त; tr. शमित.
शस to praise, शस्त, प्रशस्त.
शिष to have, शिष्ट; to distinguish, विशिष्ट.
शी to sleep, शयित.
शुध to be pure, शुद्ध.
शुष to dry, शुष्क.
शूर to injure, शूर्ण.
शॄ to injure, शीर्ण.
श्रम to be weary, श्रान्त.
श्रा to cook, श्राण.
श्रै to cook, श्राण.
श्लिष to embrace, श्लिष्ट.
श्वस to breathe; with वि, विश्वस्त trusted in: but श्वसित breathed.

श्वि to increase, शून or श्वयित.
सञ्ज to adhere to, सक्त.
सद to faint, सन्न.
सिध to become perfect, सिद्ध.
सूर to be brave, सूर्ण.
स्निह to be bland, स्निग्ध.
स्वञ्ज to embrace, स्वक्त.
स्वन to sound, स्वान्त or स्वनित; to adorn, with आ prefixed, आस्वान्त or आस्वनित.
स्वप to sleep, सुप्त.
स्विद to sweat, स्विन्न.
सृज to let go, to create, सृष्ट.
सृप to creep, सृप्त.
स्कन्द to go, स्कन्न.
स्तॄ to cover, स्तीर्ण.
स्पृश to touch, स्पृष्ट.
स्फाय to swell, स्फीत or स्फात.
स्फुर्ज to thunder, स्फूर्ण.
हद to void ordure, हन्न.
हन to strike or kill, हत.
हृष to be glad, हृष्ट.
ह्री to be ashamed, ह्रीण or ह्रीत.
ह्लाद to rejoice, ह्लन्न.

Future Participles active.

240. The active future participles are two, one in each Pada, and bear the same relation to the present participles as the indefinite future does to the present tense; the terminations being the same, with स्य prefixed. Thus the terminations of the participles are स्यतृ or स्यत् and स्यमान; and the insertion or omission of the augment इ, or any other modification of the base, follows the analogy of the indefinite future tense; as, भू 'to be,' भविष्यत् 'what will be;' गम 'to go,' गमिष्यत्;

जि 'to conquer,' जेष्यत् 'what will conquer;' श्रु 'to hear,' श्रोष्यत् 'what will hear.' This participle is declined like the present participle in अत्; as, m. भविष्यन्, f. भविष्यन्ती, n. भविष्यत्.

So एध, 'to increase,' makes एधिष्यमाण 'what will increase;' तुद 'to torture,' तोत्स्यमान 'what will torment;' मुच 'to liberate,' मोक्ष्यमाण 'what will liberate;' कृ 'to do,' करिष्यमाण 'what will do,' &c. These are declinable like nouns in अ.

Future Participles passive or neuter.

241. A class of future participles, most extensively employed, is formed by adding to verbs the affixes तव्यत्, अनीयर्, यत्, क्यप्, or ण्यत्. Of these, the two first reject the final, leaving तव्य and अनीय; whilst the three last leave only य. The participles thus formed express not only the sense of futurity, but the conditions of fitness, probability, or necessity; or that which is to be, which ought to be, which may be, or which must be: भवितव्य, भवनीय, भव्य, and the like.

a. The participles thus formed are declinable in the three genders like nouns in अ; and in one or other gender, but especially the feminine and neuter, they assume very commonly the office of nouns: thus कृत्य 'to be made or done,' from कृ 'to do,' becomes कृत्या f. 'a magical rite,' and कृत्यं n. 'motive' or 'cause.' Further instances will be specified.

242. तव्यत् is attached to the base analogously to the mode in which the ता of the first future is connected with it. If the verb prefixes इ, so does the participle; as, भू 'to be,' भवितव्य 'what is or ought to be;' एध 'to increase,' एधितव्य 'to be increased:' otherwise, as, जि 'to conquer,' जेतव्य 'to be conquered;' कृ 'to make,' कर्तव्य 'to be made;' रुध 'to oppose,' रोद्धव्य 'to be opposed;' षह 'to bear,' सोढव्य 'to be borne;' &c.

243. अनीयर्, is attached to the final consonants of verbs without change, and to final vowels agreeably to the rules of Sandhi. Short medial vowels are changed to their Guńa substitutes: thus, of the verbs above cited, भू makes भवनीय; एध, एधनीय; जि, जयनीय; कृ, करणीय; रुध, रोधनीय; षह, सहनीय,

&c.; 'to be,' 'to be increased,' 'to be conquered,' &c. This and the preceding termination, तव्य, is annexed to all verbs indiscriminately.

244. The participles formed with य are not so indiscriminately applied, but are restricted, with exceptions, to certain verbs or classes of verbs. They affect the base also differently, according to the letters with which the य is combined.

245. यत् is added to verbs ending in vowels, when it requires a final आ or a diphthong, to become ए, and other vowels to be changed to their Guńa equivalents; as, दा, देय 'to be given;' गै, गेय 'to be sung;' छो, छेय 'to be cut;' जि, जेय 'to be conquered;' णी, नेय 'to be guided.' In some cases the final vowel being changed to the Guńa letter, combines with य, as if it were a vowel: thus जि, 'to be conquered,' may be जेय्य (see rule 5, *a.* p. 13).

a. यत् is added to verbs ending with a labial consonant, प, फ, ब, भ, म, if preceded by अ; as, शप, शप्य 'to be sworn;' लभ, लभ्य 'to be acquired;' रम, रम्य 'to be agreeable:' but लभ, preceded by आ, requires the insertion of म before य; as, आलम्भ्य 'to be killed:' also when preceded by उप in the sense of 'commending;' उपलम्भ्यः साधुः 'the virtuous man is to be praised:' but not in its primitive sense; as, उपलभ्यं धनं 'wealth is to be acquired.' जप 'to pray silently,' and नम 'to bow,' preceded by आ, take ण्यत्, as well as यत्, making जाप्य or जप्य, आनाम्य or आनम्य. The following verbs also, although ending in labials, form their participles with ण्यत्: चम 'to eat,' with आ prefixed, आचाम्य 'to be sipped' or 'tasted;' त्रप, त्राप्य 'to be ashamed;' दम, दाम्य 'to be tamed;' रप, राप्य 'to be spoken;' लप, लाप्य 'to be spoken;' वप, वाप्य 'to be sown.'

b. यत् is affixed to the following verbs: यत 'to seek,' यत्य; तक 'to laugh,' तक्य; भज 'to worship,' भज्य; यज 'to worship,' यज्य; शक 'to be able,' शक्य; शस 'to slay,' शस्य; सह 'to endure,' सह्य; and वध substituted for हन 'to kill,' वध्य. Of these, भज, यज, and हन, may also take ण्यत्, making भाग्य 'to be divided' or 'portioned,' याज्य 'to be worshipped,' घात्य 'to be slain.' यत् is also affixed to the following: गद् 'to speak,' चर् 'to go,' मद् 'to be wild,' यम 'to restrain,' if not preceded by a preposition; गद्य 'to be spoken,' चर्य 'to be gone' or 'practised,' मद्य 'to be made frantic or drunk,' यम्य 'to be restrained:' but आ may be prefixed to चर्, if not meaning a spiritual teacher; as, आचर्यो देशः 'a country to be gone to;' otherwise, आचार्यः 'an A'chárya' or 'religious instructor.'

c. The following words are considered as irregularly formed with यत्, and are used as nouns, as well as participles:

अजर्यः mfn. 'imperishable;' but restricted to companionship or friendship;' as, अजर्यं संगतं 'uninterrupted association;' from जॄ 'to decay.'

अर्यः 'a master,' 'a Vaisya;' from ऋ 'to go:' otherwise, आर्यः 'a respectable man.'

अवद्यः -द्या -द्यं 'improper,' 'bad,' 'what is not fit to be said,' 'reprehensible,' 'blamable;' from वद् 'to speak,' which more regularly takes क्यप्, making अनूद्य mfn. 'not to be uttered.'

उपसर्या 'A female fit for impregnation;' उपसर्या गौः 'a cow fit for the bull;' from सृ with उप: otherwise, उपसार्य mfn. 'to be gone to' or 'approached.'

पण्यः -ण्या -ण्यं 'To be bought' or 'marketed,' 'to be pledged;' from पण 'to praise:' otherwise, पाण्य mfn. 'to be praised.'

वर्य -र्यः -र्या -र्यं 'Fit to be chosen' or 'solicited;' वर्या f. 'a maiden to be sought;' from वृ 'to choose as a bride' (a maiden): otherwise, वृत्य 'to be chosen,' with क्यप्; or वार्य mfn. 'to be appointed or selected generally,' with ण्यत्.

वह्यं 'a conveyance,' 'a vehicle,' 'that by which any thing is borne;' from वह: but with ण्यत् it makes वाह्यः mfn. 'to be carried.'

246. The termination क्यप् intimates by its initial क, that in affixing य, the radical vowel is not to be changed to its Guńa or Vṛiddhi equivalent, although it may be liable to such other changes as its conjugational inflexion prescribes; it also shews

that a radical nasal penultimate is to be dropped: whilst प requires the insertion of त in some cases before य. This termination forms participles with verbs ending in consonants having a penultimate ऋ; as, वृत 'to choose,' वृत्य 'to be chosen;' वृध 'to increase,' वृध्य 'to be increased:' except ऋच 'to praise,' चृत 'to injure,' and कृप 'to make,' which take यत्, making अर्च्य 'to be praised,' चर्त्य 'to be injured,' कल्प्य 'to be made.' So सृज, with the preposition अव or सं, or पाणि 'the hand,' prefixed, takes ण्यत्; as, अवसर्ग्य or संसर्ग्य 'to be let go,' पाणिसर्ग्य 'to be let go by the hand.'

a. क्यप् is added to the following verbs ending in vowels: इ, इत्य 'to be gone;' दृ, with आ prefixed, आदृत्य 'to be respected;' वृ (वृञ्), वृत्य 'to be chosen;' स्तु, स्तुत्य 'to be praised.' Also to these ending in consonants: कृत, कीर्त्य 'to be celebrated:' जुष, जुष्य 'to be pleased; शास, शिष्य 'to be governed.' When annexed to खन 'to dig,' ए is substituted for अन; as, खेय 'to be dug.' क्यप् is optionally affixed to form the following words:

कृ 'to make,' कृत्य; or with ण्यत्, कार्य्य 'to be made.'

गुह 'to hide,' गुह्य; or with यत्, गोह्य 'to be hid' or 'kept secret.'

ग्रह 'to take,' with अपि or प्रति prefixed, अपिगृह्य, प्रतिगृह्य 'to be received;' or with ण्यत्, अपिग्राह्य, प्रतिग्राह्य.

दुह 'to milk,' दुह्य; or with यत्, दोह्य.

भृञ् 'to nourish,' भृत्य; or with ण्यत्, भार्य्य 'to be nourished.'

मृज 'to cleanse,' literally or metaphorically, मृज्य; or with ण्यत्, मार्ग्य 'to be cleansed,' 'to be purified.'

वद 'to speak,' उद्य; or with यत्, वद्य: with any term signifying 'falsely' prefixed, it is only उद्य; as, अनृतोद्य, मृषोद्य, &c.: with a preposition it takes ण्यत्; प्रवाद्य 'to be declared.'

वृष 'to rain,' वृष्य; or with यत्, वर्ष्य 'to be rained.'

शंस 'to praise,' शस्य; or with यत्, शंस्य.

b. A number of words are considered to be irregularly formed with this affix; as the following:

अव्यथ्यः -थ्या -थ्यं 'Suffering no pain' or 'fatigue;' from व्यथ 'to pain.'

आज्यं 'Clarified butter;' from अञ्ज 'to anoint.'

उद्ध्यः The name of a river; from उज्झ 'to leave (its bed).'

कुप्यं Any valuable metal except gold or silver; from गुप 'to hide.'

कृष्टपच्यः -च्या -च्यं 'Ripening or flowering in cultivated ground:' so अकृष्टपच्य 'growing wild,' &c.; from पच 'to ripen.'

गृह्यः -ह्या -ह्यं 'Dependent,' 'servile,' 'confined;' गृह्याः शुकाः 'the encaged parrots:' attached to as a partisan, देवगृह्यः 'a friend of the gods:' with प्र prefixed, प्रगृह्यं a term in grammar, an exception. Fem. only, and combined with other words, 'without;' as, ग्रामगृह्या सेना 'the army outside of the village;' from ग्रह 'to take.'

चित्या 'A funeral fire;' अग्निचित्या 'maintaining a sacred fire;' from चि 'to gather.'

जित्यः 'A plough;' from जि 'to conquer.'

तिष्यः One of the lunar constellations; from तुष 'to please.'

पुष्यः One of the lunar constellations; from पुष 'to nourish.'

भार्या A proper name. When meaning 'a wife,' it is formed with ण्यत्, from भृ 'to nourish.'

भिद्यः The name of a river; from भिद् 'to break (its banks).'

युग्यः -ग्या -ग्यं To be used as a conveyance or carriage; a horse, an ox, a car, &c.; from युज 'to join,' 'to yoke.'

रुच्यः -च्या -च्यं 'Agreeable,' 'liked;' from रुच 'to please.'

विनीयः 'Refuse,' 'sediment;' from नी with वि prefixed, 'to take away.'

विपूयः 'Munja grass;' from पू with वि prefixed, 'to purify.'

सिध्यः A lunar mansion; from सिध 'to accomplish.'

c. भू with क्यप् forms भूय, to denote, in combination with other words, 'state' or 'condition;' as, देवभूयं 'divinity,' 'the being a god:' and हन with क्यप् forms हत्या 'killing,' which is also used in composition; as, रिपुहत्या 'slaughter of an enemy,' ब्रह्महत्या 'murder of a Brahman,' नृहत्या 'homicide.'

d. The following participial nouns are considered as being formed with this affix, which in the feminine gender become denominations:

इज्या worship, from यज to worship.
इत्या a litter — इण to go.
निपत्या muddy earth — पत to go.
निषद्या an assembly — षद् to sit.
भृत्या livelihood — भृञ to nourish.
मन्या the jugular vein — मन to know.
विद्या knowledge — विद् to know.
व्रज्या wandering about as a mendicant — व्रज to go.
शय्या a court, from शी to sleep.
समज्या an assembly — अज to go.
सुत्या ablution, bathing — षु to bathe.

247. The last of these terminations, ण्यत्, indicates by its initial that the radical vowel is to be changed to its Guńa or Vṛiddhi equivalent. It may be affixed—to verbs ending in उ or ऊ, when 'necessity' is implied; as, भू, भाव्य 'what is to be, necessarily;' otherwise भव्य:—to यु, याव्य 'to be mixed;' and षु, with आ prefixed, आसाव्य 'to be stirred up:' to verbs ending in ऋ or ॠ; as, कृ, कार्य्य 'to be made;' दॄ, दार्य्य 'to be torn:'—also to verbs ending in consonants not labials; as, वह, वाह्य 'to be borne.' As noticed above, it is also annexed to some verbs ending in labials.

a. When ण्यत् is added to verbs ending in palatals, they are usually changed to gutturals, or च to क, and ज to ग; as, पच, पाक्य 'to be cooked;' रुज, रोग्य 'to be made sick:' but there are many exceptions. It does not effect this change if the verb takes the augment इ before the त of the passive past participle; nor when 'necessity' is implied; as, पाच्य 'what must be cooked;' त्याज्य 'what must be abandoned;' याज्य 'what must be worshipped;' प्रवाच्य 'what must be said.' Some verbs optionally admit the change in different acceptations; as, भुज 'to enjoy' makes भोग्य 'what is to be enjoyed;' but भुज 'to eat' makes भोज्य: युज, with नि prefixed, 'to appoint,' makes नियोग्य 'what or who is fit to be employed;' नियोज्य

'what or who may be employed:' so वच, 'to speak,' makes वाच्य 'what may be said;' but वाक्य 'a sentence.'

b. The following are considered as irregularly formed with ण्यत्:

अमावस्या or अमावास्या 'Day of conjunction of the sun and moon;' from अमा 'together,' and वस 'to dwell.'

आनाय्यः 'To be brought from a particular fire,' the Dakshinágni; applicable only to a form of sacrificial fire; from णी, 'to take,' with आ prefixed: otherwise, आनेय.

उपचाय्यः A kind of sacrificial fire; from चि 'to collect,' with उप prefixed.

कुण्डपाय्यः A kind of sacrifice; from कुण्ड 'an altar,' and पा 'to drink;' in which the Soma juice is drunk.

धाय्या 'A sacred text;' from धा 'to have' or 'hold.'

निकाय्यः 'A dwelling;' from चि 'to collect,' with नि.

परिचाय्यः 'To be brought as fire for a sacrifice;' from परि and चि 'to collect.'

पाय्यं A sort of liquid measure; from मा 'to measure;' म being changed to प.

प्रणाय्यः -य्या -य्यं 'Adverse,' 'disliked,' 'disagreeable,' 'not approved of' or 'agreed with;' from णी 'to guide.'

याज्या 'A sacred text;' from यज 'to sacrifice.'

राजसूयं 'A royal sacrifice,' held by a paramount sovereign; from राजा and षु 'to bring forth.'

समूह्यः 'To be carried as sacrificial fire;' from सम and वह 'to bear.'

संचाय्यः A sort of sacrifice.

सान्नाय्यं 'Clarified butter;' from सम् and णी 'to take.'

248. An affix of similar import, though not much employed, is केलिमर्, which leaves एलिम, attached to verbs ending in consonants without change of the radical vowel: thus पच makes पचेलिम -मः -मा -मं 'what is to be cooked' or 'ripened;' भिद्, भिदेलिम -मः -मा -मं 'what is to be, or may be, broken' or 'divided.'

Indeclinable Participles.

249. There are two participles of the past tense, which are very extensively used, and which admit of neither gender, number, nor case. They are formed by adding to the verbal base the terminations क्त्वा leaving त्वा, or ल्यप् leaving य. The latter is affixed in the place of त्वा only when the verb is a compound, or is preceded by a preposition. In either case the accompanying letters are indicatory, and denote that the radical vowel is not changeable to the corresponding Guṅa or Vṛiddhi letter, and that a penultimate nasal is to be rejected. When however the augment इ is inserted before क्त्वा, the Guṅa substitute should take the place of the radical vowel.

a. Although implying past time, or something that has been, the participles thus formed with त्वा and य have not an absolutely past signification: they rather suspend the meaning, importing that although something has been, yet that something else is immediately to follow; as, स भुक्त्वा पीत्वा व्रजति 'having eaten and drunk, he goes;' इत्याकर्ण्य हिरण्यको ऽब्रवीत् 'having heard this, Hiraṅyaka said.' The designation of indeterminate past participles would therefore perhaps better express their character than that of Gerund, by which, as ordinarily employed, something remaining to be done is alone intended.

b. As a general rule, whatever form the base assumes before क्त, the sign of the indefinite past, it also takes before क्त्वा, that of the indeterminate past; as, कृ; कृतः, कृत्वा, 'having done:' श्रु; श्रुतः, श्रुत्वा, 'having heard:' पा; पीतः, पीत्वा, 'having drank:' दा; दत्तः, दत्त्वा, 'having given:' धा; हितः, हित्वा, 'having held:' स्था; स्थितः, स्थित्वा, 'having stood:' वच; उक्तः, उक्त्वा, 'having said:' वस; उषितः, उषित्वा, 'having dwelt:' क्षुध; क्षुधितः, क्षुधित्वा, 'having hungered:' अद; जग्धः, जग्ध्वा, 'having eaten:' गम; गतः, गत्वा, 'having gone:' नम; नतः, नत्वा, 'having bowed to:' खन; खातः, खात्वा, 'having dug:' शी; शयितः, शयित्वा, 'having slept:' मुद; मुदितः or मोदितः, मुदित्वा or मोदित्वा, 'having been pleased:' षिव; सेवितः, सेवित्वा, 'having served:' ग्रह; गृहीतः, गृहीत्वा, 'having taken:' and the like.

c. The deviation from general rules affects chiefly the influence of the indicatory क upon a penultimate nasal and the augment इ.

d. Thus, although a penultimate nasal should be rejected, the following are instances of its being retained: स्कन्द्, 'to go,' makes स्कंत्वा; and स्यन्द् 'to go,' स्यंत्वा, or with इ, स्यन्दित्वा 'having gone.' A verb ending with थ or फ, preceded by a nasal, and which inserts इ, optionally rejects the nasal; as, ग्रन्थ, 'to arrange,' makes ग्रथित्वा or ग्रन्थित्वा; श्रन्थ 'to loosen,' श्रथित्वा or श्रन्थित्वा; and गुम्फ 'to tie together,' गुफित्वा or गुम्फित्वा. The same with वञ्च 'to deceive,' which makes either वचित्वा or वञ्चित्वा; and लुञ्च 'to cut,' लुचित्वा or लुञ्चित्वा. Verbs ending with ज, preceded by a nasal, optionally reject it; as, भञ्ज 'to break,' भक्त्वा or भंक्त्वा; रञ्ज 'to colour,' रक्त्वा or रंक्त्वा; अञ्ज, 'to anoint' or 'to worship,' makes अक्त्वा, अंक्त्वा, or अञ्जित्वा; णश, 'to perish,' may retain the nasal which it inserts in conjugation; as, नंष्ट्वा or नष्ट्वा, or with इ, नशित्वा.

e. With regard to the change of the radical vowel when इ is inserted, all verbs beginning and ending with a consonant, excepting a final य or व, and having a penultimate इ or उ, optionally take the Guṅa vowel; as, लिख, 'to write,' makes लिखित्वा or लेखित्वा; द्युत 'to shine,' द्युतित्वा or द्योतित्वा; क्षुध 'to be hungry,' क्षुधित्वा or क्षोधित्वा. A vowel initial has but one form; इष 'to go,' एषित्वा; and so has a final व; as, षिव 'to serve,' सेवित्वा. विद 'to know,' and रुद 'to weep,' are exceptions to this rule having but one form; विदित्वा, रुदित्वा. The following are additional instances to those already specified, of the vowel being unchanged when the augment इ is inserted: कुष 'to embrace,' कुषित्वा; गुध 'to ply,' गुधित्वा; मुष 'to steal,' मुषित्वा; मृड 'to be glad,' मृडित्वा; मृद 'to trample,' मृदित्वा.

f. In the following, the vowel is optionally changed before इ: ऋ 'to go,' ऋतित्वा or अर्तित्वा; कृश 'to be thin,' कृशित्वा or

कर्शित्वा; कृष 'to draw,' कृषित्वा or कर्षित्वा; तृष 'to thirst,' तृषित्वा or तर्षित्वा; मृष 'to endure,' मृषित्वा or मर्षित्वा.

g. Verbs having an indicatory उ optionally insert इ (p. 106); as, शमु, 'to be tranquil,' makes शमित्वा or शान्त्वा; a final म requires the radical vowel to be made long, when इ is not inserted: but क्रम, 'to go,' has different forms; क्रमित्वा, क्रन्त्वा or क्रान्त्वा; दिव, 'to play,' makes द्यूत्वा or देवित्वा; पू, 'to purify,' पूत्वा or पवित्वा; अञ्च 'to go,' makes अक्त्वा, but when it means 'to worship,' अञ्चित्वा; लुभ, 'to beguile,' forms लोभित्वा, but 'to be covetous,' लुब्ध्वा; क्लिश 'to be distressed,' क्लिशित्वा or क्लिष्ट्वा; &c.

250. The termination ल्यप् is used when the verb is a compound, particularly when it is preceded by a preposition. The radical vowel is unchanged.

a. When affixed to a base ending in a short vowel, त is commonly prefixed to य; as, कृ 'to make,' अनुकृत्य 'having made like' or 'after;' जि 'to conquer,' पराजित्य 'having 'defeated;' स्तु 'to praise,' प्रस्तुत्य 'having celebrated:' and this prevails though the radical vowel become long by combination; as, इ 'to go,' with अधि prefixed, अधीत्य 'having studied;' or with प्र, प्रेत्य 'having deceased.' When य is attached to a base ending in a long vowel, no change takes place: स्था 'to stay,' प्रस्थाय 'having gone forth;' डी 'to fly,' उड्डीय 'having flown up;' भू 'to be,' अनुभूय 'having perceived.' ॠ is commonly changed to ईर्; as, तॄ 'to cross,' अवतीर्य 'having come down.' जागृ, 'to wake,' changes its vowel, उज्जागर्य 'having woke up.' Diphthongs, as in other instances, are usually changed to आ; as, धे 'to suck,' प्रधाय; गै 'to sing,' प्रगाय; छो 'to cut,' प्रछाय.

b. Some verbs ending in vowels or diphthongs modify their finals in a special manner before य. Thus क्षि, 'to decay,' makes विक्षित्य or विक्षीय; दी 'to waste,' प्रदाय; ली 'to dissolve,' प्रलीय or प्रलाय; मे 'to barter,' अनुमित्य or अनुमाय. वे 'to weave,' and व्ये 'to cover,' make प्रवाय and प्रव्याय; but after परि or सं, व्ये may make either परिवीय, संवीय, or परिवाय, संवाय.

c. Verbs ending in nasals occasionally change them to त,

or admit some other modification of the base. Thus खन, 'to dig,' makes either प्रखन्य or प्रखाय; गम 'to go,' आगम्य or आगत्य 'having come;' जन 'to produce,' संजन्य or संजाय; णम 'to bow,' प्रणम्य or प्रणत्य; तन 'to stretch, वितत्य; मन 'to mind,' अनुमत्य 'having assented;' यम 'to refrain,' नियम्य or नियत्य; रम 'to sport' or 'rest;' विरम्य or विरत्य; हन 'to kill,' आहत्य 'having beaten' or 'slain.' कम, 'to desire,' makes its vowel long, प्रकाम्य 'having desired much:' so does चर 'to go,' विचार्य्य 'having considered.' आप, 'to obtain,' may substitute अय्य; as, प्राप्य or प्रापय्य 'having obtained.'

d. Causal verbs, and those of the tenth conjugation which do not make the radical vowel long by virtue of a grammatical rule, or in which it is not long naturally or by position, prefix अय् to य; as, विगणय्य 'having caused to compute;' प्रणमय्य 'having made to stoop,' 'having bent' or 'bowed;' प्रकथय्य 'having declared' (from कथ, tenth conj.): but धृ 'to hold cause,' धारयति, makes सन्धार्य्य 'having caused to hold;' and भूष 'to adorn,' tenth conj., भूषयति, makes अनुभूष्य 'having similarly adorned.'

Participles of repetition, or Adverbial Participles.

251. In one form the indeclinable participle of repetition is nothing more than the indeterminate participle past repeated —गत्वा गत्वा 'having gone repeatedly,' कृत्वा कृत्वा 'having done repeatedly'—and is rather a case of grammatical construction, than part of conjugation. There is another form, no doubt of an analogous character, although specially provided for by adding the termination णमुल् to the verbal base: this leaves अम्, whilst the initial ण indicates the change of a final vowel to the Vṛiddhi equivalent, to be again changed before the vowel of अम् agreeably to the rules of Sandhi: thus चि, 'to gather,' becomes चै, which makes चायं चायं 'having collected repeatedly;' श्रु, 'to hear,' becomes श्रौ, and भू 'to be,' भौ, thus making श्रावं श्रावं 'having heard repeatedly,' भावं भावं 'having been repeatedly:' स्मृ, 'to remember,' makes स्मारं स्मारं

'having remembered repeatedly.' A final आ inserts य before the termination; as, दा 'to give,' दायं दायं 'having given repeatedly.' When the verb ends in a consonant, a radical अ, if not preceding a compound consonant, is changed to आ, and any other short vowel to its Guńa equivalent: vowels long by nature or position are unchanged: thus पच makes पाचं पाचं 'having cooked repeatedly;' शास, शासं शासं 'governing repeatedly;' विद, वेदं वेदं 'knowing or having known repeatedly;' भुज, भोजं भोजं 'eating or having eaten repeatedly;' &c.

a. The reiterated form of this participle is however by no means the mode in which it most frequently occurs, and it is much more often found singly in particular senses or combinations in which it offers an analogy to an adverb. Thus it occurs with words signifying 'first,' as पूर्वं भोजं or अग्रे भोजं or प्रथमं भोजं—व्रजति 'having first eaten, he goes.' कृ, 'to do,' employs this form when used transitively, and with a verb signifying 'to call;' चौरं कारमाक्रोशति 'he calls out, having made, or imputed, theft;' i. e. he calls out, 'Stop thief.' The same verb also uses it connected with कथम् 'how,' or इत्थम् 'thus;' कथङ्कारं or इत्थङ्कारं भुङ्क्ते 'having done, thus or how he eats:' or with स्वादु 'sweet;' स्वादुकारं भुङ्क्ते 'having sweetened it, he eats.' जीव, 'to live,' takes this form in conjunction with यावत्; यावज्जीवमधीते 'having lived so long, he studies;' i. e. he studies during life.' पूर, 'to fill,' takes it with चर्म्म or उदर; चर्म्मपूरं 'having filled the skin;' उदरपूरं 'having filled his belly.' हन also takes it; as, समूलघातं हन्ति 'killing all entirely, or to the very root, he slays;' or पादघातं हन्ति 'he strikes, kicking with his foot.' Instances might be infinitely multiplied of the use of the indeclinable or adverbial participle employed without repetition to signify an action indeterminately past.

SECTION II.

Verbal Nouns.

252. The nouns that are derived immediately from verbs

comprehend a great variety of terms, for which an unexceptionable classification can scarcely perhaps be proposed. There are two principal classes into which they might be divided, as adjectives or attributives, and substantives or names; but the same word is very frequently used in either form, the quality or attributive constituting the appellation of the individual: thus कर or कार in their generic acceptation signify 'any thing or person that does an action, or makes any thing;' whilst in combination, किङ्करः means 'a servant,' कुम्भकारः 'a potter;' and singly करः has for one of its meanings 'toll' or 'tax,' and कारः 'a letter of the alphabet.' To distinguish derivative words therefore according to their import, would lead at least to much inconvenient repetition.

253. These different nouns are formed, agreeably to the usual scheme of Sanskrit grammar, by affixing certain terminations to the crude verb, which is modified in a greater or lesser degree, and then forms the inflective base. These terminations are very numerous; but the greater number have a very limited, in some instances almost an individual, application; others comprehend a large class of words. It would be inconsistent with the object of the present grammar to furnish very numerous examples of these derivatives; nor is such detail necessary, as they will be found, where they seem to be most appropriately placed, in the Dictionary. It will be sufficient therefore to give here a selection of such words as may appear to be most useful, or as may best exemplify the principles upon which they are constructed; classing them under the terminations by which they are formed, and arranging them in alphabetical order, as has been done by Professor Bopp. He has, however, taken only the essential letters of the affixes; but I prefer exhibiting them as they occur in original grammars, as from the letter or letters by which the essential element is accompanied, a clue is usually obtained to the modification to which the inflective base, or some word compounded with it, is subjected.

अ is added to derivative verbs to form abstract nouns, declinable only in the feminine gender, and which therefore add the feminine termination (टाप्) आ; as, चिकीर्ष् 'to wish to do,' चिकीर्षा 'the desire to do;' पुत्रकाम्य् 'to desire a son,' पुत्रकाम्या 'desire of a son.' It is also added to verbs ending with consonants preceded by a vowel long either by nature or position, to form similar substantives: ईह् 'to endeavour,' ईहा 'effort' or 'wish;' ऊह् 'to reason,' ऊहा 'reasoning.'

अङ्, leaving अ to be added to the verb, forms feminine abstract nouns from verbs which have an indicatory ष्, and भिद् 'to break,' and others, forming the class भिदादि. The nasal prevents the change of the radical vowel; as, भिदा 'rupture;' चिन्ता 'reflection,' from चिन्ति 'to think;' पूजा 'worship,' from पूज 'to worship;' मृजा 'cleaning,' from मृज 'to cleanse:' except in the case of a final ॠ; as, जॄ, 'to decay,' makes जरा 'decay.' त्रप (त्रपूष्), 'to be ashamed,' makes त्रपा 'modesty.' कृप्, 'to have compassion,' changes its र to ऋ; as, कृपा 'clemency.' अङ् is also added to verbs in आ when preceded by a preposition or analogous term; as, दा 'to give,' प्रदा 'a gift;' भा 'to shine,' प्रभा 'light;' and श्रद्धा 'faith,' and अन्तर्द्धा 'disappearance,' from धा 'to have' or 'hold,' preceded by श्रत् or अन्तर्.

अच्, leaving अ, is one of the most widely applicable affixes. 1. It is added to the class of verbs called पचादि, or, according to most authorities, to all verbs whatever, to signify the agent; forming attributives which may take the three genders, but which are commonly used in some one gender as appellatives. A final vowel is changed before अ, according to the rules of Sandhi; as, पच् 'to cook,' पच 'who or what cooks' or 'ripens;' चर् (चरट्) 'to go,' चर 'who or what goes;' अनुचरः 'a male follower,' अनुचरी 'a female attendant;' चुर् (चुरट्) 'to steal,' चोरः 'a thief;' भू 'to be,' भव 'what is,' भवः 'the world,' or a name of S'iva; नद् (नदट्) 'to sound,' नद 'what sounds;' नद 'a male river,' नदी 'a female river.' (Obs. Those verbs of the class

पचादि which have an Anubandha ट् require the feminine to be formed with ई, not आ; as, चरी, चोरी, नदी, &c.)

2. अच् is also added to certain verbs compounded with their objects in restricted acceptations: as to हृ 'to take,' bodily exertion being omitted; as, अंशहर: 'an heir,' 'one who takes his portion;' but भारहार: 'a porter,' 'one who takes a load:' also with आ prefixed; पुष्पाहर 'having flowers,' 'blossoming.' It is also added to ग्रह, 'to take,' in a similar manner; as in शक्तिग्रह: 'a spearman,' 'one who holds a pike:'—to अर्ह 'to be worthy;' पूजार्हा 'a female Brahman,' 'one worthy of reverence:'—to जप 'to whisper,' and रम 'to sport,' compounded with कर्ण 'the ear,' and स्तम्ब 'a bush,' put in the locative case; as, कर्णेजप: 'an informer;' स्तम्बेरम: 'an elephant:'—to verbs compounded with शम् to form proper names; शम्भव: S'ambhava:—to शी 'to sleep,' compounded with various terms;' as, खशय: 'who sleeps in the air,' 'a divinity;' हृच्छय: 'who sleeps in the heart,' 'Cupid;' उत्तानशय: 'one who sleeps supine.'

3. Verbs ending in इ take अच् to form abstract masculine and neuter nouns; as, जि 'to conquer,' जय: 'victory;' चि 'to gather,' चय: 'collection;' भी 'to fear,' भयं 'fear,' 'peril.' It is also added to a few other verbs, with a similar effect; as, वृष 'to rain,' वर्ष: 'rain,' or 'the rainy season.'

अण्, leaving अ, with the change of a short radical vowel to Vṛiddhi, is added to verbs to express the agent when compounded with the object; as, कृ 'to make,' कुम्भकार: 'a potter,' 'one who makes pots;' हृ 'to take,' भारहार: 'a porter,' 'one who takes a load.' When added to हन 'to strike' or 'kill,' ट is substituted for the final in certain combinations; as, दार्वाघाट: 'who strikes the tree,' 'a woodpecker.' When सम् is prefixed, the final may be त्; as, वर्णसङ्घाट: or वर्णसङ्घात: 'a collection of letters,' 'an alphabet.'

अथुच्, leaving अथु, is added to a few verbs, distinguished by an Anubandha ट्, to form masculine abstract nouns: वेप (टुवेपृ)

'to tremble,' वेपथुः 'a trembling;' श्वि (टुश्वि) 'to increase,' श्वयथुः 'intumescence;' दु (टुदु) 'to be distressed,' दवथुः 'anxiety,' 'pain.'

अनि is added to verbs to form masculine nouns implying imprecation; as, from जीव 'to live,' अजीवनिस्ते भूयात् 'may loss of thy life be;' 'mayest thou perish.'

अप्, leaving प, forms masculine appellative and abstract nouns from verbs ending in उ, ऊ, ऋ, ॠ; as, स्तु 'to praise,' स्तवः 'praise;' यु 'to join,' यवः 'barley;' पू 'to purify,' पवः 'winnowing corn;' कृ 'to make,' करः 'the hand;' गॄ 'to swallow,' गरः 'poison;' स्तॄ 'to spread,' preceded by वि, makes विस्तरः 'prolixity,' 'diffuseness;' but विष्टरः 'a bed,' 'a tree.' It may also be added to ग्रह 'to take;' as, ग्रहः 'a planet:—to चि 'to collect,' preceded by निर्; निश्चयः 'certainty:'—to गम 'to go;' गमः 'going:'—also to घस्, substituted for अद 'to eat,' preceded by a preposition; as, निघसः, प्रघसः, विघसः, 'food' or 'eating:'—to जप 'to meditate,' and व्यध 'to pierce,' not compounded with a preposition; जपः 'silent prayer,' व्यधः 'wounding:'—to स्वन 'to sound;' स्वनः 'sound:'—हस 'to laugh;' हसः 'laughter:'—to यम 'to refrain,' either singly or preceded by उप, नि, वि, and सम्; as, यमः 'restraint,' उपयमः 'marriage,' नियमः 'fixed rule,' वियमः 'cessation,' संयमः 'restraint:'—to गद 'to speak,' नद 'to sound,' पठ 'to read,' स्वन 'to sound,' preceded by नि; as, निगदः 'speaking,' &c.:—also क्वण 'to sound,' either singly or with नि when it means 'to sound as a lute;' क्वणः निक्वणः 'the sound of the Viñá. There are other combinations with this affix, of which it may be observed, that its use very commonly alternates with that of घञ्, which latter makes the vowel long. Thus optionally with the preceding words we may have, निघासः, यामः, ग्राहः, स्वानः, हासः, क्वाणः, which are formed with घञ्.

आरु is added to शॄ 'to injure,' and वन्द 'to praise;' as, शरारु 'mischievous,' वन्दारु 'praising,' वन्दारुः 'a bard.'

आलुच् is added to a few verbs to form attributives implying

possession of the quality signified by the verb: thus ग्रह 'to take,' tenth conj., गृहयालु 'greedy,' 'insatiable;' दय 'to be compassionate,' दयालु 'kind,' 'pitiful;' निद्र 'to sleep,' निद्रालु 'sleepy,' 'slothful;' स्पृह 'to envy,' स्पृहयालु 'envious.'

इ is added to a class of verbs called कृषादि to form masculine or feminine abstract or appellative nouns; as, कृष 'to plough,' कृषिः 'ploughing' or 'agriculture;' गॄ 'to swallow,' गिरिः 'a mountain:' and the same affix, or इ, as derived from the technical affixes इञ् and इण्, forms similar nouns with the classes वपादि and अजादि; as, वापिः 'a pond,' from वप 'to sow;' and आजिः 'war,' from अज 'to go.'

इत्र is added to a few verbs to form neuter nouns chiefly signifying an instrument;' as, खनित्रं 'a spade,' from खन 'to 'dig;' लवित्रं 'a sickle,' from लू 'to cut:' but चर 'to go,' चरित्रं, means 'instituted observance,' also 'a history' or 'narrative;' and पू 'to purify,' पवित्रं 'the sacrificial thread,' 'a prayer of the Vedas,' or 'sacrificial fire.'

इनि, leaving इन्, is added to various verbs, either single or compounded, to form attributives; as, जि, जयिन् 'conquering,' 'victorious;' भू with परि prefixed, परिभविन् 'who is disgraced;' जु 'to be quick,' प्रजविन् 'who is quick.' These, when inflected, form जयी, जयिनी, जयि (see p. 63). To form masculine appellatives इनि is added to विक्री 'to sell,' preceded by the article sold, as तैलविक्रयी 'a vender of oil;' and sometimes in a depreciatory sense, as सोमविक्रयी 'a low Brahman,' 'a vender of the Soma juice,' which is used at sacrifices.

इष्णुच्, leaving इष्णु, forms attributives, declinable in three genders, from various simple and compound verbs; as, from चर, चरिष्णु 'going,' 'what goes;' from सह, सहिष्णु 'what endures;' from कृ with अलं, as अलङ्करिष्णु 'what adorns,' or with निर् and आ, as निराकरिष्णु 'what annihilates' or 'makes nothing of,' &c.

उ forms attributives with desiderative verbs; as, चिकीर्ष् 'to wish to do,' चिकीर्षु 'desirous of doing:' also with a few others;

as, इष ‘to wish,’ इच्छु ‘wishful;’ विद ‘to know,’ विन्दु ‘knowing;’ आशंस ‘to wish,’ आशंसु ‘desirous;’ and भिक्ष ‘to beg,’ भिक्षु ‘begging,’ भिक्षुः ‘a mendicant.’

उकञ् forms attributives after various verbs; the final indicates the lengthening of the radical vowel; as, from लष ‘to desire,’ लाषुक ‘wanton;’ कम ‘to desire,’ कामुक ‘desirous;’ भू ‘to be,’ भावुक ‘existing;’ पत ‘to fall,’ पातुक ‘falling;’ हन ‘to kill,’ घातुक ‘destroying,’ ‘destructive.’

उण्, leaving उ, forms a number of appellative nouns of various genders and purports: the radical vowel is made long by virtue of the final ण्. Thus with कृ ‘to make,’ कारुः ‘an artisan;’ जि ‘to overcome (disease),’ जायुः ‘a drug;’ वा ‘to blow,’ वायुः ‘the wind;’ अश ‘to pervade,’ आशु ind. ‘quickly,’ or आशुः m. ‘a sort of rice;’ जन ‘to be born,’ जानु n. ‘the knee.’ The chief importance of उण् is, however, its standing at the head of a very numerous class of terminations, thence called Uńádi, or Uń and others; the effect of which, as will be observed even in the few examples above given, is confined to no particular signification, and which form derivatives not always bearing an obvious relation to the verbs whence they are derived. The principle of the Uńádi derivatives is in fact merely their resolution into conjectural etymological elements, without much regard to the sense either of the primitive or derivative. The terms are too numerous to be further particularized in this place, and they will all be found in the Dictionary, which contains the whole of those specified in the five Uńádi chapters of the Siddhánta Kaumudí.

क, leaving अ, forms attributives after verbs having any penultimate vowel except अ or आ; the change of which is barred by the initial क्; as, from लिख ‘to write,’ लिख ‘who or what writes;’—from बुध ‘to know,’ बुध ‘who or what knows.’ It is also added to प्री ‘to please,’ प्रिय ‘what pleases,’ ‘dear,’ ‘loved,’ ‘liked;’—to कॄ ‘to scatter,’ किर ‘who or what throws.’ It is also added to verbs ending in आ, either as a radical letter, or as a substitute for a diphthong, and with or without a preposition, when the final आ is cut off; as, from ज्ञा 'to know,' ज्ञ or प्रज्ञ 'who or what knows,' ह्वे 'to call,' आह्व 'who or what calls.' It forms appellatives or attributives with verbs in आ, preceded by a subordinate term; as, दा 'to give,' गोद 'who gives a cow;' त्रा 'to preserve,' पार्ष्णित्रं 'the rear of an army;' and from पा 'to drink,' द्विपः 'an elephant,' who drinks with two things, his mouth and his trunk. It is added to स्था 'to stay or be,' in various forms and senses; as, समस्थ 'who or what is level' or 'at ease,' विषमस्थ 'who or what is uneven' or 'in difficulty;' प्रष्ठ 'what goes first,' or प्रस्थः 'a measure;' the sibilant being unchanged in this as in some other derivatives of the same class. ग्रह, 'to take,' changes its र to ऋ before क, forming appellatives; as, गृहं 'a house,' गृहाः (always m. pl.) 'a wife.'

कञ्, leaving अ, is added to दृश, when compounded with pronominal nouns, to denote 'likeness;' as, सम् and दृश make सदृशः; whilst क्स, leaving स, is added to the same verb, similarly compounded, when the two sibilants form क्ष; as, सदृक्षः &c.: so तादृश, तादृक्ष, &c.: see p. 83.

कि, leaving इ, which is substituted for the radical final vowel, is added to verbs in आ, or those which substitute आ for a diphthong, when preceded by a preposition, to form appellatives; as, from धा 'to have,' निधिः 'a treasure;' सन्धिः 'a joint,' &c.: also when preceded by a subordinate term; as, जलधिः 'what holds water,' i. e. the ocean.

कुरच्, leaving उर, forms attributives from भिद 'to break,' विद 'to know,' छिद 'to cut;' as, भिदुर 'who or what breaks:' विदुर 'who or what knows,' छिदुर 'who or what cuts.'

क्तिन्, leaving ति, is added to verbs to form feminine abstract or appellative nouns. There is a general analogy between the mode of attaching the final to the base, with the formation of past participles with क्त: thus कृ forms कृतिः 'act,' 'action;' स्तु, स्तुतिः 'praise;' श्रु, श्रुतिः 'hearing' or 'the Veda;' पद 'to go,' with सम् or वि prefixed, सम्पत्तिः 'prosperity,' विपत्तिः 'calamity.' यज, 'to sacrifice,' makes इष्टिः 'sacrifice;' स्था 'to stay,' स्थितिः

'staying,' 'station;' गै 'to sing,' गीतिः 'singing;' पा 'to drink,' पीतिः 'drinking;' पच 'to cook,' पक्तिः 'cooking,' 'maturity;' गम 'to go,' गतिः 'going,' 'motion;' रम 'to sport,' रतिः 'pleasure.' Verbs ending with ऋ or ॠ change the त to न; as, धू 'to be anxious,' धूनिः 'anxiety;' कॄ 'to scatter,' कीर्णिः 'scattering.' षो, 'to destroy,' makes सातिः 'destroying;' हन 'to kill,' हेतिः 'a weapon;' and कृत 'to celebrate,' कीर्त्तिः 'fame,' 'reputation.'

क्त्रिम forms adjectives from verbs which have an Anubandha डु; as पच (डुपच) 'to ripen,' पक्त्रिम 'what ripens' or 'is ripe.'

क्नु, leaving नु, forms attributives from क्षिप, गृध, त्रस, and धृष; as, क्षिप्नु 'who or what throws;' गृध्नु 'greedy;' त्रस्नु 'fearful;' धृष्णु 'arrogant.' भी, 'to fear,' takes क्रु, क्रुकन्, or क्लुकन्, in all which the क is indicatory, to form adjectives;' as, भीरु, भीरुक, or भीलुक, 'timid,' 'fearful.'

क्मरच् forms adjectives with अद or its substitute घस 'to eat;' as, अद्मर, घस्मर, 'voracious;' and सृ 'to go,' सृमर 'movable,' 'moving.'

क्वनिप्, leaving वन्, forms adjectives with a few words in particular combinations; as दृश 'to see,' with the object prefixed,' पारदृश्वन् 'who has seen across;' also युध 'to fight,' and कृ 'to make;' as, राजयुध्वन् 'who has fought the king;' राजकृत्वन् 'who has made a king;' सहयुध्वन् 'who has fought with;' सहकृत्वन् 'who has done any thing along with (another).' These words are declined like nouns in अन्, p. 59.

क्वरप् forms adjectives with इण 'to go,' जि 'to conquer,' णश 'to perish,' and सृ 'to go;' as, इत्वर 'what goes,' जित्वर 'victorious,' नश्वर 'perishing,' सृत्वर 'moving,' 'going:' also with गम, which changes its final to त; as, गत्वर 'what goes.' These adjectives form the feminine with ई; as, इत्वरी, जित्वरी, गत्वरी, &c.

क्विन्, leaving a blank, or, in other words, annexing no additional letter to the final of the verb to form its derivative, is subjoined to स्पृश, 'to touch,' to denote the agent combined with the object or instrument, when the former is not water;

a final श before this affix is changed in inflexion to क (see r. 119, p. 65): घृतस्पृश् (-स्पृक्) 'who touches Ghee;' मन्त्रस्पृश् 'who touches (fire, &c.) by prayer:' but उदकस्पर्शः 'who touches water;' the affix being घञ्. The following nouns are irregularly formed with this affix: ऋत्विज् 'a priest,' from यज 'to sacrifice;' दधृश् 'arrogant,' from धृष 'to be proud;' स्रज् 'a garland,' from सृज 'to quit;' दिश् 'a quarter,' from दिश 'to shew;' उष्णिह् 'a kind of metre,' from ष्णिह 'to be bland:' these form their nominatives in क्. The derivatives of अञ्च 'to go,' as प्राञ्च् 'east,' &c., and the words युज् 'who joins,' and क्रुञ्च् 'a curlew,' are also formed with this affix (see nouns in च &c., p. 48).

क्विप् is an affix of very extensive application; its effect is precisely the same as that of the preceding, which is separated from it only to mark the peculiarities of inflexion to which nouns formed with क्विन् are subject. क्विप् adds nothing to the verb. The derivative ends with the same final as the primitive, modified occasionally, but never by the addition of a vowel. The nouns it forms are both attributives and appellatives; as, प्रसूः 'a mother,' from षु 'to bring forth;' द्युसत् m. 'one who goes in the sky,' 'a deity,' from षद् 'to go;' प्रद्विष् (प्रद्विट्) 'an enemy,' from द्विष 'to hate;' अश्वयुज् (युक्) 'a lunar mansion,' from अश्व 'a horse,' and युज 'to join;' सेनानीः 'a general,' from सेना 'an army,' and णी 'to lead;' विराज् (राट्) 'Brahmá,' from राज 'to shine.' Verbs ending in short vowels add त् before क्विप्, as the प् indicates: thus चि, 'to collect,' makes अग्निचित् 'who collects the fire,' 'a householder;' जि, 'to conquer,' जित्, as इन्द्रजित् 'the conqueror of Indra,' a proper name; ष्टु 'to praise,' स्तुत्, as देवस्तुत् 'who praises the gods;' षु 'to sprinkle,' as सोमसुत् 'who sprinkles the Soma juice;' कृ 'to make,' as कर्म्मकृत् 'who does the work,' 'an artificer;' भाष्यकृत् 'who makes the gloss,' 'a scholiast.' दृश 'to see,' स्पृश 'to touch,' सृज 'to leave,' take क्विप् to express the agent when combined with the object, as सर्व्वदृश् (-दृक्) 'all-seeing;' मर्म्मस्पृश् (-स्पृक्) 'sharp,' 'corrosive;' विश्वसृज् (-सृक्) 'all-creating,' 'the

Creator:' so does अद् 'to eat,' as क्रव्याद् 'who eats flesh,' 'a goblin;' and हन 'to kill,' as ब्रह्महन् (हा) 'who kills a Brahman.' The following are modifications to which the base is in some instances liable: छाद, 'to cover,' makes its vowel short; as, तनुछद् 'what covers the body,' 'a garment:' verbs ending in a nasal, on the contrary, lengthen the vowel; as, शम 'to be tranquil,' प्रशाम् (प्रशान्) 'who is tranquil;' तन 'to stretch,' प्रतान् 'who extends.' तन, नम, गम, and यम, however, may change their finals to त्, and then the vowel remains short; as, अध्वगत् 'who goes along the road;' परीतत् 'every way extended;' सुनत् 'humble,' 'lowly;' संयत् 'self-restrained.' शास, 'to instruct,' substitutes इ for its penultimate: मित्रशिष् (शीः) 'who instructs a friend:' also with आ prefixed; as, आशिष्, nom. आशीः, 'a blessing.' गॄ, 'to swallow,' makes गिर् 'speech.' भ्रंश, स्रंस, ध्वंस, 'to fall,' &c., drop their nasals, and substitute त् for the final; as, वाहभ्रत् 'falling from a car;' उखास्रत् 'falling from the pot;' पर्णध्वत् 'falling from the leaf.' व in various combinations as a radical letter is changed to उ or ऊ, when क्विप् follows a verb: thus दिव, 'to play,' makes द्युत्, as अक्षद्युत् 'who plays with dice,' 'a gambler:' अव 'to preserve,' makes ऊः 'a preserver;' which with a preceding अ substitutes the Vṛiddhi letter, as जनौः 'who preserves mankind:' वे, 'to weave,' becomes ऊः 'a weaver:' ज्वर and त्वर make जूर् 'one who is ill;' तूर् 'one who is quick.' छ and व final, preceded by र are rejected; as, मुर्छा, 'to faint,' makes मूर् 'who faints;' and धुर्व 'to injure,' धुर्, nom. धूः, 'who injures;' as, अक्षधूः 'a load,' 'what injures the axle of a cart.' Some verbs form nouns as it is considered irregularly with this affix; as, वच 'to speak,' वाच 'speech;' प्रच्छ 'to ask,' प्राच्छ्, nom. प्राट्, 'who inquires;' प्रु 'to move,' कटप्रूः 'a worm;' श्रि 'to serve,' श्रीः 'prosperity;' व्रज 'to go,' प्रव्राज् 'who wanders about,' 'an ascetic;' दिव 'to shine,' विद्युत् 'lightning;' गम 'to go,' जगत् 'the world;' ध्यै 'to meditate,' धीः 'understanding;' and many others, for which the Dictionary must be referred to.

वुन् is added to रञ्ज 'to colour,' रजकः 'a washerman,' रजिका 'a washerwoman;' but if the derivative be formed with ष्वुन्, or the feminine noun signify 'a wife,' the form is रजकी.

खच् and its analogous affix खश्, each leaving अ, form a number of attributive and appellative nouns, compounded with the object or instrument of the action, which the letter ख indicates is to retain the terminations of the accusative case. The श् of the one indicates that the form of the derivative is analogous to that of the conjugation: the च् of the other, that the radical vowel must be always short. Words formed with खच् are, from वद 'to speak,' प्रियम्वदः 'who speaks kindly;' वशम्वदः 'who speaks authoritatively:' from गम 'to go,' विहङ्गमः 'who goes in the sky:' from कृ 'to make,' भयङ्कर 'fearful,' 'alarming;' अभयङ्कर 'what removes fear;' क्षेमङ्कर 'what brings good:' from भृ 'to nourish,' विश्वम्भर 'what nourishes all;' विश्वम्भरा 'the earth:' from तप 'to scorch,' परन्तपः 'who scorches or subdues an enemy,' 'a hero:' from यम 'to restrain,' वाचंयमः 'an ascetic,' 'one who restrains his speech' or 'observes a vow of silence:' from दृ 'to tear,' पुरन्दरः (not पुरन्द्वार) 'who tears or destroys a town,' a name of Indra. भू 'to be,' with आशित 'fed,' makes आशितम्भवः 'food' or 'satiety.' Of words formed with खश् the following are examples: from एजय 'to cause to tremble,' जनमेजयः 'who awes mankind,' the name of a prince: from अज 'to go,' वातमजः 'who goes with the wind,' 'a deer:' from धे (धेट) 'to suck,' स्तनन्धयः, fem. यी, 'who sucks the breast,' 'an infant:' from ध्मा 'to blow,' नाडिन्धमः 'a piper:' from तुद 'to torment,' विधुन्तुदः 'who tortures the moon,' 'the planet Ráhu;' अरुन्तुदः 'what afflicts the marrow,' 'what is very painful:' from पच 'to cook,' मितम्पचः 'who cooks by measure,' 'a niggard:' from तप 'to scorch;' ललाटन्तपः 'what scorches the forehead,' 'the sun:' from मद 'to be or make mad,' इरम्मदः 'what maddens or shines upon the water,' 'lightning.' From मन 'to mind' or 'think,' implying conceit or imagination, come such compounds as पण्डितम्मन्यः 'one who thinks himself a Pañdit;' गाम्मन्यः 'who fancies himself a cow.' It is unnecessary to multiply examples further.

खल्, leaving अ, is added to verbs preceded by ईषत्, दुर्, or सु, to form adjectives implying the mode of the action; as, ईषत्कर 'that which is made by a little at a time;' दुष्कर 'what is made with difficulty;' सुकर 'what is made with ease.' This affix is sometimes used indiscriminately with घञ्: see below.

खिष्णुच् and खुकञ् are attached to भू 'to be,' and ख्युन् to कृ 'to do,' compounded with certain words, which, as in the case of खच् and खश्, the ख indicates must terminate in a nasal: thus आढ्यम्भविष्णुः and आढ्यम्भावुकः 'a man who becomes wealthy,' 'not having been so before,' are formed with the two first affixes; and आढ्यम्करणं 'the means of becoming wealthy,' with the last: so अन्धम्भविष्णुः, अन्धम्भावुकः, 'becoming blind;' अन्धम्करणं 'means of blinding;' &c.

घ, leaving अ, forms nouns, for the most part masculine, implying place, or instrument, or appellation; as, from कृ, आकरः 'a mine,' 'where men work;' छद 'to cover,' दन्तच्छदः 'the lip,' 'that by which the teeth are covered;' खन 'to dig,' आखनः 'a spade;' पण 'to deal,' आपणः 'a market;' कष 'to touch,' निकष 'a touchstone;' चर 'to go,' गोचरः 'pasture-land;' वह 'to bear,' वहः 'a conveyance;' &c.

घञ् is one of those affixes of which the application is most extensive, and it forms a number of very useful masculine nouns, signifying the act, the agency, the instrument, the thing, or the abstract property. The essential element is अ; but the घ indicates that a final palatal is to be changed to a guttural; and the ञ्, that a radical medial अ is to be made long, and a final vowel to take its Vṛiddhi element, whilst any medial vowel but अ is changed to the Guña equivalent: a penultimate nasal is, with a few exceptions, rejected. Thus पच, 'to cook,' makes पाकः 'cooking' or 'maturity;' पद 'to go,' पादः 'a foot;' कम 'to desire,' कामः 'desire,' 'love;' श्रम 'to be weary,' विश्रामः 'rest;' सृ 'to go,' सारः 'strength,' 'essence,' अतीसारः

'diarrhœa;' हृ 'to take,' हारः 'a necklace,' आहारः 'food;' रु 'to cry,' with सम्, संरावः 'roaring;' भू 'to be,' भावः 'nature,' 'condition;' विश 'to enter,' वेशः 'an abode;' रुज 'to be sick,' रोगः 'disease;' स्पृश 'to touch,' स्पर्शः 'touch;' इन्ध 'to kindle,' एधः 'fuel;' श्रन्थ 'to loosen,' प्रश्रथः 'flaccidity,' the vowel remaining short; रञ्ज 'to colour,' रागः 'passion,' but रङ्गः 'a theatre:' स्यद, 'to go,' makes either स्यदः 'speed,' or स्यन्दः 'dropping:' स्फुर् and स्फुल्, 'to throb,' make स्फारः and स्फालः 'throbbing:' चि, 'to collect,' changes its initial to क; as, कायः 'the body,' निकायः 'a habitation.' Many words formed with घञ् admit of अप् also, as observed above; taking one or other in different senses or combinations; as, णी, 'to guide,' makes नायः 'leading;' but प्रणय 'affection,' परिणाय 'throwing round,' परिणयः 'marriage:' ग्रह 'to take,' with अव and नि prefixed, to form terms of imprecation, makes अवग्राहः 'dishonour,' निग्राहः 'death,' as अवग्राहस्ते भूयात्; but अवग्रहो धनस्य 'acceptance or seizure of the wealth,' चोरस्य निग्रहः 'confinement of the thief.' Some of the distinctions are very fanciful: thus चि compounded with पुष्प, 'a flower,' takes घञ् when it means 'gathering by hand,' as पुष्पचायः; but अप् when it means gathering in any other way, as पुष्पचयः 'gathering flowers (with a stick).'

घिनुण् forms attributives in इन्, requiring the change of अ to आ, and of any other short vowel to its Guṅa substitute: त्यज 'to leave,' त्यागिन् 'who leaves;' युज 'to join,' योगिन् 'who joins,' योगी 'a religious man;' द्विष 'to hate,' द्वेषिन् 'who or what hates;' क्रीड 'to play,' क्रीडिन् 'who plays;' पृच् 'to touch,' सम्पर्किन् 'what touches' or 'is close to;' वद 'to speak,' परवादिन् 'who contradicts.' The class of verbs शमादि (see p. 224.) do not change the vowel; शमिन् 'who is calm;' except मद, with उत् or प्र prefixed, उन्मादिन् or प्रमादिन् 'mad,' 'intoxicated.'

घुरच्, leaving उर, is added to मिद 'to be unctuous,' भास 'to shine,' भञ्ज 'to break;' as, मेदुर 'unctuous,' भासुर 'splendid,' भङ्गुर 'fragile.'

ट, leaving अ, is added to कृ 'to do,' सृ 'to go,' and चर 'to go,' to form attributives and appellatives in composition with other words. ट indicates the formation of the feminine in ई; as, किङ्करः 'a servant,' किङ्करी 'a female servant.' When the feminine is किङ्करा, the derivative कर has been formed with अच्: so दिवस्करः 'who makes the sky,' 'the sun;' भास्करः 'who makes light,' 'the sun:' यशस्करः -री -रं 'what makes fame,' 'honourable,' 'glorious:' so also अग्रेसरः 'one who goes before,' 'a leader;' भिक्षाचरः 'one who goes for alms,' 'a mendicant;' &c.

टक्, leaving अ, is added to हन् in certain compounds, when घ् is substituted for the root, to signify the agent; as, जायाघ्नः 'a man who kills his wife;' पतिघ्नी 'a woman who kills her husband;' कपाटघ्नः 'one who destroys or breaks open a door,' 'a thief;' पित्तघ्नं 'what destroys bile,' 'clarified butter.' Compounded with पाणि and ताड, in the sense of 'manufacture' or 'art,' घ् is substituted for the root; as, पाणिघः or ताडघः 'a mechanic,' 'an artisan.' It is also added to गै 'to sing,' and पा 'to drink,' in certain combinations; सामगः, सामगी, 'a male or female chaunter of the Sáma;' सुरापः -पी 'a winebibber:' but पा, 'to preserve,' takes क; as, क्षीरपा ब्राह्मणी 'a female Brahman, who keeps the milk.'

ड, leaving अ, is added to गम 'to go,' and हन 'to kill,' to form attributives and appellatives: the ड indicates the elision of the radical final: सर्वत्रग 'who or what goes every where;' विहगः 'who goes in the air,' 'a bird;' उरगः 'what goes on its belly,' 'a snake;' शत्रुह 'a destroyer of an enemy;' तमोपहः 'what drives away darkness,' 'the sun.'

डु forms nouns with भू 'to be,' preceded by वि, प्र, and सं; as, विभुः 'who is every where,' 'a deity;' प्रभुः 'a master;' सम्भुः 'a progenitor:' also with द्रु 'to flow,' preceded by its object; मितद्रुः 'what runs in a measured course,' 'the ocean;' शतद्रुः 'what runs in a hundred (streams),' 'a river.' शम्भुः, a name of Śiva, is considered to be formed also with this affix, from शं 'auspicious,' and भू 'to be.'

ण, leaving अ, is added to verbs ending in आ to form nouns of various kinds;' as, दा 'to give,' दायः 'a portion;' धा 'to hold,' धाय: 'a possessor,' 'one who has' or 'holds;' श्यै 'to go,' अवश्याय: 'frost:' also to इर 'to go,' स्रु 'to ooze,' षो 'to destroy,' हृ 'to take,' preceded by prepositions; as, अत्याय: 'going away,' 'end,' 'destruction;' आस्राव: 'trickling;' अवसाय: 'end,' 'conclusion,' or 'who or what ends;' अवहार: 'a shark,' also 'who or what takes away:' also to णी 'to guide,' नाय: 'a means;' लिह 'to lick,' लेह: 'licking;' श्लिष 'to embrace,' श्लेष: 'embracing;' ग्रह 'to take,' ग्राह: 'an alligator; व्यध 'to pierce,' व्याध: 'a hunter.' It is also added to जन 'to be born,' preceded by nouns or particles in various senses; as, अज 'unborn;' द्विज 'twice born;' द्विज: 'a Brahman;' अनुज 'born after;' अनुज: 'a younger brother;' सरसिजं 'a lotus,' 'born in a pool;' मन्दुरज: 'a monkey,' 'one born in a stable;' अहहज 'born from accident,' or 'what has not been foreseen.' From खन, 'to dig,' it forms परिखा 'a ditch.' It is also added to अद 'to eat,' preceded by नि; as, न्यद: 'food:' and to शील 'to be possessed of,' कम 'to desire,' भक्ष 'to eat,' preceded by their objects;' as, मांसशील 'having flesh,' 'stout;' मांसकाम 'desirous of flesh;' मांसभक्ष 'eating flesh:' also to ईक्ष 'to see,' and चर 'to go,' preceded by आ; as, सुखप्रतीक्ष 'expecting happiness;' कल्याणाचार 'one of good habits.' These make their feminines in आ; as, मांसशीला &c.

णिनि is an affix of extensive use to form attributives from verbs. The essential termination is इन्; the initial ण prolonging in most cases a radical short vowel. Nouns thus formed are mostly declinable in three genders as nouns in इन् (p. 63). It is affixed to a class of words called ग्रहादि; as, ग्राहिन् 'who or what takes;' स्थायिन् 'who or what stays' or 'is stationary;' निरक्षिन् 'preserving,' 'protecting;' अपराधिन् 'who or what offends;' परिभाविन् 'what disgraces.' It is also added to हन्, preceded by कुमार or शीर्ष; as, कुमारघातिन् 'who strikes the boy;' शीर्षघातिन् 'who strikes the head:' —to verbs preceded by nouns; as, उष्णभोजिन् 'who eats his meal hot;' साधुकारिन् 'who does what is right;' ब्रह्मवादिन् 'who declares Brahma' (the Vedas or the true god). It is also added to them to form attributives implying 'similarity,' as उष्ट्रक्रोशिन् 'who cries like a camel;' or to denote a religious obligation, as स्थण्डिलशायिन् 'who sleeps on the ground,' in consequence of a vow.

ष्युट् is affixed to a few verbs to form appellatives or attributives: ष prolongs the radical vowel; ट indicates the feminine termination to be ई; and यु, wherever it occurs, indicates the final of the derivative to be अन: thus, from गै 'to sing,' गायनः, गायनी, 'a male' or 'female singer;' from हा 'to abandon,' हायनः 'a year,' or 'a kind of rice.'

ण्वि is added to भज 'to take,' with the effect of क्विप्, except that it prolongs the vowel; as, अंशभाज् (nom. भाक्) 'one to take his share,' 'an heir.'

ण्वुल् is an affix to verbs in general to form nouns attributive of agency: ण, as usual, lengthens the vowel; whilst वु indicates the termination of the derivative to be अक: thus कृ, 'to do,' makes कारक 'who or what makes;' पच 'to cook,' पाचक 'who or what cooks' or 'ripens;' हन 'to kill,' घातक 'who or what destroys;' दा 'to give,' दायक 'a giver.' Some verbs do not make the vowel long;' as, दम, दमक 'who tames;' वध, वधक 'who kills;' जन, जनकः 'who begets,' 'a parent.' Feminine nouns usually substitute इ for the penultimate vowel; as, कारिका, पाचिका, &c.: so do some feminine nouns, names of diseases, formed with this affix; as, प्रच्छर्दिका 'vomiting,' प्रवाहिका 'diarrhœa:' they are considered irregular: so are आसिका 'sitting,' and शायिका 'lying down.'

तृच् is an affix of extensive use to form appellatives of agency; it leaves तृ, and nouns formed with this affix are declined like nouns in ऋ in the three genders (see p. 42): thus कृ 'to make,' कर्तृ 'a maker,' 'a doer;' गम, गन्तृ 'a goer;' पच, पक्तृ 'a cooker,' 'a ripener.' It follows the analogy of the original verb in inserting or omitting इ before त; as, सोढृ or सहितृ 'who bears;' एषितृ or एष्टृ 'who wishes;' क्रन्तृ, क्रान्तृ, or क्रमितृ, 'who goes;' &c. After some verbs, तृन् is said to be used instead of तृच्; as, from हु 'to sacrifice,' होतृ 'the ministering priest.'

नङ्, leaving न, forms substantives from यज 'to worship,' याच 'to ask,' 'यत 'to strive,' विश 'to shine,' प्रछ 'to ask;' as, यज्ञः 'sacrifice,' याच्ञा 'solicitation,' यत्नः 'effort,' विश्नः 'shining,' and प्रश्नः 'a question. स्वप्नः, 'sleep' or 'a dream,' is formed from स्वप 'to sleep,' with नन् affixed.

नजिङ् forms adjectives from स्वप 'to sleep,' तृष 'to thirst,' धृष 'to be proud;' as स्वप्नज् 'sleepy,' तृष्णज् 'thirsty,' धृष्णज् 'arrogant:' they are declined in three genders like nouns in ज् (p. 48).

मनिन् forms attributives and appellatives from verbs ending in vowels; as, from दा 'to give,' सुदामन् a proper name;' शॄ 'to injure,' शर्म्मन् a title proper for a Brahman.

युच्, which, as remarked under the head of ल्युट्, leaves, for the termination of the derivative, अन, forms attributives of agency and appellatives after verbs that signify 'motion,' 'sound,' 'ornament,' or 'anger;' as, चलन 'who or what is going;' कम्पन 'who or what is shaking;' रवण 'who or what is sounding;' भूषण 'who or what is adorning;' क्रोधन 'who or what is in a passion:' also after verbs beginning with a consonant, and having the indicatory vowel gravely accented; as, वृ 'to be,' वर्त्तन 'who or what is abiding;' वृध 'to increase,' वर्द्धन 'who or what is increasing:' also after various other verbs; as, जु 'to be quick,' जवन 'fleet;' ज्वल 'to burn,' ज्वलन 'burning,' 'shining;' &c. The feminine termination of nouns formed with युच् is टाप्; as, चलना, कम्पना, &c.: it also forms feminine nouns signifying the act, after verbs of the tenth conjugation or causals; as, कारणा 'causing to do;' हारणा 'causing to take:' also after a few other verbs; as, आस, आसना 'sitting;' श्रन्थ्, श्रन्थना loosing;' घट्ट, घट्टना 'effort,' 'exertion;' वदि, वन्दना 'praising;' विद, वेदना 'perception.'

र forms attributives with नम 'to bow,' कम्प 'to tremble,' स्मि 'to smile,' कम 'to desire,' हिंसि 'to injure,' दीप 'to shine;' as,

नम्र 'bent,' कम्प्र 'tremulous,' स्मेर 'smiling,' कम्र 'desirous,' हिंस्र 'mischievous,' 'cruel,' दीप्र 'radiant.' It also forms the indeclinable noun अजस्रं 'continual,' from जस 'to let loose,' with the negative prefixed.

रु forms attributives with certain verbs; as, दा 'to give,' दो 'to cut,' षि 'to bind,' शद 'to decay,' षद 'to go:' दारु 'who or what gives,' or 'who or what cuts;' सेरु 'who or what binds;' शद्रु 'decaying;' सद्रु 'what goes.'

ऊक forms appellatives with जागृ, 'to wake,' and verbs in the frequentative mode; as, जागरूक 'vigilant,' and यायजूक 'who worships frequently,' दन्दशूक 'who bites keenly,' दन्दशूकः 'a snake;' from यज 'to worship,' दंश 'to bite;' &c.

ल्यु forms nouns of agency from a class of verbs called नन्द्यादि, and from a variety of others: for the effect of यु, see ल्युट् and युच् above: नन्द 'to delight,' नन्दन 'who or what is delighted;' मद 'to madden,' मदन 'who or what maddens;' साध 'to accomplish,' साधन 'who or what effects;' षह 'to bear,' सहन 'who or what bears.' These nouns are very commonly used in the masculine gender as appellatives; as, नन्दनः 'a son,' मदनः 'Love,' मधुसूदनः 'the destroyer of Madhu,' a name of Vishńu; and the like.

ल्युट् is an analogous termination to the preceding, and also forms derivatives ending in अन; but they are not nouns signifying an agent; they denote the object, the act, the instrument, the site, or the abstract condition; and although sometimes masculine or feminine, are more usually neuter nouns: भोजनः 'an article of food,' भोजनं 'food in general' or 'feeding,' from भुज 'to eat;' जल्पनं 'chattering,' from जल्प 'to talk;' हसनं 'laughing,' 'laughter,' from हस 'to laugh;' साधनं 'accomplishing,' or 'means,' 'instrument,' from साध 'to effect;' पानं 'drinking' or 'drink,' from पा 'to drink;' प्रव्रश्चनः 'an implement of cutting,' 'an axe,' from व्रश्च 'to cut;' गोदोहनी 'an implement of milking,' 'a milk pail,' from दुह 'to milk.' The ट of the affix denotes the feminine formation in ई.

वरच् forms attributives, which in one or other gender become appellatives, from different verbs; as, ष्ठा 'to stay,' स्थावर 'who or what is stationary,' स्थावरं 'an inanimate product of nature;' ईश 'to be powerful,' ईश्वर 'who is powerful,' ईश्वरः 'God;' भास 'to shine,' भास्वर 'radiant,' &c. It is also added to या, 'to go,' in the frequentative mode; यायावर 'who or what goes repeatedly.'

वुञ् is added to निन्द, 'to abuse,' and other verbs, to form attributives signifying the agent;' as, निन्दक 'who or what reviles;' हिंसक 'who or what injures:' also to दिव 'to play,' and क्रुश 'to cry,' preceded by आ; as, आदेवक 'who sports' or plays;' आक्रोशक 'who calls out' or 'cries.'

वुन्, like the preceding, leaving अक, forms attributives with प्रु 'to go,' सृ 'to go,' and लू 'to cut;' as, प्रवक 'who or what goes;' सरक 'who or what moves;' लवक 'who or what cuts.' It also forms benedictory nouns; as, जीवक, 'living,' is used as wishing long life to; जीवकस्त्वं भूयाः 'Mayest thou be a liver,' i. e. live long.

श, leaving अ, is added to different verbs to form attributives and appellatives. The श indicates that the derivative follows the conjugational form of the verb; as, पा, पिबति 'to drink,' पिब 'who or what drinks,' दृश, पश्यति 'to see,' पश्य 'who or what sees;' धे, धयति 'to suck,' धय 'who sucks,' धयः 'a boy,' धया 'a girl.' So दा 'to give,' and धा 'to hold,' third conj.; दद 'who or what gives;' दध 'who or what holds.' So लिप 'to smear,' and विद 'to know,' of the sixth conjugation, make लिम्प and विन्द; as in निलिम्पाः 'the unsoiled,' 'the gods;' गोविन्दः 'who tends the cattle,' a name of Vishńu. So derivatives from verbs of the tenth conjugation and causals retain the sign; as, चित 'to think,' चेतय 'who or what reflects;' पॄ, पारय 'who or what fills;' उद् and एज, उदेजय 'what causes to tremble.' श is also added to various verbs to form feminine abstract nouns; as, क्रिया 'act,' 'action,' इच्छा 'wish,' परिचर्य्या 'worship,' परिसर्य्या 'wandering,' मृगया 'hunting,' अटाट्या 'roaming,' जागर्य्या 'waking,' 'vigilance.'

णाकन्, leaving आक, forms attributives from a few verbs; as,

जल्पाक 'prattling,' 'a babbler,' from जल्प 'to talk idly;' भिक्षाक 'begging,' from भिक्ष 'to seek alms;' &c. The feminine is formed with ई—जल्पाकी, भिक्षाकी, &c.—by virtue of the indicatory initial ष.

ष्वुन्, like ण्वुल् &c., as above, leaves षन, and forms attributives denoting the practiser of any art or business: the feminine, in consequence of ष, ends in ई: thus नृत, 'to dance,' makes नर्त्तकः, नर्त्तकी, 'a male or female dancer;' खन 'to dig,' खनकः, खनकी, 'a male or female ditcher.'

ष्ट्रन्, leaving त्र, forms neuter and feminine nouns from various verbs, signifying the instrument or means by which any end is effected; as, दो 'to cut,' दात्रं 'a sickle;' षिच 'to sprinkle,' सेक्त्रं 'a bucket;' यु and युज 'to join,' योत्रं or योक्त्रं 'fastening of a yoke;' शस 'to injure,' शस्त्रं 'a weapon;' णी 'to guide,' नेत्रं 'the eye;' दंश 'to bite,' दंष्ट्रं 'a tooth;' शास 'to govern,' शास्त्रं 'a scripture.' पू, 'to purify,' makes पोत्रं 'the snout of a hog,' or 'the shaft of a plough.' धे, 'to suck,' makes धात्री 'a nurse;' and धा 'to have (health by it),' धात्री a particular shrub.

ण्यकन् is added to the verb गै, 'to sing,' to form गायकः 'a singer.'

SECTION III.

Nominal Derivatives.

254. Having formed primitive nouns from verbs, other nouns may again be derived from the primitive nouns, to imply every possible relation to the things, actions, or notions, which the primitives express. These derivative nouns, called, as already mentioned, Tad-dhita ('relating or belonging to that' which is primitive), are formed in the usual mode by attaching certain affixes to the base, and modifying the latter agreeably to special rule, or to the indications afforded by the letter or letters accompanying the essential elements of the termination.

255. The difficulty of an unexceptionable classification of the Taddhita derivatives is still greater than even that of the classification of Kṛidanta words, inasmuch as the former are still more diversified in form and purport, and as many of the affixes are applicable in a greater variety of acceptations. We must therefore have recourse again to the alphabetical arrangement of the terminations, distinguished under a few different heads, and occasionally associating a few of an analogous and limited application.

256. Some of the most extensively useful of the Taddhita affixes are connected by an analogous diversity and extent of application. They are mostly employed in forming words which are one or other, or sometimes all, of the following: 1. Patronymics and terms denoting lineal descent, or community of origin; 2. Attributives of a variety of qualities and circumstances; 3. Appellatives, or names of persons and things; 4. Nouns of aggregation; and 5. Abstract nouns. These may therefore be classed under one head, as Miscellaneous nouns. Another considerable class of terminations is employed to denote possession of a thing or property by an individual object; and they may constitute another class, as Possessives. The terminations forming the superlative and comparative degrees are included amongst the Taddhita affixes; and so are those which form various pronominal derivatives, and terms connected with number, as ordinals, &c.: these may be grouped together. Finally, there are various indeclinable and adverbial terms. Thus making four classes of nominal derivatives; in each of which the terminations may be alphabetically arranged. With exception of the last of the above classes, Taddhita derivatives are declinable in either one or all of the genders.

257. The letter or syllable which forms the essential adjunct to the base, is sometimes merely added to it agreeably to the laws of combination; but it more usually takes the place of the last vowel of the primitive, and if that be followed by न्, of the consonant also. Thus from शिव comes शैव; from विकर्ण, वैकर्णि; from विनता, वैनतेय. A final उ or ऊ

may be changed to its Guṅa equivalent, and thus combined with the vowel of the affix, as कुरु, कौरव; but it may be sometimes cut off, as इक्ष्वाकु, ऐक्ष्वाक. अश्मन्, 'a stone,' makes आश्म 'stony;' ब्रह्मन् 'the Vedas' or 'Brahma,' ब्राह्म 'relating to Brahma' or 'the Vedas;' but as a generic term of descent, it makes ब्राह्मण: 'a Brahman.' So nouns ending in इन् usually preserve the final; as, चक्रिन् 'a car,' चाक्रिण 'belonging to a car.' There are many varieties, however, in the annexation of the affix to the base, for which the Dictionary must be consulted.

258. It is also a general rule, that all those terminations which contain an indicatory ण, ञ, or क, require that the first vowel of the base, whether it be a simple or compound term, substitute the Vṛiddhi equivalent; as, चक्षुष् 'the eye,' चाक्षुष 'relating to the eye.' In some polysyllabic words the Vṛiddhi letter is repeated; as, सुहृद् 'a friend,' सौहार्द 'friendship;' and from अग्नि and मरुत् combined, comes आग्निमारुतं 'sacred to Agni and Marut' (fire and wind). If the primitive begins with a compound letter, of which the second member is य or व, the Vṛiddhi diphthong ऐ or औ is commonly prefixed to the semivowel; as, from न्याय, 'logic,' comes नैयायिक: 'a logician;' from व्याघ्र 'a tiger,' वैयाघ्र 'covered with a tiger's skin;' from श्वस् to-morrow, शौवस्तिक 'of, or relating to, to-morrow.'

259. In some instances, nominal derivatives retain the form of the primitives unaltered; as, पञ्चाल: 'a native of Panchála,' otherwise पाञ्चाल:; यवन 'belonging or relating to the Yavanas,' otherwise यावन. In these cases, it is affirmed, that the usual affix had been attached to the primitive, but again rejected, together with its effects: this is called Taddhita-luk.

260. Attributives formed with affixes containing an indicatory ण, ञ, ठ, ढ, ष, and taking the three genders, form, with a few exceptions, the feminine with ई; as, पाञ्चाली, वैदर्भी, चाक्षुषी, मानुषी, &c.

Class I. *Miscellaneous affixes.*

अञ्, leaving अ, forms, 1. Patronymics; as, औरस: 'a son' or

'male descendant,' of उपगु: also generic terms of descent; as, दैव 'any divine being,' from देव 'a deity:' 2. Attributives in certain senses; as, द्वैप 'covered with an elephant's hide,' from द्वीप 'an elephant;' हारिद्र 'dyed with turmeric,' from हरिद्रा; दैवदारव 'made of the wood of the Devadáru pine:' 3. Appellatives; as, नृ 'a man,' नारी 'a woman;' पृथिवी 'the earth,' पार्थिवः 'a prince:' 4. Nouns of aggregation; as, कापोतं 'a flock of pigeons,' from कपोत: and 5. Abstract nouns in certain senses; as, आश्वं 'the nature of a horse.' In general, अञ् may be considered as forming similar derivatives with the analogous termination अण्, and to be applicable to the same primitives, although theoretically it is limited to words of which the first vowel is gravely accented, which terminate in उ, or which belong to certain specified classes; as, खण्डिकादि or खण्डिक, and others.

अठच् forms from कर्म्मन्, 'act,' the attributive कर्म्मठ 'active,' 'energetic.'

अण्, leaving अ, is an affix of very universal application. It forms, 1. Patronymics; as, औपगवः 'a son or descendant of उपगु;' वासुदेवः 'the son of Vasudeva' वसुदेवः, that is, Krishńa: also terms of descent in general; as, ब्राह्मणः 'a Brahman,' from ब्रह्मन्. A final ऋ is changed to उर् before the अ of अण् in this sense; as, द्वैमातुरः 'the son of two mothers,' from द्वि and मातृ 'a mother.' 2. Attributives; as, मंजिष्ठा 'Madder,' मांजिष्ठ 'of the colour of, or dyed with, Madder;' वस्त्र 'cloth,' वास्त्र 'made of, or covered with, cloth,' &c.; शैव 'relating or belonging to, or a worshipper of, S'iva;' वैष्णव 'relating or belonging to, or a worshipper of, Vishńu;' नैषध 'belonging to, or produced in the country of, Nishadha.' अश्व, 'a horse,' makes आश्व 'belonging or relating to a horse,' 'drawn by horses;' शर्करा 'sugar,' शार्कर 'sugary,' 'made of sugar,' or 'as sweet;' और्ण 'woollen,' 'made of wool,' from ऊर्णा 'wool;' ग्रैष्म, हैमन्त, हैमन, 'produced in the hot or cold weather,' 'summer,' 'winter;' आह्न 'diurnal,' from अहन् 'a day;' नैश 'nocturnal,' from निशा 'night;' सांवत्सर 'annual,' from संवत्सरः 'a year;' शारीर 'bodily,' 'corporeal,' from

शरीरं 'the body.' It also forms possessive attributes; as, प्रज्ञा 'wisdom,' प्राज्ञ 'having wisdom,' 'wise.' 3. Many of the attributives already given are also appellatives: thus शैवः and वैष्णवः mean severally 'a follower of S'iva or Vishńu;' नैषधः is a proper name, 'king of Nishadha;' आश्वः 'a carriage drawn by horses.' पौष, relating to the asterism पुष्य, is in the masculine पौषः, the name of a month, when the moon is in that asterism; and in the feminine, पौषी 'day of full moon in the month of Paush.' 4. Aggregates; as, वाकं 'a flight of cranes,' from बकः 'a crane;' भैक्षं 'a troop of beggars,' from भिक्षुः 'a beggar.' 5. Abstract nouns; as, शुचिः 'who is pure,' शौचं 'purification;' मुनिः 'a silent sage;' मौनं 'silence;' युवन् 'young,' यौवनं 'youth;' पुरुषः 'a man,' पौरुषं 'manliness,' 'manhood,' 'manly stature,' &c.; पृथु 'large,' पार्थवं 'bulk,' 'bigness.' अण् is also sometimes used pleonastically; as, बन्धुः or बान्धवः 'a kinsman;' ओषधिः or औषधं 'a drug;' देवता or दैवतः 'a divinity.'

इञ्, leaving इ, forms patronymics only; as, दाक्षिः 'a descendant of Daksha;' वैयासकिः 'a descendant of Vyása' (क being inserted).

इनच् and analogous terminations, क and पिटच्, are added to चिक् and चि, substituted for नि, to form चिकिन, चिक्क and चिपिट signify 'flat, as the nose,' चिकिना नासिका; or 'flat-nosed,' चिपिटः पुरुषः, &c.

इनि is added to a class of words to form nouns of multitude; as, खलिनी 'a number of mills:' also to कर्म्मन्द and कृशाश्व, severally authors of rules for an order of mendicants, and for acting; to imply their disciples; कर्म्मन्दिन् 'a mendicant,' कृशाश्विन् 'an actor.' इनि is of more extensive application as a possessive affix.

इमनिच्, leaving इमन्, forms abstract masculine nouns from attributes of sensible properties; as, शुक्ल 'white,' शुक्लिमन् 'whiteness;' पृथु 'large,' प्रथिमन् 'bulk;' मृदु 'soft,' म्रदिमन् 'softness;' महत् 'great,' महिमन् 'greatness;' गुरु 'heavy,' गरिमन् 'heaviness;' &c. These form their nominatives in आ; as, शुक्लिमा, &c. (see p. 59).

एण्य is added to प्रावृष् 'the rainy season,' forming प्रावृषेण्य 'what grows or is produced in the rains.'

कटच् is added to appellatives to signify 'multitude;' अविकटः 'a flock of sheep:' also to various prepositions to form attributives conveying their general purport; प्रकट 'manifest;' विकट 'large,' 'extended;' संकट 'contracted;' उत्कट 'much;' निकट 'near.'

कत्यच् added to रथ forms रथकत्या 'a multitude of carriages.'

कन्, that is, क, forms a variety of derivative words, mostly attributives; as, मद्रक 'produced or born in the country of Madra,' स्थूलक 'stout,' पीतक 'dyed yellow,' मामक 'belonging to me,' त्वाक 'belonging to thee,' उत्क 'sad,' पञ्चक 'bought with five,' 'bearing or receiving five,' as tax or interest. It forms also attributives implying 'skill;' as, केशक 'one skilled in dressing hair:' or 'limitation;' as, छिन्न 'cut,' छिन्नक 'a little cut:' also 'likeness;' as, शीतक 'cold, as it were,' i. e. dull, slow; उष्णक 'hot, as it were,' i. e. quick, smart. It is added to prepositions; as, to अधि 'over,' अधिक 'more than;' and to अनु 'after,' and अभि 'near;' अनुक, अभिक or अभीक 'lustful.' It forms also appellatives; as, अंशकः 'an heir,' 'one who takes his portion,' from अंशः 'a part;' particularly when pity or contempt is intended; as, वृक्षकः 'a stumpy tree;' शूद्रकः 'an inferior S'údra;' पुत्रकः 'the poor child;' देवदत्तकः 'the unhappy Devadatta;' अश्वकः 'a vile horse.' It sometimes implies 'doubt;' as, अश्वकः 'the horse (of whom is this).' It is frequently pleonastic; as, अविः or अविकः 'a sheep;' मणिः or मणिकः 'a jewel;' &c.

कल्प and the analogous terminations देश्य and देशीयर् are affixed to nouns to form appellatives implying 'inferiority;' विद्वत्कल्पः, विद्वद्देश्यः, विद्वद्देशीयः, 'an inferior scholar.' They are also attached in an adverbial form to verbal inflexions; as, पचतिकल्पं &c. 'he cooks incompletely,' 'he does not finish cooking.'

ख and खञ् are analogous terminations, of which the essential adjunct is ईन; the second requires the Vṛiddhi vowel: they form, 1. Words implying 'descent;' as, from कुल 'a race,'

कुलीन or कौलीन 'sprung from a good family:' 2. Attributives; as, अहन्, 'a day,' makes अहीन 'to be done in a given number of days;' अवारपार: 'either bank of a river,' अवारपारीण 'who or what goes or extends to both banks;' ग्राम: 'a village,' ग्रामीण 'rustic' 'village:' आत्मन् makes आत्मनीन 'what is fit or good for oneself;' विश्वजन 'all mankind,' विश्वजनीन 'what is fit or good for all:' 3. Appellatives; तिल, 'Sesamum,' makes तैलीनं 'a field of Sesamum;' सप्तपदं 'seven steps,' साप्तपदीनं 'friendship,' 'intimacy;' हैयङ्गवीनं 'fresh butter,' from ह्यस् 'to-day,' and गो 'a cow.'

घ, leaving इय, forms, 1. words of descent; as, from क्षत्र: 'a man of the military caste,' क्षत्रिय: the same, as sprung from him: 2. Attributives; as, राष्ट्र: 'a country,' राष्ट्रिय 'relating or belonging to it.'

छ and छण् are analogous affixes, both leaving ईय: the one requires Vṛiddhi; the other not: they form, 1. words of descent in general; as, स्वस्रीय: 'a sister's son,' पैतृस्वस्रीय: 'the son of a father's sister:' 2. Attributives; महेन्द्रीय or माहेन्द्रीय 'relating to Mahendra;' वत्सीय 'suited to, or fit for, a calf;' प्राकारीय 'fit for a wall:' क is inserted before the affix after some words; as, स्वकीय 'own,' राजकीय 'royal:' 3. Appellatives; as, पर्व्वतीय: 'a mountaineer.'

चणप् and चुञ्चु are two affixes to nouns to form attributives implying 'being known by;' as, विद्याचण or विद्याचुञ्चु 'known by, or on account of, learning.'

ञ, leaving अ, forms feminine nouns of descent; as, पार्थिवा 'a female descendant of पृथिवी;' and nouns of action, compounded with पात 'falling;' as, दाण्डपाता 'falling of an hour,' 'a lunar day.' After श्येन 'a hawk,' and तिल 'Sesamum,' a nasal is inserted; as, श्यैनम्पाता 'hawking;' तैलम्पाता 'an oblation' (in which Sesamum is scattered).

ञिठ् alternates with ठञ् after a few words, and like it leaves इक for the termination; but it differs in forming the feminine with आ; as, काशि 'a city' (Benares), काशिक 'belonging to Káśi;' fem. काशिका; with ठञ् it would be काशिकी.

ष्य, leaving य, forms a few appellative and abstract nouns; वैदूर्य्यं 'the lapis lazuli,' from विदूर a mountain so named; गाम्भीर्य्यं 'depth,' from गम्भीर 'deep;' आनन्त्यं 'infinity,' from अनन्त 'endless;' आतिथ्यं 'hospitality,' from अतिथि 'a guest;' and others.

टीटच् with the analogous terminations नाटच् and भ्रटच् are added to the preposition अव to form attributives implying 'flat,' as the nose; अवटीटा, अवनाटा, or अवभ्रटा, नासिका, 'a flat nose;' अवटीटः, अवनाटः, अवभ्रटः—पुरुषः 'a flat-nosed man.'

ट्यु or ट्युन्, is an affix, leaving अन, to form attributives from adverbs importing 'time:' त is inserted: as सायं 'evening,' सायन्तन 'what is of the evening;' अद्य 'to-day,' अद्यतन 'what is of to-day;' प्राह्णे 'in the forenoon,' प्राह्णेतन 'what is of the forenoon;' चिरं 'long,' चिरन्तन 'lasting' or 'delayed long;' &c.

ठक् is an affix forming a number of words, substituting इक for the finals of nouns ending in अ or आ, or in अन्, and adding क to others: it forms, 1. a few patronymics from feminine nouns in ई, the final of which is also cut off; as, रैवतिक 'a descendant of रेवती:' but it also implies inferiority in this form; as, गार्गिक 'an inferior,' 'a young or silly descendant of गार्गी.' 2. Attributives; as, लाक्षा makes लाक्षिक 'dyed with Lac;' दधि, दाधिक 'made with, or fed with, curds;' धर्म्म, धार्म्मिक 'virtuous,' but आधर्म्मिक 'wicked;' मास, मासिक 'given or lasting for a month;' वर्ष, वार्षिक 'annual,' 'lasting for a year;' सेना, सैनिक 'belonging to an army.' 3. Appellatives; आक्षिकः 'a gambler,' from अक्ष 'dice;' नैयायिकः 'a logician,' from न्याय 'logic;' आस्तिकः 'a believer,' नास्तिकः 'an atheist,' from अस्ति 'what is:' असि, 'a sword,' makes आसिकः 'a swordsman;' धनुष् 'a bow,' धानुष्कः 'a bowman.' 4. Aggregates of inanimate objects; as, साक्तुकं 'a heap of parched grain:' but also of elephants, हास्तिकं; and of kine, धैनुकं.

ठञ् forms similar derivations as the preceding, but is mostly limited to attributives, which sometimes become appellatives; as वैदिक 'relating to the Vedas,' वैदिकः 'a Brahman who studies or teaches them;' सांग्रामिक 'relating to war or battle,'

सांग्रामिकः 'a soldier.' It is extensively used to form adjectives relating to measures of value, quantity, number, or time: नैष्किक 'bought with, or of the value of, a Nishka;' अर्द्धद्रौणिक or आर्द्धद्रौणिक 'containing, or relating to, half a droṅa' (a measure of grain); वैंशतिक 'bought with, or of the value of, twenty;' आह्निक 'daily' or 'lasting for a day;' मासिक 'monthly' or 'lasting for a month;' द्वैरात्रिक 'lasting for two nights;' कालिक 'continuing for a time.' Some terms of philosophy are also formed with it; as, आधिदैविक, आधिभौतिक, आध्यात्मिक, relating to that which is celestial, elemental, or spiritual. It also forms nouns of aggregation; as, केदार: 'a field,' कैदारिकं 'a number of fields.'

ठन्, like the two preceding, supplies इक for the termination of similar nouns, but it does not require the Vṛiddhi change of the vowel; as, घट 'a jar,' घटिक 'what is placed in a jar;' नौ 'a boat,' नाविक 'who or what goes in a boat, relating or belonging to it;' क्रयिक 'who sells,' विक्रयिक 'who buys,' क्रयविक्रयिकः 'a dealer,' 'a tradesman;' शत 'a hundred,' शतिक 'worth, or bought with, a hundred.' It is affixed to अर्द्ध and भाग to signify 'rate of interest;' अर्द्धिकं or भागिकं शतं 'half per cent.' It is also a possessive affix; as, दण्ड 'a staff,' दण्डिक 'one who bears a staff;' केश 'hair,' केशिक 'one who has much hair;' गो and शत 'a hundred,' गोशतिक 'one who has a hundred cows.'

डामहच् is considered as an affix forming the words पितामहः -मही, मातामहः -मही 'paternal and maternal grandfather and grandmother,' from पितृ and मातृ. डुलच् added to मातृ forms मातुलः 'a maternal uncle;' व्यत् to पितृ, पितृव्यः 'a paternal uncle;' and व्य to भ्रातृ, भ्रातृव्यः 'a brother's son.'

ढक् is a useful affix: it leaves एय, and forms, 1. Patronymics and terms of descent; as, आग्नेयः 'the son of Agni;' वैनतेयः name of Garuḋa, 'the son of Vinatá;' मैत्रेयः 'son of Mitrayu;' the final of the primitive being cut off: sometimes इनङ् is prefixed to the termination; as, कौलटेयः or कौलटिनेयः 'the son of a respectable woman,' कुलटा; when कुलटा means 'a harlot,' the derivative implying 'her son' is कौलटेर, being formed with the analogous affix द्रक्. So either of these, forms words implying 'descent' from a disfigured or a base person; as, काणेयः or काणेरः 'the son of a one-eyed man;' दासेयः or दासेरः 'the son of a slave.' स्वसृ, 'a sister,' in combination rejects its final before ढक्; as, पितृस्वसेयः 'the son of a father's sister,' मातृस्वसेयः 'the son of a mother's sister.' 2. ढक् also forms attributives signifying 'produced in,' or 'derived from;' नादेय 'aquatic,' from नदी 'a river;' माहेय 'earthen,' from मही 'the earth:' and 3. a few appellatives; as, from व्रीहिः 'rice,' व्रैहेयं 'a rice-field.'

ढकञ् is analogous to the preceding, adding क to the termination; as, कौलेयक 'belonging to, or derived from, a family;' otherwise कौलेय. It is also added to a few words in a contemptuous sense; as, ग्राम, 'a village,' makes ग्रामेयकः 'a clown;' नगर 'a city,' नागरेयकः 'a libertine,' 'a profligate.'

ढञ् is another termination allied to the preceding; differing from ढक् only in being restricted to certain words; as, पुरुष, 'a man,' in particular acceptations; as, पौरुषेयो वधः 'a killing of men;' पौरुषेयः समूहः 'an assemblage of men;' पौरुषेयो विकारः 'mortal or human change;' पौरुषेयः -यी -यं 'done by a man' or 'human being.'

णा, leaving आ, forms a few feminine nouns that signify 'striking in sport;' as, दाण्डा 'quarter-staff,' and मौष्टा 'boxing,' from दण्ड 'a staff,' मुष्टि 'the fist:' also some attributives; as, सर्व्व 'all,' सार्व्व 'fit or good for all.'

ण्य, leaving य, forms words implying 'descent;' as, दैत्यः 'a demon,' 'a son of Diti;' आदित्यः 'an Áditya,' 'son of Aditi;' कौरव्यः 'a descendant of Kuru.' It is added to पति, when preceded by a noun; as, प्राजापत्यः 'son or descendant of प्रजापति;' and to words signifying 'an artisan;' as, तन्तुवाय, 'a weaver,' makes तान्तुवाय्यः 'a weaver's progeny:' it also forms appellatives; as, परिषद् makes पारिषद्यः 'an assistant at an assembly.'

तल् forms feminine nouns signifying, 1. Aggregation; ग्रामता 'a number of villages;' जनता 'a number of men;' गजता 'a herd of elephants:' 2. Abstract property; स्त्रीता 'womanhood,' गोता 'cowhood,' पुत्रता 'childhood.' It is also added pleonastically to देव; as, देवता 'a divinity.'

त्न is added to some words to denote 'time;' as, परुत्न 'of last year;' परारित्न 'of the year before last;' चिरत्न 'of a long time ago:' also to नू substituted for नव, नूत्न 'new:' the latter takes तनप् in the same sense, नूतन, and, as above, नवीन.

त्यक् is added to terms of place to form attributives; दाक्षिणात्य 'produced in the south,' 'a native of the south,' &c.: so पाश्चात्य, पौरस्त्य, 'produced in the west, east,' &c.

त्यकन् forms feminine appellatives after the prepositions अधि and उप; as, अधित्यका 'an acclivity;' उपत्यका 'land, the foot of a mountain.'

त्यप् is affixed to indeclinables to form attributives implying 'production;' as, क्कत्य 'produced where;' तत्रत्य 'born or produced there;' इहत्य 'born or produced here:' with अमा, 'together,' it forms अमात्यः 'a minister.'

त्र is added to गो, 'a cow,' to denote 'multitude;' गोत्रा 'a herd of cattle.'

त्व forms neuter abstract nouns from any other nouns; ब्राह्मणत्वं 'Brahmanhood,' बालत्वं 'childhood,' पुण्यत्वं 'holiness.'

दघ्नच् and द्वयसच् are added to nouns to denote 'measure of height;' ऊरुदघ्न, ऊरुद्वयस 'as high as the thigh.'

दूस is added to अवि in the sense of 'milk;' अविदूसं 'ewe's milk.' मरीस and सोढ, equally anomalous affixes, and probably obsolete words, meaning 'milk,' are similarly employed; as, अविमरीसं and अविसोढं.

नञ् and the analogous affix स्नञ् are added severally to स्त्री and पुंस् to form appellatives; स्त्रैण 'produced from, or by, a woman;' पौंस्न 'produced of, or by, a man.' In the neuter gender they may be abstract nouns; स्त्रैणं 'womanhood,' पौंस्नं 'manhood.'

पाशप् forms attributives from nouns in the sense of 'inferiority;' as, भिषक्पाशः 'an indifferent physician:' compounded with केश it signifies 'quantity;' केशपाशः 'abundant hair:' केशपक्षः has a similar purport.

पिञ्ज and पेज are added to तिल to denote 'barrenness;' तिलपिञ्जः or तिलपेजः 'barren Sesamum,' 'not bearing seed.'

फक् and फिञ् are affixes forming principally patronymics or terms implying 'descent:' the former furnishes the terminaton आयन, the latter आयनि; as गार्ग्यायणः or गार्ग्यायणिः 'a descendant of the sage गर्गः.' Analogous to them is ष्फक्, forming attributives of which the feminine takes ई, as denoted by the sibilant: thus from कपिशा, 'a country,' comes कापिशायन 'produced in it;' as, कापिशायनं मधु 'honey of Kapiśá;' कापिशायनी द्राक्षा 'a grape of the same.'

मयट् is added to nouns to import 'made or consisting of;' as, अश्ममय 'made or consisting of stone,' 'stony,' 'marble;' काष्ठमय 'wooden,' 'made of wood;' मृण्मय 'earthen,' 'made of earth or clay:' it also implies 'containing' or 'abounding with;' as, अन्नमय 'containing food' (a dish, &c.); मोदकमय 'containing sweetmeats' (a shop or the like); घृतमयो यज्ञः 'a sacrifice abounding with clarified butter,' i. e. one in which many oblations are offered. It also forms with गो, 'an ox,' the term गोमयः, which may mean either 'cow-dung,' or 'the nature or property of a cow.'

मात्रच् is added to words to denote 'measure,' either of height, capacity, or number; जानुमात्र 'as high as the knee;' प्रस्थमात्र 'as much as a Prastha;' पञ्चमात्र 'five in tale;' तावन्मात्र 'so much.'

य is added to a few words to form, 1. Attributives; as, ग्राम 'a village,' ग्राम्य 'rural,' 'rustic;' मुख 'the face,' मुख्य 'principal;' दण्ड 'punishment,' दण्ड्य 'deserving punishment;' अर्घ 'respect,' अर्घ्य 'deserving respect;' वध 'killing,' वध्य 'deserving death:' 2. Abstracts; as, सखि 'a friend,' सख्यं 'friendship;' दूत 'a messenger,' दूत्यं 'mission:' वणिज्, 'a merchant,' makes वणिज्या 'trade:' स्तेन 'a thief,' makes स्तेयं 'theft,' 'thieving.' य is more frequently combined with other letters, as in ण्य, ष्य, यक्, यञ्, and यत्.

यक् forms a few abstract nouns: राजन्, 'a king,' makes राज्यं 'kingdom;' सेनापति 'a general,' सैनापत्यं 'command;' पुरोहित 'a family priest,' पौरोहित्यं 'priesthood.'

यञ्, leaving य, forms, 1. Patronymics or terms of descent; as, अभिजित् 'a proper name,' आभिजित्यः 'the son of Abhijit;' दैव्य 'sprung from a god;' बाह्य 'a native of the outer (बहिस्) country:' 2. Attributives; as, द्वैप्य 'is produced in or on an island,' द्वीप: 3. Aggregates; as, केदार 'a field,' कैदार्यं 'a number of fields;' केशः 'hair,' कैश्यं 'a quantity of hair;' पाशः 'a noose,' पाश्या 'a number of snares;' &c.

यत्, leaving य, and requiring no change of the radical vowel, is of much more extensive application than either of the preceding: it forms a few terms of descent; as, राजन्यः 'a man of the military tribe, sprung from a Raja;' कुल्य 'of a good family:' but its chief application is to form attributives implying derivation, relation, or fitness, becoming frequently appellatives; as, रथ्य 'what is fit for a carriage;' रथ्यः 'a horse fit for harness;' रथ्यं 'a carriage-wheel:' मूल relating to the root, or to original price; मूल्यः 'price,' मूल्यं 'profit;' वयस्य 'suited in age,' वयस्, whence वयस्यः 'a friend.' Of other attributives formed with this affix are तुल्य 'like,' न्याय्य 'suitable,' पथ्य 'appropriate,' हृद्य 'agreeable,' धन्य 'wealthy,' अग्र्य 'chief,' धर्म्य 'virtuous,' जन्य 'relating to the people,' 'popular,' 'current,' यशस् 'fame,' यशस्य 'famous,' शीर्षच्छेद्य 'deserving decapitation,' from शीर्ष for शिरस् and छेद 'cutting.' Nouns ending in उ and the word गो take Guṇa before यत्; as, शङ्कु 'a stake,' शङ्कव्य 'fit for a stake' (wood); गव्य 'relating to a cow' or 'derived from one,' गव्यं 'cow's milk:' श्वन्, 'a dog,' changes the semivowel; as, शुन्य or शून्य 'canine:' नाभि, 'the nave of a wheel,' makes नभ्य 'fit for the nave;' and नास 'the nose,' नस्य 'fit for the nose,' नस्यं 'a nozzle:' यशस्, 'fame,' makes यशस्य 'famous;' भाग 'a part,' भाग्यं 'half' (at interest),' भाग्यं शतं 'half per cent.' Of the appellatives, besides those specified, are, जन्या 'a bridemaid,' from जनी 'a wife;' धेनुष्या 'a milch cow,' from धेनु, the same, with ष inserted;' वेष्यः 'an actor,' from वेष 'dress;' कार्म्मीण्यं 'vigour,' from कर्म्मन् 'act;' and द्रव्यं 'thing,' 'wealth,' from द्रु 'a tree.'

र is added to nouns to form diminutives; कुटी 'a house,' कुटीरः 'a small house;' शमी 'the S'amí tree,' शमीरः 'a small S'amí tree.'

रूप्य is added to words to imply 'cause' or 'origin,' if the latter be man; as, समरूप्य 'what proceeds from the same cause;' देवदत्तरूप्य 'what originates with Devadatta.'

ल is added to चिल्, चुल्, and पिल्, substituted for क्लिन्न 'moist,' making चिल्ल, चुल्ल, and पिल्ल, to signify 'blear-eyed.'

बिडच् and बिरीसच् are added to the preposition नि to form attributives; as, निबिड, निबिरीस, 'thick,' 'coarse;' also 'flat or crooked nosed.'

वुञ् is a useful affix: वु always, as in the Kṛidanta derivatives, denotes the addition of अक. It forms attributives signifying chiefly 'produced in' or 'from;' as, ग्रीष्म 'the hot season,' ग्रैष्मक 'growing or produced in summer;' उष्ट्र 'a camel,' औष्ट्रक 'produced from a camel;' कौलालक 'made by a potter,' कुलाल; आरण्यक 'produced in a wood,' 'wild.' It is also added to names of countries to signify either the place or people; पाटलिपुत्रकाः is synonymous with पाटलिपुत्राः 'Palibothra;' आङ्गकाः means 'the people of An̍ga:' also any thing peculiar to the country; as, from कच्छ, 'Cutch,' comes काच्छको मनुष्यः 'a man of Cutch;' काच्छकं हसितं 'a Cutch laugh.' It also forms nouns of aggregation;' as, औक्षकं, from उक्षन् 'an ox,' 'a herd of oxen;' औपगवकं 'a number of the descendants of Upagu,' or 'his family or tribe collectively.'

वुन्, like the preceding, adds अक, but does not change the vowel of the primitive. It forms such attributives as क्रमक, from क्रम 'order,' 'one who knows the order;' पन्थक 'produced in or on the road;' पथक 'one who knows the road;' पूर्वाह्णक 'produced in the forenoon:' also a few feminine nouns in particular acceptations; as, from पद for पाद, 'a quarter,' comes पदिका 'quarter,' when succession is implied; as, द्विपदिकां ददाति 'he gives two and two quarters;' द्विशतिकां ददाति 'he gives two and two hundreds:' or when succession is not implied, but legal proceedings are; as, द्विशतिकां दण्डितः 'fined two hundred.'

वुन् also forms feminine nouns from compounds implying 'enmity between the objects;' as, काकोलूकिका 'the natural hostility of the crow and the owl.'

शालच् forms an attributive noun with the preposition वि; विशाल 'large,' 'extensive.'

शाकट and शाकिन are added to names of vegetable substances to denote 'a field;' as, इक्षुशाकटं or इक्षुशाकिनं 'a field of sugar-cane.'

ष्टरच् is added to nouns to form appellatives with the sense of 'diminutiveness' or 'inferiority:' गोणी 'a sack,' गोणीतरी 'a small sack;' वत्सतरः 'a young calf;' अश्वतरः 'a foal,' also 'a mule;' ऋषभतरः 'an ox unfit for the yoke.'

ष्टन् forms attributive nouns analogous to those formed with ठन्, as above, but in particular senses; and the feminine termination is ई. The words imply, 1. 'Who or what goes by means of;' as, आश्विक 'one who goes on a horse;' पर्पिकः -की 'a cripple,' 'one who goes by means of a wheel-chair,' पर्पः; पथिकः -की 'a traveller,' 'one who goes along the road;' or, as applied to inanimate things, वारिपथिकं 'what comes, or is brought, by water:' 2. 'Who or what takes by means of;' as, भस्त्रा 'an inflated skin,' भस्त्रिकः 'a ferryman,' 'one who takes passengers or goods across a river on a skin;' विवधः or वीवधः 'a yoke for carrying burdens by a rope at each end,' विवधिकः or वीवधिकः 'a porter carrying loads by a yoke:' and 3. Containing a given measure; as, द्व्याढकिक 'containing two Árhakas of grain,' 'a field,' &c.

ष्टल is similarly applied to a few words; as, आकर्षिकः -की -कं 'who or what goes by being dragged.'

ष्लच् is added to शमी, 'the S'amí tree,' to signify 'made of its wood,' शामिलः -ली -लं.

ष्यञ् forms abstract neuter nouns from a variety of words; as, शुक्ल 'white,' शौक्ल्यं 'whiteness;' दृढ 'firm,' दार्ढ्यं 'firmness;'

मधुर 'sweet,' माधुर्य्यं 'sweetness;' मूर्खः 'a blockhead,' मौर्ख्यं 'folly;' चोरः 'a thief,' चौर्य्यं 'stealing;' स्तेनः 'a thief,' स्तैन्यं 'stealing;' पिशुनः 'a knave,' पैशुन्यं 'dishonesty;' ब्राह्मणः 'a Brahman,' ब्राह्मण्यं 'the nature or office of a Brahman;' चतुर्वर्णाः 'the four castes,' चातुर्वर्ण्यं 'the duties or institution of the four castes;' परम्परा 'successively,' पारम्पर्य्यं 'succession,' 'tradition.' If taking the feminine gender, these nouns reject य before ई; as, उचित 'right,' 'fit,' makes औचित्यं or औचिती 'fitness.'

सा and स्ना are added pleonastically to मृद् 'earth;' so is तिकन्, making मृत्तिका, मृत्सा or मृत्स्ना, 'earth.'

Class II. *Possessives.*

अच्, leaving अ, is substituted for the terminations of a few words ending in vowels, and added to others ending in consonants, to form possessive adjectives; as, जटा makes जट 'who has braided hair;' उरस् 'the breast,' उरस 'breasted;' अघ 'sin,' अघ 'sinful;' अर्शस 'who has hæmorrhoids,' from अर्शस्; &c.

आटच् and आलच् are added to nouns to signify possession or use of the object they denote, but in a depreciatory sense; as, वाच्, 'speech,' makes वाचाट or वाचाल 'one who speaks much and nonsensically.'

आमिनच् added to स्व, 'property,' makes स्वामिन् -मी -मिनी 'a master' or 'mistress,' 'an owner of property.'

आरकन् is added to शृङ्ग 'a horn,' and वृन्द 'a heap,' to form attributives; as, शृङ्गारक 'horned,' वृन्दारक 'preeminent.'

आलुच् forms attributives of possession, with the sense of 'non-endurance;' with शीत 'cold,' उष्ण 'warm,' and तृप्र 'oiled butter;' as, शीतालु 'suffering from cold,' 'freezing;' उष्णालु 'suffering from heat;' तृप्रालु 'having, but not liking, oiled butter.' हृदय, 'the heart,' forms हृदयालु 'kind-hearted.'

इतच् forms possessive attributives from the class of words called तारकादि; as, तारका 'a star,' तारकित 'starred,' 'starry;' पुष्प 'a flower,' पुष्पित 'flowered,' 'flowery;' कुसुम 'a flower,' कुसुमित 'having flowers;' खण्ड 'a part,' खण्डित 'parted,' 'divided,' 'having parts;' पिपासा 'thirst,' पिपासित 'thirsty;' दुःख 'pain,' दुःखित 'afflicted,' 'pained;' सुख 'pleasure,' सुखित 'happy,' 'at ease;' &c.

इनच् forms फलिन 'fruitful,' from फल 'fruit;' and बर्हिण 'peacock-tailed,' or बर्हिणः 'a peacock,' from बर्ह 'the tail of that bird.' मल, 'dirt,' makes मलिन, or with ईमसच्, मलीमस 'dirty,' 'foul,' 'wicked.'

इनि is affixed to nouns ending in अ to denote possession actual or figurative; दण्ड 'a staff,' दण्डिन् 'one who carries a staff;' धन 'wealth,' धनिन् 'wealthy;' सुख 'happiness,' सुखिन् 'happy;' दुःख 'pain,' दुःखिन् 'sorrowful:' also to पूर्व in particular meanings; पूर्विन् 'one who has priority,' i. e. one who has done (eaten or drank) any thing on a former occasion; कृतपूर्वी कटं 'he formerly made the mat.' श्राद्ध makes श्राद्धिन् 'one who has partaken of a S'ráddha' or 'funeral feast;' and साक्ष 'visible,' साक्षिन् 'one who has seen any occurrence,' 'a witness.' It is also added to certain words in आ or ई; as, शिखा 'a crest,' शिखिन् 'crested,' शिखी 'a peacock;' माला 'a garland,' मालिन् 'having a garland,' माली 'a gardener;' व्रीहि 'rice,' व्रीहिन् 'having rice:' also to numerals connected with age; as, पञ्चमिन् 'having the fifth (month or year);' पञ्चमी बालः 'a boy in his fifth year.' Occasionally क is prefixed to इनि; as, वातकिन् 'one who suffers from disordered wind.' It forms various feminine nouns of locality; as, पुष्करिणी 'a pool having the lotus:' so पद्मिनी, कुमुदिनी, &c. It forms various appellatives, as above, and as हस्तिन् 'an elephant,' from हस्त 'his trunk.'

इलच् is affixed to a class of words termed पिच्छादि to form possessives; as, पिच्छा 'mud,' पिच्छिल 'muddy;' उरस् 'the chest,' उरसिल 'broad-chested;' प्रज्ञा 'knowledge,' प्रज्ञिल 'wise:' also to फेन 'froth,' फेनिल 'frothy:' to सिकता 'sand,' and शर्करा 'gravel,' as epithets of place; सिकतिला or शर्करिला भूमिः 'sandy or gravelly soil:' also to तुन्द and other words; तुन्दिल 'corpulent,' उदरिल 'big-bellied,' &c.

उरच् is added to दन्त, 'a tooth,' to form दन्तुर 'having large or prominent teeth.'

ऊलच् is added to बल 'force,' and वात 'wind,' to signify 'impatience;' बलूल 'not enduring force;' वातूल 'not bearing wind:' the latter is also an appellative; वातूलः 'a gale,' 'a whirlwind.'

ग्मिनि forms वाग्मिन् 'eloquent,' 'well spoken,' from वाच् 'speech.'

ड्वलच् is added to नड and शाद; as, नड्वल 'abounding with reeds;' शाद्वल 'abounding with young grass' (a field, a country, &c.)

न, as a possessive affix, is added to a class of words termed पामादि, and which imply 'diseased;' as, पामन् 'itch,' पामन 'itchy;' कृमि 'a worm,' कृमिन 'affected with worms.' It also forms irregularly ज्योत्स्ना 'moonlight,' from ज्योतिष् 'light.'

भ is added to the words तुन्दि, वटि, and वलि; as, तुन्दिभ 'having corpulence,' 'corpulent;' वटिभ 'lousy;' वलिभ 'wrinkled.'

मतुप् is in an especial degree the affix implying possession: the essential element is मत् or वत्, inflected as मान्, मती, मत्, or वान्, वती, वत् (see p. 55). The म is changed to व after a final or penultimate अ or आ, and after any consonant except a nasal or a sibilant: it is so changed after a final or penultimate म; it is unchanged after any other vowel than अ or आ, and after a nasal or a sibilant: but there are special exceptions to these changes: thus किम् makes किंवत् 'having something;' यशस् 'fame,' यशस्वत् 'famous;' लक्ष्मी 'prosperity,' लक्ष्मीवत् 'prosperous.' A great variety of attributives and appellatives are formed with this affix; as, धनवत् 'wealthy,' रसवत् 'flavoured,' मेधावत् 'intelligent,' गोमत् 'having cows,' भूमिमत् 'having land.' राजन् retains its final, if meaning 'well governed,' राजन्वती भूः 'a well governed country;' but राजवत् 'having a king.' उदक, 'water,' substitutes उदन् before मतुप्; as, उदन्वत् 'having water,' उदन्वान् 'the ocean.' The following are irregularly formed with this affix: अष्ठीवान् 'the knee' (having a bone); चक्रीवान् the name of a king (having a country); रुमण्वान् the name of a mountain (having salt); चर्मण्वती 'the river Chambal' (having a skin or hide). In their literal acceptation these are regular; as, अस्थिवत्, चक्रवत्, &c. In place of मतुप्, the affix in certain senses is termed इमतुप्, the initial इ causing the elision of the final vowel of the primitive; as, कुमुद 'a lotus,' कुमुद्वती 'a place abounding in lotuses;' महिष 'a buffalo,' महिष्मती the name of a city.

यप् is added to a few words to form attributives; as, हिम्य 'snowy;' गुण्य 'excellent,' 'having merit;' रूप्य 'having a handsome form:' also रूप्यः 'a coin,' i. e. having an impression.

युस् is added to ऊर्णा 'wool,' ऊर्णायु 'woolly:' also to अहम् 'I,' अहंयु 'arrogant;' and शुभम् 'good,' शुभंयु 'lucky:' also to कं and शं; as, कंय्यु, शंय्यु 'happy,' 'prosperous.'

र forms attributives and appellatives after certain words; पाण्डु 'paleness,' पाण्डुर 'pale;' मधु 'honey,' मधुर 'sweet,' 'honied;' सुषि 'a hole,' सुषिर 'perforated;' ऊष 'saline soil,' ऊषर 'having or abounding with such soil.' नग, 'a mountain,' makes नगरं 'a city' (having houses as lofty as mountains); and तमस् 'darkness,' तमिस्रं or तमिस्रा the same; the penultimate being changed to इ.

लच् forms attributives with various words; अंस 'the shoulder,' अंसल 'strong;' वत्स 'a child,' वत्सल 'affectionate;' चूडा 'a crest,' चूडाल 'crested;' फेन 'froth,' फेनल 'frothy.'

व is added to केश 'hair,' केशव 'having fine or abundant hair;' in which sense it may be also केशिन्, केशिक, or केशवत्; as a name of Krishńa, it is केशवः alone. It is added to a few other words; as, to मणि 'a jewel,' and हिरण्य 'gold,' to form मणिवः 'a particular Nága;' हिरण्यवः 'one of the treasures (personified) of the god of wealth:' also to अर्णस् 'water,' which rejects its final, अर्णवः 'the ocean.'

वलच् forms attributives, used chiefly as appellatives, after certain words; शिखावल 'crested,' शिखावलः 'a peacock.' A final short vowel becomes long before it; as, दन्त 'a tooth,' दन्तावलः 'an elephant;' कृषि 'culture,' कृषीवलः 'a husbandman;' आसुति 'spirit,' आसुतीवलः 'a distiller;' परिषद् 'a court,' परिषद्वलः 'a Raja;' रजस् 'menstrual excretion,' रजस्वला 'a woman at that period.' ऊर्जस्, 'strength,' makes ऊर्जस्वल 'strong.'

विनि is added to words ending with अस्; as, तपस् 'penance,' तपस्विन् 'who practises penance,' 'an anchorite;' यशस् 'fame,' यशस्विन् 'famous:' also to माया 'illusion,' मायाविन् 'deceptive,' मेधा 'apprehension,' मेधाविन् 'intelligent;' स्रज् 'a garland,' स्रग्विन् 'having a garland;' and आमय 'sickness,' with the final made long, आमयाविन् 'sick,' 'ill.'

श forms attributives from a class of words termed लोमादि; as, लोमन् and रोमन् 'hair of the body,' लोमश, रोमश, 'hairy;' कपि 'an ape,' कपिश 'tawny;' &c.

CLASS III. *Degrees of Comparison: Pronominals: Numerals.*

261. The affixes which form the comparative and superlative degrees have already been specified, as तरप् or तमप्, and ईयस् or ईयसुन्, and इष्ठ or इष्ठन्; they are noticed here only as belonging to the class of Taddhita affixes (see p. 74).

262. Pronouns take some of the preceding affixes, with the same effect and signification as those already specified: thus अण् is added to the possessive cases plural of अस्मद् and युष्मद्, making आस्माक, यौष्माक, 'what belongs or relates to us' or 'to you:' also to the same cases singular, with क inserted; as, तावक, मामक, 'what relates or belongs to thee' or 'me.' छ is also added to अस्मद्; as, अस्मदीय 'relating or belonging to me;' and to भवत् 'you' (respectfully); भवदीय 'yours' or 'your honour's.' Besides these, they have some peculiar to themselves.

अकच् is sometimes substituted for the proper terminations of किम्, यद्, and तद्; as, कक 'which,' यक 'who,' सक 'that.'

डतरच् and डतमच् are added to the same pronouns, also to एक, to form comparisons between two or many; as, कतर, यतर, 'which of two;' कतम, यतम, 'which of many;' ततर, ततम, 'that of two' or 'of many;' एकतर, एकतम, 'one of two' or 'of many.'

डति is added to किम्, forming कति 'how many.'

वतुप् is added to several of the pronouns to imply 'quantity:' it leaves वत्, as already noticed (p. 83). To these may be added तियुक्, forming attributives from them; यावतिथ 'having or being how many;' तावतिथ 'having or being so many.'

263. Nouns of number take Taddhita affixes to denote ordinals and other modifications: some of them have been already noticed (p. 89).

ड is added to दशन् and its compounds, to विंशति and the decimals ending in शत्, to form numerals in addition to others with which they are inflected. ड, leaving अ, causes the elision of the final letter; एकादशं शतं 'one hundred and eleven;' विंशं शतं 'a hundred and twenty.'

डट् forms ordinals from cardinals for all above ten; एकादश 'eleventh,' विंश 'twentieth,' &c.; or those from twenty upwards prefix तमट् to डट्, making विंशतितम, &c. (p. 90).

डिमच् added to आदि, 'first,' forms the ordinal आदिम 'first:' it also forms terms signifying 'relative order,' either in place, degree, or time, with अग्र 'before,' अन्त 'end,' and पश्चात् 'after;' as, अग्रिम 'first,' 'prior;' अन्तिम 'subsequent;' पश्चिम 'posterior.'

तयप् added to numerals implies 'division;' as, पञ्चतयं दारु 'wood in five pieces,' or 'five pieces of wood.' It forms similar derivatives with द्वि and त्रि in alternation with अयच्; as, द्वितय or द्वय, त्रितय or त्रय, 'two' or 'twofold,' 'three' or 'threefold.'

तीय is added to द्वि and त्रि, the latter of which changes रि to ऋ, to form ordinals; as, द्वितीय 'second,' तृतीय 'third:' to these, अन्, that is, अ, taking the place of the primitive अ, is added, to imply 'division;' as, द्वितीयो भागः 'a second part,' 'a half;' तृतीयो भागः 'a third:' so चतुर्थ पञ्चम 'a fourth, a fifth,' &c.; ordinals being in fact the same as fractionals. षष्ठ and अष्टम take optionally अ, making either षष्ठ or षाष्ठ 'a sixth,' अष्टम or आष्टम 'an eighth.'

सुच् is added to द्वि, त्रि, and चतुर्, making द्विस्, त्रिस्, चतुस्, 'in value twice,' 'thrice,' 'four times.' स् becomes Visarga, and that again र् before a sonant; as, द्विर्भुङ्क्ते 'he eats twice.'

अण् is added to शत and सहस्र to signify 'bought with' or

worth:' शात 'bought with a hundred;' साहस्र 'bought with a thousand:' also to signify general relation to those numbers.

कन् may be added to numerals not ending with शत् or ति to signify 'bought with;' पञ्चक 'bought with five:' the exceptions take ठक्; वैंशतिक 'bought with twenty;' चात्वारिंशत्क 'bought with forty.' It may be added to them to form denominatives; as, विंशतिकः 'a book containing twenty (chapters).' It is also added to terms of quantity, formed with वतु; as, तावत्क, or with इट् inserted, तावतिक 'bought with so much.' कन् is added to numerals forming attributives to imply a sum given, either as interest, tax, profit, or bribe; as, पञ्चको राजा 'the king, who has received a tax of five;' पञ्चको देवदत्तः 'Devadatta has taken five (per cent. interest);' &c. Derivatives with other affixes are similarly employed; as, शतिकः शत्यः 'one to whom a hundred has been given,' &c.

ख may be added to विंशति when preceded by a numeral or by अध्यर्द्ध 'plus a half:' to signify 'value;' क is inserted; as, द्विविंशतिकीन 'worth twenty-two;' अध्यर्द्धविंशतिकीन 'worth twenty plus a half,' i. e. worth thirty.

ठन् or यत् may be added to शत to signify 'being worth' or 'bought with;' शतिक or शत्य 'what is worth a hundred;' also, as above, 'he to whom a hundred is given.'

डुन् is added to numerals ending in ति or शत् to signify 'value;' विंशक, त्रिंशक, चत्वारिंशक, 'bought with, or worth, twenty,' &c.

मयट्, added to numerals, implies 'equal or equivalent to in value; as, द्विमयमुदश्वित् यवानां 'the butter-milk is worth two (it is twice the value) of the barley.'

Class IV. *Indeclinables.*

264. A variety of indeclinable words, chiefly significant of time or place, are formed with affixes considered as belonging to the class of Taddhita terminations.

अ is affixed to किम् 'what,' which is changed to कु in the sense of 'place;' as, क्व 'where.'

अतसुच् forms with उत्तर 'north,' and दक्षिण 'south,' or 'on the right,' the indeclinables उत्तरतः 'in or from the north,' दक्षिणतः 'in or from the south,' or 'on the right hand.'

असि and अस्ताति form adverbs of place or time with पुर्, अध्, and अव्, considered as substitutes for पूर्व, अधर, and अवर; as, पुरः, पुरस्तात् 'before,' 'prior,' 'in front,' 'in or on the east;' अधः, अधस्तात् 'down,' 'below,' 'inferior;' अवः, अवस्तात् 'behind,' 'after,' 'in the west:' the latter is also optionally अवरस्तात्. पर optionally takes अतसुच् or अस्तात्; as, परतः, परस्तात् 'after,' 'subsequent.'

अधुना is considered as irregularly substituted for इदम्, 'this,' 'in this time,' 'now.'

अर्हिल् is added to different pronouns to signify 'time;' एतद् 'this,' as एतर्हि 'in this time,' 'now;' कर्हि and यर्हि 'when;' तर्हि 'then,' 'at that time.'

आच् is added to उत्तर and दक्षिण to signify 'in' or 'from;' उत्तरा or दक्षिणा वसति 'he dwells in the north' or 'in the south;' उत्तरा or दक्षिणा पुनरागतः 'returned from the south.' They take आहि in the same sense; उत्तराहि, दक्षिणाहि.

एनप् is added to the same words; उत्तरेण, दक्षिणेन, 'in or on the north' or 'the south.'

कृत्वसुच् is added to numerals and to बहु to signify 'times,' when alluding to the reiteration of an act essential to life; द्विकृत्वो भुंक्ते 'he eats twice:' so पञ्चकृत्वस्, शतकृत्वस्, बहुकृत्वस्, and the like.

च्वि converts into indeclinables, nouns compounded with any of the derivatives or inflexions of अस or भू 'to be,' or कृ 'to make,' to imply that the object is, or is made, what it was not before. A final अ or आ, except when the word is already an indeclinable terminating with the latter, is changed to ई; इ and उ are made long; and ऋ is changed to री; as, कृष्णीकृत 'made black,' 'blackened;' शुक्लीकरोति 'he makes white' or 'whitens;' दोषाभूतमहः 'the day has become evening;' शुचीभवति 'he becomes pure;' पटूसन् 'becoming eloquent;' मात्रीभूता

'become a mother.' अरुस्, मनस्, and चक्षुस् drop their finals; अरूकरणं 'making sore;' उन्मनीस्यात् 'he will become mad;' उच्चक्षूकरोति 'he looks upwards.'

डाच् is an affix similar to the preceding, attaching आ to the end of a word joined to the derivatives or inflections of the verb कृ 'to make;' as, दुःखाकरोति 'he pains' or 'distresses;' सुखाकरोति 'he makes happy;' प्रियाकरोति 'he pleases:' also after reiterated words expressing inarticulate sound; पटपटाकरोति 'he makes the sound paṭ paṭ:' also after particular words used in the sense of 'ploughing;' द्वितीया or तृतीयाकरोति 'he ploughs (a field) twice or thrice;' शम्बाकरोति 'he ploughs (a field) back again;' बीजाकरोति 'he ploughs (a field) with the seed,' 'he drill-sows it.'

तसि is substituted for the terminations of the instrumental and ablative cases; the former implying 'cause:' चरित्रतः 'by, or on account of, behaviour;' वृत्ततः 'by or on account of, its rotundity;' ग्रामतः 'from the village;' आदितः 'from the first;' मध्यतः 'from the middle:' also as implying 'descent;' कृष्णतः प्रद्युम्नः 'Pradyumna was descended from Krishña.' It is added to the names of diseases, to imply their removal;' तं प्रवाहिकातः कुरु 'make him (free) from flux.' It is considered to represent the genitive case in such sentences as देवा अर्जुनतोऽभवन् 'the gods were (on the side) of Arjuna.'

तसिल्, which, like the former, leaves तस्, is added to pronouns and pronominals in the sense of the ablative and locative cases: अतस् or इतस् 'hence' or 'here;' ततस् 'thence,' 'therefrom,' also 'therefore' or 'there;' यतस् 'whence,' 'wherefrom,' 'wherefore,' 'where;' इतस्ततस् 'here and there,' 'every where.' किम् before an affix beginning with त or ह becomes कु; कुतस् 'whence,' 'wherefrom,' or 'wherefore,' 'when;' सर्वतस्, विश्वतस्, 'every where;' उभयतस् 'on both sides:' so अभितस् 'on both sides;' परितस् 'all around;' बहुतस् 'in many places' or 'ways.'

त्रल् is affixed to pronouns and pronominals in the sense of 'locality;' as, कुत्र 'where,' यत्र 'where,' तत्र 'there,' सर्व्वत्र 'every where.' अ is substituted for एतद्; as, अत्र 'in this place,' 'here.'

त्रा is added to certain words with the sense of the accusative or locative case: देवत्रा वन्दे 'I salute the gods;' मनुष्यत्रा रमे 'I delight in the men;' बहुत्रा 'in many ways.'

थाल् is affixed to pronouns and pronominals to denote 'manner,' 'kind;' as, यथा 'as,' 'in what manner;' तथा 'so,' 'thus,' 'in this manner;' कथा 'how.'

थमु is added to इदम् and किम्, substituting severally इद् and क in the same acceptation: इत्थम् 'thus,' कथम् 'how.'

दा is added to pronouns and pronominals to imply 'time;' as, यदा 'at what time,' 'when;' तदा 'at that time,' 'then;' कदा 'when;' एकदा 'once;' अन्यदा 'at another time;' सर्व्वदा 'always:' also स being substituted for सर्व्व, सदा.

दानीम् is added to इदम् and तद् to signify 'time:' the initials of the primitives only are retained; इदानीम् 'now,' 'at this time;' तदानीम् 'then,' 'at that time.'

धा is affixed to numerals to imply 'numeration;' as, एकधा 'once,' 'one,' 'singly;' द्विधा or द्वेधा 'twice,' 'twofold;' त्रिधा or त्रेधा 'thrice,' 'threefold;' पञ्चधा 'five times' or 'fivefold' or 'five parts;' as, एकं राशिं पञ्चधा कुरु 'make one heap into five.' The analogous affix धमुञ् is added to द्वि and त्रि, making द्वैधम्, त्रैधम्, 'twofold,' 'threefold.' ध्यमुञ् may be added to एक, making ऐकध्यम्.

ना is added to the preposition वि, making विना 'without,' 'except;' and नाञ् to the negative नञ्, नाना 'manifold,' 'various.'

रिल् and रिष्टातिल् are added to उप, substituted for उर्द्ध्वेस्; as, उपरि or उपरिष्टात् 'up,' 'above.'

वत् affixed to words forms indeclinables implying 'resemblance in act;' as, ब्राह्मणवत् 'like a Brahman;' क्षत्रियवत् 'like a Kshetriya:' also denoting 'fitness,' 'suitableness;' राजवत् 'fit for, or worthy of, a king:' also if the preceding word have the sense of the genitive or locative case; मथुरावत् 'as in Mathurá;' देवदत्तवत् 'like (the figure of) Devadatta.'

शस् is added to अल्प and बहु to imply 'degree;' अल्पशः 'a little;' बहुशः 'much,' 'abundantly,' 'for the most part:' also to numerals and terms of measure, to denote 'successive order;' द्विशः 'two and two;' माषशः 'Másha by Másha.'

साति is added to words like च्वि to signify a thing's becoming what it was not before, in combination with the same verbs; also with verbs signifying 'production;' as, भस्मसात् करोति 'he reduces to ashes;' शस्त्रमग्निसात् सम्पद्यते 'the weapon is produced as fire,' or 'is in a blaze;' also अग्निसाद्भवति 'is fire.' It also means 'dependence;' as, राजसाद्भवति राष्ट्रं 'the country becomes dependent wholly on the king:' or 'appropriation;' as, दानं विप्रसात् करोति 'he makes the gift wholly the property of the Brahmans.

CHAPTER VII.

COMPOUND WORDS.

265. The composition of words prevails in Sanskrit to an extent that much exceeds its occurrence in any other language. It is termed in original grammars, Samása समासः.

266. When a greater or lesser number of words are combined, so as to form one new term, the characteristic signs of case and number are, with occasional exceptions, rejected by all the members of the compound except the last.

267. Compound words are arranged, agreeably to the nature of this construction, under four classes.

1. The first class consists of substantive nouns simply aggregated under one head, which, if not compounded, would be held together by the intervention of a copulative; as, 'Ráma and Lakshmaña,' रामश्च लक्ष्मणश्च, make, when united, रामलक्ष्मणौ. This is termed Dwandwa, 'doubling' or 'aggregation.'

2. The second class, termed Tatpurusha, is not confined to substantives, but combines nominal and verbal derivatives in

different relations; such as that of the object and the act, as कृष्णाश्रयः 'dependence upon Kṛishṅa;' that of the object and the agent, as ग्रामप्राप्त 'arrived at the village;' or that of the attribute and the object, as नीलोत्पलं 'a blue lotus.' It also comprises adjectives, participles, and particles aggregated, so as to form compound attributives or appellatives; as, कृष्णशुक्ल 'black and white;' कृताकृत 'done and not done;' अतिराज 'surpassing the king.' The two last are, however, considered as forming either a subdivision of this class, or a separate class termed Karmma-dháraya, कर्म्मधारयः; and so is the combination of a numeral with a noun; which subdivision is termed द्विगुः. Of these terms, Tatpurusha, 'the man of him,' refers to a word that commonly exemplifies this kind of compound, or राजपुरुषः 'the king's man.' Karmma-dháraya implies 'that which comprehends (dhárayati) the object (karmma).' Dwigu is a technical word derived from Dwi 'two.'

3. The third class of compounds, called बहुव्रीहि, is the association of any given number of terms, simple or compound, to form an epithet to a noun, of which the word Bahuvríhi furnishes an example: as separated, it means 'much rice;' as compounded, 'that which has much rice,' a field or the like. In compounds of this class, the last member, whatever its original gender, takes that of the noun with which it is connected; as, दर्शनीयभार्य्यः '(a man) who has a beautiful wife.' These epithets are sometimes used absolutely as appellatives; as, पुण्डरीकाक्षः 'having eyes like the lotus;' a name of Vishṅu. As an instance of the multiplication of terms in a Bahuvríhi compound, we may take जनकतनयास्नानपुण्योदकः '(a place) of which the waters were sanctified by the bathing of the daughter of Janaka.'

4. The last class is termed Avyayí-bháva, अव्ययीभावः, being the construction of indeclinable or adverbial compounds (Avyaya), consisting for the most part of a preposition and the noun governed by it in the objective case neuter, as उपकृष्णं, and requiring a verb or verbal derivative, expressed or understood,

to complete the sense; as, उपकृष्णं तिष्ठति 'he stays near to Krishńa;' उपकृष्णमर्जुनः 'Arjuna (is) near to Krishńa.'

268. In forming these several kinds of compounds, various peculiarities occur, the most important of which we shall specify under their respective heads.

SECTION I.

Dwandwa Compounds.

269. When words are combined in this form of compound, the final usually takes the sign of the dual number where there are two objects, as हरिहरौ 'Vishńu and S'iva;' and that of the plural if there are more than two, as कामधर्म्मार्थमोक्षाः 'desire, virtue, wealth, liberation' (the four objects of human existence).

270. The following words, when compounded, terminate in the neuter singular: terms for parts of the body, as पाणिपादं 'the hand and foot:' players on musical instruments, मार्द्दङ्गिकपा-णविकं 'players on different kinds of drums:' component parts of an army, रथिकाश्वारोहं 'the chariots and horse:' members of different trades, रजकतन्तुवायं 'a washerman and weaver:' specific terms not signifying living things, धानाशष्कुलि 'fried grain and barley water:' names of small insects, यूकालिक्षं 'flies and lice:' names of animals, natural enemies, अहिनकुलं 'the snake and ichneumon:' a class of words beginning with गवाश्वं 'the cow and horse:' names of rivers and countries, if in different genders, कुरुकुरुक्षेत्रं 'Kuru and Kurukshetra;' but if the genders are the same, then they vary the number, as गङ्गायमुने 'the Ganges and Yamuná.' Some words take either form, when more than one is meant, as प्लक्षन्यग्रोधं or प्लक्षन्यग्रोधौ 'Plaksha and Nyagrodha trees;' but it is confined to the dual to signify a Plaksha and a Nyagrodha tree; पूर्व्वापरं or पूर्व्वापरे 'first and last; अधरोत्तरं or अधरोत्तरे 'upper and lower,' 'many or one of each.' Qualities, if contrariety be meant, take either form, शीतोष्णं or शीतोष्णे 'cold and hot.' A compounded word preceded by a definite number takes only the first form, as दशदन्तोष्ठाः 'ten teeth and lips:' but if the number is indefinite, and the numeral is converted into an attributive which is not part of the compound, the form is optional, उपदशं दन्तोष्ठं or उपदशा दन्तोष्ठाः 'about ten teeth and lips.'

271. Various rules are given for the order in which the words are to be arranged in Dwandwa compounds; but they are liable to many exceptions. Thus in general the shortest term should come first, as ईशकेशवौ 'Śiva and Vishńu:' so should words ending in इ or उ, as हरिहरौ, or गुरुशिष्यौ 'teacher and pupil.' Names of seasons and asterisms, if of equal length, follow the natural order, as हेमन्तशिशिरवसन्ताः 'winter, 'dewy season, spring;' but ग्रीष्मवसन्तौ 'summer and spring,' the first being the shorter. When names of castes or persons come together, the precedence is to be given to the most worthy or the senior; ब्राह्मणक्षत्रियविट्शूद्राः 'the Brahman, Kshatriya, Vaiśya, and Śúdra;' युधिष्ठिरार्जुनौ 'Yudhishṫhira and Arjuna. आ is sometimes interposed, as मित्रावरुणौ 'Mitra and Varuńa.

272. In some compounds different terms are occasionally substituted for the first member; as, जम् or दम् for जाया, 'a wife,' in जम्पती or दम्पती 'wife and husband; द्यावा for दिव् in द्यावापृथिव्यौ 'heaven and earth:' so द्यावाभूमी, द्यावाक्षमे, &c. उषासा is substituted for उषस् in उषासासूर्यं 'the dawn and the sun;' and अन्यं repeated makes अन्यस्, as अन्योन्यं 'one and another,' 'one another;' and पर, परस्परं 'mutually' or 'in succession.'

273. Single words have sometimes the force of Dwandwa compounds: thus रामौ means 'the two Rámas;' रामाः 'the three Rámas,' who were Paraśuráma, Rámachandra, and Balaráma. A masculine noun in the dual comprises the feminine: thus हंसौ is put for हंस and हंसी, or 'the gander and the goose:' so भ्रातरौ means 'sister and brother;' पुत्रौ 'daughter and son;' पितरौ, 'parents,' may be used for मातापितरौ 'mother and father;' and श्वशुरौ, 'parents-in-law,' for श्वश्रूश्वशुरौ.

SECTION II.

Tatpurusha Compounds.

274. This class includes, as above remarked, three subdivisions; to the first of which the term Tatpurusha may be for the present restricted. In compounds of this order, the words stand in a relation to each other which would require, if they were separated, the use of different cases; the one exercising a syntactical government over the other, and not being connected, as in the preceding class, by copulatives understood, nor, as in the subdivision Karmmadháraya, by simple concordance. The words thus formed are mostly attributives and appellatives.

275. The following are arranged in the order of the cases.

a. Words in the sense of the objective case are mostly compounded with the past participle as the governing member; as, ग्रामप्राप्त 'one who has reached the village;' दुःखातीत 'one who has overcome pain;' खट्वारूढः 'a fool,' 'one who lies in his bed: in the literal sense it is not compounded; खट्वामारूढः 'mounted or lying on the couch.' They may also be compounded with verbal derivative nouns denoting the agent; as, कुम्भकारः 'a potter;' तन्तुवायः 'a weaver.'

b. With the instrumental case nouns as well as participles are combined; as, शङ्कुलाखण्डं 'a piece cut by the nippers;' धान्यार्थः 'wealth acquired by grain;' पितृसदृशः '(a son) like his father;' मासपूर्व्व 'prior by a month;' वाक्कलहः 'dispute by or with words;' दध्योदनः 'rice sprinkled by curds,' 'dressed with them;' गुडधान्यं 'rice mixed with sugar:' also अहिहत 'killed by a snake;' दात्रच्छिन्न 'cut by a sickle;' काकपेय 'to be drunk by a crow,' as काकपेया नदी 'a river with muddy water, fit only for a crow's beverage.' In some combinations the third case is retained; as, ओजसाकृत 'done by force;' पुंसानुजः 'younger by a male' (having an elder brother); मनसादेवी 'a goddess mentally,' a proper name; जटाभिस्तापसः 'a penitent, by his braided locks.' Where these and similar combinations with the third or any other case retaining its inflexion are used as appellatives, they may be admitted to be compound terms; but where the latter member is a participle or adjective, which qualified by the preceding term forms an attributive declinable in the three genders, it must be regarded as constituting an exception to composition; ओजसा कृत, for instance, cannot be considered as properly a compound term.

c. Compounds are formed with words in the sense of the dative case, as expressed not so much by the sign 'to,' as by that of 'for' or 'on account of;' as, यूपदारु 'timber for a stake:' this sense is also conveyed by अर्थ, with which words in the dative case form attributives; as, द्विजार्थः सूपः, द्विजार्था यवागूः, द्विजार्थं पयः 'broth, gruel, or milk, for, or on account of, the Brahman.' The grammatical terms परस्मैपदं and आत्मनेपदं are compounds of this class retaining the sign of the case.

d. Attributives are formed with participles preceded by nouns having the sense of the ablative case; as, सुखापेत 'removed from happiness,' 'unhappy;' स्वर्गपतित 'fallen from heaven.' Composition does not take place after words signifying 'near,' 'far,' 'a little,' or कृच्छ्र in the ablative case; as, अन्तिकादागत 'brought from near;' दूरादागत 'come from afar;' स्तोकान्मुक्त 'loosed from a little;' कृच्छ्रात्प्राप्त 'obtained from penance;' &c.

e. There are many compound terms, in which the first word has the sense of the genitive case; as, राजपुरुषः 'the king's man;' आम्रवणं 'a grove of Mango trees;' इध्मव्रश्चनः 'a cutter of wood,' i. e. a hatchet; बुद्धिमान्द्यं 'dulness of intellect.' Verbal derivatives terminating in तृ or अक, and denoting the agent, do not form compounds with words in the sense of the sixth case, with the exception of words belonging to the class याजकादि; as, देवयाजकः 'a worshipper of the gods;' ब्राह्मणपूजकः 'a reverencer of the Brahmans;' भूभर्त्ता 'a lord of the earth.' If the agent is not meant, composition may take place; as, इक्षुभक्षिका 'eating of the sugar-cane:' also if play or profession be intended; as, पुष्पभञ्जिका 'who breaks the flowers (in sport);' दन्तलेखकः 'a cleaner of teeth,' 'a dentist.' The sign of the sixth case is retained in these compounds; दिवस्पतिः 'lord of heaven,' 'Indra;' वाचस्पतिः 'lord of speech,' a name of Vṛihaspati,' the preceptor of the gods;' दिवोदासः 'the servant of heaven,' a proper name.

f. Compounds in which the first member has the sense of the locative case are formed with शौण्ड and other words; as, अक्षशौण्डः 'a gambler,' 'one skilled in dice;' शास्त्रपण्डितः 'one learned in the S'ástras;' कर्म्मकुशलः 'one skilled in work,' 'an artisan;' ईश्वराधीनः 'one dependent on, or trusting in, God;' आतपशुष्क 'what is dried in the sun;' स्थालीपक्क 'what is boiled in a pot;' मासजात 'born or produced in a month;' तत्रकृत 'done there,' 'in that place;' पूर्व्वाह्णकृत 'done in the forenoon.' Terms of ridicule are formed in this manner; as, तीर्थकाकः 'a crow at a holy pool,' i. e. a man out of his place; कूपमण्डूकः 'a frog in a well,' i. e. a man ignorant of the world. In this sense it is also usual to form compounds retaining the sign of the case; गेहेशूरः 'a hero in his house,' 'a cot-quean;' पात्रेकुशलः 'one dexterous in his dish,' 'a gourmand.' Various nouns ending with अ or a consonant, and forming appellatives or proper names, retain the sign of the seventh case; as, स्तम्बेरमः 'who sports in a clump of grass,' 'an elephant;' खेचरः 'who goes in the sky,' 'a deity;' कर्णेजपः 'who whispers in the ear,' 'a spy,' 'an informer;' जलेशयः 'who sleeps in water,' 'a fish;' युधिष्ठिरः 'the firm in battle,' 'the elder of the Páńd́us:' so गो, 'a cow,' makes गविष्ठिरः 'firm in cattle,' a proper name. Some words take both forms, त्वचिसारः or त्वक्सारः 'what has strength in its skin,' 'a kind of deer;' सरसिजं or सरोजं 'born in a lake,' 'a lotus;' द्युषद् or दिविषद् 'who resides in heaven,' 'a deity.'

g. Certain words which imply the part of any thing, when compounded with the word signifying that whole of which it is a part, are prefixed to it; as, पूर्व्वकायः 'the front of the body;' अपरकायः 'the back of the body.' If it is a part of a part only, composition does not take place; as, पूर्वं नाभेः कायस्य 'the front of the navel of a body.' अर्द्धं in the neuter gender, but dropping the sign, is also prefixed; as, अर्द्धपिप्पली 'a half of the pepper:' but not if used in the masculine; as, ग्रामार्द्धः 'half a village.' Fractional numbers may be placed first or last; as, भिक्षाद्वितीयं or द्वितीयभिक्षा 'half of the alms;' प्राप्त and आपन्न governing the objective case, may take either form; as, प्राप्तजीविकः or जीविकाप्राप्तः 'a man who has obtained a livelihood:' so आपन्नजीविकः or जीविकापन्नः.

Karmmadháraya Tatpurusha Compounds.

276. Compounds of the Karmmadháraya division of Tatpurusha do not require that the members of which they consist should exercise any government the one over the other; they are connected together by implied, though not expressed concordance, or by copulatives understood.

a. The most numerous series of Karmmadháraya compounds is that in which the attribute is combined with the object; as, नीलोत्पलं 'a blue lotus;' कृष्णसर्प्पः 'a black snake;' महाराजः 'a great king;' प्रियभार्य्या 'a dear wife;' उत्तरकुरवः 'the northern Kurus' (a country); सप्तर्षयः 'the seven Rishis,' 'the constellation of the Great Bear.'

b. Compounds of this class may consist of attributives only; as, कृष्णशुक्ल 'black and white;' स्नातानुलिप्त 'anointed after being bathed;' तुल्यश्वेत 'equally white;' भोज्योष्ण 'warm enough to be eaten;' ईषद्रक्त 'a little red:' or of substantives and attributives forming attributives to a third term; as, घनश्याम 'black as a cloud;' राशिकृत 'made as a heap;' पण्डितमत 'considered as a Pańdit;' निधनगत 'gone to death,' 'deceased;' &c.

c. When the sense of the term is complete in itself, combining the object and the attribute, the latter usually precedes the former, as in the instances नीलोत्पलं, &c. When it forms an attribute to a third term, the adjective or participle is usually placed last, as in राशिभूत and the like: but there are many varieties in this respect. Words denoting 'excellence,' or used metaphorically for that purpose, are placed after the object; as, नृपवृन्दारकः 'an excellent king;' गोमतल्लिका 'a capital cow;' पुरुषव्याघ्रः or पुरुषसिंहः 'a man-tiger,' 'a man-lion,' i. e. a superior man. पूर्व्व and other terms implying 'relative position' or 'merit' precede the object; पूर्व्वपुरुषः 'a preceding or superior man;' अपरपुरुषः 'a subsequent or inferior man;' मध्यमपुरुषः 'a middle man,' 'an impartial one,' or 'a middling man,' 'one of indifferent character:' so वीर, 'a hero,' forms वीरपुरुषः 'a heroic man.' पूर्व्व, forming an attributive of time, is placed after a participle; दृष्टपूर्व्व 'formerly seen;' भूतपूर्व्व 'formerly been.' Terms of depreciation require the object to be placed first; as, वैयाकरणखसूचिः 'a very bad grammarian:' except when compounded with पाप or अणक; as, पापनापितः 'a vile barber;' अणककुलालः 'a bad potter.' किम्, also used in a depreciatory sense, precedes the object; as, किंराजा 'what sort of a king is this,' यो न रक्षति प्रजाः 'who does not protect his subjects.' कुमार 'young,' or 'a boy,' precedes certain terms; as, कुमारमृदुः 'a gentle boy;' कुमारमृद्वी 'a tender girl:' so it does when substituted for कुमारी 'a girl;' as, कुमारदासी 'a slave girl;' कुमारबन्धकी 'a young harlot.' युव is placed before जरत्, पलित, and वलित, to form युवजरत् 'an aged or infirm youth;' युवपलितः 'a grey-haired youth;' युववलितः 'a wrinkled young man.' On the other hand, धेनु and others are always last; as, गोधेनुः 'a milch cow;' इभयुवतिः 'a young elephant;' अग्निस्तोकः 'a little fire;' &c.

d. In Tatpurusha compounds, of whatever class, certain words, forming the second member of the compound, undergo changes of termination; टच्, that is, a final अ, being substituted for इ or for अन्, or added to a final स्: thus सखि, 'a friend,' forms विबुधसखः 'a friend of the gods;' रात्रिः 'night;' पुण्यरात्रः 'a holy night;' सक्थि, 'the thigh,' when similitude is implied, मृगसक्थं 'a thigh like that of a deer;' राजन्, as परमराजः 'a supreme king;' अहन् 'a day,' सुदिनाहः 'a fine day;' or अह्न is sometimes substituted, as सर्व्वाह्नः 'the whole day,' or 'lasting for the whole day:' अश्मन् makes शुक्लाश्मः 'a white stone:' ब्रह्मन् becomes ब्रह्म in such terms as गौडब्रह्मः 'a Brahman of Gaur.' After कु and महत्, implying 'baseness,' the change is optional; कुब्रह्मः or कुब्रह्मा, महाब्रह्मः or महाब्रह्मा, 'a low Brahman;' महत् being used ironically. श्वन् 'a dog,' preceded by an indeclinable, takes टच्; as, अतिश्वो वराहः 'a boar swifter than a dog;' अतिश्वी सेवा 'service worse than that of a dog:' but not if similitude to living beings is implied; as, मनुष्यश्वा 'a dog-like man,' 'a cynic;' अयस्, 'iron,' makes कालायसं 'black iron;' अनस् 'food;' महानसः 'a kitchen.' टच् is added to गो, as परमगवः 'an excellent ox;' and to नौ compounded with अर्द्ध, as अर्द्धनावं 'half a boat;' or with numerals, द्विनावं 'two boats collectively,' when even combined with a Taddhita affix, as द्विनावरूप्यः 'what comes from two boats.' When सु or अति or a negative, however, are prefixed to these words, forming appellatives, the finals are unchanged; as, सुसखिः 'a good friend;' अतिसखिः 'an excellent friend;' असखिः 'not a friend,' 'an unfriend;' or सुहस्ता &c.: so सुराजन्, अतिराजन्, अराजन्, &c. महत्, being the first member of a Tatpurusha compound, becomes महा; as, महादेव 'the great deity Śiva;' महाराजः 'a great king;' &c.

e. The following are considered by some as irregular compounds of the Karmmadháraya class: उच्चावचं 'high and low;' निश्चप्रचं 'picked out and heaped up;' अकिञ्चन 'having nothing,' 'poor;' अकुतोभय 'fearless;' चिन्मात्रं 'the mind alone;' अश्नीतपिबता 'drinking after eating.' Derivatives of कृ 'to do,' combined with अहं 'I,' as, अहंकार, अहंकृति, 'self sufficiency,' 'egotism;' also अहंपूर्व्विका, अहमहमिका, 'contending to be first' or 'foremost.' Compounds with एहि 'come;' as, एहिस्वागता 'come and welcome;' एहिवाणिजिका 'come and trade;' अपेहिवाणिजिका 'go and leave trade:' also with जहि, 'abandon,' in particular acceptations; as, जहिस्तम्बः 'one who cries, Leave the clump of grass.' These and others of a like anomalous character very rarely occur.

Dwigu Tatpurusha Compounds with Numerals.

277. Compounds are formed with numerals to signify attributes of weight, measure, or number; as, पञ्चकपाल 'measured by five cups;' पञ्चकपालः पुरोडाशः 'butter offered at sacrifice to the extent of five cups;' अष्टगु सुवर्णं 'gold of the value of eight oxen;' द्व्यङ्गुल 'of the measure of two inches.'

a. Aggregates of any given number of things are formed in the same manner, when the final takes either the neuter gender or the feminine, with the termination ई; as, त्रिभुवनं 'three worlds;' त्रिलोकी the same; चतुर्युगं 'the four ages;' पञ्चाध्यायी 'a work in five chapters;' त्रिखट्वं or त्रिखट्वी 'a collection of three bedsteads.'

b. The changes to which finals are subjected, as enumerated above, are of course applicable here; as, त्रिराजं 'three kings collectively;' पञ्चगवं 'five cows;' त्रिसखं 'three friends;' पञ्चरात्रं 'a term of three nights;' चतुष्पथं 'a meeting of four roads;' अष्टनावं 'an assemblage of eight boats.'

c. These same compounds may be used as possessive attributives; as, द्विनाव 'who or what has three boats;' पञ्चगव 'who or what has three cows;' द्विरात्र 'what lasts for two nights.'

d. The combinations of cardinal numbers to form multiples are considered to be compound Tatpurusha terms; as, एकादश, एकविंशति, &c.

Tatpurusha Compounds with Particles and Prepositions.

278. Besides the two subdivisions usually specified, the class of Tatpurusha compounds comprises a number of words formed with nominal or verbal derivatives, preceded by particles and prepositions, which may be conveniently separated from those compounds which are formed with nouns alone.

a. Compound attributives and appellatives are formed with negatives prefixed to nouns; as, अब्राह्मणः or नब्राह्मणः 'a man not a Brahman;' अनश्वः 'an animal not a horse:' असत् 'who or what is not;' असत्य 'untrue,' नासत्यौ 'who are not untrue,' 'the Aswini Kumáras:' नखः 'what has not space,' 'a finger nail:' अगः or नगः 'what does not go,' 'a mountain' or 'tree;' न-अक 'what does not depart,' नाकः 'sky:' अक्षर 'what does not decay;' अक्षरः 'a letter of the alphabet;' नक्षत्रं 'a constellation:' नपुंसकं 'not male,' 'neuter:' and in short, most words to which a negative is prefixed, retaining either their literal, or assuming some conventional, meaning.

b. The combination of the indeclinable words comprehended under the term Gati with the verbal derivatives of the verbs अस or भू 'to be,' or कृ 'to do,' is considered to form a class of Tatpurusha compounds; as, उरीकरणं 'promising,' उरीकृत्य 'having promised,' उरीभूत 'promised,' &c.; of which examples have already been given (see p. 100). To which may be added the following: अस्तङ्गत्य 'having set;' अच्छगत्य 'having met;' अच्छोद्य 'having spoken to;' पुरस्कृत्य 'having placed before;' तिरोभूय 'having disappeared;' साक्षात्कृत्य 'having made present' or 'visible.' Analogous compounds are formed with the derivatives of कृ and भू, with nouns retaining the inflections of case; as, लवणंकृत्य 'having made salt;' मनसिकृत्य or कृत्वा 'having made up the mind,' 'having determined;' उरसिकृत्य or कृत्वा 'having placed on the breast;' हस्तेकृत्य or पाणौकृत्य 'having placed in the hand,' i. e. having married or promised to marry.

c. The following are Tatpurusha compounds with prepositions: अतिराज 'surpassing the king;' अत्यह्न 'more than a day;' अतिमाल 'exceeding the necklace (in beauty);' अवकोकिल 'overcome by the cry of the Koïl;' निष्कौशाम्बि 'gone from Kausámbi;' पर्य्यध्ययन 'weary of study;' प्राचार्य्य 'over whom the teacher has authority.' These are attributives; as, अतिराजो मन्त्री 'the minister more powerful than the king;' अवकोकिलं मनः 'the mind overpowered by the Koïl's song;' &c.

279. Tatpurusha compounds, when attributives, take the gender of the substantives with which they agree; but when they form appellatives, adopt for the most part the gender of the concluding member of the compound, in which respect Dwandwa compounds agree with them. There are, however, a few exceptions: thus, in the latter class, अश्व 'a horse,' and वडवा 'a mare,' form अश्ववडवौ; and अहन् 'a day,' and रात्रि 'night,' अहोरात्रः. रात्रि with numerals in the sense of 'aggregation' becomes neuter, as द्विरात्रं 'a term of two nights;' and अहन् masculine, as द्व्यहः 'a period of two days:' so अह्न, substituted for अहन् is masculine, as मध्याह्नः 'midday;' when joined with an adjective, it may be neuter, as पुण्याहं 'a lucky day.'

a. Nouns of aggregation are formed with numerals; the gender is either neuter or feminine, as already noticed. पथिन्, preceded by a preposition to form an appellative, is neuter; as, विपथं 'a cross-road,' 'a by-way.'

b. सभा, preceded by a word meaning 'king,' except राजन्, and one not meaning 'man,' implying 'an assembly,' is neuter; as, ईश्वरसभं 'an assemblage of princes;' स्त्रीसभं 'a company of women:' but राजसभा, मनुष्यसभा. When it signifies the place of assembly, it remains feminine; as, इन्द्रसभा 'the hall of Indra;' धर्म्मसभा 'a hall of justice.'

c. सेना 'an army,' शाला 'a hall,' छाया 'shade,' सुरा 'wine,' निशा 'night,' when members of a Tatpurusha compound, retain the feminine, or adopt the neuter gender; as, वीरसेना -नं 'an army of heroes;' गोशाला -लं 'a cow-house;' वृक्षछाया -यं 'the shade of a tree;' यवसुरा -रं 'barley wine,' i. e. beer.

SECTION III.

Bahuvríhi Compounds.

280. Two or more words, or two or more compound terms, may be put together to form the attribute or epithet of an object. There is no limit to the component members of such a compound, and the final may be a noun of any gender; but it loses its own distinctive mark, as it takes, like all attributives, the gender of the word to which it is related: thus उदकं, 'water,' makes प्राप्तोदको ग्रामः 'a village at which the water has come;' प्राप्तोदका कलशी 'a pitcher which has been filled;' प्राप्तोदकं सरस् 'a pool with water in it.' भार्य्या, 'a wife,' may become masculine; as, रूपवद्भार्यो मनुष्यः 'a man who has a handsome wife:' गो 'a cow,' masculine or neuter; as, चित्रगुः पुरुषः a man 'who has a brindled cow;' चित्रगु क्षेत्रं a field 'in which such a cow is feeding.' Compounds of this class may be formed with particles; as, अपुत्रः अपुत्रा 'a childless (man or woman);' प्रपर्णो वृक्षः a tree 'of which the leaves are fallen;' अस्तिक्षीरा गौः a cow 'in whom there is milk:' also with numerals; as, उपविंश 'near to twenty,' &c. Nouns implying 'intermediate space' are also compounds of this class, the substantive दिश्, 'quarter,' being either expressed or understood; as, दक्षिणपूर्वा 'the south-east,' पश्चिमोत्तरा 'the north-west.'

a. In general the order of the words of which a Bahuvríhi compound consists places the term indicating the principal subject of attribution, and which will be the substantive, last; as in the preceding instances. When the principal term retains the sign of the case, it may be put first; as, कण्ठेकालः 'who is black in the throat,' S'iva: otherwise, कालकण्ठः. Pronominals and numerals are usually put first; as, सर्वश्वेत 'who is white all over;' द्विशुक्ल 'what is white in two places:' when they are combined, the numeral precedes; as, द्व्यन्य 'having other two.' Participles are usually put first; as, कृतकृत्य 'one by whom what was to be done has been done;' कृतकट 'one who has made the mat;' पीतोदक 'by whom water has been drunk:' but not always, when connected with words implying 'species' or 'time,' or the term सुख; as, सारङ्गजग्ध 'by whom venison has been eaten;' मासजात 'produced in a month;' सुखजात 'produced easily.' In the compound signifying 'one (a Brahman) by whom a domestic fire is maintained,' the participle takes either place; as, आहिताग्निः or अग्न्याहितः. Forms implying 'using a weapon' place the participle last; as, अस्युद्यतः '(a soldier) lifting up a sword (to strike):' but विवृतासिः 'one who has his sword sheathed.'

b. As an epithet is commonly formed by a feminine substantive, preceded by its adjective, and the former being changed according to the gender of the new term to which it is attached, it becomes a question what is to be done with the latter: thus, for instance, चित्रा गौः being converted to an epithet, गौ becomes गु, and may be masculine, गुः, as the epithet of a man having cattle. In that case is चित्रा to remain feminine? So रूपवती भार्य्या becoming an attribute of a man 'having' a handsome wife, and भार्य्या accordingly becoming भार्य्यः, what is to be done with रूपवती? In general, adjectives so circumstanced are reduced to their crude forms, and in the examples given the compounds are चित्रगुः, रूपवद्भार्य्यः. There are, however, exceptions to this rule.

1. When a compound epithet, of which the final was originally feminine, is preceded by more than one adjective, all except that preceding the final retain the feminine termination; as, चित्राजरद्गुः or जरतीचित्रगुः 'one who has an old brindled cow.' According to some authorities, both should be feminine, as चित्राजरतीगुः; but this appears questionable.

2. When the preceding term is necessarily feminine, it retains its termination; as, गङ्गाभार्य्यः 'he who has the river-goddess Gangá to wife:' also if it ends in ऊ feminine; as, वामोरूभार्य्यः 'one who has a wife of elegant shape' (handsome thighed): also if the first term have no necessary relation to the second; as, कल्याणीप्रधानं 'having for its head an illustrious woman' (a family); स्त्रीप्रमाणः 'having a woman for witness or authority' (a suit, &c.) Feminine nouns having a penultimate क preserve their final; as, पाचिकाभार्य्यः 'one who has a wife that can cook.' दत्ता, used either as an attribute or as a name, retains a feminine termination; as, दत्ताभार्य्यः 'one who has a wife given,' or 'whose name is Dattá.' Ordinal numbers do the same; as, पञ्चमीभार्य्यः 'he who has a fifth wife:' so do nouns ending in ई implying part of the body; as, सुकेशीभार्य्यः 'who has a wife with fine hair:' so do nouns implying caste; as, शूद्राभार्य्यः ब्राह्मणीभार्य्यः 'one who has a wife of the Śúdra or the Brahman caste.'

c. The final members of Bahuvríhi compounds occasionally undergo some modification.

1. The most common is the substitution of अ for the final vowel, or in some cases for the penultimate vowel and final consonant of the last member of a compound epithet; as, सक्थि 'a thigh,' दीर्घसक्थ 'long-thighed;' (but not if used figuratively, as दीर्घसक्थि शकटं 'a cart with long axle;') अक्षि 'the eye,' पुण्डरीकाक्ष 'lotus-eyed;' अङ्गुलि 'a finger,' when applied to any thing of wood, पञ्चाङ्गुलं दारु 'a rake;' but पञ्चाङ्गुलिर्हस्तः 'the hand.' नाभि 'the navel,' and other words, optionally change इ to अ; as, ऊर्णनाभ or ऊर्णनाभि 'having a woolly or hairy navel:' so हलि 'a furrow,' सक्थि 'the thigh,' or, according to some, शक्ति 'utility,' optionally change the final after a negative, दुर् 'bad,' or सु 'good;' as, अहल or अहलि 'unfurrowed,' दुर्हल or दुर्हलि, &c. Numerals preceded by particles or by other numerals, to signify 'approximation,' take अ for their finals; उपदशाः those which are 'near ten,' i. e. nine or eleven; द्वित्राः 'two or three;' पञ्चषाः 'five or six;' द्विविंशाः 'twice twenty.' It is added to चतुर्, preceded by certain particles; अचतुर 'what is not four;' उपचतुर 'what is about four.' नेतृ, 'a leader,' takes अ when preceded by the name of a constellation; as, मृगानेत्र 'what has Mṛigá for a leader.' After a numeral, मूर्द्धन् substitutes अ for its final syllable; द्विमूर्द्ध, त्रिमूर्द्ध, 'two-headed, three-headed:' so does लोमन् after अन्तर् and वहिर्; as, अन्तर्लोम 'hairy internally;' वहिर्लोम 'hairy externally.' The following are considered as irregularly taking अ; प्रातर् 'morning,' सुप्रात 'having a good morning;' दिवस् 'a day;' सुदिव 'having a good day;' श्वस् 'morrow,' सुश्व 'having a good morrow;' कुक्षि 'the belly,' हरिकुक्ष 'green-bellied,' as हरिकुक्षः शुकः 'the green-bellied parrot;' अस्रि 'an angle,' चतुरस्र 'quadrangular.'

2. In a few instances a final अ is changed to another vowel, or substitutes अन् or अस्; thus गन्ध, 'smell,' makes with उत्, पूति, सु, and सुरभि, उद्गन्धि 'emitting smell,' सुगन्धि and सुरभिगन्धि 'fragrant,' पूतिगन्धि 'fetid:' also in compounds implying 'a little;' as, घृतगन्धि 'smelling slightly of Ghee:' and intending similitude; as, पद्मगन्धि 'fragrant as a lotus:' but not if the odour is separated from the object; as, सुगन्ध आपणिकः 'a shop

of fragrant things,' 'a perfumer's.' ईर्म, 'a wound,' in one combination takes अन्; as, दक्षिणेर्म्मा मृगः 'a deer wounded by a hunter:' so does जम्भ, 'a tooth' or 'food,' after सु, हरित, तृण, or सोम; as, सुजम्भन् 'having good teeth;' हरितजम्भन् 'having green teeth;' तृणजम्भन् 'eating grass;' सोमजम्भन् 'eating the Soma plant:' but not after any other term; as, पतितजम्भ 'toothless.' धर्म्म takes अन् in composition; as, कल्याणधर्म्मन् 'who performs his duty well.' प्रजा 'offspring,' and मेधा 'understanding,' take अस् when compounded with a negative or with दुर् or सु; as, अप्रजस् 'without progeny;' अप्रजाः पुरुषः 'a childless man,' अप्रजाः स्त्री 'a childless woman:' so दुष्प्रजस् सुप्रजस् 'having bad or good children;' अमेधस् 'stupid,' दुर्मेधस् 'dull,' सुमेधस् 'intelligent.'

3. In various instances the final term of a Bahuvríhi compound substitutes a different form, and especially when the word signifies a part of the body: thus नस् is put for नासिका; as, उन्नस 'high-nosed,' प्रणस 'prominent-nosed.' With खर and खुर the substitute may also be नस्; as, खरणसः or खरणाः, खुरणसः or खुरणाः पुरुषः 'an ass-nosed or hoof-nosed man.' After स्थूल the primitive is unchanged; as, स्थूलनासिक 'large-nosed.' After वि the syllables ख, ग्र, and खु may be substituted; as, विख, विग्र, विखु; also विनस 'noseless.' पाद् is substituted for पाद when 'resemblance' is implied; as, व्याघ्रपाद् 'having a foot like a tiger:' but not after the class हस्त्यादि; as, हस्तिपाद 'elephant-footed.' After numerals and सु the substitute is used; as, द्विपाद्, त्रिपाद्, 'biped, triped,' &c.; सुपाद् 'well-footed.' पदी is used in the feminine after कुम्भ 'a jar,' एक 'one,' निर् 'without,' and other words; as, कुम्भपदी, एकपदी, निष्पदी, '(a woman) having a foot like a water-jar,' &c. If masculine, the form is as in कुम्भपाद, 'jar-footed' (a man). दतृ, making in inflection दन्, is substituted for दन्त 'a tooth,' preceded by सु; as, सुदत् 'having good teeth:' by a numeral when age is implied; as, द्विदत् 'having two teeth;' द्विदन् बालः 'a child old enough to have two teeth:' but द्विदन्तो हस्ती 'an elephant with two teeth.' The feminine is formed with ई; as, द्विदती बाला 'a two-toothed

female infant.' In feminine appellatives the same form is used; as, अपदती a proper name: but समदन्ती स्त्री 'a woman with even teeth.' दत् is substituted after certain other words, as, शुभ्र, अग्र, and गर्द्दभ, and others; as, शुभ्रदत् 'white-toothed;' कुशाग्रदत् 'having teeth as sharp as the tip of Kuśa grass;' गर्द्दभदत् 'ass-toothed,' &c.: also optionally after श्याव and अरोक; as, श्यावदत् or श्यावदन्त 'black-toothed;' अरोकदत् or अरोकदन्त 'having discoloured teeth.' ज्ञु is substituted for जानु, 'the knee,' after प्र, सम्, and optionally after ऊर्द्ध्व; as, प्रज्ञु 'prominent-kneed,' संज्ञु 'compact-kneed,' ऊर्द्ध्वज्ञु or ऊर्द्ध्वजानु 'high-kneed.'

4. In words not signifying parts of the body we have जानि put optionally for जाया 'a wife;' as, युवजानिः or युवतिजायः 'a man who has a young wife:' ऊध्न for ऊधस् 'an udder;' as, घटोध्नी '(a cow) having a large udder:' धन्वन् for धनुष् 'a bow;' as, शार्ङ्गधन्वन् 'having a bow of horn:' optionally if the compound is a proper name; as, शतधन्वा or शतधनुः the name of a prince, 'he who has a hundred bows.' ककुद, 'a hump' or 'a peak,' drops its final when denoting age; as, अजातककुद् 'a young ox,' 'one whose hump has not grown:' or when signifying a mountain; त्रिककुद् 'a three-peaked mountain.' काकुद, 'the palate,' drops its final after उत् or वि, and optionally after पूर्ण; as, उत्काकुद् or विकाकुद् 'without the hard palate;' पूर्णकाकुद or पूर्णकाकुद् 'having a complete palate.' हृद् is substituted for हृदय, 'the heart,' after सु and दुर्; as, सुहृद् 'kind-hearted,' i. e. a friend; दुर्हृद् 'bad-hearted,' i. e. a foe: in a literal sense the compounds would be सुहृदय, दुर्हृदय.

5. क, technically termed कप्, is added to many Bahuvríhi compounds; as, to उरस् 'the breast,' व्यूढोरस्क 'broad-chested;' to सर्पिस् 'ghee,' प्रियसर्पिष्क 'fond of ghee:' to अर्थ, 'object,' after a negative, अनर्थक 'useless,' and optionally after a preposition, अपार्थ or अपार्थक; to यशस्, 'fame,' optionally, as महायशस् or महायशस्क 'very famous.' It is substituted for the finals in इन् to form feminine attributives; as, from दण्डिन् 'an ascetic bearing a staff,' 'a Dańḋi,' come बहुदण्डिका नगरी 'a city having many Dańḋis;' बहुवाग्मिका सभा 'an assembly of many eloquent

persons.' If masculine, क may be optionally substituted for the final nasal; as, बहुदण्डी or बहुदण्डिको ग्रामः 'a village with many Daṇḍis.' When added to feminine nouns in आ, the final is optionally short; as, माला 'a garland,' बहुमालाक or बहुमालक 'having many garlands.' नाडी and तन्त्री do not take क when used anatomically; as, बहुनाडिः कायः 'the many-vesselled body;' बहुतन्त्री ग्रीवा 'the many-fibred neck:' but they may add it in other senses; as, बहुनाडीकः स्तम्भः 'a clump with many pipes' or 'reeds;' बहुतन्त्री वीणा 'a many-stringed lute.' क is added to भ्रातृ in a depreciatory sense; as, मूर्खभ्रातृकः 'one who has a foolish brother:' otherwise प्रशस्तभ्रातृ 'having an excellent brother.'

d. सह 'with,' forming the first member of a compound, is commonly changed to स; as, सपुत्र 'having a son,' 'being with a son;' सकर्मक 'having an office or object, occupied,' 'transitive;' सलोमक 'being with hair,' 'hairy.' When the compound is connected with a term of benediction, सह is retained; as, स्वस्ति राज्ञे सहपुत्राय 'health to the king, along with his son:' but not before the words गो 'a cow,' हल 'a plough,' or वत्स 'a calf;' as, सगवे, सहलाय, सवत्साय. महत् usually substitutes महा in a similar situation in this as well as in other kinds of compounds; as, महात्मन् 'great-souled,' 'magnanimous;' महाकाय 'great-bodied;' महाबल 'very strong:' but महत् is unchanged before words signifying 'become grown' or 'made;' as, महद्भूत 'become large' or 'great.'

e. Words implying 'mutual striking,' when repeated, prolong the final of the first member, and substitute इ for that of the last; as, केशाकेशि 'pulling hair,' दण्डादण्डि 'cudgelling,' मुष्टीमुष्टि 'boxing.' Although these words are used adverbially, without a substantive, they are Bahuvríhi compounds, and regarded as epithets of युद्धं, 'fighting,' understood.

SECTION IV.

Avyayí-bháva—Indeclinable Compounds.

281. Indeclinable words are formed by combining a noun

with a preposition or particle, when the former is put in the accusative case neuter. These compounds being in fact compound adverbs, and like all adverbial terms, when not otherwise inflected, taking the sign of the invariable neuter accusative.

a. The following are examples of indeclinable compounds formed with prepositions and particles, which, it will be observed, retain their own sense, and exercise the same effect upon the purport of the noun which they would do if uncompounded. The sense of each term is complete in itself, but, agreeably to its adverbial character, requires a verb, either present or understood, to connect it with a substantive.

1. Prepositions.

अति 'beyond:' अतिगङ्गं 'beyond the Ganges,' अतिगङ्गं ग्रामः 'the village (that is) beyond the Ganges;' अतिहिमं 'after the cold weather,' अतिहिममागच्छति वसन्तः 'spring comes after the cold weather;' अतिनिद्रं 'after sleep,' अतिनिद्रमुत्तिष्ठति पुरुषः 'the man gets up after sleep.' These examples will sufficiently explain the relation in which this sort of adverbial compound stands to the other members of a sentence.

अधि 'upon,' 'near to:' अधिहरि 'upon Hari or Vishńu;' अध्यग्नि 'near to or upon the fire.'

अनु 'after,' 'according to,' 'near to:' अनुविष्णु 'after Vishńu' (following or worshipping); अनुक्रमं 'according to order;' अनुज्येष्ठं 'according to seniority;' अनुवनं 'near to the wood;' अनुगङ्गं 'near to or upon the Ganges.'

अप 'off,' 'from;' as, अपदिशं 'in the off-point,' i. e. in the intermediate point; अपविष्णु 'from Vishńu,' 'withdrawn from,' 'hostile to.'

आ, limitative; as, आमुक्ति 'until final liberation;' आसमुद्रं 'unto the sea;' आबालं 'to the boys,' as, आबालं हरिभक्तिर्भवति 'faith in Hari extends even to the children.' The termination of the fifth case may be also used with this preposition; as, आमुक्तेः, आसमुद्रात्, आबालेभ्यः.

उप 'near to:' उपकृष्णं 'near to Kṛishṅa;' उपग्रामं 'near to the village.'

निर् 'out of,' 'exempt from:' निर्जनं 'lonely,' 'void of men;' निर्मक्षिकं 'free from flies.'

परि 'about' or 'against:' परिविष्णु 'about or against Vishṅu.' It follows numerals and the words अक्ष 'dice,' शलाका 'a man (at draughts, &c.),' or a numeral, when signifying 'loss at play;' as, एकपरि 'losing one;' अक्षपरि 'having the dice against one;' शलाकापरि 'losing a man.'

प्रति 'to' or 'towards:' प्रत्यग्नि शलभाः पतन्ति 'the grasshoppers go towards the fire.' It also implies 'severalty' or 'succession;' as, प्रत्यर्थं 'according to each several object or signification;' प्रतिजन्म 'birth after birth.'

स is usually substituted for सह, signifying 'similarity' or 'sameness,' as सहरि 'like Hari;' also 'association,' implying 'finality,' as सतृणमत्ति 'he eats with the grass,' i. e. even to the grass; also 'possession,' as a property, as सक्षेत्रं 'having, or rich in, fields.'

2. Particles.

इति, implying 'so,' 'such,' and the like; as, इतिहरि 'such is (the word) Hari.'

दुर् 'bad,' and सु 'good;' as, दुर्यवनं 'bad with the Yavanas;' सुमद्रं 'well or prosperous with the Madras.'

यथा, 'according to;' as, यथाशक्ति 'according to power or ability:' but not when it signifies 'analogy;' as, यथा हरिस्तथा हरः 'such as Hari is, such is Hara.'

यावत् 'as many as;' as, यावदन्नं ब्राह्मणान् आमन्त्रयस्व 'as far as there may be food (for them), invite the Brahmans.'

निकषा and समया 'near;' as, निकषालङ्कं 'near to Lanká;' समयापुरं 'near the city.'

b. The derivatives of अञ्च 'to go,' implying 'direction,' optionally form indeclinables; as, प्राग्वनं or प्राग्वनात् 'east from the wood:' so does बहिर् 'out of,' 'without;' as, बहिर्ग्रामं or बहिर्ग्रामात् 'out of the village.'

c. Indeclinable compounds may be formed with numerals, except एक 'one,' referring to families or classes; as, द्विमुनि त्रिमुनि 'born in or belonging to a family in which there have been two or three Munis:' so त्रिमुनि व्याकरणं 'the grammar of which the three Munis (Pánini, Patanjali, Kátyáyana) are the authors.' Names of rivers are also combined with numerals to indicate the place of junction; as, द्विगङ्गं 'at the meeting of the two Ganges;' त्रियमुनं 'at that of the three Yamunas.' They are also combined with other words in a like acceptation; as, उन्मत्तगङ्गं 'at the place where the Ganges is furious;' लोहितगङ्गं 'where the Ganges is red;' as, शीघ्रगङ्गं वाराणशी 'Benares (stands) where the Ganges is rapid.'

d. In this, as in preceding forms of composition, the finals of the last member of the compound are sometimes changed. When the final is a long vowel or a diphthong terminating a feminine noun, its change to a corresponding short vowel is nothing more than the alteration required by the substitution of the neuter gender (p. 41); as, स्त्री, 'a female,' makes अतिस्त्रि 'surpassing the woman;' नौ 'a boat,' अतिनु 'beyond the boat.' But the more special alteration is analogous to that which occurs so frequently in Bahuvríhi compounds, the substitution of अ for a final vowel, or a final अन्; or its addition to words ending in consonants; as, उपगिरं or उपगिरि 'near the mountain;' उपनदं or उपनदि 'near the river;' उपराजं 'under the king;' अध्यात्मं 'over or in the spirit.' If the noun ending in अन् be already neuter, it may retain its own termination; as, अपचर्म or अपचर्मं 'off the skin.' शरद् 'the autumn,' and other words, add अ; as, उपशरदं 'near the autumn:' or sometimes words with final consonants, not nasals, semivowels, or sibilants, add अ optionally; as, उपदृशद् or उपदृशदं 'near to the stone.' अक्षि, 'the eye,' substitutes अ when compounded with the prepositions अनु, पर, प्रति, or सम्; as, अन्वक्षं 'according to the eye,' 'visibly,' 'perceptibly.' पर substitutes ओ for its own final, whether in a Tatpurusha or Avyaya compound; as, परोक्षं 'away from the eye,' 'absent,' 'invisible;' प्रत्यक्षं

'before the eye,' 'present;' and समक्षं also 'before the eye,' 'visible' or 'present.'

e. अग्रे 'in front,' मध्ये 'in the midst,' पारे 'on the further side,' may be compounded with nouns in this form; as, अग्रेरामं 'in the presence of Ráma;' मध्येगङ्गं 'in the midst of the Ganges;' पारेसमुद्रं 'beyond the ocean:' or the terms may be optionally used with the signs of the case, either their own or the noun which they govern; as, पारेसमुद्रात् or समुद्रस्य पारात् 'from beyond the ocean.'

f. The following words are considered as forming indeclinable compounds of an anomalous description: अहन् 'a day,' as प्राह्णं 'in the forenoon;' गो 'a cow or ox,' तिष्ठद्गु 'at cow-standing (time),' i. e. when they stand to be milked, वहद्गु 'at ox-bearing,' i. e. ploughing (time), आयतीगवं 'at cattle-coming,' i. e. at the time of their coming home; दक्षिण 'the right hand,' प्रदक्षिणं 'walking round a person or thing, keeping it on the right;' पदाति 'a foot-soldier,' समम्पदाति 'at drill-time,' or when the soldiers are in line; भूमि 'earth,' समम्भूमि '(at a place) where it is level;' मृग 'a deer,' प्रमृगं 'at deer-coming,' विमृगं 'at deer-going;' यव 'barley,' खलेयवं 'when barley is on the threshingfloor' (the season), लूनयवं 'at barley-cutting;' and other compounds: so बुष 'chaff,' खलेबुषं 'at chaff on the floor' (time), &c.; रथ 'a car,' प्ररथं 'at chariot-going;' समा 'a year,' पापसमं 'during a wicked year,' पुण्यसमं 'during a virtuous year;' सम 'equal,' सुषमं 'level' or 'even,' विषमं 'uneven.' सम् is compounded with प्रति, as सम्प्रति 'now,' 'at present.'

SECTION V.

General Rules.

282. There are some changes which are common to all or most of the classes of compounds. Some, as the substitution or addition of a final अ, have been noticed: the most useful of the others are the following, affecting either the final member of the compound or the initial:

a. 1. अप् 'water,' is changed to अप; as, विमलाप 'having pure water,' विमलापं सरः 'a clear lake.' After द्वि, अन्तर्, or a preposition ending in any vowel except अ, the initial अ is changed to ई; as, द्वीपं 'an island,' 'having water on both sides;' also अन्तरीपं 'an island,' 'in the midst of water;' प्रतीप, 'reverse.' सम with अप् makes समीप 'near;' but in a literal sense समाप 'having water equally.' After अनु the vowel becomes ऊ, if applied to a country; as, अनूपो देशः 'marshy land:' but अन्वीपं 'upon or along the water.' After a preposition ending with अ, the change to ई is optional; as, परा and प्र make either पराप or परेप 'where the water has retired;' प्राप or प्रेप 'where it has gone forth.'

2. पथिन्, 'a path,' is changed commonly to पथ; as, महापथः 'a great road;' चतुष्पथ 'a place where four roads meet;' रम्यपथो देशः 'a place having a pleasant road;' उपपथं 'near to the road.'

b. 1. कु, a particle implying 'inferiority,' 'vileness,' or sometimes 'a little,' is variously modified before different words. In a Tatpurusha compound, and preceding a word beginning with a vowel, it is changed to कत्; as, कदश्वः 'a bad horse,' 'a hack;' कदुष्ट्रः 'a bad camel;' but कूष्ट्रो राजा 'a prince who has a bad camel:' also before रथ and वद्; as, कद्रथः 'a bad chariot;' कद्वदः 'one who speaks ill:' before तृण, signifying 'a species,' कत्तृणं 'a kind of grass;' but कुतृणं 'bad grass in general.' कु is changed to का before पथिन्, as कापथः 'a bad road;' अक्षि 'the eye,' as काक्षः 'a tear,' and optionally before पुरुष; as कापुरुषः or कुपुरुषः 'a mean despicable man,' 'a coward.' का is also a diminutive; as, कामधुर 'a little sweet;' काम्ल 'a little sour:' before उष्ण, 'hot,' either कत्, कव, or का may be used; as, कदुष्ण, कवोष्ण, कोष्ण, 'a little hot,' 'tepid.'

2. The infinitive mood is used as the first member of a compound with काम and मनस्, when it optionally rejects the nasal; as, ज्ञातुकाम or ज्ञातुङ्काम 'desirous to know;' कर्तुमनस् or कर्तुम्मनस् 'inclined to do.'

3. अवश्यं, 'certainly,' optionally rejects its nasal when com-

pounded with a future participle; as, अवश्यकार्य्यं or अवश्यंकार्य्यं 'what is necessarily to be done.' मांस, 'flesh,' compounded with पाक or पचन 'cooking,' optionally rejects its final vowel; as, मांसपाकः or मांस्पाकः, मांसपचनं or मांस्पचनं 'cooking meat.'

4. अन्य becomes अन्यत् before various words, if not in the sense of the instrumental or genitive cases; as, अन्यदाशा 'hope in something else;' अन्यदाशीः 'benediction in or on another;' अन्यत्कारकः 'one who does something different.'

5. The substitution of स for सह has already been noticed; but it is also substituted for समान 'same,' 'like;' as, सपक्ष 'being of the same party;' सधर्म्मा 'observing the same duties:' whence साधर्म्म्यं 'community of the duties of caste, profession,' &c.; सब्रह्मचारी 'a fellow-student,' 'one studying under the same teacher:' so सतीर्थः also 'a fellow-student,' 'having the same holy object' or 'preceptor.' स is substituted for समान before दृश 'to see;' as, सदृशः 'like,' 'similar,' 'of like appearance:' so सदृक् and सदृक्षः. It is also substituted before the following words in the sense of either class of compounds: ज्योतिस् 'light,' जनपद 'country,' रात्रि 'night,' नाभि 'navel,' बन्धु 'a relative,' गन्ध 'smell,' पिण्ड 'a lump of rice,' &c.; लोहित 'blood,' कुक्षि 'side,' वेणी 'braided hair,' पत्नी 'a wife;' as, सज्योतिः 'equal in lustre;' सजनपद 'of the same country;' सपिण्ड 'of the same cake;' सपिण्डः 'a relative connected by offerings to the same ancestors;' &c.

The following take either स or समान; रूप 'form,' नाम 'name,' गोत्र 'family,' वर्ण 'caste,' वयस् 'age,' वचन 'speech,' धर्म्म 'duty,' जातीय 'specific,' उदर्य्य 'uterine;' as, सरूप or समानरूप 'of the same form;' सगोत्र or समानगोत्र 'of the same race;' सोदर्य्य or समानोदर्य्य 'related in the female line,' as सोदर्य्यो भ्राता 'a brother by the same mother;' &c.

CHAPTER VIII.

SYNTAX.

283. The great body of Sanskrit composition is in metre, and the construction of sentences has consequently been subordinate to the necessities of rhythm. Examples therefore of syntactical arrangement are not so diversified as might be expected; and it is not always certain, whether any unusual combination may not be a license of the poet, rather than a law of the language. The use of protracted compounds also in a very great degree supersedes the occasion of individual inflexion; as a sentence or a stanza, embracing a great variety of circumstances, may be made up of a nominative and accusative, with a single copulative, the rest of the words, however numerous, being compound epithets of one or other of the nouns. There also prevails very commonly an elliptical style of construction, in which the verb is altogether omitted, or its tenses are supplied by participles and analogous words.

In the following line from the Mahábhárata we have two sentences without a verb or any other copulative, and only a nominative case: पिता गुरुर्न सन्देहो वेदविद्याप्रदः प्रभुः 'A father (or) a spiritual preceptor (is) the lord, the giver (of) knowledge, of the Vedas: (there is) no doubt (of this).' Instances of the absence of a verb are numerous in the didactic verses of the Hitopadeśa. कोऽर्थः पुत्रेण जातेन यो न विद्वान् न धार्म्मिकः । काणेन चक्षुषा किंवा चक्षुः पीडैव केवलं ॥ 'What (is) the use of a son (being) born, who (is) neither learned nor pious? What (benefit is there) from a sightless eye? (such) an eye (is) even only pain.' In the following stanza from the Kumára Sambhava there is only one verb, and one change of inflexion from the nominative to the instrumental, which, if the metre had not needed a long syllable, would probably have been dispensed with: विरोधिसत्त्वोज्झितपूर्व्वमत्सरं । द्रुमैरभीष्टप्रसवार्च्चितातिथि ॥ नवोटजाभ्यन्तरसम्भृतानलं । तपोवनं तच्च बभूव पावनं ॥ 'And that grove of penitents was pure; (for in it) animals of hostile natures (had) abandoned their former animosity; guests (were) reverenced by its trees with desired fruits; and within its new-reared cottages the (holy) fires (were) enshrined.' There is a little more variety of inflexion in the following verse from the Raghu Vanśa; but it is sufficiently rare to show how much syntactical construction has been set aside for rhythmical disposition, even in the works of authors who have not indulged in that abuse of elaboration which characterises later and inferior writers. अथ स विषयव्यावृत्तात्मा यथाविधि सूनवे । नृपतिककुदं दत्वा यूने सितातपवारणं ॥ मुनिवनतरुच्छायां देव्या तया सह शिश्रिये । गलितवयसामिक्ष्वाकूणामिदं हि कुलव्रतं ॥ 'He then, whose mind was liberated from objects of sense, having delivered to his young son the symbol of royalty, the shelter of the white umbrella, with the usual solemn rites, repaired together with his queen to the shade of the trees of the grove of hermits: for such is the observance of the princes of the race of Ikshwáku, when in the decline of life.' In this long stanza we have but one verbal inflexion, शिश्रिये, besides the indeclinable participle दत्वा.

Although however in this manner dispensed with in composition to a great extent, yet the relations of words in sentences are expressed in modes analogous to those adopted in other cultivated languages; as the following rules will exemplify.

SECTION I.

Nouns.

284. The noun substantive expresses as usual the subject or object of a proposition by the different modifications of number, gender, and case. Its relations to other parts of a sentence depend especially upon the latter, and will therefore be better explained, as in native grammars in the chapter to which the title of कारक: is attached, in the order of the cases. When, as not unfrequently happens, more than one case may be employed to convey a similar relation, the alternatives will be found, with some exceptions, under that case which is subsequent in order, according to the scheme given under the head of declension (rule 46).

285. Nominative case (कर्त्ता or प्रथमा). The nominative case declares the simple sense of a word; as, मनुष्यः 'a man,' स्त्री 'a woman,' ज्ञानं 'knowledge.' Its employment in a definite or indefinite manner is usually indicated by the context, as there is no article. The numeral एक, or a pronoun, however, sometimes performs the same office; as, एकः पुरुषः 'a man,' स पुरुषः 'the or that man,' कश्चिन्नृपः 'a certain king,' एको वृद्धव्याघ्रः 'an old tiger.'

a. Two substantives may be connected absolutely in the nominative case; as, द्रोणं व्रीहिः 'rice a droṅa (in measure);' क्रोशो गिरिः 'the mountain a kos (in extent);' माता शत्रुः 'a mother an enemy;' पिता वैरी 'a father an enemy;' विषं सभा दरिद्रस्य 'Society (is) poison to the poor:' but in these cases the copulative 'is' must be understood, as in similar phrases it is expressed; भवत्यधर्म्मो धर्म्मः 'iniquity becomes virtue.' The nouns in apposition may be in different genders and numbers: वैदिकानि कर्म्माण्यस्य स्वर्ग्यः पन्थाः 'The acts of the Vedas (are) his path to heaven;' के वा न स्युः परिभवास्पदं निष्फलारम्भयत्नाः 'Who engaged in unprofitable undertakings do not become a subject of disgrace?'

b. The nominative case is connected with the active verb, or governs it, when it expresses the agent, and with the passive when it signifies the object: देवदत्तः कटं करोति 'Devadatta makes the mat;' देवदत्तेन क्रियते कटः 'The mat is made by Devadatta.' It is also put absolutely sometimes in a sentence, as the object of an action, but where the accusative that should express that object is omitted: विषवृक्षोऽपि संवर्द्ध्य स्वयं छेत्तुमसाम्प्रतं 'Even a poison-tree, having reared (it), one should not of oneself cut (it) down.' In this the complete construction should be, वृक्षं संवर्द्ध्य तं छेत्तुमसाम्प्रतं योऽपि विषवृक्षः स्यात् 'Having reared a tree, it is not proper to cut it down, even though it be a poison-tree.'

c. When various nouns, separated by a disjunctive particle expressed or implied, occur in a sentence with a common verb, that which is nearest to the verb may become its nominative: अहं रामो वा राजा लक्ष्मणो वा मरिष्यति 'I or Ráma, the king, or Lakshmaṅa, will die:' न चैनमशकद् भानुरहम् वा स्नेहकारणैः । पुरा प्रत्यनुनेतुं वा गन्तुं वाऽप्येकतां त्वया ॥ 'Neither was the sun able, nor I, by motives of affection, to conciliate him, or (induce him) to enter into amity with thee:' न तथा सुखयत्यग्निः न प्रावारा न कम्बलः । शीतवातार्द्दितं लोकं यथा तव मरीचयः ॥ 'Fire gratifies not, neither do clothes nor a blanket, the region that is afflicted with cold breezes, so much as thy rays (O sun).'

d. When two or more nouns are joined together by a copulative conjunction, they usually govern a verb in the plural number: ततः कुन्ती च राजा च भीष्मश्च सह बन्धुभिः । ददुः श्राद्धं तदा पाण्डोः स्वधामृतमयं तदा ॥ 'Then afterwards Kuntí and the king and Bhíshma, with the kinsmen, gave to Páṅḋu the obsequial offerings, with libations to the manes.' This is not invariably the case, however, and the verb may have for its nominative only the nearest of the nouns combined by copulative conjunctions: सा च सत्यवती देवी कौशल्या च यशस्विनी । राजदारैः परिवृता गान्धारी चापि निर्ययौ ॥ 'And the queen Satyavatí and the illustrious Kauśalyá, and also Gándhárí, attended by the wives of the king, went forth:' आदित्यचन्द्रावनिलोऽनलश्च द्यौर्भूमिरापो हृदयं यमश्च । अहश्च रात्रिश्च उभे च सन्ध्ये धर्म्मोऽपि जानाति नरस्य वृत्तं ॥ 'The sun and moon, wind and fire, the sky, earth, waters, the heart and Yama, and day and night, and both dawn and evening, and also Dharma, knows the conduct of a man.'

286. Accusative case (कर्म्म or द्वितीया). The accusative expresses, after a transitive verb, the object of the action: कुम्भं करोति कुम्भकारः 'The potter fabricates the vessel;' हरिं भजति भक्तः 'The votary worships Hari.'

a. The accusative follows a neuter or intransitive verb, when it denotes place or time: कुरून् स्वपिति 'He sleeps in the country of the Kurus;' क्रोशं प्रतिष्ठते 'He proceeds for a Kos;' कियन्तं कालमवसन् पर्व्वते गन्धमादने 'They dwelt for some time on the mountain Gandhamádana;' मासौ गुरुगृहे स्थितः 'He stayed two months in the house of his preceptor.'

b. Verbs signifying 'motion to,' literally or figuratively, govern the accusative case: ग्रामं गच्छति 'He goes to the village;' मनसा कृष्णमेति 'He goes mentally to Krishńa,' he worships him; विस्मयं परमं ययौ 'He went to (or felt) great astonishment.' The accusative is also employed when 'going along a road' is intended; पन्थानं याति पथिकः 'The traveller goes along the road:' but not if 'going to a road' is meant; उत्पथेन पथे गच्छति 'He goes by a byeway to the road.' The dative case may also be used optionally, when actual 'motion to' is signified; ग्रामाय गच्छति.

c. The accusative case follows verbs of giving, to signify the thing given; ग्रामं ब्राह्मणेभ्यो ददामि 'I give the village to the Brahmans:' also verbs of hearing, to denote the thing heard; आसुरं मे शृणु 'Hear from me the Ásura (creation).'

d. A double accusative follows a number of verbs, when the thing done, and the thing or person that is the object of the action, are both designated. These are mostly verbs that signify, 1. speaking, 2. asking, 3. instructing, 4. knowing, 5. conquering, 6. leading, 7. dragging, 8. taking, 9. collecting, 10. stealing, 11. fining, 12. cooking, 13. milking, 14. churning, and 15. obstructing; whether they have these meanings literally or metaphorically. 1. राजानं सर्वं ब्रूते चारः 'The spy tells the whole to the king;' तमब्रवीत् कुन्ती वचनमर्थवत् 'Kuntí said to him words full of meaning:' 2. सोऽपृच्छल्लक्ष्मणं सीतां 'He asked Lakshmańa (after) Sítá:' 3. शिष्यान् धर्मं गुरुः शास्ति 'The Guru teaches the disciples virtue:' 4. दण्डं धर्मं विदुर्बुधाः 'The wise know punishment (to be) virtue:' 5. जित्वा राज्यं नलं नृपं 'Having conquered his kingdom (from) Nala the king:' 6. ग्राममजान् नयति गोपालः 'The shepherd leads the goats to the village:' 7. चोरं कारागारं कर्षति दण्डपालः 'The officer of justice drags the thief to prison:' 8. स जहाराराण्यमाभीरीः 'He took the Ábhíra women to the forest:' 9. वृक्षमवचिनोति फलानि बालः 'The boy gathers the fruit (from) the tree:' 10. देवदत्तं धनं मुष्णाति धूर्तः

'The rogue robs Devadatta (of) his wealth:' 11. अधमर्णिकं शतं दण्डयति राजा 'The king fines the debtor a hundred (rupees):' 12. तण्डुलानोदनं पचति सूपकारः 'The cook dresses the grain (and) the boiled rice:' 13. गां दोग्धि पयः 'He milks the cow (for) milk;' प्राणान् दुहन्निवात्मानं 'Milking (abandoning) life (from) himself:' 14. सुधां क्षीरनिधिं ममन्थुः सुरासुराः 'The gods and Asuras churned the milky ocean (for) ambrosia:' 15. गोविन्दो व्रजमवरुणद्धि गाः 'Govinda shuts up the cows (at) the cow-pens;' शोकं चित्तमवारुधत् 'He confined his grief (in) his heart.' वह, 'to bear,' is sometimes similarly used; कन्यां गृहमवहत् or गृहायावहत् 'He bore the damsel to the house.' In common with other transitive verbs, these verbs may govern a single accusative, when only one object is designated; मातरमुवाच वीरः 'The hero said to his mother.' Several of them may govern the object in other cases also, as will be subsequently noticed.

e. The causal modes of verbs signifying, 1. motion, 2. speaking or articulate sound, 3. or eating; 4. the causals of intransitive verbs, and 5. of ग्रह 'to take,' दृश 'to see,' and श्रु 'to hear,' govern a double accusative, when the object and the subject of the act are both expressed. 1. शत्रूनगमयत् स्वर्गं 'He caused the enemies to go to heaven:' 2. वेदानध्यापयद् द्विजं 'He caused the Brahman to read aloud the Vedas:' 3. आशयच्चामृतं देवान् 'He caused the gods to eat nectar:' 4. आसयत् सलिले पृथ्वीं यः स मे श्रीहरिर्गतिः 'That Hari is my refuge, who placed (caused to sit) the earth upon the waters;' प्रीतोऽहम् भोजयिष्यामि भवतीं भुवनं त्रयं 'If I am pleased, I will cause thee, lady, to enjoy the three worlds:' 5. बालमग्राहयद्विद्यां 'He made the boy take learning;' दर्शयाञ्चक्रिरे रामं सीतां 'They shewed (caused to see) Sítá to Ráma;' श्रावय पारिषदान् नाटकं 'Recite (cause to hear) the drama to the company.'

f. There are some exceptions to the preceding rule. The causals of अद and खाद, 'to eat,' require the instrumental case for the subject of the action; खादयति or खादयत्यन्नं बटुना गुरुः 'The Guru causes the rice to be eaten by the pupil.' So भक्ष, when it means 'eating;' गोपैरभक्षयदिश्भक्षं 'He caused the food they liked to be eaten by the cowherds:' but if it means destroying by the act of eating, it may be followed by a double accusative; भक्षयति बलीवर्दान् शस्यं 'He makes the oxen eat up the corn.' शब्द, 'to sound,' in the causal mode requires the subject to be put in the instrumental case; शब्दयति शब्दं देवदत्तेन 'He causes the sound to be uttered by Devadatta.' जल्प and some other verbs, signifying 'articulate sound,' are similarly combined. The causal of वह 'to bear,' when it implies 'driving,' governs a double accusative; वाहयति रथमश्वान् सूतः 'The charioteer makes the horses draw the car:' otherwise the subject is put in the instrumental case; स्वामी वाहयति भारं भृत्येन 'The master makes the load be borne by the hireling.'

g. The causal modes of कृ 'to make,' हृ 'to take,' वद 'to speak' with अभि prefixed, and of दृश 'to see' in the Átmanepada, may take either a second accusative or the instrumental case for the agent or subject of the action: कारयति कटं शिल्पिनं or शिल्पिना 'He causes the workman to make the mat,' or 'he causes it to be made by the workman:' so हारयति दौत्यं दूतं or दूतेन 'He causes the messenger to take the message,' &c.; अभिवादयते देवं भक्तं or भक्तेन 'He makes the devotee salute the deity,' &c.; दर्शयते कृष्णमर्जुनं or अर्जुनेन 'He makes Arjuna see Krishńa,' &c. The fact being, that when the causal is used in a passive sense, the subject or subordinate agent is specified in the instrumental; when it is used in an active sense, it is specified in the accusative case.

h. A second accusative may sometimes follow a verb, as a qualification of the first, being put absolutely or in apposition: मेदिनीं दानवपते देहि मे त्रिक्रमत्रयं 'Give me, O lord of the Dánavas, earth, three paces.'

i. The accusative case may follow various prepositions and indeclinable words or particles. Of the former class are अति, अधि when reiterated, अभि, अनु, उप, परि, and प्रति. अति देवान् हरिः 'Hari is beyond the gods;' अतिरामं 'Superior to Ráma' (अहं, 'I am,' understood); अध्यधिलोकं वर्त्तते विष्णुः 'Vishńu abides over and above the worlds;' नदीमनुवसिता सेना 'The army will halt at or along the river;' जपमनु प्रावर्षत् 'It rained after the prayer;' अनुपितरम् गच्छति पुत्रः 'The son goes after, or imitates, the father.' अनु and उप, indicating 'inferiority,' also govern the accusative: न भवाननुरामं चेत् 'If you are not inferior to Ráma;' उपशूरं न ते वृत्तं 'If thy conduct is not beneath a hero.' अनु, परि, and प्रति govern accusatives designating any particular object; as, गिरिमनु (परि or प्रति) विद्योतते विद्युत् 'The lightning flashes at or toward the mountain;' चिन्तयामास तत्कार्य्यं सुमहत् स्वां सुतां प्रति 'He considered that grave matter concerning his daughter:'—a part of any thing or person; लक्ष्मीर्हरिमनु (हरिं परि or प्रति) 'Lakshmí is part of Hari:'—and several and successive order; वृक्षमनु (परि or प्रति) सिञ्चति माली 'The gardener waters tree by tree;' परि स्त्रीं (अनु or प्रति स्त्रीं) जातमन्मथः 'In love with every (successive) woman.' The indeclinable words governing accusatives are अधोऽधः, उपर्य्युपरि, अन्तरा, अन्तरेण, अभितः, परितः, उभयतः, सर्व्वतः, समया, निकषा, धिक्, हा; as, अधोऽधः भूमिं पातालः 'Pátála is below the earth;' उपर्य्युपरि पृथिवीं द्यौः 'The sky is above the earth;' त्वामन्तरा कृष्णस्तिष्ठति 'Kṛishńa tarries away from thee;' खड्गं समुद्यम्य रावणः क्रूरविग्रहः वैदेहीमन्तरा 'Rávańa, of dreadful form, having raised up his sword (to cut) Vaidehí in two;' प्रियामन्तरेण न सुखं 'There is no happiness without a mistress;' अभितो (or परितो) राममद्रवन् राक्षसाः 'The Rákshasas ran upon or around Ráma;' उभयतः कृष्णं गोपाः 'The cow-herds (were) on both sides of Kṛishńa;' सर्व्वतः प्रासादं जाग्रति दण्डधारिणः 'All around the palace watch the staff-bearers;' समया ग्रामं निकषा पुरं गच्छति 'He goes near to the village,' 'near to the city;' धिक् कृष्णमभक्तं 'Fie on one not devoted to Kṛishńa;' हा देवशत्रुं 'Alas! (for) the enemy of the gods.' Several of these may be combined with other cases; as, उपर्य्युपरि सर्व्वेषामादित्य इव तेजसा 'Above and over all, like the sun in splendour;' उपशूरेषु वा 'or inferior to heroes.'

j. The neuter verbs शी 'to sleep,' स्था 'to stay' or 'be,' and आस 'to sit,' when compounded with अधि, govern the noun expressing the site of the action in the accusative: अधिशेते पर्यङ्कं कुमारी 'The maiden sleeps upon the couch;' अधितिष्ठत्यात्मानं केशवः 'Keśava presides in (or over) the soul;' अध्यास्ते वैकुण्ठं हरिः 'Hari abides in Vaikuṅṭha.'

k. विश, 'to enter into,' as a transitive verb, governs an accusative; गेहं प्रविशति 'He enters the house.' When preceded by अभि and नि, it may govern either the accusative or locative; as, अभिनिविशति सन्मार्गं 'He enters upon a good path;' अभिनिविशति पापे 'He enters upon (or falls into) wickedness.' When preceded by उप, and implying 'to sit,' it is followed by the locative only; आसनेऽस्मिन्नुपविशत 'Sit down on this seat.'

l. वस 'to dwell,' preceded by अधि, अनु, आ, or उप, may govern an accusative case; अधिवसति (अनुवसति, &c.) वनं रामः 'Ráma inhabits the wood;' शून्यमन्ववसद्वनं 'He inhabited a lonely wood;' पुरीमयोध्यामवात्सीत् 'He dwelt at the city Ayodhyá;' ग्राममुपवसति 'He inhabits the village:' but when उपवस means 'to fast,' the site is expressed in the locative only; उपवसति वने रामः 'Ráma fasts in the forest.'

287. Instrumental case (करणं or तृतीया). This case expresses the agent, the implement, or the means by which any thing is done, or any end is accomplished, whether active effort is implied or not: अजानता मया भ्राता घातितः 'By me, unknowing, my brother has been slain;' रामेण बाणेन हतः 'Killed by Ráma with an arrow;' पुण्येन दृष्टो हरिः 'Hari is seen by (or through) virtue;' अध्यापनेन वर्त्तते 'He subsists by teaching;' प्रकृत्या चारुः 'Beautiful by nature.' It also expresses the manner or degree in which any object is effected: सुखेन जीवति 'He lives with ease' (happily); दुःखेन याति 'He goes with difficulty;' प्रायेण याज्ञिकः 'For the most part (usually) a sacrificer.' It also denotes any mark or circumstance by which an object is characterised: जटाभिस्तापसः 'He is an ascetic, by his clotted hair;' जात्या ब्राह्मणः 'a Brahman by caste;' गोत्रेण गार्ग्यः 'a descendant of Garga by family.'

a. The instrumental case may be employed with words signifying 'object' or 'result:' उद्यमेन कोऽर्थः 'What is the object of effort?' परिदेवनेन किं फलं 'What is the fruit of lamenting?'

b. Words implying 'bodily deformity' require the instrumental case for the organ or member in which the defect occurs: चक्षुषा काणः 'blind by an eye;' पादेन खञ्जः 'lame by a foot.'

c. Prepositions signifying 'with,' 'along with,' are connected in sentences with the instrumental case: आस्स्व साकं मया 'Stay along with me;' हीयते हि मतिस्तात हीनैः सह समागमात् 'The mind is depraved, O sire, from association with the base.' Verbs signifying 'association' also govern the object in the same case: त्वया साधो समागम्य 'Having met, O pious man, with thee.'

d. The particle अलम्, implying 'enough of,' governs the instrumental case: अलमतिविस्तरेण 'Enough of prolixity.'

e. The instrumental case may be used optionally with the accusative in various instances; as after the verb दिव 'to play,' अक्षान् or अक्षैर्दीव्यति द्यूतकारः 'The gambler plays dice,' or 'with dice:' also after ज्ञा 'to know,' preceded by सम्; as, तव पितरं (or पित्रा) संजानीष्व 'Recognise thy father.' When it signifies 'calling to mind' or 'thinking upon,' it governs the accusative only: संजानीष्व विष्णुं 'Meditate on Vishńu.' When 'space' or 'time' are spoken of, in connexion with an act or event completed, the instrumental case is employed: अह्ना or क्रोशेन गत्वा ग्रहमागच्छत् 'Having gone for a day, or for a Kos, he arrived at home.' But if the act or event is incomplete, the accusative: मासम् प्रस्थितो न त्वायातः 'He has been travelling (for) a month, but is not arrived.'

f. Words signifying 'weight,' 'measure,' or 'number,' when succession or repetition is also implied, are put after verbs either in the instrumental or accusative case: शतेन शतेन (or शतं शतं) वत्सान् पाययति पयः 'He gives milk to the calves to drink, by a hundred at a time;' द्विद्रोणेन or द्विद्रोणं क्रीणाति धान्यं 'He buys corn by two Drońa (measures) at once.'

288. Dative case (सम्प्रदानं or चतुर्थी). This case expresses

the object or recipient of a gift, either literal or figurative: ब्राह्मणेभ्यो निष्कान् ददौ 'He gave Nishkas (gold coins) to the Brahmans;' पशुं शिवाय ददाति 'He offers an animal to S'iva;' न शूद्राय मतिं दद्यात् 'Let him not give understanding to a S'údra:' and it may be used after verbs which imply 'presenting' or 'offering,' although not bearing such import originally; as, रामाय पूजां चक्रे महामुनिः 'The great sage made (or offered) worship to Ráma.'

a. Although, however, the fourth or dative case most appropriately follows verbs that imply 'giving,' of some kind or other, yet the genitive case is frequently used with a similar purport, and sometimes also the locative: राष्ट्रं शिवीनां वृद्धं वै ददानि तव खेचर 'Spirit of air, I may give thee the prosperous kingdom of the S'ivis;' दत्त्वाऽतिथिभ्यो देवेभ्यः पितृभ्यः स्वजनस्य च 'Having given (food) to guests, gods, ancestors, and his own household;' यस्त्वं रामे पृथिवीं दातुमिच्छसि 'Thou who wishest to give the earth to Ráma.' When the genitive case is thus used, however, an ellipse is implied, to be filled up by a noun understood in the dative case: तव हस्तेभ्यः 'to the hands of thee;' स्वजनस्य व्यक्तिभ्यः 'to the persons of his own family.'

b. Nouns expressing 'cause' or 'purpose,' that for or on account of which a thing is done, or that for which a thing is fit or suitable, follow verbs in the dative case: मुक्तये हरिं भजति साधुः 'The pious man worships Hari for the sake of liberation;' भक्तिर्ज्ञानाय कल्पते 'Devotion is practised for the sake of holy knowledge;' वाताय कपिला विद्युत् 'The pale lightning is on account of (it is a sign of) a gale;' प्रभवन्त्युग्रकर्माणः क्षयाय जगतोऽहिताः 'The unfriendly performers of cruel acts are born for the destruction of the world;' ब्राह्मणाय हितो धर्मः 'Virtue is fit for a Brahman.'

c. Connected with this application of the dative case, is its optional substitution for the infinitive after a verb: फलेभ्यो गच्छति 'He goes for fruit,' for फलान्याहर्तुं गच्छति 'He goes to bring fruit;' यागायाज्ञापयति 'He gives orders for a sacrifice,' for यष्टुमाज्ञापयति 'He gives orders to sacrifice.'

d. Intransitive verbs signifying 'to be agreeable' or 'acceptable' govern the dative case: हरये रोचते भक्तिः 'Devotion is acceptable to Hari;' बालाय स्वदते मोदकः 'The sweetmeat is pleasant to the boy.'

e. The verbs श्लाघ 'to praise,' ह्नु 'to conceal, स्था 'to stay,' शप 'to curse,' may be connected with the object of the act in the dative case, when some particular feeling is implied by it: गोपी स्मरात् कृष्णाय श्लाघते ह्नुते तिष्ठते शपते 'The Gopí praises, hides from, stays with, vows by Kṛishṅa, through love.' When no such feeling is implied, such of them as are transitive govern the accusative: राजानं श्लाघते मन्त्री 'The minister flatters the king.'

f. With a similar kind of relation, verbs signifying 'desire,' 'anger,' 'wrong,' 'jealousy,' or 'detraction,' govern the object in the dative case: तस्मै स्पृहयमाणोऽसौ 'He being filled with desire for her;' सीतायै नाक्रुध्यन्नाप्यसूयत 'He was not angry with Sítá, nor did he revile her;' अशप्त निह्नुवानसौ तस्मै 'He vowed to her, dissembling with her.' When the feeling is not excited by the object, they govern the accusative: भार्य्यामीर्ष्यति पतिः 'The husband is jealous as to his wife,' that is, he cannot endure that others should look at her; तन्नद्रुह्येत् कदाचन 'Let (the pupil) never offend him.' क्रुध and द्रुह preceded by prepositions govern the accusative: किं मां संक्रुध्यसि 'Why art thou angry with me?' मा परस्वमभिद्रोग्धाः 'Commit not violence against another's property.'

g. धृ, 'to hold,' in the causal mode, having the sense of 'owing,' literally or figuratively, governs the person to whom the debt or obligation is due in the dative case: देवदत्ताय शतं धारयति 'He owes a hundred to Devadatta;' भक्ताय मोक्षं धारयति हरिः 'Hari owes liberation to his worshippers.'

h. श्रु preceded by आ or प्रति, signifying 'to promise,' governs the person or thing to which the promise is addressed in the dative: विप्राय गामाशृणोति or प्रतिशृणोति राजा 'The Rájá promises a cow to the Brahman;' शृण्वद्भ्यः प्रति शृण्वन्ति मध्यमाः 'Common persons promise assent to those who counsel them.'

i. गॄ, 'to sound,' preceded by अनु or प्रति, implying 'to conform to' or 'comply with,' governs the dative case: होत्रे प्रतिगृणाति or अनुगृणात्यध्वर्युः 'The Adhwaryu (or reciter of the prayers of the Yajur-veda) acts in conformity to the Hotri (or Brahman of the Rig-veda);' गृणद्भ्यो ऽनुगृणन्त्यन्ये न मद्विधाः 'Others, such as I am, do not conform to those who flatter us.'

j. राध 'to accomplish,' and ईक्ष 'to see,' when signifying 'to think or consider about,' govern the object in the dative: कृष्णायराध्यति or कृष्णायेक्षते गर्गः 'Garga considers concerning or about Kṛishṇa.'

k. Forms of reverential address or religious invocation, such as नमस्, स्वस्ति, स्वाहा, स्वधा, &c. are followed by nouns in the dative case: नमः शिवाय 'Salutation to Śiva;' महाराजाय स्वस्ति 'Health to the king;' स्वाहा देवेभ्यः 'Salutation to the gods;' स्वधा पितृभ्यः 'Salutation to the manes.' नमस् compounded with कृ governs either the accusative or dative: नमस्कुर्मो देवेभ्यः or नमस्करोति देवान् 'We make, or he makes, salutation to the gods.'

l. अलम्, when signifying 'to be sufficient for' or 'equal to,' governs the dative: नालं सुखाय सुहृदो नालं दुःखाय शत्रवः 'Friends are not (alone) sufficient for happiness, nor enemies for misery;' अलं मल्लो मल्लाय 'One wrestler is a match for the other;' दैत्येभ्यो ऽलं विष्णुः 'Vishṇu is equal to, or a match for, the Daityas.' Compounded with a transitive verb, it governs the accusative: पापं नालंकर्तुं समर्थो ऽस्ति 'He is not able to be a match for, or overcome, sin.'

m. The prohibitive मा may be used with the dative case, with the verb understood: मा चापलाय 'Be not for unsteadiness,' i. e. do not act unsteadily.

n. Verbs of motion, as noticed above (rule 286, *b*), are most usually followed by the noun in the accusative case; but they may also be associated with the dative: ग्रामाय गच्छति 'He goes to the village.'

o. मन, 'to mind' or 'think,' when of the fourth conjugation, and implying 'disrespect,' governs a subsidiary noun, signifying 'degree' or 'comparison,' in either the dative or accusative case: न त्वां मन्ये तृणाय or तृणं 'I value thee not a straw.' मन of the eighth conjugation is followed by the accusative only: न त्वां मन्ये तृणं. If the comparison be intimated by the terms नौः 'a boat,' काकः 'a crow,' अन्नं 'food,' शुकः 'a parrot,' or शृगालः 'a jackal,' the accusative only is employed: न त्वां नावं मन्ये 'I hold thee not of the value of a boat,' &c. If 'disrespect' be not intended, the accusative only follows the verb: मन्ये काष्ठमुलूखलं 'I suppose the mortar to be wood.'

p. When a term of number or quantity is used to signify 'rate of wages' or 'hire,' it takes either the dative or instrumental case: शताय or शतेन भृत्यान् परिक्रीणाति 'He hires servants by or for a hundred.'

q. दाण्, 'to give,' preceded by सम्, and implying 'cohabitation,' governs the dative when the act is legal; the instrumental when criminal: भार्यायै संयच्छते दास्या संयच्छते पतिः 'The husband cohabits with his wife,' 'with his bondswoman.'

289. Ablative case (अपादानं or पञ्चमी). This case denotes 'a taking away,' 'a separating of or from,' 'removal' or 'departure' of any kind; as, ग्रामादायाति 'He comes from the village;' उत्ततार गङ्गायाः सलिलादाकुलेन्द्रियः 'He returned from the water of the Ganges afflicted;' धावतोऽश्वात् पतति 'He falls from a galloping horse.' It also implies metaphorical disjunction; as, पापाद्विरमति 'He refrains from sin;' धर्मात्प्रमाद्यति 'He strays from virtue.'

a. The ablative case has also an inceptive signification, implying the cause or motive of any act or feeling, or the origin from which any thing proceeds, literally or figuratively: चोराद्बिभेति स्त्री 'The woman is afraid of (or from) the thief;' चोरेभ्यस्त्रायते राजा 'The king protects from thieves;' भीतो रणे श्वेतवाहादिति मां मंस्यते जनः 'People will think of me thus, he is afraid of Arjuna in battle;' ब्रह्मणः प्रजाः प्रजायन्ते 'Progeny are born from Brahmá;' अर्थेभ्यः क्रिया सर्वाः प्रवर्तन्ते पर्वतेभ्य इवापगाः 'Religious acts proceed from wealth, like rivers from mountains.'

b. Verbs signifying, 1. hinderance, 2. disappearance or concealment, 3. being ashamed of, 4. acquiring knowledge from, 5. being averse to, govern nouns in the ablative case. 1. यवेभ्यो गावो वारयति गोपालः 'The cowherd keeps off the cows from the barley:' 2. मातुर्निलीयते कृष्णः 'Kṛishṅa hides from his mother: 3. श्वशुराज्जिह्रेति 'He is ashamed of his father-in-law:' 4. उपाध्यायादधीते शिष्यः 'The pupil (reads with or) acquires learning from the teacher:' 5. अध्ययनात् पराजयते शिष्यः 'The pupil is averse from (or tired of) reading;' सा पराजयमाना दशाननात् 'She (Sítá) averse to (or abhorring of) Rávaṅa.' When जि with परा prefixed is used transitively, it of course requires the accusative: शत्रून् पराजयते वीरः 'The hero overcomes the enemies.'

c. The ablative is used to express the site from which any act is performed: प्रासादादीक्षते 'He looks from the palace;' आसनादुदतिष्ठत् 'He rose from his seat.' Also a place or period from which distance or time is computed: वनात् पुरं योजनं 'From the wood the city is a Yojana distant;' कार्त्तिक्या अग्रहायणीमासे 'From Kártik into the month Agraháyaṅa.'

d. The ablative is also sometimes used to express the means by which any end is accomplished: कृतं पापं कल्याणेन हन्यते । निवृत्त्या तीर्थगमनाच्छ्रुतिस्मृतिजपेन च ॥ 'Committed sin is destroyed by good acts, by refraining from it, by (from) visiting holy places, and by repeating texts of the Vedas and the institutes:' द्रोहाद्देवैरवाप्तानि दिवि स्थानानि सर्व्वशः 'Their places in heaven have been obtained by the gods through violence.'

e. The words अन्य, इतर, आरात्, ऋते, प्रभृति, वहिर्, terms significant of relative place or time, and compounds ending in words derived from अञ्च 'to go,' are connected with nouns in the ablative case: अन्यो हरेः 'other than Hari;' इतरो कृष्णात् 'different from Kṛishṅa;' आराद्वनात् 'near to the wood;' ऋते पुरुषात् 'without the man;' ततः तदा or तस्मात् प्रभृति 'thenceforth,' 'thereafter;' वर्षात् प्रभृति 'from after a year;' नगराद्वहिः 'out from the city;' ग्रामात् पूर्व्वो वृक्षः 'a tree east from the village;' चैत्रात् पूर्व्वः फाल्गुनः 'The month Phalguna is before Chaitra;' पुरं प्राग्वनात् 'a city east of the wood;' ग्रामात् प्रत्यग्गिरिः 'a mountain west from the village.' When पूर्व्व and similar terms denote 'a part' of any thing, they require the genitive case: पूर्वः कायस्य 'the fore part of the body;' अह्नः पश्चिमो भागः 'the latter part of the day.'

f. The preposition आङ् requires the ablative case in the sense of 'limitation,' either of place, time, events, or things: आसमुद्रात् 'as far as to the ocean;' आयुगान्तात् 'to the end of the age;' आमुक्तेः संसारः 'Repeated birth occurs until final liberation;' आसकलाद् ब्रह्म 'Brahma extends unto (or comprehends) all things;' भैक्ष्यमेवाचरिष्यामः शरीरस्याविमोक्षणात् 'We will practise mendicity even until liberation from the body.'

g. अप and परि implying 'separation,' and प्रति signifying 'substitution' or 'equivalent,' require the ablative case: अप लोकेभ्यो लङ्कायां वसतिः 'Dwelling in Lanká, away or apart from the world;' परित्रिगर्तेभ्यो वृष्टो देवः 'The god (Indra) sent rain away from Trigartta;' प्रद्युम्नः कृष्णात् प्रति 'Pradyumna is the substitute or representative of Krishńa;' तिलेभ्यः प्रति यच्छति माषान् 'He gives Másha (pulse) in place of, or return for, sesamum.'

h. Words implying 'bound on account of a debt' may be connected with the ablative, when the reason, not the debt, is intended: शताद्बद्धं द्रव्यं 'Property pledged on account of a hundred;' ऋणाद्बद्ध इव 'Like one bound on account of debt:' but शतेनबद्धः 'Bound by a debt, held in bond, or indebted, by a hundred.' Either the instrumental or ablative case may be used, when the state or circumstance of the person is the result of some property, not expressed by a feminine noun: जाड्येन or जाड्याद्बद्धः 'Bound by or from stupidity;' वनं मौर्ख्यात् प्रतिष्ठसे 'Thou goest to the wood through folly.'

i. The words स्तोक, अल्प, कृच्छ्र, कतिपय, may be used after a verb, either in the instrumental or ablative case, to imply 'degree' or 'manner;' as, स्तोकेन or स्तोकान्मुक्ता 'left or liberated a little;' कृच्छ्रेण or कृच्छ्रात् कृतः 'made with difficulty;' कृच्छ्रात् समासाद्य 'having come with difficulty;' कतिपयेन or कतिपयात्प्राप्तः 'obtained in some degree.' When used with a substantive, they agree with it in case; as, स्तोकेन विषेण हतः 'killed by a little poison.' When employed adverbially, and not signifying 'instrumentality,' they are put in the accusative neuter; as, स्तोकं गच्छति अल्पं करोति 'he goes or does a little,' 'a short way,' or 'for a short time,' or 'a small quantity.'

j. The particles पृथक्, नाना, and विना, govern either the accusative, instrumental, or ablative case: पृथग्रामं रामेण or रामात् 'separate from, or without, Ráma;' विना or नाना देवं देवेन or देवात् 'without a deity;' विना वधं न कुर्वन्ति तापसाः प्राणयापनं 'Penitents do not practise emission of breath without destruction of life;' सुखं दुःखैर्विना न लभ्यते 'Pleasure is not obtained without pain;' पृथक् छलेन कृतं 'done without deceit;' पृथङ्नभस्वतः 'except the wind.'

290. Genitive case (शेषः or सम्बन्धः or षष्ठी). This case is employed when one noun follows another, expressed or understood, having a different meaning, and to which the latter intimates some relation; as, राज्ञः पुरुषः 'the man of the king;' पुत्रस्य माता 'the mother of the boy;' धनिनो धनं 'the wealth of the rich man;' द्रव्यस्य गुणः 'the quality of the thing.' The prior noun may be understood: अभयं सत्त्वसंशुद्धिः । भवन्ति सम्पदं दैवीमभिजातस्य ॥ 'Fearlessness, purity of nature, &c., are of a man born to a heavenly condition:' they are the qualities, गुणाः understood.

a. Verbal derivatives signifying 'the agent' are followed by the object in the genitive case; as, जगतः स्रष्टा 'the creator of the world;' सतां पालकः 'the protector of the good;' नरकस्य जिष्णुः 'the victor of (over) hell.' Those formed with उ from desiderative verbs govern the accusative; राजा त्वां दिदृक्षुः 'The king is desirous of seeing thee.' So do those with उक; as, दैत्यान् घातुको हरिः 'Hari is the destroyer of the demons:' but not when the root is कम्; कान्तायाः कामुकः 'the lover of the beloved.'

b. Similar derivatives, implying 'the act,' may be followed by the agent or the object of the act in the genitive: पुरुषस्य क्रिया 'the act of a man;' ब्राह्मणानां धर्म्मः 'the duty of Brahmans;' पयसः पानं 'the drinking of milk;' गवां दोहः 'the milking of kine.' The subject also may follow the property in the genitive; as, अश्वस्य वेगः 'the speed of a horse;' मधुनः स्वाद्यं 'the sweetness of honey.' When the act is followed by both the agent and the object, each may be put in the genitive case; जगतः सृष्टिर्ब्रह्मणः 'the creation of the world of (by) Brahmá:' or the agent or instrument may take the instrumental case; जगतः सृष्टिर्ब्रह्मणा. A term expressing 'aggregation' is followed by the objects collected in the genitive: राज्ञां सभा 'an assemblage of princes;' पशूनां समाहारः 'a flock of cattle;' धूमज्योतिः सलिलमरुतां सन्निपातः 'a collection of wind, water, light, and smoke.'

c. Verbs of 'speaking to,' 'communicating or representing to,' 'conveying to, as speech and the like,' are commonly followed by the person spoken to in the genitive case: तन्मे वद 'Tell me that;' कथयिष्यामि ते 'I will tell thee;' आचक्ष्व मे महाबाहो सर्वज्ञो ह्यसि मे मतः 'Tell me, mighty armed, for thou art thought of me to be all-wise;' निवेदयामास चित्रसेनाय स न्यवेदयच्च शक्रस्य 'He represented to Chitrasena, and he to (of) Indra;' प्रियायाः सन्देशं मे हर 'Bear news of me to my beloved.' Instances of their occurrence with similar terms in the accusative and dative cases have already been given. नाथ, 'to ask' for any thing, governs the object in the genitive: धृत्या नाथस्व 'Ask for firmness;' धनस्य नाथते 'He asks for wealth.' But when the person is designated, it governs an accusative: नाथन्ति के नाम न लोकनाथं 'Who do not implore the lord of the world?' प्रच्छ, 'to ask,' may govern the person in the genitive, the thing in the accusative: अपृच्छन् कस्यचिन्मार्गं 'not asking the way from any one.' It also governs a double accusative, the person being one: कुशलं पृच्छति त्वां 'He asks thee after thy health.'

d. The verb श्रु, 'to hear,' governs the genitive case of the person speaking; as, पृच्छन्नपि मे शृणु 'Asking, hear of me;' मार्गं तावच्छृणु कथयतः (मे) 'Hear from me, describing it, the road:' but this is considered as an elliptical form of expression, the word वचनं, or some synonyme of words or speech, being understood. The verb governs also the ablative: श्रोष्यत्यस्मात् परमवहिता 'She will hear very attentive from me.'

e. भू, 'to be,' preceded by प्र, signifying 'to have power or authority over,' may govern the object in the genitive case: प्रभवति निजस्य कन्याजनस्य महाराजः 'The prince has power over his own daughter;' प्रजानां प्रभवति राजा 'The king is lord over the people.' Verbs expressing 'to be stronger than,' or 'to prevail over,' govern the genitive: नाप्रोषीदस्य कश्चन 'No one prevailed over him.' Verbs signifying 'to be angry with,' 'to do violence or injury to,' or 'to desire,' may govern the genitive: न कुप्ये तव धर्म्मिष्ठ न त्वं दूषयसे मम 'I am not angry with thee; thou hast done no wrong to me:' यदाऽसौ सर्व्वभूतानां न द्रुह्यति न काङ्क्षति। कर्म्मणा मनसा वाचा ब्रह्म सम्पद्यते तदा॥ 'When a man neither does wrong to, nor wishes for, all beings, either in act, thought, or speech, he obtains Brahma' (final felicity). These latter verbs may also govern other cases (rule 288, *f.*)

f. ज्ञा 'to know,' when signifying something else than true knowledge, and when knowledge is not a property of the thing known, governs the genitive case: सर्प्पिषो जानीते 'He knows ghee.' दय 'to have pity on,' ईश 'to be lord of,' and कृ 'to make,' implying some particular effort, and verbs signifying 'to remember,' also govern the genitive: दीनानां दयस्व 'Have pity on the wretched;' धनानामीशते यक्षाः 'The Yakshas rule over riches;' एधोदकस्योपस्कुरुते 'He prepares the fuel and water for an oblation;' उपास्कृषाताम् राजेन्द्रावागमस्येह 'The two princes have made preparations for coming hither;' मातुः स्मरति 'He remembers his mother;' कश्चिद्दुःखे वर्त्तमानः सुखस्य स्मर्त्तुमिच्छति 'Who, being in pain, wishes to remember pleasure?' अध्येति तव लक्ष्मणः 'Lakshmaṇa thinks of thee.' In these cases, however, an ellipse is supposed, a prior substantive in the accusative case being understood: सर्प्पिषो गुणान् जानीते 'He understands (the properties of) ghee;' दीनानामवस्थां दयस्व 'Pity the condition of the wretched,' &c. Otherwise these verbs govern the accusative:' सर्प्पिषं जानीते, दीनान् दयते, लोकानीष्टे, मातरं स्मरति.

g. दृश, 'to see,' in the causal may govern the person in the genitive instead of the accusative (r. 286, *g*): स भ्रातुर्दर्शयामास तौ करौ 'He shewed of (to) his brother those two hands.'

h. Verbs implying 'sickness,' except from fever, govern the person in the genitive: पुरुषस्य रुजयत्यतिसारः 'Dysentery affects the man:' but तं रुजयतिज्वरः 'Fever affects him.'

i. जस 'to hurt,' literally or figuratively, हन 'to kill,' preceded by नि or प्र, or both, नाट and क्राथ 'to hurt,' and पिष 'to pound,' when it implies 'hurting,' govern the object in the genitive case: चोरस्योज्जासयति राजा 'The king punishes the thief;' मन्योरुज्जासयात्मनः 'Remove or destroy thy sorrow;' राक्षसानां प्रणिहनिष्यति (प्रहणिष्यति or निहनिष्यति) रामः 'Ráma will destroy the Rákshasas;' वृषलस्योन्नाटयति or क्राथयति 'He destroys the outcaste;' साहसिकस्य पिनष्टि गजः 'The elephant grinds the felon.' If injury is not meant, पिष governs the accusative: धानाः पिनष्टि 'He grinds the corn.' Other verbs signifying 'to injure' usually govern the object in the accusative: पथिकं हिनस्ति व्याघ्रः 'The tiger destroys the traveller.'

j. The compound verb व्यवहृ 'to transact business,' and पण 'to deal,' or 'engage in any office,' govern the word signifying the terms of the transaction in the genitive: शतस्य व्यवहरति or पणते 'He sells or buys or deals for, or stakes, a hundred;' प्राणानामपणिष्टासौ रावणस्त्वामिहानयन् 'Rávańa, bringing thee hither, has trafficked for (or staked) his life.' So दिव 'to play,' meaning 'to deal,' or 'pledge:' अदेवीद्बन्धुभोगानां 'He has played for his kindred and enjoyments.' But when दिव is preceded by a preposition, it may govern either the accusative or the genitive; प्रादेवीदात्मसम्पदम् or सम्पदः 'He has staked, or has trafficked for, his own fortune.'

k. Participles, whether past or future, having a present application, govern the object in the genitive case: राज्ञः सम्मतो or पूजितो विप्रः 'The Brahman is esteemed or reverenced of the king;' यो धर्म्मः स सतां मतः 'that which is thought virtue of (by) the good;' अभिज्ञानं ददौ रामस्य सम्मतं 'He gave the signet, recognised or cherished of Ráma;' तस्य लोकावुभौ जितौ 'Both worlds are conquered of or by him;' वन्द्यैः पुंसां रघुपतिपदैः '(marked) by the feet of the chief of Ráma's race, praised of (by) men.' Participles of the neuter gender, signifying 'site' or 'circumstance,' have a similar government: रामस्य शयितं भुक्तं जल्पितं हसितं स्थितं प्रक्रान्तञ्च मुहुः पृष्ट्वा हनुमन्तं व्यसर्ज्जयत् 'Sítá having repeatedly inquired after the sleeping, eating, talking, laughing, staying, going of Ráma, dismissed Hanumán.' (The participles are in fact used as nouns, and are consequently followed by the noun to which they relate in the genitive.)

l. The word हेतु, 'cause,' 'motive,' or 'object,' follows a verb in the genitive case: अन्नस्य हेतोरनुगच्छति 'He follows for the sake of food;' हेतोर्बोधस्य मैथिल्याः प्रास्तावीद्रामसंकथां 'He repeated the praise of Ráma, for the purpose of apprising Maithilí.' It is also used interrogatively and responsively in this and in other cases, with a pronoun; as, कस्य हेतोः, केन हेतुना, 'For what reason?' 'why?' 'wherefore?' तस्य हेतोः, तेन हेतुना, तस्माद्धेतोः, 'For this or that reason,' 'thus,' 'therefore.' Its synonymes may be similarly used; as, कस्य निमित्तस्य, कस्य प्रयोजनस्य, &c.: but they are more usually employed adverbially in the accusative neuter; as, किं निमित्तं, किं प्रयोजनं, and the like.

m. Indeclinable words formed with the affix कृत्वसु govern the genitive case: शतकृत्वस्त्वैकस्याः स्मरत्यह्नो रघूत्तमः 'The best of the race of Raghu thinks of thee alone a hundred times of a day.' Numerals in a similar sense of repetition have a similar government: द्विरह्नोऽधीते 'He reads twice a day.'

n. Indeclinable words, or words so used, being terms of relative site, may govern the genitive (as well as the ablative) case: तस्य स्थित्वा कथमपि पुरः 'Having stood in some manner before (it) the cloud;' त्वमसि पुरो मे 'Thou art before or in front of me;' सखीनां पुरस्तात् 'before your friends;' ग्रामस्य पुरतः 'in front, or on the east, of the village;' वृक्षस्योपरि or उपरिष्टात् 'above the tree.' When such words are formed with एन, they may govern the accusative: ग्रामं or ग्रामस्य दक्षिणेन 'south of the village.'

o. Words implying 'propinquity' or 'distance' may govern a genitive case: प्रत्यासन्नो माधवीमण्डपस्य 'near to the Mádhaví bower;' सा गता तस्य सकाशम् 'she having gone near him;' दमयन्त्यास्तदन्तिके निपेतुस्ते 'They alighted near to Damayantí;'

नगरस्य दूरं गतः 'He went far from the city.' They also govern the accusative: कदाचिद्रामस्तु चरन्नाश्रमनिकात् 'Once Ráma rambling about from the neighbourhood of the hermitage.'

p. Words implying 'likeness' or 'equality' may govern either the genitive or instrumental case: यस्य नास्ति समो वीर्ये पृथिव्यामपि कश्चन 'The equal of whom in valour is no one upon earth;' कोऽन्योऽस्ति सदृशो मम 'Who else is like me?' or न त्वया सदृशः कश्चित् त्रिषु लोकेषु विद्यते 'The like to thee is not known in the three worlds;' धर्म्मेण हीना पशुभिः समानाः 'Devoid of virtue, (men) are like beasts.' The substantives तुला 'equality,' उपमा 'resemblance,' are followed by the genitive only: स कृष्णस्य तुलां or उपमां न प्राप्तः 'He has not the equality or similitude of Kṛishṅa.'

q. Neuter or indeclinable nouns importing 'benediction' are followed by the object in either the dative or genitive case: आयुष्यं देवदत्तस्य or देवदत्ताय 'Long life (be) of or to Devadatta.'

r. The genitive case is used absolutely with a participle: गच्छतस्तस्य 'as he was going;' मिषतां नः 'as we were looking on;' वैदर्भ्याः प्रेक्षमाणायाः 'whilst Vaidharbhí was beholding.' It is also used with the auxiliary verb अस in the sense of 'possession:' अस्ति मे 'there is of me,' i. e. I have; अस्य जनस्य किञ्चिदस्ति प्रभुत्वं 'There is of this person some power,' i. e. I have some power.

s. The term कृते governs a genitive case: अल्पकालस्य राज्यस्य कृते 'for the sake of a brief dominion.'

291. Locative case (अधिकरणं). This case expresses the site or receptacle of any object, whether substantial or ideal, that, in or upon or over which, any other thing is situated, any act performed, any property exhibited, or any notion comprehended, &c. भूमौ तिष्ठति नरः 'The man stands on the ground;' वने चरति सिंहः 'The lion roams in the forest;' कटे आस्ते ब्राह्मणः 'The Brahman sits on a mat;' स्थाल्यामन्नं पचति 'He boils the rice in a pot;' कर्णे कथयति 'He speaks or whispers in the ear;' भीतो रणे 'timid in war;' विपदि धैर्यं 'fortitude in

adversity;' हंसे शुक्लता 'whiteness in the swan;' आत्मन्यात्मानं स पश्यति 'He beholds spirit in himself.'

a. This case is sometimes used to express the thing or purpose for which any act is performed, when it is essentially connected with some other thing, the object of the act: चर्मणि द्वीपिनं हन्ति दन्तयोर्हन्ति हस्तिनं । केशेषु चमरीं हन्ति सीम्नि पुष्कलको हतः ॥ 'He kills the tiger for its skin; the elephant for its two tusks. He kills the Yak for the long hair: the musk-deer is slain for its musk.' If the connexion is not intimate, that for or on account of which the act is done requires the dative case (288, *b*). The locative is also used when the object is of a more general nature: यथासृष्टोऽसि धात्रा कर्मसु तत्कुरु 'As thou art made by the Creator for acts, perform them.'

b. The locative case is usually required in connexion with prepositions signifying 'being over' or 'upon' in any manner: उपपरार्द्धे हरेर्गुणाः 'The virtues of Hari are above infinite number;' अधि भुवि रामः 'Ráma is over the world:' but both these may signify 'inferiority' also; as, उप शूरेषु 'inferior to heroes;' अधि रामे भूः 'The earth is under Ráma.' When अधि is compounded with कृ, and the verb implies 'subjection,' it governs the accusative case: यदि मामधिकरिष्यति कर्मणि विनियोक्ष्यते 'If he will acknowledge me superior (lit. If he will make me over him), he shall be appointed to the work.' In the sense of 'superiority' the ablative case may be also used: लोके or लोकादधिको हरिः 'Vishńu is greater than the world.'

c. The words साधु and निपुण are followed by the object in the locative case, unless the prepositions अनु, परि, or प्रति intervene: मातरि साधुः 'pious to his mother;' पितरि निपुणः 'dutiful to his father:' but मातरं प्रति साधुः पितरमनु निपुणः.

d. The locative case is sometimes used to signify that from which any result may be expected, in the like manner as the ablative; as, विनाशे (or विनाशात्) धृतराष्ट्राणां किं फलं लभ्यते 'In (or from) the destruction of the sons of Dhṛitaráshṭra what advantage is obtained?'

e. A frequent use of the locative case is its employment as the ablative case absolute, in connexion with a participle in the same case: मयि गते 'I being gone;' तस्मिन्सति 'that being so;' प्रत्यासन्ने नभसि 'The month S'rávańa being at hand;' काले शुभे प्राप्ते 'A lucky time being arrived.' More than one substantive may be thus connected with the participle, when the latter will agree in number and person with the substantive nearest to it: अभिमन्यौ हते बाले द्रौपद्यास्तनयेषु च 'The boy Abhimanyu being slain, and the sons of Draupadí:' (हतेषु being understood). As mentioned above, the genitive is similarly employed;' as, रुदतः पुत्रस्य or रुदति पुत्रे प्राव्राजीत् '(Though) his son was weeping, he went forth (to lead a life of mendicity).'

f. Words signifying 'proximity' or 'distance' may be used adverbially in the locative case: तस्याः समीपे गत्वा 'having gone near her' (in her vicinity); दूरे ग्रामस्य 'at a distance from the village.' These and similar words may be used in like manner in other cases; as, ग्रामस्य दूरं दूरात् &c. मध्य takes only the locative case: भैमी सखीमध्ये राजते स्म 'Bhaimí was resplendent amongst (in the midst of) her companions.'

g. The names of asterisms, employed to signify the period of their being above the horizon, may follow a verb either in the locative or instrumental case: मूले (or मूलेन) आवाहयेद्देवीं श्रवणे (or श्रवणेन) विसर्जयेत् 'Let a man invoke Deví at the time (or rising) of the lunar constellation Múla, and dismiss her at that of S'ravańa.' If the asterism itself is intended as the site or receptacle of a planet, the locative alone, of course, is used: पुष्ये चन्द्रः 'The moon is in Pushya.'

h. The locative case is used to designate any given period: तस्मिन् काले 'at that time;' अस्य वाक्यस्य निधने 'upon the close of this speech;' साभ्रेऽह्नीव स्थलकमलिनी न प्रबुद्धां न सुप्तां 'like the Sthala-padma flower on a cloudy day, neither awake nor asleep.' It is also optionally used with the ablative to denote any intervening term, either of time or space: अद्य भुक्त्वाऽयं द्व्यहे (or द्व्यहाद्) भोक्ता 'Having eaten to-day, he will eat in or after two days;' इहस्थोऽयं क्रोशे (or क्रोशात्) लक्ष्यं विध्यति 'Standing here, he pierces the mark at (or from) a Kos.'

i. The words प्रसित and उत्सुक govern either the instrumental or locative case: प्रसितो हरिणा or हरौ 'attached to Hari;' पत्या प्रस्थितेन or पत्यौ प्रस्थिते योषिदुत्सुका 'The wife is anxious for her absent husband.'

j. The words आयुक्त and कुशल govern either the genitive or the locative case, when not used literally: आयुक्तो हरिपूजनस्य or पूजने 'intent upon worshipping Hari:' so कुशलः पूजने or पूजनस्य 'happy in worshipping.' If literally employed, they govern the locative only: आयुक्तो वृषभः शकटे 'the bullock harnessed to the cart;' कर्म्मणि कुशलः 'skilful in work.'

k. A noun following either of the words स्वामी, ईश्वरः, अधिपतिः, दायादः, साक्षी, प्रतिभूः, or प्रसूतः, is put in either the genitive or locative case: गवां or गोषु स्वामी 'the owner of kine;' पृथिव्याः or पृथिव्यामीश्वरः 'lord in or of the world;' ग्रामेषु or ग्रामाणामधिपतिः 'chief in or over the villages;' पित्र्यंशस्य or पित्र्यंशे दायादः 'heir of the paternal portion;' व्यवहारे or व्यवहारस्य साक्षी 'witness in or of a suit;' दर्शनस्य or दर्शने प्रतिभूः 'a surety in or of (for) appearance;' गोषु or गवां प्रसूतो गोपः 'the cowherd born amongst or for cattle,' i. e. to tend them.

292. Vocative case (सम्बोधनं). This is considered in native grammars to be not a distinct case, but the nominative employed in addressing or calling, with a slight modification of the singular number only. Its use is the same as in other languages: इन्द्र एहि 'O Indra, come;' उत्तिष्ठोत्तिष्ठ गान्धारि 'Gándhári, rise up.'

a. The vocative case is commonly used without any interjection; but it is also frequently employed with one, when, as above stated (r. 162, *a*), different particles are employed to signify respectful or disrespectful address: भो भोः पण्डिताः 'O Pańḋits;' रे पान्थ 'Ho, traveller.'

SECTION II.

Adjectives.

293. The adjective agrees with a corresponding substantive noun or pronoun, expressed or understood, in gender, number, and case: बलवान् पुरुषः 'a strong man;' रूपवती स्त्री 'a beautiful woman;' श्वेतं छत्रं 'a white umbrella;' सिंहाविव बलोत्कटौ 'like two mighty lions;' अभ्यगच्छत् कृशानश्वान् समर्थान् अध्वनि क्षमान् 'He approached the steeds, spare, vigorous, and able for the road.'

a. When a common adjective occurs in a sentence with more than one noun or pronoun, it may take the plural number and the prevailing gender, and agree with them collectively: अहं मदीयाश्च सर्व्वे तवानुगाः 'I and mine are all dependent upon thee;' वृद्धौ च मातापितरौ साध्वी भार्य्या सुतः शिशुः अप्यकार्य्यं शतं कृत्वा भर्त्तव्या मनुरब्रवीत् 'Manu has said, that both parents when aged, a virtuous wife, and an infant son, are to be nourished, even if they do a hundred improper acts.' If the words admit of the disjunctive copulative, expressed or understood, the adjective will be put in the singular number, and agree in gender with the word nearest to it: उद्वेगः कलहः कण्डूः सेव्यमाना च वर्द्धते 'Sorrow, strife, or itching, being yielded to, augments.'

b. Many words properly attributives are used as substantives: मर्त्या अमर्त्याः संवृत्ता न विशेषोऽस्ति कश्चन 'Mortals are become immortals (or immortal); there is no difference whatever.' Most attributives of agency, derived from verbs, admit of this application; जगत्कर्त्ता 'the maker of the world,' 'a deity;' सेनानां नेता 'the leader of armies,' 'a general,' &c.; as has already been intimated in considering the cases of the nouns.

c. Adjectives, when expressing degrees of comparison, influence the inflexions of the nouns with which they are connected. When they express the comparative degree, the noun is put in the ablative case: न ज्यायोऽस्ति धनात् 'There is nothing better than wealth;' अर्जुनाद्युधिष्ठिरो ज्येयान् 'Yudhishṫhira is older than Arjuna.' When the superlative, the noun takes either the genitive or the locative case: धार्त्तराष्ट्रेषु or धार्त्तराष्ट्राणां दुर्योधनः पापिष्ठः 'Duryodhana was the wickedest of the sons of Dhṛitaráshṫra.' The comparative may also be used with the instrumental case: को नु स्वन्ततरो मया 'Who has a more ḥappy ending than I?' स चेन्ममार सृञ्जय चतुर्भद्रतरस्त्वया पुत्रात्पुण्यतरश्चैव मा

पुत्रमनुतप्यथाः 'If he has died who was four times more prosperous than thou, and more virtuous than thy son, grieve not for thy son.' The termination of degree may convert a substantive into an adjective: सन्तोषः स्वर्गतमः 'Contentment is most heavenly.'

d. The adjective is sometimes employed in a comparative signification, whilst retaining its positive form; as, पाषाणात् कठिनं हृदयं 'a heart hard (or harder) than stone;' छात्राणां or छात्रेषु मैत्रः पटुः 'Maitra is clever (the cleverest) of, or amongst, the scholars.'

e. वर, either singly or compounded, expresses the superlative degree, and governs either the genitive or locative case: चतुष्पदां गौः प्रवरा लोहानां काञ्चनं वरं 'The cow is the best of quadrupeds; gold the best of metals.' This word may be similarly used in the neuter gender and singular number in apposition with nouns in any gender or number, and in connexion with a negative: अजातमृतमूर्खाणां वरमाद्यौ न चान्तिमः 'Of (sons) unborn, dead, or silly, the two first are the best, not the last;' वरमेको गुणी पुत्रो न च मूर्खशतैरपि 'One son of good qualities is better than a hundred blockheads.'

f. Terms implying 'less' or 'more,' either in quantity or degree, and used in a comparative relation, govern the ablative case: शतादूनं 'less than a hundred;' शतादधिकं 'more than a hundred;' कान्तोदन्तः सङ्गमात् किञ्चिदूनं 'Intelligence from a lover is something less than a meeting.' अधिक may also be connected with the noun in the genitive and locative case: कूडवे ऽधिकः प्रस्थः 'A Prastha is more than a Kúdava;' तेषामप्यधिका मासाः पञ्च 'five months more than those (years).'

g. The government of numerals has already been adverted to (p. 88); to which it may be added, that their Taddhita derivatives may be used analogously to शतं, with the invariable neuter termination, with nouns of any gender and in any case: ततो पञ्चाशतं कन्याः पुत्रिका अभिसन्दधे 'After that, he had fifty maiden daughters;' पञ्चाशतं मनोः पुत्रास्तथैवान्येऽभवन् क्षितौ 'Fifty other sons of the Manu were upon the earth.'

SECTION III.

Pronouns.

294. Personal pronouns of the first or second person have but one gender: those of the third, and pronouns of the other classes, vary their gender according to the noun to which they relate, expressed or understood: स पुरुषः 'that man;' एषा नारी 'this woman;' तेन शिल्पिना कृतं 'made by that artist.'

a. The optional inflexions of the two first personal pronouns, मा, मे, नौ, नः, त्वा, ते, वाम्, वः, are not used indiscriminately, but with certain limitations. They are not to be used at the beginning of a metrical foot or period, nor in construction with the conjunctions च, एव, वा, or the expletives ह and अह, nor with a word meaning 'seeing,' used metaphorically: तव शत्रवो राजन् मम तेऽप्यतिशत्रवः 'Thy enemies, O king, they are still more mine,' not ते शत्रवः at the head of the line, even if the metre allowed it; आवयोर्युवयोश्च, not नौ and वां with च, 'of us two, and of you two;' हरिर्मामेव रक्षतु 'May Hari even preserve me,' not मा; अस्मभ्यं वा युष्मभ्यं दीयतां 'Let it be given to us or to you,' not नो वा वो वा; सम्पत्तिस्तव ह वृथा 'Thy wealth is in vain,' not ते ह. In these prohibitions euphony is consulted, and also distinctness. When 'seeing' is intended in any other than a literal sense, the substitutes are not employed: चेतसा त्वामीक्षते 'He sees thee by his mind.' When the 'seeing' is literal, either form may be allowed, मा or मां, त्वा or त्वां पश्यति 'He beholds me,' &c.; पश्यतु त्वाचिलम्बितं 'Let him see thee without delay.'

b. These substitutes may not be used after a noun in the vocative case, being the first in a sentence, unless an epithet intervene: गुरो मम नमस्तुभ्यं 'O my Guru! salutation to thee;' but हरे कृपालो नः पाहि 'O merciful Hari! protect us.'

c. The relative pronoun agrees with its antecedent in number and gender: the case is determined by its connexion with other parts of the sentence: यद् येन युज्यते लोके बुधस्तत् तेन योजयेत् 'Let a wise man associate that with that, with which any thing in the world corresponds;' पुरुषः स परः पार्थ यस्यान्तस्थानि भूतानि येन सर्वमिदं ततं 'He is the supreme male, O Pártha, in whose interior all beings abide, by whom the universe is pervaded.'

d. The masculine and feminine inflexions of the third personal pronoun are not unfrequently used in combination with the pronouns of the first and second person, or as substitutes for them, like 'ipse,' 'ipsa,' in Latin: सोऽहमेतां गतिं प्राप्तः 'I (ego ipse) have come to this condition;' साऽहं सर्वाधमा लोके स्त्रीणां 'I (ego ipsa) am the vilest of women in the world;' स त्वं भ्रातॄनिमान् प्रति नन्दयस्व 'Do thou (tu ipse) console these thy brothers;' ते वयं दमयन्त्यर्थं चरामः पृथिवीमिमां 'We (nos ipsi) traverse this earth in search of Damayantí.' It is used sometimes without the proper personal pronoun: सा क्षिप्रमातिष्ठ गजं रथं वा 'Do thou (ipsa) quickly mount either an elephant or chariot;' स गत्वा बाहुदां शीघ्रं तर्पयस्व यथा विधि । देवान् । 'Do thou (ipse), having gone quickly to the Báhudá river, offer fit libations to the gods.' The third personal pronoun may be also used in a similar manner with a demonstrative pronoun: सोऽयं विपुलमध्वानं नरोऽभ्येति 'That very man approaches to an extended road.'

e. A relative pronoun may be sometimes used in like manner with a personal pronoun, when the sentence is interrogative: तथा विनाकृता पुत्रैर्योऽहमिच्छामि जीवितुं 'Thus bereft of my children, who (am) I, (that I should) wish to live?'

f. The relative and interrogative pronoun, the latter in combination with the particles चित् or चन, are sometimes used together to form an indefinite distributive pronoun: कर्मणा येन केनचित् 'by some act or other;' याः काश्चिज्जीवता शक्याः कर्तुमभ्युदयक्रियाः 'Whatever acts of enjoyment may be done by a living man.'

SECTION IV.

Indeclinables.

295. Adverbs. The greater number of these, as already observed, are merely nouns in an invariable neuter inflexion;

most commonly that of the accusative neuter, although other cases are sometimes admitted; as, चिरं or चिरेण ध्यात्वा 'Having meditated for a long time;' त्वद्धितार्थं सुरेन्द्रेण भिक्षिते कुण्डले 'The two earrings were begged by the king of the gods, for the good of thee;' राजानः कन्यार्थे समुपागमन् 'The kings came for the maiden;' अन्यान् हस्तमर्दमवीमृदत् 'He kneaded others, kneadingly with his hands;' यथर्तु ववर्ष पर्जन्यः 'Indra was raining, according to the season;' अवसत्तत्र प्रच्छन्नं 'He dwelt there privately.'

a. A number of adverbs are formed of nouns in the invariable neuter, compounded with यथा; as, यजस्व यथाविधि 'Offer sacrifice according to rule;' पूजां यथान्यायं कृत्वा 'Having made worship as was fitting;' तस्मै यथावृत्तं कथयामास 'He told him as it had happened;' यथाशक्ति कुर्य्यात् 'Let him do according to his ability.' विधि 'sort,' 'kind,' becoming in composition विध, is also used adverbially with बहु, नाना and the like; as, नानाविधं 'in various ways;' and so is पूर्व्वं, 'before,' combined with a noun, to express something prior to an act done; as, इत्युक्ता बहुविधं सान्त्वपूर्व्वं 'Being thus addressed in many ways, preceded by acts of conciliation;' अबुद्धिपूर्व्वं भगवन् धेनुरेषा हता मया 'Through (previous) ignorance, thy cow, O sage, was killed by me;' त्वां मोचयिष्यामीति शपथपूर्व्वं तेन सन्धाय 'Having been promised by him, I will liberate thee, preceded by an oath.'

b. Many adverbs are also formed from pronouns, or are the pronouns themselves, in the invariable neuter accusative, or in some other case; as, यत्, येन, यस्मात्, 'wherefore,' 'whence;' तत्, तेन, तस्मात्, 'therefore,' 'thence.' They are frequently put correlatively, as in a familiar verse in the Hitopadeśa, which exhibits most of them: यस्माच्च येन च यथा च यदा च यच्च । यावच्च यत्र च शुभाशुभमात्मकर्म्म । तस्माच्च तेन च तथा च तदा च तच्च । तावच्च तत्र च विधातृवशादुपैति । 'Whence, and wherefore, and as, and when, and what, and how much, and where, one's own acts are good or evil; thence, and therefore, and so, and then, and that, and so much, and there, (the condition of a man) proceeds from subjection to destiny.'

c. The adverb इति 'thus,' 'so,' 'ita,' is of constant use, not only in its own sense, as इत्युक्त्वा 'having so said,' इत्याकर्ण्य 'having thus heard,' but to mark a quotation or a parenthesis, or separate one part of a sentence from another: न शास्त्रं पठतीति कारणं 'He reads the S'ástras: this is not the cause:' इन्द्रो हि राजा देवानां प्रधान इति नः श्रुतं 'Indra is the chief king of the gods: so it has been heard by us:' आस्यतामित्यथोचुस्ते 'Be seated: thus they said:' इत्येते देवगन्धर्वा जगुः 'In this manner sang the quiristers of the gods:' कोऽत्रेत्यहमिति ब्रूयात् सम्यगादेशयेति 'Who waits (so)? I am here; (thus) let him say; and, Give your commands' (thus let him speak): अतोऽहं ब्रवीमि कङ्कणस्य तु लोभेन इत्यादि 'Therefore I say, By desire of a bracelet,' and so forth. इति in combination with तथा forms an adverb of assent, 'so be it,' the verb being understood: विदुरस्तं तथेत्युक्त्वा 'Vidura having said to him, So be it.'

The influence of adverbs on the cases of nouns has already been indicated. The manner in which they are connected with verbs will be presently adverted to.

296. Prepositions. It is unnecessary to make any further remarks upon their government, as, whether singly or in connexion with verbs, sufficient instances have already been given (p. 97).

297. Conjunctions. The employment of copulatives of this description requires no particular observation, as they fulfil their usual offices, and being sometimes omitted, or sometimes multiplied, for the sake of emphasis or perspicuity.

a. The copulative conjunction in most frequent use is च 'and;' which, when it connects words in the same sentence, connects nouns either in the same cases or in those having a similar government, and verbs in the same tenses or in different ones of like purport. आदाय पाण्डोर्दारांश्च पुत्रांश्च ते शरीरे च प्रतस्थिरे 'Having taken the wives and sons of Páńdu, and those two (dead) bodies, they set out:' धनुर्वेदपरत्वाच्च तपसा विपुलेन च 'From his proficiency in the science of arms, and by his intense devotion:' कुट्टिनी च शासिता गोपी च निःसारिता कन्दर्पकेतुश्च पुरस्कृतः

'And the harlot was punished, and the cowherd's wife was banished, and Kandarpaketu was honoured:' सान्त्वयामासुरव्यग्रा वचनं चेदमब्रुवन् 'Tranquil they consoled her, and said these words.' When the sentences are different, they have their several construction, although connected by the copulative: तस्मिन्नेव वनोद्देशे स्थापितः कुरुनन्दनः । ते चान्तर्दधिरे नागाः पाण्डवस्यैव पश्यतः । 'The son of Kuru was left in that wood, and the Nágas disappeared even as the Páńđava was looking.' The conjunction is sometimes repeated, either for emphasis or to imply immediate connexion: ते च प्रापुरुदन्वन्तं बुबुधे चादिपूरुषः 'And they reached the ocean, and Vishńu woke;' i. e. 'as soon as.' च is frequently combined with other copulatives, either for the sake of emphasis or for the convenience of the rhythm: स रामस्य धनुर्वेदं दिव्यान्यस्त्राणि चैव ह । श्रुत्वा तेषु मनश्चक्रे नीतिशास्त्रे तथैव च । 'He having heard of the science of arms, and also the heavenly weapons of Ráma, fixed his mind upon them, and also upon the science of polity.'

b. Disjunctive copulatives may likewise combine words in similar inflexions: अस्त्राणि वा शरीरं वा वरय 'Choose the arms or my person;' आत्मा पुत्रः सखा भार्या कृच्छ्रन्तु दुहिता किल 'A man's self, a son, a wife, or in difficulty (in their absence) even a daughter;' उपपन्नं सतामेतद् यद् ब्रवीषि तपोधन । न तु दुःखमिदं शक्यं मानुषेण व्यपोहितुं । 'That which thou sayest, O rich in devotion, is the progeny of the benevolent; but this grief is not to be removed by a human being.'

c. The connexion of certain of the conjunctions with particular tenses of the verbs will be subsequently explained.

298. Interjections. These are used sometimes with nouns in the vocative case, or sometimes in the accusative or dative, as already intimated. They also occur singly as exclamations. The following verse from Bhatti collects some of either kind: आः कष्टं बत ही चित्रं हूं मातर्दैवतानि धिक् । हा पितः क्वासि हे सुभ्रु बह्वेवं विललाप सः 'Ah sad! O! alas! strange! O mother! Shame on the gods! O father! Where art thou, O lovely-browed? Thus he frequently exclaimed.' Various nouns and phrases are also

employed as interjections: साधु 'well done!' 'bravo!' भद्रं or कुशलं 'good luck!' स्वागतं 'welcome!' स्वस्ति 'hail!' दिष्ट्या 'lucky,' 'prosperous,' and the like: and also others which are specially employed in offering libations to the gods or manes, as noticed above.

SECTION V.

Verbs.

298. The different voices in which the active verb may be conjugated have been already described (p. 113), as well as the changes to which either may be subjected when a verb is compounded with an inseparable preposition (p. 259). Besides those distinctions, and their derivative forms or modes, the verb occurs also in construction in the passive voice, and as transitive, intransitive, or neuter, impersonal or reflective; as, महानागं सुपर्णः सहसाऽहरत् 'Suparna quickly seized the large serpent;' प्राकम्पत महाशैलः 'The vast mountain shook;' पणवानां निस्वनः श्रूयते 'The sound of drums is heard;' सर्वाणि भूतानि गृहस्थैर्धार्यन्ते 'All beings are supported by householders;' मया क्रियते 'It is done by me;' 'I do or have done:' त्वया गम्यते 'It is gone by thee;' 'Thou goest or art gone:' इन्दुनोदैयत 'It was risen by the moon;' 'The moon rose:' नाकालतो म्रियते जायते वा 'It is not (by any one) deceased or born out of season:' भिद्यते काष्ठं 'The wood breaks;' it breaks of itself: तण्डुलं पच्यते 'The rice boils;' it boils of itself. When a verb is not impersonal it agrees with a nominative, expressed or implied, in number and person, as exemplified under the nominative case of nouns. When impersonal, it may be considered that a nominative, the name of the thing or action intended by the verb, is understood. Thus त्वया क्रियते, 'It is done by thee,' is nothing more than the ellipse of the perfect sentence, त्वया क्रियते कर्म्म 'The act is done by thee;' कर्म्म being understood.

The powers of the different tenses have also been already

described (p. 111); but their application in construction is subject to some modifications, which it is necessary to notice.

299. Present tense (वर्त्तमाने लट्). This tense indicates present time, actual or continuous, that which is now, or which is occasionally or always: अस्मिन् क्षणे शास्त्रमधीते 'At this moment he reads the S'ástra:' मांसं खादति 'He eats flesh;' he does so habitually: इह कुमाराः क्रीडन्ति 'Here the boys play;' either now or occasionally: आ प्रलयकालाज्जगद्वर्त्तते 'The world lasts until the time of dissolution.'

a. The present tense may also express other modifications of time, or the absence of any distinction; as when used with अपि or जातु to intimate 'censure' or 'condemnation:' पुरुषोऽपि जायां त्यजति 'A man even abandons a wife;' he either does so now, or has done or will do it।' जातु तत्रभवान् वृषलान् याजयति 'Your reverence ever conducts sacrifices for S'údras.'

b. The present tense may be used in reply to a question referring to either past or future time, when not remote: कदागतोऽसि 'When hast thou come?' एषोऽहमागच्छामि or आगमम् 'I come, or I have come, now;' कदा गमिष्यसि 'When wilt thou go?' एषोऽहं गच्छामि or गमिष्यामि 'I go, or I shall go, now.' It may also be used in reply to a question referring to time past, when it is preceded by ननु; as, किमकार्षीः 'What hast thou done?' ननु करोमि कर्म्म 'Verily I perform an action;' instead of अकार्षं 'I did.' It may be used in the same way, it is said, when preceded by न or by नु; कटमकार्षीः किं 'What hast thou made the mat?' न करोमि 'I do not make (for, I have not made) it;' नु करोमि 'Verily I make (for, have made) it.' The present tense may be used with a past signification when connected with पुरा; as, वसन्तीह पुरा ब्राह्मणाः 'Brahmans formerly dwell (for, dwelt) here.'

c. The present tense may be used for the future in connexion with the particles यावत्, पुरा, कदा, or कर्हि; as, यावद् भुंक्ते तावद् देहि 'Give him as long as he will eat;' न गच्छामि पुरा लङ्कामायुर्यावद् दधाम्यहं 'I go not (I will not go) again to Lanká as long as I have (shall have) life;' कदा or कर्हि पश्यामि गोविन्दं 'When do I (shall I) see Govinda?' It may also be used for the future when in connexion with a word expressing a short time to come: ऊर्ध्वं म्रिये मुहूर्त्तात् 'I die (shall die) after an hour.'

d. When deliberation or election is intended, the present tense may be used for the future: किं करोमि 'What do I?' for किं करिष्यामि 'What shall I do?' एतयोः कतरं or एतेषां कतमं वृणोषि or वरिष्यसि 'Which of these two, or of these, wilt thou choose?' कं नु पृच्छामि दुःखार्त्ता 'Whom sorrowful do I (for shall I) ask?' It may also be used for the future, when conditional consequence is implied: योऽन्नं ददाति स स्वर्गं याति 'Who bestows food goes (for, will go) to heaven.' And it may be employed in a future sense with the usual signs of the conditional mood, यदि and चेत्; as, देवश्चेद्वर्षति धान्यं वपामः 'If the heaven rains, we sow (for, shall sow) the corn.' In such a sort of phrase the future or the past may also be employed. The present may alternate with the future also, in a similarly constructed sentence, with यदि or चेत्, when the consequence is expressed by the imperative: यद्युपाध्याय आगच्छति (or आगमिष्यति) त्वं वेदमधीष्व 'If the teacher comes (or will come), do thou read the Veda.'

e. A more remarkable modification of the present, and one of frequent occurrence, is effected by the addition of the particle स्म, which gives it a past signification. This particle appears to be derived from the first person plural of the present tense of the auxiliary verb, स्मः 'sumus,' 'we are,' rejecting the Visarga. It is used, however, indifferently in all the persons and numbers of the verb to which it is attached. यजति स्म युधिष्ठिरः 'Yudhishṭhira sacrificed;' अभिधावन्ति स्म पौराः 'The citizens ran quickly;' येन स्थीयते स्म 'by whom it was stood.' It may precede the verb, either immediately or in a different part of the sentence: त्वं स्म वेत्थ महाराज यत् स्माह न विभीषणः 'Thou didst not acknowledge, O great king, what Vibhíshaṅa said;' मन्त्रे स्म हितमाचष्टे 'He said in council what was good.'

300. First præterite or imperfect (अनद्यतने लङ्). As already remarked (p. 111), this tense indicates action that has taken place at any time prior to the current day; and although it is very commonly used in a vague manner, yet the past is in general not absolute or perfect, but implies continuity or connexion with some other action: प्रायच्छदाज्ञाम् 'He gave command (to do something):' यावज्जीवम् भिक्षामदात् 'He gave alms as long as he lived;' the giving was continuous: येयं पौर्णमास्यतिक्रान्ताग्नीनधीत सोमेनायष्ट 'This full moon being passed, he read the Agni prayers, and sacrificed with the Soma juice;' these acts were dependent upon a period not remotely past: ततो मायामयीं सीतां घ्नन् खड्गेन वियद्गतः। अदृश्यतेन्द्रजिद्वाक्यमवदत्तं मरुत्सुतः। 'After that Indrajit was seen ascended into the air, striking the illusory Sítá with his sword, the son of the wind spake to him.'

a. The imperfect may be used in connexion with the present tense of verbs implying 'recollection,' if preceded by यत्; अभिजानासि देवदत्त यत् काश्मीरेष्ववसाम 'Thou knowest, Devadatta, how we did dwell in Káśmira:' or यद् may be dispensed with, if a connected action is also described; as, स्मरसि काश्मीरेष्ववसाम तत्रौदनमभुञ्ज्महि 'Thou rememberest we did dwell in Káshmir, and did eat rice there.'

b. Either the imperfect or the perfect may be used with the expletive ह; इति ह अकरोत् or चकार 'Thus he did:' also after शश्वत् 'continually;' शश्वदकरोत् शश्वच्चकार 'He did continually.' They may also be optionally used in question and answer, if the time be not long past; as, अगच्छत् किं 'Did he go?' अगच्छत् 'He did go:' जगाम किं 'Has he gone?' जगाम 'He went.' But if the time of the act be remote, the perfect only is used: कृष्णः कंसं जघान किं 'What? slew Kṛishńa, Kansa?' तं जघान सः 'He slew him.'

c. The negative मा, derived from माङ्, may be conjoined with स्म, and attached to the imperfect, to which it gives the sense of the prohibitive-imperative. When माङ् is used in this manner, the temporal augment अ is rejected: मास्मभवः 'Be thou not;' मास्म करोत् 'Let him not do;' मास्म प्रहृदितं युवां 'Do not you two weep;' मास्म तिष्ठत 'Do not ye tarry.' The negative is also used without the particle स्म; but not in the imperative sense, although it causes the loss of the augment: मच्छीलं मा बुध्यथाः 'Thou hast not known my disposition.'

301. Præterite (परोक्षे लिट्). This tense denotes something absolutely past: चकार 'he made;' पपाच 'he cooked;' ततो निर्याय नगरात् प्रययौ पुरुषोत्तमः 'Krishńa having gone forth from the city departed;' ताडकाख्यां निजघान रामः 'Ráma killed the female demon called Táďaká;' तमृषिः पूजयामास विशेषप्रतिपत्तिभिः 'The Rishi did him honour with particular attentions.' The tense may also be used when mental absence or unconsciousness is implied: सुप्तोऽहं किल विललाप 'Whilst I slept he still talked.' It is employed in construction, however, without much attention to any particular specification of past time, and alternates, at the convenience of the writer, with both the imperfect and the indefinite past.

302. Indefinite past (सामान्ये लुङ्). This is properly used in a general and indefinite manner for time past, whether proximate or remote. सोऽध्यैष्ट वेदांस्त्रिदशानयष्ट पितॄनतार्प्सीत् सममंस्त बन्धून् । अजेष्ट षड्वर्गमरंस्त नीतौ समूलघातं न्यवधीदरींश्च । 'He studied the Vedas, he sacrificed to the gods; he made libations to the manes, he respected his kinsmen; he subdued the class of six (evil feelings), he delighted in regal polity, and utterly destroyed his foes:' अभूद्वृष्टिरद्य 'Rain was, or it rained, to-day:' तां दृष्ट्वा हृष्टोऽभूत् 'Having seen her, he was happy:' अपृच्छत कस्मान्मामप्राबोधीद्राक्षसान् 'He asked the Rákshasas, Why have ye awakened me?'

a. This form of the præterite, or either of the others, may be used as well as the present (see r. 299, *b*) when preceded by पुरा; as, अवात्सुरिह पुरा द्विजाः 'Brahmans formerly dwelt here:' also अवासन् or ऊषुः as well as वसन्ति, as above. It may be used also optionally with the future or present, when the conditional consequence of a past action is expressed: देवश्चेदवर्षीद् धान्यमवाप्स्म: 'If it had rained, we had sown the grain.'

b. मा, derived from माङ्, is frequently used with the indefinite past, when it gives it the force of the imperative, and causes the rejection of the temporal augment: मा भैषीः 'Do not fear;' मा शुचः 'Do not grieve;' मा भूत् 'Let it not be;' मैवं कार्षीः पुनः क्वचित् 'Never do so again;' मा चाधर्मे मनः कृथाः 'Do not give your mind to wickedness.' It may also be employed with स्म; as, मा स्म क्रंस्थाः 'Do not go.' It is also used in the same manner with another negative, in an affirmative sense: मा द्विषो न वधीर्मम 'Do not not-kill (i. e. kill) my foes.' There are examples, however, especially in the older writers, of the use of this negative with the indefinite past, in which the augment is retained; as, मा निषाद प्रतिष्ठां त्वमगमः 'Do not thou ever obtain reputation, O barbarian?' Rámáyana: and when the verb is compounded with a preposition, the augment of the imperfect and the indefinite past may be retained; as, श्रद्धा च नो मा व्यगमत् 'Let not faith depart from us;' Manu: मा मन्युवशमन्वगाः 'Do not be subject to wrath;' Mahábhárata. On the other hand, it is rejected in compounds also; as, मावमंस्था स्वमात्मानं 'Do no disrespect to thy own soul.' The difference is explained by affirming that a different negative, मा not माङ्, is employed; the former not requiring the elision of the augment. It, and not माङ्, is also said to be used with other tenses; as with the imperative, मा भवतु, or the future, मा भविष्यति 'Let it not be.'

303. Definite future (अनद्यतने लुट्). This tense indicates future time, defined either expressly, as in the example above given (p. 112), or by some circumstance or event not immediately proximate, or, as it is expressed, not of day; as in the following example from Bhatti: आनन्दितारस्त्वां दृष्ट्वा प्रष्टारश्चावयोः शिवं। मातरः सह मैथिल्यास्तोष्टा च भरतः परं। 'Our mothers having seen thee shall be delighted, and shall ask after the welfare of us both, along with Maithilí; and Bharata will rejoice exceedingly.'

a. This form of the future is used optionally with the indefinite future or the present in certain phrases or combinations; as with कदा or कर्हि; कदा भोक्ता or भोक्ष्यते, कर्हि स्याता or स्यास्यति,

'When will he eat? Where will he remain?' also with the interrogative implying 'preference;' किं कतरं or कतमं वरीतासि or वरीष्यसि 'What or which wilt thou choose?' also when it denotes the consequence of a conditional act; यो भिक्षां दाता or दास्यति स स्वर्गं याता or यास्यति 'He who shall give alms will go to heaven.'

304. Indefinite future (लृट् शेषे). The time expressed by this tense may be either immediately or remotely future: नाहं संदर्शिष्येऽद्य 'I shall not be seen to-day;' मरिष्यामि विजेष्ये वा हताश्चेत्तनया मम 'Since my sons are slain, I will die or conquer.'

a. When connected with verbs implying 'recollection,' this tense may be used with a past signification; as, स्मरसि कृष्ण गोकुले वत्स्यामः 'Rememberest thou Kṛishṅa; we shall dwell (for, we were dwelling) at Gokula:' also optionally, when one action is dependent upon another; as, स्मरसि देवदत्त काश्मीरेषु वत्स्यामस्तत्रौदनं भोक्ष्यामहे 'Rememberest thou Devadatta; we dwell in Káshmir, and dressed (shall dress) rice there:' otherwise the imperfect may be used, as above.

b. It alternates, as above remarked, with the definite future after कदा and कर्हि; also when 'choice' or 'consequence' is signified, or when an act contingent upon some event is predicated: देवश्चेद्वर्षिष्यति धान्यं वप्स्यामः 'If it shall rain we will sow the corn.'

c. The indefinite future is to be used where dispatch is signified; as, दूतः शीघ्रं गमिष्यति 'The messenger will go swiftly:' also when continuous action is implied; यावज्जीवमन्नं दास्यति 'As long as life lasts he will give food:' also when an act is followed for a certain time without interruption; येयममावास्यागामिनी तस्यामग्नीनध्येष्यते सोमेन च यक्ष्यते 'When this future day of new moon (is), on that (day) he will read the prayers to Agni, and sacrifice with the Soma juice.' It is used in like manner when अवर, 'after,' is employed to denote immediately subsequent place or time: योऽयमध्वा गन्तव्य आपाटलिपुत्रात् तस्ययदवरं कौशांब्यास्तत्रौदनं भोक्ष्यामहे 'This is the road to Pátaliputra, (and having gone) subsequently by that of Kauśámbí, we will there eat food:' योऽयं सम्वत्सर आगामी तस्य यदपरमाग्रहायण्यास्तत्र युक्ता अध्येष्यामहे 'When the future (next) year (is arrived), then immediately, on the full moon of the month Ágraháyańa, we, entering upon devotion, will study (the Vedas).' If परम् be used instead of अवरं the definite future may be used; परमाग्रहायण्यास्तत्र अध्येतास्महे or अध्येष्यामहे; and the latter only is to be employed if days or nights be specified; as, योऽयं मास आगामी तस्यावरः पञ्चदशरात्रस्तत्राध्येतास्महे 'When the future (next) month (is arrived), and fifteen days after it (have passed), then we will study.'

d. When disbelief, doubt, or intolerance is signified, and especially if put interrogatively, the indefinite future may be used optionally with the potential: न सम्भावयामि, or न मर्षये भवान् हरिं निन्देत् or निन्दिष्यति 'I cannot believe, or I cannot endure, that you revile Vishńu,' i. e. either should or shall revile or have reviled: को कतरो or कतमो हरिं निन्देत् or निन्दिष्यति 'Who or which may or will revile Hari?' कं वृषलं भवान् याजयेत् or याजयिष्यति 'For what Śúdra may or will your reverence perform sacrifices?' If preceded by the compound particle किंकिल or by अस्ति or its synonymes in these senses, the future only, not the potential, is employed: न सम्भावयामि भवान् किंकिल वृषलं याजयिष्यति 'I cannot think it possible your reverence will sacrifice for a Śúdra:' also अस्ति, भवति or विद्यते, भवान् वृषलं याजयिष्यति 'Is it (possible, can it be) your reverence will sacrifice for a Śúdra?' The same tense may be used optionally with the potential when possibility is admitted or expected: सम्भावयामि भोक्ष्यते (or भुञ्जीत) भवान् 'I think it possible your excellency will eat;' केन सम्भावितं तात कुम्भकर्णस्य राघवः। रणे कर्त्स्यति गात्राणि मर्म्माणि च वितर्स्यति। 'By whom is it supposed, that in battle Rághava will cut to pieces the limbs, or scatter the members, of Kumbhakarńa.'

e. The indefinite future is used with exclamations of astonishment, if any conditional particle, as यच्च or यदि, be not inserted: आश्चर्य्यमन्धो कृष्णं द्रक्ष्यति 'Wonderful! the blind man will see (can see) Kṛishńa.' It may also be used with the particles उत and अपि when implying 'doubt;' उत दण्डो पतिष्यति 'Will the staff fall (or not)?' अपिधास्यति द्वारं 'Will he shut the door?' and must be used with अलम् when it signifies 'certainty' or 'capability;' अलं कृष्णो हस्तिनं हनिष्यति 'Certainly Kṛishṅa will kill (that is, is able to kill) the elephant.'

305. Imperative (विधिलोट्). The uses of the imperative tense require no particular illustration. It has, however, a first as well as a third person; to which, 'command' or 'injunction' is not applicable: but as the powers of this mood correspond with those of the potential, and consequently comprehend 'permission' and 'capability,' as signified by 'may,' 'let,' 'can,' there is no difficulty in understanding their applicability to any person indifferently. नहि प्रेष्यवधं घोरं करवाण्यस्तु ते मतिः 'Let this be thy determination, I may not cause the dreadful destruction of the servants:' दूधि कार्य्यस्करस्त्वं मे गत्वा प्रवद राघवं 'Be thou my messenger; and having gone, say (thus) to Rághava.'

a. The imperative is very frequently used in the third person singular of the passive, either with a nominative expressed, or with the agent in the instrumental case expressed or understood; in which latter case it is used indefinitely: आनीयतां देवी 'Let the queen be brought;' भो भोः पण्डिताः श्रूयतां 'Ho Pańḍits, be it heard,' i. e. युष्माभिः 'by you;' क्रीयतां 'Let it be done;' आगम्यतां 'Let it be come,' i. e. केनचित् 'by some one;' सीते गम्यतामतः 'Sítá, let it be gone hence,' i. e. by thee, or 'Go thou away;' रथः स्थीयतां 'Let the carriage be stopped,' or रथेन स्थीयतां 'Let it be stopped by the carriage;' मुच्यन्तामाशाः 'Let all hopes be dismissed,' तैः 'by them.'

b. When any act enjoined is to be done after a short time, the imperative may be used in relation to the future, the present or the potential: उपरिमुहूर्त्तादुपाध्यायश्चेदागमिष्यति (आगच्छति or आगच्छेत्) त्वं वेदमधीष्व 'If the teacher shall (does or may) come after an hour, do thou (then) read the Veda.' Or it may be used where time shortly past is implied, without any condition, when स्म may be combined with it: ऊर्द्ध्वं मुहूर्त्तात्

स्वामिनी स्म भव क्षितेः 'After an hour be mistress of the earth.'

c. The imperative may be used optionally with the potential to express 'wish:' इच्छामि भवान् भुञ्जीत or भुंक्तां 'I wish your worship may, or would, eat.' So with कामये, प्रार्थये, 'I desire,' 'I beg,' or other synonymous verbs.

d. When desire to have any thing done that should be performed is expressed, स्म is used with the imperative: त्वं बालमध्यापय स्म 'Do thou cause the boy to read; do thou teach him.'

e. The third person singular of the imperative of the substantive verb is often used with the particle एवं 'so,' 'thus,' absolutely, to signify 'assent;' as, एवं भवतु, एवमस्तु, 'So be it;' एवमस्त्विति तं चापि प्रत्युवाच युधिष्ठिरः 'And Yudhishṫhira also thus replied to him, So be it.'

f. The negative मा is prefixed to the imperative sometimes, with a sense equivalent to that of the present tense: मा भवतु 'there is not;' मा च ते निघ्नतः शत्रून् मन्युर्भवतु पार्थिव 'There is not (or may not be) any crime in thee, O prince, killing thy foes.'

g. तात् is substituted for the terminations of the second and third persons singular of the imperative, when used in a benedictory sense: भवतादवियुक्ता त्वमत ऊर्ध्वं स्ववेश्मनि 'Mayest thou be undivided from thy husband henceforth in thine own dwelling.'

306. Potential mood (विधि निमन्त्रणामन्त्रणाधीष्टसंप्रश्नप्रार्थनेषु लिङ्). The senses of the potential mood, as detailed in the citation from Páṅini, have been explained above (p. 112). It is sufficient here to add a few examples of its application. हर्षयेद्ब्राह्मणांस्तुष्टो भोजयेच्च शनैः शनैः 'Let a man pleased make the Brahmans happy, and feed them deliberately:' तस्माद्धीरो नैव हृष्येन्न शोचेत् 'Therefore let a man of fortitude neither rejoice nor grieve:' न वारयेद्गां धयन्तीं न चाचक्षीत कस्यचित्। नदिवीन्द्रायुधं दृष्ट्वा कस्यचिद्दर्शयेद्बुधः। 'Let not a wise man disturb a cow drinking, nor tell of it to another; nor, having seen a rainbow in the sky, let him point it out to another.'

a. The potential mood is very commonly employed as the

conditional or subjunctive mood in combination with particles indicating 'condition,' 'contingency,' 'alternative,' 'uncertainty,' 'doubt,' 'astonishment,' and the like; as, यदि, चेत्, 'if;' यद् 'as,' 'since;' यच्च 'as;' यथा 'as,' 'so,' 'that;' यत्र 'where,' 'how;' यदा 'when;' जातु 'ever;' अपि 'although,' 'since;' वा or उत or उतापि 'whether;' किं 'what;' कथम् 'how;' चित्रम् 'wonderful;' &c. ममत्वं न प्रजानीयुर्यदि दण्डो न पालयेत् 'If punishment does not protect, people may not recognise property:' दण्डश्चेन्न भवेल्लोके विनश्येयुरिमाः प्रजाः 'If there were not punishment in the world, the people would perish:' अहो दुःखं—यत्कृत्वा मानुषं कर्म्मत्यजेथाः श्रियमुत्तमां 'O grief! that, having done manly deeds, thou (shouldest) abandon glorious fortune:' यच्च त्वमेवं कुर्य्याः न श्रद्दधे 'I did not believe that thou couldest act thus:' जातिष्वन्येष्वपि यथा न भवेयं कुलान्तकृत् । न भोक्ष्ये न च पानीयमुपभोक्ष्ये कथञ्चन । 'So that I may not be also in other races a destroyer of my kin, I will not eat, nor partake in any way of drink:' यदा मन्येत हृष्टं पुष्टं बलं स्वकं । परस्यविपरीतं च तदा यायाद्रिपुं प्रति । 'When he may judge his own army in good condition, and that of his adversary in the reverse, let him march against the enemy:' परदुःखेन यो दुःखी न स जातु सुखी भवेत् 'He who is distressed by the grief of others can never be happy:' यत्तादृशाः कृष्णं निन्देरन् आश्चर्य्यं 'That such persons should revile Kṛishṅa, astonishing!' or यदि may be used with similar exclamations; चित्रं यदि सोऽधीयीत 'Surprising! if he read.' उत and अपि may be used to imply 'doubt of will,' or 'capability:' उत or अपि हन्यादघं हरिः 'Will Hari destroy sin?' 'Will he be pleased to do so?' अपि गिरिं शिरसा भिन्द्यात् 'Can he indeed break a mountain with his head?' किमनुशोचेयं 'Why should I grieve?' कथं, when used reproachfully, may be connected with the present or the potential:' कथं त्वं धर्म्मं त्यजेः or त्यजसि 'How canst thou, or dost thou, abandon virtue?'

These particles may be also understood, or dropped altogether, when the condition can be expressed by the use of correlative terms, or by a preceding phrase: दशाननो हरेत् सीतां बन्धनं स्यान्महोदधेः '(Since) Rávaṅa carries (may carry) off Sítá, (so) the binding of the great sea may occur:' ध्रियमाणे तु पितरि पूर्वेषामेव निर्वपेत् 'But if the father be living, let him offer libations to those prior to him.'

b. The potential mood is also used to intimate 'fitness,' 'propriety,' or 'capability:' त्वं कन्यां वहेः 'Thou shouldest or oughtest to marry the damsel;' स भारमाहरेत् 'He may or can carry the load;' कर्णार्जुनसहायोऽहं जयेयमपि वासवं 'Aided by Karña and Arjuna, I could conquer even Indra.'

c. Verbs signifying 'to wish' or 'desire' may use the potential optionally with the present: गन्तुमिच्छेत् or इच्छति 'He wishes to go;' तामालिङ्गयितुं कामयेत or कामयते 'He desires to embrace her.' The object of the wish may also be expressed in the potential, instead of the infinitive; as, तामालिङ्गयेत् कामयते 'He wishes he may or might embrace her.'

d. The potential often takes the place of the imperative, with a similar signification; तोयमादाय गच्छेः 'Having taken water, thou mayest go,' i. e. go thou: especially when preceded by आशंस 'to order' or 'enjoin;' गुरुश्चेदुपेयादाशंसे त्वमधीयीथाः 'If the teacher come, I desire that thou read.'

e. The potential may be used with a present or future sense when time not remote is specified: प्राप्तःकालस्ते तपः कुर्य्याः 'The time is come that thou perform thy penance;' मुहूर्त्तादूर्द्ध्वं यजेत् 'Let him sacrifice after an hour.'

f. In didactic and injunctionary sentences the potential is constantly employed without a nominative expressed, referring either to a noun previously enunciated, or to such words as 'some one,' 'any one,' 'a man,' or the like, understood: आपदर्थे धनं रक्षेद्दारान् रक्षेद्धनैरपि । आत्मानं सततं रक्षेद्दारैरपि धनैरपि । 'Let a man preserve his wealth against misfortune; but his wife even by his wealth: let him even preserve himself by a wife even, or also, by wealth:' यद्यद्रोचेत विप्रेभ्यस्तत्तद्दद्यादमत्सरः 'Let (one) not a niggard give to the Brahmans that which may be agreeable to them.'

g. The potential is used in a future sense to signify the conditional result of an act which a person may perform:

स्कन्दस्य य इदं विप्रः पठेज्जन्मसमाहितः । श्रावयेद्वा ब्राह्मणेभ्यो य शृणुयाद्द्विजेरितं । स पुष्टितुष्टी सम्प्राप्य स्कन्दमालोक्यमाप्नुयात् । 'Whatever Brahman may read attentive this Birth of Skanda, or may cause it to be heard by Brahmans, or may hear it repeated by a Brahman, he, having obtained abundance and happiness, may obtain the heaven of that divinity.'

307. Benedictive mood (लिङाशिषि). The term by which the power of this mood is defined imports 'blessing;' but as there is also connected with it the notion of 'wish,' and as this wish or desire may concern oneself as well as another, the term 'optative' would better indicate its character; as, तन्नो देवा विधेयासुर्येन रावणसन्निभं । सपत्नांश्चविजीयास्म संग्रामे च मृषीमहे । 'May the gods direct us, so that we may either conquer such enemies as Rávaňa, or die.' It is used sometimes optionally with the imperative in a benedictory sense: चिरं जीव्यात् or चिरं जीवतु भवान् 'May your excellency live long.'

308. Conditional mood (लिङ् निमित्ते लृङ्). This mood is considered as the equivalent of the potential when cause is indicated as well as consequence, or when one act or condition is contingent upon another act or condition, and whether the cause and consequence be future or past. Like the potential, it is commonly used with the same conditional particles, यदि, चेत्, &c., as specified above; as, सुवृष्टिश्चेदभविष्यत् तदा सुभिक्षमभविष्यत् 'If there shall be abundant rain, then there will be plenty;' यदि स मया दृष्टोऽभविष्यत् ततोऽभोक्ष्यत 'If he had been seen by me, he should have been devoured (by me).'

a. Although the same notion of contingency prevails, yet this mood is also used analogously to the potential, to signify 'uncertain consequence,' 'doubt,' 'suspicion,' 'possibility,' 'inquiry,' and the like; as in this exemplification of its application from Bhatti: अपि तस्य रिपुः सीतां प्रार्थयिष्यत दुर्मतिः । क्रुरं जात्वर्दयिष्यच्च जात्वस्तोष्यत श्रियं स्वकां । सङ्कल्पं नाकरिष्यच्चात्त्वेयं शुद्धमानसा । मृषामर्षमवाप्स्यस्त्वं राम सीतानिबन्धनं ॥ 'O Ráma, unjustly thou wouldest entertain suspicion of Sítá; for although the vile enemy warmly solicited her, and sometimes menaced and sometimes vaunted his own magnificence, yet she, pure of mind, would never bestow a thought upon him.'

b. The conditional mood, like the potential, is employed with exclamations of surprise, but they require the addition of यच्च or यत्र; as, आश्चर्यं यच्च or यत्र स्त्री कृच्छ्रेऽवर्त्स्यत तव 'Strange that a woman should in any way abide in thy evil opinion.' When used interrogatively, it requires an interrogative adverb; as, किं नारायणमात्मानं नाभोत्स्यत भवानजं 'What! do you know yourself to be the unborn Náráyaña?' त्रासादस्यां विनष्टायां किं किमलप्स्यथाः फलं 'She being dead through fright, what then? what benefit wouldest thou obtain?' In the following example many of the particles with which this mood or the potential may be connected, are illustrated: दैत्यक्षये महाराज यच्च यत्राघटिष्यथाः । समाधिं जातु तत्रापि किं नानेष्यस्त्वमीहितं । 'Mighty king, as whatever and however thou mayest have (or hast) accomplished in the destruction of the demons, what! wouldest thou not ever thus also bring (or have brought) thy desired purposes to fulfilment.'

309. Infinitive mood. This, as shewn above (p. 369), is considered to be a verbal derivative noun, and is attached in the invariable accusative apparently to a verb; as, श्रोतुमिच्छामि 'I wish to hear;' कथयितुमर्हसि 'Thou art able to tell;' प्रोत्सहिष्ये न जीवितुं 'I will not endure to live.'

a. Like other verbal derivatives, the infinitive may exercise a similar government as one of the moods or tenses of the verb from which it is formed: मेनिरे सहिता गन्तुं पाञ्चाल्याः स्वयम्वरं 'They resolved to go together to Draupadi's marriage election.' It cannot as a noun, however, admit the difference of active and passive voices, and the effect of the latter is given to it by its association with participles, and especially with the future participle of the verb शक 'to be able,' in connexion with the object; the agent, when expressed, being in the instrumental case: अथ मूढोऽसौ जेतुं शक्यश्च भवति 'Now that blockhead is to be conquered;' न त्वेवमनेन विभीषणेन शक्या वयं त्रासयितुं त्वयाऽद्य 'We are not to be intimidated to-day by thee with this terror;' कथं रिपुः द्रष्टुं शक्यः 'How is the enemy to be seen;' नैते देवर्षिपितरस्तथाऽद्य शक्यास्त्वया भर्तुं 'Nor can these gods, sages, and progenitors, be thus now nourished by thee.'

b. The infinitive is also used after nouns and participles; as, वेला भोक्तुं 'time to eat;' कर्तुं समर्थः 'able to do;' द्रष्टुं गतः 'gone to see:' but these are evidently elliptical phrases, in which the verbal copulative is understood; कालोऽस्ति गन्तुं 'It is time to go.' The same may be said of the like combination of the infinitive with adverbs or adverbial nouns; as, न न्याय्यं निहतं शत्रुं भूयो हन्तुं नराधिपाः '(It is) not right, O princes, to slay again a slain enemy;' प्रासादास्त्वां तुलयितुमलम् 'Palaces (are) fit to be compared to thee;' तस्माद्योगः प्रधानेष्टः स तु दुःखं प्रबोधितुं 'Therefore Yoga is the desired object of the eminent; but it (is) to be made known with difficulty.'

SECTION VI.

Derivative Verbs.

310. The derivative forms of the verb are not of common occurrence, with exception of the causal, which is of very frequent use. As this must from its nature be a transitive verb, it will govern an accusative case, either singly or doubly, as exemplified above (r. 286, *g*). The following are a few additional illustrations of its use: तीक्ष्णा इति वयं ख्याता भवन्तं ज्ञापयामहे 'We are called severe; this we apprise you' (cause you to know); विज्ञापयति देवी 'The queen represents;' नन्वाज्ञापयति 'Nay, she commands;' ते त्वां विभेदयिष्यन्ति दुःशीलाश्च मदन्तरं 'Those evil disposed ones will alienate thee from me' (will cause to separate from); तां श्वभिः खादयेद्राजा 'Let the king cause her to be devoured by dogs;' मूर्द्धानं ते पातयिष्यति विक्रम्य शत्रुः 'The enemy, being valiant, shall strike off thy head' (cause it to fall); आनययामास सपरिच्छदा स्त्रियः 'He caused the women, with their attendants, to be brought;' प्राणैरेनमव्ययूयुजत् 'He did not cause him to be disunited from his life' (he did not put him to death).

a. The desiderative form is also from its nature transitive, and has the government of transitive verbs: प्रादिदृक्षत नो नृपं

नाशुश्रूषत गायनान्। रामं सुस्मूर्षमाणोऽसौ कपि र्विरहदुःखितं। 'The monkey (Hanumán) did not wish (or would not) look at the dance, nor hear the singers, desirous of remembering Ráma, suffering the pain of absence.' This form of the verb implies 'volition' as well as 'wish;' as, याच्यमानं मया मूढ पित्र्यमंशं न दित्ससि 'Thou wilt not give my father's share, being asked for by me.' The desiderative form of श्रु, 'to hear,' implies not only 'to wish to hear,' but 'wait upon' or 'obey;' that is, to wish to please by service: आसमाप्तेः शरीरस्य यस्तु शुश्रूषते गुरुं। स गच्छत्यञ्जसा ब्रह्मणः सद्म शाश्वतं। 'He who until the end of his life waits upon his Guru, goes assuredly to the eternal mansion of Brahma.'

b. The frequentative mode expresses either repetition or intensity—the doing of an act repeatedly or energetically—but it is of very unfrequent use in either: स्तोकका इव रारास्यमानास्तिष्ठन्ति 'They stand, like Chátakas, crying aloud repeatedly;' भूयस्तं बेभिदाञ्चक्रे खगः 'Again the bird eagerly assailed him;' पक्षौ लोलूयाञ्चक्रे पतत्रिणः 'He cut the wings of the bird to pieces.' With verbs of motion this form may also imply 'going crookedly' or 'badly;' as, यावज्यते खञ्जः 'The lame man goes awry.' With certain verbs it also intimates 'defect' or 'impropriety;' as, जञ्जप्यते ब्राह्मणः 'The Brahman prays hypocritically.'

c. From a desiderative verb others may be formed; as, शिश्रावयिषति पुराणानि 'He wishes to cause the people to hear the Puráñas;' किं मामधः प्रापयिषसि 'Why dost thou wish to cause me to go downwards?' A desiderative may not be formed from a desiderative, unless some other mode intervene; as, ज्ञानिनं बोभूयिषयिषति मूर्खः 'The blockhead wishes to cause the desire of frequent existence in the sage.' And in this manner the forms might be compiled without end; but the practice is not adopted.

d. The conversion of substantives into verbs is not unfrequent, and depends apparently upon the pleasure of the writer. A few examples of the use of such verbs in construction will be sufficient to illustrate their application. निरस्तपादपे देशे

एरण्डोऽपि द्रुमायते 'In a spot destitute of trees the castor oil plant becomes a tree;' उष्णो दहति चाङ्गारः शीतः कृष्णायते करं 'A burning coal burns the hand; when cold it blackens it:' उपांशुक्रीडितोऽमात्यः स्वयं राजायते यतः 'A minister who is made the companion of (a king's) private amusements, if active, kings it himself:' मतिर्दोलायते नूनं सतामपि खलोक्तिभिः 'The mind of the virtuous oscillates (or swings) by the speech of the wicked:' दुःखायते सर्व्वजनः स एवैकः सुखायते 'All men are in sorrow; he alone is happy:' नोदकण्ठयिष्यतात्यर्थं त्वामैक्षिष्यत चेत् स्मरः 'If the god of love should see thee, he would not grieve much (for his absent bride):' इयं व्याधायते बाला भूरस्याः कार्म्मुकायते कटाक्षाश्च शरायन्ते मनो मे हरिणायते 'This maiden is the hunter; her eyebrow is her bow, her glances are arrows, and my heart is the deer.'

SECTION VII.

Participles.

311. Those participles which are declinable are, like adjectives, inflected in the gender, number, and case of the noun with which they are connected in construction. Both the declinable and indeclinable may exercise the same government as the verbs from which they are derived.

312. The present participles active of transitive verbs ordinarily govern the noun in the accusative case: कुर्व्वन् or कुर्व्वाणः सृष्टिं ब्रह्मा 'Brahmá is making (or makes) creation;' वेदानधीयानश्छात्रः 'The pupil is reading the Vedas;' आत्मानं मण्डयमाना स्त्री 'The woman (is) decorating herself;' समुत्तरन्तौ नदान् 'They two (were) crossing rivers;' ते विचिन्वानास्तमाश्रमं 'They searching that hermitage;' स बलं भीमसेनस्य चिन्तयानः व्यदह्यत 'He, considering the strength of Bhímasena, was consumed (with envy).' The participle present of द्विष, 'to hate,' optionally governs the genitive case: मुरं or मुरस्य द्विषन् हरिः 'Hari (is) hating (of) Mura.' The participles of verbs of remembering may also govern the genitive; as, मां or मम स्मरन्ती 'remembering (or thinking of) me.' The present participle may be used with particles in the sense of the potential mood; as, शृणुष्वैव यथा कुर्व्वन् धर्म्मान्न च्यवसे 'Listen, that so acting (for, that you may so act that) you will not fall from duty.'

a. The present participle of the passive voice involves no notion of past time, but implies the continuance of the state or thing suffered. Thus स दश्यमानस्तु कृमिणा तथा 'He also being thus bitten by the reptile,' signifies that the biting has not ceased, but is going on: so यदा त्वबुध्यतात्मानं भक्ष्यमाणं 'When he perceived himself being devoured;' अनुसार्य्यमाणो बहुभीरक्षिभिः 'Being pursued by numerous guards.'

313. The participles of the perfect tense are not of very frequent occurrence: they follow the general rules relating to concord and government, and are not unusually employed without a verb in the sense of the perfect tense: ते तिरश्चामुपसेदुषां निधनमैषिषुः 'They desired the death of the animals that were near (them);' त्वमुपेयिवानसि 'Thou art arrived;' पुरो निषेदिवान् कंसकृषः स विस्तरे 'He (was) seated (or sat down) on a couch in the presence of the destroyer of Kansa.'

313. The indefinite past participles are of much more universal use than the preceding, and bear an important part in the formation of sentences: they take the variations of inflexion according to the noun or pronoun with which they are connected, expressed or understood.

a. The active indefinite past participle governs the same cases as its verb, and may be used absolutely, with the auxiliary verb implied: ततो राममुक्तवान् शङ्करः 'Then S'ankara said to Ráma;' दैत्यान् हतवान् कृष्णः 'Krishńa slew the demons.'

b. The passive indefinite past participle is ordinarily connected with the agent in the instrumental case; रावणेन हृता सीता लङ्कां नीता 'Sítá, seized by Rávańa, (was) conveyed to Lanká:' but in some cases it may be optionally connected with the agent in the genitive; as, राज्ञः or राज्ञा मतो विप्रः 'The Brahman is respected by or of the king;' तस्य or तेन महीयं जिता This earth is conquered of or by him.' It also governs the agent in either case, when signifying the site or subject of the action; as, इदमेतेषां or एतैः शयितं 'This was (the) slept of or by them;' i. e. the place where, or the time when, they slept: इदमेतस्य or एतेन गतं 'This was (the) gone of or by him;' i. e. the time or manner of his departure.

c. When derived from neuter or intransitive verbs, this participle may be used with a noun in the place of the past tense of the verb: प्ररुदितो राजा राक्षसां 'The king of the Rákshasas wept;' आ स्वयं मृतोऽयं 'Ah! he has died (or is dead) of himself.'

d. The indefinite past participle of verbs of motion, and of others already specified (p. 275), takes an active sense, and is used in place of the past tense, governing a noun in the same manner as a transitive verb: हिरण्यको विवरं प्रविष्टो वायसः स्वस्थानं गतः 'Hiranyaka entered his hole; the crow went to his own nest:' न शोच्यः स नरव्याघ्रो युधि निधनं गतः 'That hero is not to be mourned (who is) departed to death.' Other verbs than those above enumerated, which bear analogous imports, may also be used in this manner: अहोऽस्म्यशुचितां प्राप्तः 'Alas! I have incurred impurity;' सा प्रसूता गर्भमुत्तमं 'She bore an excellent offspring.' The time expressed may also be indefinite; as, राजानो दक्षिणामाश्रिताः 'Kings (affecting) dwelling in the south. The past indefinite participle of intransitive verbs may also be used to denote time indefinitely present or continuous; as, तद्दिनान्ते सुप्तो ब्रह्मा 'At the end of his day Brahmá sleeps.'

e. The past participles of verbs signifying 'to speak,' 'to ask,' and the like, when used with a masculine or feminine noun, imply 'spoken to,' 'inquired of,' referring the object to the noun with which they agree, and being followed by the agent or speaker, when specified, in the instrumental case: स एवमुक्तस्तु मुनिः 'That sage thus spoken to;' तेन भाषिता सा 'She addressed by him;' स तैः पृष्टः 'He inquired of by them.' The participle may also govern the matter of the speech, like an active verb, in the accusative: कृष्णेन वाक्यमुक्तोऽसि 'Thou art spoken to, a speech by Krishńa;' इत्युक्ता सिन्धुराजेन वाक्यं हृदयकम्पनं 'Thus spoken to by the king of Sindhu, a heart-agitating speech.'

f. The indefinite participle past is often used for a noun, the noun or pronoun being understood: दण्डः सुप्तेषु जागर्ति 'Punishment watches over those who sleep;' जनेषु, 'people,' understood: पक्वापक्वेन वर्त्तयन् 'subsisting by ripe and unripe;' फलेन, 'fruit,' understood. In the neuter gender it is used, not only as an abstract noun (p. 275), but absolutely or adverbially: यथोक्तं 'as it is said;' तथाकृतं 'so it is done;' यथायुक्तं 'as it is proper,' 'fitly,' 'rightly.'

g. Both the past participles indefinite are commonly used with the different tenses of the auxiliary verbs अस and भू, forming in fact compound tenses, which might be comprised within the scheme of conjugation with as much, or rather perhaps with as little, propriety in Sanskrit as in other languages; as, गतोऽस्मि or गतवानस्मि 'I am or have gone;' गत आसं गतोऽभवं, गतवानासं, गतवानभवं, 'I was or had gone;' गतो भवितास्मि or भविष्यामि, or गतवान् भवितास्मि 'I shall be or have gone;' गतो or गतवान् भवेयं 'I may be or have gone,' &c.; कृतवानस्म्यकार्याणि 'I have done improper acts;' गतो वनं श्वो भवितेति रामः 'Ráma will be gone to-morrow to the forest;' सम्प्राप्तः कीर्त्तिमतुलां भविष्यसि 'Thou shalt have obtained unequalled fame.' When used alone, either absolutely or transitively, it may be inferred that the form is elliptical, and that the verb is understood; as, हिरण्यको विवरं प्रविष्टोऽभूत् 'Hirańyaka was or had entered his hole.'

314. The indefinite past participles indeclinable are also of very extensive and important application. They are especially used to suspend the close of a sentence, acting at the same time as copulatives, and connecting something which precedes with something which is to follow;' as, इत्युक्त्वा स गतः 'Having so spoken, he went away;' चिरमालोच्य मया कृतं '(I) having long considered, it was done by me.' They may be repeated, to imply a succession of actions preparatory to some final one: इति प्रबोध्यातिथ्यं कृत्वालिंग्यच सम्प्रेषितः 'Having thus discoursed (to them), treated (them) with hospitality, and embraced them, he sent (them) away.'

a. As ordinarily employed, these participles undergo and exercise the same government as the tenses of the verb; that is, they are connected with the subject in the nominative, and the object in the accusative or some other case: ब्राह्मणेभ्यो राजा दक्षिणां दत्त्वा 'The king having presented gifts to the Brahmans;' हिरण्यको विवरं कृत्वा निवसति 'Hirańyaka, having made a hole, dwelt;' कथयस्व भयं त्यक्त्वा 'Speak, having dismissed fear.'

b. It often occurs, however, that these participles are used elliptically or parenthetically, and in appearance absolutely or without government; whence it has been inferred*, that they are rather gerunds than participles. It is doubtful, however, if in any case the deficient nouns may not be readily supplied: thus, तेन व्याधेन तण्डुलकणान् विकीर्य जालं विस्तीर्णं 'By that fowler, (he) having scattered the grains of rice, a net was spread:' इति सर्वैः पक्षिभिर्निश्चित्य गृध्रो व्यापादितः 'The vulture was killed by all the birds, (they) having thus concluded:' अबुद्धैरात्मा संस्कृत्य संस्कृत्य परोपकरणीकृतः 'By the unwise, the self or person, (they) having diligently adorned (it), is made the tool of another.' This sort of construction is, no doubt, often complicated, but it may perhaps be always unravelled in this manner: इत्यालोच्य तेन सिंहेन ग्रामं गत्वा दधिकर्णनामा विडालो मांसाद्याहारं दत्त्वा प्रयत्नादानीय स्वकन्दरे धृतः 'The cat named Dadhikarńa was placed by that lion in his cave; (he) having thus reflected, and having gone to the village, and having given (the cat) flesh and other kinds of food, and brought (him) thence with much trouble.'

315. The participles of the future tense are said to have these significations in common with the imperative mood, 'directing,' 'commanding,' and indication of season or opportunity: कटः कर्त्तव्यः करणीयः कार्य्यः 'The mat is to be made; it must be made; it is time for it to be made.' They also intimate 'fitness' or 'propriety;' कन्या वोढव्या 'The girl is to

* This was first proposed in a very elaborate and interesting investigation of these and some other verbal forms, by the late Baron W. Humboldt, published in the Indische Bibliothek.

be married;' she is marriageable: धर्म्मोऽनुसरणीयः 'Duty is to be observed:' and they denote 'ability' or 'competency;' त्वया भारो वहनीयः 'The load is to be borne by thee;' यद्यहं वध्यस्तदा हन्तव्यः 'If I am fit to be killed, I am to be killed.' In these and the like phrases they agree with the object, and are used without a verb, although it is evident that the verb is understood; कटः कर्त्तव्यः being properly कटः कर्त्तव्योऽस्ति; so हन्तव्यः is properly हन्तव्योऽस्मि.

a. Future participles are used absolutely in the neuter gender, either in place of a noun, or with the noun implied: यथा भवितव्यं तद्भवतु 'As it is to be, so be it;' प्रष्टव्यं पृच्छतस्तस्य कथनीयमवाचयत् 'He caused to be said what was to be said to him asking what was (fit) to be asked.'

b. These participles, when capable of a transitive effect, govern the object in the same case as the verb to which they belong;' as, तेन ग्रामं गन्तव्यं 'It is to be gone by him to the village;' नेतव्या गावो व्रजम् कृष्णेन 'The cows are to be taken to pasture by Kṛishṅa;' दण्ड्यः स्ववित्तस्यांशमष्टमं 'He is to be fined an eighth part of his property;' गद्यमेतत्त्वया मम 'That is to be said by thee of (to) me.' The agent, agreeably to their passive signification, is usually in the instrumental case; but it may be also sometimes in the genitive; मया or मम सेव्यो हरिः.

316. Some verbal derivatives of a participial character exercise the like government upon nouns as already noticed (r. 290, *a*). To the examples there adduced the following may be added. The derivative from कृ with अलम् prefixed, and ष्णु affixed, governs an accusative: पत्नीमलङ्करिष्णुर्भर्त्ता 'The husband adorns, or is the adorner of, his wife.' Derivatives from कृ with the affix खल् may require the instrumental case; ईषत्करः प्रपञ्चो हरिणा 'The material world is easily made by Vishṅu:' or the genitive; न हि दुष्करमस्तीह किञ्चिदध्यवसायिनां 'Nothing here is difficult to the persevering.' Derivatives with तृन् are followed by nouns in the accusative; विष्णुः कर्त्ता लोकान् 'Vishṅu is the maker of the worlds:' but considered as substantives, such derivatives may be followed by other substantives in the genitive case, and कर्त्ता लोकानां is equally allowable. Words formed with इन्, when 'futurity' is implied, govern the object in the accusative: व्रजङ्गामी 'Who is going (will go) to the pasture?' शतन्दायी 'Who is giving (will give) a hundred?' A noun formed with इनि from the indefinite past participle may be connected with another in the locative case: अधीती व्याकरणे 'well read in grammar.'

CHAPTER IX.

PROSODY.

SECTION I.

General Rules.

317. It would be inconsistent with the plan and limits of the present work to attempt any lengthened detail of the infinite varieties of the metrical system of the Hindus; but a brief description of the principles by which it is regulated, and their illustration by a few examples of the most frequently occurring kinds of metre, will not be out of place, and may be of use.

318. The essential element of Sanskrit prosody is Quantity. As the long and short vowels have distinct symbols, their value is at once determined. A short vowel, however, is considered to be prosodially long when it precedes a conjunct consonant, also when it precedes Anuswára or Visarga. At the end of a line or stanza, also, the last vowel is regarded as long or short according to the exigence of the metre.

319. Syllables of various quantities are arranged in certain definite groupes to form prosodial feet. This is effected according to two different methods.

a. The first method is that which is employed in the greatest number of popular metres, and is the formation of trisyllabic feet. Of these, eight varieties are enumerated. Each has its equivalent denomination in Greek prosody; but by native writers each is designated by a distinct syllable, having the term गण, 'class' or 'number,' attached to it, as in the following list:

1. Na-gaṅa नगणः ⏑⏑⏑ Tribrach.
2. Ma-gaṅa मगणः – – – Molossus.
3. Ja-gaṅa जगणः ⏑–⏑ Amphibrach.
4. Ra-gaṅa रगणः –⏑– Cretic.
5. Bha-gaṅa भगणः –⏑⏑ Dactyl.
6. Sa-gaṅa सगणः ⏑⏑– Anapæst.
7. Ya-gaṅa यगणः ⏑– – Bacchic.
8. Ta-gaṅa तगणः – –⏑ Antibacchic.

With given numbers of these feet a monosyllable or dissyllable may be further necessary to complete a line, but they are regarded as supplementary syllables, not feet, and are specified accordingly as one or two long or short syllables, or one long and one short, as the case may be.

b. In the second method of forming prosodial feet, which characterises a peculiar class of metres, the element is a syllabic instant, or short syllable: of these, four constitute a foot; that is, a foot consists of either four short syllables or their equivalents, viz. two long or one long and two short syllables.

c. There is another mode of measuring verse, which dispenses with, or only partially permits, the use of regular feet. In this a definite number of short syllables, or their equivalents, without further subdivision, constitutes a verse; certain portions of which, however, commonly consist of feet of the first class.

320. A varying number and disposition of these several feet, or syllabic instants, form a verse, which differs as to length and proportions. This verse is a stanza or S'loka, which, with some exceptions, consists of two lines or hemistichs: each of these is again subdivided into two parts: so that the entire stanza is for the most part a tetrastich, composed of four Pádas or Charañas, literally 'feet,' or, in our understanding of the term, lines or semi-hemistichs: the intervals between the first and second, and third and fourth of which are not always so distinctly marked, as that between the second and third.

a. When the metre consists of feet of the first order, and is single, the Pádas are of equal length, and of corresponding quantities. Sometimes, however, two or more kinds of metre may be mixed in one stanza, and then the hemistichs or Pádas may vary in length and in quantity. When feet of the second kind are used, the Pádas are of different, though definite lengths.

b. Rhyme is not employed in any of the older, or in the higher order of, writings. It is met with in poems of a lyrical character, and of later date; and in them also great inequality of metre is introduced. In the best and oldest compositions great regularity prevails, although the metre is occasionally varied even in the same work.

SECTION II.

Varña-vritta.

321. Of the two classes of measures which depend upon feet, the larger and more popular is also regulated by another principle, viz. the number of syllables contained in the stanza. The class is thence denominated Varña-vritta or Akshara-Chhandas, 'Literal or syllabic metre.'

a. The number of syllables in a verse of this class may vary from four to nearly four thousand; but of the prevailing orders of this class few contain less than twenty-four syllables, or six syllables in a line; or more than one hundred and four in a verse, or twenty-six in a line. Within these limits twenty-one orders are specified, each of which, by the varying disposition of the feet, and of the pause or cæsura, comprises different species. The number of species ordinarily enumerated is above two hundred; but of these, many are of rare use, although the whole number is infinitely less than the possible combinations of this class of metre, which, as a matter of arithmetical computation, is reckoned at many millions of millions. The forms in popular use do not perhaps exceed twenty or thirty, and range from thirty-two syllables to fifty-six in the verse. When they exceed the latter number, the verse is very rarely employed in continuous passages of any length, but is inserted occasionally, or occurs at the close of a canto or section, as a more stately and sonorous close. We shall specify the different orders of this class, with a notice of their varieties, and exemplifications of a few of their most ordinary species.

1. Gáyatrí, $6 \times 4 = 24$. Eleven varieties. This metre is not of frequent occurrence in profane versification, and when used, as it is in the hymns of the Vedas, it is most commonly a triplet, somewhat varying in length. The most usual form is a triplet of three lines of eight syllables each, as in the following, which is the most sacred verse of the Vedas, and known emphatically as 'the' Gáyatrí. It is held in such reverence, that it is never to be uttered in the hearing of ears profane.

ओम् तत्सवितुर्वरेण्यं । भर्गो देवस्य धीमहि । यो नः प्रचोदयात् ।

'Om! let us meditate on the glorious splendour of that divine sun, that he may inspire us.'

2. Ushńih, $7 \times 4 = 28$. Eight varieties; none of frequent occurrence, except in the Vedas.

3. Anushťubh, $8 \times 4 = 32$. Twelve varieties. This is by far the most frequent and useful form of Sanskrit verse. It is that in which the great body of metrical composition, whether narrative or didactic, exists. All works of considerable extent are written in it, relieved by the occasional introduction of other measures. It is the prevailing form of metre in the laws of Manu, the Mahábhárata, the Rámáyańa, and the Puráńas.

a. The Anushťubh or (in the nominative inflexion) Anushťup stanza is divided into four Pádas, of eight syllables each. In its most regular form the first foot is any one except a tribrach; the second may be a dactyl, a tribrach, cretic, or anapæst; the other two syllables are indifferently long or short. In the twelve species, however, other dispositions occur. Thus in that termed Vidyunmálá the whole stanza consists of long syllables, or is a verse of molossi and spondees: in another, Pramáńí, we have alternately short and long syllables, a stanza of amphibrachs or iambics: in a third, Samání, long and short syllables alternate, forming a verse of cretics or trochees: whilst in a fourth, Tuńgá, the first six syllables of each line are short, or two tribrachs.

b. Another rule given for the formation of the Anushťup verse is, that the fifth syllable of each line shall be short, the sixth long, and the seventh alternately long and short; whilst the four first syllables and the eighth are arbitrary. This will be found to be usually the form adopted, with occasional exceptions. The following are examples.

– – ⏑ | – ⏑ – | – – ‖ – – – | ⏑ ⏑ – | ⏑ – ‖ – ⏑ – | ⏑ ⏑ ⏑ | – – ‖ ⏑ – ⏑ | ⏑ ⏑ – | ⏑ – ‖

आसीदिदं तमोभूतमप्रज्ञातमलक्षणं । अप्रतर्क्यमविज्ञेयं प्रसुप्तमिव सर्वतः ।

'This universe had become darkness, undiscerned, uncharacterised, indescribable, incomprehensible, as if every where in a deep sleep.' Manu.

– ⏑ – | – ⏑ – | – ⏑ ‖ ⏑ ⏑ – | – ⏑ – | ⏑ – |
मा निषाद प्रतिष्ठां त्वमगमः शाश्वतीः समाः
– – ⏑ | ⏑ ⏑ – | – ⏑ | ⏑ ⏑ – | – ⏑ – | ⏑ – ‖
यत् क्रौञ्चमिथुनादेकमवधीः काममोहितं

'Never, barbarian, mayest thou acquire fame for endless years, since thou hast slain one of these birds, heedless through passion.' Rámáyańa.

Tradition affirms of this, that it is the first S'loka or Anushťup verse ever composed.

– – – | – ⏑ ⏑ | ⏑ – ‖ ⏑ – ⏑ | ⏑ ⏑ – | ⏑ – ‖ ⏑ – – | ⏑ ⏑ – | – – ‖ ⏑ ⏑ – | – ⏑ – | ⏑ – ‖

गङ्गाद्वारं प्रति महान् बभूव भगवानृषिः । भरद्वाज इति ख्यातः सततं शंसितव्रतः ।

'At Gańgádwára was a great holy sage, Bharadwája by name,

ever engaged in devotion.' Máhábhárata. In the first Páda the sixth syllable is short; and the seventh is short in the first, second, and fourth.

– – –|⏑ ⏑–|– –‖⏑⏑ –|⏑⏑ –|⏑–‖ –⏑–|⏑ ⏑–|– –‖⏑⏑– |⏑⏑ –|⏑–‖
दृशिं देहि पुनर्बाले कमलायतलोचने । श्रूयते हि पुरा लोके विषस्य विषमौषधं ।

'Maid with the long and lotus eyes, O look upon me again. It is an ancient saying, that in the world poison is the antidote of poison.' S'ringára Tilaka.

The following is given in the S'ruta Bodha both as the rule and the example of a verse of long syllables:

– – –|– – –|– –‖– – –| – – –|– –‖
सर्व्वे वर्णा दीर्घा यस्यां विश्रामःस्यात् पादे पादे ।
– – –|– – –|– –‖– – –| – – –|– –‖
विद्वद्वृन्दे वीणावाणि व्याख्याता सा विद्युन्माला ।

'That (verse) in which all the vowels are long, and there is a pause at each Páda, is called, O lute-voiced, Vidyunmálá by the learned.'

4. Vṛihatí, 9 × 4 = 36. Twelve varieties: not much used.

5. Pankti, 10 × 4 = 40. Fourteen varieties: not much used alone, but sometimes mixed with the following.

6. Trishťubh, 11 × 4 = 44. Twenty-two varieties. Some of the species of this order are next in frequency of use to the Anushťubh, and are generally employed, even in poems written for the most part in the latter metre, in passages affecting a more elevated or animated tone. Many parts of the Mahábhárata, the Puráńas, and the plays, and the greater portion of the Raghu Vans'a, Kumára Sambhava, Bhaťťi Kávya, Mágha, Kirátárjuníya, and other popular poems, are written in one or other form of the eleven-syllable metre, either singly or alternating with other kinds, especially with the next or twelve-syllable metre; or sometimes mixed with it or with the ten-syllable metre in the same stanza; but then it is considered to belong to the third class of metres, under the name of Vaitálíya or Aupachchandasika, as will be subsequently noticed.

a. The most frequent form of the order Trishťubh is that

called Indravajrá, a verse of four Pádas, each of which contains two antibacchics, an amphibrach, and two long syllables. Instead of a double antibacchic, the first foot may be an amphibrach, when the metre is termed Upendravajrá: and a third variety, named Upajáti, is said to be formed when these two are, as is very commonly the case, mixed in different Pádas of the same stanza, as in the following examples; the first of which is in the Indravajrá, the second in the Upendravajrá, and the third in the Upajáti metre.

– – ⏑|– – ⏑|⏑ – ⏑|– – ‖ – – ⏑|– – ⏑|⏑ – ⏑|– – ‖
सेनानिवेशान् पृथिवीक्षितोऽपि । जग्मुर्विभातग्रहमन्दभासः ।
– – ⏑|– – ⏑|⏑ – ⏑|– – ‖ – – ⏑|– – ⏑|⏑ – ⏑|– – ‖
भोज्यां प्रति व्यर्थमनोरथत्वात् । रूपेषु वेषेषु च साभ्यसूयाः ।

'These princes returned to their tents, displaying in their appearance and attire the vexation which their disappointed love for Bhojyá had excited, resembling planets, whose lustre fades before the dawn of day.' Raghu Vanśa.

⏑ – ⏑|– – ⏑|⏑ – ⏑|– – ‖ – – ⏑|– – ⏑|⏑ – ⏑|– – ‖
हृतेन राज्येन तथा धनेन । रत्नैश्च मुख्यैर्न तथा बभूव ।
⏑ – ⏑|– – ⏑|⏑ – ⏑|– – ‖ – – ⏑|– – ⏑|⏑ – ⏑|– – ‖
यथात्रपाकोप समीरितेन । कृष्णाकटाक्षेण बभूव दुःखं ।

'The grief that was felt (by Yudhishṫhira) for the loss of his most precious jewels, his treasure, or his kingdom, was not so severe as that which was inflicted by the glances of Krishṅa, darting anger and shame.' Mahábhárata.

⏑ – ⏑|– – ⏑|⏑ – ⏑|– – ‖ – – ⏑|– – ⏑|⏑ – ⏑|– – ‖
कुवेरगुप्तां दिशमुष्णरश्मौ । गन्तुं प्रवृत्ते समयं विलंघ्य ।
– – ⏑|– – ⏑|⏑ – ⏑|– – ‖ ⏑ – ⏑|– – ⏑|⏑ – ⏑|– – ‖
दिग्दक्षिणा गन्धवह मुखेन । व्यलीकनिःश्वासमिवोत्ससर्ज ।

'When the sun, having completed his (southern) sojourn, commenced to travel towards the quarter protected by Kuvera (the north), the region of the south breathed forth a fragrant zephyr, like a sigh of regret.' Kumára Sambhava. In this the first and fourth Pádas are in the Upendravajrá, the second and third in the Indravajrá metre.

7. Jagatí, $12 \times 4 = 48$. Thirty varieties. This order of metres is also of frequent employment, and very commonly

alternates with the preceding in the same passages, or in separate cantos. The most common variety of it is the Vanśastha, a stanza in which each line consists of an amphibrach, an antibacchic, an amphibrach, and a cretic.

⏑ – ⏑| – – ⏑|⏑ – ⏑| – ⏑ – ‖ ⏑ – ⏑| – – ⏑|⏑ – ⏑| – ⏑ – ‖
विलासवापीतटवीचिवादनात् । पिकालिगीतेः शिखिलासलाघवात् ।
वनेऽपि तौर्य्यत्रिकमररराधतं । क्क भोगमाप्नोति न भाग्यभाग्जनः ।

'With the music of the waves that murmured against the borders of the pool, with the songs of the flocks of koïls, and the graceful dance of the peacock, an entertainment was prepared for him in the forest. Where is it that the man who is prosperous meets not with delight?' Naishadha.

Another variety, the Indravanśá, differs from this only in the first foot, which may be an antibacchic as well as the second; and these two being mixed in the same stanza, as in the foregoing order, form a species of Upajáti. They may both, again, be blended with the two first varieties of the Trishťubh, as in the following, in which the first Páda is in the Indravajrá metre, the second in the Indravanśá, the third in the Upendravajrá, and the fourth in the Vanśastha.

– – ⏑| – – ⏑|⏑ – ⏑| – – ‖ – – ⏑| – – ⏑|⏑ – ⏑| – ⏑ – ‖
विद्या प्रबोधोदय जन्मभूमिः । वाराणसी मुक्तिपुरी निरत्यया ।
⏑ – ⏑| – – ⏑|⏑ – ⏑| – – ‖ ⏑ – ⏑| – – ⏑|⏑ – ⏑| – ⏑ – ‖
अतः कुलोच्छेदविधिं विधित्सुः । निवस्तुमत्रेच्छति नित्यमेव सः ।

'Váráńasí, the eternal, is the city of salvation, the native land of the acquirement of true wisdom: hence he wishes to dwell perpetually here, being desirous of observing the practices that cut off (the bonds) of family attachment.' Prabodha Chandrodaya.

8. Atijagatí, $13 \times 4 = 52$. Sixteen varieties. In the earlier writers this order of metres is not common, although occasional stanzas occur in the plays. In works of later date, and especially in the Mágha and Kirátárjuníya, whole cantos are composed in one or other of its varieties.

a. One species, the Manjubháshińí, consists of an anapæst and an amphibrach, each repeated, and a long syllable; as,

⏑ ⏑ –|⏑ – ⏑|⏑ ⏑ –|⏑ – ⏑|– ‖ ⏑ ⏑ –|⏑ – ⏑|⏑ ⏑ –|⏑ – ⏑|– ‖

अचिरप्रभाविलसितैः पताकिना । सुरकार्म्मुकाभिनव चित्रशोभिना ।

गमितेन खेलगमने विमानतां । नय मां नवेन वसतिं पयोमुचा ।

'Waft me home upon the new cloud, converted into a chariot for our happy journey, decorated with the many-coloured bow of Indra, and waving the swift gleaming lightning for its banner.' Vikramorvasí.

b. Another species, the Praharshińí, consists of a molossus, a tribrach, an amphibrach, a cretic, and a long syllable:

– – –|⏑ ⏑ ⏑|⏑ – ⏑|– ⏑ –|– ‖ – – –|⏑ ⏑ ⏑|⏑ – ⏑|– ⏑ –|– ‖

उल्लोलस्खलितकपालकण्ठमाला । सङ्घट्टक्कणितकरालकिंकिणीकः ।

पर्य्याप्तं मयि रमणीयडामरत्वं । सन्धत्ते गगणतल प्रयाणवेगः ।

'The speed of my flight through the sky invests me with terror as well as grace, being musical, instead of with bells, with the fierce clanging sounds of the skulls that form my necklace, striking against each other in my undulating motion.' Málatí Mádhava.

c. A metre composed of twelve and of thirteen-syllable lines is also to be found in some extended passages in the same works in which other varieties of this order are used. This, however, which is termed Pushpitágrá, is also considered to be a variety of the third class of metres, or of those regulated by syllabic instants.

9. S'akkarí, 14 × 4 = 56. Twenty varieties. The forms of this order are also not unfrequent, and one of them especially, the Vasantatilaka, is often used. This contains in each Páda an antibacchic, a dactyl, two amphibrachs, and two long syllables.

– – ⏑|– ⏑ ⏑|⏑ – ⏑|⏑ – ⏑|– – ‖ – – ⏑|– ⏑ ⏑|⏑ – ⏑|⏑ – ⏑|– – ‖

राज्याच्च्युतस्य बहुशः परिवाररामाः । कोषादि तस्य रिपवो व्रजतो निजहुः ।

उर्व्वीरुहो विगलितस्य नगेन्द्रशृङ्गाद् । वल्लीफलादिरभसादिव गण्डशैलः ।

'The enemy, hastening from many parts, seized the women of his family, and plundered the treasures of the king, thus fallen from his throne, as a rocky fragment carries away the fruit and flowers of a tree that has been hurled from the summit of a mighty mountain.' Rája Tarańgińí.

10. Atiśakkarí, $15 \times 4 = 60$. Eighteen varieties. They occur occasionally, though not in passages of any length. The most common is the species termed Máliní, which consists of two tribrachs, a molossus, and two bacchics.

⏑⏑⏑ | ⏑⏑⏑ | – – –| ⏑ – – | ⏑ – – ‖ ⏑⏑⏑ | ⏑⏑⏑ | – – – | ⏑ – – | ⏑ – – ‖
स्मरसि सुतनु तस्मिन् पर्वते लक्ष्मणेन । प्रतिविहितसपर्य्यासुस्थयो स्तान्यहानि ।
स्मरसि सरसतीरं तत्र गोदावरीं वा । स्मरसि च तदुपान्तेष्वावयो र्वर्त्तनानि ।

'Rememberest thou, O lovely-formed, those days which we passed happily together in that mountain, when all our service was performed by Lakshmańa? Rememberest thou the borders of the lake, or the Godaverí river? Rememberest thou our habitation upon its shore?' Uttara Ráma Charitra.

11. Ashŕi, $16 \times 4 = 64$. Twelve varieties. They are very rarely met with.

12. Atyashŕi, $17 \times 4 = 68$. Seventeen varieties. Some of these are popular, occurring principally in short passages at the close of a section, although sometimes forming the only metre of entire poems, when they are not of great extent. Thus the whole of the Ánanda Laharí is written in a popular variety of this metre, termed Śikhariñí, in which each Páda contains a bacchic, a molossus, a tribrach, an anapæst, a dactyl, and one short and one long syllable.

⏑ – – | – – – | ⏑⏑⏑ | ⏑⏑ – | – ⏑⏑ | ⏑ – |
सुधासिन्धोर्मध्ये सुरविटपवाटी परिसरे
मणिद्वीपे नीपोपवनवति चिन्तामणिगृहे
शिवाकारे मञ्चे परमशिवपर्य्यङ्कनिलयां
भजन्ति त्वां धन्याः कतिचन चिदानन्दलहरीं

'Some blessed sages worship thee, the wave of spiritual felicity, having thy resting place with the supreme Śiva upon the throne in which his fivefold form is typified, in the temple of the all-bestowing jewel, which stands in a grove of Kadamba trees, near a lake surrounded by the trees of heaven, on the island of gems, in the midst of the sea of ambrosia.'

Another variety of this order, the Mandákrántá, forms also the metre of the whole of the Megha Dúta. It consists of a molossus, a dactyl, a tribrach, two antibacchics, and two long syllables or a spondee.

– – –|– ⏑⏑|⏑⏑⏑|– – ⏑|– – ⏑|– – |

ब्रह्मावर्तं जनपदमधश्छायया गाहमानः
क्षेत्रं क्षत्रप्रधनपिशुनं कौरवं तद्भजेथाः
राज्यानां शितशरशतैर्यत्र गाण्डीवधन्वा
धारापातैस्त्वमिव कमलान्यभ्यवर्षन्मुखानि

'Enveloping with thy shade the region Brahmávartta beneath thee, go thence to the field of Kuru, infamous for the slaughter of heroes, and with thy falling rain-drops pelt the lotus flowers, as the wielder of the bow Gáńdíva here showered his sharp and countless arrows upon the faces of the warriors.'

13. Dhrití, $18 \times 4 = 72$. Seventeen varieties, but of rare occurrence: and of all these higher numbers it may be observed, that they are seldom used in books, except in occasional and closing stanzas, and that it is only in elaborate and commonly turgid panegyrical inscriptions that they extend to wider limits. The concluding verse of the twelfth book of the Raghu Vanśa is an example of the variety of this order termed Mahámáliká, in which the Páda is formed of two tribrachs and four cretics.

⏑⏑⏑|⏑⏑⏑|– ⏑ –|– ⏑ –|– ⏑ –|– ⏑ – |

रघुपतिरपिजातवेदोविशुद्धां प्रगृह्य प्रियां

⏑⏑⏑|⏑⏑⏑|– ⏑ –|– ⏑ –|– ⏑ –|– ⏑ – |

प्रियसुहृदि विभीषणे सङ्गमय्य श्रियं वैरिणः
रविसुतसहितेन तेनानुयातः ससौमित्रिणा
भुजविजितविमानरत्नाधिरूढः प्रतस्थे पुरीं

'Ráma having received his bride, purified by fire, and transferred the kingdom of his foe to his friend Vibhíshańa, set out, accompanied by the son of the sun and Saumitra to his city, in the heavenly car which his arm had won.'

14. Atidhrití, $19 \times 4 = 76$. Thirteen varieties. One of these is a favourite metre as an occasional stanza. This is the Śárdúla víkŕídita, in which the Páda consists of a molossus, an anapæst, an amphibrach, an anapæst, two antibacchics, and a long syllable.

— — — | ⏑ ⏑ — | ⏑ — ⏑ | ⏑ ⏑ — | — — ⏑ | — — ⏑ | —

संक्षिप्याथ तनुं निरीक्ष्य सकलां लङ्कां शरच्चन्द्रिका

निर्धौताखिलसौधमण्डलमहोद्युतप्रसन्नान्तरां

दृष्ट्वाशोकवने सराक्षसवधूसंवेष्टितां जानकीं

आरूढो निभृतं स्थितः पवनजः कङ्केल्लिभूमीरुहं

'Having contracted his body, and examined the whole of Lańká, whose rows of white palaces shone with augmented beauty, as glistening in the autumnal moonlight, and having beheld Jánakí in the Aśoka garden, surrounded by Rákshasa females, the son of air ascended a Kańkelli tree, and there remained concealed.' Hanumán Nátaka.

15. Kṛiti, $20 \times 4 = 80$. Four varieties: not often used.

16. Prakṛiti, $21 \times 4 = 84$. Three varieties; of which one, the Sragdhará, is met with in an occasional verse. The Páda comprises a molossus, a cretic, a dactyl, a tribrach, and three bacchics; as,

— — — | — ⏑ — | — ⏑ ⏑ | ⏑ ⏑ ⏑ | ⏑ — — | ⏑ — — | ⏑ — — |

सर्व्वोत्कर्षस्य धात्रा निधय इव कृता केऽपि कस्याऽपि हेतोर्

— — — | — ⏑ — | — ⏑ ⏑ | ⏑ ⏑ ⏑ | ⏑ — — | ⏑ — — | ⏑ — — |

जेतारः स्वेन धाम्ना मदसलिलमुचां नागयूथेश्वराणां

दंष्ट्राभंगं मृगाणामधिपतय इव व्यक्तमानावलेपा

नाज्ञाभङ्गं सहन्ते नृवरनृपतयस्त्वादृशाः सार्व्वभौमाः

'Who are they, and for whose use created, who were formed by Brahmá treasures of every excellence; surpassing in their splendour the lords of the elephant herd, when shedding the dews of passion from their brows? Like the haughty and proud monarch of the forest tribes, who submits not to have his teeth broken, so sovereigns such as those emperors of the world suffer not their orders to be disobeyed.' Mudrá Rákshasa.

17. Ákṛiti, $22 \times 4 = 88$. Three varieties.

18. Vikṛiti, $23 \times 4 = 92$. Six varieties.

19. Sańkṛiti, $24 \times 4 = 96$. Five varieties.

20. Atikṛiti, $25 \times 4 = 100$. Two varieties.

21. Utkṛiti, $26 \times 4 = 104$. Three varieties.

22. Dańḍaka is the general name given to all metres of this class exceeding the Utkṛiti measure.

SECTION III.

Gańa-vritta.

322. The second class of metres consists of those in which the feet are formed of four short syllables or their equivalents. There are sixteen classes of this metre, and each of them admits of sixteen species; but it will be sufficient to notice the five principal classes.

1. *Áryá.* This is a stanza of four Pádas, the first of which contains twelve short syllables, the second eighteen, the third twelve, and the fourth fifteen. As regulated by the feet, however, the division is best adapted to the hemistich, and the Áryá stanza may be more conveniently regarded as a couplet; the first half of which contains thirty syllabic instants, distributed amongst seven feet and a half; and the second, twenty-seven syllabic instants, distributed also amongst seven feet and a half, but in which the sixth foot consists of one short syllable only; as in the following:

– ⏑ ⏑|– ⏑ ⏑|– –|– –|⏑ ⏑ –|⏑ – ⏑|– –|–
वत्सविवृद्धिनिमित्तं क्षीरस्य यथा प्रवृत्तिरज्ञस्य
⏑ ⏑ ⏑|⏑ – ⏑|⏑ – –|⏑ – ⏑|– –|⏑|– –|–
पुरुषविमोक्षनिमित्तं तथा प्रवृत्तिः प्रधानस्य

'In like manner as the secretion of the unconscious milk occurs for the nutriment of the calf, so the activity of (ignorant) matter takes place for the liberation of spirit.' Sánkhyá Káriká.

– ⏑ ⏑|– –|– –|– –|⏑ ⏑ –|⏑ – ⏑|⏑ ⏑ –|–
स्त्रीषु न रागः कार्य्यो रक्तं पुरुषं स्त्रियः परिभवन्ति
– –|⏑ ⏑ –|– –|⏑ – ⏑|– –|⏑|– –|–
रक्तैव हि रन्तव्या विरक्तभावा नु हातव्या

'Fall not in love with women, for they disdain the man who loves. If one should bear you affection, love her; if she be scornful, let her go.' Mrichchakatí.

a. The disposition of the feet in the Áryá verse is not

altogether arbitrary: in the first hemistich the sixth foot must either be a long syllable between two short, that is, an amphibrach, or else four short syllables. In the second hemistich the sixth foot consists of one short syllable. The odd feet in either hemistich, the first, third, fifth, and seventh, should never be amphibrachs.

b. A variety of the Árya, and of the other classes also, is termed Chapalá; in which it is required that the second and fourth feet should be amphibrachs, the first a spondee or an anapæst, and the fifth a dactyl or spondee. This rule may apply to both hemistichs, or to the first or to the second only; constituting thus three varieties in addition to the regular one, or four in all.

c. In like manner, when the pause occurs after the third foot, the verse is termed Pathya; when after any other, Vipula: and this variation may prevail in either hemistich or in both, forming therefore four modifications of the pause; which being applied to the four modifications of the metre, compose the sixteen varieties of each order of this class of metres.

d. The Árya metre is in general employed only in occasional verses; but the whole of the Sánkhyá Káriká is composed in it, as is the Nalodaya of Kálidása.

2. Udgítí. This differs from the Árya only in inverting the order of the second and fourth Pádas. The first contains, as before, twelve short syllables; the second, fifteen; the third, as before, twelve; and the fourth, eighteen.

3. Upagítí. In this class each hemistich consists of but twenty-seven short syllables; the second as well as the fourth containing but fifteen; the first and third are unaltered.

4. Gítí. Both hemistichs consist of thirty short syllables; the fourth Páda as well as the second consisting of eighteen.

5. Áryagítí. In this class each hemistich consists of eight full feet, or thirty-two short syllables, divided into Pádas of twelve and twenty syllabic instants.

SECTION IV.

Mátrachhandas.

323. The third class of metres is regulated in the first instance by the number of short vowels or syllabic instants, or Mátras, as in the preceding class; not by the number of syllables, without regard to their syllabic length, as in the first. It so far partakes, however, of the character of the first class, that, after having defined the number of short syllables, or their equivalents, which the stanza shall contain, they may be, either wholly or partially, distributed into trisyllabic feet; so that the verses may in many instances be identified with recognised varieties of the first class of metres, more or less intermixed in the same stanza. The principal orders of this class are the following.

1. Vaitálíya. This is a stanza of four Pádas; the first and third of which contain the time of fourteen short syllables; the second and fourth, sixteen. Each Páda should end in a cretic and iambic, or else in a dactyl and spondee. Of the remaining moments, which are six in the first and third, and eight in the second and fourth Pádas, neither the second and third, nor the fourth and fifth, should be combined in the same long syllable; nor, in the second and fourth Pádas, should the sixth and seventh Mátra be combined in one long vowel. There are exceptions, however, to these rules, which constitute varieties of the class. Entire cantos in this form of metre occur in the Mágha, Kirátárjuníya, and Naishadha; and occasional verses in it are found in other works; as in the following, in which the last syllables of the three first Pádas are long by position.

⏑⏑– ⏑⏑–⏑–⏑ – ⏑⏑ – –⏑⏑– ⏑–⏑ –
नृपतेः प्रतिषिद्धमेवतत् । कृतवान् पंक्तिरथो विलंघ्य यत् ।
⏑⏑– ⏑⏑–⏑– ⏑ – ⏑⏑– – ⏑ ⏑–⏑–⏑ –
अपथे पदमर्पयन्ति हि । श्रुतवन्तोऽपि रजोनिमीलिताः ।

'This was (an act) prohibited to a king; but Daśaratha (did

it), having transgressed the prohibition. Those even who are learned in the Vedas, when they are blinded by passion, set their feet on a forbidden path.' Raghu Vanśa.

The first and third Pádas of this stanza correspond to the Sanyuktá species of the Paṅkti, or ten-syllable metre; the second and fourth to an undefined variety of the Trishṭubh, or eleven-syllable.

a. A variety of the Vaitálíya in not unfrequent use, termed Aupachchhandasika, is formed by merely adding a long syllable to each Páda; making the first and third therefore contain sixteen, and the second and fourth eighteen, syllabic instants.

य इहात्मविदो विपक्षमध्ये सहसंवृद्धियुजोऽपि भूभुजः स्युः
बलिपुष्टकुलादिवान्यपुष्टैः पृथगस्मादचिरेण भाविता तैः

'Those princes who are now joined in alliance with the enemy, but who know themselves, will quickly fall from him, like cuckoos soon deserting the nest of the crow.' Mágha.

This stanza might be resolved into a verse of mixed metre, in which the first and third Pádas would belong to the eleven syllable order, and the second and fourth to the twelve; in each corresponding Páda admitting of precisely the same disposition of the syllables into trisyllabic feet.

b. There are several sub-species of each variety of the Vaitáliya; and one of the Aupachchhandasika, termed Pushpitágrá, is of frequent occurrence. The whole of the tenth Sarga of the Kirátárjuníya, from which the following is taken, is composed in it.

तनुमवजितलोकसारधाम्नीं त्रिभुवनगुप्तिसहां विलोकयन्त्यः ।
अवययुरमरस्त्रियोऽस्ययत्नं विजयफले विफलं तपोधिकारे ॥

'The celestial nymphs, beholding the form (of Arjuna), effacing the splendour of the universe, and capable of protecting the three worlds, felt that all attempts to distract the penance in which he was immersed, for the sake of victory, would be in vain.'

The verse, in fact, is a compound of the twelve and thirteen-syllable metres, and the trisyllabic feet in each Páda are regular, and correspond throughout.

2. Mátrasamaka. This, which is the second order of the class, consists of a verse of four Pádas, each of which contains sixteen short syllables, or their equivalents: the ninth syllabic instant must be single, and of course short, and the last long. Varieties are made by restricting other syllabic instants, as the fifth, eighth, and twelfth, to single or short quantities, or by allowing the ninth to form part of a long syllable. The following is an example of this metre:

⏑ ⏑ – ⏑ ⏑ ⏑ ⏑ ⏑ ⏑ ⏑ – ⏑ ⏑ – | – – – ⏑ ⏑ ⏑ ⏑ ⏑ ⏑ ⏑ ⏑ ⏑ – |
नलिनीदलगतजलवत्तरलं तद्वज्जीवनमतिशयचपलं
⏑ ⏑ ⏑ ⏑ – ⏑ ⏑ – ⏑ ⏑ – – | ⏑ ⏑ ⏑ ⏑ – ⏑ ⏑ ⏑ ⏑ – – – |
क्षणमिहसज्जनसङ्गतिरेका भवतिभवार्णवतरणे नौका

'Life is as unstable as the water that trembles on the leaf of the lotus. Association with the virtuous, although for a moment, is the only vessel to bear us across the ocean of existence.' Moha Mudgara.

3. Gityáryá. This is, like the preceding, a verse of which each Páda contains sixteen Mátras, or syllabic instants; but they are all short, except sometimes the last of each hemistich, which may be long. Varieties are also formed by constructing one hemistich entirely of long syllables, and the other of short, or by slightly altering the number of short syllables in the stanza; so that each hemistich may contain but twenty-nine, or the first may contain twenty-nine, and the second thirty-one; or the first thirty, and the second thirty-two. These forms of metre are not often met with in works of standard reputation.

As a specimen of irregular metre, as well as of rhyme, the following stanza is inserted from the Gíta Govinda, in which lyrical poem a great variety of anomalous, but exceedingly melodious versification is exemplified. The passage is left untranslated, as a short exercise for those who may have accompanied this Grammar to its termination.

ललितलवङ्गलतापरिशीलनकोमलमलयसमीरे
मधुकरनिकरकरम्बितकोकिलकूजितकुञ्जकुटीरे
विहरति हरिरिह सरसवसन्ते
नृत्यति युवतिजनेन सम सखि विरहिजनस्य दुरन्ते

INDEX I.

INDEX II.

VERBS IN THE DIFFERENT CONJUGATIONS.

CORRECTIONS.

Page	Line				
4	5	*for*	chchhra	*read*	chhra
4	8		ña		ñña
7	2		है		हे
11	21		उपकोरयीति		उपकोरीयति
13	16		है		हे
14	32		सिवायोन्नमः		शिवायोन्नमः
16	26		ककुब्भि		ककुब्भिः
21	18	*for*	such a ढ is changed to	*read*	it is changed to ष, which becomes
23	20	*for*	विष्णु	*read*	विष्णुः
24	5		पाश		पाश
24	5		पशस्पाश		यशस्पाश
27	5	*dele*	Section I.		
29	14	*for*	Section II.	*read*	Section I.
39	27		अभ्यिः		अीभ्यः
40	10		वध्वैः		वध्वै
49	20		भश्च्		भश्न्
51	9		प्राङ		प्राङ्
51	9		प्रत्यङ		प्रत्यङ्
51	27		तिर्य्यङ		तिर्य्यङ्
55	4		यकृद्भ्याः		यकृद्भ्यः
55	7		पकनि		यकनि
88	23		प्रियतिसृणा		प्रियतिसृणि
90	12		एककृत्व		एककृत्वः
95	5		माङ		माङ्
97	30		अतित्नमः		अतिक्रमः
101	7		with verbs		the verbs भू, अस, and कृ
108	11		चुरादि		चुरादि
111	14		अभिगभ्येदं		अभिगम्येदं
123	9		सिधु		सिधुः
123	31		सखा		सखाः
124	33		अपुष्पीत्		अपुष्पीत्
130	9		तात		तात्

Page	Line				
133	28	*for*	भवेतं	*read*	भवेतां
134	27		अभाविषत:		अभाविषत
136	32		रापयति		रोपयति
141	27		पपाच्यते		पापच्यते
143	2		पचूर्य्यते		पञ्चूर्य्यते
143	2		पंकुल्पते		पंफुल्यते
146	8		बुभूषाञ्चक्रासे		बुभूषाञ्चक्राते
146	10		अबुभूषिष्व:		अबुभूषिष्व
146	10		अबुभूषिष्म:		अबुभूषिष्म
146	31		बुभूषिषीयाथां		बुभूषिषीयास्थां
156	9	*dele*	अर्हर्य्यते		
157	3		अवूयते		
157	33		अर्जार्ज्यते		
171	5	*for*	देद्यतीति	*read*	देद्योतीति
171	12		अदूद्रवत्		अदिद्रवत्
171	31		दधोर्त्ति		दुधोर्त्ति
172	20		'to go'		'to go;' 'to fall.'
173	2		अपास्यत		अपास्यत्
175	5		भेमतु		भेमतुः
175	7		विभ्रमिषति		विभ्रमिषति
176	27		अयाक्षीत		अयाक्षीत्
178	7		अलब्ध		अलब्ध
180	18		अवर्त्तत्		अवर्त्तत
181	26		आशसंसे		आशशंसे
181	27		शंसिष्यते		आशंसिष्यते
184	7		ससिज्यते		सासिज्यते
190	10		असुसुवत्		असुसुवत्
191	7		जोहाति		जोहोति
202	17		ह्रिद्दि		ह्रिड्ढि
202	17		ह्रिद्ढ्वं		ह्रिड्ढ्वं
203	16		मृड्ढि		मृड्ढि
214	28		श्यमादि		शमादि
214	28		श्यम		शम
216	6		ऐयत्		ऐयत
221	24		श्यमादि		शमादि

Page	Line			
227	16	*for* सोषूये	*read*	सोषूयते
228	32	देभतु		देभतुः
238	5	[illegible]		हंभ्वहे
244	2	in vowels		in long vowels
249	28	अस्कुनात्		अस्कुनात्
253	2	चौरयामहै		चोरयामहै
254	13	अकाखिष्यत्		अकाणयिष्यत्
254	22	चिकथ्यिषति		चिकथयिषति
254	27	गुण		गण
256	32	अचीचहृत्		अचीचहत्
262	23	वाष्प		वाष्प
271	7	तिस्यत्		तिष्ठत्
273	8	विविदित्		विव्विदिवत्
291	20	भुक्ते		भुंक्ते
291	21	भुक्ते		भुंक्ते
345	18	सुहस्ता		सुसत्ता
345	20	महादेव		महादेवः
348	31	प्रामोको		प्रामोदको
351	23	वहिर		वहिर्
352	16	नस्		नस
361	30	वार्षिता		वार्धिता
369	15	-ध्यामवाप्सीत्		-ध्यामावास्सोत्
374	16	संपच्छते		संयच्छते
375	3	गावो		गा
375	20	नाछुति		नाच्छुति
375	28	इतरो		इतरः
383	6	केषेषु		केशेषु
386	8	ग्रहं		अहं
391	4	म		स
394	12	पुरुषी		पुरुषो
396	7	मास्य		मास्य
397	34	वाप्स्नः		वाप्स्न
400	8	ध्येतामहे		ध्येतास्महे
411	29	उक्त		उक्त
422	6	कमरराध		कमारराध

WORKS BY THE SAME AUTHOR,

To be had of Messrs. Madden and Co.

DICTIONARY, Sanskrit and English. 2d edition. Calcutta, 1832. *5l. 10s.*

SELECT SPECIMENS of the THEATRE of the HINDUS. 2 vols. 8vo. 2d edition. Allen and Co. *1l. 1s.*

SANKHYA KARIKA. Hindu Philosophy. London, 4to. *10s. 6d.*

VISHNU PURANA. Hindu Mythology and History. 4to. J. Murray, 1840. *2l. 2s.*

MILL'S BRITISH INDIA, with Notes. 6 vols. 8vo. Madden and Co. *14s.* per vol.

In the Press.

ARIANA ANTIQUA. Antiquities of Afghanistan, with Plates. 4to. *2l. 2s.*

HISTORY OF BRITISH INDIA, in continuation of MILL'S HISTORY. 2 vols. 8vo.

Also lately published by Madden and Co.

HITOPADESA; First Book: Sanskrit Text, with Glossary. By PROFESSOR JOHNSON. 4to. *15s.*